RIDLEY'S LAW OF THE CARRIAGE OF GOODS BY LAND, SEA AND AIR

RIDLEY'S LAW OF THE CARRIAGE OF GOODS BY LAND, SEA AND AIR

EIGHTH EDITION

by
BRIAN HARRIS
Nottingham Trent University

SWEET & MAXWELL

THOMSON REUTERS

First edition 1957
Second edition 1965
Third edition 1971
Fourth edition 1975
Fifth edition 1978
Sixth edition 1982
Seventh edition 1992

Published in 2010 by Thomson Reuters (Legal) Limited
(Registered in England & Wales, Company No 1679046.
Registered Office and address for service:
100 Avenue Road, London NW3 3PF)
trading as Sweet & Maxwell

*For further information on our products and services, visit
www.sweetandmaxwell.co.uk

Typeset by YHT Ltd
Printed in the UK by CPI William Clowes, Beccles, NR34 7TL

No natural forests were destroyed to make this product;
only farmed timber was used and re-planted

A CIP catalogue record for this book is available from the British Library.
ISBN: 978-0-414-04502-6

Preface

The law relating to the international carriage of goods by land, sea and air raises many interesting issues and I have very much enjoyed working in this field, both previously in legal practice and now in higher education. I am indebted both to those clients who instructed me in this area, whilst I was in practice with Clyde & Co and DLA, and also to those students at Nottingham Trent University, to whom it has been my privilege to teach this subject over the past few years.

Brian Harris
Senior Lecturer in Law
Nottingham Trent University

TABLE OF CONTENTS

Table of Cases

TABLE OF STATUTES

TABLE OF STATUTORY INSTRUMENTS

TABLE OF EUROPEAN CASES

Table of European Legislation

TABLE OF CONVENTIONS, ETC.

TABLE OF UNIFORM RULES, TRADE TERMS, ETC.

TABLE OF WEBSITES

http://ec.europa.eu/transport/index_en.htm
http://www.bifa.org
http://www.bimco.org/
http://www.bolero.net/index.htmland
http://www.comitemaritime.org
http://www.dft.gov.uk/
http://www.easa.europa.eu/ws_prod/index.html
http://www.emsa.europa.eu/
http://www.era.europa.eu/Pages/Home.aspx
http://www.erscharter.eu/.
http://www.eurotunnel.com
http://www.fiata.com
http://www.freightliner.co.uk
http://www.globaltradecorp.com
http://www.iata.org
http://www.icao.int/icao/en/leb/treaty.htm
http://www.ilo.org/global/lang–en/index.htm
http://www.imo.org
http://www.justice.gov.uk/civil/procrules
http://www.londonchamber.co.uk/lcc
http://www.marisec.org/
http://www.otif.org
http://www.otif.org/en/law.html
http://www.parismou.org/
http://www.rail.dbschenker.co.uk
http://www.rail-reg,gov.uk
http://www.uncitral.org
http://www.uncitral.org/uncitral/en/uncitral
http://www.unctad.org
http://www.unece.org
http://www.unece.org/trans/conventn/legalinst
http://www.unece.org/trans/welcome.html.

TABLE OF ABBREVIATIONS

ACMI	Aircraft, crew, maintenance and insurance
ADR	Agreement concerning the International Carriage of Dangerous Goods by Road
APTU	Uniform Rules concerning the Validation of Technical Standards and the Adoption of Uniform Technical Prescriptions applicable to Railway Material intended to be used in International Traffic
ATA	A mnemonic of "Admission Temporaire" and "Temporary Admission" representing the customs procedures adopted pursuant to the Customs Convention on the ATA Carnet for the Temporary Admission of Goods 1961 and the Istanbul Convention on Temporary Admission 1990
ATMF	Uniform Rules concerning the Technical Admission of Railway Material used in International Traffic
AWB	Airline air waybill
BALTIME	The charterparty form codenamed BALTIME 1939 recommended by BIMCO for use in connection with non-demise time charter arrangements
BARECON	The charterparty form codenamed BARECON recommended by BIMCO for use in connection with bareboat demise charter arrangements
BIFA	British International Freight Association
BIMCO	Baltic International Marine Cargo Organisation
CCT	Common customs tariff
CIM	Contract for International Carriage of Goods by Rail
CIV	Contract for International Carriage of Passengers and Luggage by Rail
CMI	Comité Maritime International
CMR	Convention Relative au Contrat de Transport International de Marchandises par Route
COGSA71	Carriage of Goods by Sea Act 1971
COGSA92	Carriage of Goods by Sea Act 1992
COLREG	Convention on the International Regulations for Preventing Collisions at Sea
COTIF	Convention concerning International Carriage by Rail
CTO	Combined transport operator

CUI	Uniform Rules concerning the Contract of Use of Infrastructure in International Rail Traffic
CUV	Uniform Rules concerning Contracts of Use of Vehicles in International Rail Traffic
CVR	Convention on the Contract for the International Carriage of Passengers and Luggage by Road
DfT	Department of Transport
EASA	European Aviation Safety Agency
ECJ	European Court of Justice
ECT	EC Treaty
EDI	Electronic data interface
EEA	European Economic Area
EEC	European Economic Community
EFTA	European Free Trade Association
EMSA	European Maritime Safety Agency
ERA	European Railway Agency
FCL	Full container load
FEU	Foot equivalent unit
FIATA	International Federation of Freight Forwarders Associations
FTA	Freight Transport Association
GHS	Globally Harmonised System of Classification and Labelling of Chemicals
HAWB	House air waybill
IATA	International Air Transport Association
ICAO	International Carriage by Air Organisation
ICC	International Chamber of Commerce
ILO	International Labour Organisation
IMF	International Monetary Fund
IMO	International Maritime Organisation
IRU	International Road Transport Union
ISC	International Chamber of Shipping
ISF	International Shipping Federation
ISM	International Safe Ship Management Code
ISPS	International Ship and Port Facility Security Code
LCL	Less than a container load
LLMC	Convention on Limitation of Liability for Maritime Claims 1976
LOF	Lloyds Open Form

MARPOL	International Convention for the Prevention of Pollution from Ships
MAWB	Master air waybill
MOU	Memoranda of understanding
MSA	Merchant Shipping Act 1995
MTO	Multimodal transport operator
NAWB	Neutral air waybill
NCTS	New Computerised Transit System
NODISP	No disposal
NYPE 93	The charterparty form codenamed NYPE 93 recommended by BIMCO for use in connection with non-demise time charter arrangements
ORR	Office of the Rail Regulator
OTIF	Organisation for International Carriage by Rail
RHA	Road Haulage Association
RID	Regulation concerning the International Carriage of Dangerous Goods by Rail
SAD	Single Administrative Document
SCOPIC	Special Compensation P&I Clubs
SDR	Special Drawing Right
SOLAS	International Convention for the Safety of Life at Sea
STWC	International Convention on Standards of Training, Certification and Watchkeeping for Seafarers
TDG	Transport of Dangerous Goods
TEU	Tonnage equivalent units
TFEU	Treaty on the Functioning of the European Union
TIR	Transports Internationaux Routiers
UCTA	Unfair Contract Terms Act 1977
UNCITRAL	United Nations Commission on International Trade Law
UNCLOS	UN Convention on the Law of the Sea
UNCTAD	United Nations Conference on Trade and Development
UNECE	United Nations Economic Commission for Europe
UN-EDIFACT	United Nations Electronic Data Interchange For Administration, Commerce and Transport standards for electronic data interchange developed under the auspices of the United Nations
UTCCR	Unfair Terms in Consumer Contracts Regulations 1999
VAT	Value Added Tax

Introduction

A single textbook that addresses the legal and regulatory concepts governing the carriage of goods by land, sea and air is perhaps even more useful now than it was when this title was originally created by Jasper Ridley over 50 years ago. Nowadays arrangements for the international carriage of goods commonly involve multimodal carriage (i.e. carriage by a combination of road, rail, inland waterway, sea and/or air). The book has been updated over the years but since the last edition in 1992, the legal framework for such carriage has changed significantly.

Now, as in 1992, the United Kingdom is an EU Member State and English law takes effect within the context of the European Economic Area (EEA) single market, both giving way to directly effective EU legislation and being interpreted, as far as possible, in conformity with all other EU legislation. However, the common transport policy for the single market has been greatly developed with concepts of the European roadway, railway, sea and sky. The common law has also seen significant developments, with various important decisions of the higher courts generally affecting contractual obligations and particularly affecting carriage obligations.

At the international level there have been many developments. In particular, significant changes have been made by the Vilnius Protocol to the CIM Convention for the international carriage of goods by rail; the new Montreal Convention is now in force (alongside the old Warsaw regime) for the international carriage of goods by air; the new Rotterdam Convention has now been adopted by the United Nations for the international carriage of goods by sea, including any ancillary carriage by any other mode; and there have been many changes to the international, EU and UK regimes regulating the carriage of goods. Commercial practices have also changed, particularly regarding electronic communication, standard contractual terms and containerisation. All of these developments, and more, have been taken into account in the comprehensive updating of this textbook.

The essential structure of previous editions is preserved in that carriage by land, sea and air are addressed in separate parts. However, the separate parts are organised rather differently as follows.

- Part One addresses general legal issues arising in respect of contracts for the carriage of goods. This provides the background knowledge for examination of each of the particular modes of carriage.
- Part Two addresses the legal issues arising in connection with

contracts for the carriage of goods by land. These issues are addressed separately in relation to road, rail and inland waterways in the context of both domestic and international movements.

- Part Three considers carriage of goods by sea. The principal issues addressed are the following: the common law principles of carriage by sea; the nature of the various contrasting forms of agreement for such carriage; the mandatory regulation of contractual terms arising under the Hague-Visby Rules; and the contrasting possible effects of the Hague, Hamburg and Rotterdam Rules.
- Part Four reviews carriage of goods by air. This addresses the general context of such carriage and then the applicable statutory terms arising under the Montreal Convention, the UK Non-International Carriage Rules and the various applicable versions of the Warsaw Convention.
- Part Five addresses the current commercial and regulatory environments for carriage in terms of: electronic commerce, multimodal carriage, the unimodal regulation of carriage and the interrelationship between contractual duties and statutory regulation at the UK and EU levels.

The eighth edition of *Ridley's Law of the Carriage of Goods by Land, Sea and Air* is designed for anyone needing to understand the applicable legal framework under English law for contracts of carriage. This includes law students and lawyers advising on carriage issues, as well as those working in the industry such as freight forwarders, carriers, insurers, claim adjustors and surveyors.

Part One: Contracts for the Carriage of Goods

1.1 Nature of a Contract for the Carriage of Goods

A contract of carriage is, like other contracts, governed by the general law of contract developed by the common law. Nevertheless, carriage contracts do have a number of unifying factors that, together, distinguish them from other commercial contracts. Generally goods are not carried simply for the purpose of moving them from A to B but for the purpose of performing discrete contractual obligations owed to others (often under contracts of sale and purchase). In consequence, persons other than the immediate contracting parties will be concerned with their proper perfomance. Where international in nature, by reason of the goods being carried across international borders, carriage operates within an international legal environment that requires inter-state agreement for the export and import of goods and the transit, loading and unloading of road and rail vehicles, ships and aircraft; however, carriage nonetheless operates by private contractual arrangement. Consequently issues of public international law have to be addressed, albeit from the perspective of private contracts governed by their own applicable law.

Only the carrier can exercise control over the performance of the carriage and the safekeeping of the goods during the carriage; so the act of the consignor in handing the goods over to the carrier involves some considerable commercial risk to the owner of the goods. Frequently, the assistance of third parties is necessary to facilitate the performance of the contract of carriage, particularly in connection with certain ancillary operations generally performed by others, such as: loading, discharging, transhipping, delivery and a variety of logistical services. In consequence, a complex patchwork of discrete contractual and non-contractual legal relationships will be created under which those third parties will provide such services, in the midst of which it may be difficult to apportion liability between the parties. This is particularly the case in connection with carriage of an international nature, since those relationships will be subject to contrasting applicable laws and jurisdictions. These, in turn, will need to be selected, in the event of dispute, by the application of those rules of private international law applied by the court or tribunal determining the dispute.

The performance of carriage contracts is attended by significant operational risk. In consequence, carriers and those undertaking ancillary operations may only be prepared to undertake performance on the basis that their liability is, at least in certain respects, excluded or limited. Those operational risks pose hazards for third parties, particularly in terms of the personal, property, financial and environmental costs potentially resulting from operational failure in the performance of carriage contracts. States have to balance those hazards against the benefits arising from facilitation of trade by commercial carriage operations. In consequence, states seek to regulate both the contractual terms of carriage and the manner in which such contractual obligations are performed. This results in diverse and wide-ranging mandatory regulation imposed by national law, albeit frequently enacted pursuant to obligations arising under international public law.

Almost invariably carriage contracts are concluded by reference to standard terms and, where goods move across international borders, statutory terms deriving from the United Kingdom's international treaty obligations. In general, these terms (whether contractual or statutory) relate to carriage to be performed by a particular mode, i.e. by road, rail, sea or air. In consequence identical principles arising under the common law (as to such matters as the incorporation and interpretation of contractual terms and the effect of similar contractual duties, rights and remedies) have to be addressed in relation to every mode of carriage. Furthermore, incidents of breach themselves have much in common since, irrespective of the mode of carriage, goods in carriage fall to be lost, damaged or delayed. However, these generally applicable principles are likely to be displaced by contractual terms and mandatory regulation unique to a particular mode of carriage by land, sea and air; thereby producing a complicated series of self-contained legal environments (which are all examined by this book) whenever goods are carried by more than one mode.

The common law itself fosters conceptual complexity by previously according some carriers the status of a "common carrier".[1] When a common carrier carries goods without entering into a special contract with the consignor; he is not deemed at common law to be carrying under an implied contract, he carries the goods by virtue of the custom of the realm as a common carrier.[2] However, as carriers invariably do carry goods under contracts of carriage rather than as common carriers; it is appropriate to

[1] As discussed at 1.10.1 below, only a carrier who held itself out to the public at large as being ready to carry goods for reward and did not reserve any right to refuse to carry could be a common carrier at common law.

[2] *London and North-Western Railway Company v Hudson and Sons* [1920] A.C. 324, 333, per Lord Dunedin.

primarily focus on the carriage contract and leave the arcane and largely redundant concept of the common carrier to be more briefly addressed at the end of Part One.[3] In consequence of the effective demise of the common carrier it is no longer necessary to address the essential nature of "a carrier". In prior centuries that issue had significance; as the common law sought to protect persons from being exposed to the significant obligations and liability of a common carrier where they only carried, or agreed to carry, goods incidentally to some other main business (such as warehousekeeping, stevedoring or freight forwarding). Nowadays, what is essential is whether or not a person has agreed to carry. Where they have so agreed to carry they will be carriers and their contract with their customer will be a contract of carriage.[4]

1.2 Regulatory and Commercial Context for the Carriage of Goods

In connection with contracts of carriage, unlike very many other commercial contracts, the contracting parties are rarely uncertain as to the scope of the contractual duties that are to be performed. In essence those duties could hardly be more straightforward, being simply those of one party transporting goods from place A to place B and of the other party paying the price ("the freight") for such transportation. However, many uncertainties do arise for the contracting parties under contracts of carriage. These are largely attributable to the complex regulatory and commercial environment in which such contracts have to be performed.

Contracts of carriage are subject to mandatory regulation over their performance and, in certain circumstances, their terms. Almost all of this regulation is unimodal in its application in that there are discrete regulatory environments for the carriage of goods on land (by road, rail and inland waterway), by sea and by air. Mandatory regulation of the terms of carriage, when applicable, has the force of law displacing contrary contractually agreed terms for the international carriage of goods by road under CMR,[5]

[3] For a detailed review of the common carrier concept and its limited current relevance see McBain "Time to abolish the common carrier" J.B.L. 2005, (Sep) 545. A summary of the concept is give at 1.10 below.

[4] *Aqualon (UK) Ltd v Vallana Shipping Corp* [1994] 1 Lloyd's Rep. 669.

[5] Pursuant to the CMR Convention, made applicable in the UK by s.1 of the Carriage of Goods By Road Act 1965, as discussed at 2.3.

rail under CIM,[6] sea under Hague-Visby[7] and air under the Montreal or Warsaw regimes[8] and for the domestic carriage of goods by air.[9] Whilst these mandatory terms are addressed in Parts Two (land), Three (sea) and Four (air), the detailed mandatory regulation applicable to the undertaking of carriage obligations, by whichever of the discrete modes of carriage (road, rail, inland waterway, sea and air) might be rendered in performance of such contracts, is discussed at Part Five. Such regulation takes effect in the context of a particular contract for the carriage of goods in one of two ways, namely either as instruments of mandatory law applied by the state in which any dispute is being determined, or as contractual terms agreed between the parties.

The commercial context of carriage is that goods, in order to be transported between sellers and buyers, are likely to be carried by various modes of carriage (e.g. land transit to the load port and from the discharge port and sea transit between the load and discharge ports). The contractual arrangements for the entire physical transportation will involve the conclusion either of discrete contracts of carriage each for only one mode (unimodal carriage), with different carriers for each discrete movement; or, alternatively, a single contract of carriage for all the various modes (multimodal carriage) with a single carrier for the entire movement irrespective of the mode. Such unimodal or multimodal carriage contracts will be entered into by whichever of the contracting parties to the contract of sale has responsibility under that contract for arranging the subject movement.

However, the responsible contracting party may engage some other person to procure the transportation and such person may perform the entire carriage as carrier or alternatively may arrange the entire carriage as an agent. Such agents, commonly called freight forwarding agents, may contract, or purport to contract, as an independent agent for consignors and consignees and may conclude contracts of carriage with carriers on

6 Pursuant to the CIM Convention, made applicable in the UK by s.103 of the Railways And Transport Safety Act 2003 and the Railways (Convention on International Carriage by Rail) Regulations 2005 (SI 2005/2092) as discussed at 2.6.2.

7 Pursuant to the Hague-Visby Convention made applicable in the UK by s.1 of the Carriage of Goods By Sea Act 1971, as discussed at 3.3.2.

8 Pursuant to whichever of the Montreal, Reamended, Amended, MP1 or Unamended Original Warsaw Conventions are in force between the states of flight departure and arrival and made applicable in the UK by s.1 of the Carriage by Air Act 1961, as discussed at Part Four.

9 Pursuant to the UK Non-International Carriage Rules, applied by s.10 of the Carriage by Air Act 1961 and SI 2004/1899, as discussed at 4.2.2.

their customer's, rather than on their own, behalf.[10] The capacity in which such a person acts will be an issue of fact in each case. Similarly, carriers undertaking carriage may contract to do so themselves in their own name; or they may contract through others, in which case the same issue arises as to whether those others are themselves undertaking performance as a contractual carrier, or simply contracting as agent for and on behalf of the carrier. Contracting carriers may themselves perform the contract of carriage or they may sub-contract its performance wholly or partly to others. Sub-contracting the performance of carriage obligations is both normal and common, not least because of the common practice of carriers hiring out and in, vehicles, vessels and aircraft (fully equipped and manned) pursuant to vehicle, vessel and aircraft chartering arrangements.

Increasingly goods, particularly manufactured goods, are carried in containers[11] in the course of multimodal carriage operations. Standard dimensions are 20 foot length containers (TEU or tonnage equivalent units) and 40 foot length containers (FEU or 40 foot equivalent units). In stark contrast to the unimodal nature of the regulatory regime, these containers are designed for multimodal carriage by sea, inland waterway, rail and road, facilitating efficient through transit from exporting manufacturers to importing distributors. Customers either consign goods to be carried in containers as entire full container loads (FCL) or as part of groupage consignments as less than a container load (LCL). The containers themselves may be owned by one or other of the parties loading (stuffing), carrying or unloading (destuffing) them. They are, however, more likely to be owned by others and then leased under container rental agreements to one or other of those persons. They are likely to be stuffed at the start and destuffed at the end of the carriage: they may be stuffed by the consignor and destuffed by the consignee or sometimes by or for the carrier, and frequently by third party packers or consolidators who might be acting for any one of them, depending on the agreement reached.

[10] The role performed by freight forwarding agents is examined in more detail in the context of multimodal carriage at 5.2.2.

[11] The growth of worldwide international container traffic, since containers were first employed on international routes in 1966, has been extraordinary. The January 13, 2003 UNCTAD report on *Multimodal Transport: the Feasibility of an International Legal Instrument* (available online at *http://www.uncitral.org*) reported at para.6 growth in port container shipments "from zero in 1965 to 225.3 million moves in 2000".

Carriage can only be performed by the carrier making use of third party facilities such as roads, railways, inland waterways, ports, airports etc. provided and maintained by others (e.g. highway, railway, inland waterway, port or airport authorities; stevedores, warehouse keepers etc.). Operational failings of facilities or services provided by such third parties may result in claims for breach against the carrier, as well as against such third party service providers. Such claims will fall to be determined by reference to the contract of carriage, which will govern the liability of the carrier and may also regulate the liabilities of any third parties to any person bound by the contract of carriage.

Frequently rights under the contract of carriage will be assigned, or otherwise transferred, along with risk or title to goods sold in the course of carriage. When goods have been sold across national borders complexities will arise as to the applicable law and jurisdiction for the determination of any disputes. Any disputes arising between the parties fall to be determined by reference to standard form contracts familiar to those operating within the industry; for reasons of economic efficiency carriage contracts must be concluded quickly, frequently by electronic communications, with limited negotiation on a basis permitting sufficient calculation of risk for carriers to arrange appropriate insurance protections. Generally such disputes require careful analysis of the contractual matrix, starting with an analysis as to precisely when the carriage arrangements were made, precisely what those arrangements were and with whom they were agreed. Those arrangements will need to be performed in compliance with the mandatory regulation applicable to the mode of carriage undertaken. The scope and detail of such regulation, which is very extensive, is the subject of some discussion in 5.3. Non-compliance can result in the criminal, civil and administrative sanctions of public law and also in private law civil sanctions resulting from contractual illegality where compliant performance is impossible,[12] or where the agreed manner of performance is prohibited.[13] Otherwise non-compliance may give rise to liability in contract for breach of some express

[12] Although it is exceptional for contracts of carriage to be prohibited per se since that demands a conclusion that an agreement to perform a particular obligation is prohibited and that the contracting parties in fact agreed to the performance of that prohibited obligation (see *Waugh v Morris* 1873 LR 8 Q.B. 202).

[13] *Ashmore Benson Pease & Co Ltd v Dawson Ltd* 1973 1 W.L.R. 828 is an example of such a case in which consignor and consignee acted in concert in overloading a vehicle pursuant to an otherwise lawful contract of carriage and in consequence rendered the contract void through illegality.

or implied contractual obligation;[14] or in tort for breach of statutory duty,[15] or for negligence for breach of an already existing duty of care.[16] These issues are discussed in more detail in 5.3.7.

1.3 Parties and Practices

Where the consignor contracts on its own behalf with the carrier for the carriage of the goods and remains the only person having a proprietary or possessory right in the goods throughout the period of the carriage, then duties under the contract of carriage will only be owed by the carrier to the consignor. However, in consequence of the commercial context described above, identifying the contracting parties to a contract of carriage is rarely so straightforward. The consignor may not be contracting solely on its own behalf, but may be someone selling the goods who intends, by handing them to the carrier, to deliver them to the buyer. If delivery to the buyer under the contract of sale is to be made by handing the goods to the carrier at the outset of the carriage, the consignor may, in the absence of an express provision to the contrary, be deemed to be entering into the contract of carriage as the agent of the consignee.[17] If delivery under the contract of sale is to be made by the transfer of constructive possession in the course of carriage, the contract of carriage is deemed to be made with the consignor, unless the contrary is expressly agreed between the consignor and the carrier. The fact that the consignor is not the owner of the goods at the time the goods are consigned does not prevent the consignor from being party to the contract of carriage opposite the carrier. Where a bailee delivers goods to a carrier to carry them back to the bailor, the contract of carriage with the carrier is made by the bailee despite its limited possessory interest in the goods.[18] Alternatively, the consignee may make

[14] For example *Golden Fleece Maritime Inc v ST Shipping and Transport Inc (The Elli)* [2009] 1 All E.R. (Comm) 908 where the Court of Appeal concluded that obligations of seaworthiness and cargo-worthiness embraced not only the physical characteristics of the chartered vessel but also legal compliance with the MARPOL convention.

[15] See K. M. Stanton, "New Forms of the tort of breach of statutory duty" L.Q.R. 2004, 120(Apr), 324 for a useful discussion of such causes of action.

[16] As the Privy Council commented in *Tan Chye Choo v Chong Kew Moi* [1970] 1 W.L.R. 147.

[17] *Dawes v Peck* (1799) 8 T.R. 330; Sale of Goods Act 1979, s.32.

[18] *Freeman v Birch* (1843) 3 Q.B. 492n. The concept of bailment (whereby the person, the bailor, in possession of goods hands them over to another, the bailee, for safekeeping and redelivery) is discussed at 1.6.1.1.

the arrangements for the carriage, having agreed to buy the goods at the point of collection by the carrier. In this case the consignor may have no involvement with the contract of carriage save in relation to loading.[19]

The person apparently accepting the obligation of carriage may be intending to sub-contract all or part of the performance of the carriage to someone else, although that person as principal contractor will nonetheless incur and retain the performance obligations of a contracting carrier. Alternatively, that person may be acting as an agent: either a forwarding agent acting on behalf of the consignor and only agreeing to arrange carriage for its client by concluding contracts with carriers on its principal's behalf; or a ship owner's or charterer's agent, undertaking carriage obligations as agent on behalf of the carrier it represents. In determining whether a person who makes such arrangements for carriage is an agent or a carrier, courts tend to focus on the following aspects of the factual matrix: what that person agreed to do; how that person's role was described by the parties; the manner in which previous contracts between the parties had been performed; the nature and basis on which that person is to be remunerated for their services; and the nature and terms of any documentation issued in respect of the carriage.[20]

1.4 Jurisdiction and Law

1.4.1 Overview

Any agreement for the carriage of goods is "anchored" by the law that governs its interpretation and performance. However, the identity of that law, as well as those of the laws applicable to non-contractual obligations and proprietary rights owed or claimed by the disputants, will be determined by the private international law rules of the forum in which any dispute is determined. In this context, whenever the formation or performance of carriage involves any potential conflict of laws, it is appropriate to identify the forum in which any disputes under the contract are to be determined first, particularly since international contracts of carriage may

[19] Although sellers participating in the contractual performance may acquire rights and incur liabilities arising in respect of the contract of carriage pursuant to the principles established in *Pyrene Co Ltd v Scindia Steam Navigation Co Ltd* [1954] 2 Q.B. 402.

[20] See the judgment of Mance J. in *Aqualon (UK) Ltd v Vallana Shipping Corp* 1994 1 Lloyd's Rep. 669 where all these factors are considered and see 5.2.2 where the role and status of freight forwarding agents is particularly discussed.

be subject to differing mandatory regulations according to whichever public international law obligations happen to be binding on the forum.

1.4.2 EU Jurisdiction Regime

Where any defendant to an action is domiciled in any of the 27 Member States of the European Union, choice of jurisdiction is governed by EC Regulation 44/2001 (often referred to as "the Jurisdiction Regulation"). Conflicts of jurisdiction between EU Member States were previously governed by the 1968 Brussels Convention (brought into force in the United Kingdom by the Civil Jurisdiction and Judgments Act 1982). The 1988 Lugano Convention governs jurisdiction between the EU Member States and the European Free Trade Association (EFTA) states of Iceland, Liechtenstein and Norway. Together the territories of the EU and EFTA Member States comprise the European Economic Area (EEA). The provisions of the Brussels and Lugano Conventions are broadly reflected in the Jurisdiction Regulation,[21] which has superseded the 1968 Brussels Convention.

It is important to appreciate that whenever R44/2001 is applicable it ousts general common law concepts entirely.[22] The effects of arts 27 and 28 of R44/2001 should also be particularly noted. These provide that any court, other than the court first seised of an action involving the same cause of action between the same parties, must stay its proceedings until the first court's jurisdiction is established. Accordingly an agreement to jurisdiction, or reference to arbitration, will have to be capable of being enforced in the EU state that is first seised of any particular dispute within the meaning of arts 27 and 28.[23]

Article 23(1) of R44/2001 provides that the parties may agree that a

[21] Albeit, there are some differences particularly in relation to consumer contracts and non-exclusive jurisdiction agreements.

[22] Such as *lis alibi pendens* and *forum non conveniens* as to which see *Owusu v Jackson* Case C-281/02 where the ECJ ruled that, where a defendant was domiciled in England, the English courts were precluded from declining jurisdiction in favour of the courts of a non-Member State; even though the English court would otherwise have taken the view that the courts of that non-Member State were the more appropriate forum.

[23] In *Allianz SpA v West Tankers Inc* Case C-185/07, the ECJ held that the previously common practice of the Commercial Court in London, to award anti-suit injunctions preventing commencement of legal action in other jurisdictions within the EU in breach of any agreement to arbitrate disputes, was unlawful under EU law by reason of arts 27 and 28.

court or courts of a particular Member State are to have jurisdiction and that such jurisdiction "shall be exclusive unless the parties have agreed otherwise". An exclusive choice is one that seeks to prevent the parties attempting to establish jurisdiction elsewhere;[24] whilst a non-exclusive choice is one that entitles the parties to determine their dispute in the chosen jurisdiction, but leaves them free to establish jurisdiction elsewhere. Article 23(1) provides that for an agreement on jurisdiction to be enforceable under the Jurisdiction Regulation it needs to be either: in writing or evidenced in writing;[25] in a form consistent with the parties' own "established practices"; or consistent with "a usage of which the parties are or ought to have been aware and which in such trade or commerce is widely known to, and regularly observed by, parties to contracts of the type involved in the particular trade".[26] Article 23 of the Jurisdiction Regulation does not entitle choice of jurisdiction for certain matters. The following are most pertinent in the context of contracts for the carriage of goods: matters relating to insurance governed by art.3, and consumer contracts governed by art.4, of R44/2001.

In the absence of any agreed choice within the meaning of art.23(1), the Jurisdiction Regulation provides at art.2 that persons domiciled in a Member State should primarily be sued in the courts of that Member State. However, the Jurisdiction Regulation also provides for certain alternative jurisdictions, some of which are particularly relevant to carriage contracts. Article 5 provides that contractual claims can be brought before "the courts for the place of performance of the obligation in question";[27] that a tortious claim can be brought before "the courts for the place where the harmful

[24] Exclusive jurisdiction clauses tend to be the norm under standard conditions of carriage and all the standard conditions reviewed in this book incorporate exclusive jurisdiction clauses.

[25] Article 23(2) stipulates that "in writing" includes any communication by electronic means providing "a durable record" of the agreement.

[26] It is clear that whether an agreement falls within art.23(1) is a matter of European Union law. In *Trasporti Castelletti Spedizioni Internazionali SpA v Hugo Trumpy SpA* C-159/97 the ECJ emphasised that the key issue is that of consent by the defendant and held that such consent can be evidenced by a generally observed practice in the international trade concerned, even though the practice might not be established in specific countries or even in all Member States.

[27] In a case under art.5(1) of the Brussels Convention, Case 12/76, *Industrie Tessili Italiana Como v Dunlop* AG 83, the Court of Justice held that the place of performance of the obligation in question is to be determined in accordance with the law governing the obligation in question as selected by the private international law rules of the forum.

event occurred or may occur"; and that a salvage claim may be brought before "the court under . . . which the cargo or freight in question" has been arrested or could have been arrested but for security having been given. Article 6 provides that where there are a number of defendants, persons may be sued before the courts for the place in which any one of them is domiciled "provided the claims are so closely connected that it is expedient to hear and determine them together to avoid the risk of irreconcilable judgments resulting from separate proceeding". Furthermore, art.71 of the Jurisdiction Regulation provides that its own provisions "shall not affect" any provisions of international public law binding on any Member States which "govern jurisdiction or the recognition or enforcement of judgments" in particular matters. Article 71 expressly permits courts to assume jurisdiction in accordance with such public international law even against persons domiciled in other Member States that are not bound by the international public law in question and requires the courts of those other Member States to enforce any resultant judgments.[28]

Accordingly, the Jurisdiction Regulation must give way to other international legislation regulating jurisdiction in respect of particular matters but only to the extent necessary to give effect to such other international legislation. Consequently, those provisions of the Jurisdiction Regulation that do not conflict with such other international legislation (such as arts 27 and 28 of R44/2001) continue to apply, even though jurisdiction can be claimed under the other international legislation. Accordingly, the jurisdictional provisions contained in CMR, CIM and the Montreal and Warsaw Conventions that are reviewed in Parts Two and Four take effect within the context of the EU jurisdiction regime.

1.4.3 EU Applicable Law Regime

As already mentioned, it is the conflict of law rules applied by the forum seised of the dispute that will determine the applicable law of the contractual obligations. For all agreements made after April 1, 1991 and before December 17, 2009, issues relating to the choice of law between the laws of different countries is governed by the 1980 Rome Convention on the Law

[28] Article 57 of the 1968 Brussels Convention, the precursor provision to art.71, was interpreted in the *Owners of Cargo Lately Laden on Board the Tatry v Owners of the Maciej Rataj*, Case C-406/92. The ECJ held specialised conventions with jurisdictional rules would preclude only those provisions within the Brussels Convention which were incompatible with the provisions of the specialised conventions and not any other provisions of the EU jurisdiction regime.

Applicable to Contractual Obligations (the Rome Convention) incorporated into English law by the Contracts (Applicable Law) Act 1990. For all agreements made after December 17, 2009 EC Regulation 593/2008/EC (the Rome I Regulation) will apply. Accordingly, for several years to come, an initial issue to be addressed in any international carriage dispute will be whether the carriage contract has been entered into before or after December 17, 2009, since that will determine whether the applicable law to be chosen by any court or tribunal of an EU Member State will be selected by reference to the Rome Convention or the Rome I Regulation. However, the two regimes are similar. As from January 11, 2009 the applicable law for obligations arising independently of contract is to be determined subject to EC Regulation 864/2007/EC (the Rome II Regulation).

The applicable law can be chosen by the parties to the carriage contract by an express agreement between them, provided that such choice is express or demonstrated with reasonable certainty by the terms of the contract, or the circumstances of the case.[29] The effectiveness of any choice of law is constrained by various stipulations to the effect that the parties cannot, by choosing an alternative law, evade mandatory regulation imposed by: the country with which, at the time of the choice, all the other elements of the contract are connected;[30] the forum in which any dispute is being determined insofar as they comprise mandatory laws (in the case of the Rome I Regulation "overriding" mandatory laws) applicable irrespective of the law otherwise applicable to the contract;[31] and, effectively, the places of performance to the extent applied by the forum of the dispute.[32] Article 3(4) of the Rome I Regulation also preserves the applicability of mandatory European Union law where "all other elements relevant to the situation at the time of the choice are located in one or more Member States"; but it is

[29] Pursuant to art.3(1) both of the Rome Convention and the Rome 1 Regulation.

[30] Pursuant to art.3(3) both of the Rome Convention and the Rome 1 Regulation.

[31] Article 7(2) of the Rome Convention and 9(2) of the Rome I Regulation, although under the Rome I Regulation "overriding" mandatory provisions are restrictively defined at art.9(1) and limited to those mandatory provisions which are "crucial ... for safeguarding its public interests, such as its political, social or economic organisation ...".

[32] Article 7(1) of the Rome Convention refers to the law of the place with which "the situation has a close connection". Article 9(3) of the Rome I Regulation refers to the law of the place "where the obligations arising out of the contract have to be or have been performed, in so far as those overriding mandatory provisions render the performance of the contract unlawful", which more closely mirrors the approach taken by the common law to such issues (see *Regazzoni v K. C. Sethia (1944) Ltd* [1956] 1 Lloyd's Rep. 435).

submitted that mandatory European Law ought, in any event, to be accorded the same effect under the Rome Convention.[33]

It is where applicable law is not agreed that there is a clear divergence between the Rome Convention and the Rome I Regulation. Under the Rome Convention, art.4(1) provides for a primary rule that the applicable law will be the law of the country with which the contract is "most closely connected" and "by way of exception" that a severable part of the contract may be governed by the law of another country with which that severable part is more closely connected. Article 4(4) provides for a "presumption" in the case of carriage contracts that the closest connection is with the country of the carrier's principal place of business if that is also the country of loading, discharge or the consignor's principal place of business; however, art.4(5) provides that the presumption is to be disregarded where "from the circumstances as a whole that the contract is more closely connected with another country". Under the Rome Convention, English courts readily disapply the presumption where it points away from some other governing law more closely connected with the contract.[34] In contrast, the primary rule under the Rome I Regulation only partially resembles the above referenced presumption. Article 5(1) of Rome I provides that in the absence of choice the applicable law for contracts of carriage shall be the "law of the country of habitual residence of the carrier, provided that the place of receipt or the place of delivery or the habitual residence of the consignor is also situated in that country"; or, where that is not the case, "the law of the country where the place of delivery as agreed by the parties is situated". Article 5(3) of Rome I provides for this primary rule only to be disapplied where "it is clear from all the circumstances of the case that the contract ... is manifestly more closely connected with" another country, in which case the applicable law will be the law of that other country.

In the case of international carriage, however, the mandatory regulation of the terms of international carriage arising from CMR, CIM, Hague-Visby and the Montreal and Warsaw Conventions, as reviewed in Parts Two to Four, is apparently preserved, since such mandatory regulation has the "force of law" in the United Kingdom. Similarly, the mandatory regulation

[33] As directly effective European law should be accorded an equivalent effect to that of English law so as to ensure the effectiveness of European law (see *Manfredi v Lloyd Adriatico Assicurazioni SpA* Case C-295/04); and English law would be considered to have such overriding effect (see *The Hollandia* [1983] 1 A.C. 565 where the Hague-Visby Rules were applied as overriding mandatory law pursuant to the Carriage of Goods by Sea Act 1971).

[34] See *Kenburn Waste Management Ltd v Bergmann* [2002] EWCA Civ 98.

arising in respect of the performance of contracts of carriage and reviewed at 5.3 can also be considered to be overriding and applicable in the UK courts in this context, irrespective of the law applicable to the contractual obligations under the Rome 1 Regulation.[35]

1.5 Contractual Terms

1.5.1 Incorporation

Carriers normally make contracts with their customers by means of a set of standard conditions of carriage, either drawn up by their legal advisors, or made available by their trade association. Contracts of carriage may be made orally or in writing; for the effective management of commercial rights and liabilities, they should always be made subject to standard carriage conditions covering all the matters likely to affect the carrier's trading relations with consignors and consignees. The identification of the contractual terms of any contractual carriage, and whether any standard carriage conditions have been incorporated into the contract, is a question of fact, which is to be determined according to the principles of the applicable law governing the formation of the contract. Under English law it is of course necessary that the terms of the contract should have been brought to the notice of the parties at the time when the contract was made.[36]

With the exception of vehicle, vessel or aircraft chartering arrangements, such as those dealt with in 3.2.1, express contract terms for carriage are generally contained in standard form terms incorporated by making express reference to them on information, consignment, delivery or invoicing documentation. It is essential for the incorporation of such standard form terms that the customer (be that the consignor, consignee or some other person) receives reasonably sufficient notice of them.[37] There are also

[35] Whilst clearly the case under art.7(2) of the Rome Convention, which refers simply to mandatory law, the wording of art.9(2) of Rome I creates some doubt by its reference to "overriding mandatory provisions". However, it is submitted that, where such mandatory regulation derives from obligations under public international law, their effect will be preserved.

[36] See *Henderson v Stevenson* (1875) L.R. 2 H.L. Sc. 470; *Parker v South-Eastern Railway Company* (1877) 2 C.P.D. 416; *Hood v Anchor Line* [1918] A.C. 837; *Thompson v London, Midland and Scottish Railway Company* [1930] 1 K.B. 41; *Chapelton v Barry Urban District Council* [1940] 1 K.B. 532.

[37] *Parker v South Eastern Railway Co Ltd* [1877] 2 CPD 416.

various categories of circumstances which, at common law, may give rise to the implication that contractual terms have been incorporated. A consistent and regular course of dealing between parties on particular conditions may result in the incorporation of those conditions in a particular contract,[38] although this will not be the case where there is insufficient consistency in the prior course of dealing.[39] Incorporation of terms can also be implied where standard conditions are customary in a particular trade.[40] Of course, where contracts for the international carriage of goods are subject to mandatory terms (imposed by the statutory implementation of public international law instruments such as the CMR, CIM, Hague-Visby, Montreal and Warsaw Conventions),[41] such terms will be implied into any contract of carriage in relation to which they have mandatory effect and will displace any contrary expressly agreed terms.

1.5.2 Interpretation

The terms in a contract for the carriage of goods are, according to English law, construed and interpreted in the same way as other contracts. The starting point is for the words used in the contract to be construed as far as possible to give effect to whatever meaning might ordinarily be given to them by a reasonable reader against the matrix of fact known to the parties at the time they entered into the contract.[42] Courts seek, however, to give effect to the parties' intentions and may apply established rules, or canons, of construction to assist them in this process.[43] One particular canon of construction frequently employed by courts in relation to a carrier's standard terms of carriage is the *contra proferentem* rule. This provides that ambiguities in contractual terms will be interpreted against both those who

38 *Circle Freight International Ltd v Medeast Gulf Exports Ltd* 1988 2 Lloyd's Rep. 427.

39 *Hertford Foods Ltd v Lidl GmbH* [2001] EWCA Civ 938.

40 *British Crane Hire Corp Ltd v Ipswich Plant Hire Ltd* 1975 Q.B. 303 where conditions commonly used in crane hire arrangements were held incorporated into dealings between crane hirers through the common understanding in the trade.

41 These mandatory terms, respectively arising in connection with international carriage by land, sea and air, will be examined in Parts Two, Three and Four.

42 Being the approach advocated by Lord Hoffman in *Investors Compensation Scheme Ltd v West Bromwich BS* [1998] 1 WLR 896, 911–918.

43 The approach taken by several of their lordships (particularly Lord Bingham and Lord Hobhouse) in the House of Lords in *Homburg Houtimport BV v Agrosin Private Ltd (The Starsin)* [2003] 1 Lloyd's Rep. 571 in giving precedence to signed and expressly written terms on the front of a bill of lading over preprinted terms on the reverse.

claim the benefit from them and those who drafted them. Accordingly, any exclusions or limitations of liability contained in a carrier's standard terms that are capable of more than one meaning will be construed as limiting the carrier's liability to a lesser, rather than greater, extent.[44] Another related rule is that a provision in the contract by which one party limits or excludes its liability in general terms, without expressly referring to any limitation or exclusion as to negligence, will be interpreted as not necessarily referring to liability for negligence where there is some other liability, not arising in negligence, for which the party may be liable.[45] As a matter of public policy a party cannot exclude liability for its own fraud or deliberate misconduct,[46] although it is clear that liability for fraud or deliberate wrongdoing by employees, agents or sub-contractors in the performance of a contract may be excluded by clear and aptly worded exclusions.[47]

Courts will also give effect to any specific meanings that words may have either at law (by reason of previously decided cases)[48] or in fact (by reason of their usage in a particular context).[49] The common incorporation of standard terms in carriage contracts means that frequently the wording at

[44] Although there are limits to the principle as indicated in *The Irbenskiy Proliv* [2005] 1 Lloyd's Rep. 383, where it was held that it does not oblige a court to construe a provision so widely that it can be seen as repugnant to the purpose of the contract when a narrower construction would be consistent with that purpose.

[45] *Canada Steamship Lines Ltd v The King* [1952] A.C. 192 where the Crown, as the landlord of a warehouse, was held liable for the destruction of its tenant's goods arising from the Crown's negligence, despite a contractual provision that its tenants should "not have any claim or demand" against it for damage to the goods; since the exclusion was held to relate to liabilities for inherent defects and the acts of third parties, rather than to the Crown's liabilities in negligence.

[46] See the House of Lords decision in *HIH Casualty and General Insurance Ltd v Chase Manhattan Bank* [2003] 2 Lloyd's Rep. 61. As Lord Bingham said in that case "fraud is a thing apart . . . .This is not a mere slogan. It reflects an old legal rule that fraud unravels all."

[47] See *Frans Maas (UK) Ltd v Samsung Electronics (UK) Ltd* [2004] 2 Lloyd's Rep. 251.

[48] See, for instance, how in *AIC Ltd v Marine Pilot Ltd (The Archimidis)* [2008] 1 Lloyd's Rep. 597 Clarke MR addressed the issue whether the express selection of "one safe port" in an Asbatankvoy charter should take effect as a warranty that the port was a safe port within the meaning determined by Sellers L.J. in *Leeds Shipping Co Ltd v Société Française Bunge* [1958] 2 Lloyd's Rep. 127.

[49] So that common trade acronyms (e.g. TEU, FEU, FCL, LCL etc.) may be used in the expectation that they will be recognised and applied by the English courts.

the centre of any dispute already has a previously defined meaning, which may well be employed by any court determining the dispute. Where certain obligations are not stated, but are a necessary incident of express terms and are so obvious that the parties should effectively be considered as being relieved from any requirement to state them expressly, they may be implied to give business efficacy to the contract. Courts do not readily imply terms on this basis, but may do so where they are satisfied that, at the time of contracting, the parties would have considered such a term obvious, had the need for it been expressly brought to their attention at that time by the so-called "officious bystander".[50] The House of Lords considered the proper approach to the implication of terms on this basis in *Attorney General of Belize v Belize Telecom Ltd*[51] where Lord Hoffmann, in giving the Privy Council judgment, reviewed the many criteria expressed by judges for the implication of terms and concluded by saying that they are "best regarded, not as series of independent tests which must each be surmounted, but rather as a collection of different ways in which judges have tried to express the central idea that the proposed implied term must spell out what the contract actually means, or in which they have explained why they did not think that it did so".[52]

The approach taken towards the interpretation of statutory terms that are imposed on the parties under national law but which derive from international treaty obligations undertaken by the United Kingdom differs from that applicable to the interpretation of contractual terms. Such public international law should be interpreted "unconstrained by technical rules of English law, or by English legal precedent, but on broad principles of general acceptation".[53] In the interpretation of public international law, the courts should adopt a purposive approach to give effect to the underlying purposes of the international treaty to be revealed not only by the wording

[50] See *Mediterranean Salvage & Towage Ltd v Seamar Trading & Commerce Inc (The Reborn)* [2008] 2 Lloyd's Rep. 628 where Aikens J. declined to imply a safe load port warranty on this basis in the context of a voyage charter and his decision was upheld by the Court of Appeal in [2009] EWCA Civ 531.

[51] [2009] UKPC 10.

[52] At para.27 of his judgment when addressing, in particular, the five criteria for implication expressed by Lord Simon in *BP Refinery (Westernport) Pty Ltd v Shire of Hastings* (1977) 180 CLR 266, 282–283.

[53] Per Lord Wilberforce in *Buchanan v Babco* [1978] 1 Lloyd's Rep. 119 in addressing the CMR.

used but also by the legislative history, academic writing and international jurisprudence relating to the treaty as required by arts 31 to 33 of the Vienna Convention on the Law of Treaties.[54]

1.6 Contractual Duties

1.6.1 Overview of Carriage Duties at Common Law

Carriers, unless extraordinarily they are common carriers, are not under any duty to carry goods for anyone unless they agree to do so. Other carriers are free in every case to make, or to refuse to make, a contract to carry goods for a consignor and only if they do agree to carry the goods to destination will they be responsible in contract for the performance of the carriage. In addition to any such contractual obligation however, by accepting possession of the goods carriers will become subject to common law duties in bailment and tort. In the event that a carrier was to agree to act as an agent on behalf of the consignor in arranging any further required carriage, storage, insurance or other service in relation to the goods, that carrier would be exposed to further duties arising in agency. The carrier will have a concurrent liability for breach of its obligations however they arise, subject of course to whatever exclusions and limitations might be effectively applied under the contract of carriage.[55]

1.6.1.1 Bailment[56]

By accepting possession of goods, private carriers become bailees of the goods delivered to them for carriage, and are liable accordingly whether the bailment is for reward or gratuitous. As bailees, carriers are not under the liability of an insurer (unlike a carrier in the extraordinary position of a common carrier) but are obliged to take reasonable care of the goods entrusted to them and to redeliver those goods in the same condition as that in which they were originally received, save for any loss or damage proved by them to have been caused notwithstanding their exercise of

[54] Per Lord Diplock in *Fothergill v Monarch Airlines* [1981] A.C. 251 in addressing the Warsaw Convention.

[55] *Henderson v Merrett Syndicates Ltd* [1995] 2 A.C. 145.

[56] For a detailed authoritative guide to the complexities of bailment see *Palmer on Bailment*, 3rd edn (London: Sweet & Maxwell, 2009).

reasonable care to safeguard the goods. The onus is on the bailee to prove the exercise of reasonable care and that any loss or damage occasioned to the goods was caused by circumstances not attributable to any want of reasonable care on the bailee's part. The bailee's possessory rights to the goods are strictly limited by the terms of the bailment and there may be no deviation by the bailee from those terms.[57] The duty to redeliver is owed by the bailee to the person (the bailor) who originally passed legal, not merely physical, possession to the bailee. By attornment, i.e. by the bailee recognising and accepting some third party as having the rights of the original bailor, rights to enforce duties in bailment may be passed to a replacement bailor.

Furthermore a carrier, as bailee, may (at least where it has the authority of the bailor to do so) pass legal possession of the goods to some sub-bailee acting as sub-contractor or agent on its behalf. The sub-bailee, simply by receipt of the goods, will not only incur obligations in bailment to its immediate bailor, the carrier (who, in consequence of the sub-bailment, would become an intermediate bailee) but also co-extensive obligations in sub-bailment to the original bailor. The carrier, as original and now intermediate bailee, would meanwhile remain responsible opposite the bailor for the proper performance of the bailment, even in the event of some deliberate breach, such as theft, by the sub-bailee.[58] An alternative scenario of course, particularly common in multimodal carriage, is that the consignor (or a forwarding agent on its behalf) arranges discrete contracts of carriage for separate movements. In such cases the end of the prior movement will determine the prior bailment, as the prior carrier is released from its obligations in bailment by delivering legal possession of the goods to the succeeding carrier who, by accepting possession of the goods, will incur obligations in bailment, not sub-bailment, directly to the person to whom the prior carrier owed their obligations of redelivery.

The degree of care which must be exercised by both a bailee and a gratuitous bailee is that degree of care which a reasonable man would exercise with his own goods. Thus where a trailer unit was left where it could be seen from the road in a compound which had only one guard, no guard dogs and no warning alarms, both the bailee carrier and the

[57] *Coggs v Barnard* (1703) Com. 133.

[58] *Morris v C. W. Martin & Sons Ltd* [1965] 2 Lloyd's Rep. 63 which, whilst concerning the theft by an employee of a cleaning firm of a valuable white mink stole, is of wider application.

gratuitous sub-bailee compound owner were held liable.[59] The standard of care required by a bailee, whether gratuitous or otherwise, is the standard demanded by the circumstances of the particular case.[60]

Duties owed in bailment may be controlled by contract whenever the carrier, as bailee, is entitled to assert the contractual conditions of carriage against the person who, as bailor or sub-bailor, is entitled to enforce those duties. The common law has developed two distinct principles protecting carriers and their sub-contractors in this respect. First, there is the principle of bailment upon terms by which a carrier may rely on its own contractual conditions, subject to which the goods were received, to regulate its liability not only to the other immediate contracting parties but also to any bailor or sub-bailor consenting to the bailment.[61] The principle of sub-bailment on terms is explained by Lord Diplock in *The Pioneer Container* where the terms of the superior bailment provided that the superior bailee "shall be entitled to sub-contract on any terms the whole or any part of the carriage ... and any and all duties whatsoever undertaken ... in relation to the goods". The Privy Council held that, by reason of this clause, a sea carrier as sub-bailee was able to rely on a jurisdiction clause against the owner of the goods, as bailor, despite the jurisdiction clause only being contained in the contract of carriage concluded by the sub-bailee with a superior intermediate bailee (i.e. the prior carrier) and the original bailor having no knowledge of the jurisdiction clause at all.[62]

Indeed, it may be possible (where there is a bailment chain resulting in a sub-bailee accepting goods under conditions protecting all intermediate bailors) for the terms of the sub-bailment (when made with the consent of the original bailor) to regulate the superior bailment relationship between the original bailor and all intermediate bailers, including the original bailee.[63]

59 *James Buchanan & Co v Hay's Transport Services and Duncan Barbour and Son* [1972] 2 Ll.L.R. 535, Sutcliffe J.

60 *Houghland v Low Luxury Coaches Ltd* [1962] 1 Q.B. 694.

61 *The Pioneer Container* [1994] 2 A.C. 324.

62 The reason for the decision being that the original bailor had authorised sub-bailment "on any terms" and that the jurisdiction clause in question was not an unusual or unduly onerous term.

63 See *Sandeman Coprimar SA v Transitos y Transportes Integrales SL* [2003] Q.B. 1270 where the Court of Appeal held intermediate bailees could claim the protection of the CMR convention reviewed at 2.3.

Secondly, there is the so-called Himalaya clause,[64] pursuant to which a succeeding carrier may rely on the contractual conditions of any prior carrier regulating the bailment of the goods to that prior carrier, to regulate the terms of the sub-bailment of the goods to itself.[65] As discussed in 1.6.1.2 below, similar protection to the Himalaya clause may now be available to sub-contractors by the operation of the Contracts (Rights of Third Parties) Act 1999 to the extent applicable and not excluded.

1.6.1.2 Contract

By agreeing to undertake the carriage of goods, the carrier accepts an absolute contractual obligation to carry the goods to the destination. In consequence of that undertaking circumscribing the terms of the bailment, a carrier has a strict duty not to deviate from the journey which the carrier has contracted to perform. By reason of s.13 of the Supply of Goods and Services Act 1982 the absolute contractual obligation to carry, being a contract for the performance of carriage services, is subject to an implied term that the carrier will exercise reasonable skill and care in the performance of that absolute carriage obligation. The implied term is relative to the carriage being performed, so a higher standard is to be expected of specialist carriers of high value cargo than of general carriers of low value cargo.

Contractual duties are owed primarily to those with whom the carrier has a contractual relationship under the doctrine of privity of contract, but contractual duties can arise outside those classic contractual relationships. The Contracts (Rights of Third Parties) Act 1999 made substantial inroads into this principle by enabling third parties to enforce contractual provisions in their own names, where the contract permits them to do so, by an express term to that effect, or by expressly conferring a benefit on them. In

[64] Being a clause fulfilling the requirements described by Lord Reid in *Scruttons Ltd v Midland Silicones Ltd* [1961] 2 Lloyd's Rep. 365 for the protection of stevedores by contractual terms contained in bills of lading (i.e. the bill of lading must specify that the stevedore is intended to be protected by the provisions limiting liability and make it clear that the carrier contracted for those provisions for himself and as agent of the stevedore; the carrier must be authorised, if necessary by subsequent ratification, by the stevedore to so contract and sufficient consideration must have moved from the stevedore to the goods owner).

[65] The effect of the Himalaya clause was considered in the context of sub-bailment on terms in *The Mahkutai* [1996] 2 Lloyd's Rep.1 where it was held that the protection extended by the prior carrier's exclusion and limitation of liability did not extend to mutual obligations such as jurisdiction clauses.

both cases, the third party's right of enforcement would depend on it being expressly identified in the contract by name, class or description. A third party will not be able to claim any benefit under the Act if a true construction of the contract indicates that the contracting parties did not intend the third party to have a personal right to enforce such a benefit. In the case of carriage, the impact of the Act is severely constrained. Whilst the Act generally applies to carriage contracts, its effect is excluded in the case of contracts for (a) carriage of goods by sea and (b) carriage of goods by rail, road, or air subject to the applicable international transport conventions (i.e. CMR, CIM, Montreal and Warsaw). However, a third party may in reliance on the Act avail itself of an exclusion or limitation of liability in such a contract.[66]

This is significant for those employees and sub-contractors responsible for the performance of all, or any part of the carriage, or for any services incidental to the carriage, as it enables them to rely upon exclusions and limitations contained in the contract of carriage in relation to any claim that may be made against them by cargo interests. Where such sub-contractors or employees cause any loss, damage or delay to the goods they will be exposed to claims arising in tort for negligence (as against anyone having a possessory or proprietary right to the goods at the time of the damage)[67]; or in bailment (as against anyone to whom the goods should be released by those sub-contractors and employees).[68] Of course, where the owner of the goods is not a party to the contract of carriage, the principal contracting carrier may also be exposed (in the event of loss, damage or delay to the goods carried) to such claims in tort for negligence and in bailment on a similar basis and should seek in its contract to protect itself from such exposure by having its customers warrant that they are entering the contract not only on their own behalf but also as authorised agents on behalf of the owner of the goods.[69]

Contractual terms for international contracts of carriage (and also domestic contracts for the carriage of goods by air) which conflict with the statutory terms provided by applicable mandatory regulation will be displaced; but such mandatory regulation takes effect within the context of the

[66] Section 6(5)(a) Contracts (Third Party Rights) Act 1999.

[67] *Leigh & Sillivan v Aliakmon Shipping Co* [1986] A.C. 785 (*The Aliakmon*).

[68] In *The Pioneer Container* [1994] 2 A.C. 324 the Privy Council referred at p.339 to the effect of a sub-bailment being that the sub-bailee "assumes towards the owner the responsibility of a bailee".

[69] Such a term can be found in all of the standard carriage terms reviewed in Parts Two to Five.

governing law of the contract. There are "strong considerations of commercial sense in favour of an interpretation which recognises and gives effect to the underlying contractual structure"[70] whenever these statutory terms are being applied to determine disputes under particular contracts. Any such contract will be governed by an applicable law, which will be selected according to the private international law rules of the forum in which the dispute is to be determined. Accordingly, the application of rules of private international law to select the place (the forum) in which the court or tribunal determining the dispute is to be situated is likely to be the crucial first step to resolving any such dispute.

The use of the Himalaya clause referred to in 1.6.1.1, expressing the apparent intention of the contracting parties that the employees, agents and independent sub-contractors of the carrier should have the benefit of contractual limitations and exclusions, resulted in consideration being given to the possible formation of contractual relationships between the sub-contractors of the carrier (being the persons actually performing some of the the carrier's obligations) and the consignor, or other contracting party (being the intended recipient of the contractual services). Concerns over the necessity in such arrangements for consideration to be exchanged between the contracting parties to satisfy the formation requirements of English contract law were initially resolved by the Privy Council in the *Eurymedon*[71], on the basis that a unilateral offer had been made by the goods' owner that could be accepted by stevedores in the actual discharge of the vessel. This resolution was then placed on a rather more secure legal platform by the House of Lords in the *Starsin*, on the basis that the contract was concluded not by an exchange of promises, but by the exchange of performances.[72] This contractual exchange of performances is sometimes called "the Barwick contract" after the Australian judge who first adopted the argument. However, to date the principle of the Barwick contract has been confined to extending the benefit of exception and limitation clauses and has not

[70] Per Mance L.J. (as he then was) at para.81 of his judgment in *Western Digital Corporation v British Airways Plc* [2000] 2 Lloyd's Rep. 142, 161 in addressing the rights of claimants to sue for causes of action in tort and bailment under contracts governed by the Warsaw Convention for the carriage of goods by air.

[71] *The Eurymedon* [1975] AC 154.

[72] *The Starsin* [2003] 1 Lloyd's Rep. 571 on the basis that the goods owner, acting via the carrier, provides consideration by presenting his goods for carriage, or discharge, on the basis of the bill of lading; whilst the sub-contractor provides consideration in return by carrying, or discharging, the goods on the basis of the bill of lading.

been applied to clauses having the character of a mutual bargain such as an agreement as to jurisdiction.[73] Although, in *Sandeman Coprimar SA v Transitos y Transportes Integrales SL*,[74] the Court of Appeal was content to apply the principle to the entirety of the provisions of the CMR convention which do contain jurisdictional provisions.[75]

The conceptual problems inherent in goods being consigned by one person who contracts with the carrier to another person who intends to take the benefit of the carriage contract but does not contract with the carrier were previously addressed by an implied contractual arrangement (often considered a legal fiction, but now being re-evaluated in the context of the Barwick contract referred to above) which originated from the decision in *Brandt v Liverpool, Brazil and Riverplate SN Co Ltd*.[76] In the *Brandt v Liverpool* case, bankers to whom the bills of lading had been pledged to secure a loan advance took delivery of the cargo in a damaged condition at the discharge port. The court held that a contract could be implied as between the carrier and the receiver of the goods from the acts of presenting the bills of lading and the delivery and acceptance of the goods specified in the bills. Subsequent cases confined the principle to cases of delivery where the receiver either pays the carrier outstanding freight, or provides the carrier with an unusual degree of assistance to facilitate the discharge operation. To imply a *Brandt* type contract the courts must consider that to be necessary, by reason of business efficacy, to give effect to the parties' intentions.[77] Furthermore, where goods are consigned in the contemplation that ownership might pass during the carriage, the consignor may claim for the loss or damage to the goods suffered by the consignee.[78]

The Carriage of Goods by Sea Act 1992 addresses similar such issues in the context of sea carriage as discussed at 3.1.7.1.

[73] See *The Mahkutai* [1996] 2 Lloyd's Rep. 1.

[74] [2003] Q.B. 1270.

[75] See para.63 of Lord Wright's judgment in *Sandeman Coprimar SA* ibid.

[76] [1924] 1 KB 575.

[77] See *The Elli* 2 [1985] 1 Lloyd's Rep. 107 where the court considered that whether it was necessary was a question of fact and that, as per May L.J., "... no such contract should be implied on the facts of any given case unless it is necessary to do so; necessary that is to say, in order to give business reality to a transaction and to create enforceable obligations between parties who are dealing with one another in circumstances in which one would expect that business reality and those enforceable obligations to exist".

[78] *Dunlop v Lambert* (1839) 6 Cl & F 600.

1.6.1.3 Tort

The carrier owes a duty of care in tort to exercise reasonable care to safeguard the goods and the carrier is susceptible to incurring liability in negligence.[79] The onus of proving negligence on the part of the carrier rests with the party making the allegation.[80] However, it has been clearly established in a series of cases that, where goods handed to a carrier in good condition have arrived damaged, the situation is one of res ipsa loquitur (the facts speak for themselves). In these circumstances, once damage has been proved, it is for the carrier to prove that the goods were not damaged as a result of negligence, but for some other reason.[81] It is clear that an employer is vicariously liable for any wrongdoing, including deliberate wrongdoing such as theft, committed by its employees in breach of their employment contract, where such wrongdoing has been committed within the general scope of the employees' duties.[82] A claim for the loss of or damage to goods in tort can only be brought in tort at the suit of the person who was the owner or was entitled to the immediate possession of the goods at the time the cause of action arose (i.e. when the damage could be seen to have occurred).[83] Carriers may also incur liability in tort by reason of deceit, or negligent misstatement, by their employees (over such matters as false statements in carriage documentation) towards those affected by the deceit, or those who ought reasonably to have been in the carrier's contemplation as likely to have been affected by any negligent misstatement.[84] The carrier may limit or exclude liability for negligence by an express term in the contract of carriage subject to the operation of principles of contractual interpretation.[85]

79 *Whalley v Wray* (1799) 3 Esp. 74.

80 ibid.

81 *Joseph Travers and Sons Ltd v Cooper* [1915] 1 K.B. 73.

82 *Lister v Hesley Hall Ltd* [2002] 1 A.C. 215 where the managers of a boarding home were held liable for personal injuries resulting from sexual abuse committed without their knowledge by the warden they had employed. The House of Lords decided the abusive misconduct was so closely connected with the tortfeasor's wrongdoing that such vicarious liability was fair and just.

83 As determined by House of Lords in *The Aliakmon* [1986] AC 789.

84 See *Standard Chartered Bank v Pakistan National Shipping Corporation* [2003] 1 Lloyd's Rep. 227, where a sea carrier incurred such liability, by reason of misstatement on the bill of lading as to the date of shipment.

85 See 1.5.2 above.

1.6.1.4 Agency[86]

Contracts of carriage do not necessarily create relationships of agency, but such relationships do frequently arise in the context of carriage. Carriers may be engaged by freight forwarders, acting as agents on behalf of cargo owners who, as the principals for whom those freight forwarders are acting, may be the contracting parties to the contract of carriage.[87] Carriers, particularly carriers by sea, frequently contract by agents. In such cases, determining on whose behalf the agent is acting, or is deemed to be acting, may determine the identity of the carrier.[88] If something untoward happens in the course of the carriage, carriers may be obliged to act as agents of necessity on behalf of the cargo owners in protecting, preserving or even disposing of the goods.[89] For an agency of necessity to arise it must be impracticable for the principal to be contacted, the steps taken must be for the benefit of the principal and the agent must be acting bona fide in the principal's interests.[90] In the context of carriage by sea, relationships of agency arise between the master and owner of the vessel[91] and, particularly in the context of time and demise charterparties, between the master and charterer[92] of the vessel. Agents are frequently appointed by carrier and/or cargo interests at load and discharge ports. Similar agency relationships can arise in the context of carriage by other modes, particularly carriage by air at airports of departure, destination and landing. For these reasons, some understanding of agency is essential to an understanding of contracts of carriage.

An agent's authority may be actual or apparent. Actual authority is the authority expressly or implicitly agreed between the principal and the agent. Express actual authority will, by implication, extend to doing anything ordinarily or necessarily incidental to that express authority, including anything usually done by such agents with such authority; such usual

[86] For a detailed authoritative guide to the complexities of agency see *Bowstead and Reynolds on Agency*, 18th edn (London: Sweet & Maxwell, 2009).

[87] See 5.2.2.

[88] *The Starsin* [2003] 1 Lloyd's Rep. 571.

[89] *Australasian SN Company v Morse* (1871–73) L.R. 4 P.C. 222 where the agency of necessity extended to the sale of the goods.

[90] *Prager v Blatspiel, Stamp and Heacock Ltd* 1924 1 K.B. 566.

[91] *The Unique Mariner* [1978] 1 Lloyd's Rep. 438 as to the ostensible authority of a master to sign a salvage agreement.

[92] Under which a master employed by the shipowner may be expressly empowered to issue bills of lading on behalf of charterers.

authority is generally referred to as ostensible authority and should be distinguished from further apparent authority. Apparent authority arises by reason of some express or implied representation by the principal that the agent is invested with authority beyond both its actual express and implied ostensible authority, which representation may, where it is relied upon by some third party to its detriment, give rise to an estoppel. Subsequent ratification by a principal of acts undertaken by the agent purportedly on its behalf, but outside the scope of the agent's actual authority, is permissible at any time; save, apparently, where it would operate so as to cause unfair prejudice to the third party with whom the agent had contracted, ostensibly on the principal's behalf.[93] Whilst conceptually distinct, both apparent and ostensible authority constitute the extent of the authority as it appears to others and, by virtue of an agent's ostensible or apparent authority, a principal may become bound to contracts entered into by the agent purportedly on behalf of the principal, but outside the scope of the express authority given by the principal to the agent.[94]

An agent may contract on behalf of a principal whose existence is not disclosed at the time of contracting. However, the agent must, at the time of contracting, be authorised by the undisclosed principal to act on its behalf since, unlike disclosed principals, an undisclosed principal cannot subsequently ratify acts alleged to have been taken on its behalf. The general nature of an agency relationship is that no rights or duties arise as between agent and third party where the agent acts within the principal's authority.[95] However, where the principal is undisclosed, the third party and the agent may each enforce the contract against the other, subject to the independent rights of both the undisclosed principal and the third party to enforce the contract against each other instead.[96]

An agent has a duty to be obedient to its principal's instructions, insofar as they may be reasonably understood rather than as intended and must

[93] *The Borvigilant* [2003] 2 Lloyd's Rep. 520, para.70 of Clarke L.J. judgment.

[94] See *The Unique Mariner* (fn. 91) in which the court held that the doctrine of ostensible authority, as well as that of apparent authority, effectively operates as an estoppel with an implied, or express, representation by the principal that it has invested the agent with authority. In consequence, third parties can only take advantage of apparent or ostensible authority where they have acted in reliance upon that representation to their own detriment.

[95] Although, of course, where the agent exceeds its authority it may incur liability to the third party for breach of warranty of authority.

[96] However, by proceeding against either undisclosed principal or agent the third party may lose its rights against the other (see art.84 of *Bowstead and Reynolds on Agency* (fn. 86).

exercise a degree of care appropriate to the duties to be undertaken. The relationship of agency may also be subject to certain loyalty obligations in the nature of fiduciary duties which oblige the fiduciary agent to act in good faith, not to make a undisclosed profit and not to permit any conflict between its own interest and its duty to its principal.[97] It is submitted that, whilst some of the various agency relationships arising in connection with contracts of carriage may give rise to such a fiduciary relationship (importing these central obligations of loyalty), more frequently they will not, because a fiduciary has been narrowly defined as "someone who has undertaken to act for or on behalf of another in a particular matter in circumstances which give rise to a relationship of trust and confidence".[98]

1.6.2 The Carrier's Duties at Common Law

1.6.2.1 As Carrier

The carrier is not necessarily liable as a carrier during the whole of the time during which the goods are in its possession under a contract of carriage. In the absence of any express term in the contract, the duty of the carrier is to use all reasonable care to deliver the goods within a reasonable time.[99] What is a reasonable time is a question of fact. The carrier is bound to carry the goods by the usual route between the points of loading and unloading; there may be more than one usual route, in which case the carrier has the choice as to which usual route is taken.[100] The carrier has no obligation to carry the goods by the shortest route.[101] However, the carrier is obliged to carry the goods in the usual way, such that a sea carrier cannot take a vessel on tow, or carry goods on deck, which should, expressly or by implication, be carried under deck.[102]

At common law the duty to load, stow and unload the cargo appears to lie on the carrier, but it is clear that by agreement it may be transferred to cargo interests.[103] Even when the cargo loading and stowage obligations

[97] *Bristol and West Building Society v Mothew* [1998] Ch.1.

[98] ibid. Millet L.J. at p.18.

[99] *Raphael v Pickford* (1843) 5 Man. & G. 551.

[100] *Davis v Garrett* (1830) 6 Bing. 716; *Indian City* [1939] A.C. 562.

[101] *Hales v London and North-Western Railway Company* (1863) 4 B. & S. 66.

[102] *Scaramanga v Stamp* (1880) 5 C.P.D. 295.

[103] See para.11 of the judgment of Lord Steyn in *Jindal Iron and Steel Co Ltd v Islamic Solidarity Shipping Co Jordan Inc* [2005] 1 W.L.R. 1363 in context of loading, stowage and discharging obligations under a voyage charterparty.

have been transferred to cargo interests, the carrier retains a right at common law (and generally also a statutory duty) to ensure the vehicle, vessel, or aircraft remain, as the case may be, roadworthy, railworthy, seaworthy or airworthy for the contemplated carriage.[104] Where there has been such a contractual transfer, the party to whom the obligation to load and/or stow has been transferred cannot hold the carrier liable for want of roadworthiness, railworthiness, seaworthiness or airworthiness by reason of its own breach.[105] Indeed, that party may be obliged to indemnify the carrier where liabilities are incurred to third parties by reason of any breach of their loading, stowage and unloading obligations.[106] It is clear beyond doubt that generally a sea carrier has an implied contractual duty to ensure the seaworthiness of the vessel provided for the carriage; but the extent to which statutory duties as to roadworthiness, railworthiness and airworthiness are applicable to contractual duties without express contractual provision being made to that effect is less certain and these issues will be explored further in 5.3.

The carrier's liability as a carrier extends only for the duration of the carriage. If the carrier is in possession of the goods before the beginning, or after the end, of the carriage, the goods are then held not as a carrier, but as a warehouseman, and the carrier is liable accordingly.[107] This distinction had a particular resonance in the nineteenth century when carriers were often held to have the status of common carriers, since the particular strict liabilities carriers were exposed to as common carriers ceased when the carriage ended and they became mere warehousemen. Even in the twenty-

[104] *Court Line Ltd v Canadian Transport Co Ltd* [1940] A.C. 934 where Lord Akin was clear that contractual rights to the same effect in a charterparty simply restated a right which "would have existed even if not expressly reserved" as regards carriage by sea.

[105] *Compania Sud American Vapores v MS ER Hamburg Schiffahrtsgesellschaft MBH & Co* KG Q.B.D. [2006] 2 Lloyd's Rep. 66 in which Morison J. quoted with approval at pp.71 and 72 the succinct observation, again in connection with carriage by sea, of Langely J. in *The Imvros* [1999] 1 Lloyd's Rep. 848 that "It would be a remarkable construction which produced the effect that so long as the loading was carried out by the charterers badly enough to put the other cargo, but not the vessel at risk the charterers would be liable and the owners would not but the moment the loading was so badly carried out that it made the vessel itself unseaworthy the entire responsibility fell upon the owners and the charterers were relieved of it".

[106] See Lord Wright's dictum to that effect in *Court Line* (fn. 104), at pp.943–45, and the Civil Liability (Contribution) Act 1978 discussed at 1.8.1 below.

[107] *Chapman v Great Western Railway Company and London and North-Western Railway Company* (1880) 5 Q.B.D. 278, 281, per Cockburn C.J.

first century the distinction is not without importance as, when the carriage ends, the contractual or statutory basis under which the carrier is holding the goods may vary.[108]

1.6.2.2 As Warehouseman

The liability of a warehouseman is that of a bailee. However, if the carrier remains in possession of the goods after the end of the carriage only because of the failure of the consignee to take delivery within a reasonable time, the carrier's duty as warehouseman is that of an involuntary bailee. The extent of the liability of an involuntary bailee has not been clearly determined. Indeed there is an inherent contradiction in the concept of "involuntary bailment" as the fundamental basis of bailment is that of voluntary assumption of responsibility. Nevertheless, various cases refer to involuntary bailment and it is best considered as a distinct principle that applies in different ways to the various types of involuntary bailment. However, the basic obligation on an involuntary bailee appears to be one of reasonable care. The onus remains on the involuntary, or gratuitous, bailee to prove the discharge of that duty by the exercise of an appropriate degree of care relative to the circumstances. Accordingly, precisely what degree of care can reasonably be said to have been expected from an involuntary bailee in any given situation remains uncertain and will vary according to the circumstances of the loss.

There is no authority as to the extent of the liability of the carrier where the contract excludes that liability in terms which can be referred only to the duration of the carriage, but the carrier remains in possession of the goods after the termination of the carriage as an involuntary bailee. It seems inappropriate that the carrier should be placed in a more onerous position than during the period of the carriage, simply through the wrongful failure of the consignee to take delivery of the goods. Nevertheless, the carrier's contractual exclusions and limitations should be expressly drawn to cover not only the period of the carriage, but also any period of gratutious bailment.

[108] For instance, the Hague-Visby Rules considered in 3.3.2 cease to apply after the discharge of the goods.

1.6.2.3 Where there are Multiple Carriers

In the absence of any agreement to the contrary, the duty of the carrier is to deliver the goods to the consignee. If the carrier delivers goods to another carrier to complete the carriage, the first carrier has not discharged the duty of delivering the goods to the consignee. Consequently, the contracting carrier remains liable for any misdelivery by the second carrier (or for any other loss or damage to the goods while in the possession of the second carrier) to the same extent as if the contracting carrier were still carrying the goods,[109] for the carrier cannot be absolved of liability by performing the contract of carriage through the means of an agent. If it is a term of the contract of carriage that the goods will be carried throughout the journey in the vehicles of the carrier, the carrier commits a breach of contract by delivering the goods to the second carrier and that would amount to a deviation from the terms on which the goods had been bailed to the carrier. In carriage by land, unlike carriage by sea, it appears that such a term in the contract cannot ordinarily be implied into the carriage contract.

If, however, the consignor has expressly or implicitly authorised the carrier to deliver the goods to a second carrier to complete the carriage, the duty of the first carrier is not to deliver the goods to the consignee but merely to deliver them to the second carrier.[110] In this case, the first carrier will have discharged its duty by delivering the goods to the second carrier, and will not be liable for misdelivery by the second carrier, or for any loss or damage to the goods whilst they are in the possession of the second carrier. It is in every case a question of fact whether it is a term of the contract of carriage that the carrier may discharge its liabilities by delivering the goods to another carrier,[111] and the onus of proving this rests on the carrier.

1.6.2.4 Termination of the Carriage

The duration of the carriage is not limited to the time during which the goods are being transported on the journey. Except where it is expressly or implicitly agreed that the carrier shall hold the goods as a warehouseman for a period before the beginning of the carriage, the carriage is deemed to

[109] *Hyde v Trent and Mersey Navigation Company* (1793) 5 T.R. 389; *Muschamp v Lancaster and Preston Junction Railway Company* (1841) 8 M. & W. 421.

[110] ibid.

[111] ibid.

begin and the carrier to be in possession of the goods as a carrier, as soon as the goods are delivered to the carrier for carriage at its receiving office, or other place.[112] This only applies if the carrier has expressly or implicitly accepted delivery of the goods. If the goods are accepted by a third party, or even by a servant of the carrier acting without express or implied authority from the carrier, the goods are deemed never to have been delivered to the carrier at all (unless, of course, the carrier has held out such person or servant as having authority to accept the goods).[113]

The carriage is not terminated until the carrier has taken all reasonable steps to deliver the goods to the consignee. It is in every case a question of fact, dependent on the provisions of the contract and on the custom of the trade, whether the carrier is bound to deliver the goods to the consignee at the consignee's address, or whether the consignee is to call for the goods at the carrier's office at the place of destination, discharge or landing.[114] If the carrier has undertaken to deliver the goods to the consignee's address, the carriage continues until the carrier arrives at this address with the goods, and tenders delivery of them to the consignee at a reasonable hour. If the hour is, in the light of all the relevant circumstances, unreasonable, the consignee is not bound to accept delivery. In such a case the carrier is not deemed to have properly tendered delivery of the goods and is still liable as a carrier.[115] If the consignee unjustifiably refuses to accept delivery of the goods, or if there is no one at the consignee's address to do so when the carrier offers to deliver them at a reasonable hour, the carriage is at an end; in this case, the carrier is under a duty to retain possession of the goods as a warehouseman, even when carrying the goods from the consignee's address back to his office, and back again to the consignee's address in a further attempt to deliver the goods. If the carrier is entitled to retain possession of the goods following the termination of the carriage (where, for example, the consignee refuses to pay freight at the time of delivery and the carrier consequently exercises any effective lien over the goods for the unpaid freight as discussed in 1.9.1.2 below), the fact that the carrier does retain possession will not prevent the carriage being at an end.

[112] As for example, in *Colepepper v Good* (1832) 5 C. & P. 380, an inn.

[113] Compare *Harrisons and Crossfield Ltd v London and North-Western Railway Company* [1917] 2 K.B. 755 (carrier not liable for fraudulent acceptance of goods by servants) and *Jenkyns v Southampton Steam Packet Company* [1919] 2 K.B. 135 (carrier liable for fraudulent acceptance of goods by servants).

[114] *Golden v Manning* (1773) 2 Wm. Bl. 916.

[115] *Chapman v Great Western Railway Company and London and North-Western Railway Company* (1880) 5 Q.B.D. 278, 281, per Cockburn C.J.

Where a seller of goods exercises a right of stoppage in transit (as discussed in 1.9.2 below), the carriage ends when the carrier re-delivers the goods to the seller; or delivers them as otherwise directed by the seller. If the seller fails thereafter to give reasonable directions to the carrier with regard to the disposal of the goods, the carriage is at an end, and the carrier apparently is no longer under any liability to take care of the goods[116] save, presumably as an involuntary bailee.

1.6.3 The Customer's Duties at Common Law

The customer, whether acting by itself, via the consignor or via the consignee, is responsible for the performance of various obligations owed to the carrier including those of: making the goods available to the carrier for carriage at the appointed time in a state of readiness for carriage; ensuring that any description provided to the carrier as to the goods is accurate; and undertaking whatever performances are required from it in the circumstances of any particular carriage as to the handing over of the goods to the carrier, the loading and stowage of the goods, the unloading of the goods and the taking of delivery of the goods from, the carrier.[117] The customer is obliged to pay the carriage charges commonly called freight as well as any further sums due under the contract of carriage.

1.7 Incidents of Breach of the Contract

1.7.1 Carrier's Breach at Common Law

1.7.1.1 Loss or Damage to Goods Carried

Whether common law claims against the carrier for the loss of or damage to goods carried are made in bailment, contract or in tort, the carrier is entitled to resist such claims where the loss or damage occurred notwithstanding the exercise by the carrier of reasonable care to safeguard the goods. Opposite those entitled to possession of the goods from the carrier, the carrier has responsibility not only for the negligence, but also the wilful

[116] *Booth Steamship Company v Cargo Fleet Iron Company* [1916] 2 K.B. 570, 601.

[117] The position in respect of sea carriage under the common law as to loading and discharging operations is usefully discussed by Lord Esher M.R. in *Petersen v Freebody & Co* [1895] 2 Q.B. 294 and *Aktieselkab Helios v Ekman & Co* [1897] 2 Q.B. 83 and by Lord Diplock (in connection with voyage charters) in *The Johanna Oldendorff* [1973] 2 Lloyd's Rep. 285.

default, of those entrusted with the safekeeping of the goods.[118] Carriers generally seek to limit or exclude their liability for loss of, or damage to, goods carried by including appropriate express terms in the contract of carriage as they are entitled to do, subject to effective incorporation and the operation of mandatory regulation by the statutory terms arising under the CMR, CIM, Hague-Visby, Montreal and Warsaw instruments reviewed at Parts Two, Three and Four and, more generally, the Unfair Contract Terms Act 1977 (UCTA)[119] and, in consumer contracts, the Unfair Terms Consumer Contract Regulations 1999 SI 1999/2083 (UTCCR).[120]

1.7.1.2 Misdelivery of Goods Carried

At common law, the duty of the carrier is to deliver the goods to the consignee; if they are delivered to any other person the carrier is liable for misdelivery. Misdelivery of goods by a carrier probably amounts not only to a breach of contract, but also to a tortious conversion of the goods.[121] Where the duty of the carrier is to deliver the goods to the address of the consignee, the carrier is liable for misdelivery if they are delivered anywhere else.[122] If the carrier delivers the goods to the consignee's address, the duty to deliver has been performed, and the carrier is not liable for misdelivery if the person who takes delivery of the goods at the consignee's address is not authorised to do so by the consignee. If the consignee unjustifiably refuses, or for any other reason fails to take delivery at its premises, when the carrier has offered to deliver the goods there at a reasonable hour, the carrier is no

[118] See *Morris v C W Martin & Sons Ltd*[1966] 1 Q.B. 716 where the Court of Appeal held that duties in bailment are non-delegable; reflecting the status of contractual duties absent any novation.

[119] UCTA applies to all contracts for the carriage of goods excepting carriage by sea and imposes a requirement of reasonableness by s.2(2) on all exclusions or limitations of liability arising in negligence and by s.3, where one party contracts on the basis of its own standard terms, on all other exclusions and limitations of liability contained in such standard terms rendering void any such terms which do not satisfy the reasonableness requirement.

[120] UTCCR derive from the Unfair Terms in Consumer Contracts Directive 1993 (D93/13/EC) and renders void any "unfair term" causing a significant imbalance in the parties' rights and duties to the detriment of a consumer.

[121] *Heugh v London and North-Western Railway Company* (1870) L.R. 5 Ex 51; *Hollins v Fowler* (1874) L.R. 7 H.L. 757.

[122] *Heugh v London and North-Western Railway Company. Stephenson v Hart* (1828) 4 Bing. 476, was decided before the law as to misdelivery was clearly settled, but it is a good example of a case in which a carrier holding goods as a warehouseman was guilty of negligence in delivering the goods to the wrong consignee.

longer under an absolute duty to deliver the goods to the consignee having discharged its contractual duty. However, the carrier remains in possession of the goods as a warehouseman, and is liable only for negligence (i.e. the carrier is liable for misdelivery only if it was negligent in delivering the goods to the wrong person).[123] Whether or not the carrier was negligent is a question of fact.

Where, owing to a fraud, the carrier is instructed to deliver the goods to a fictitious consignee, and the carrier delivers the goods at the stated address to a rogue who falsely claims to be the fictitious consignee, there is no question of misdelivery at all, for the carrier delivered the goods to the address as instructed, and the carrier is not liable.[124] There is no direct authority for the extent of the carrier's liability for misdelivery where it is the carrier's duty to deliver the goods to the consignee at the carrier's office. If the consignee does not take delivery of the goods at the carrier's office within a reasonable time, the carrier is no doubt liable, as a warehouseman, only for negligence. If, before a reasonable time has elapsed, some person other than the consignee takes delivery of the goods, it is not certain whether the carrier is liable in the absence of negligence. The issue may turn on whether, in the particular facts of any case, the carrier has agreed to deliver to a particular person at a particular place or just to a particular place for collection, as in the latter circumstances the carrier would probably not be liable.

The carrier may limit or exclude its liability for misdelivery by an express term in the contract of carriage, provided that the limitation unambiguously extends to cover misdelivery, for such a term (although still subject to the above-referenced mandatory regulation) is apparently not void as being repugnant to the fundamental purpose of the contract.[125] However, very clear words indeed would be necessary to exclude liability for failing to deliver against any bill of lading issued for the subject carriage.[126]

[123] The situation is otherwise where the carrier is obliged to deliver against a bill of lading as discussed in 3.2.3.4.

[124] *McKean v McIvor* (1870) L.R. 6 Ex. 36.

[125] *Hollins v J. Davy Ltd* [1963] 1 Q.B. 844 and Hunt and *Winterbotham v British Railways Services (Parcels) Ltd* [1962] 1 Q.B. 617; but note to the contrary *Alexander v Railways Executive* [1951] 2 K.B. 882.

[126] *Trafigura Beheer BV v Mediterranean Shipping Co SA* [2007] 2 Lloyd's Rep. 622 discussed in 3.2.3.4.

1.7.1.3 Delay to Goods Carried

In the absence of any express term in the contract, the duty of the carrier is to use all reasonable care to deliver the goods within a reasonable time.[127] What is a reasonable time is a question of fact. In order to render a carrier liable for damages for delay the plaintiff must establish that the carrier failed to deliver the goods within a reasonable time, and that this was due to the carrier's negligence.[128] If the delay is due, wholly or in part, to the fact that the carrier has deviated from the route, negligence need not be proved and the carrier's liability will be attributable to the deviation, as discussed below, that has caused the delay. It is, of course, open to the parties to agree, by an express provision in the contract, that the carrier will deliver the goods by a given date or time, and if the carrier fails to do so it is liable for breach of that absolute contractual obligation.[129]

1.7.1.4 Deviation in Carriage

If the carrier leaves the route which was expressly or implicitly agreed, the carrier is said to deviate. The carrier also deviates if it goes past the destination,[130] or takes a vessel in tow in the carriage of goods by sea.[131] There is virtually no authority as to when a carrier by land is entitled to depart from the route without performing a deviation. A carrier by sea is entitled to depart from the route in order to avoid imminent peril, or to save life or the property carried and, presumably, a carrier by land is entitled to do so for the same reasons. A departure from the route in order to save life is unlikely to arise in the carriage of goods by land; but a carrier by land is probably entitled to depart from the route in order to avoid travelling through a district which is rendered unsafe by war, civil war, riot or flood, thereby protecting the property carried.

127 *Raphael v Pickford* (1843) 5 Man. & G. 551.

128 *Hales v London and North-Western Railway Company* (1863) 4 B. & S. 66; *Taylor v Great Northern Railway Company* (1866) L.R. 1 C.P. 385.

129 *Hadley v Baxendale* (1854) 9 Ex. 341 is a good example of an agreed delivery period since in that case the carrier had agreed, and failed, to deliver the broken shaft "on the second day after" receipt.

130 *Cunard Steamship Company v Buerger* [1927] A.C. 1, 13, per Lord Parmoor.

131 *Scaramanga v Stamp* (1880) 5 C.P.D. 295.

The traditional view is that if the carrier deviates, the action amounts to a repudiation of the contract by the carrier.[132] As all the terms of the contract of carriage have been repudiated along with the contract itself, the carrier cannot rely on any of the terms in the contract which limit its common law liability. Moreover, as the carrier is not in possession of the goods under any contract, it is deemed to be a wrongful possessor of the goods, and is consequently under an even heavier liability than that of the common carrier at common law. These principles are thrown into some doubt by the 1980 decision of the House of Lords in *Photo Productions v Securicor.*[133] In that case the House of Lords held that a fundamental contractual breach did not disentitle the guilty party from claiming the protection of the contractual exclusions and limitations contained in the contract, notwithstanding the termination of the contract by reason of acceptance of the guilty party's fundamental breach as a repudiation of the contract. Whether the concept of deviation as being a fundamental breach of a carriage contract primarily derives from contract law or bailment,[134] modern judicial dicta suggest the concept should be embraced within current contractual principles so that express contractual exclusion and limitation clauses (restrained only by normal principles of contractual construction) may survive contractual repudiation notwithstanding deviation.[135]

However, it currently remains the case that a carrier who has agreed to carry goods by sea may lose the benefit of exclusion and limitation clauses where they deviate unlawfully from the intended voyage. At common law a carrier by sea who has deviated is liable for all loss or damage to the goods

[132] *London and North-Western Railway Company v Neilson* [1922] 2 A.C. 263; affirming *Mallet v Great Eastern Railway Company* [1899] 1 Q.B. 309, and overruling *Foster v Great Western Railway Company* [1904] 2 K.B. 306. *Hain v Tate and Lyle* (1936) 55 Ll. L. Rep. 159 and *Stag Line v Foscolo, Mango and Co* [1932] A.C. 328.

[133] [1980] A.C. 367; a security guard employed to make four vists a night to guarded premises deliberately set them alight. His employers successfully claimed the benefit of clauses both excluding their liability entirely, except where they themselves had failed to exercise due diligence, and limiting their liability in the event of any such failure on their part.

[134] See Christopher M.C. Cashmore, "The legal nature of the doctrine of deviation" [1989] JBL 1989 Nov 492–496.

[135] *Kenya Railways v Antares Co Pte Ltd (The Antares) (Nos 1 and 2)* [1987] 1 Lloyd's Rep. 424 where Lloyd L.J., in declining to equate deviation by carriage on deck with "deviation cases strictly so-called" expressed the view that they should be "assimilated into the ordinary law of contract" as had previously been advocated by Lord Wilberforce in *Suisse Atlantique Société d'Armement Maritime SA v Rotterdamsche Kolen Centrale* [1966] 1 Lloyd's Rep. 529.

unless it can be proved that the loss or damage were caused by either an act of God or the Queen's enemies, or by the fault of the owner or consignor, or by the inherent vice of the goods; and, furthermore, that the damage so caused would also have occurred even if the carrier had not deviated.[136] Deviation amounted likewise to a repudiation of the contract, and the carrier who has deviated is in wrongful possession of the goods by having strayed from the terms of the bailment. It had previously been held that deviation repudiated the contract of carriage ab initio, not only from the moment when the deviation occurs.[137] It is difficult to see how such an approach is consistent with contractual repudiatory breach as it is now understood, which discharges the parties from their future obligations only when the guilty party is advised, by the innocent party, of the acceptance of the fundamental breach as a repudiation of the contract.[138]

In any case a carrier who has deviated is apparently entitled to a reasonable sum as freight.[139] This may or may not be the sum which was agreed as freight in the repudiated contract and this issue may turn on whether or not freight is deemed due and owing on shipment. A carrier who deviates will obviously be liable in damages for loss caused by the breach of contract, whether such damages are attributable to delay or some other consequence of the deviation. Carriers frequently stipulate in their standard form conditions, or expressly agree by special express terms, that the carrier may deviate, either generally or for agreed reasons. In this case, the carrier incurs no liability by the deviation, and as the deviation is permitted in the contract, there has been no breach and no repudiation of the contract by the carrier. Such stipulations are commonly called "liberty clauses" as they give the carrier liberty to deviate; but such stipulations are subjected to a narrow restrictive interpretation by the courts, and printed clauses may be set aside if they are thought to defeat the main purpose of the contract of carriage.[140]

[136] See *Morrison v Shaw, Savill and Company* [1916] 2 K.B. 783.

[137] *Internationale Guano v Macandrew and Company* [1909] 2 K.B. 360.

[138] See *Hongkong Fir Shipping Co Ltd v Kawasaki Kisen Kaisha Ltd* [1961] 2 Lloyd's Rep. 478 and Diplock L.J.'s assertion that in the event of a breach "going to the root of the contract" the common law recognises the right of the injured party to treat the contract as discharged.

[139] *Hain Steamship Company v Tate and Lyle Ltd* [1936] 2 All E.R. 597 (House of Lords), at p.612, per Lord Wright (Lord Atkin dub., at p.601).

[140] *Leduc v Ward* [1888] 20 QBD 475.

1.7.2 Customer's Breach at Common Law

In the event that the consignor or the consignee should fail to perform their respective obligations, whatever they might be, in connection with the collection, loading, unloading and receipt of cargo, the customer will, at common law, be responsible for the cost of any delay caused to the carrier. The customer is permitted a reasonable time for such performance in the absence of any specific time for performance being agreed.[141] The cost of delay is often the subject of express contractual provisions commonly described as demurrage charges in the case of carriage by sea or rail. Where there is some misdescription of the goods, or of the places of loading or discharge, and such misdescription causes loss to the carrier by reason of delay or damage to the transport conveyance, the carrier may recover damages by reason of any express or implied warranty;[142] or in tort for negligent misstatement pursuant to the rule in *Hedley Byrne & Co Ltd v Heller & Partners Ltd.*[143]

1.7.3 Repudiatory Breach

Contractual terms are frequently referred to as conditions, innominate terms and warranties following the judgment of Lord Justice Diplock in *Hong Kong Fir Shipping Co Ltd v Kawasaki Kisen Kaisha Ltd*;[144] but, in the thoughtful subsequent analysis of Lord Diplock in *Photo Production Ltd v Securicor Transport Ltd*[145] there are really only two types of terms. The first type are fundamental terms, or conditions, any breach of which can, at the election of the innocent party, be accepted as bringing the contract to an end. The second type are ordinary terms, or warranties, breach of which can only be accepted as bringing the contract to an end where the breach has the effect of depriving the innocent party of "substantially the whole

[141] See *Postlethwaite v John Freeland and Alexander Freeland* (1879–80) L.R. 5 App. Cas. 599 in which Lord Selbourne said in connection with the discharge of cargo following sea carriage "If ... there is no fixed time, the law implies an agreement ... to discharge the cargo within a reasonable time; that is ... as was said by Mr Justice Blackburn ... a reasonable time under the circumstances."

[142] Such implied terms arise only when a necessary inference from, or to give business efficacy to, the contract as confirmed by the Court of Appeal in *Mediterranean Salvage & Towage Ltd v Seamar Trading & Commerce Inc* (*The Reborn*) [2009] EWCA Civ 531.

[143] [1964] A.C. 465.

[144] [1962] 1 All E.R. 474.

[145] See fn. 133.

benefit" of the contract and it is convenient to describe such breach as being a fundamental breach. Accordingly a repudiatory breach capable of being accepted by the innocent party as bringing the contract of carriage to an end can be either any breach of a fundamental term or a fundamental breach of any term. It is important to recognise that faced with a repudiatory breach the innocent party must elect whether to accept the breach as bringing the contract to an end or continue with its own performance of the contract. In either event the innocent party may also sue for damages, but the need for an election remains. Where contractual performance by the innocent party or its continued acceptance of contractual performance by the guilty party continues, following a repudiatory breach, such continued performance or acceptance is likely to amount to an affirmation of the contract. Effectively, by such continued contractual performance, a final and binding election will have been made in favour of the contract's continuance.[146] On the other hand, should a party purport to accept a breach of contract as bringing a contract to an end when it was not in fact a repudiatory breach, such party will be exposed to claims for wrongful termination. Such issues are likely to require careful consideration in the context of delayed loading and discharging, the hire of vessels under charterparty arrangements and long-term distribution contracts and will be particularly revisited in 3.1.6.3.

Contractual repudiation should be clearly contrasted from any expiry or cancellation of the contract within the contractual terms and from common law principles by which contracts may be void, frustrated, or voidable. Contracts may be completely void by reason of mistake when, unbeknown to the parties, unforeseen circumstances in existence at the time the contract is made render the contemplated performance of the contract wholly impossible.[147] Should future performance of the contract become impossible by reason of the occurrence of such unforeseen circumstances after the contract is made the contract will be rendered legally frustrated.[148] In

[146] See the analysis of Lord Goff in *Motor Oil Hellas (Corinth) Refineries SA v Shipping Corp of India (The Kanchenjunga)* [1990] 1 Lloyd's Rep. 391, 398–399.

[147] *The Great Peace* [2002] 3 W.L.R. 1617.

[148] With regard to frustration, see *Jackson v Union Marine Insurance Company*; *Tamplin Steamship Company v Anglo-Mexican Petroleum Company* [1916] 2 A.C. 397; *Bank Line v Capel and Company* [1919] A.C. 435; *Joseph Constantine Steamship Line v Imperial Smelting Corporation* [1942] A.C. 154; *Blane Steamship Ltd v Minister of Transport* [1951] 2 K.B. 965; *Carapanayoti v E. T. Green Ltd* [1959] 1 Q.B. 131; *The Eugenia* [1964] 2 Q.B. 226; *Tsakiroglou and Company Ltd v Noblee Thorl GmbH* [1962] A.C. 93; *The Wenjiang (No.2)* [1983] 1 Ll.L.R. 400.

contrast, otherwise valid contracts may become voidable and capable of rescission at the unilateral option of one or other of the contracting parties by reason of such matters as duress, undue influence or misrepresentation.

1.8 Liability for Breach

1.8.1 Rights to Claim

At common law only parties to contracts of carriage have contractual rights of action in respect of their breach; however, as discussed at 1.6.1.2 above, there are now many circumstances when persons other than a contracting party to the carriage contract might have a contractual right of action against the carrier. These circumstances include those provided for by The Contracts (Rights of Third Parties) Act 1999, the mandatory terms for international carriage by road, rail and air and agency principles as well as common law rules to which reference has already been made.[149] Claims in bailment or sub-bailment may be made against the carrier as bailee by those entitled to immediate possession of the goods from the carrier as original bailor, or sub-bailor, or by reason of the carrier having attorned to them by recognising their immediate right of possession.[150] Claims in tort for negligence for damage to the goods carried may be made by any person with proprietary or immediate possessory rights over the goods.[151] Where loss is caused by misstatement on carriage documentation, or elsewhere, claims for loss may be recovered pursuant to the torts of deceit or of negligent misstatement. Loss caused by any deceit may be claimed by anyone suffering loss in consequence.[152] Claims for loss caused by negligent misstatement may be claimed under the principles of *Hedley Byrne v Heller*,[153] pursuant to the test laid down in *Caparo v Dickman*:[154] i.e. where the loss claimed was reasonably foreseeable to the person liable for the misstatement, a sufficient relationship of proximity existed between the claimant relying on the misstatement and the person liable and it is fair, just and

[149] See 1.6.1.2 and 1.6.1.4 above.
[150] *The Pioneer Container* [1994] 2 AC 324.
[151] *The Aliakmon* [1986] 1 AC 785.
[152] *Standard Chartered Bank v Pakistan National Shipping Corporation* [2003] 1 Lloyd's Rep. 227.
[153] [1964] A.C. 465.
[154] [1990] 2 A.C. 605.

reasonable to impose a duty of care.[155] Claims for contribution or indemnity may be brought pursuant to the Civil Liability (Contribution) Act 1978 where the person claiming contribution, and the person from whom contribution is claimed, are each liable to compensate the same person for the same damage.[156] By s2(1) of the 1978 Act the level of contribution recoverable is determinable by an assessment of what is "just and equitable", by reference to the extent of responsibility of the person liable to make contribution, for the damage in question.

1.8.2 Value of Claim

The amount that may be claimed for breach of the contract of carriage (commonly called the measure of damages)[157] is governed, as in all other contracts, by the rule in *Hadley v Baxendale*,[158] which itself concerned a claim made under a contract of carriage. The damages are limited to those which flow naturally from the breach of contract (generally characterised as direct loss), save where the parties had in their contemplation at the time they entered into the contract that some extraordinary further damage would be the result of its breach (generally characterised as indirect loss).[159] The test is not now one simply of causation flowing from foreseeable consequences, but one which requires the parties to have had, at the time they entered into the contract, the particular loss (whether direct or indirect) generally in their mutual contemplation as the probable financial consequence of a contemplated breach.[160] The normal measure of damages for breach of

[155] In *The David Agmashenebeli* [2003] 1 Lloyd's Rep. 92 Colman J. held that it was not "fair, just and reasonable" to impose a duty of care on a carrier as to the clausing of a bill of lading governed by the Hague or Hague-Visby Rules.

[156] See ss.1(1) and 6(1) of the 1978 Act. What constitutes liability "in respect of the same damage" was considered by the House of Lords in *Royal Brompton Hospital NHS Trust v Hammond (No.3)* [2002] 1 W.L.R. 1397 when, in dismissing a claim for contribution by an architect liable for professional negligence against a contractor liable for delay, they favoured a narrow interpretation respecting the notion of a common shared liability rather than a broad notion of connected liability.

[157] A full discussion on the measure of damages would be outside the scope of this book.

[158] *Hadley v Baxendale* (1854) 9 Exch. 341.

[159] ibid. See also *Victoria Laundry (Windsor) Ltd v Newman Industries Ltd* (1949) 2 K.B. 528.

[160] See *Transfield Shipping Inc v Mercator Shipping Inc (The Achilleas)* [2008] 2 Lloyd's Rep. 275.

contract is the expectation measure which requires that the innocent party should receive sufficient compensation from the guilty party to be placed "in the same situation ... as if the contract had been performed".[161]

In the case of non-delivery of goods, the measure of the direct loss is generally the normal market value of the goods assessed at the place and time at which the goods should have been delivered. If the value of the goods at the place of destination has fallen as a result of delivery being delayed, the measure of damages is the difference between the price which the consignee could have obtained on a resale of the goods if they had been delivered on time, and the price which the consignee in fact received by selling the goods when they were delivered.[162] Under normal principles the innocent party must act reasonably in mitigation of the loss which has been suffered.

Irrespective of the measure of damages for tort in general, it seems that when an action is brought against a carrier in tort or bailment by the owner of the goods, or by the other party to the contract of carriage, the amount of damages recoverable is the same as would be awarded, under the rule in *Hadley v Baxendale*, if the action were founded on breach of contract.[163] The parties may agree in the contract on a sum to be payable as liquidated damages for breach of contract, but if such sum is in fact a penalty, that is, not a genuine pre-estimate of damages, it is void.[164]

The parties may also agree that the party in breach provides an indemnity for loss or damage suffered instead of, or more likely in addition to, the guilty party's liability to pay damages by way of compensation. Any party entitled to an indemnity is not subject to the usual rules as to remoteness. It is not necessary that the type of loss should be in the contemplation of the indemnifying party when the indemnity is agreed and the claimant under an indemnity is under no obligation to mitigate its loss unless expressly required to do so by the terms of the indemnity. However, any claim for indemnity is subject to the usual rules as to causation.

[161] Being the formulation used by Parke B. in *Robinson v Harman* (1848) 1 Exch. 850 Ex Ct; although Adam Kramer proposes at L.Q.R. 2009, 125(Jul), 408–415 that this seminal formulation should be redrawn in the light of the *Achilleas* decision (ibid.) to provide that the guilty must put the innocent "... in the same situation in all respects protected by the contract (but not others) as if the contract had been performed".

[162] *C. Czarnikow Ltd v Koufos* [1969] 1 A.C. 351.

[163] *The Arpad* [1934] P. 189, Greer, Maugham, L.J.J., Scrutton, L.J., diss.

[164] See *Magee v Lavell* (1874) L.R. 9 C.P. 107, per Lord Coleridge C.J.; *Dunlop Pneumatic Tyre Company v New Garage Company* [1915] A.C. 79.

Accordingly the party claiming an indemnity must prove the amount of the loss for which the indemnity is sought and that the loss is one which must be indemnified under the terms of the indemnity.

In claims for damages in tort caused by negligence, the measure of damages is determined by the objective concept of forseeability of loss on the part of the tortfeasor (as a notional reasonable person) at the time of the negligent act, as expressed by the House of Lords in the *Wagon Mound*.[165] Forseeability of the general nature of the damage that might result may be sufficient, even if the full extent of such damage was not; unless such full extent could be seen to be "different in kind from that which should have been foreseen".[166] The proper measure of damages in bailment appears to be calculated by reference to the market value of the goods at the time and place at which they were lost or damaged, with the claimant in bailment being able to recover the full value of the goods lost irrespective of their financial interest, if any, in those goods.[167] Consequently, the bailee has a right to insure the goods for their full insurable value, albeit the insured bailee is obliged to hold any amount received in excess of their own financial interest in trust for the owner of the goods.[168] Liability for negligent misstatement pursuant to the principles in *Hedley Byrne*[169] sounds in damages measured by contractual principles as the basis of such claims is considered to be analogous to contractual claims.[170] However, such claims should be contrasted from claims made in tort for deceit to which tortious principles apply.[171]

1.8.3 Claim Time Limitation

Claims made in contract, tort or bailment in connection with the defective performance, or non-performance in whole or part, of carriage contracts are subject to the same statutory periods of time to sue—commonly called suit time periods—as other claims under English law pursuant to the relevant statute of limitations.[172] Generally a period of six years applies to

[165] (No.1) [1961] A.C. 388.
[166] Lord Hoffman in *Jolley London Borough of Sutton* [2000] 2 Lloyd's Rep. 65, 76.
[167] *The Winkfield* [1902] P. 42.
[168] *Hepburn v A Tomlinson (Hauliers) Ltd* [1966] A.C. 451.
[169] *Hedley Byrne & Co Ltd v Heller & Partners* [1964] A.C. 465.
[170] Per Lord Devlin ibid. 530.
[171] See *Standard Chartered Bank v Pakistan National Shipping Corporation (No.2)* [2003] 1 Lloyd's Rep. 227, which concerned the deliberate misdating of a bill of lading.
[172] Currently the Limitation Act 1980 as amended.

claims for loss of or damage or delay to goods or other chattels whether made in contract, bailment or tort, or to claims for economic loss resulting from contractual breach, negligent misstatement or deceit.[173] Determining when suit time commences is somewhat more complex. In contract suit time begins to run as soon as the breach occurs; in tort all the elements of the cause of action must first be in place, so that suit time only commences when actual damage or loss has occurred in claims for negligence or negligent misstatement. In the event of fraudulent concealment of facts giving rise to the cause of action, time will not start to run until the fraud is discovered; or, if earlier, such time as the fraud would with reasonable diligence have been discovered.[174] Under English law suit time may be extended or curtailed by agreement; contractual terms imposing shorter limitation periods will be subject to the requirement of reasonableness imposed by the UCTA provisions in the circumstances previously discussed at 1.7.1.1 above.[175]

1.9 Miscellaneous Carriage Contract Rights

1.9.1 Carriers' Rights

1.9.1.1 Right to Freight

The carrier has the right to be paid the price charged for the carriage services commonly called freight. Freight may be payable by the customer as consignor, or the goods may be shipped on a freight collect basis, whereby the freight will be payable by the consignee on delivery. Irrespective of whether payment is made on shipment or delivery, it is generally the case that freight is earned by the carrier on shipment. The obligation to pay freight is absolute irrespective of what loss, damage or delay may be occasioned to the goods during carriage. In the words of Lord Wilberforce

[173] Except in the case of contracts made under deed when the suit time period is 12 years (s.8 ibid.), or for negligence in tort within three years from the date of knowledge where the damage is latent subject to a 15-year long stop date (s.14A and s.14B ibid.), or for contribution or indemnity within two years of liability being established under the Civil Liability (Contribution) Act 1978.

[174] See s.2 (tort), s.5 (contract), s.32 (fraudulent concealment) ibid.

[175] See fn. 119 and *Granville Oil & Chemicals Ltd v Davies Turner & Co Ltd* [2003] 2 Lloyd's Rep. 356 where the the nine-month suit time limitation provision under cl.30(B) of the BIFA (British International Freight Association) Standard Trading Conditions (1989 edition) was held to satisfy the requirement of reasonableness in the international carriage context.

"That a claim in respect of cargo cannot be asserted by way of deduction from the freight, is a long established rule in English law".[176] Accordingly, in the absence of express agreement to the contrary, the customer liable for the payment of freight may not withhold from, delay or claim set off against, the due payment of freight by reason of any claim defence or counterclaim arising in connection with the performance of the contract of carriage. In consequence, summary judgment is readily obtainable by carriers in the event of any non-payment of freight.[177]

1.9.1.2 Right to Lien

Common carriers are entitled to exercise a lien over goods at common law, to retain possession of them until the freight owing for the carriage of those goods is paid.[178] Such common law lien is in the nature of a particular lien as it only extends over the subject goods for the freight due for their carriage and is discussed further in respect of common carriers in 10.4. However, it seems clear that no carrier other than a common carrier or a sea carrier is entitled to exercise such a lien at common law.[179] Carriers other than common carriers are certainly not entitled at common law to exercise a lien against the lawful owner of the goods where the consignor was in wrongful possession of the goods at the time they were consigned.[180] Accordingly, where a consignor lawfully in possession of goods under a contract of hire purchase defaulted in payment and forfeited the right to retain possession of the goods, the carrier with whom the goods had been consigned was not entitled to retain them, by way lien for freight, against the hire purchase company, which owned the goods.[181] Statute has, however, created certain particular liens in the particular circumstances of international carriage by road and rail as discussed in Part Two.

The parties may also agree, by express contractual provision, for the

[176] *Aries Tanker Corporation v Total Transport Ltd (The Aries)* [1977] 1 Lloyd's Rep. 334, 338.

[177] See judgment of Simon J. in *Cover Version Ltd v DHL Logistics (UK) Ltd* [2007] EWHC 562 (Comm) where the common law rule is discussed in the context of express terms to the same effect.

[178] *Skinner v Upshaw* (1702) 2 Ld. Raym. 752.

[179] See *Hirst v Page and Company* (1891) 7 T.L.R. 537; *Electric Supply Stores v Gaywood* (1909) 100 L.T. 855 and see 3.1.8.2.

[180] *Electric Supply Stores v Gaywood* (1909), 100 L.T. 855.

[181] *United States Steel Products Company v Great Western Railway Company* [1916] 1 A.C. 189.

carrier to exercise a lien. Such an agreement may be for a particular lien as described above. Alternatively, it may be for a lien over goods not only for freight due in relation to the carriage of those goods but also for sums owing for the carriage of other goods for the same owner, or in respect of any other debt due from the owner to the carrier. Such an extended lien is usually known as a general lien. A general lien may be implied by a prolonged course of dealing between the parties,[182] but the onus of proving that it has been expressly or implicitly agreed rests in every case on the carrier.[183] The parties may also agree that the carrier may sell the goods on which he holds a lien in order to raise the money owed by the owner; such a lien is usually known as an active lien. Where statutory terms of carriage impose liens and prohibit derogation, such statutory liens may displace otherwise agreed general or active liens.[184]

Legal difficulties can arise for carriers in the exercise of liens against persons, entitled to possession of the goods, who are not parties to the contract of carriage. Many standard contractual conditions seek to protect against these difficulties by providing for both a warranty of authority to contract as agents on behalf of such persons and an indemnity for any loss occasioned to the carrier by reason of that warranty being untrue.[185] Further protection is provided by the concept of sub-bailment on terms under which any such person claiming delivery of goods may be bound as original bailor to the terms of any agreed sub-bailment, provided that such sub-bailment was expressly or by implication consented to by the bailor.[186]

A carrier who lawfully exercises lien over goods is in possession of the goods as a bailee, and is liable accordingly.[187] The carrier is not, in the absence of express agreement to the contrary, entitled to charge the owner of the goods for the cost of warehousing them while they are being held under the carrier's lien, for they are then retained by the carrier without the owner's consent.[188] However, the carrier may charge the owner with the

[182] *Aspinall v Pickford* (1800) 3 Bos. & P. 44n.; *Rushforth v Hadfield* (1806) 7 East 224.

[183] *Rushforth v Hadfield* ibid.

[184] *T Comedy (UK) Ltd v Easy Managed Transport Ltd* [2007] 2 Lloyd's Rep. 397 where the combination of the statutory particular lien arising under art.13.2 of the CMR and the non-derogation provision at CMR art.41 displaced the general lien otherwise arising pursuant to standard carriage conditions.

[185] See for instance cll.3 and 20(A) of BIFA 2005A Conditions discussed at 5.2.2.2.

[186] *Lukoil-Kalingradmorneft Plc v Tata Ltd (No.2)* [1999] 1 Lloyd's Rep. 365 where a lien was successfully claimed on this basis under a towage contract.

[187] See 1.6.1.1 above generally for duties in bailment.

[188] *Somes v British Empire Shipping Company* (1860) 8 H.L.C. 338.

cost of preserving the goods when it is reasonably necessary for the carrier to spend money for this purpose. The carrier may consequently charge the owner with the cost of feeding animals retained under his lien.[189]

1.9.1.3 Dangerous Goods

Are goods "dangerous" only when they are capable of causing direct physical damage to property in the carrier's possession, or physical injury to persons in the carrier's employ? Or can they be considered dangerous simply because they expose the carrier to some potential hazard or inconvenience? In *Effort Shipping Co Ltd v Linden Management SA*[190] the characteristics of dangerous goods within the specific context of art.IV, r. 6 of the Hague Rules was considered by the House of Lords in the context of the shipment of ground-nut extraction meal pellets with Khapra beetle infestation. In that case, the infested cargo was considered dangerous simply because it exposed an accompanying consignment of wheat pellets to the risk of being condemned by port authorities and dumped at sea. The infested cargo was considered dangerous although it was not itself capable of directly damaging the other cargo or the ship.

As a variety of contractual and legislative provisions address the carriage of dangerous cargo by road, rail, sea and air, it is perhaps inappropriate to seek to draw a general formulation of what might constitute dangerous goods. Instead this issue will be more particularly addressed in Parts Two, Three and Four. It is worth noting however that the common law tends to give a broad interpretation to the word "dangerous" in the context of the carriage of goods.[191] In the *Effort Shipping Co Ltd* case[192] the House of Lords did not confine dangerous goods to goods of an inflammable or explosive nature but appeared to extend the concept to any goods which, from their nature, are liable to constitute a physical danger to some person or some thing (be that property, or some part of the natural environment) in which the carrier has some interest (by way of existing right or potential liability). An equivalent term, used almost exclusively in the United States, is hazardous material (hazmat).

189 *Great Northern Railway Company v Swaffield* (1874) L.R. 9 Ex. 132.

190 [1998] A.C. 605.

191 *Chandris v Isbrandsten-Moller Co Inc* [1951] 1 K.B. 240 in which Devlin J. adopted a broad definition of dangerous goods to include turpentine notwithstanding the ejusdem generis rule of construction pointing to a narrower construction.

192 See fn. 190 in which Lord Lloyd at p.612 approved the above approach of Devlin J.

Where goods are delivered to a carrier, who is under neither a common law nor a statutory duty to carry, the consignor may be subject to an implied term that goods known to have a dangerous nature will not be consigned without bringing that dangerous nature to the attention of the carrier.[193] Where such an implied term arises and the consignor consigns goods without advising the carrier of their dangerous nature, the consignor will be liable for any damage caused by the dangerous goods, even if the consignor neither knew, nor even had the means of knowledge, that the goods were dangerous.[194] The consignor's liability for dangerous goods is a matter which is generally dealt with expressly by whatever specific contract terms may have been incorporated, or applied by statute, into the contract of carriage.

Where dangerous goods cause damage to other goods of another owner, which the carrier is carrying together with the dangerous goods, the carrier may incur liability to the owner of the other goods and may need to exercise rights of recourse against the owner of the dangerous goods. The carrier's right to recover damages from the owner of the dangerous goods is not, however, a mere right of indemnity, as the carrier has a possessory interest in the damaged goods as bailee. By reason of this bailment, the carrier may make full recovery for the loss or damage to the goods from the owner of the dangerous goods. Such full recovery may be made even where the carrier is not in fact liable to the owner of the damaged goods, whether the absence of liability is attributable to some contractual exclusion or limitation in place between the carrier and the owner of the damaged goods, or to some other reason.[195] If the carrier succeeds in recovering damages from the owner of the dangerous goods, the carrier holds the sum recovered as a trustee for the owner of the damaged goods[196] and must pay it to the owner, even though the carrier was not directly liable to the owner for the damage to the goods.

[193] Such an implied term was held to arise in *Brass v Maitland* (1856) E. & B. 470 in a case of contractual carriage of goods by sea; which case was approved in, and applied by, *Bamfield v Goole and Sheffield Transport Co Ltd* [1910] 2 K.B. 94 and *Great Northern Railway Co v L.E.P. Transport and Depository Ltd*[1922] 2 K.B. 742, albeit, in connection with carriage by land by common carriers.

[194] *Effort Shipping Co Ltd* (fn. 190) in which the House of Lords expressed a clear obitur dictum to this effect with Lord Lloyd expressing the view of the House in the following terms "... the liability of a shipper for shipping dangerous goods at common law, when it arises, does not depend on his knowledge or means of knowledge that the goods are dangerous".

[195] *The Winkfield* [1902] P.42.

[196] ibid.

1.9.2 Customers' Stoppage Rights

The right of an unpaid seller of goods to stop the goods in transit is of considerable importance, not only to the buyer and the seller, but also to the carrier. The right is regulated by ss.44–46 of the Sale of Goods Act 1979. Section 44 stipulates that the unpaid seller who has parted with the possession of the goods has the right, in the event of the buyer's insolvency, of "stopping the goods in transit", which right is explained by the section as the right to "resume possession of the goods as long as they are in course of transit". The significance of the right is that in the event of the buyer's insolvency (even though the goods have been consigned with an independent carrier for delivery to the buyer and legal title to the goods has passed to the buyer, whether by negotiation of the bill of lading or by some other means) the seller has a statutory right to reacquire possession of the goods and continue to hold them subject to the unpaid seller's possessory lien.[197] The right is extinguished where a buyer lawfully in possession of the bill of lading transfers the document to a person who takes it in good faith and for valuable consideration.[198]

This *stoppage* right only subsists whilst the goods are in transit, which is a concept entirely distinct from goods being in the course of carriage, since the period of transit is determined not by the contract of carriage but rather by the consignment and delivery of goods under the contract of sale. Accordingly, the "transit" for the purpose of the seller's right of stoppage in transit is a different thing from the "carriage" for the purpose of determining whether the carrier is in possession of the goods as a carrier or as a warehouseman. The references to a "carrier or other bailee" in ss.45 and 46, and to the carrier remaining in possession of the goods "as a bailee" in s.45(3) does not affect the distinction in the functions, as carrier and warehouseman, of the carrier. Goods are in the course of transit under the contract of sale from the time they are delivered to a carrier, for onward transmission to the buyer, until the time the buyer (or an agent on behalf of the buyer) takes legal (as opposed to physical) delivery of them. This may take place before the goods arrive at the intended destination. Transit under the contract of sale will also come to an end where the carrier wrongfully refuses to make delivery to the buyer.[199]

[197] Pursuant to s.41 of the Sale of Goods Act 1979 as confirmed by s.44.
[198] Section 47(2) ibid. confirming the principle in *Lickbarrow v Mason* (1794) 5 T.R. 683.
[199] As defined by s.45 ibid.

Where part of the goods have been legally delivered under the contract of sale, s.45(7) preserves rights of stoppage over any part of the goods still undelivered unless the circumstances point to an agreement to give the buyer legal possession of the undelivered goods as well. Even once the goods arrive at their intended destination, transit will continue unless and until the carrier acknowledges to the buyer, or an agent on behalf of the buyer, that the goods are held on the buyer's behalf and will be delivered to, or to the order of, the buyer. Once the carrier has so attorned to the buyer the transit will come to an end, despite the carrier continuing in physical possession of the goods and/or the carriage continuing on to some further destination nominated by the buyer.[200] A particularly difficult issue arises in connection with carriage on ships chartered by the buyer, as s.45(5) provides that it is a question of fact in each case whether the goods have been delivered into the possession of the master of the ship as a carrier, or as agent to the buyer.

Rights of stoppage in transit can be exercised by the unpaid seller either taking actual possession of the goods, or giving notice of the exercise of the right to a carrier in possession of the goods. Where notice is given to the principal of the person in actual possession of the goods, rather than that person directly, the notice is only effective insofar as the principal can, by the exercise of reasonable diligence, communicate it to the person in actual possession in time to prevent delivery to the buyer. On receipt of an effective notice the carrier must redeliver the goods to, or to the order of, the seller with the carrier's expenses as to redelivery being borne by the seller.[201] If a seller who is entitled to stop the goods in transit gives notice to the carrier, in accordance with the provisions of s.46(1), that he is exercising this right, the carrier is guilty of conversion of the goods if he delivers them to the consignee.[202] If, however, the transit has already terminated when the seller gives notice to the carrier to stop the goods in transit, the carrier will be liable to the buyer for conversion if the carrier re-delivers the goods to the seller, or as directed by the seller.[203] In cases of doubt, the carrier should interplead.[204] Interpleader proceedings are proceedings where a party appears before the court to explain that whilst the party has no interest in

[200] ibid.

[201] s.46 ibid.

[202] *Litt v Cowley* (1816) 7 Taunt. 169; *The Tigress* (1863) 32 L.J. (Ad.) 97, 102, per Dr. Lushington.

[203] This was clearly accepted in *Taylor v Great Eastern Railway Company* (1901) 70 L.J. (K.B.) 499 (not reported on this point in [1901] 1 K.B. 774; see p.777 (note 3)).

[204] *Wilson v Anderton* (1830) 1 B. & Ad. 450; *The Tigress*, per Dr. Lushington.

the action concerned and will deal with the matter as the court directs, he is in a difficulty because other parties are disputing the matter and he does not know how to resolve the difficulty. The court will then summon the interested parties, hear their cases and dispose of the matter.[205] Where the seller exercises the right of stoppage in transit but refuses to take delivery of the goods, or to give instructions to the carrier as to how to dispose of them, the carrier remains in possession of the goods as an involuntary bailee. In such circumstances the seller is liable to the carrier for any expenses or damages which the carrier may have suffered through remaining in possession of the goods.[206] For the carrier's right of lien for carriage charges against a seller who has exercised the right of stoppage in transit, see 1.9.1.2.

1.10 Common Carriers

1.10.1 Nature of a Common Carrier

The concept of a "common carrier" still resonates in many judgments of the higher courts[207] but it seems that in recent times courts have not held carriers to be common carriers.[208] The legal concept now seems largely redundant as carriers either operate by private contractual arrangements or under legislation, providing that they are not common carriers. Contractually carriers avoid the status of common carriers by the simple expedient of making express provision to that effect in their contractual conditions, ensuring that those carriage conditions reserve to themselves whether or not to accept goods for carriage and provide that all goods are carried under contractual arrangements concluded pursuant to those

[205] Interpleader proceedings are governed by Sch.1 RSC Order 17 as per Pt 50 of the Civil Procedure Rules.

[206] *Booth Steamship Company v Cargo Fleet Iron Company* [1916] 2 K.B. 570.

[207] For instance in *Effort Shipping Co Ltd v Linden Management SA* (fn. 190) where Lord Lloyd addressed at p.619 the contention that certain prior authorities on dangerous goods be distinguished from contractual carriage as they involved common carriers.

[208] The most recent English authority coming to the attention of the author where a carrier was found to be a common carrier is *A Siohn & Co Ltd v RH Hagland & Son (Transport) Ltd* [1976] 2 Lloyd's Rep. 428 where Cusack J. held that carriers advertising themselves as "hanging garments transport specialists" were common carriers carrying goods for anyone on request against a published tariff otherwise than under private contractual arrangements.

conditions.[209] Statutory terms of carriage, when applicable, displace the common carrier concept in respect of international carriage of goods by road, rail and sea and any carriage by air; much domestic UK carriage (e.g. carriage by anyone by rail and by certain statutorily empowered carriers such as the British Waterways Board) is performed subject to express statutory provision to the effect that the carriers are not common carriers.[210] The legal status of the common carrier is now so divorced from the current regulatory and commercial context for the carriage of goods that a strong case could be made for its complete abolition.[211] However, for the time being, the common carrier status remains an effective legal status and some understanding of it is necessary; firstly, for the interpretation of prior authorities, statutes and contracts referring to the concept; secondly, so that carriers can by contract effectively avoid the status of a common carrier and the strict liabilities arising in consequence of that status.

At common law there was no third class of carrier of goods by land (although the position might be otherwise as to carriers by sea and by inland waterway).[212] Every carrier of goods by land in England and Wales was either a common carrier carrying goods under the common law or a contractual carrier carrying goods under a carriage contract. In the case of a common carrier, there was no contract of carriage at all and the liability of the carrier as to loss, damage, or delay to the goods during the carriage was apparently a liability in tort to the owner of the goods. The position of a common carrier differs from that of a contractual carrier in the following five respects.

(i) A common carrier is under a legal duty to carry goods for anyone if required to do so, except where lawfully entitled to refuse to carry. A contractual carrier is under no such duty.

(ii) A common carrier is, save in five exceptional circumstances, strictly liable for any loss or damage to the goods during the carriage. A contractual carrier is only liable if the goods are lost or damaged through want of reasonable care.

[209] See for example the following preamble to the Road Haulage Association Limited 2009 Conditions of Carriage "[the Carrier] is not a common carrier and accepts goods for carriage only upon that condition and the Conditions set out below".

[210] See s.123 Railways Act 1993 and Transport Act 1962 s.43(6) as amended.

[211] The case persuasively put by Mcbain in "Time to abolish the common carrier" J.B.L. 2005, September, 545–96.

[212] *Watkins v Cottell* [1916] 1 K.B. 10.

(iii) Express terms of limitation, or exclusion, of liability are interpreted differently according to whether the carrier is a common or a contractual carrier.
(iv) The common carrier has a common law lien. A contractual carrier probably has no lien in the absence of a contractual or statutory lien.
(v) The Carriers Act 1830 applies to common carriers but not to contractual carriers.

Carriers who held themselves out as being ready to carry goods for the public at large for hire or reward were common carriers. Carriers might still be common carriers if they limited the kind of goods which they were ready to carry for the public, or limited the route over which they were prepared to carry, or both.[213] In every case, they would be common carriers to the extent that they held themselves out as ready to carry goods for the public, and no further. In order for carriers who held themselves out as ready to carry goods for the public to be common carriers, they must have accepted reward for the carriage.[214]

Where a common carrier of goods, which was also a public carrier of passengers, allowed passengers to carry a certain amount of personal luggage free of charge, that carrier was a common carrier of the goods which comprised the passengers' luggage since it was deemed to be carrying the luggage for reward. The fact that the luggage was accompanied by the passenger did not prevent the carrier from being a common carrier of the goods.[215] This doctrine did not, however, apply unless the public carrier of passengers was also a common carrier of goods. Where a public corporation permitted passengers in its trams to carry a certain amount of luggage, it was held that the corporation was not a common carrier of the luggage; as it did not hold itself out as ready to carry goods except when accompanied by a passenger and did not comply with the definition of a common carrier. To be a common carrier, the carrier had to hold itself out as ready to carry goods for the public irrespective of whether they were accompanied by a passenger or not.[216] Of course, carriers of passengers by air and rail are, by statute, not now common carriers; whilst passengers by

[213] *Johnson v Midland Railway Company* (1849) 4 Exch. 367, 373, per Parke B. See also *Belfast Ropework Co v Bushell* [1918] 1 K.B. 210.
[214] See *Benett v Peninsular Steamboat Company* (1848) 6 C.B. 775, 787, per Wilde C.J.
[215] *Munster v South-Eastern Railway Company* (1858) 4 C.B. (N.S.) 676, 703.
[216] *Rosenthal v London County Council* (1924) 131 L.T. 563.

road and sea will be carried pursuant to passenger conditions (agreed by contract or, in international carriage, imposed by statute) effectively displacing the common carrier concept in connection with the carriage of passenger luggage.

Carriers were not common carriers if they held themselves out as ready to carry goods for the public at large only in connection with some other business to which the carriage of goods was merely ancillary. Thus, where a wharfinger held himself out as ready to carry goods from ships to his warehouse for all persons who agreed to place their goods in the warehouse, the wharfinger was not a common carrier. Although he held himself out as ready to warehouse goods for the public at large, the wharfinger was only prepared to carry goods for cargo owners who had agreed to warehouse their goods at his wharf, and the carriage of goods was merely ancillary to his business as a wharfinger.[217]

Courts are now reluctant to hold that a carrier is a common carrier.[218] If a carrier reserved the right to refuse to carry goods, and in each case exercised a choice whether to carry or not, it was not a common carrier even if, invariably, it did decide to carry for commercial reasons.[219] Choice could be evidenced by the carrier, before agreeing to carry, providing estimates as to the cost of carriage for agreement, or negotiating the price to be paid; if a carrier, who would otherwise be a common carrier, only provided such an estimate for certain goods, it might still be a common carrier of other goods for which it did not give an estimate.[220] The issue as to whether a carrier was a common carrier depended in every case on whether it held itself out as ready to carry goods of the class in question on the route in question for the public at large. This was, in every case, a question of fact to be evaluated in all the circumstances of the particular case.[221]

1.10.2 Liability of Common Carrier for Refusing Carriage

The common carrier is under a duty to carry all goods, for the carriage of which it is a common carrier, that are delivered to it for carriage. If it refuses without lawful justification to accept goods for carriage, it is liable in

[217] *Consolidated Tea and Lands Company v Oliver's Wharf* [1910] 2 K.B. 395.
[218] For example, *Webster v Dickson* [1969] 1 Lloyd's Rep. 89.
[219] *Belfast Ropework Company v Bushell* [1918] 1 K.B. 210.
[220] *Electric Supply Stores v Gaywood* (1909) 100 L.T. 855.
[221] *Belfast Ropework Company v Bushell* (fn. 219).

tort for damages,[222] apparently both to the owner and to the consignor, and possibly to anyone else who has suffered damage by its refusal to carry. Previously, it was even accepted judicially that a common carrier unjustifiably refusing to carry was also guilty of a criminal misdemeanour under the common law.[223] However, there is no reported case of an indictment of a common carrier for refusal to carry and any such criminal liability is now unrealistic. If the common carrier demands an unreasonably high freight,[224] this is tantamount to a refusal to carry, and the common carrier is liable accordingly.[225] There is no obligation, however, on a common carrier to charge all consignors the same freight. If a common carrier can establish that it habitually charges less than a reasonable freight, it is entitled to make a particular consignor pay more than the usual freight, provided that this does not amount to more than a reasonable freight.[226] All relevant circumstances are to be taken into account in determining the amount which constitutes reasonable freight. A common carrier is entitled to demand higher freight for delivering two packages to different consignees than for delivering the same two packages to one consignee.[227] The common carrier may demand a higher freight for carrying goods through a district where they are particularly likely to be stolen, since the common carrier would be liable for the loss in this event.[228] At common law, the common carrier was entitled to demand higher freight for the carriage of valuables to defray increased insurance costs,[229] but this rule of common law has probably been abrogated by the common carrier having a statutory right to limit liability for the carriage of valuables under the Carriers Act 1830 as discussed at 2.2.3.

A common carrier is justified in refusing to carry in any of the following circumstances.

[222] *Jackson v Rogers* (1683) 2 Show. 327, per Jeffreys C.J.

[223] *Pozzi v Shipton* (1838) 1 Per. & Dav. 4, 12, per Patteson J.

[224] Freight is defined in *Kirchner v Venus* (1859) 12 Moo. P.C.C. 361, as "the reward payable to the carrier for the safe carriage and delivery of the goods".

[225] *Harris v Packwood* (1810) 3 Taunt. 264, 272; *Garton v Bristol and Exeter Railway Company* (1861) 1 B. & S. 112, 162, per Cockburn C.J.

[226] *Baxendale v Eastern Counties Railway Company* (1858) 4 C.B. (N.S.) 63, 78; *Great Western Railway Company v Sutton* (1868) L.R. 4 H.L. 226, 237, per Blackburn J.

[227] *Baxendale v Eastern Counties Railway Company* ibid.

[228] *Gibbon v Paynton* (1769) 4 Burr. 2298, per Lord Mansfield C.J., where it was noted that for this reason freights were high in the case of goods to be carried in the vicinity of Birmingham.

[229] *Gibbon v Paynton* ibid.; *Riley v Horne* (1828) 5 Bing. 217.

(i) The common carrier may refuse to carry through a district which is unsafe on account of riot[230] and probably also where it is unsafe on account of war, or act of God, since the common carrier is not liable for loss or damage caused to the goods by such events. There is no authority as to whether the common carrier is entitled to refuse to carry on account only of the risk to its vehicle in such circumstances.

(ii) The common carrier is entitled to refuse to carry dangerous goods, being any goods likely to cause damage either to persons, or to the carrier's vehicle, or to the goods of other persons that the carrier is also carrying in the vehicle.[231]

(iii) The common carrier is entitled to refuse to carry goods if they are delivered to it not properly packed, or in a state in which they cannot be carried in the carrier's vehicle with reasonable convenience.[232]

(iv) The common carrier is entitled to refuse to carry goods if its vehicle is full[233] and the common carrier is not bound to run a special vehicle, or service, in order to carry goods for a consignor.

(v) The common carrier is entitled to insist that the consignor should pay the freight when the goods are handed over for carriage, otherwise the carrier is entitled to refuse to carry;[234] however, the carrier may not, as a condition of carriage, require payment before the goods are handed over to the carrier, since that would constitute an unlawful refusal to carry.[235]

(vi) The common carrier is apparently entitled to refuse to carry if the consignor refuses to inform it, on request, as to the nature of the goods to be carried.[236]

The common carrier may, of course, accept goods for carriage in those

[230] *Edwards v Sherratt* (1801) 1 East 604.

[231] It may now, in the light of *Effort Shipping Co Ltd v Linden Management SA* (fn. 190), be appropriate to consider goods dangerous if they are likely to be an indirect cause of damage (e.g. goods that fail to conform with applicable regulation that are likely to result in delay with a consequent risk of damage to other goods).

[232] *Munster v South-Eastern Railway Company* (1858) 4 C.B. (N.S.) 676, 701.

[233] *Riley v Horne* (1828) 5 Bing. 217 at p.224, per Best C.J.

[234] *Wyld v Pickford* (1841) 8 M. & W. 443.

[235] This seems to be the rule laid down in *Pickford v Grand Junction Railway Company* (1841) 8 M. & W. 372.

[236] *Riley v Horne* (fn. 233).

cases where it would be justified in law in refusing to carry. If this is the case, the carrier is under his ordinary liability as a common carrier, subject to any special contract which it may make.[237]

1.10.3 Liability of Common Carrier for Damage to Goods Carried

1.10.3.1 Strict Liability

The common carrier is liable for any loss or damage to the goods while it is in possession of them as a carrier, except where the damage is caused by one of the excepted events discussed below. This doctrine of the strict liability of the common carrier, effectively as an insurer of the goods, was clearly established by the beginning of the eighteenth century.[238] Holt C.J. summarised the status of the common carrier for reward as being that of someone:

> "entrusted to carry goods against all events but acts of God and of the enemies of the King. For though the force be never so great, as if an irresistible multitude of people should rob him, nevertheless he is chargeable. And this is a politic establishment contrived by the policy of the law for the safety of all persons, the necessity of whose affairs oblige them to trust these sorts of persons, that they may be safe in their ways of dealing; for else these carriers might have an opportunity of undoing all persons that had any dealings with them, by combining with thieves, etc., and yet doing it in such a clandestine manner as would not be possible to be discovered".[239]

The onus of proving that the damage to the goods was caused by one of the excepted causes for which the common carrier is not liable rests on the common carrier.[240] The following are the excepted causes, for the consequences of which the common carrier is not liable.

(i) An act of God, being an operation of natural forces so unexpected that no human foresight or skill could reasonably be

[237] See 1.10.3.3.
[238] *Coggs v Bernard* (1703) 2 Ld. Raym. 909.
[239] ibid. 918.
[240] *Forward v Pittard* (1785) 1 T.R. 27, 33, per Lord Mansfield C.J.

expected to anticipate it.[241] For example, a fall of rain heavier than any within living memory is an act of God.[242] It is unnecessary for the carrier to prove that the occurrence was altogether unheard of, or that it was impossible to guard against it: it is sufficient to establish that it was sufficiently unusual that the carrier could not reasonably be expected to guard against it.[243] However, the defence of act of God is not open to the carrier where the proximate cause of the damage was the act of the carrier, or of the carrier's servants or agents, even where the more remote cause was an act of God and the carrier may not have acted negligently.[244]

(ii) An act of the Queen's enemies, being for most practical purposes limited to acts of enemy soldiers in time of war; however, the acts of the rebels during the insurrection in Dublin in 1916 were held to be an act of the King's enemies in the Irish courts,[245] and has been held to be an act of war for the purpose of an express term in a contract of insurance by the English courts.[246] The acts of bandits and armed robbers, even if acting in large bands by open violence, or of rioters or strikers, are not acts of the Queen's enemies.[247]

(iii) Inherent vice, being damage to goods caused by some defect inherent in the goods. Thus the common carrier is not liable where fruit rots during the carriage owing to some latent defect in the fruit;[248] where animals injure themselves during carriage by reason of their savage or capricious instincts;[249] or where couplings of a carriage break during loading owing to a latent defect.[250] The defence of inherent vice is only open to the common carrier where the goods are damaged through their own inherent vice. It has no application where goods are damaged by

241 *Winfield & Jalowicz on Torts*, 17th edn (Sweet & Maxwell, 2006) p.712.
242 *Nichols v Marsland* (1876) 2 Ex. D. 1.
243 *Nugent v Smith* (1876) 1 C.P.D. 423, 434–8, per Cockburn C.J.
244 *Smith v Shepherd* (1796).
245 *Secretary of State for War v Midland Great Western Railway Company of Ireland* [1923] 2 I.R. 102.
246 *Curtis and Sons v Mathews* [1919] 1 K.B. 425.
247 *The Marshal of the Marshalsea's Case* (1455) Y.B. 33 Hen. VI, 1 pl. 3.
248 *Bradley v Federal Steam Navigation Company* (1927) 137 L.T. 266 (House of Lords).
249 *Blower v Great Western Railway Company* (1872) L.R. 7 C.P. 655.
250 *Lister v Lancashire and Yorkshire Railway Company* [1903] 1 K.B. 878.

the inherent vice of other goods, which the carrier is carrying in the same vehicle irrespective of whether their ownership is the same, or different; in this event, the carrier will have a remedy against the owner of the goods which caused the damage if these are dangerous goods.

(iv) Fraud, or fault of the owner, consignor or their respective agents. In the event of fraud, the carrier is relieved from all liability for damage to the goods, howsoever caused, during the carriage; so that a common carrier was not liable for damage to valuables where the consignor deliberately misled the carrier as to their nature and value.[251] In the event of fault, the carrier is not liable if the damage was caused by the fault of the consignor or the owner, or their servants or agents. Accordingly, where a common carrier accepts goods for carriage that are improperly packed, the carrier is not liable for damage caused by the faulty packing.[252] The carrier is, however, liable where the damage is caused by faulty covering of the carrier's vehicle and, in this case, the carrier may be liable to the consignee even if the faulty covering was placed on the vehicle by the consignor.[253]

1.10.3.2 Negligence Liability

If goods are damaged by an act of God or of the Queen's enemies, or by the fault of the owner or consignor or by the inherent vice of the goods, the common carrier is nevertheless liable if it has contributed to the loss or damage by negligence. Thus where goods are damaged by an act of God but the damage would have been avoided if the carrier had taken all reasonable steps to prevent it, the carrier is liable.[254] The duty of the common carrier to avoid or mitigate the loss or damage in these cases is not, however, an absolute one; it is only obliged to take all reasonable steps to do so, and is liable only for negligence.[255] Where the carrier has established that the damage to the goods was caused by an act of God or the

[251] *Titchburne v White* (1719) 1 Stra. 145, per Lord King, L.C.; *Gibbon v Paynton* (1769) 4 Burr. 2298, 2300, per Lord Mansfield C.J; but see the Carriers Act 1830 as to the road carriage of valuables by common carriers addressed in 2.2.3.

[252] *Hart v Baxendale* (1867) 16 L.T. 390; *Barbour v South-Eastern Railway Company* (1876) 34 L.T. 67.

[253] *London and North-Western Railway Company v Hudson and Sons* [1920] A.C. 324.

[254] See *Amies v Stevens* (1718) 1 Stra. 127.

[255] *Nugent v Smith* (1876) 1 C.P.D. 423.

Queen's enemies, the fault of the owner or consignor, or inherent vice, the onus of proof that the carrier was negligent rests on the party making that allegation.

1.10.3.3 Special Contract Liability

It is lawful for common carriers to make special contracts of carriage limiting or excluding their liability as common carriers, and also their liability for negligence, at least in cases where the carrier is entitled to refuse to carry the goods. Thus where the consignor has failed to offer to pay the freight in advance, the common carrier may refuse to carry unless the consignor enters into a special contract.[256] It has never been held judicially that a common carrier is entitled to exclude its liability as a common carrier by a special contract in those cases where it is under a duty to carry, but it appears to have been accepted in cases that it may do so.[257] The liberty to exclude is subject to the test of reasonableness under the Unfair Contract Terms Act 1977.[258] As it is now clearly settled that a common carrier may limit its liability by a special contract, the fact that a carrier habitually does so is no evidence that it is not a common carrier.[259] From this it follows that a condition in a contract couched in identical terms may be interpreted differently according to whether the carrier is a common or a contracting carrier. If a common carrier limits or excludes its liability in general words, without expressly referring either to its liability as an insurer or for negligence, the contract will be interpreted as limiting or excluding only its liability as an insurer, and the carrier will therefore remain liable for negligence.[260] A common carrier may only limit its liability for negligence by a contractual term referring unambiguously to that liability.[261] Moreover, a provision in the contract limiting the liability of a common carrier for the negligence of its servants will be interpreted as not extending to its personal

[256] *Wyld v Pickford* (1841) 8 M. & W. 443.

[257] See especially the judgments in the Court of Appeal in *Great Northern Railway Company v L.E.P. Transport and Depository Ltd* [1922] 2 K.B. 742.

[258] See s.2 of that Act regarding exclusion of liability for negligence. Section 3 subjects "written standard terms of business" proffered in a contract, to the reasonableness test, for which see s.11 and Sch.2 of the Act.

[259] See *Great Northern Railway Company v L.E.P. Transport and Depository Ltd* [1922] 2 K.B. 742; *Belfast Ropework Company v Bushell*; disapproving *Scaife v Farrant* (1875) L.R. 10 Ex. 358.

[260] *Price and Company v Union Lighterage Company* [1904] 1 K.B. 412.

[261] *Phillips v Clark* (1857) 2 C.B. (N.S.) 156.

negligence.[262] However, a contractual provision that a common carrier will not be liable for loss or damage "howsoever caused" has been held to exclude its liability for negligence.[263]

1.10.4 Common Carriers' Rights

1.10.4.1 Common Law Lien

The common carrier is entitled to exercise a particular lien over all the goods it is carrying in the same vehicle on the same journey for the same owner under the same contract[264] to secure payment of unpaid freight relating to the carriage of all those goods consigned together.[265] The lien may only be exercised in respect of sums owing as freight, and the common carrier may not exercise its lien in respect of sums owing to it for weighing the goods,[266] or incurred in connection with the carriage otherwise than as freight for carrying the goods. The common carrier is not entitled to exercise a lien to secure payment of sums due to it for warehousing the goods,[267] unless under a statutory duty to warehouse the goods.[268] Neither is the carrier entitled to retain possession of goods in order to secure payment of sums due to it in respect of freight due for the carriage of other goods for the same owner,[269] or for a previous carriage of the goods on which it is exercising the lien, or for any other debt due from the owner of the goods.[270]

The carrier's lien merely permits it to retain possession of the goods until the owner has paid the freight due. The goods cannot be sold by the carrier

[262] *City of Lincoln (Master and Owners) v Smith* [1904] A.C. 250.

[263] *Joseph Travers and Sons Ltd v Cooper* [1915] 1 K.B. 73.

[264] *Prenty v Midland Great Western Railway Company* (1866) 14 W.R. 314.

[265] *Mulliner v Florence* (1878) 3 Q.B.D. 484, so held in respect of an inn-keeper's lien, and the reasoning of the learned Lords Justices would equally apply to the common carrier's lien; the principle has been held to apply in the case of the carrier of goods by sea.

[266] *Lambert v Robinson* (1793) 1 Esp. 111.

[267] *Great Northern Railway Company v Swaffield* (1874) L.R. 9 Ex. 132, 137, per Pollock B.

[268] *Singer Manufacturing Company v London and South-Western Railway Company* [1894] 1 Q.B. 833.

[269] *Prenty v Midland Great Western Railway Company* (1866) 14 W.R. 314.

[270] *Rushforth v Hadfield* (1806) 7 East 224.

in order to raise the money,[271] nor may the carrier use the goods in any way while they are in its possession. The carrier may not exercise its lien unless the sum to be paid as freight is already owing at the time. The common carrier is entitled to refuse to carry unless paid the freight in advance; if the carrier does not insist upon this, the liability of the consignee to pay the freight does not arise until the carrier offers to deliver the goods.[272] The common carrier is therefore liable for damages if it seeks to exercise its lien before this time. Where it is a term of the contract that the carrier will give credit to the consignee, the carrier is not entitled to enforce its lien if the consignee fails to pay the freight at any earlier time such as when delivering the goods to the consignee.[273]

Where the unpaid seller exercises its right of stoppage in transit (see 1.9.2), the carrier may exercise its common law lien against the seller, and retain possession of the goods until the freight and the costs of re-delivering the goods to the seller or according to the seller's instruction have been paid. However, the common carrier may not exercise against the seller any general or active lien granted under the terms of the contract of carriage. This applies even if the contract of carriage was made with the seller as the consignor of the goods; any general or active lien given by the contract will be interpreted as extending only against the consignee, and not against a seller exercising the right of stoppage in transit, unless the contrary is unambiguously clear from the contract.[274] A common carrier may exercise its common law lien against all comers and is therefore entitled to exercise it against the lawful owner of the goods even in respect of freight incurred for goods consigned by a thief, or any other wrongful possessor of the goods.[275]

[271] *Jones v Pearle* (1723) 1 Stra. 556, which concerned an innkeeper's lien, has always been accepted as laying down this proposition for all liens.

[272] *Barnes v Marshall* (1852) 18 Q.B. 785, 789, per Crompton J.

[273] *Raitt v Mitchell* (1815) 4 Camp. 146.

[274] *United States Steel Products Company v Great Western Railway Company* [1916] 1 A.C. 189.

[275] *The Exeter Carrier's Case*, referred to in *Yorke v Grenaugh* (1703) 2 Ld. Raym. 867.

1.10.4.2 Carriage of Dangerous Goods

The consignor is liable to a common carrier for all damage caused by dangerous goods[276] which it has delivered to the carrier for carriage, except where the dangerous nature of the goods was declared to the carrier when they were handed over and the carrier has taken over the goods knowing of their dangerous propensities.[277] Where other goods are damaged by being carried together with dangerous goods, the common carrier is liable to the owner of the damaged goods for the damage caused, unless this liability has been excluded by a special contract; the common carrier can recover any damages paid to the owner of the damaged goods from the owner of the dangerous goods.

1.10.5 Avoiding Common Carrier Status

From the above it can be seen that the responsibilities of any common carrier are onerous, since its status at common law is that of an insurer of the goods, liable for every loss that occurs unless the loss arose in circumstances covered by the common law exceptions. To avoid these onerous responsibilities most carriers issue conditions of carriage in which they specify that they are not common carriers, and will accept goods for carriage only as contractual carriers on the conditions laid down in the document. A common carrier may cease at any time to be a common carrier by giving notice that it is no longer prepared to carry for the public at large any, or any particular, goods. Where the common carrier simply gives such notice as to goods of a particular kind, the carrier only ceases to be a common carrier for that kind of goods and retains any existing common carrier status for other goods carried for the public at large.[278]

[276] See cl.3 Road Haulage Association Ltd Conditions of Carriage 1982 (but due for revision 1992) and cl.1 (Definition) and cl.9 of British Rail Board's General Conditions of Carriage of Goods (1992).

[277] *Brass v Maitland* (1856) 6 E. & B. 470; *Bamfield v Goole and Sheffield Transport Company* [1910] 2 K.B. 94; and see *Burley v Stepney Corporation* [1947] 1 All E.R. 507, per Hallett J.

[278] *Johnson v Midland Railway Company* (1849) 4 Exch. 367, 373, per Parke B.; *Sutcliffe v Great Western Railway Company* [1910] 1 K.B. 478, 495, per Buckley L.J.

1.11 International Carriage

1.11.1 General Context

If any carriage is to be undertaken internationally, the agreement of the carrier to undertake the contract of carriage must be supplemented by the agreement of the countries between or within which the carriage is to be performed. The export and import of goods from one state to another requires the authorisation of the respective states of export and import. The carriage or transit through the territory of a state, other than that in which the goods originated, requires the permission of that "transit" state. Similarly, for all or part of the carriage to be undertaken in a "foreign" state by a carrier domiciled in another state (an activity known as "cabotage"), the permission of that "foreign" state will be required; and, in addition, the carrier will need to comply with any mandatory regulation imposed by that 'foreign' state as to the performance of the carriage activity. The latter issue of cabotage is addressed in 5.3; the former issue concerning the export, import and transit of goods is addressed here.

1.11.2 Export, Import and Transit

A principal source of revenue for states is the taxation of exports and imports from and into their territory. Taxation of the export and import of goods creates particular difficulty where the route of carriage, between the country of original export and ultimate import, involves the goods being moved through the territory of another state or several other states; without international agreement, the carrier would be exposed to the risk of having to pay customs' duty at every international border. The EEA incorporates a customs union that for the last 40 years or so has applied a common customs tarrif (CCT) to any goods being exported from or imported into the various EEA contracting states (which now total some 30, including Iceland, Liechtenstein and Norway as well as the EU and its 27 Member States). Goods originating within the EEA may be transported within the EEA free of duty and border controls.[279] Goods originating from outside but imported into the EEA will, by reason of their lawful importation into

[279] Article 30 of the Treaty on the Functioning of the European Union (TFEU) (ex art.25 EC Treaty).

the EEA and the payment of duty falling due under the CCT, be released for free circulation within the EEA.[280]

Whilst this solves the transit state difficulty referred to above in relation to goods travelling only within the EEA, that difficulty remains for goods that have neither originated within the EEA nor been released for free circulation within it and which are either travelling to importing states through territories within the EEA, or to importing states through the territories of non-EEA states. The issues arising in the former situation are discussed below in the context of community/common transit procedures, whilst the issues arising in the latter are discussed under the TIR/ATA transit procedures.

1.11.3 Community/Common Transit Procedures

Under these procedures[281] custom duties on goods imported into the EEA may be suspended during their transit by land, sea or air (the community transit) through the EEA on the basis that both the importer of the goods and the person (the community transit principal) undertaking the community transit—under such duty suspension arrangements—are responsible for its proper performance. Often, the community transit principal is also a freight forwarder or a carrier, either arranging or undertaking the carriage of the goods; however, obligations undertaken by community transit principals, for the regular completion of a community transit, are distinct from obligations undertaken as to carriage. Whatever independent contractual obligations they might owe as to carriage, community transit principals incur statutory obligations to complete the community transit in regular fashion: in particular to present the goods, as sealed by customs, intact along with the community transit declaration at the custom's office at the EEA place of destination within the prescribed time limit. Community transit principals incur liabilities for the payment of

[280] Article 79(2) of the Community Customs Code (R2913/92/EEC) to be replaced in due course by the Modernised Customs Code R450/2008/EC.

[281] Being the procedures for community transit (i.e. transit throughout the territories of EU Member States) pursuant to the Community Customs Code; and common transit (i.e. transit throughout the territories not only of EU Member States but also those of the three EFTA countries and Switzerland) pursuant to the Conventions on Common Transit and on Simplification of Formalities in Trade in Goods of 20 May 1987. However, for all practical purposes they are indistinct and in this book are both referred to as "community transit".

custom duties and similar taxes due for the importation of goods should they fail to discharge these statutory obligations.

Community transit procedures are provided for by Regulation 2454/93/EEC of 2 July 1993 as amended. This lays down distinct procedures for the implementation of the Community Customs Code for external community transit using the so-called T1 declaration for the movement of non-community goods through the EEA for the purpose of import or mere transit,[282] and internal community transit using the so-called T2 declaration for the movement of community goods through the EEA for the purpose of export.[283] In return for being allowed to undertake a community transit, the community transit principal is obliged to provide: either, an individual guarantee for the particular movement for the full amount of any customs duties and other similar charges (such as VAT or excise duties) at risk during the community transit calculated at the highest rate applicable to the goods in the country of departure;[284] or a comprehensive guarantee covering a number of movements undertaken by a community transit principal who is regularly responsible for such transits. By a comprehensive guarantee, for which very strict criteria must be met, multiple transits may be covered by a single guarantee given to cover the entire custom charges at risk, or a proportion of them.[285] The community transit ends when the goods are properly presented at the customs' office of destination. However, the community transit principal is not discharged from its liabilities until the customs' office of departure has confirmed that the community transit obligations have indeed been discharged. For the customs' office of departure to give that confirmation, it must first have been advised by the

[282] The T1 declaration is also used for the export of particular community goods to which specific community measures apply, such as certain agricultural products subject to subsidy under the common agricultural policy.

[283] A T2F declaration is used for goods originating from those customs territories of EU Member States in respect of which there is no harmonisation e.g. the Channel Islands.

[284] The country of the departure is the EEA country where the community transit, under arrangements for duty suspension, commences. Minimum rates are specified for particular goods involving an increased fraud risk (such as tobacco and alcohol products)—see Annex 44C of R2454/93.

[285] The amount of the comprehensive guarantee will be calculated as being 100 per cent, 50 per cent, 30 per cent or 0 per cent (i.e. a complete waiver) of the maximum amount at risk (the reference amount) in respect of all movements over a period of at least one week taking account of the community transit principal's anticipated trading trends depending on the risk profile of the community transit principal for the goods in question.

customs' office at destination of the completion of the community transit and, under the original paper-based system, have compared the customs' certifications issued at the start and end of the community transit by reference to the applicable Single Administrative Document (SAD). If such official certification of the end of the community transit is not forthcoming within four months of commencement of the community transit, the customs' office at the place of departure initiates enquiries to ascertain whether or not the community transit has been regularly performed. In the absence of official certification of the end of the community transit, the community transit principal, along with the person making the original import declaration to the country of departure, will incur liabilities to the state authorities in the country of departure for the payment of the suspended customs' debt.

This original paper system was and is unsatisfactory in many ways. Customs' offices at destination might fail to return SAD certifications, or return them late, or they might be lost or delayed in the post. As a result, the customs' authorities at departure would be uncertain as to which community transits had and had not been completed. The resulting administrative confusion could facilitate fraudulent activities, so that goods being moved under duty suspension arrangements might "disappear" and be sold for consumption in the EEA without any customs', excise or VAT duty ever being paid.[286] As a result, a new computerised transit system (NCTS) has been introduced,[287] which currently operates as an alternative system. The NCTS facilitates the electronic issue, transmission and certification of SAD for community transits between customs' offices of departure and destination where all parties have the required electronic data interface capabilities. Incorporated within NCTS is a new simplified procedure by which authorised consignors and consignees complying with strict criteria may create and transmit SAD information electronically from their own premises without physically having to present goods at the departure and destination customs' offices.

[286] The European Commission in a 1997 communication (COM(97) 188 final—Official Journal C 176 of 10.06.1997) put the tax revenue lost by such fraud at some ECU 1.27 billion over the period 1990 to 1996.

[287] Pursuant to R515/97/EC of 13 March 1997 as amended.

1.11.4 TIR and ATA Transit Procedures

TIR and ATA transit procedures may be available for goods that are to be carried across states outside the EEA.

The Transports Internationaux Routiers (TIR) procedure applies, by international public law in the form of the amended TIR Convention 1975,[288] to exported goods travelling by land through states other than the states of export and import, for the purpose of transit. The 1975 TIR Convention replaced the 1959 Convention, which remains in force in countries such as Japan. The TIR procedure now encompasses Europe (including the EU), North Africa and the Middle East and extends to other more distant countries such as the USA, Canada and certain parts of South America. The TIR procedure suspends the payment of duties and taxes against a chain of guarantees issued by national guaranteeing associations for transit irregularities occurring within the territory of a particular state,[289] provided goods travel in approved vehicles or containers sealed by customs and are accompanied by the internationally recognised TIR carnet.[290] The procedure involves states of transit and destination accepting the custom control measures taken by the states of departure. Transit states match the entry and exit vouchers taken from the TIR carnet. The EEA is considered a single territory for operation of the TIR and its procedures can only be used for a customs' transit movement beginning or ending outside that territory or moving, in the course of carriage between departure and destination within that territory, through the territory of some third country. Fraud has been a real problem in connection with the operation of the TIR for goods, such as tobacco and alcohol, which are subject to high rates of duties and charges; national associations have withdrawn their TIR guarantees from use for many such goods.

The ATA procedure applies to the temporary admission of goods for

[288] Agreed under the auspices of UNECE by 67 (as at 8 February 2010) contracting states plus the EU, of which some 56 (as of 28 November 2008) have established procedures to facilitate the operation of a TIR transit within their territories according to the UNECE depositary information available at *http://www.unece.org.*

[289] In the UK the authorised guaranteeing associations are the Road Haulage Association and the Freight Transport Association, to which reference is also made at 2.2.2. The amount of each national guarantee is set by the state concerned, but the recommended maximum is US$50,000.

[290] Printed by the International Road Transport Union (IRU) for use by national guaranteeing associations for individual transits only and issued in the form of multiple vouchers to verify exit from and entry to successive states up to a maximum of four.

specifc purposes such as displays, exhibitions, samples or as professional equipment. Again the procedure applies by international public law, now in the form of the ATA and Temporary Admission Conventions of 1961 and 1990 respectively,[291] both of which require the use of the ATA carnet, issued under the auspices of other national guaranteeing authorities which generally comprise national chambers of commerce.[292]

[291] Agreed under the auspices of the World Customs Organisation: the later convention was intended to replace the earlier but has not done so; the later convention only has 34 contracting states, the earlier ATA convention.

[292] The UK guaranteeing association is the London Chamber of Commerce and Industry and details of the procedures for their issue are available at *http://www.londonchamber.co.uk/lcc.*

Part Two: Contracts for the Carriage of Goods by Land

2.1 Overview of Contracts for Land Carriage

The legal complexities associated with contracts for the carriage of goods by land sometimes appear disproportionate to the operational simplicity of carrying goods from A to B. Land carriage may be domestic or international and involve carriage by road, rail and/or inland waterway, each being addressed at 2.2 to 2.7 below. However, it is in connection with road movements where the disconnection between contractual complexity and operational simplicity appears most obvious and that aspect will be addressed first in the context of domestic carriage by road.

2.2 Domestic Road Carriage

2.2.1 Contractual Context

Contracts concluded for the carriage of goods wholly in the United Kingdom may indeed be simply contracts between road carrier and goods owner for the movement of goods from A to B, subject to the common law and any incorporated contractual terms. Alternatively, they may be incorporated within an international movement of goods with collection and delivery within the United Kingdom either at the end, the beginning, or in the middle of the international movement. Where the UK road carriers actually become international road carriers pursuant to art.34 of the CMR, by the acceptance of the goods and the consignment note, the carriage will be governed by the CMR Convention as further discussed in 2.3. Otherwise the UK road carrier will be acting as sub-contractor to the principal carrier responsible for the international movement, or possibly as principal contractor for part only of an entire movement organised by some intermediary (typically a freight forwarding agent) acting as agent.[1] In this event, were the goods to be lost, damaged or delayed, the UK road carrier may be able to claim protection from liability either under its own conditions of carriage by reference to the doctrine of sub-bailment on terms or, possibly, under any combined transport document issued for the entire movement

[1] It is of course commonly the case that persons contracting ostensibly as freight forwarding agents conclude contracts as principals as discussed in 5.2.2; a fact expressly acknowledged by BIFA 2005A Conditions clause 4(A).

by reference to arguments arising under the Contracts (Rights of Third Parties) Act 1999 and/or any Himalaya type clause.[2] It is in connection with such combined movements by sea carriers that the United Nations Convention on Contracts for the International Carriage of Goods Wholly or Partly by Sea (the Rotterdam Rules)[3] could have a significant effect were the convention to take effect as a legislative instrument of public international law (by being subjected to ratification, acceptance, approval or accession by at least 20 states),[4] be applied into national law and be recognised and applied by courts exercising jurisdiction over any dispute.[5]

As with all carriage obligations, the carrier may be collecting from and/or delivering to persons other than those owning the goods or those with whom the contract for carriage was made. As a result the road carrier is always exposed to third party liability in bailment and tort. Provided that the owner of the goods expressly or implicitly consented to their bailment to the carrier and the carrier's carriage conditions are not unduly onerous or unusual, the carrier will be able to claim the protection of those carriage conditions as against the third party claimants pursuant to the doctrine of sub-bailment on terms.[6]

In the absence of any specific authority to the effect that the common law draws any conceptual distinction between the loading and unloading of vehicles and vessels it would appear that prima facie responsibility for loading and unloading in connection with road carriage lies with the carrier where no special equipment is required beyond that provided by the carrier pursuant to the contract. Goods should be handed over for carriage properly packed for the contemplated movement in a state in which they

[2] As discussed in 1.6.1.2.

[3] Adopted by the United Nations on 11 December 2008, opened for signature from 23 September 2009 and some 21 states have, as at 26 October 2009, signified an intention to ratify in due course.

[4] Article 94(1) providing for its coming into force after the expiry of one year from the twentieth such ratification.

[5] The potential effect of the Rotterdam Rules is reviewed in 3.3.5.

[6] See *Sandeman Coprimar SA v Transitos y Transportes Integrales SL* [2003] Q.B. 1270 where, even in the absence of a CMR note (and the consequent loss of successive CMR carrier status under art.234 of the CMR), third party carriers were able to secure the protection of the CMR.

can, with reasonable convenience, be loaded and carried;[7] with the carriage ordinarily being subject to the implied warranty on the part of the consignor that the goods are fit and proper for carriage and are not dangerous.[8] Holders of the road freight vehicle and freight operator's licences for the operation of the vehicle have statutory obligations to maintain the vehicle in a roadworthy condition; however, the carrier has no implied contractual obligation at common law to provide a roadworthy vehicle.[9] There is no authority indicating that the consignor is generally under any implied obligation as to the safety of the places of collection or delivery of the goods, but the occupiers of those premises have a statutory duty to exercise the common duty of care to ensure the safety of their premises for visitors (such as the carrier). Breach of this statutory duty is actionable in tort by anyone suffering damage in consequence.[10]

The carrier may deliver to its own premises for collection by the consignee, or to some other place such as a port for collection or onward movement, most commonly, however, the carrier will deliver to the premises of the consignee. Where the obligation of the carrier is to deliver the goods to the consignee at the carrier's premises, the carrier is under a duty to inform the consignee of the arrival of the goods, unless the contrary has been expressly agreed or is to be implied.[11] The consignee must then take delivery of the goods within a reasonable time, and if it fails to do so, the carriage is at an end when a reasonable time has elapsed after the carrier has given notice to the consignee of the arrival of the goods.[12] The question as to what is a reasonable time for the consignee to take delivery is a question of fact. Whether the carrier is obliged to deliver to the consignee's premises, or to some other place, the carriage is at an end when the goods are presented within normal working hours, irrespective of whether or not

7 *Munster v South-Eastern Railway Company* (1858) 4 C.B. (N.S.) 676, 701. Indeed, a seller of goods, who is also a consignor of those goods, should note that deficient packing may also be a breach of the condition implied in the contract of sale by s.14 of the Sale of Goods Act 1979 (*Mash & Murrell Ltd v Joseph I. Emanuel Ltd* [1961] 1 W.L.R. 862).

8 See 1.9.

9 See 1.2 and 1.6.1.2.

10 Occupiers' Liability Act 1957 ss.1 to 3.

11 *Mitchell v Lancashire and Yorkshire Railway Company* (1875) L.R. 10 Q.B. 256, 260, per Blackburn J.; see *Chapman v Great Western Railway Company and London and North-Western Railway Company* (1880) 5 Q.B.D. 278, at pp.280, 282, per Cockburn C.J.

12 *Chapman v Great Western Railway Company and London and North-Western Railway Company* ibid. at p.282, per Cockburn C.J.

they are accepted. Should the carrier remain in possession of the goods after the carriage has come to an end, the carrier would continue to hold the goods as bailee, but only as a warehouseman and not as a carrier. The only significance in the change of status (unless, extraordinarily, the carrier is a common carrier)[13] will lie in the carriage and/or storage conditions governing the carrier's relationship with the consignor and any third party such as consignee.[14] Given that many forwarders, road carriers and warehousemen have adopted industry-wide standard carriage conditions it is appropriate now to consider them.

2.2.2 Industry Standard Conditions

There are only a few conditions which are used in common across the many providers of road carriage services and these are all prepared by industry associations for the use of their members only. The most relevant associations meeting the needs of those businesses entering into contracts of carriage with others for the carriage of goods by road are the Road Haulage Association (RHA), the Freight Transport Association (FTA) and the British International Freight Association (BIFA) who, respectively, make the following conditions available to their members for the carriage of goods by road: the RHA Conditions of Carriage 2009 Edition (RHA 2009), the FTA Conditions for the Carriage of Goods by Road in the United Kingdom 2002 Edition (FTA 2002) and the revised BIFA Standard Trading Conditions 2005 Edition (BIFA 2005A).

The focus of each of these associations is different. The membership of the RHA comprises some 10,000 independent haulage businesses operating commercial vehicles and predominantly engaged in the carriage of goods for reward by road for customers under contracts of carriage. In contrast the membership of the FTA consists of some 12,000 or so businesses with a wider logistical focus engaged in the carriage of goods for themselves or their customers (both under carriage and sale contracts) by means of road, rail, sea and air movements. The 1,400 or so members of BIFA tend to be businesses predominantly arranging for the carriage of goods by land, sea and air by others on behalf of customers. The BIFA members either enter

13 See 1.10. Also see 2.2.3 below for the effect of the Carriers Act 1830 on the duties and liabilities of common carriers by road.

14 See 1.2.

into contracts with carriers as agents on behalf of their customers or, as principal carriers, sub-contract the actual performance to others. BIFA is an association member of the international FIATA body which in turn represents the interests of some 40,000 freight-forwarding businesses worldwide.

The contrasting commercial focus of their respective memberships explains why the standard trading conditions of these associations are so distinct from each other, even though any one or more of them may apply in connection with UK road carriage. Of course, all limitations and exclusions of liability contained in RHA 2009, FTA 2002 and BIFA 2005A Conditions can only take effect subject to the common law rules as to the contractual incorporation and interpretation of those conditions, the general statutory regulation of contractual exclusions and limitations and the particular statutory regulation of carriage conditions arising under the international carriage conditions.[15] Whilst RHA 2009 and FTA 2002 conditions are discussed respectively at 2.2.2.1 and 2.2.2.2 below, BIFA 2005A conditions are discussed in the context of freight forwarding services at 5.2.2.

2.2.2.1 RHA 2009 Conditions[16]

The RHA is an association primarily representing the interests of UK road hauliers carrying goods for others for reward. Consequently, it is not surprising that the standard conditions of carriage published for its members' use should state by way of introduction that the "carrier" (defined by the member's description of itself in the box provided) "is not a common carrier". Clause 2 addresses the identity of the parties to the contract of carriage in various ways: at 2(1) by providing for a warranty on the part of the "customer" (defined as the person contracting with the carrier) that it is the owner of the goods to be carried or whoever has the authority of the owner to agree to the conditions on behalf of the owner; at 2(2) by permitting the carrier to sub-contract performance to other carriers; at 2(3) by providing that the carrier also contracts as agents on behalf of its own agents, employees and sub-contractors so as to extend the benefit of the conditions to them; and at 2(4) by purporting to provide that where the carrier arranges rail, sea, inland waterway or air carriage it does so as agent

[15] See 1.5.

[16] Formerly issued in the form of the prior RHA 1998 edition.

of the customer who, in consequence, is to become subject to the conditions of the performing carrier.[17]

The structure of the liability provisions under RHA 2009 conditions at cll.9(2)(b), 9(3) and 10 follows the liability framework for common carriers, albeit with significant additional protections for carriers. As with common carriers the RHA 2009 carrier is an effective insurer of the goods and generally responsible for any loss, damage or misdelivery occasioned to them during transit.[18] As with common carriers, the RHA carrier is exempted from strict liability arising from particular excluded causes, albeit the carrier nevertheless has a duty to exercise reasonable care to minimise their effects. The excluded causes referred to at cl.2(b)(i) to (ix) (relating to such matters as acts of God, etc., acts of war etc., inherent vice etc., or fault of the consignor or owner of the goods) largely restate, in the context of private contracts of carriage, the exclusions applicable to common carriers. However, the exceptions at (iii) for seizure or forfeiture under legal process and (viii) in respect of riot etc. under RHA 2009 Conditions are exceptions not available to a common carrier. Clause 10 expressly relieves the carrier of liability for loss in the event of fraud by the customer or owner or their respective employees and agents unless contributed to by the complicity of the carrier or its employees. Additional protection is provided in respect of valuable goods and live animals as cl.9(1) provides that the carrier shall only be liable for loss, damage or misdelivery of such goods where the carrier has agreed in writing to carry the goods, the customer has agreed to writing to reimburse the additional cost of carriage of such goods and any loss, damage or misdelivery of them is caused by the negligence of the carrier, its agents, employees or sub-contractors. The period of transit defined by cl.6 is distinct from the period of carriage under common law discussed at 1.6.2.[19] It covers the period from when the carrier has first taken possession

[17] These provisions engage the protection for carriers of the various principles discussed at 1.6.1.2 as arising under the Contracts (Rights of Third Parties) Act 1999 and Himalaya clauses. The effect of the express authority to sub-contract engages the principles of sub-bailment on terms since, as per Lord Goff in the *Pioneer Container* (fn. 61 in Part One), authority of the owner to any sub-bailment engages "all the terms of the sub-bailment, warts and all". The principles of *Aqualon v Vallana* (fn. 20 in Part One) must be applied when considering whether a road carrier can really disclaim responsibility pursuant to cl.2(4) for carriage by other modes which it has procured.

[18] As defined by cl.6

[19] That is the period from the acceptance by the carrier of the goods for carriage until the time of either delivery, or once all reasonable steps to achieve delivery have been undertaken.

of the goods under cl.6(1) until the carrier tenders the goods at the place of delivery "within the customary cartage hours of the district"; or until the expiry of one day's written or, pursuant to prior written agreement, telephone notice that "no safe and adequate access or adequate unloading facilities" are available; or until the expiry of a "reasonable time" where goods are held by the carrier to await collection. The RHA 2009 carrier purports by cl.9(3) to exclude liability for any loss or damage (but not apparently misdelivery) occurring after the defined period of transit has ended, even if caused by act or omission on the part of the carrier, its employees, agents or sub contractors. Since as a matter of public policy a carrier cannot exclude liability for its own fraud or deliberate wrongdoing, uncertainty arises as to the proper interpretation of this exclusion.[20]

The concept of dangerous goods in RHA 2009 Conditions is not determined by their nature under common law,[21] but is a more restrictive concept defined by reference to the international ADR Agreement.[22] The uncertainty at common law as to loading and unloading operations[23] is removed by cl.4 of RHA 2009 Conditions which provides, in the absence of contrary written agreement that: the carrier has no obligation to provide "plant, power or labour, other than that carried by the vehicle"; "any plant, power or labour" not carried by the vehicle, which is required for loading and unloading, will be provided by the customer; the carrier shall have no liability for "any damage whatsoever, howsoever caused" where such "plant, power or labour" is not provided by the customer and the carrier is nonetheless instructed to load or unload; and should the carrier "provide service beyond the usual place of collection and delivery" such service shall be at the "sole risk" of the customer. Clearly these provisions are an improvement on the RHA 1998 Conditions, which referred to the uncertain concept of "special appliances" for loading and unloading, but they are equally unlikely to assist a road carrier in defending a claim for damage caused or contributed to by the driver's negligence for reasons discussed at 1.5.2.

The financial limitation provisions for any liability arising on the part of the carrier is at the heart of the contractual protection which the RHA 2009 Conditions seek to provide to association members. Any direct or indirect

20 Such issues are discussed at 1.5.2.
21 As to which see 1.9.1.3.
22 Discussed at 5.3.2.1.
23 Addressed at 1.6.2.1.

damages arising at common law[24] are subjected to financial limitation by cl.11, which provides that: claims for loss, damage or misdelivery to goods are limited to the lower of their value, the cost of repair, or a sum calculated at the rate of £1,300 per tonne of the gross weight of the goods lost, damaged or misdelivered. By cl.11(2) other claims, not arising by reason of loss damage or misdelivery, such as claims for delay, are limited to the value of the carriage charges. Provision is made by cll.11(1)(iv) and 11(2) for higher limits to apply on the customer both making written request and agreeing to pay a proportionate surcharge. The absolute common law right to freight discussed at 1.9.1.1 is, by cl.8, extended to all charges of the carrier. The consignor cannot avoid liability for freight by consigning it on the basis the consignee will pay; albeit, where the carrier accepts goods for carriage on that basis, the consignor has no payment obligation unless and until the consignee shall have failed to pay on reasonable demand. The common law right of the carrier to claim damages for any delay caused to its vehicle in consequence of breach by the customer is preserved, but not quantified, by cl.15. In place of the position at common law that a private carrier by road may not even have a particular lien over the goods in the event of non-payment of the carriage charges, RHA 2009 Conditions provide at cl.14 for a general lien and right of sale as against the customer and for a particular lien as against any owner of the goods who is not the customer. The particular lien is capable of being enforced against any owner pursuant to the doctrine of sub-bailment on terms, always provided of course that such owner has expressly or by implication consented to the sub-bailment.[25]

RHA 2009 Conditions contain express choices in favour of English law and the jurisdiction of the UK courts which are capable, subject to effective incorporation as discussed in 1.5.1, of constituting effective choices of law and jurisdiction for the purposes of art.23(1) of R44/2001 and art.3(1) of the Rome Convention (and the Rome 1 Regulation) subject to the restrictions as to choice discussed at 1.4. Unlike the position at common law,[26] claims must be issued within one year from the commencement of the transit, otherwise the carrier is "discharged from all liability whatsoever and howsoever arising".[27] Furthermore the carrier is expressed to "not be liable" for loss, damage or misdelivery unless that is notified in writing to

[24] Concepts addressed in 1.8.2.

[25] See 1.6.1.1.

[26] Discussed at 1.8.3.

[27] See cl.13.2 of RHA 2009 Conditions.

the carrier within seven days of, and any consequent claim is made in writing to the carrier within 14 days of, the termination of the transit. Under RHA 2009 Conditions, certain acts of default by the customer result in an indemnity rather than merely damages[28] and the indemnity at cl.12(2) extends to any liabilities incurred by the carrier in connection with the consignment in excess of the liabilities imposed on the carrier under the RHA 2009 Conditions.

2.2.2.2 FTA 2002 Conditions

The structure of the FTA 2002 Conditions is in many respects similar to that of the RHA 2009 Conditions. There is an introductory stipulation that the carrier (similarly defined) is not a common carrier. The provisions at cl.2 as to the parties bound by the conditions adopt a similar approach by affording the benefit of the conditions to the carrier's sub-contractors, providing that the carrier may sub-contract performance and providing for the customer to warrant it has authority to accept the conditions on behalf of the owner of the goods should the customer not be the owner. However, it should be noted that the FTA 2002 Conditions do not purport to make the carrier an agent of the customer in connection with the procurement by the carrier of carriage by means other than road and do not permit the sub-contracting of carriage of dangerous goods without the written consent of the customer. Dangerous goods are again defined by reference not to the broad common law concept but to particular statutory concepts to be understood in the light of current enactments.[29] The liability provisions at cl.9 again accept liability for loss or damage to any goods carried, excluding valuable goods and live animals (other than in the circumstances outlined in cl.9.3) arising from any cause excepting those excluded as stated at cl.9.4. The excepted causes again broadly track the common law exclusions to the liability of the common carrier. Similarly to the RHA 2009 Conditions, they include additional exclusions at (c) for seizure or forfeiture under legal process and (i) in respect of riot etc. Additional specific exclusions, particularly significant in the context of cargo handling operations on loading and unloading, are also stipulated in connection with (h) special handling

[28] See cll.4(2) and 12 of the RHA 2009 Conditions.

[29] Referring to an approved carriage list previously maintained by the Health and Safety Commission, which merged with the Health and Safety Executive on April 1, 2008. The approved carriage list formerly had statutory effect under UK delegated legislation, but has now been overtaken by the Carriage of Dangerous Goods and Use of Transportable Pressure Equipment Regulations 2009/1348.

requirements not notified to the carrier; (j) defects in customer's equipment or negligence on the part of the customer's servants or agents; and (k) delay in providing the carrier with "safe and adequate access" for loading and unloading.

The concept of a period of "carriage" as at common law (or of "transit" under the RHA 2009 Conditions) is replaced by the concept of "Carrier's responsibility" provided for by cl.6 of the FTA 2002 Conditions. The carrier is expressed to have no liability "for loss, damage or delay" to the goods where carried at "owner's risk" under cl.6.1. Otherwise the carrier's responsibility commences when it takes "physical control" of the consignment on collection or receipt. The carrier's responsibility ends when it, or its agents or sub-contractors, relinquish "physical control ... at the proper place of delivery", or present the consignment at that place within normal business hours allowing for "sufficient" unloading time as provided for by cll.6.2 and 6.3. The carrier's responsibility for the goods may be ended by the carrier giving 24 hours written notice to the consignee and/or the consignor within cl.6.4, in circumstances where the consignee is to collect the goods from the carrier, or where the carrier is unable to deliver the goods in the absence of safe adequate access or unloading facility. Clause 3.1 provides that, in the absence of the customer's request and the carrier's written agreement, the carrier has no responsibility to provide any services other than carriage of the goods from and to the designated places of loading and unloading; cll.3.2 to 3.6 seek to make the customer responsible for the provision and operation of all loading and unloading equipment and activities, apart from the residual obligation on the carrier under cl.3.5 to make goods reasonably accessible on the vehicle.

Financial limitation provisions at cl.10 are at the same level as those available under the RHA 2009 Conditions except that the limitation fund calculated by reference to the £1,300 per tonne rate is subject to a minimum fund value of £500 for the entire consignment. Unlike the RHA 2009 Conditions, cl.7 of the FTA 2002 Conditions does not give the carrier an absolute right to the payment of freight without deduction; nonetheless, the carrier may seek to argue for the payment of freight without deduction or set off pursuant to the common law. A general lien and power of sale over the consignment are provided for by cl.13 where the customer is the owner of the consignment. Clause 13.3 provides that where the consignment is owned by someone else, the customer warrants that it has the authority of that owner to agree to the carrier having a bare particular lien over the consignment without any further right beyond holding the goods against the owner for payment of the carrier's charges in respect of that consignment. Clause 16 provides for English law to be the applicable law governing the contractual obligations and for an exclusive choice of jurisdiction in favour of the courts of England; this choice of jurisdiction is subject to the operation of alternative dispute resolution procedures pursuant to cll.15.1 and 15.2 and to the reference to arbitration at cl.15.3. As there is an express choice of English jurisdiction it may be intended that the lex arbitri, or legal seat of the arbitration, would be England.[30]

FTA 2002 Conditions do not limit the period of time arising under the statute of limitations for the commencement of proceedings, but do stipulate at cl.12.1 that the carrier will not be liable for: (a) loss or damage to the whole consignment unless written notice and written claim (stating weight, value and date of collection) is given to the carrier within 14 days of the carrier taking physical control of the consignment; (b) loss or damage to part of the consignment unless written notice is given within seven days and written claim (stating weight, value and date of collection) is given within 14 days of the carrier's responsibility for the consignment ending; (c) any damage unless made available for inspection within a reasonable period; (d) delay unless written notice is given within three days of the agreed delivery date or, where no delivery date is agreed, 63 days of the carrier taking physical control of the consignment. As with the RHA 2009 Conditions, express provision is made for the recovery of unquantified "cost or expense" occasioned by improper or excessive detention of the carrier's vehicles and for the customer to indemnify the carrier in respect of particular incidents of loss or damage suffered by the carrier in consequence of the customer's default, third party claims in excess of the liability provided for in the FTA 2002 Conditions and/or claims made by HM Revenue and Customs in respect of dutiable goods.[31]

2.2.3 Common Carriers by Road—The Carriers Act 1830

2.2.3.1 Application

The Carriers Act 1830 gave statutory recognition to the common law right of the common carrier to demand an increased freight for the carriage of valuable goods (see 1.10.2), and contains provisions exempting the

[30] Although that may not always be the case as cl.15.3 provides for the physical location of the arbitration to be "in the town" where the carrier's main administrative office is located and that office may well be located outside England.

[31] Clauses 14 and 11 of FTA 2002 Conditions.

common carrier from all liability in respect of valuables not declared by the consignor. It also prohibited a common carrier from limiting liability with respect to any goods other than valuables by means of a public notice. The Act applies to carriage of goods by land by "mail contractors, stage coach proprietors or other common carriers". It is thus clear that, whilst the Act would still apply to any common carriers, it cannot apply to any contractual carrier.

Furthermore, it does not now apply to the carriage of mail by the Post Office or any other provider of universal postal services under the Postal Services Act 2000.[32] The Carriers Act does not apply to the carriage of goods by sea and were a common carrier to carry goods partly by land and partly by sea, the statute would only apply to that part of the carriage on land.[33] The Carriers Act originally applied to carriage by railway, for the railway companies were common carriers and the Railways Act 1921 made special provisions with regard to the application of the Carriers Act to railways. However, the Transport Act 1962, s.43 enacted that the Railways Board should not be regarded as a common carrier. This change of status is maintained by current legislation,[34] with the consequence that the Carriers Act does not apply to carriage by railway.

As will be appreciated from the above, the Carriers Act 1830 is now largely of academic interest only and a strong case could be made for its repeal. However, as the legislation is still in force, road carriers could still undertake carriage for reward as common carriers and Carriers Act provisions are replicated in aspects of the standard carriage and forwarding conditions reviewed above, it is still appropriate to deal with its provisions.

2.2.3.2 Provisions relating to Valuables

The Carriers Act provides that where goods of a class specified in s.1 of the Act exceeding £10 in value are contained in a package, the common carrier shall not be liable for any loss or damage to the goods, except where caused by the felony of his servants, unless the consignor has made a declaration of the nature and value of the goods at the time of the delivery of the goods to the carrier, and has paid an additional sum, over and above the freight, as

[32] Section 99 Postal Services Act 2000.

[33] In *London and North-Western Railway Company v Ashton and Company* [1920] A.C. 84 it was decided that the common carrier has the onus of proving that any loss or damage occurred on land so as to entitle it to rely on the provisions of the Carriers Act.

[34] See 1.10.1.

insurance money if such sum is demanded by the carrier. Goods of the class specified in s.1 have usually been referred to, both judicially and otherwise, as valuables, although this term is not used in the Carriers Act.

The specified goods are: gold or silver coins of this realm or of any foreign state, or any gold or silver in a manufactured or unmanufactured state, or any precious stones, jewellery, watches, clocks or time-pieces of any description, trinkets, bills, notes of the Governor and Company of the Banks of England, Scotland and Ireland respectively, or of any other bank in Great Britain or Ireland, orders, notes or securities for payment of money, English or foreign, stamps, maps, writings, title deeds, paintings, engravings, pictures, gold or silver plate or plated articles, glass, china, silks in a manufactured or unmanufactured state and whether wrought up or not wrought up with other materials, furs or lace. The Carriers Act Amendment Act 1865 enacted that machine-made lace should no longer be included as valuables for the purposes of the Carriers Act. The meaning of the words used in the definition of valuables should be interpreted in the popular sense, and not in a stricter sense. Thus "paintings" are limited to works of an artistic nature, and does not include painted patterns carried by a commercial traveller to show to customers.[35]

The provisions of s.1 of the Carriers Act apply only where valuables are contained in a parcel or package to a value exceeding £10. Where the value of the valuables in the package is exactly £10 s.1 of the Carriers Act does not apply. The value is apparently to be taken as the value to the consignor at the time of the carriage. Where the consignor, who had bought valuables for £9.95, sold them to the consignee for over £10 and sent the goods to him by a carrier, the goods were within s.1 of the Carriers Act as the value of the goods to the consignor was the sum that the consignee had agreed to pay for the goods.[36] Although the Act refers to a "parcel or package" containing the valuables, s.1 applies where the valuables are placed without any wrapping in a truck.[37]

For the purpose of ascertaining whether the Act applies to goods, it is the value of the valuables contained in any one package which must be

[35] *Woodward v London and North-Western Railway Company* (1878) 3 Ex. D. 121.

[36] *Blankensee v London and North-Western Railway* (1881) 45 L.T. 761.

[37] *Whaite v Lancashire and Yorkshire Railway Company* (1874) L.R. 9 Ex. 67; but in *Studebaker Distributors v Charlton Steam Shipping Company* [1938] 1 K.B. 459, which concerned the interpretation of a contract of carriage by sea containing a term requiring the consignor to declare the value of valuables in a "package", Goddard J. held that a motor car which was shipped without any packing at all could not be deemed to be a package.

considered. Thus where a package contains both valuables and other goods, the value of the other goods is disregarded, as is the value of the packing or case, unless the packing or case itself is made of a material classed as valuables. If the aggregate value of all the valuables contained in the package exceeds £10, the Act applies to these goods. It does not apply to goods other than the valuables contained in the same package.[38] Where a package contains only valuables, and the aggregate value of the valuables exceeds £10, the case or bag or other material in which the goods are contained is within the provisions of s.1, although it is not made of a material classed as valuables.[39] However, if the package contains both valuables and non-valuables, the bag or packing is excluded from the provisions of s.1 along with the non-valuables, unless the bag or packing itself is classed as valuables.[40]

Where an object is made of two or more materials, some of which are valuables and others non-valuables, the whole object, together with those parts made of non-valuable materials, is within the provisions of s.1 if it is contained in a package in which the value of the valuables exceeds £10, unless the nature of the object is such that the non-valuable materials may be said to have a separate identity from the valuables; if the non-valuables have such a separate identity, they will be excluded from the provisions of s.1. Thus where a lace garment was contained in a frame which was not made of valuable material, the frame was not within the provisions of s.1, because the lace could be removed without destroying the identity of the frame.[41] However, where a picture was encased in a frame which was not of valuable material, the owner was unable to recover damages in respect of the frame where the picture and frame were contained in a package which was subject to the provisions of s.1, for the frame was held to be an integral part of the picture.[42]

2.2.3.3 Common Carriers' Liability

If the consignor fails to make a declaration to the carrier of the nature and value of goods within s.1, the consignor is unable to recover any damages whatsoever for loss or damage to the goods, howsoever caused otherwise

[38] *Treadwin v Great Eastern Railway Company* (1868) L.R. 3 C.P. 308.
[39] *Wyld v Pickford* (1841) 8 M. & W. 443.
[40] *Treadwin v Great Eastern Railway Company* (fn. 38).
[41] ibid.
[42] *Henderson v London and North-Western Railway Company* (1870) L.R. 5 Ex. 90.

than by the felony of the carrier's servants. The carrier is not even liable up to £10 if the valuables in a package exceed £10 in value and are consequently subject to the provisions of s.1. There is no provision in the Act as to the form in which the declaration is to be made, and it may therefore be made verbally. Where the consignor makes a declaration that a package contains valuables and states their value as exceeding £10, the carrier is entitled to demand a further sum over and above the freight to procure insurance (insurance premium). The Act does not provide that the sum demanded as an insurance premium must be reasonable; presumably this is to be implied, and the carrier is presumably entitled to demand a reasonable sum to procure insurance in addition to the reasonable freight which it is entitled to demand as a common carrier.

If, after the consignor has made the declaration, the carrier does not demand any insurance premium, the consignor is not obliged to pay it, and failure to do so will not preclude the consignor from recovering damages for loss or damage to the valuables.[43] However, if the carrier demands the insurance premium, the failure of the consignor to pay it will debar the owner from recovering in respect of any loss or damage other than felony by the carrier's servants, to the same extent as if the consignor had not made the declaration. Refusal by the consignor to pay the insurance premium will not, however, entitle the carrier to refuse to carry the goods.[44] The obligation of the consignor to make the declaration is not limited to cases where the goods are delivered to the carrier at the carrier's receiving office, it also applies if the goods are delivered to the carrier at the consignor's house,[45] or any other place. Section 9 of the Act enacts that the owner of the goods is estopped from alleging that the value of the goods exceeds the sum which the consignor stated as being their value in the declaration to the carrier, although the carrier is entitled to allege that the true value of the goods is less than that stated in the consignor's declaration. Section 7 of the Act enacts that where the goods are lost or damaged during the carriage, the consignor is entitled to recover the insurance premium as well as damages for the loss or damage to the goods.

[43] *Behrens v Great Northern Railway Company* (1861) 3 L.T. 863.

[44] This was laid down obiter in *Hart v Baxendale* (1851) 6 Exch. 769, 788, by Maule J., and in *Behrens v Great Northern Railway Company* ibid. at p.865, per Channell B.; but if this is so, the Act has adversely affected the position of the carrier in this respect, for at common law the carrier was entitled to demand an additional sum as freight for the carriage of valuables, and to refuse to carry if this reasonable freight was not paid when the goods were delivered.

[45] *Hart v Baxendale* (1851) 6 Exch. 769.

Section 3 of the Act requires the carrier to exhibit in its receiving office a public notice referring to the obligations of the consignor to declare the nature and value of the goods and to pay the insurance premium and requires the carrier, on demand by the consignor, to give a receipt for the payment of the insurance premium. Whilst there is no clear authority, it seems that notwithstanding breach of these provisions, the common carrier will nonetheless be entitled to take the benefit of the Act; so that where the carrier fails to affix the notice and the consignor fails to make the declaration, the common carrier is still not liable for any loss or damage to valuables exceeding £10 in one package, save in the case of felony by its servants.[46]

Section 8 of the Carriers Act provides that, notwithstanding anything in the Act, the carrier shall be liable for loss to the goods where this is caused by the felonious act of any "coachman, guard, bookkeeper, porter or other servant in his employ". Consequently, where the goods are proved to have been stolen by a servant of the carrier, the owner can recover damages for the theft of the valuables, even if the consignor failed to make the declaration or pay the insurance premium demanded. The onus of proving that the goods were stolen by a servant of the carrier rests on the claimant. It is not enough to raise a presumption that larceny was committed, and that the thief was the carrier's servant, or to rely on the doctrine of res ipsa loquitur where the goods are shown to have been in the custody of the carrier's servants at the time of the theft; the fact that the thief was a servant of the carrier must be strictly proved.[47] If it were clear that the goods had been stolen by one of two servants of the carrier, but neither could be convicted of larceny because it was impossible to prove which was the thief, the owner would be entitled to recover from the carrier under s.8.[48] The words in s.8 referring to any "coachman, guard, bookkeeper, porter or other servant in his employ" have been extended to cover any servant of an agent employed by the carrier,[49] and any person acting in one of the above-mentioned capacities for the carrier, although the relation of master and servant did not exist in law between the carrier and the thief. Thus where the carrier regularly used an inn as a receiving office for goods, and the

[46] *Hart v Baxendale* (1851) 6 Exch. 769, 789–90, per Patteson J.; *Rosenthal v London County Council* (1924) 131 L.T. 563, where Bailhache J, stated that he would have been reluctantly bound to adhere to this view had it been necessary for the determination of the action.

[47] *M'Queen v Great Western Railway Company* (1875) L.R. 10 Q.B. 659.

[48] See *Vaughton v London and North-Western Railway Company* (1874) L.R. 9 Ex. 93.

[49] *Machu v London and South-Western Railway Company* (1848) 2 Exch. 415.

goods were stolen by the innkeeper's son, who regularly assisted his father in receiving and handling the goods, the carrier was liable under s.8.[50]

Section 1 of the Carriers Act refers only to loss and damage to the goods, and not to delay. The failure of the consignor to make the declaration of the nature and value of the goods does not prevent the recovery of damages for delay to valuables exceeding £10 in value in a package.[51] Section 1 has, however, been held to apply to a temporary loss of the goods as well as to a permanent loss. The distinction between goods temporarily lost and goods delayed depends on whether or not the carrier knew where they were during the relevant period. If the carrier, or its servants, knew where the goods were to be found, they were not temporarily lost, and the owner can recover; but if they did not know where the goods were, the goods were temporarily lost, and the owner cannot recover damages for the ensuing delay, as this would evade the purposes of the Act.[52] The provisions of the Carriers Act are statutory, and do not depend for their validity on the contract of carriage. A carrier who has deviated may rely on the provisions of the Carriers Act 1830,[53] and no doubt on any other statute, for the fact that the contract has been repudiated does not affect the operation of statutory enactments. Consequently, a carrier who has repudiated the contract by deviation and is in possession of the goods as a wrongful possessor, can still rely on the statute, and the owner of goods within s.1 cannot recover if the consignor failed to make the declaration of nature and value.[54]

Section 4 of the Carriers Act enacts that save as provided in the Act, a common carrier may not limit its liability at common law by means of a public notice exhibited in its receiving office. This applies to all goods delivered to a common carrier for carriage, and not only to valuables. The section does not restrict the right of the common carrier to limit or exclude liability by a special contract[55] but merely provides that it shall be conclusively presumed that the consignor did not, at the time of contracting, have notice of such conditions merely displayed in the carrier's receiving office. However, where the consignor's attention is specifically drawn to the public notice and he thereafter delivers the goods to the carrier, this may be

[50] *Stephens v London and South-Western Railway Company* (1886) 18 Q.B.D. 121.

[51] *Hearn v London and South-Western Railway Company* (1855) 10 Exch. 793.

[52] *Millen v Brasch and Company* (1882) 10 Q.B.D. 142.

[53] *Morritt v North-Eastern Railway Company* (1876) 1 Q. B.D. 302.

[54] ibid.

[55] *Walker v York and North Midland Railway Company* (1853) 2 E. & B. 750.

deemed to constitute a special contract binding the consignor.[56] Section 6 of the Act provides that the parties shall be free to enter into a special contract varying the provisions of the Act. It is therefore open to the parties to agree that the common carrier shall be liable for undeclared valuables, or shall not be liable even for theft by his servants of undeclared valuables,[57] or will not be liable for valuables even when duly declared by the consignor. Any such contract is valid, provided that the common carrier draws the attention of the consignor to its terms by some means other than a public notice at its receiving office.

Although the statute only applies to common carriers it is possible for a private carrier to adopt the Act contractually by stating in its conditions of carriage that it is agreed that the private carrier shall have the protection of the Act even though it is not a common carrier. Where international carriage of goods by road is governed by the CMR pursuant to the Carriage of Goods by Road Act, even though the UK carriage might be performed by a common carrier (or by a contractual carrier adopting the Act), the provisions of the Carriers Act would be displaced by the CMR.

2.3 International Carriage of Goods by Road—The CMR

2.3.1 Scope of Application

The Carriage of Goods by Road Act 1965 (which was brought into force by an Order of the Queen in Council on June 5, 1967) provided that in all cases of international carriage by road for reward (other than carriage of postal packets, funeral consignments, and furniture removal) the contract of carriage should be governed by the provisions of the international Convention of Geneva of 1956, the Convention Relative au Contrat de Transport International de Marchandises par Route (the CMR). The CMR does not apply to domestic carriage within the United Kingdom; nor, by reason of the protocol to it, to carriage between the United Kingdom and the Republic of Ireland. It was entered into in Geneva on May 19, 1956 in English and French on the basis that each version would be equally

[56] *Peek v North Staffordshire Railway Company* (1863) 10 H.L.C. 473, 507, per Blackburn J.; *Shaw v Great Western Railway Company* [1894] 1 Q.B. 373, 381, per Wright J.

[57] *Shaw v Great Western Railway Company* ibid.

authentic. Whilst English courts are cognisant of their duty[58] to interpret the CMR purposively to give effect to the underlying purposes of the treaty and to achieve international consistency there is nonetheless a significant lack of consistency in the jurisprudence of the respective contracting states regarding the interpretation of its various provisions.[59]

The CMR applies to any contract for the carriage of goods by road in vehicles for reward from a place in one state to a place in another state, where at least one of those two states is a party to it. It continues to apply where part of the journey is by sea, rail, inland waterways or air, if the goods remain loaded to the road vehicle while they are on the ship, railway, watercraft or airplane. It is clear that the CMR applies as much to framework or umbrella agreements for multiple contracts of carriage by road as it does to single contracts of carriage by road and equally to written and oral contracts.[60] If any actual carriage is subject to the CMR, it makes no difference that the carriage has not commenced; or that the carrier might, under its own standard conditions, have a right to refuse to carry the goods.[61] Neither does it make any difference if the contracting carrier does not in fact carry the goods, since the person or entity who contracts with the sender to carry the goods is the carrier, even if that person or entity does not undertake any stage of the carriage.[62]

The United Kingdom (for itself and certain of its dependant territories including Gibraltar, Guernsey and the Isle of Man) is a party to the CMR.

[58] See 1.5.2.

[59] See, for instance, the brief discussions below as to the meaning of the financial limitation provisions at arts 23(4) and 29(1); for a more detailed analysis of the many inconsistencies arising in the interpretation of the CMR see Hill and Messent, *CMR: Contracts for the International Carriage of Goods by Road*, 3rd edn (LLP Professional Publishing, 2000) or Malcolm A. Clarke, *International Carriage of Goods by Road: CMR*, 4th edn (Mansfield Press, 2003).

[60] See *Gefco UK Ltd v Mason* [1998] 2 Lloyd's Rep. 585 where logistical arrangements for the regular carriage of goods by road from UK to France for Marks & Spencer were held to be subject to the CMR; although it should be noted that framework agreements for carriage will not constitute CMR contracts where, as was found in *Datec Electronic Holdings Ltd v United Parcels Service Ltd* [2007] 1 W.L.R. 1325, there is no binding commitment by the parties to consign, or carry, goods by road.

[61] See *Datec Electronic Holdings Ltd v United Parcels Service Ltd* (ibid.) where the House of Lords held that a contractual reservation, by a carrier under a contract for carriage, of a right to refuse carriage would not disapply the CMR.

[62] See the decision of Donaldson J. in *Ulster-Swift Ltd v Taunton Meat Haulage* [1977] 1 Lloyd's Rep. 346 approved by the Court of Appeal as reported at [1975] 2 Lloyd's Rep. 502.

The other parties are Albania, Armenia, Austria, Azerbaijan, Belarus, Belgium, Bosnia and Herzegovina, Bulgaria, Croatia, Cyprus, Czech Republic, Denmark, Estonia, Finland, France, Georgia, Germany, Greece, Hungary, Iran, Ireland, Italy, Jordan, Kazakhstan, Kyrgyzstan, Latvia, Lebanon, Lithuania, Luxembourg, Malta, Moldova, Mongolia, Montenegro, Morocco, Netherlands, Norway, Poland, Portugal, Romania, Russia, Serbia, Slovakia, Slovenia, Spain, Sweden, Switzerland, Syria, Tajikistan, The Former Yugoslav Republic of Macedonia, Tunisia, Turkey, Turkmenistan and Ukraine.[63] Ratifications are collated by the UN Treaty Depositary, but s.2 of the Carriage of Goods by Road Act 1965 provides for the UK Government by Order in Council to certify conclusively, from time to time, who are the contracting states to the CMR. The latest such published certification is by the Carriage of Goods by Road (Parties to Convention) (Amendment) Order 1980/697 which is now considerably out of date.

As the CMR applies to international carriage where only one or other of the places of departure or destination need be in contracting states to it, any contract for the carriage of goods in a road vehicle between the United Kingdom and any foreign country (except Ireland), is governed by the CMR. For the CMR to apply the goods must not be unloaded from the road vehicle on which they are carried, but it does not matter how the road vehicle carrying the goods may have been transported to, or from, the United Kingdom. Neither does it matter whether or not the foreign country is a party to the CMR. By CMR art.1(2) "vehicles means motor vehicles, articulated vehicles, trailers and semi-trailers"; so, if goods remain loaded on a road trailer during carriage by other means or modes, they remain "unloaded" from the road vehicle and, in consequence, are carried subject to the CMR.[64] However, by art.2(1), the liability of the carrier by road may in certain circumstances be determined in the manner in which the liability of a carrier by the other means of transport would have been determined had a separate contract of carriage been made only for that mode. The required circumstances are that: (i) it is proved loss, damage or delay to the goods occurred during carriage by some other mode of carriage; (ii) such loss, damage or delay was not caused by any act or omission of the carrier by road, but instead was caused by an event "which could only have occurred in the course of and by reason of" the carriage by that other mode; and (iii) other conditions of carriage were "prescribed by law"

[63] From UNECE website *http://www.unece.org/trans/conventn/legalinst_25_OLIRT_CMR.html* accessed on July 15, 2009.

[64] As is clearly stated by the first sentence of CMR art.2(1).

for carriage by that other mode.[65] Otherwise contracts for such international carriage of goods by road will remain subject to the CMR during the transit of the road vehicle by some other mode. The fact that a carrier might have agreed to carry by some other mode (e.g. air) would not prevent any actual international carriage by road from being governed by the CMR where the carrier had reserved to itself the right or liberty to carry the goods wholly or partly by some mode other than that for which it originally contracted.[66]

When applicable, the CMR applies to contracts between the consignor and the contracting carrier and may be enforced by either consignor or consignee pursuant to arts 12 and 13. It applies also to any performance of the carriage by any other carrier who is a successive carrier by reason of carriage under a single contract performed by successive road carriers, each becoming a party to the contract of carriage by their acceptance of the goods and the consignment note under art.34.[67] The protection of the CMR extends to "agents and servants and . . . .any other persons of whose services [the carrier] makes use for the performance of the carriage" pursuant to art.28(2) and to non-contractual claims pursuant to art.28(1) whether such non-contractual claims arise in bailment or tort. Article 36 provides that, in the case of successive road carriage under art.34, legal proceedings for loss, damage or delay to the consignment may only be brought against the first carrier, the last carrier or the carrier performing the carriage at the time of the event, which caused such loss, damage or delay.

In *Sandeman Coprimar SA v Transitos y Transportes Integrales SL*,[68] the Court of Appeal held that, in a contractual chain where carriers were authorised to sub-contract carriage, the common law concepts of sub-bailment on terms and authorised sub-contracting would have the effect of binding the consignor (as original bailor) to all the contracts of carriage entered into, with their consent, by the carriers in the contractual chain, irrespective of whether or not the requirements of art.34 were satisfied by the creation and

65 In *Thermo Engineers Ltd and Anhydro A/S v Ferrymasters Ltd* [1981] 1 Lloyd's Rep. 200 Neill J. held these conditions to be satisfied where stevedores were responsible for a collision between the consignment loaded to a road trailer and a ship's bulkhead during loading to the ship under a bill of lading in circumstances where the Hague-Visby Rules were applicable.

66 *Quantum Corp Inc v Plane Trucking* [2002] 2 Lloyd's Rep. 25.

67 The attendant liabilities and rights to claim of carrier and cargo interests are respectively discussed at 2.3.6 and 2.3.7.

68 [2003] Q.B. 1270.

passing on of the CMR note. In this context it should be appreciated that the CMR is only a partial code sitting within the legal framework applied by the courts or tribunals exercising jurisdiction over any dispute which may arise for determination.[69] This point has been repeatedly emphasised by judges when tackling various diverse issues not addressed by the CMR[70] which nonetheless arise for determination in particular contracts that are subject to the CMR. The approach of the common law to the CMR was neatly expressed by Lord Wilberforce in *James Buchanan & Co Ltd v Babco Forwarding and Shipping (UK) Ltd* when he said "... the contract of carriage seems to have incorporated contractually the English text [of the CMR]";[71] those contractual terms have overriding effect as, by s.1 of the Carriage of Goods By Road Act 1965, they have "the force of law" and are applicable as mandatory statutory terms.

The Carriage by Air and Road Act 1979, which applied the SDR protocol into UK law to give rise to the claim limitation values referred to at 2.3.4 below, provides for the Carriage of Goods by Road Act 1965 to be further amended by Order in Council as and when further protocols of amendment to the original convention require amendments to be made to the 1965 Act. This streamlines the procedure for updating the UK law as and when the 1956 CMR convention is revised and is likely to be used to apply into UK law any changes thought necessary by reason of the e-CMR protocol referred to at 2.3.2 below.

2.3.2 Documentation

The sender and the carrier must make out a consignment note in three parts. One part is handed to the sender, one retained by the carrier, and one accompanies the goods. It is clear that the absence, irregularity or loss of the consignment note does not affect the validity of the contract of carriage which nevertheless remains subject to the CMR.[72]

Article 6(1) of the CMR provides that the consignment note shall contain:

[69] For which see 1.4.

[70] For instance see *Shell Chemicals UK Ltd v P&O Roadtanks Ltd* [1993] 1 Lloyd's Rep. 114, which concerned claims for damage caused by a carrier to some property of the consignee other than the consigned goods; where Saville J. permitted recovery, under tortious principles at common law, notwithstanding the application of the CMR to the consigned goods.

[71] [1978] AC 141 at p.152.

[72] This being expressly stated by art.4 of the CMR.

"(a) the date of the consignment note and the place at which it is made out;
(b) the name and address of the sender;
(c) the name and address of the carrier;
(d) the place and the date of taking over of the goods and the place designated for delivery;
(e) the name and address of the consignee;
(f) the description in common use of the nature of the goods and the method of packing, and, in the case of dangerous goods, their generally recognised description;
(g) the number of packages and their special marks and numbers;
(h) the gross weight of the goods or their quantity otherwise expressed;
(i) charges relating to the carriage (carriage charges, supplementary charges, customs duties and other charges incurred from the making of the contract to the time of delivery);
(j) the requisite instructions for Customs and other formalities;
(k) a statement that the carriage is subject, notwithstanding any clause to the contrary, to the provisions of this Convention."

Whilst the parties may, if they wish, insert any other useful matter in the consignment note, art.6(2) of the CMR provides further that the consignment note shall contain, "where applicable", these additional particulars:

"(a) a statement that transhipment is not allowed;
(b) the charges which the sender undertakes to pay;
(c) the amount of 'cash on delivery' charges;
(d) a declaration of the value of the goods and the amount representing special interest in delivery;
(e) the sender's instructions to the carrier regarding insurance of the goods;
(f) the agreed time-limit within which the carriage is to be carried out;
(g) a list of the documents handed to the carrier."

Article 7 provides that the sender shall be responsible for all expenses, loss and damage sustained by the carrier because of the inaccuracy or inadequacy of: the particulars specified in subsections (b), (d), (e), (f), (g), (h) and (j) of the first paragraph of art.6; any of the particulars specified in the second paragraph of art.6; any other particulars or instructions provided to enable the consignment note to be made out. However, if the consignment note does not contain the statement required by art.6(1)(k), that "the carriage is subject, notwithstanding any clause to the contrary, to the provisions of this Convention" the carrier is liable for all expenses, loss and damage sustained through such omission by the person entitled to dispose of the goods. By art.9 of the CMR the consignment note is designated "prima facie evidence of the making of the contract of carriage, the conditions of the contract and the receipt of the goods by the carrier".[73]

An additional protocol to the CMR was signed by some seven contracting states to the CMR on May 27, 2008 (with a further seven states, including the United Kingdom, being expected to sign shortly thereafter) to give formal recognition to the widespread use of electronic forms of the consignment note. The protocol (likely to be known as the e-CMR protocol), is to enter into force once five of the contracting states have completed the process of ratification. The e-CMR protocol entitles parties to issue the CMR consignment note, as well as any other communication envisaged by the CMR, in electronic form. Pursuant to art.5 of the e-CMR protocol it will be for the parties to any carriage contract to agree various matters contemplated by the protocol including:

> "(a) The method for the issuance and the delivery of the electronic consignment note to the entitled party; (b) An assurance that the electronic consignment note retains its integrity; (c) The manner in which the party entitled to the rights arising out of the electronic consignment note is able to demonstrate that entitlement; (d) The way in which confirmation is given that delivery to the consignee has been effected; (e) The procedures for supplementing or amending the electronic consignment note; and (f) The procedures for the possible replacement of the electronic consignment note by a consignment note issued by different means".

Pursuant to art.6 of the e-CMR protocol the carrier must provide the consignor, at the consignor's request, with a receipt for the goods and all information necessary for identifying the shipment and giving access to the

[73] Evidence considered by Mance J. in *Aqualon (UK) Ltd v Vallana Shipping Corp* [1994] 1 Lloyd's Rep. 669 when addressing the identity of the carrier by road to be of some probative value, but certainly not to be conclusive as to the issue to be determined.

electronic consignment note. The requirements as to the content of the CMR consignment note remain the same for an e-CMR note as for a hard copy as stipulated by CMR art.6. The e-CMR protocol may have little impact under English law, which does not generally distinguish between, or adopt different evidential rules as to, paper documents and e-documents.[74]

2.3.3 Liability of Carrier

Article 17(1) makes the carrier liable for any loss or damage to the goods incurred between the time of taking them over until the time of delivery. It also makes the carrier liable for delay. Particular exemptions from this general liability arise under various provisions of the CMR. Article 17(2) provides exemption from liability

> "if the loss, damage or delay was caused by the wrongful act or neglect of the claimant, by the instructions of the claimant given otherwise than as the result of a wrongful act or neglect on the part of the carrier, by inherent vice of the goods or through circumstances which the carrier could not avoid and the consequences of which he was unable to prevent".

Article 18 places on the carrier the onus of proving exemption from liability under art.17(2); if the carrier succeeds in proving that the loss, damage or delay might be attributed to one of the exempted causes, the onus of proof shifts to the claimant to prove that the loss, damage or delay was not, in fact, wholly or partly caused by one of these causes.

The shifting evidential burden under art.18 appears to reflect ordinary English common law rules whereby the onus of proof lies on the party making the allegation. However, the exemptions under art.17(2) tend to be construed restrictively, as shown by the interpretation of "circumstances which the carrier could not avoid and the consequences of which he was unable to prevent" as being limited to those that "even with the utmost

[74] See, for instance, the statutory definitions of "writing" at Sch.1 to the Interpretation Act 1978 "Writing includes typing, printing, lithography, photography and other modes of representing or reproducing words in a visible form, and expressions referring to writing are construed accordingly" and "document" by s.13 of the Civil Evidence Act 1995 as meaning "anything in which information of any description is recorded, and *copy*, in relation to a document, means anything onto which information recorded in the document has been copied, by whatever means and whether directly or indirectly".

care"[75] could not be avoided and prevented. Defences on this basis are very difficult to substantiate since, in the event of loss, damage or delay to cargo, it is generally the case that such consequences could have been averted by the road carrier taking or avoiding some action. Nevertheless such a defence has succeeded in two reported cases.[76] Coincidentally, both involved the hijacking of vehicles by armed and determined robbers at lorry park facilities in Italy and the theft of animal pelt consignments considered judicially to be of low to medium value and at low risk of such organised attack. In each case the respective judges concluded that, notwithstanding the carriers' duty to exercise the utmost care in the commercial context of the respective carriage movements and losses, there was nothing further that the carriers could have done to prevent such an attack or to mitigate its consequences. Article 17(3) provides that the carrier shall not be relieved of liability because of the defective condition of the vehicle used to perform the carriage, or because of the wrongful act or neglect of either the person from whom the vehicle has been hired, or that person's agents or servants.

Article 17(4) provides that the carrier shall not be liable when loss or damage arise from the special risks involved by reason of carriage being performed in particular circumstances including:

> "(a) use of open unsheeted vehicles, when their use has been expressly agreed and specified in the consignment note; (b) the lack of, or defective condition of packing in the case of goods which, by their nature, are liable to wastage or to be damaged when not packed or when not properly packed; (c) handling, loading, stowage or unloading of the goods by the sender, the consignee or persons acting on behalf of the sender or the consignee; (d) the nature of certain kinds of goods which particularly exposes them to total or partial loss or to damage, especially through breakages, rust, decay, desiccation, leakage, normal wastage, or the action of moth or vermin; (e) insufficiency or inadequacy of marks or numbers on the packages; (f) the carriage of livestock".

[75] Per Mustill J. in *Silber v Islander Trucking* [1985] 2 Lloyd's Rep. 243, 247 where this phrase was used to describe a standard of care considered to fall somewhere between taking "every conceivable precaution, however extreme" and "a duty to do no more than act reasonably in accordance with prudent current practice".

[76] Namely, *Silber v Islander Trucking* ibid. and *GL Cicatiello Srl v Anglo European Shipping Services Ltd* [1994] 1 Lloyd's Rep. 678.

Under art.17(5) the carrier remains liable to the extent that other factors for which it is liable have contributed to the loss, damage or delay. Article 18(2) provides that where the carrier proves loss or damage "could be attributed" to any one or more of these special risks a rebuttable presumption arises in favour of them being the cause, subject to the claimant proving the contrary.

However, the carrier loses the protection of these special risks in various circumstances. Article 18(3) removes the rebuttable presumption in special risk (a) where there is an abnormal shortage, or loss, of a package from an unsheeted vehicle. Article 18(4) provides that when the carriage is performed in vehicles which are specially equipped to protect the goods from the effect of heat, cold, temperature variations or humidity of the air, the carrier can only take advantage of special risk (d) where the carrier proves that all reasonable steps to maintain the vehicle in a suitable condition have been taken, and that any special instructions issued were complied with. Article 18(5) provides that in order to claim the protection of special risk (f) the carrier must prove that it took "all steps normally incumbent on him in the circumstances" and complied with any special instructions. Furthermore all such defences for the carrier will be lost in the event of wilful misconduct being proved as against the carrier, or its agents, employees or sub-contractors as discussed at 2.3.4.3 below.

Delay in delivery for the purposes of art.17(1) is defined by art.19 as being when the goods are not delivered within the agreed time-limit, or within a reasonable time if there is no agreed time-limit. Article 6(2)(f) provides that where there is an agreed time-limit within which the carriage is to be carried out, it must be stated in the consignment note. Article 7(1)(b) provides that "the sender shall be responsible for all expenses, loss and damage sustained by the carrier by reason of the inaccuracy or inadequacy" in the consignment note particulars as to, among other matters, the agreed time-limit. Uncertainty could arise in this context where the parties have agreed on a time limit in the contract of carriage but have not inserted it in the consignment note, and the carrier, although delivering the goods within a reasonable time, has not delivered them within the agreed time-limit. The carrier may be able to avoid liability for any delay where the liability has arisen from the sender's failure to insert the agreed delivery time in the consignment note. In any event the carrier is exempted from liability for delay where the carrier establishes that such delay was caused by the narrowly defined art.17(2) events.

According to art.20, if the goods are not delivered within 30 days of the agreed time-limit, or, if there is no agreed time-limit, within 60 days of the time when the carrier took over the goods, it will be conclusively presumed that the goods are lost. The owner of the goods is then entitled to demand compensation for their loss from the carrier. The owner may choose to request in writing notification from the carrier if the goods are found within a year. In this case, if the goods are found within the year, the carrier will be obliged to deliver the goods to the owner. The owner will then be required to repay the compensation received for the loss of the goods and to pay the charges of the carriage; albeit without prejudice to the owner's right to claim compensation for the delay to the goods. If the owner of the goods does not give such a notice in writing to the carrier, or if the goods are found after more than a year, the carrier is entitled to deal with the goods according to the law of the place where they are found, and the consignee retains the compensation for the loss of the goods. There are no provisions with regard to deviation in the CMR. It is therefore clear that the doctrine does not apply to international carriage of goods by road within the context of the CMR, not least because, as the doctrine of deviation is not expressly included in the CMR, it cannot deprive the carrier of the rights granted by the CMR which are given the force of law in the United Kingdom by s.1 of the Carriage of Goods by Road Act 1965.

2.3.4 Value of Claims

2.3.4.1 Financial Valuation

Article 23(1) provides that the damages recoverable for total or partial loss of the goods shall be calculated by reference to the value of the goods at the place and time when they were accepted for carriage, with such value being fixed by art.23(2) as being:

> "the commodity exchange price or, if there is no such price, according to the current market price or, if there is no commodity exchange price or current market price, by reference to the normal value of goods of the same kind and quality".

This contrasts sharply with the expectation loss recoverable under common law as discussed at 1.8.2 pursuant to which the relevant valuation is at the intended time and place of delivery and not, as in the CMR, the time and place of receipt. Pursuant to art.23(4) the carrier is liable "in addition" to refund "all carriage charges, customs duties and other charges" and under English jurisprudence difficult issues of interpretation have arisen as to whether this provision operates independently of the CMR claim limitation provisions at art.23(3) as discussed at 2.3.4.2 below in relation to the *James Buchanan & Co Ltd v Babco Forwarding and Shipping (UK) Ltd* case.[77] Article 25 provides that in case of damage, the carrier shall be liable for the diminution in value, with value being calculated by reference to the provisions at art.23(1), (2) and (4) referred to above, subject to compensation not exceeding the amount payable in the case of total loss, or, where damage is only to part of the consignment, the amount payable for loss of that part.

2.3.4.2 Financial Limitation

Under the original convention, damages were limited by art.23(3) to 25 gold francs per kilogram of gross weight short, but by international protocol applied in the United Kingdom by s.4 of the Carriage by Air and Road Act 1979, this was changed to "8.33 units of account per kilogram of gross weight short" ending the difficulty arising from frequent changes in the valuation of gold. The unit of account referred to is defined as "the Special Drawing Right as defined by the International Monetary Fund". The Special Drawing Right is a notional currency introduced in 1969. Its value is calculated daily by reference to the relative daily values of currencies in a weighted currency basket comprising, as from January 1, 2006, 44 per cent US dollar, 34 per cent euro, 11 per cent Japanese yen and 11 per cent British pound sterling. The composition of the basket is subject to periodic review every five years with the next review planned to take place in late 2010; its value is published by the International Monetary Fund daily and quoted in the currency markets, national press and various internet resources. Under art.23(7) of the CMR the SDR limit is converted into national currency on the day of judgment, or the date agreed upon by the parties. The calculation of the limitation fund by reference to "gross weight short" is significant as it is against the gross weight of the goods lost, damaged or delayed that the limitation fund is to be calculated.

As mentioned above difficult issues have arisen as to whether this limitation fund is inclusive or exclusive of the carrier's obligation under art.23(4) to refund "all carriage charges, customs duties and other charges". In 1978 the House of Lords decided in *James Buchanan & Co Ltd v Babco Forwarding and Shipping (UK) Ltd*[78] that duty charged in consequence of the

[77] [1978] AC 141.
[78] ibid.

theft of a consignment of whisky (being carried under excise duty suspension arrangements) was recoverable under art.23(4) and was not subject to the limitation at art.23(3). The duty would not have been chargeable had the goods, instead of being stolen, been exported as intended to Tehran and so, the duty was not part of the value of the goods stolen, but rather a liability incurred by the exporter in consequence of the theft from the carrier. This much criticised[79] majority decision of the House of Lords remains binding on the English courts, but was distinguished and not followed by the Court of Appeal in the *Sandeman Coprimar* case,[80] which concerned liability for duty following the loss of custom seals.[81] Article 23(5) of the CMR limits claims for delay to the amount of the carriage charges.

The CMR does permit the sender to declare in the consignment note a value for the goods, and a higher level of compensation, in excess of the limits specified in arts 23(3) and (5). Such declaration may only be made pursuant to an agreement with the carrier on payment of such surcharge as may be agreed between sender and carrier pursuant to arts 24 and 26. By art.27 the carrier is liable to pay interest on any compensation at the rate of 5 per cent per annum from the day when the claim was first made in writing, to the carrier, or, in the absence of such claim, from the day legal proceedings began. In contrast to its limited liability for loss or damage to the goods, the CMR provides little protection to a carrier who agrees with the sender, under the contract of carriage, to collect from the consignee any "*cash on delivery* charge"; since, by art.21, the carrier's liability in the event of the goods being delivered without collection of such charge is limited only to "compensation not exceeding the amount of such charge". The carrier is given an independent right of action against the consignee to recover that charge but, by art.21, is completely exposed both to the cost of funding that "*cash on delivery* charge" for the benefit of the sender and to the risk that reimbursement, for whatever reason, may not be forthcoming from the consignee.

[79] Malcolm A. Clarke, *International Carriage of Goods by Road: CMR*, 4th edn (Mansfield Press, 2003), p.371, para.98; Hill and Messent's *CMR: Contracts for the International Carriage of Goods by Road*, 3rd edn (LLP Professional Publishing, 2000), p.204, para.9.31.

[80] *Sandeman Coprimar SA v Transitos y Transportes Integrales SL* [2003] Q.B. 1270.

[81] On grounds that such a loss was both too remote at common law and not a "charge incurred in respect of the carriage of the goods" under art.23(4); see para.39 of Lord Phillips judgment ibid. at para.39.

2.3.4.3 Disapplication of Limits and Defences

Pursuant to art.29 of the CMR, the limitation on the amount recoverable as damages for goods which are lost, damaged or delayed, does not apply where the cause of the damage is attributable to wilful misconduct on the part of either the carrier or of those employees, agents, or sub-contractors of the carrier engaged in the performance of the carriage, provided such wilful misconduct arises in the course of their employment. Several issues arise in the context of art.29, namely: what conduct will amount to wilful misconduct; for whose wilful misconduct will the carrier be responsible; and what provisions of the CMR will be disapplied in the event such wilful misconduct is proved.

As Lord Justice Beldam said in *Laceys Footwear (Wholesale) Ltd v Bowler International Freight Ltd*:[82] "Few phrases have been more fully considered in decisions of the Courts than wilful misconduct". It has been considered in various distinct carriage contexts including the following: special contracts agreed with common carriers; particular contracts agreed with private carriers; particular contracts for international carriage by air under the 1929 Warsaw Convention; and particular contracts for international carriage by road under the CMR. Whilst the concept of *wilful misconduct* has been described in the various cases in differing formulations and contrasting contexts, the concept has nonetheless received a broadly consistent interpretation from the courts of England and Wales as being some conscious act or default proved, by objective inference from the evidence or by admission, to have been committed by the perpetrator in the subjective knowledge that such conscious act or default (a) was wrong and (b) was exposing the goods to additional risk; or recklessly without any thought being given to (a) and (b).[83]

The onus of proving wilful misconduct lies on the party making the allegation. Whilst the onus can be discharged under English law on the

[82] [1997] 2 Lloyd's Rep. 369, 374.

[83] See, to mention but a few, the judgments of Lord Alverstone C.J. in *Forder v Great Western Railway Co* [1905] 2 K.B. 532; Popplewell J. in *Jones v Bencher Ltd* [1986] 1 Lloyd's Rep. 54; Lord Justice Taylor in *Circle Freight International Ltd v Medeast Gulf Exports Ltd* [1988] 2 Lloyd's Rep. 427; Tudor Evans J. in *Texas Instruments Ltd v Nason (Europe) Ltd* [1991] 1 Lloyd's Rep. 146; Longmore J. in *National Semiconductors (UK) Ltd v UPS Ltd* [1996] 2 Lloyd's Rep. 212; Beldam L.J. in *Laceys Footwear* ibid.; Lord Mance in *Datec Electronic Holdings Ltd v United Parcels Service Ltd* [2007] 1 W.L.R. 1325; and Waller L.J. in *Denfleet International Ltd v TNT Global SPA* [2007] 2 Lloyd's Rep. 504.

balance of probabilities, the legal test for ascertaining the boundary between innocent and negligent misconduct on the one hand (liability for which is subject to financial limitation under the CMR) and wilful misconduct on the other hand (liability for which is not subject to financial limitation under the CMR), makes the onus difficult to discharge in any given case before the courts of England and Wales.[84] The difficulty arises from the fact that the evidential issue turns on the degree of awareness in the commission of the wrongdoing, rather than on the seriousness of the wrongdoing itself. Accordingly, a driver who had been instructed to make an urgent delivery to a consignee at a particular address (and not to permit off loading of the goods anywhere else) was found guilty of wilful misconduct[85] although he had been fooled, by an elaborate and sophisticated charade,[86] into believing that it was the consignee who required delivery elsewhere. Conversely, a driver who had actually fallen asleep at the wheel whilst driving was found not guilty of wilful misconduct,[87] despite the fact that the judge had found, as a matter of fact, that the driver "was aware that he was sleepy and made a conscious and deliberate decision to continue his journey".[88] The contrasting approaches to these different facts has been criticised as punishing the actions of an apparently careful driver who became the victim of a sophisticated fraud and relieving the grossly negligent driver of CMR liability, notwithstanding his serious wrongdoing.[89]

In the context of wilful misconduct, it is the subjective obviousness of the breach to the wrongdoer, rather than the objective seriousness of the breach to the reasonable man, which is the critical issue for the English

[84] Professor Malcolm Clarke maintains in "The Convention on the Contract for the International Carriage of Goods by Road 1956: wilful misconduct again—and again" J.B.L. (2008) 2, 184–190 that in certain other contracting states to the CMR, and unlike the UK, rules of evidence may oblige the carrier to show cause why it should not be considered guilty of wilful misconduct.

[85] *Laceys Footwear (Wholesale) Ltd v Bowler International Freight Ltd* [1997] 2 Lloyd's Rep. 369.

[86] The fraudsters operated from immediately outside and within the consignee's premises at the identified delivery address and ultimately convinced the suspicious driver (who even took the step of telephoning UK agents of the consignor in an unsuccessful attempt to clarify his instructions) into off loading the goods directly into another vehicle located elsewhere.

[87] *Denfleet International Ltd v TNT Global SPA* [2007] 2 Lloyd's Rep 504.

[88] Despite the driver's conduct in ignoring signs of his own fatigue being characterised in the Court of Appeal by Waller LJ as "grossly negligent" (ibid. para.18 Waller L.J.'s judgment).

[89] See, for instance, the views of Professor Malcolm Clarke in the article referred to at fn. 84.

courts. However, this is by no means an approach universally applied by courts in other contracting states to the CMR. Indeed, internationally courts adopt widely divergent approaches to the concept of wilful misconduct.[90] CMR art.29(1) itself promotes such divergent approaches by authorising any court or tribunal to extend the concept of wilful misconduct to

> "... such default ... as, in accordance with the law of the court or tribunal seised of the case, is considered as equivalent to wilful misconduct".

For this reason the extent of a carrier's liability for loss in excess of the CMR financial limitations is determined less by the circumstances giving rise to the claim than by the forum in which the claim is to be determined.

The carrier is responsible for its own wilful misconduct as well as for wilful misconduct committed "within the scope of their employment" by its "agents or servants" and by those "of whose services [the carrier] makes use for the performance of the carriage". Where the carrier is a corporation the carrier itself can only be guilty of wilful misconduct where someone's wilful misconduct can be attributed to the company. As Lord Hoffman commented in *Meridian Global Funds Management Asia Ltd v Securities Commission*[91] the concept of attribution "is one of construction rather than metaphysics [and] varies according to the context in which the concept is to operate". As CMR art.29(2) specifically provides for "agents or servants" and those "of whose services [the carrier] makes use for the performance of the carriage", it would appear that the wider concepts of "general principles of agency, vicarious liability and so forth"[92] should be disregarded in determining attribution under art.29(1). On this basis only what Lord Hoffman characterised as the "company's primary rules of attribution"[93] contained in its articles of association (e.g. decisions of the board of directors or of shareholders in general meeting), or implied under company law (e.g. unanimous decision by all shareholders of a company or a decision by the controlling mind, or alter ego, of the company) should automatically

[90] Various divergent approaches evident in international jurisprudence are examined by Malcolm A. Clarke in *The International Carriage of Goods by Road: CMR*, 4th edn (London: Sweet & Maxwell, 2003).

[91] [1995] 2 A.C. 500, 509.

[92] Per Lord Hoffman ibid. 506.

[93] ibid.

be applied to attribute acts of wilful misconduct to the company under art.29(1) of the CMR.

Article 29(2) applies principles of agency and vicarious liability (extended to encompass not only employees but all those "of whose services [the carrier] makes use for the performance of the carriage") only where the wilful misconduct in question was committed "within the scope of their employment". At first instance in *Datec Electronic Holdings Ltd v United Parcels Service Ltd*[94] Andrew Smith J. appeared to approach the issue from the perspective of what the culpable individuals had actually been employed to do by the carrier, without regard either to the agreement between the carrier and the customer or any breach by the culpable individual of the terms of their employment. His decision on this aspect was not reviewed by the higher courts on appeal. This contextual approach to the concept of acts within the scope of employment is consistent with the common law jurisprudence discussed at 1.6.1.1 and 1.6.1.3 as to any deliberate breach of duties in bailment and tort committed by those who have been particularly entrusted with the performance of the subject duty. For the purpose of CMR art.29(2) the issue is whether the general tasks entrusted to the servant, agent or independent contractor in question encompassed the safeguarding of the goods and the performance of the carriage contract, not whether the particular act alleged to constitute wilful misconduct was actually committed in performing those tasks.

The CMR provisions to be disapplied in the event of wilful misconduct are referred to by art.29(1) as being "the provisions *of this chapter* which exclude or limit his liability or which shift the burden of proof" [emphasis added]. The reference to "this chapter" can only be a reference to CMR Chapter IV including CMR arts 17 to 28; however, the Court of Appeal held in *Laceys Footwear (Wholesale) Ltd v Bowler International Freight Ltd*[95] that certain of these CMR articles did not "exclude or limit liability" but instead fixed the compensation due. In this respect the Court of Appeal distinguished between CMR art.23(1) and (2)—which it decided was not disapplied by wilful misconduct as it "fixed" the value of the goods as being the value "at the place and time at which they were accepted for carriage"—and art.23(3) and (4)—which it disapplied as limiting the compensation due. Similar differentiations could be drawn in relation to other CMR articles within Chapter IV such as in relation to art.27 which appears to fix interest at 5 per cent p.a. to run from the sending of a written

94 [2005] 1 Lloyd's Rep. 470, at para.69.
95 fn. 85.

claim and to require the currency conversion of losses to be effected at the date of payment. It should not be overlooked that in the event of wilful misconduct the carrier will also be deprived of the benefit of the various provisions within Chapter IV that would otherwise give rise to defences on liability or raise rebuttable presumptions in the carrier's favour (e.g. arts 17(2), 17(4), 18(2) etc).

2.3.5 Time to Claim

Article 30(2) provides that if the consignee and the carrier have checked the goods before the consignee takes delivery of them, no evidence contradicting the result of the checking will be admissible to prove any loss or damage which would have been apparent on such checking. In the case of loss or damage which was not apparent, evidence contradicting the result of the checking is admissible, but only if the consignee has sent reservations in writing to the carrier within seven days of the date of the checking (excluding Sundays and public holidays). However, if the consignee takes delivery of the goods without checking them, failure to point out any apparent loss or damage at the time of taking delivery is, under art.30(1), only prima facie evidence that no apparent loss or damage occurred during the carriage; similarly, failure to make reservations in writing to the carrier within seven days of taking delivery of the goods (excluding Sundays and public holidays) is only prima facie evidence that no loss or damage, which was not apparent, had occurred during the carriage. In the case of delay, pursuant to art.30(3) no damages are obtainable unless the consignee gives notice in writing to the carrier within 21 days of the time when the goods are placed at its disposal (excluding Sundays and public holidays). Article 30(5) provides that the carrier and the consignee are to afford every "reasonable facility" to the other to make the contemplated checks whilst art.30(6) provides that the various time periods referred to exclude the day on which they commence.

The statutory limitation periods reviewed in 1.8.3 take effect subject to art.32. Article 32(1) provides that actions become barred by lapse of time unless they are brought within one year, extended to three years in the event of wilful default. The commencement date for the one-year period (and for the three-year period applicable only in the event of wilful default) varies in any particular case according to whether the loss is partial (or attributable to damage or delay), total, or attributable to some other claim. In the case of partial loss, damage or delay, the period commences from the date of delivery to the consignee. In the case of total loss the period commences, if there was an agreed time-limit for the delivery of the goods, within 30 days of the date when the goods should have been delivered, or if there was no agreed time-limit, within 60 days of the date when the carrier took over the goods. "In all other cases", the period commences from the end of three months after the contract of carriage was made. Although this provision has been expansively interpreted by the UK courts to date,[96] there seems no good reason why it should be applied to claims arising other than in relation to the contemplated contractual performance, which is subject to the CMR. According to art.32(1), the day from which the time is reckoned is not included in the number of days fixed, and the period begins to run from the next following day.[97]

The suit-time provided for by art.32(1) may be prolonged by a written claim pursuant to art.32(2), which provides that a written claim suspends the period of limitation until the claim is rejected by the carrier "by notification in writing": the carrier must also return any documents received. The onus of proof as to receipt, reply and return rests on the party seeking to rely on the relevant communication (i.e. in order to secure suspension or termination of suspension as the case may be). The concept of suspending time by making a formal claim is familiar to lawyers in several civil law jurisdictions, but is generally unfamiliar to English lawyers and English law. The suspension arises by reason of the simple receipt of the written claim and operates only against the particular carrier to whom the written claim is directed and by whom it has been received. The suspension is only terminated by a written rejection of the claim *and* the return of all documents submitted with the claim. Article 32(4) provides that a right of action barred by lapse of time may not be exercised by way of counter-claim or set-off, so it is critical for all parties to protect their own rights of action in respect of any claim they might wish to assert (whether as claimant, defendant or third party) against anyone involved in any CMR contract where loss, damage or delay have occurred.

[96] In *Shell Chemicals UK Ltd v P & O Roadtanks Ltd* [1993] 1 Lloyd's Rep. 114 Saville J. appeared to accept that a claim for lost production by an oil refinery (following contamination caused to it by a CMR road carrier who, having collected the wrong goods, discharged detergent into the refinery's storage tanks) fell within the scope of CMR art.31(c), although the cause of action arose under the common law and not under the CMR.

[97] *Poclain SA v S.C.A.C. SA* [1986] 1 Lloyd's Rep. 404; *ICI Plc v MAT Transport Ltd* [1987] 1 Lloyd's Rep. 354.

2.3.6 Successive Carriage

Article 35 provides that when a carrier takes over the goods from a previous carrier during the carriage, that carrier shall give a dated and signed receipt for the goods to the previous carrier, and shall enter its name and address on the second copy of the consignment note. This applies regardless of how many carriers are successively involved in the carriage. Article 34 provides that where the goods are carried during the carriage by more than one carrier, every carrier who accepts the goods and the consignment note shall be deemed to become a party to the original contract of carriage, and shall be liable to the owner of the goods in respect of the whole duration of the carriage. Such carriers, accepting the goods and the consignment note from a previous carrier are generally referred to as "successive carriers". Where a carrier takes over the goods from a previous carrier but does not accept the consignment note, the carrier will not become party to the original CMR contract as a successive carrier under art.34. In such circumstances the contract between the carriers may be categorised as one of three distinct types as follows: (a) it may comprise another entirely separate CMR contract within art.1 where it is for the carriage of goods across international border; (b) it may comprise a contract for domestic carriage unregulated by the CMR where it is for the carriage of goods by road entirely within one state[98] subject to whatever conditions may be applicable to such contract; or (c) it may by virtue of the normal English law contract and bailment principles[99] incorporate all the terms of the CMR including those terms relating to successive carriage at Chapter VI of the CMR at arts 34 to 40 where the bailor has, expressly or by implication, authorised the sub-contracting of performance of the carriage on the basis of the CMR.[100] Article 36 provides that, except in a case of a counter-claim or set-off, legal proceedings for loss, damage or delay to the goods may be brought only against the first carrier, the last carrier, or the carrier who was carrying the goods when the loss, damage or delay occurred and only those carriers can have liability to cargo interests in the event of successive carriage.

[98] Or, by the protocol discussed at 2.3.1, for such carriage between the UK and Ireland.

[99] Discussed in 1.6.1.1 and 1.6.1.2.

[100] The conclusion reached at first instance and upheld by the Court of Appeal in *Sandeman Coprimar SA v Transitos Y Transportes Integrales S.L.* [2003] 2 Lloyd's Rep. 172.

2.3.7 Rights to Claim

The CMR is not definitive as to who has rights to claim. Article 12 refers to the sender[101] and the consignee as each having rights of disposal in relation to the goods either from the outset, in the case of the sender or, in the case of the consignee, from the sender endorsing the consignment note to that effect. As already discussed, carriers, successive carriers and their respective agents, employees and sub-contractors are bound to, and accorded rights by, the CMR. The CMR does not, however, use consistent terminology to describe who may be claimants.[102] All of the parties bound by rights and duties under the CMR (senders, consignees, carriers/successive carriers and their respective agents, employees and sub-contractors) can assert the rights accorded to them; the CMR does not expressly remove rights to claim arising under the applicable laws applied by the forum. Indeed, it clearly contemplates such rights will continue to subsist, albeit regulated by the CMR.[103] For these reasons, those common law and statutory rights to claim reviewed in 1.6.1 and 1.8.1 appear to be applicable notwithstanding the application of the CMR, at least to the extent that such rights are not expressly or implicitly curtailed by the CMR.[104] Such an interpretation tends to be supported by cases such as *Sandeman Coprimar SA v Transitos Y Transportes Integrales SL*[105] and *Western Digital Corp v British Airways Plc*,[106] in which common law causes of action in contract, tort and/or bailment were held to continue to subsist despite the mandatory application of the CMR and Warsaw unimodal conventions.

[101] Albeit only until the arrival of the goods at the consignee's premises and control of the goods being taken by the consignee pursuant to art.12(2).

[102] As noted by Lord Justice Lawrence Collins at paras 46 and 47 of his judgment in *Hatzl v XL Insurance Co Ltd* [2009] 1 Lloyd's Rep. 555 in the course of dismissing attempts by claimants to found CMR jurisdiction on the basis of the cargo insurers' domicile.

[103] See, for instance, CMR art.28 which, in expressly extending to carriers and those for whom they are responsible under art.3 the benefit of provisions under the CMR that exclude liability, or fix or limit compensation in relation to "non-contractual claims", clearly contemplate the making of such claims.

[104] As, for instance, those rights to contribution that carriers otherwise would have had under the Civil Liability (Contribution) Act 1978 as discussed in 2.3.11.

[105] See fn. 100.

[106] [2000] 2 Lloyd's Rep. 142.

2.3.8 Jurisdiction for Determination and Enforcement

Article 31 provides that an action arising out of carriage under the CMR may be brought before any court or tribunal in any one of a number of permitted jurisdictions. These are those jurisdictions designated by agreement between the parties that are within contracting states to the CMR; or where the defendant is ordinarily resident, or has its principal place of business, or branch or agency through which the carriage contract was made; or where the carrier took over the goods; or where the place of destination was situated. No action may be brought in the courts of any other country. Under art.33, the parties may agree to refer the case to arbitration, provided that by their agreement the arbitrator is required to apply the provisions of the CMR. Under art.31(2), the court that is first seised of jurisdiction in an action has exclusive jurisdiction and no other action may be commenced "between the same parties on the same grounds", unless for some reason any judgment from that jurisdiction would not be enforceable in the jurisdiction in which fresh proceedings are brought. For the reasons discussed in Part One, sub-part 4.2, the EU jurisdiction regime takes effect subject to the jurisdictional rules of the CMR; unless the jurisdictional issues are all clearly determined by the CMR the EU jurisdictional regime will need to be considered and applied.[107] Exclusive jurisdiction agreements are not permitted and are rendered void by the operation of the non-derogation provisions discussed at 2.3.9 below.

By reason of the significant differences in interpreting and applying the CMR across contracting states (e.g. as discussed in 2.3.4.3 in relation to wilful misconduct), forum shopping is a significant aspect of CMR litigation. As a result, in the interests of securing their most favoured jurisdiction under the CMR, carriers and their liability insurers frequently issue proceedings for declarations of non-liability or limited liability in advance of the issue of proceedings by cargo interests for compensation.[108] Under s.4 of the 1965 Act, foreign judgments given in actions commenced pursuant to art.31 are capable of registration under the Foreign Judgments (Reciprocal Enforcement) Act 1933, and thus become matters of record enforceable in the United Kingdom. Insofar as the states in which those judgments are

[107] As in *Sony Computer Entertainment Ltd v RH Freight Services Ltd* [2007] 2 Lloyd's Rep. 463: proceedings commenced in England were stayed, although they involved different parties to an existing Dutch action, since the English proceedings were considered to be related to the prior Dutch action under art.28 of Regulation 44/2001/EC.

[108] ibid., an approach which succeeded.

obtained are also bound by the EU jurisdiction regime, their judgments can in any case be registered and enforced within the United Kingdom pursuant to Regulation 44/2001/EC as discussed in 1.4.2.

2.3.9 Contractual Derogation of Convention Provisions

Article 41 provides that the parties are not entitled to contract out of the terms of the CMR, and any contract purporting to do so is void. This restriction of contractual autonomy is very widely drawn as it states "... any stipulation which would directly or indirectly derogate from the provisions of this Convention shall be null and void". The use of the word "derogate" is significant as, unlike other carriage conventions, the prohibition on contracting out extends to the entirety of the CMR (excepting only those specific instances of autonomy expressly permitted by the CMR),[109] irrespective of who is to benefit from the derogating provision. Accordingly, increasing and decreasing the rights, duties and liabilities of the carrier, sender and consignee are all equally prohibited, save to the extent expressly permitted by the CMR.

2.3.10 Rights of Carriers

2.3.10.1 Liens

The carrier has the right to exercise a particular lien over the goods being carried against the consignee pursuant to art.13(2) for "the charges shown to be due on the consignment note". In *T Comedy (UK) Ltd v Easy Managed Transport Ltd*[110] Jonathan Hirst Q.C., sitting as a deputy judge of the Commercial Court, held that a lien against the consignee would only arise where such charges were shown to be due by the consignment note. In the case before him, as the consignment note did not show any charges to be due, he found no particular lien arose against the consignee. He dismissed the suggestion that rights to lien under national law would continue to be applicable, notwithstanding the CMR; as discussed in 1.9.1.2 a contractual carrier by land probably has in any event no right to a lien under the

[109] For instance art.40 provides that successive carriers may, as between themselves, vary the rights of contribution and indemnity provided for at arts 37 and 38 and a higher value for the goods, or a special interest in their delivery, may be agreed pursuant to arts 23(6), 24 and/or 26.

[110] [2007] 2 Lloyd's Rep. 397.

common law. The carrier had sought to rely on the general and particular liens arising under RHA Conditions[111] but these were considered to be in derogation from the CMR and, in consequence, null and void under art.41.[112] Accordingly on the basis of the *T Comedy (UK) Ltd* authority,[113] the CMR carrier can only have a particular lien for unpaid freight as against the consignee (as art.13(2) provides) where the particulars of the unpaid charges relating to the carriage are contained in the consignment note (as art.6(1)(i) provides). The carrier cannot provide for any further lien as that would derogate from the CMR (as art.41 provides). A common carrier, or a sea carrier, undertaking part of a CMR movement and entitled to exercise particular liens under the common law[114] or statute[115] would not, on the basis of this judgment, be in a better position, although there is nothing in the CMR which expressly requires the suppression of such rights.

2.3.10.2 Dangerous Goods

Article 22 provides that the sender is obliged to inform the carrier of the exact nature of any dangerous goods which it delivers to the carrier. If the sender delivers dangerous goods to the carrier without telling the carrier that they are dangerous, the carrier may unload or destroy the goods or render them harmless without being liable for any compensation. If the nature of the dangerous goods is not stated in the consignment note, the onus of proof that the carrier has been informed rests on the sender. Article 7 read in conjunction with art.6(f) provides that the sender is responsible for all

> "expenses, loss and damage sustained by the carrier by reason of the inaccuracy or inadequacy of ... the description in common use of the nature of the goods and the method of packing, and, in the case of dangerous goods, their generally recognised description".

The CMR does not contain a definition of dangerous goods. Given the attempts to harmonise the carriage of dangerous goods by road by the European Agreement of 30 September 1957 concerning the International

[111] See 2.2.2.1.
[112] As discussed at 2.3.9.
[113] See fn. 110.
[114] See 3.1.8.2.
[115] ibid.

Carriage of Dangerous Goods by Road (ADR), as revised by the protocol of 28 October 1993, it is likely that the concept of dangerous goods would be determined by the contents of annexes A and B to the ADR Convention,[116] rather than by reference to the broader common law concept discussed in 1.9.1.3.

2.3.11 Claims among Carriers

Article 37 provides that a carrier "who has paid compensation in compliance with the provisions of this Convention" has a right to recover it from other carriers involved in the carriage on the following basis: (a) the carrier "responsible" for the loss is solely liable; (b) where the loss "has been caused" by more than one carrier each of the responsible carriers shall pay an amount "proportionate to his share of liability" or, if it is "impossible" to apportion the liability, an amount "in proportion to" their share of the carriage carriages; (c) where it "cannot be ascertained" which carriers were responsible for the loss it is to be apportioned between all carriers as per (b). Article 38 provides that in the event of insolvency, the share payable by the insolvent carrier is to be divided between the other carriers in proportion to their share of carriage charges. These express Convention rights for the recovery of contribution or indemnity from the other carriers responsible for the damage effectively oust the provisions for contribution and/or indemnity under the Civil Liability (Contribution) Act 1978,[117] insofar as the claim for which such contribution or indemnity is sought is regulated by the CMR.[118]

Article 39 provides that when a carrier has been given "due" notice of proceedings brought against another carrier and afforded the opportunity of entering an appearance, that carrier may not afterwards dispute the validity of any judgment given against the other carrier in those proceedings. Where the original claim giving rise to derivative claims for contribution and indemnity between successive carriers is one which is regulated by the CMR, the provisions of Chapter VI of the CMR have been interpreted as constituting a self-contained code for contribution or indemnity, so that carriers paying claims under collateral obligations to customers without liability under art.36 will have no rights of recourse

[116] Discussed at 5.3.2.

[117] Discussed at 1.8.1.

[118] *ITT Schaub-Lorenz GmbH v Birkart Johann Internationale Spedition GmbH* [1988] 1 Lloyd's Rep. 487.

against other carriers.[119] However, carriers do have the right under art.40 of the CMR "to agree among themselves" provisions other than arts 37 and 38 for the regulation of claims for contribution and indemnity. Claims between successive carriers are according to art.39(2) subject to the suit time provisions contained in art.32, although the one or three year period of limitation only commences when the CMR compensation has been fixed by final judicial decision or, in the absence of such decision, by payment. Claims between successive carriers are also, according to art.39(2), subject to a discrete jurisdictional regime. This provides that carriers wishing to enforce recovery rights against other carriers may proceed in any country "in which one of the carriers concerned is ordinarily resident, or has his principal place of business or the branch or agency through which the contract of carriage was made" and all carriers against whom such action is taken may be joined as defendants to the same action.

2.4 International Road Carriage—Passengers' Luggage (CVR)

The CMR governs contracts for the international carriage of goods for reward and not contracts for the international carriage of passengers and their luggage. The latter is the subject of the Convention on the Contract for the International Carriage of Passengers and Luggage by Road 1973 (the CVR) to which there are some eight contracting states. However, the Convention has not been ratified by any of these states and, in consequence, has not come into force as an instrument of public international law.[120] The UK government prepared for it to be brought into force in the United Kingdom by the Carriage of Passengers by Road Act 1974. This Act never came into force so far as its substantive provisions were concerned and was repealed by the Statute Law (Repeals) Act 2004. Accordingly, at least until the EU legislates on the terms of carriage for the transportation of passengers' luggage by road across international borders in the EEA, it seems unlikely that national rules concerning the carriage of passengers' luggage will be harmonised. Currently, under English law, the rights and

[119] *Rosewood Trucking Ltd v Brian Balaam* [2006] 1 Lloyd's Rep. 429 where an intermediate carrier who had indemnified a first CMR carrier, by reason of a non-CMR contractual obligation, was unable to recover indemnity from the responsible carrier under art.37.

[120] According to art.25 of the CVR, ratification by five contracting states was required for entry into force.

duties of such passengers and road carriers are governed by the principles described in Part One.

2.5 Domestic Rail Carriage

2.5.1 Contractual Context

The privatisation of the UK rail industry introduced in the early 1990s has affected the contractual arrangements for the carriage of goods and passengers' luggage in different ways. The National Rail Conditions of Carriage represent a minimum level of protection for the customer irrespective of the identity of the train operating company.[121] For the carriage of goods there is no minimum level of protection. The various different freight operating companies contract on the basis of their own carriage conditions, thereby enabling them to compete with road carriers on equal terms as regards contractual conditions. Unlike road carriage, there are no industry standard terms for the carriage of goods by rail. The conditions of DB Schenker Rail (UK) Ltd (DB Schenker) and Freightliner Ltd (Freightliner) are discussed in 2.5.2 below, as contrasting examples of the various rail carriage conditions currently used by the five freight operating companies licensed by the Office of the Rail Regulator (ORR) to operate rail services for the carriage of goods on the UK rail network.[122] Unlike passenger services, the licences are not exclusive and the freight operating companies compete freely for any business that they are licensed to undertake.[123] DB Schenker predominantly undertake discrete rail freight movements, having taken over the rail freight operations of their predecessor, English Welsh & Scottish Railway International Ltd. Freightliner mainly undertakes intermodal rail movements, having taken over the intermodal operation of British Railway. However, before reviewing the substantive provisions of these companies' respective carriage conditions, it

[121] Accordingly, train operating companies may grant their customers more but not less extensive rights, except in cases where expressly permitted by the National Rail Conditions of Carriage for certain reduced fare tickets.

[122] The five licensed rail operators are DB Schenker Rail (UK) Ltd; Freightliner Ltd; Direct Rail Services Limited; Fastline Ltd trading as Fastline Freight; and GB Railfreight Ltd; DB Schenker and Freightliner have the largest shares of the market. Source: ORR website *http://www.rail-reg.gov.uk* (accessed February 8, 2010).

[123] Subject of course to competition regulation in their various markets by the ORR, the Office of Fair Trade and the European Commission.

is appropriate to give a little historical background, so that the present contractual arrangements can be considered in the context of the previously applicable regimes.

When railways first came into existence after 1825, a railway company was held, at common law, to be a common carrier of all goods which it held itself out as ready to carry for the public, within the area of its operations. The railway companies' status as common carriers continued until the Transport Act 1962, s.43(6), enacted that the Railways Board should not be regarded as a common carrier. The rights and liabilities of the railway companies were, however, regulated by their private statutes, and by the Railways (Consolidated Clauses) Act 1845, and the Railway and Canal Traffic Acts 1854–88. The Railway and Canal Traffic Act 1854 enacted that any contract of carriage by which the railway company limited its liability for negligence must be in writing, signed by the owner of the goods or the consignor, and must also be just and reasonable. If a rail carrier offered to the consignor a fair alternative of carriage, at a reasonable additional charge, under a contract by which the carrier would be liable for its negligence, that was held strong evidence that a contract of carriage, by which the rail carrier limited its liability for negligence, was just and reasonable.[124]

This led to the railway carriers offering consignees two alternative contracts of carriage: carriage at the company's risk and carriage at the owner's risk. In carriage at the company's risk, the company was liable, with certain exceptions, unless it could prove that it had not been negligent. In carriage at owner's risk, it was only liable, again subject to certain exceptions, if the owner of the goods could prove that the railway company's servants had been guilty of wilful misconduct. The effect of the Railways Act 1921 was that these conditions of carriage at company's and owner's risk applied in almost every case after January 1, 1928, not by virtue of a contract between the parties but by the provisions of the standard terms and conditions, which were given force of law by a Statutory Rule and Order made under the provisions of the Railways Act 1921. The Transport Act 1962 abolished these standard terms and conditions, enacting that, after September 1, 1962, the conditions of carriage by railway should be settled by private contract between the parties. At that time the carriage of goods by rail in the United Kingdom was dominated by the public sector in the form of the British Railways Board. The contracts used by British

[124] *Peek v North Staffordshire Railway Company* (1863), 10 H.L.C. 473, 511–12, per Blackburn J.; *Lewis v Great Western Railway Company* (1877), 3 Q.B.D. 195; *Manchester, Sheffield and Lincolnshire Railway Company v Brown* (1883), 8 App. Cas. 703.

Railway, latterly contained in the *Book of Rules of British Railways*, were almost identical to the former standard terms and conditions, which themselves were largely the same as the old contractual conditions for carriage at company's risk and owner's risk in force between 1863 and 1928. In carriage at the Board's risk, the Railways Board was liable, subject to various exceptions, unless it could prove that it was not negligent. In carriage at the owner's risk, the Board was liable only for "wilful default".[125]

Armed with that background it is appropriate to turn to consideration of carriage conditions now in use for the carriage of goods by rail following privatisation of the UK rail industry.

2.5.2 Specified Contractual Terms

Obviously anyone can agree to carry goods by rail, just as they can agree to carry goods by any other mode. Contracts are governed by the contractual principles reviewed in Part One and any such person contracting to carry goods by rail has the benefit of the s.123 Railways Act 1993 stipulation that "No person shall be regarded as a common carrier by railway". However, unless that person is a licensed rail freight operator, any such person will need to sub-contract performance to a rail freight operator who is likely only to agree carriage by rail subject to its own carriage conditions; such conditions also take effect subject to the principles reviewed in Part One.

Whilst the significant differences in carrier liability exposures under the various applicable carriage conditions may reflect various commercial factors (such as contrasting levels of perceived risk from carriers' respective carriage operations, contrasting insurance protections, contrasting customer attitudes, and so on), they also increase the legal complexity of carriage cargo operations by multiple carriers, particularly when subjected to different modes of carriage. In that respect, and from the perspective of the customer consigning goods from A to B, the contractual environment for the carriage of goods by rail in the United Kingdom can be compared unfavourably with mandatory, or even industry standard, carriage terms.

This is the context in which each of the general carriage conditions at 2.5.2.1 and 2.5.2.2 below, respectively those of DB Schenker and Freightliner, will take effect.

[125] A term reviewed in the context of the CMR at 2.3.4.3 above.

2.5.2.1 Rail Bulk Carriage Conditions[126]

The DB Schenker conditions mirror the RHA 2009 conditions reviewed at 2.2.2.1 in many respects. They state that the carrier is not a common carrier (relevant only for carriage performed other than by rail);[127] provide at cl.4.1 for the customer to warrant it is either the owner of the goods, or that it has authority to accept the conditions from all persons interested in them and by cl.2.2 that DB Schenker is expressly permitted to sub-contract performance (albeit not expressly on any terms);[128] accept liability for any loss or damage to goods occurring whilst the goods are in transit subject to certain similar exceptions;[129] apply a limitation fund by cl.8.4 for such claims to be calculated at the rate of £1,300 per tonne of "the goods" (unlike the RHA conditions, the limit appears calculable by reference to the weight of the goods to be carried under the contract rather than of those goods lost or damaged); define dangerous goods specifically, rather than by reference to the wider common law context (although, unlike the RHA conditions, by reference to "the Carriage of Dangerous Goods and Use of Transportable Pressure Equipment Regulations 2004 as amended or replaced from time to time").[130] The conditions place extensive obligations on the customer as to the packaging, labelling, and consigning of goods at cl.4 and as to dangerous goods at cl.5 with the carrier only having liability in respect of dangerous goods where the customer has complied with its obligations and DB Schenker has not only received in writing "precise and correct" identification of the dangerous goods but has also agreed in writing to accept them for carriage; provides at cl.12 that after transit has ended and whilst transit is suspended the carrier has no liability whatever for the goods; provide at cl.10.3.4 that any liability for delay is limited to the carriage charges; provide at cl.7.2 for the carrier to have a general lien and power of sale in relation to the goods in the event of any non-payment by the customer (but unlike RHA conditions do not provide for a particular lien against any owner of the goods other than the customer). Various

[126] DB Schenker website *http://www.rail.dbschenker.co.uk* (accessed August 30, 2009).
[127] See s.123 Railways Act 1993.
[128] Which, as discussed at 1.6.1.1, is significant to sub-bailment terms.
[129] See cll.8.1 and 8.2 with "transit" being defined by reference to the departure and arrival points for the carriage contemplated by the carriage contract.
[130] A definition pointing to the current enactment of this provision by The Carriage of Dangerous Goods and Use of Transportable Pressure Equipment Regulations 2007 No.1573, which incorporates goods encompassed by both ADR and RID discussed in 5.3.2 and 5.3.3.

indemnities are provided for against the customer at cll.3.2.5, 4.4, 5.3 and 10.2 which are similar to those contained in RHA conditions. The DB Schenker conditions also provide clear stipulations as to loading and unloading at cl.3 albeit, unlike the RHA conditions, predicated on an assumption that either the carrier or the customer may undertake such obligations; and, finally in the context of these similarities, the conditions incorporate at cl.19.11 an exclusive English law and jurisdiction clause.

Unlike the RHA conditions however, the DB Schenker conditions contain provisions reflecting the rail freight operator's use of rail facilities owned and operated by Network Rail in a regulated rail environment, requiring the customer to undertake additional liabilities or provide the rail carrier with enhanced security and protection from service default. Additional customer liabilities can be seen in the provision of indemnities at cl.16.8 for any damage sustained to equipment or sidings not owned by the customer and at cl.16.6 for any failure of DB Schenker to meet Network Rail performance standards by reason of the customer providing faulty equipment. Increased protection for the rail carrier can be seen in the reservation by DB Schenker at cl.7 of a right to require financial security for such liabilities; the obligation on the customer to maintain liability insurance covering all liabilities to which the customer is exposed by the conditions, up to the value of the per occurrence financial limitation of £5,000,000 as provided for by cll.10.4 and 13.1; the wide ranging force majeure protection for the carrier for service failure pursuant to cl.9 and the broad definition at cl.1.1 of circumstances force majeure. It is noteworthy that, unlike the RHA, the DB Schenker conditions do not contain any regulation of suit time or seek to supplement by express terms the absolute right of a carrier to receive carriage charges notwithstanding any rights of set off or counterclaim that might otherwise arise.

2.5.2.2 Intermodal Rail Carriage Conditions[131]

The conditions used by Freightliner have much in common with those used by DB Schenker. For instance, the Freightliner conditions also assert by cl.24 that they are not common carriers; contain at cl.25 a choice of English law; provide at cl.3 that the sender warrants it has authority "of all persons owning or interested in the Consignment"; provide at cl.4(c) that anyone claiming through the customer is bound to the conditions; expressly permit Freightliner by cl.4 to sub-contract performance to others and to extend the

[131] Freightliner website *http://www.freightliner.co.uk* (accessed August 30, 2009).

benefit of the conditions to its "servants and agents"; and, substantively, apply the same definition of dangerous goods.

However, in other respects the Freightliner conditions are completely unlike the DB Schenker and RHA conditions, presumably so as to reflect the intermodal nature of the operations for which they have been prepared. The choice of jurisdiction is in favour of the "United Kingdom courts";[132] Freightliner's liability will only be engaged by its own default of the various obligations described at 1.8.1, which arise under the common law and statute with very few exclusions of liability being expressly stipulated.[133] There is no concept of any period of responsibility and no indemnity provisions are stipulated against the customer (other than in respect of duty payable to HM Revenue and Customs under cl.22). The financial limitation provisions at cl.17 appear to follow broadly the structure of RHA conditions but the limitation fund is calculated "... at a rate of £1,500 per tonne gross weight of the Container and in so far as it is in respect of the whole contents of a Container or the whole of goods not in a Container to a sum calculated at a rate of £1,500 per tonne of such contents or goods ..."; so that, in contrast to RHA conditions, the limit appears calculable by reference to the weight of the goods to be carried under the contract rather than of those goods lost or damaged.[134] The Freightliner conditions make no provision for any general or particular lien.

2.5.3 Standard Contractual Terms for Domestic Carriage of Passengers' Luggage

As the railway companies were held to be common carriers at common law, they were also liable as common carriers for luggage which the passengers were permitted to take with them on the journey.[135] There were no standard terms and conditions for the carriage of passengers' luggage. As the railway companies did not make any special contract with passengers limiting their liability as common carriers for the luggage, they were under the full liability

[132] Which do not form part of a single jurisdiction, but invite proceedings anywhere in England and Wales, Scotland or Northern Ireland.

[133] Exclusions are however stipulated under cll.16.2, 16.3(c) and 17(d) as to, respectively, liabilities in the event of customer fraud, delay to customer equipment and loss or damage to any property of the trader, apart from the goods, left with the carrier.

[134] The per tonne limitation rate is of course higher than under RHA and DB Schenker conditions.

[135] *Richards v London, Brighton and South Coast Railway Company* (1849), 7 C.B. 839.

of common carriers. The Transport Act 1962, in s.43, enacted that the Railways Board was not to be regarded as a common carrier and consequently, as from September 1, 1962, the British Railways Board was liable only as a contracting carrier for want of reasonable care in contract, tort and bailment. The Board limited this liability by special contract. The contracts between the Railways Board and passengers for the carriage of passengers' luggage were contained in the *Book of Rules*, which made the Railways Board liable only for negligence and wilful default. The National Rail Conditions of Carriage provide the minimum level of protection to be afforded by the passenger train operating companies as discussed at 2.5.1 and maintain that position in relation to the carriage of passengers' luggage, with Condition 50 providing that

> "A Train Company will only be liable for any loss or damage to luggage, articles, animals or cycles in its trains or on its premises if the loss or damage was caused by the negligent or wilful acts or omissions of its, or a Rail Service Company's, staff or agents."

although that condition goes on to provide for a maximum liability for any single item of £1,000. Apart from that limitation, this provision reflects the liability attaching to the passenger train operating company under its common law and statutory obligations as a contracting carrier.[136]

2.6 International Rail Carriage: CIM and CIV

2.6.1 General Context of CIM and CIV Conventions

International carriage of goods and passengers by rail across the European and Asian landmass is governed by uniform rules of public international law originally contained in two freestanding conventions, the CIM (Convention Internationale de Marchandises) and the CIV (Convention Internationale de Voyageurs). These uniform systems of law for the international carriage of goods and passengers by rail have been in operation for very many years; the first international convention concerning the international carriage of goods by rail was signed in 1893. They have

[136] Since the rail carrier would in any case be liable only for a want of reasonable care so that, apart from the financial limitation, the practical significance of the contractual provision lies in the passenger now having to prove negligence, rather than the carrier as bailee having to disprove negligence (see 1.6).

now been subsumed within the Convention Concerning International Carriage by Rail (COTIF) signed at Berne on May 9, 1980 and originally enacted in the United Kingdom by the International Transport Convention Act 1983, s.1. COTIF came into force on May 1, 1985 and originally comprised three separate parts: the COTIF Convention itself containing general provisions primarily addressed to the Contracting States; Appendix A, dealing with the uniform rules concerning the Contract for International Carriage of Passengers and Luggage by Rail (CIV); and Appendix B, dealing with the uniform rules concerning the Contract for International Carriage of Goods by Rail (CIM).

COTIF was the subject of significant revision by a protocol of June 3, 1999 (the Vilnius Protocol) materially affecting the uniform rules appended to it and introducing the following further appendices: Appendix C Regulation concerning the International Carriage of Dangerous Goods by Rail (RID); Appendix D Uniform Rules concerning Contracts of Use of Vehicles in International Rail Traffic (CUV); Appendix E Uniform Rules concerning the Contract of Use of Infrastructure in International Rail Traffic (CUI); Appendix F Uniform Rules concerning the Validation of Technical Standards and the Adoption of Uniform Technical Prescriptions applicable to Railway Material intended to be used in International Traffic (APTU); and Appendix G Uniform Rules concerning the Technical Admission of Railway Material used in International Traffic (ATMF). The changes made by the Vilnius Protocol were applied into UK law by s.103 of the Railways and Transport Safety Act 2003 and the Railways (Convention on International Carriage by Rail) Regulations 2005 (SI 2005/2092); these changes came into force in the United Kingdom on July 1, 2006.

COTIF is administered by the Intergovernmental Organisation for International Carriage by Rail (OTIF) which was set up on May 1, 1985 and operates from headquarters in Berne, Switzerland. OTIF currently has 43 Member States which include all the European states, other than certain successor states of the Soviet Union, four Middle Eastern and three North African states. Whilst this book is not concerned with the carriage of passengers, those provisions of CIV dealing with the carriage of registered luggage (as opposed to hand luggage) will be considered at 2.6.3; but CIM must be the primary focus and these uniform rules for the international carriage of goods by rail are now addressed at 2.6.2 below.

2.6.2 CIM

2.6.2.1 Scope of Application

Before the changes made by the Vilnius Protocol, CIM only applied to contracts for international carriage by railway operators over designated railways, pursuant to through transit rail consignment notes for international carriage, with disputes being determined by the states in which those railway operators were domiciled. As a result, the CIM uniform rules have not previously featured significantly in English court decisions, particularly since passenger and freight services through the Channel Tunnel did not constitute rail carriage under CIM as the cross-channel rail link was not a designated railway for its purposes. The Vilnius amendments to CIM have removed the requirement of designation and CIM may now apply for cross-border international rail freight movements through the Channel Tunnel subject to the terms of the derogation agreed between the French and UK governments pursuant to art.4.1 of CIM and communicated to OTIF on June 29, 2006. The derogation relates to

> "carriage by means of rail shuttle services carrying road vehicles and their passengers performed exclusively between the Channel Tunnel terminals at Cheriton in Kent and Coquelles in the Pas-de-Calais, being stations situated on either side of a frontier with no other station between them".[137]

Goods may either be transported through the tunnel on road vehicles via the roll on/roll off shuttle service, or on freight trains travelling to and from UK rail freight terminals. In the former case, the CIM is disapplied by the derogation above. For the reasons discussed at 2.3.1, the movement of goods through the Channel Tunnel where the shuttle service is used is governed by the CMR.[138] Only in the latter case, where freight trains operate from and/or to UK rail freight terminals, could movement through the Channel Tunnel be governed by the CIM Convention.[139] As and when the English courts come to apply CIM their interpretation of its provisions

[137] See the OTIF website *http://www.otif.org/en/law.html.*

[138] Although the movement of the road vehicle itself will be governed by the carriage conditions of the shuttle service see the Eurotunnel partnership website *http://www.eurotunnel.com.*

[139] Although the application of CIM would depend upon the international rail movement beginning and ending in a COTIF convention country; see fn. 141.

is likely to be influenced by their previous CMR jurisprudence, since many CIM provisions have been incorporated into the subsequent CMR convention. Indeed, the similarities between the respective uniform terms have become more pronounced as a result of the changes made by the Vilnius Protocol to the scope of the CIM uniform rules, which now broadly mirror the scope of CMR.[140]

The scope of CIM extends to every contract for carriage by rail for reward where the place of taking over the goods and the place designated for delivery are in two different contracting states.[141] The following are listed by OTIF[142] as being Member States and thus contracting states to COTIF: Albania, Algeria, Austria, Belgium, Bosnia and Herzegovina, Bulgaria, Croatia, Czech Republic, Denmark, Estonia, Finland, France, Germany, Greece, Hungary, Iran, Iraq, Ireland, Italy, Latvia, Lebanon, Liechtenstein, Lithuania, Luxembourg, Former Yugoslav Republic of Macedonia, Monaco, Morocco, Netherlands, Norway, Poland, Portugal, Romania, Serbia, Slovakia, Slovenia, Spain, Sweden, Switzerland, Syria, Tunisia, Turkey, Ukraine, and United Kingdom.

According to art.1.3, CIM also applies to supplementary carriage by road or inland waterway in the internal traffic of a Member State when such carriage is performed under a single contract for transfrontier carriage by rail. Pursuant to art.1.4, CIM also extends to supplementary transnational carriage by sea and/or inland waterway performed on the same basis under a single contract for transfrontier carriage by rail, but only where such carriage is performed on services designated by Member States to OTIF under COTIF art.24.1. As with road carriage under the CMR, the absence of a consignment note does not affect the application of CIM (art.6) and the carrier of the goods by rail for the purposes of CIM now comprises under art.3 the contractual carrier with whom the consignor has concluded the contract of carriage as well as any "substitute carrier".[143] CIM now

[140] With the obvious substitution of rail for road carriage and the reduction of geographic breadth consequent upon CIM only having some 43 contracting states, whilst there are over 60 contracting states to the CMR.

[141] Pursuant to CIM art.1.1; it should be noted that, unlike the CMR, the place of taking over and the place of delivery of the goods must *both* be within OTIF Member States.

[142] See the list of Member States provided on their website *http://www.otif.org* (accessed August 2, 2009). The membership of Iraq and Lebanon was referred to as having been suspended until "international rail traffic is restored".

[143] A status defined by art.3, as that of any sub-contractor entrusted, entirely or in part, with performance of the carriage by rail, discussed at 2.6.2.6 below.

extends to all goods; but, by art.2, carriage remains subject to "prescriptions of public law"[144] generally and particularly those relating to dangerous goods, customs law and animals. When the contract comes into being and what charges are payable for the carriage are matters which now, following the Vilnius Protocol, can be determined by the governing laws applicable to determine the dispute.[145] When applicable, CIM applies to "any action in respect of liability, on whatever grounds" against the carrier or "servants or other persons for whom the carrier is liable".[146]

2.6.2.2 Documents

Articles 6, 7, 8 and 12 together prescribe the responsibilities for the creation and accuracy of the consignment note and regulate its status, content and evidential value. The consignor is obliged to present a separate consignment note duly completed for each consignment, which in the absence of a contrary agreement may not relate to more than a single wagon load. The consignment note must contain details of the place and date on which it was made out; the name and address of the consignor; the name and address of the carrier; where the goods have been handed over to anyone other than the carrier the name and address of that person; details of the place and date on which the goods were taken over; the place of delivery; the name and address of the consignee; the description of the goods (including required particulars as to dangerous goods);[147] the gross mass, or quantity, of the goods; the number of packages and information necessary for the identification of consignments in less than wagon loads; the number of the wagon for full wagon loads; the number of any railway vehicle "running on its own wheels" if it is handed over for carriage "as goods"; information necessary for the identification of any consigned intermodal transport units; a detailed list of the documents required by Customs or other administrative authorities (which are to be attached to the

[144] Presumably any international or national mandatory regulation, such as that discussed in 5.3.3.

[145] See 1.4; the jurisdictional provisions of the CIM are discussed at 2.6.2.8 below.

[146] Per art.41; the persons for whom the carrier is responsible defined by art.40 are discussed at 2.6.2.3 below. As discussed in relation to the CMR at 2.3.1 above, the references to "any action" and "liability" must be taken to exclude claims not contemplated by CIM.

[147] The required particulars are determined by reference to the regulation as to the International Carriage of Dangerous Goods by Rail (RID) forming appendix C to the COTIF convention which is discussed in 5.3.3.

consignment note or to be held at the disposal of the carrier or other agreed designated body); any costs of carriage payable by the consignee; and a statement that carriage is subject to the CIM uniform rule.

The following particulars should also be contained "when applicable": in the event of successive carriage the name of the successive carrier who is to deliver the goods;[148] any costs which the consignor undertakes to pay; the amount of any cash on delivery charge to be collected by the carrier;[149] any declaration of value, or special interest in delivery, of the goods; any agreed transit period;[150] any agreed route;[151] a list of any documents handed over to the carrier; and the number and description of any seals affixed by the consignor to the wagon.

The consignor is responsible for making out the consignment note and, pursuant to art.8, is also responsible for all costs, loss or damage sustained by the carrier because of any irregularity, inaccuracy or incompleteness of the consignor's entries and also for any failure to make entries prescribed by RID for the carriage of dangerous goods. Where the carrier is asked by the consignor to complete all or any part of the consignment note, it is assumed that this has been done, unless the contrary is proved by the consignor under art.8(2). However, should the consignment note not contain the statement that the carriage of the goods is subject to CIM uniform rules, art.8(3) provides that the carrier shall be liable for all costs, loss or damage sustained by anyone else. Article 6(4) obliges the carrier to "certify ... in an appropriate manner", on a duplicate of the consignment note, the taking over of the goods. This is significant as only from that time does the "transit" commence under art.16(4) and the carrier become responsible for the goods under art.14(1).

Significantly, art.6(5) stipulates that the consignment note does not have "effect as a bill of lading". This suggests that, unlike a bill of lading,[152] the consignment note does not symbolically represent the goods to which it refers. Accordingly, legal possession of the consignment note does not give constructive possession of the goods, title to the goods will not be

[148] Successive carriage is discussed at 2.6.2.6 below.

[149] Pursuant to CIM art.17(6) the position under CIM is the same as under CMR: if the carrier agrees to collect any "cash on delivery charge", the carrier will be obliged to compensate the consignor for the amount of that charge in the event of non-collection of the charge and delivery of the goods; with the carrier having an independent right of action against the consignee to recover that charge.

[150] Discussed at 2.6.2.3 below.

[151] Significant for the "transit period" in art.18 discussed at 2.6.2.3.

[152] See 3.2.3.4.

transferred by the negotiation of it and it cannot be presented to the carrier by way of an exchangeable receipt for the goods. The evidential value of the consignment note is that, by art.12(1), it affords prima facie evidence of the making and content of the contract of carriage and the taking over of the goods by the carrier. It is also prima facie evidence as to the apparently good condition of the goods when taken over by the carrier and of the accuracy of the contents of the consignment note as to the description, packing and quantity of the goods, unless reasoned reservations are expressed. Where the consignor has loaded the goods, this presumption only works against the carrier where the carrier has examined the goods and recorded a result of this examination on the consignment note.[153] Article 12(4) entitles the carrier to make a reservation on the consignment note where the carrier is without "the appropriate means" to examine the goods.

It should be remembered that whilst art.6(2) provides that the contract of carriage "must be confirmed by a consignment note which accords with" CIM, it goes on to state that "the absence, irregularity or loss of the consignment note shall not affect the existence or validity of the contract", which remains subject to the CIM.[154]

2.6.2.3 Liability of Carrier

As discussed above, the carrier is liable from the time of taking over the goods to the time of delivery but, whilst the concept of delivery of the goods to the consignee is regulated by art.17, the handing over of the goods to the carrier is not particularly defined. The sender is obliged to stipulate in the consignment note when, where and by whom the goods were taken over and the carrier is obliged to certify those facts.[155] The consignment note is only prima facie evidence of the factual information, that it contains and its "absence, irregularity or loss" does not detract from the application of the CIM. For these reasons how, when and where goods are handed over to a carrier in the context of any particular contract are matters to be determined by the court or tribunal exercising jurisdiction over any dispute in the light of the evidence presented, although it would be consistent with CIM for the carrier to be given the benefit of any doubt arising because of

[153] See art.12(2) and 12(3).
[154] Reflecting the status of the consignment note under the CMR.
[155] See 2.6.2.2 above.

any "irregularity, inaccuracy or incompleteness" in the consignment note.[156] According to art.13 responsibility for loading and unloading the goods is a matter for agreement between the carrier and the consignor: however, in the absence of agreement, the carrier has responsibility for the handling of "packages" and the consignor and consignee are responsible for, respectively, the loading and unloading of "full wagon loads". The concept of "packages" has, rather unhelpfully, been left undefined but a purposive construction would suggest all goods should be considered either "packages" or "full wagon loads" and interpreted accordingly in the context of each particular contract. The consignor is liable under art.13(2) for all the consequences of "defective loading" with the onus of proof being on the carrier.

Delivery to the consignee is regulated by art.17, which provides that the carrier is obliged to hand over the consignment note and deliver the goods to the consignee at the place designated for delivery against a receipt and payment of any amounts due according to the contract. Delivery will take place as determined by the prescriptions in force at the destination. Where those prescriptions require delivery to customs or similarly entitled authorities, this will be the equivalent of delivery to the consignee. The consignee is entitled by art.17(4) to refuse to accept the goods unless and until the carrier accedes to any demand of the consignee for an examination of the goods to establish any alleged loss or damage. Delivery will be deemed to have taken place when the goods are handed over. Where circumstances arise preventing delivery, under art.20 the carrier must, where so requested by the consignor in the consignment note, redeliver the goods to the consignor. Otherwise the carrier must revert for instructions to the consignor or, where the consignee has previously modified the contract of carriage pursuant to art.18(3)–(5), the consignee.[157]

Similar provisions apply under art.21 when circumstances arise which prevent the carriage of the goods, save that the carrier has the option of modifying the route. The consequences of circumstances preventing delivery or carriage under arts 20 and 21 are that the carrier, broadly, is entitled to: (a) recover costs incurred by it without any fault on its part in

[156] See art.8 and 2.6.2.2 above.

[157] In the event of "fault" by the carrier as to the modification of the contract of carriage in response to instructions from either the consignor or the consignee, the carrier is liable for the consequences of any failure in the carrying out, or improper carrying out, of such instructions pursuant to arts 19(6) and 19(7): the complex relationship of the consignor's and the consignee's modification rights under CIM are discussed below at 2.6.2.7.

consequence of such circumstances; (b) terminate the transit and unload the goods; (c) either hold them on behalf of the person entitled to them or hand them to a third party to hold them in which case the carrier's only duty as to such safekeeping is the exercise of reasonable care in the selection of such third party; and (d) sell them without instructions, when this is justified by their perishable nature or by the fact that storage costs would be out of proportion to their value and account to the person entitled to them any net sale proceeds in excess of the carrier's recoverable charges and costs, or render an account to the consignor for any net deficit.[158]

Article 23 provides that the carrier shall be liable for loss or damage to the goods between the time of taking them over for carriage and the time of delivery, and for loss or damage resulting from the transit period[159] being exceeded. Article 40 provides that the carrier shall be liable for its servants, and for any other persons whose services it uses for the carriage,[160] when acting "within the scope of their functions".[161] The carrier is relieved of such liability by art.23(2) if the loss or damage, or the exceeding of the transit period, were caused by certain excepted causes. These comprise: fault on the part of the person entitled; order of the person entitled, other than as a result of a fault on the part of the carrier; inherent vice of the goods (decay, wastage, etc.); or, circumstances which the carrier could not avoid and the consequences of which it was unable to prevent.[162]

The carrier is also relieved of such liability by art.23(3) when the loss or

[158] Pursuant to CIM art.22.

[159] Article 16(1) contemplates the transit period being agreed between the consignor and the carrier, but in the absence of agreement the period is calculated pursuant to sub-clauses (2)–(4) of art.16 by reference to: the distance the goods are to be carried; whether the goods comprise full or part wagon loads; additional transit periods fixed by the carrier in its general carriage conditions in the event of certain particular circumstances prescribed by CIM; any extension for "a stay" caused without fault of the carrier; and any applicable suspensions for Sundays and bank holidays.

[160] The "managers of the railway infrastructure on which the carriage is performed" are specifically identified as being such persons of whom the carrier makes use for the carriage.

[161] As discussed at 2.3.4.3 above, CMR art.29(2) contains in the same context the word "employment" rather than "functions" but, as previously discussed, a purposive interpretation would suggest the same meaning for each of those words in this context.

[162] The interpretation of the equivalent provision under the CMR is discussed at 2.3.3 above and the same exception applies to the carrier's liability under art.15(3) for adverse consequences arising from the carrier's loss or misuse of documents.

damage arise from the special risks inherent in one or more of the following circumstances: (a) insofar as atmospheric influences cause damage, carriage in open wagons[163] at the consignor's risk under the carrier's general carriage conditions, or pursuant to a special agreement made between the consignor and the carrier referred to in the consignment note; (b) the absence or inadequacy of packing in the case of goods which by their nature are liable to loss or damage when not packed or not properly packed; (c) loading by the consignor or unloading by the consignee; (d) the nature of certain goods which renders them inherently liable to total or partial loss or damage, especially through breakage, rust, interior and spontaneous decay, desiccation or wastage; (e) irregular, incorrect or incomplete description or numbering of packages; (f) carriage of live animals; and (g) carriage of accompanied goods if the loss or damage results from any risk which the attendant was intended to avert.

According to art.25 the carrier has the onus of proving that the loss, damage or delay was attributable to one of the excepted causes but, where the carrier establishes loss or damage could be attributable to one of the art.23(3) special risks, a rebuttable presumption arises that it was so caused, subject either to the contrary being proved, or the presumption being disapplied pursuant to art.25(3) where an "abnormally large quantity" or an entire "package" has been lost. Article 31 permits the carrier certain allowances for wastage in respect of goods, which "by reason of their nature, are generally subject to wastage in transit by the sole fact of carriage".

Discrete liability regimes apply in certain circumstances. For the carriage of railway vehicles as goods "running on their own wheels", liability is governed by art.24, which provides that the carrier is responsible for loss, damage or delay unless it can prove that such loss or damage "was not caused by his fault". The carrier is not liable for the loss of accessories unless mentioned on both sides of the vehicle and the accompanying inventory. For rail-sea traffic (made subject to the CIM by the relevant sea link being designated by Member States to OTIF under COTIF art.24.1) liability is covered by art.38. This allows Member States designating certain services as rail-sea links to stipulate (by requesting a suitable notation in the OTIF list of rail-sea links subject to CIM) the following additional grounds for exemption: (a) fire, if the carrier proves that it was not caused by the carrier's act or fault, or that of the master, a mariner, pilot or the carrier's servants; (b) saving or attempting to save life or property at sea; (c) the

[163] Excepting goods loaded in intermodal transport units or closed road vehicles.

loading of goods on the deck of the ship, if they are so loaded with the consent of the consignor given in the consignment note and are not in wagons; and (d) perils, dangers and accidents of the sea or other navigable waters. However, the carrier can only use the art.38 exemption grounds where it can be proved that the loss, damage or delay occurred in the course of the sea journey between the loading and discharging of the ship and, notwithstanding reliance on such exemptions, the carrier remains liable if the person entitled proves that the loss, damage or delay is due to the fault of the carrier, the master, a mariner, the pilot or the carrier's servants. In the case of nuclear incidents art.39 provides that the carrier is relieved of liability where, by applicable national law, liability for the subject loss and damage attaches to the operator of a nuclear installation, or a substitute for such operator.

2.6.2.4 Value of Claim

The financial limitation provisions for loss and damage are very similar to those contained in the CMR. Article 30(1) provides that in the event of total or partial loss of the goods the carrier's liability "to the exclusion of all other damages" is compensation calculated according to: (a) the commodity exchange quotation; or, if none (b) the current market price; or, if neither (c) the normal value of goods of the same kind and quality at the time and place at which the goods were accepted for carriage. Article 30(2) provides that such compensation "shall not exceed 17 ... [SDRs] ... per kilogramme of gross mass short".[164] By art.32, in the case of damage to the goods, the compensation is tied to the loss in value of the goods calculated by applying the percentage of loss in value (as noted at the place of destination) to the value of the goods (as defined in art.30): provided that the compensation cannot exceed the amount that would have been payable either in the case of total loss, or had only the damaged part of the goods been lost. Where the consigned goods comprise "a railway vehicle running on its own wheels", or an intermodal transport unit, art.32(3) limits compensation to the cost of repair limited to the amount payable for total loss under art.30(2).

According to art.30(4) the carrier is also obliged in the case of loss and damage to the goods carried to "refund the carriage charge, customs duties

[164] The limit for total loss, being the generally applicable limit for the carrier's liability, is also applied by arts 15(3), 19(6) and 19(7) for any liability (as discussed at 2.6.2.3 above) incurred under those provisions.

already paid and other sums *paid* in relation to the carriage of the goods lost *except excise duties for goods carried under a procedure suspending those duties*" [emphasis added]. The italicised words do not appear in the broadly equivalent CMR provision at art.23(4) discussed at 2.3.4.2 and make it clear that, in contrast to the decision in *Buchanan v Babco*[165] under the CMR, a carrier by rail has no obligation to indemnify a consignor in respect of liability for duty incurred in consequence of the loss of the goods.

Article 33 limits compensation for delay to an amount "not exceeding four times the carriage charge". However, this amount is not payable at all where the goods have been lost and is calculated pro rata on delayed goods in the event of partial loss. In the event of damage being caused to the delayed goods, the compensation for delay is payable "where appropriate" in addition to sums payable for damage, always provided that the aggregate amount payable does not exceed the amount payable for total loss under art.30(2).

Compensation is to be converted into other currencies at the rates applicable as at the date of payment pursuant to art.37. As with the CMR, interest is payable at the rate of 5 per cent calculated from the date of written claim or, in the absence of such written claim, from the date proceedings are instituted. However, unlike the CMR, no interest accrues from the expiry of a reasonable time for the submission to the carrier of the required supporting documents until such documents have been submitted.[166]

The various limits of liability provided for in arts 15(3), 19(6), 19(7), 30 and 32 to 35 are disapplied by art.36 in the event that the loss or damage results from any act or omission committed by the carrier "either with intent to cause such loss or damage, or recklessly and with knowledge that such loss or damage would probably result". This provision appears effectively to express the interpretation placed by English law on the concept of "wilful misconduct" (employed in the same context by art.29 of the CMR Convention)[167] that requires proof of the subjective obviousness of the breach to the wrongdoer, rather than the objective seriousness of the breach to the reasonable man. The CIM provision is, however, distinct from CMR art.29 in at least three respects. First, the particular reference to knowledge that "such loss or damage would probably result" appears to require contemplation not only of loss or damage in general but of the

[165] 2.3.4.2 at fn. 77.
[166] See art.37(3).
[167] Discussed at 2.3.4.3.

particular loss or damage actually suffered.[168] Secondly, there is no apparent distinction (unlike the CMR) between provisions fixing and limiting the compensation.[169] Thirdly, the provision does not (unlike the CMR) expressly refer to conduct of employees, agents and sub-contractors. However, as already mentioned at 2.5.2.3 above, CIM art.40 does expressly make the carrier liable "for his servants and other persons whose services he makes use of for the performance of the carriage, when these servants and other persons are acting within the scope of their functions". There is no apparent reason why that liability should not extend to such persons' deliberate or reckless acts or omissions within the meaning of art.36 committed "within the scope of their functions".[170]

Pursuant to art.34, the limit for total loss[171] may be replaced with any higher limit which is agreed between the consignor and the carrier *and* declared in the consignment note and, similarly, by art.35 all limits for delay[172] may be supplemented by such further amount (representing the consignor's "special interest in delivery" of the goods) as may be both agreed between the consignor and the carrier *and* declared "in figures" in the consignment note.

2.6.2.5 Time to Claim

Like the CMR, CIM imposes time limits in relation to the submission of claims and the issue of proceedings.

However, unlike the CMR, late submission of claims gives rise to extinguishment of the claim rather than a mere presumption. Article 47 provides that acceptance of the goods by the person entitled generally extinguishes all rights of action against the carrier arising from the contract of carriage in case of partial loss, damage or exceeding the transit period, except in certain limited circumstances. Rights of action are not extinguished in the following circumstances: (a) partial loss or damage ascertained before

[168] See *The Leerort* [2001] 2 Lloyd's Rep. 291 discussed in 3.1.7 where the Court of Appeal considered a similar provision, in art.4 of the Convention on Limitation of Liability for Maritime Claims 1976, to require foresight of the very loss actually occurring and not merely the general type of loss.

[169] See the discussion at 2.3.4.3 above as to art.29 of the CMR.

[170] In contrast to art.4 of the 1976 Limitation Convention ibid. which refers to a "personal act or omission".

[171] i.e. the limit provided for in art.30(2).

[172] i.e. those variously provided for in arts 30, 32 and 33.

acceptance,[173] or not ascertained solely through the fault of the carrier; (b) non-apparent loss or damage ascertained only after acceptance of the goods where claimant requests ascertainment within art.42 not only immediately after discovery of the loss or damage but also within seven days of acceptance of the goods and furthermore proves that the loss or damage occurred during transit; (c) the transit period has been exceeded and the claimant asserts its rights within 60 days against the first carrier, the last carrier or the performing carrier at the material time; and (d) the cause of the loss or damage is attributable to reckless default as described in art.36.

The periods of time available for the commencement of proceedings under CIM are very similar to the equivalent provisions under the CMR, although particular periods of limitation do differ in various respects. The basic limitation period provided for by art.48 is one year. However, a period of two years is applicable where the action is: (a) to recover a cash on delivery payment collected from the consignee by the carrier; (b) to recover proceeds of a sale effected by the carrier; (c) to recover loss or damage caused by reckless default as described in art.36; (d) the action arises from a contract of carriage subject to re-consignment pursuant to art.28. These periods for the commencement of proceedings may, as with the CMR, be extended by submission of written claims to the carrier with the period of suspension continuing until written rejection is made and supporting claim documents returned.[174]

2.6.2.6 Successive and Substitute Carriage

As discussed, anyone may be an international carrier by rail within CIM by agreeing to undertake the carriage of goods by rail for reward between different states, both of which are contracting states to the COTIF Convention.[175] As with the CMR, where carriage governed by a single contract is performed by several carriers, subsequent carriers by taking over the goods *with* the consignment note[176] become parties to the original contract of carriage as successive carriers responsible for the carriage over the entire

[173] Article 42 provides the framework for such ascertainment.

[174] CIM art.48(3) which, in substance, replicates CMR art.32(2) discussed at 2.3.5.

[175] See CIM arts 1(1) and 3(a).

[176] Although CIM art.45(1) appears to provide that, where the final carrier who is to deliver the goods consents to be entered on the consignment note, the final carrier becomes a successive carrier even where the final carrier receives neither goods nor consignment note.

route up to delivery.[177] However, CIM also provides for other carriage contractors (defined as "substitute carriers") who are entrusted with the performance of all or part of the carriage to be subject to the provisions of CIM for their own performance of the carriage.[178] There are important distinctions between the liability of successive carriers (who must take over the goods with the consignment note) and substitute carriers (who need only be entrusted with performance in whole or in part) in that, whilst the successive carrier is exposed to liability under the original carriage contract in common with the original and any other successive carriers, the substitute carrier is only liable for its own default.[179] As under the CMR, claims against successive carriers under CIM may, by art.45(1), only be brought against the first carrier, the last carrier or the performing carrier at the time of the loss. There are certain exceptions to that principle under CIM, however, in that actions may be brought: (a) against the carrier who collected the sum in question, for recovery of payments made to it; (b) against the first carrier who took over the goods from the consignor, for actions for recovery of cash on delivery payments; and (c) against other carriers by way of action for counterclaim or set off. Despite apparent ambiguity in references to "carriers" and "successive carriers" in art.45, it is clear that all such claims may also be brought against any liable substitute carriers.[180] Where the claimant has a choice between several carriers, art.45(7) extinguishes that right as soon as the claimant brings an action against any one of them.[181]

[177] As so provided by CIM art.26, which is in substantively identical terms to art.34 of the CMR and which, for that reason, should take effect as already discussed at 2.3.6.

[178] As provided by CIM art.27, which has no direct parallel in the CMR save that it reflects the concept in CMR art.28 that all "other persons of whose services [the carrier] makes use for the performance of the carriage" may claim the protection of the CMR.

[179] It is notable that such liability for substitute carriers is wholly governed by CIM, as distinct from CMR art.28 which simply entitles sub-contracted carriers to claims the benefit of CMR exclusions and limitations.

[180] See art.45(6). Whether art.45 otherwise applies to all carriers or only successive carriers remains uncertain on the text of CIM as, whilst successive carriers are only specifically referred to in art.45(2), the concept underlying that article appears to be actions based on a single contract of carriage only achieved by successive carriage.

[181] In the context of English jurisprudence it is generally possible to assert alternative claims against several defendants, thereby reserving election until judgment on liability. There appears no reason to interpret art.45(7) as prohibiting this practice in claims against carriers under CIM.

2.6.2.7 Rights to Claim

Under CIM the issue of rights to claim must be addressed in the context of the respective rights of consignors, consignees and persons designated by consignees to dispose of the goods and/or modify the contract of carriage during transit. By arts 18 and 19 the consignor has the primary right to dispose of the goods and/or modify the contract of carriage during transit. These rights extend to requiring the carrier to discontinue carriage of the goods; delay delivery of the goods; deliver the goods to a different consignee; and deliver the goods at a different place. However, by art.18(2) the consignor's right to modify the contract of carriage is extinguished if and when the consignee has taken possession of the consignment note; accepted the goods; or asserted rights against, or become entitled to delivery from, the carrier by reason of the arrival of the goods at the place of destination under art.17(3). By art.18(3) the consignee also has an independent right to modify the contract from the time the consignment note is drawn up, unless the consignor has indicated the contrary on the consignment note. Such contrary rights of the consignor are extinguished where the consignee has taken possession of the consignment note; accepted the goods; asserted rights under art.17(3); or when a person designated by the consignee to take delivery of the goods has asserted rights under art.17(3).

To exercise rights to modify the contract of carriage[182] the duplicate of the consignment note (originally retained by the consignor) duly endorsed with the required modifications must be produced to the carrier under art.19(1). Unlike a bill of lading[183] the transfer of the duplicate of the consignment note to another person is not capable of passing constructive possession in the goods, but does extinguish the rights to modify the contract of carriage otherwise attaching to the party transferring it, insofar as that person is the consignor or the consignee.[184] If the carrier implements

[182] Under art.19 the carrier is to be compensated for modifications causing cost and prejudice to it and is not obliged to carry out impossible, unlawful and unreasonable modifications or modifications which would cause interference to the carrier's normal working or prejudice the consignor's or consignee's other consignments.

[183] The status of which is discussed in 3.2.3.

[184] CIM art.18(5) provides that any person designated by the consignee to receive delivery of the goods does not themself acquire any such modification rights; thereby confirming that, unlike a bill of lading, the duplicate of the rail consignment note is not a negotiable document.

modifications requested, other than pursuant to the duplicate of the consignment note, it is exposed to the risk of incurring liability under art.19(7).

Article 44 addresses specific and general rights to claim against the carrier. Those claims dealt with specifically are: (i) claims for the recovery of a sum paid under the contract of carriage, which may under art.44(3) only be brought by the person who made the payment in question; and (ii) claims in respect of "cash on delivery payments", which may under art.44(4) only be brought by the consignor. Other claims are subject to the general rights provided for in art.44, which provides that actions arising from the contract of carriage may be brought: (a) by the consignor, until such time as the consignee has: taken possession of the consignment note, accepted the goods, or asserted its rights under arts 17(3), 18(3) or 24; (b) by the consignee, from the time when it has taken possession of the consignment note, accepted the goods, or asserted its rights under art.17(3), 18(2) or 18(3).

As the (a) and (b) circumstances referred to above and in art.44(1) are clearly mutually exclusive, so are the rights of the consignor and consignee to claim. Just as the consignor's right of action will be extinguished by the rights of the consignee, so the consignee's right of action will in turn be extinguished by someone else, designated by them under art.18(5), taking possession of the consignment note, accepting the goods or asserting their rights pursuant to art.17(3).[185] The production of the consignment note is necessary to establish right of action under CIM and its absence or loss will need to be justified if it cannot be produced.[186] Difficulties arise if no consignment note was ever created. Whilst CIM art.6(2) provides that the "absence, irregularity or loss of the consignment note shall not affect the existence or validity of the contract which shall remain subject to [CIM] ...", CIM gives no clear direction as to the interpretation of the articles reviewed in 2.6.2.7 in the absence of a CIM consignment note. In the absence of the consignment note, courts might decide either that: there can be no transfer of rights by the consignor; or modification of the carriage, which is dependent on transfer of the consignment note; or, that such transfer of rights or modification of the carriage takes effect as if there had

[185] As provided for in CIM art.44(1b).

[186] As provided for at paras 5 and 6 of CIM art.44.

been such transfer.[187] As discussed in relation to the CMR at 2.3.7, common law and statutory rights to claim reviewed in 1.6 and 1.8.1 appear also to be applicable to claims under CIM. However, insofar as they would comprise rights arising under the contract of carriage to claim for loss, damage or delay to the goods consigned, it may be contended that such common law rights have been expressly or implicitly curtailed by CIM art.44.

2.6.2.8 Jurisdiction for Determination and Enforcement of Claims

The jurisdictional provisions in CIM art.46 reflect those provided for under CMR art.31 already discussed at 2.3.8. As with CMR, actions under CIM may be brought before any court or tribunal in any one of a number of permitted jurisdictions of the countries: designated by agreement between the parties; or where the defendant is ordinarily resident, has its principal place of business or place of business, branch or agency through which the carriage contract was made; or where the carrier took over the goods; or where the place of destination was situated. However, CIM art.46 provides that other courts or tribunals may not be seised of proceedings and, unlike the CMR, does not provide for arbitration.

2.6.2.9 Contractual Derogation of Convention Provisions

As with CMR it is not possible to contract out of the provisions of the CIM convention. CIM art.5 provides for CIM to operate as mandatory law so that "any stipulation which, directly or indirectly, would derogate from ... [CIM is] ... null and void". However, CIM art.5 goes on to provide that "a carrier may assume a liability greater and obligations more burdensome than those provided for in" CIM; so it is possible to derogate from CIM to the prejudice of the carrier, unlike the CMR.

[187] The latter interpretation appears preferable as it respects more precisely the requirements of art.6(2). Where the absence of the consignment note causes prejudice to the contracting carrier (or any successive or substitute carrier) the provisions of art.8 may require the consignor, or even (where the prejudice is that of successive or substitute carriers) the contracting carrier, to be responsible for all costs, loss or damage suffered in consequence.

2.6.2.10 Rights of Carrier as to Liens and Dangerous Goods

The only lien and power of sale envisaged by CIM is that referred to above at 2.6.2.3 in the event of circumstances preventing carriage and delivery as provided for in CIM art.22.[188] As discussed at 2.6.2.2 above, the consignor is obliged to enter on the consignment note such description of dangerous goods as provided for in RID. CIM art.9 provides that where the consignor fails to make those entries, the carrier may unload, destroy or make "innocuous" the goods except where the carrier was in any event "aware of their dangerous nature on taking them over". Any costs, loss or damage sustained by the carrier as a consequence of RID entries not being made by the consignor in the consignment note should be recoverable from the consignor under art.8(1) as already discussed in 2.6.2.2 above. As the definition of dangerous goods is tied to the provisions of RID, the wider common law concept of dangerous goods discussed at 1.9.1.3 appears inapplicable to carriage pursuant to CIM.

2.6.2.11 Claims among Carriers

Relations between carriers are governed by CIM arts 49 to 52. By art.49(1) any carrier responsible for collecting charges, or other costs attributable to the carriage at departure or on arrival, is liable to all other carriers for their respective shares. The provisions for contribution and indemnity contained in art.37 of the CMR (discussed at 2.3.11) are substantively replicated for rail carriage under CIM by the provisions of CIM art.50. Accordingly (a) the carrier causing the loss or damage is solely liable for it; (b) where caused by several carriers, each is liable for their proportion but if their proportion is impossible to assess the compensation is apportioned between those carriers responsible; (c) where the responsible carriers cannot be identified compensation is apportioned between all carriers (in proportion to their respective shares of the carriage charge) except those proving they were not responsible. Article 49(2) provides that any insolvent carrier's unpaid contribution is to be apportioned between all carriers in proportion to their respective shares of the carriage charge. Carriers liable for contributions may not dispute the liability of the carrier claiming contributions when they

[188] Article 22 does not refer expressly to any lien, but art.22(4) appears to envisage one arises.

have been duly served with notice of the proceedings by the cargo claimant and been given the opportunity to intervene in those proceedings.[189]

As with the CMR the applicable jurisdiction for contribution claims between carriers under CIM is specifically determined. Article 51 of CIM provides that contribution claims cannot be joined to proceedings by the cargo claimant for compensation but instead must be commenced separately against all those carriers with whom no settlement has been reached. Such proceedings must take place in the courts or tribunals of any state in which any one of the carriers either has its principal place of business, or a branch or agency through which the contract of carriage was concluded.

2.6.3 CIV

Appendix A, Title II, Chapter II, art.17 indicates what constitutes acceptable articles for carriage, namely, articles contained in trunks, baskets, suitcases, travelling bags and other similar receptacles, as well as the articles themselves. Article 18 provides that articles which are unacceptable include: articles the carriage of which is prohibited in any one of the territories in which the luggage would be carried; articles the carriage of which is a monopoly of the postal authorities in any one of the territories in which the luggage would be carried; goods intended for sale; bulky or excessively heavy articles; dangerous substances or articles—in particular loaded firearms, explosive or inflammable substances, or articles likely to cause infection.

The relevant document is defined in art.20 as the luggage registration voucher which is to be issued to the passenger at the time the luggage is registered. This voucher will bear the initials CIV and, except where international tariffs provide otherwise, will indicate the following: the forwarding and destination stations; the route; the day on which the luggage is handed in for carriage; the train by which it is to be despatched; the number of passengers; the number of items of luggage and their mass (which is analogous to weight for the purpose of the convention within the United Kingdom); and the carriage and other charges.

If the luggage is damaged, then Title IV, art.48 applies. Article 48 provides that when partial loss of or damage to registered luggage is discovered or presumed by the railway or alleged by the person entitled, the railway must (without delay, and if possible in the presence of the person entitled) draw up a report stating the condition of the registered luggage, its mass and, as far as possible, the extent of the loss or damage, its cause and the

[189] As so provided in art.51(1).

time of its occurrence. A copy of the report must be supplied free of charge to the person entitled. Should the person entitled not accept the findings in the report, that person may request that the condition and mass of the registered luggage and the cause and amount of the loss or damage be ascertained by an expert appointed either by the parties or by a court.

Article 50 defines who may bring an action. An action may be brought against the railway by the person who produces the ticket or luggage registration voucher, as the case may be, or failing that, furnishes other proof of the right to sue. Article 51 indicates who will be the defendant of that action. Actions may be brought against the railway of departure, the railway of destination or the railway on which the event giving rise to the proceedings occurred.

The forum for the action is provided for in art.52. Actions may only be instituted in the competent court of the state having jurisdiction over the defendant railway, unless otherwise provided in agreements between states or in acts of concession. The right to pursue will be lost if the person accepts luggage which has been damaged. The limitation period for bringing an action is one year unless fraud or wilful damage is alleged in which case the relevant limitation period is two years (art.55). In the case of total loss or non-delivery, the limitation period expires 14 days after a sufficient time after the arrival of a train (art.23(3)). If partial loss has occurred time runs from the day of delivery.

The railway can escape liability if the loss, damage or delay in delivery was caused by a fault on the part of the passenger, by an order given by the passenger other than as a result of a fault on the part of the railway, by inherent vice of the registered luggage or by circumstances which the railway could not avoid and the consequences of which it was unable to prevent. The railway shall also be relieved of such liability when the loss or damage arises from the special risks inherent in one or more of the following circumstances: (a) the absence or inadequacy of packing; (b) the special nature of the registered luggage; (c) the despatch as registered luggage of articles not acceptable for carriage.

Article 38(1) provides that in case of total or partial loss of registered luggage, the railway shall pay, to the exclusion of all other damages: (a) if the amount of the loss or damage suffered is established: compensation equal to that amount but not exceeding 34 units of account per kilogramme of gross mass missing, or 500 units of account per item of luggage; (b) if the amount of the loss or damage suffered is not established: liquidated damages of 10 units of account per kilogramme of gross mass missing or 150 units of account per item of luggage. The method of compensation, by mass or by item of luggage, shall be determined by the international tariffs. The railway shall in addition, pursuant to art.38(2), refund carriage charges, customs duties and other sums incurred in respect of carriage of the lost item of luggage.

2.7 Inland Waterways Carriage

The law relating to the domestic carriage of goods by inland waterway is virtually the same as that applicable to the domestic carriage of goods by road, save for the addition of certain concepts generally applicable in the case of carriage of goods on water that are discussed in the context of the carriage of goods by sea. Accordingly, it is possible for certain carriers by water (such as hoymen[190] and ferrymen[191]) to be common carriers where they hold themselves out as ready to carry goods for the public and do not contract as carriers under contracts of carriage. Any such common carriers are subject to the same liabilities as a common carrier by land and may likewise limit their liability by special contract. The largely academic ambiguity (discussed at 3.1.9) as to whether there are two or three classes of carriers by sea applies likewise to carriers by inland waterways. Common carriers by inland waterways are liable as insurers for passengers' luggage, except where the passengers retain possession of the luggage and do not entrust it to the carrier.[192] The Carriers Act 1830 does not apply to common carriers by water.

For carriers concluding a private contractual arrangement for the carriage of goods by inland waterway, the seaworthiness concept discussed at 3.1.4.1 applies and carriers by inland waterways implicitly warrant that their craft is seaworthy, the warranty of seaworthiness being interpreted as a warranty that the ship is fit for the purpose for which it is to be used.[193] Otherwise the liability of a carrier by inland waterway for domestic UK carriage under a private contract of carriage is governed by the same principles arising in respect of land carriage by other modes,[194] notwithstanding that for regulatory purposes carriage by inland waterway resembles sea rather than land carriage.[195]

[190] *Dale v Hall* (1750) 1 Wils. K.B. 281 and *Rich v Kneeland* (1613) Cro. Jac. 330.

[191] *Southcote's Case* (1601) 4 Co. Rep. 83b.

[192] *Willoughby v Horridge* (1852) 12 C.B. 742.

[193] There is no direct authority for this proposition, but it has never been doubted. See *Paterson Steamships v Canadian Co-operative Wheat Producers* [1934] A.C. 538, 545, per Lord Wright.

[194] See 2.1 and 2.2.1.

[195] See 5.3.5.

Liability for the luggage of passengers carried by inland waterway is not generally subject to regulation by the Athens Convention[196] and this remains the case notwithstanding Regulation 392/2009/EC, the scope of which appears to be confined to carriage on vessels engaged in sea carriage.[197] The concept of international carriage of goods by inland waterway is inapplicable to the United Kingdom as any water carriage across international borders must involve sea carriage. In consequence, the United Kingdom is not a contracting state to the Budapest Rules,[198] which seek to harmonise contractual terms for the carriage of goods by inland waterway across international borders in mainland Europe by adopting financial limits of liability consistent with sea carriage under the Hague-Visby Rules (see 3.3.2) within a scheme of liability more consistent with road and rail carriage under, respectively, the CMR and CIM (see 2.3 and 2.6.2 above).[199]

[196] See 3.3.6.

[197] See art.2 of R392/2009/EC incorporating the definitions in art.4 of D98/18/EC on safety rules and standards for passenger ships.

[198] The Budapest Convention on the Contract for the Carriage of Goods by Inland Waterway, which entered into force as an instrument of public international law on April 1, 2005, and, as at February 5, 2010, has been ratified and given the force of national law by 13 European states.

[199] See arts 20 and 16 of the Budapest Convention available from the website of UNECE at *http://www.unece.org.*

Part Three: Contracts for the Carriage of Goods by Sea

3.1 Overview of Sea Carriage

3.1.1 Nature

Whilst this book deals only with contracts for the carriage of goods by sea governed by the law of England as interpreted in the courts of England and Wales, it is appropriate to reflect that the business of carrying goods by sea is, and has been for very many centuries, international in nature. Goods are commonly carried by sea in performance of contracts for the international sale of goods as vessels transporting them travel between states of export and import across international waters. Other goods, exchanged between other sellers and buyers from other states, may also be carried at the same time in the same vessel with that vessel possibly calling at the ports of many different states in the course of a single voyage. Vessels are themselves subject to the laws of the state in which they are registered (the flag state). The flag state of a vessel need not necessarily be the same state as that in which the vessel's owner or manager is domiciled. The master, officers and crew of any vessel are, collectively, unlikely to be of any single common nationality or domicile and may have little, if any, connection with the flag state of the vessel or any of the various states of domicile of persons interested in the vessel or the goods. The person undertaking to carry the goods by sea as the contracting carrier may well not own the vessel, but may merely have hired it, or hired space on it, for the carriage of the goods. Accordingly, none of those involved in the performance of the carriage of goods by sea need have any connection with the places in which the subject goods are to be loaded onto and discharged from the vessel. It is therefore inappropriate to draw any general distinction between domestic and international sea carriage.[1]

As with carriage by any other mode, a contract for the carriage of goods by sea[2] is an autonomous contractual relationship to be interpreted

[1] A commercial state of affairs recognised by the provision at s.1(3) of the Carriage of Goods By Sea Act 1971 that the Hague-Visby Rules shall have the force of law in the context of carriage between two UK ports as well as international carriage.

[2] Contracts for the hire of a ship, or the hire of space on a ship, are also called contracts of affreightment and, since hire of space is generally essential for carriage of goods on a particular ship, references to contracts "of affreightment" or "for carriage" are generally synonomous with each other.

according to its applicable governing law and enforced subject to whatever mandatory regulation might be applied by the forum in which any dispute is to be resolved.[3] The mandatory regulation applicable in the United Kingdom to carriage by sea extends to such matters as: the rights of cargo interests to claim; the rights of carriers to limit the value of claims and the suit time period for claims; the terms of carriage contracts governed by bills of lading; and all aspects of the performance of sea carriage.[4] Where such regulation prescribes the contractual terms of carriage, the extent to which the regulation is of mandatory effect varies according to the nature of the contract of carriage. There are important regulatory distinctions between contracts of carriage by way of: charterparty (the charter of the vessel by way of demise, bareboat, time or voyage); carriage undertaking (a promise to deliver embodied in such documents as sea waybills, other non-negotiable receipts, ship's delivery orders, consignment notes etc.); or bill of lading (a document of title controlling the constructive possession of the goods and capable of passing legal title to the goods). The nature of these various contracts of carriage is examined in more detail in 3.2 below and the regulation prescribing the contractual terms of, in particular, bills of lading is examined in 3.3 below.

A contract of carriage has a particular status under English law and needs to be distinguished from other contracts for the carriage of goods (i.e. contracts for carriage by some mode of transportation other than by sea). This distinct nature can be readily discerned from the extent to which the law applicable to contracts of carriage by sea diverges (as discussed at 3.1.2 to 3.1.9 below) from those more generally applicable contractual principles discussed at Part One.

3.1.2 Parties and Practices

A person consigning goods by sea is commonly referred to as the person "shipping" or as "the shipper" of the goods. It is the usual practice for a mate's receipt, as to the goods, to be given to the shipper when the goods are handed over to the carrier at the port of loading (either by being brought alongside the ship for loading by the carrier or by being loaded on board the ship by the shipper). Any defects in the external condition of the goods should be noted on the mate's receipt. The mate's receipt is subsequently surrendered to the master in exchange for the bill of lading. The

[3] Pursuant to the principles reviewed at 1.4 above and 3.1.3 below.

[4] As discussed variously at 3.1.7, 3.3.2 and 5.3.5.

holder of the mate's receipt is prima facie entitled to be issued with the bill of lading;[5] where no bill of lading has been issued, the holder of the mate's receipt is prima facie entitled to claim delivery of the goods,[6] but this presumption may be rebutted. The mate's receipt is not a document of title, and the holder of it acquires no rights whatsoever against the person entitled to the goods from the carrier.[7] The statements contained in the mate's receipt are prima facie evidence of the truth of such statements[8] but do not operate as an estoppel against either party.[9] A mate's receipt is a document often associated with certain types of F.O.B. contracts of sale and given to the seller when the seller loads goods on a ship nominated by the buyer.[10]

As ships are frequently chartered and many non-vessel owning carriers agree to carry goods by sea in ships owned and operated by others, it is often difficult to determine the identity of the carrier by sea. Bills of lading and other carriage documents may simply be signed "as agent" without any clear designation either of the agent or of the principal for whom the agent is purporting to act. The difficulty may be compounded by inconsistencies in the terms appearing on the front and reverse sides of carriage documents. Identifying the contracting carrier in such circumstances may be difficult and the interpretative approach to be taken as to that issue was the subject of an authoritative ruling in the *Starsin* case.[11] In that case the House of Lords held that the key is to identify from the front of the bill of lading on whose behalf the bill of lading has been issued, i.e. whether it has been issued on behalf of the master of the vessel (who can be assumed to be the designated agent of the owner, or charterer by demise, of the vessel) or by some other party contracting as carrier (e.g. a time or voyage charterer). If that is clear from the front of the bill then any indications to the contrary appearing on the reverse side of the bill of lading may be ignored. Their Lordships advanced divergent reasons to justify their decision in this significant case but there were two dominant strands of analysis as follows: (a) the modern approach that, as various persons would have needed to have relied on the bill of lading in connection with the underlying contracts for

5 *Nippon Yusen Kaisha v Ramjiban Serowgee* [1938] A.C. 429.

6 *Craven v Ryder* (1816) 6 Taunt. 433, 435, per Gibbs C.J.; *Evans v Nichol* (1841) 3 Man. & G. 614.

7 *Nippon Yusen Kaisha v Ramjiban Serowgee* (fn. 5), at p.445, per Lord Wright.

8 ibid.

9 *Biddulph v Bingham* (1874) 30 L.T. 30.

10 See *Pyrene v Scindia Navigation* [1954] 2 Q.B. 402 at p.424.

11 (2003) 1 Lloyd's Rep. 571.

the sale of the goods being carried and such persons would reasonably have expected only to rely on the front of the bill of lading, such an interpretation gave effect to the reasonable expectations of any reasonable reader of the bill; and (b) the traditional approach that, applying various canons of construction (such that precedence be given to specially agreed words and signed terms over pre-printed text), such an interpretation gave effect to the intention of the contracting parties as objectively understood by the words they used. Accordingly, applying both modern and traditional interpretative approaches, the impact of the decision is that effect should be given to the agency expressed by the front of the bill, rather than any contrary identity of carrier clause on the reverse.[12]

3.1.3 Jurisdiction and Law

The question as to which law is to govern the contract is determined by the principles of private international law and mandatory regulation applicable in the forum of any dispute.[13] The mandatory regulation of applicable law discussed at 1.4.3 applies to a contract for the carriage by sea as it applies to carriage by other modes. In the absence of any express agreement as to the applicable law, the law of the flag of the carrying vessel (or the choice of the English courts or London as the seat of any arbitration, to determine disputes) is now of limited relevance in determining applicable law, being simply factors that a court may take into account in determining, insofar as appropriate, the country with which the contract is most closely connected.[14] Where, in accordance with these principles, a contract is deemed in English law to be governed by English law it is immaterial that by the law of a foreign state the contract is held to be subject to foreign law and the English courts will disregard any foreign statute or law which, by the law of

[12] In the *Starsin* (ibid.) the bill of lading was apparently signed on its front side by an agent on behalf of a time charterer, whilst on the reverse of the bill of lading the owner or demise charterer of the vessel was identified as carrier.

[13] *Lloyd v Guibert* (1865) L.R. 1 Q.B. 115, 120, per Willes J. and the mandatory regulation of applicable law discussed at 1.4.3 is equally applicable to carriage by sea.

[14] *Coast Lines v Hudig and Veder Chartering NV* [1972] 1 Ll.L.R. 53; *Campagnie d'Armenent Maritime SA v Campagnie Tunisienne de Navigation SA* [1971] A.C. 572. As to the difficulties the courts face in determining the proper law, see *The Wahab: Amin Rasheed Shipping Corp v Kuwait Insurance Co* [1984] A.C. 50.

some foreign state, may seek to regulate the terms of the contract.[15] The parties may, however, expressly or implicitly agree to incorporate the provisions of a foreign statute into a contract which is governed by English law. In this case the English courts will enforce the foreign statute to the extent that it is a term of the contract agreed between the parties. Furthermore, contractual obligations will not be enforced in English courts where their performance is rendered illegal by the law of the state in which performance is to take place.[16]

In the case of claims for the loss of or damage to goods carried by sea, English jurisdiction may, in addition to the circumstances outlined at 1.4.2, be secured by ship arrest. The 1952 Ship Arrest Convention[17] provides for a degree of international recognition for and harmonisation of rights of ship arrest; although the United Kingdom is a party to this convention it has not been given the force of law in the United Kingdom. Instead the right of ship arrest arises in England and Wales pursuant to s.20(2)(g) of the Supreme Court Act 1981 as one of a number of claims that may be brought in rem against a ship as well as in personam against the person liable for the claim. UK legislation grants a right to arrest the vessel in which the goods were carried, or any sister ship of the carrying vessel. The right attaches to any person entitled to claim (whether in contract, tort or bailment) for loss or damage to goods carried in a ship but the right may only be exercised against a vessel that is owned by, or chartered by demise to, the party liable for the claim. Difficulties frequently arise in establishing both (a) that the registered owner of the ship has any liability as carrier for the claim and (b) that the claimant is in fact the party entitled to claim. Where these issues can be proved, the right to arrest is itself established and can be exercised by a summary process.

The procedure provided for at Pt.61 of the Civil Procedure Rules involves the issue of a claim form and lodgment of declarations (as to the

[15] See *Vita Food Products v Unus Shipping Company* [1939] A.C. 277; *OT Africa Line Ltd v MAGIC Sportswear Corporation* [2005] E.W.C.A. Civ 710.

[16] *Regazzoni v K. C. Sethia (1944), Ltd* [1956] 1 Lloyd's Rep. 435 and see art.9(3) of the Rome 1 Regulation.

[17] The International Convention Relating to the Arrest of Sea-Going Ships concluded at Brussels on May 10, 1952. A further convention was adopted by the United Nations/International Maritime Organisation Diplomatic Conference on Arrest of Ships on March 12, 1999 but this convention will only enter into force as an instrument of public international law when at least 10 states have agreed to be bound by it. As at September 2009, the 1999 convention only had seven contracting states.

ownership of the vessel by the person liable for the claim) to establish the right to the issue of a warrant of arrest.[18] The warrant of arrest is enforced by the Admiralty Marshal through officers of HM Revenue and Customs if and to the extent that the vessel is present within the jurisdiction of England and Wales. The vessel will be released as and when security satisfactory to the claimant, or the court, is provided by way of cash deposit, or bank or insurer guarantee, against the maximum value of the claim. Such security will then remain in place to await either agreement as to liability or the determination of liability by the applicable forum for the resolution of the dispute. A claimant has no liability for an invalid arrest unless the arrest was carried out in bad faith (where the arresting claimant has no honest belief that it is entitled to arrest) or with gross negligence (where the arresting claimant has no real basis for believing itself entitled to arrest).[19]

Ship arrest in England and Wales is capable both of establishing security and securing jurisdiction for any maritime claim but, where the person who would be liable for the claim in personam is domiciled within the EEA, the right to found jurisdiction by arrest is subject to the operation of the EU jurisdiction regime reviewed at 1.4.2.[20] Accordingly, whilst vessels owned by, or demise chartered to, persons domiciled in the EEA may always be arrested in England and Wales to obtain security for claims falling within s.20(2)(g) of the Supreme Court Act 1981 the arrests will only be effective to found jurisdiction in the circumstances outlined in 1.4.2, where English jurisdiction is applicable pursuant to EC Council Regulation 44/2001.[21]

3.1.4 Contractual Terms

3.1.4.1 The Warranty of Seaworthiness

At common law, there is implied in every contract for the carriage of goods by sea a warranty by the carrier that the ship is seaworthy, unless the warranty is expressly excluded.[22] The warranty implies that the ship is reasonably fit for the particular voyage which she is to make, taking into

[18] Further details of the procedure are available from the Ministry of Justice website *http://www.justice.gov.uk/civil/procrules_fin/contents/parts/part61.htm.*

[19] *The Kommunar (No.3)* [1997] 1 Lloyd's Rep. 22.

[20] *The Anna H* [1995] 1 Lloyd's Rep 11; *The Maciej Rataj* C-406/92 ([1995] 1 Lloyd's Rep. 302.

[21] Or the Lugano convention when applicable.

[22] *Bank of Australasia v Clan Line* [1916] 1 K.B. 39, 55, per Bankes L.J.

account the geographical regions in which the voyage is to be made and the cargo which the ship is to carry and all other relevant factors.[23] The carrier does not warrant that the ship is absolutely safe, but only that it has "that degree of fitness which an ordinary careful owner would require his vessel to have at the commencement of her voyage having regard to all the probable circumstances of it".[24] The fact that the vessel is not as safe as other ships does not amount to a breach of the warranty.[25] The implied duty of seaworthiness is often described as a relative duty in that "it is relative to the nature of the ship, to the particular voyage and even to the particular stage of the voyage on which the ship is engaged ... judged by the standards and practices of the industry at the relevant time, at least so long as those standards and practices are reasonable".[26]

The factors to be taken into account in determining whether or not the ship is seaworthy are not limited to those directly affecting the state of the ship herself. Thus the ship is unseaworthy if the crew is insufficient,[27] if the master is unable to perform his duties owing to illness[28] (or drunkenness)[29] and there is no one else on board capable of carrying out those duties, or if inadequate training has been provided and the crew is not competent to carry out its duties.[30] The ship is presumably also unseaworthy if she is not equipped with sufficient provisions[31] or medicines[32] for the crew during the voyage. The fact that a vessel must be seaworthy in a physical sense is not, of itself, sufficient; the vessel must also be legally compliant with all applicable mandatory regulations relating to the performance of the carriage obligation.[33] Bad stowage does not necessarily make a ship unseaworthy but may do so if, in consequence of bad stowage, the ship

[23] *Stanton v Richardson* (1872) L.R. 7 C.P. 421 (affirmed (1874), L.R. 9 C.P. 390).

[24] Per Lord Justice Scrutton in *F.C. Bradley & Sons Ltd v Federal Steam Navigation Co* (1926) 24 Ll.L.Rep 446 at p.454, approving a statement from Carver on *Carriage by Sea*.

[25] *Burgess v Wickham* (1863) 3 B. & S. 669.

[26] Per Cresswell J. in *The Eurasian Dream* [2002] 1 Lloyd's Rep. 719.

[27] *Forshaw v Chabert* (1821) 3 B. & B. 158.

[28] *Rio Tinto Company v Seed Shipping Company* (1926) 134 L.T. 764.

[29] *Moore v Lunn* (1923) 39 T.L.R. 526.

[30] *The Eurasian Dream* (fn. 26).

[31] *The Wilhelm* (1865) 14 L.T. 636, which did not directly deal with the warranty of seaworthiness.

[32] *Woolf v Claggett* (1800) 3 Esp. 257, which was apparently decided on the basis of deviation.

[33] *Golden Fleece Maritime Inc v ST Shipping and Transport Inc (The Elli)* [2009] 1 All E.R. (Comm) 908 discussed at 1.2.

commences the voyage in a condition which is not fit for the voyage in question.[34] Thus, where owing to bad stowage the crew's view of a porthole was obscured and the ship sailed with the porthole open, the carrier was liable for a breach of the warranty of seaworthiness.[35] However, in a case where a ship's cargo of coal was too great to allow passage through the Panama Canal it was held that this did not make her unseaworthy, although the master was at fault in overloading her.[36]

At common law the carrier's warranty of seaworthiness is an absolute one. Once the ship is found not to have been seaworthy for the voyage applying the objective test (i.e. it did not have the relative degree of fitness that would have been required by an ordinary careful owner at the commencement of the voyage given its probable circumstances) the carrier will be liable for breach of the implied term, even if the carrier was not negligent and did, in fact, use all reasonable diligence to ensure seaworthiness.[37] The absolute nature of the seaworthiness obligation under common law should be contrasted with the slightly qualified duty arising under contracts of carriage subject to the Hague-Visby Rules.[38]

At common law the warranty of seaworthiness implies that, when the ship sails at the beginning of the voyage, she is seaworthy for the duration of the voyage. Thus if, at the moment of sailing, the ship is not reasonably fit to complete the voyage, the carrier is liable for a breach of the warranty of seaworthiness.[39] However, the carrier is not liable if, although the ship was reasonably fit to complete the voyage at the moment of sailing, she becomes unseaworthy during the course of the voyage.[40] The duty at common law is not a continuing duty; it only arises at the commencement of each stage of a sea carrier's discrete performance obligations. The vessel must be seaworthy at the commencement of loading operations and each intermediate stage of a voyage; where a voyage includes calling at several ports, the various intermediate voyages between each port may be

[34] *Kopitoff v Wilson* (1876) 1 Q.B.D. 377; *Elder Dempster and Company v Paterson, Zochonis and Company* [1924] A.C. 522.
[35] *Steel v State Line Steamship Company* (1877) 3 App. Cas. 72.
[36] *Actis Co v Sanko Steamship Co (The Aquacharm)* [1982] 1 W.L.R. 119.
[37] *The Glenfruin* (1885) 10 P.D. 103; *McFadden v Blue Star Line* [1905] 1 KB 697.
[38] Discussed at 3.3.2.3.
[39] *McFadden v Blue Star Line* [1905] 1 K.B. 697, 703, per Channell J.
[40] ibid. at p.703.

considered a separate stage.[41] Accordingly, where a ship is unseaworthy at the time of sailing there has been a breach of the warranty, even if the ship has been repaired and rendered seaworthy during the voyage before the damage to the cargo is caused.[42] Where a voyage can naturally be divided into stages—for example, from the port down river to the open sea, or from one bunkering port to another—the warranty of seaworthiness is interpreted as a warranty that, when the ship sails on each stage of the voyage, she is fit for the duration of that particular stage.[43] There is then no breach of warranty if the ship is not fit for the whole voyage when she sails on one particular stage, provided that she is fit for the whole of this stage. The doctrine of stages has no application to the warranty of seaworthiness in a time charterparty[44] and does not apply to contracts of carriage governed by the Hague-Visby Rules.

The ship is deemed to sail on the voyage or on a stage of the voyage, for the purpose of the warranty of seaworthiness, when it leaves its moorings for the commencement of the voyage with its master having no intention of returning.[45] If the ship is unseaworthy the carrier is liable for any loss or damage caused by, or contributed to by, the unseaworthiness. The carrier is not, however, liable if the unseaworthiness played no part in causing the loss or damage[46] or if the damage resulting from the unseaworthiness was too remote.[47] Although there have been conflicting expressions of judicial opinion in the House of Lords, it appears that the warranty of seaworthiness is not necessarily to be construed as a condition precedent to a contract or as a fundamental term of a contract. Where, in a time charterparty for 24 months, the ship was unseaworthy (by the drunkenness of the ship's chief engineer and other reasons), the court held that the

[41] *The Vortigern* [1899] p.140 in which a coal burning ship, obliged to burn some of the coal it was carrying as cargo to complete a voyage, was held not to be unseaworthy when it had bunkered sufficient coal to reach an intermediate port at which there was a reasonable expectation that the vessel would be able to rebunker sufficient coal to complete the voyage.

[42] *Quebec Marine Insurance Company v Commercial Bank of Canada* (1870) L.R. 3 P.C. 234.

[43] *Dixon v Sadler* (1839) 5 M. & W. 405, 414, per Parke B.

[44] Discussed at 3.2.1.3.

[45] *The Rona* (1884) 51 L.T. 28.

[46] *Baumwoll Manufactur v Gilchrist* [1892] 1 Q.B. 253, 257Ð8, per Lord Esher M.R., in the Court of Appeal (affirmed on other grounds, sub. nom. *Baumwoll Manufactur v Furness* [1893] A.C. 8).

[47] *Elder Dempster and Company v Paterson, Zochonis and Company* [1924] A.C. 522, 549, per Lord Sumner.

charterers were not entitled to treat the charterparty as repudiated when the ship was not ready to sail throughout a period of some four months: instead the charterers were only entitled to damages for breach of the charterparty.[48]

In contracts which are not governed by the Hague-Visby Rules, the carrier may limit or exclude its liability for unseaworthiness, provided that the provisions in the contract are unambiguous. An ambiguous provision will, however, be construed against the carrier. Accordingly, contractual terms excluding the liability of the carrier in general terms (or excluding liability only for negligence) will be interpreted as not affecting liability for unseaworthiness;[49] similarly, contractual terms limiting the amount of damages recoverable by the cargo owner,[50] or even referring disputes to arbitration,[51] may be interpreted as not extending to damages or disputes arising from a breach of the implied warranty of seaworthiness, unless the contractual term unambiguously extends to include liability arising under the implied term. The onus of proof that the ship was unseaworthy rests on the cargo owner,[52] although the fact that the ship sinks, for no apparent reason, soon after leaving port may be relied upon as evidence that she was unseaworthy at the time of sailing.[53]

There is an implied warranty by the carrier, arising at the time when loading begins, that the ship is seaworthy for the purpose of taking on to it the goods to be loaded.[54] This is distinct from the warranty of seaworthiness for the voyage, and has been referred to as a warranty that the ship is cargoworthy, and fit for the reception of the goods.[55] The warranty is implied in every contract of carriage unless expressly excluded by words which refer unequivocally to seaworthiness for loading.[56] The warranty is that, at the beginning of the loading of goods for the shipper concerned, the ship will remain cargoworthy for the duration of the loading.[57] For this purpose, the beginning of the loading is the time when the operation of

[48] *Hongkong Fir Shipping Co Ltd v Kawasaki Kisen Kaisha* [1962] 2 Q.B. 26; and see *Kish v Taylor and Company* [1912] A.C. 604, 617, per Lord Atkinson; *Atlantic Shipping Company v Dreyfus and Company* [1922] 2 A.C. 250, 257 per Lord Dunedin.

[49] *Lyon v Mells* (1804) 5 East 428.

[50] *Tattersall v National Steamship Company* (1884) 12 Q.B.D. 297.

[51] *Atlantic Shipping Company v Dreyfus and Company* [1922] 2 A.C. 250.

[52] *Minister of Food v Reardon Smith Line* [1951] 2 T.L.R. 1158.

[53] *Ajum Goolam v Union Marine Insurance Company* [1901] A.C. 362.

[54] *McFadden v Blue Star Line* [1905] 1 K.B. 697.

[55] *Reed v Page* [1927] 1 K.B. 743, 755, per Scrutton L.J.

[56] *Steel v State Line Steamship Company* (1877) 3 App. Cas. 72, 86, per Lord Blackburn.

[57] *McFadden v Blue Star Line* (fn. 54), at p.704, per Channel J.

loading begins and not when the goods cross the ship's rail.[58] If the ship is cargoworthy at the beginning of the loading, there is no breach of the warranty if she becomes uncargoworthy before the loading is completed.[59] As the warranty that the ship is seaworthy for the voyage arises only when the ship sails, the fact that, at the beginning of the loading, the ship is unseaworthy for the voyage is not a breach of warranty.[60] At the beginning of the loading the warranty is only that the ship is seaworthy for the loading of the cargo, not that it is seaworthy for the voyage. In effect, loading is considered to be a separate stage of the carriage obligation undertaken by the contract of carriage. Consequently where, after loading, the ship proceeds to a different part of the port there may be a warranty that, at the time when the ship leaves the place of loading, she is seaworthy for the purpose of moving to the other part of the port, as the movement in the port may be considered a separate stage of carriage, distinct from the loading operation.[61]

The warranty of cargoworthiness is that the ship is cargoworthy for the purpose of receiving the particular cargo to be loaded. There is therefore a breach of warranty if the ship is not properly equipped with refrigerators to take the cargo, if it needs refrigeration.[62] All relevant factors must be taken into consideration for the purpose of ascertaining whether the ship is seaworthy for loading. However, circumstances will only be relevant where they are pertinent to the loading operation, so that matters relating to voyage provisions (such as for the crew and bunkers etc.) are irrelevant to the warranty of cargoworthiness for loading (despite being highly relevant to the warranty of seaworthiness for the voyage). Where the state of the ship is unfit both to receive the cargo and to carry the cargo throughout the whole of the voyage (e.g. by reason of the vessel requiring fumigation which would injure the cargo, or where the vessel has not been adequately fumigated after carrying diseased cattle)[63] there may be a breach of the warranty of seaworthiness for loading, as well as a breach of the warranty of seaworthiness for the voyage.

Where the Hague-Visby Rules apply to the contract of carriage, the distinct common law stage of cargoworthiness is encompassed by the

[58] *Svenssons Travaruaktiebolag v Cliffe Steamship Company* [1932] 1 K.B. 490.

[59] *McFadden v Blue Star Line* (fn. 54), at p.704, per Channell J.

[60] *Annen v Woodman* (1810) 3 Taunt. 299.

[61] *Reed v Page* (fn. 55).

[62] *The Maori King (Cargo Owners) v Hughes* [1895] 2 Q.B. 550.

[63] *Ciampa v British India Steam Navigation Company* [1915] 2 K.B. 774; *Tattersall v National Steamship Company* (fn. 50).

continuing qualified duty of seaworthiness, which is provided for in the Rules and arises on the commencement of loading.[64]

3.1.4.2 Deviation

As discussed in 1.7.1.4 the traditional view is that a carrier of goods by sea who deviates thereby repudiates the contract of carriage and is deemed to be in possession of the goods as a wrongful possessor of the goods. It is the duty of the carrier to take the "usual route", although there may be more than one and the usual route is not necessarily the most direct geographical route.[65] For there to be a deviation in the usual route some intentional change of route is required and an inadvertent change of route is insufficient.[66] The carrier of goods by sea is entitled to depart from the route in two circumstances, namely: (i) to save life, or to attempt to save life; (ii) to avoid imminent peril to the ship and to the cargo.

While the carrier is entitled to deviate in order to attempt to save life—for example, to proceed to the help of a ship in distress if there are reasonable grounds for believing that life may be in danger—the carrier is not entitled to deviate merely in order to save property.[67] If the only reasonable way in which the lives of the crew of the ship in distress can be saved is by towing the ship, the carrier is entitled to tow but if, after taking the crew on board, the carrier remains to tow the ship, or to save property, this amounts to a deviation.[68] The carrier may deviate in order to avoid an imminent peril of such a nature as would cause apprehension of loss or serious damage to the ship or cargo to a reasonably courageous master.[69] Thus the carrier may change course in order to avoid a storm, or put into port and wait there until the danger has passed, or until the ship has been repaired and rendered seaworthy. The principle applies where the cause of the imminent peril is apprehended capture by ships of a state at war with the state of the ship's flag[70] as well as to natural perils. The fact that the necessity of saving life, or the imminence of the peril, has only arisen because of a breach of the warranty of seaworthiness does not render the

[64] Discussed at 3.3.2.3 below.
[65] The *Indian City* [1939] AC 562.
[66] *The Majorie Seed* [1926] 24 Lloyd's Rep. 316.
[67] *Scaramanga v Stamp* (1880) 5 C.P.D. 295, per Cockburn C.J.
[68] ibid.
[69] *The Teutonia* (1872) L.R. 4 P.C. 171.
[70] ibid.

deviation unjustifiable[71] except, perhaps, where the carrier had noticed that the ship was unseaworthy before beginning the voyage.[72]

Where the deviation was induced by the fault of the owner of the goods, it appears that, as against this cargo owner, the contract of carriage is not repudiated by the deviation. Thus, in a charterparty, the shipowner was not liable for deviation when departing from the route to call at a port to load a full cargo because the charterer, in breach of its stipulation in the charterparty, had failed to load a full cargo.[73] If the carrier deviates unjustifiably, the carrier is liable, as a wrongful possessor of the goods, for any loss or damage to the goods, unless it can be proved that the damage was caused by an act of God or the Queen's enemies, the fault of the owner of the goods or the shipper, or inherent vice, and that the loss or damage would also have occurred even if the carrier had not deviated. The onus of proof is on the carrier. Thus, where the carrier deviated and the cargo was lost when the ship was sunk by an enemy submarine, the carrier was liable for the loss of the cargo since the carrier was unable to prove that this loss would also have occurred if there had been no deviation from the usual route.[74] However, the carrier would have no liability if it could establish that the damage would have occurred in any case. Where a cargo of fruit rotted on account of its inherent vice during a voyage on which the carrier deviated, the carrier was only held liable for the additional degree of decomposition resulting from the delay caused by the deviation as it was clear that some damage from inherent vice would have occurred, even if there had been no deviation.[75]

It is usual for the parties to agree, by some express contractual provision, for the carrier to be permitted to deviate for the purpose of saving, or attempting to save property as well as life and to tow ships in distress. It is also often agreed that the ship may deviate in order to call at any port. Such a term is interpreted as permitting the ship to call in order at any port en route,[76] unless it is customary, on the route in question, for ships to call at ports in some other order.[77] The contract may, however, expressly authorise the carrier to call at any port "in any order" and such a term is sometimes

[71] *Kish v Taylor and Company* [1912] A.C. 604.

[72] *Monarch Steamship Company v Karlshamns Oljefabriker A/B* [1949] A.C. 196, 212, per Lord Porter.

[73] *Wallems Rederij A/S v Muller and Company* [1927] 2 K.B. 99.

[74] *Morrison v Shaw, Savil and Company* [1916] 2 K.B. 783.

[75] *Internationale Guano v Macandrew and Company* [1909] 2 K.B. 360.

[76] *Leduc v Ward* (1888) 20 Q.B.D. 475, 482, per Lord Esher, M.R.

[77] *Frenkel v MacAndrews and Company* [1929] A.C. 545.

referred to as a general liberty clause. All such general liberty clauses are strictly construed and are invariably interpreted so as not to defeat the main purpose of the contract of carriage.[78] Accordingly, a contractual provision authorising the ship to call "at any port" is interpreted as meaning any port in reasonable geographical proximity to the route in question; thus where the carrier was entitled to call at any port in any order on a voyage from Fiume to Dunkirk, the carrier was held to have deviated when the ship called at Glasgow.[79]

In the absence of any express provision to the contrary, it is an implied term of the contract of carriage that the cargo is to be carried throughout the voyage in the same ship, unless special circumstances make it impossible for the carrier to carry the goods in the same ship to the port of discharge.[80] The law relating to transhipment in the carriage of goods by sea is thus different from that relating to the right of a carrier of goods by land to transfer the goods to another vehicle during the carriage; the prohibition of transhipment in carriage by sea is due to the risks to which the cargo is subjected in the operation of transhipment, and to difficulties in connection with insurance.[81] The common law is, in this respect, out of step with commercial practice attending the shipment of goods in containers, as transhipment of containers is now an extremely common practice; so much so that it must be reasonably likely that in the future an English court might refuse to recognise the implied "no transhipment" term in relation to container shipments.[82]

However, the carrier is, in the absence of express provisions to the contrary in the contract, entitled to tranship if the ship is unable to continue the voyage, and to repair it would take an unreasonably long time or would involve the carrier in unreasonable cost.[83] The cost of repairs will be

[78] *Leduc v Ward* [1888] 20 QBD 475.

[79] *International Guano v MacAndrew & Co* [1909] 2 KB 360.

[80] *Shipton v Thornton* (1838) 9 Ad. & El. 314, 333, per Lord Denman C.J.

[81] ibid.

[82] Particularly given that the UCP 600 standard terms for bankers documentary credits now provides at art.19(c) that "(i) A transport document may indicate that the goods will or may be transhipped provided that the entire carriage is covered by one and the same transport document. (ii) A transport document indicating that transhipment will or may take place is acceptable, even if the credit prohibits transhipment."

[83] *Hunter v Prinsep* (1808) 10 East 378, 394, per Lord Ellenborough C.J.; *Moss v Smith* (1850) 9 C.B. 94, 102Ð3, per Maule J.; *Assicurazioni Generale v Bessie Morris Company* [1892] Q.B. 652.

deemed unreasonable if that cost would exceed the value of the ship when repaired.[84] In all other cases, the carrier is not permitted to tranship but must repair the ship and proceed in her with the cargo to the port of discharge, or else offer to deliver the goods to the consignee at the place where the ship is stranded.[85] Where the carrier can repair the ship in a reasonable time, and elects to do this and to proceed in the ship to the port of discharge and deliver there, the carrier may do so. The consignee is not entitled to require the carrier to deliver the goods at the place where the ship is stranded on payment of pro rata freight,[86] unless there is an express term to this effect in the contract. Conversely, where the carrier wishes to deliver to the consignee at the place where the ship is stranded, the carrier is not entitled to any freight, or to any pro rata freight, in the absence of an express term in the contract to that effect.[87] Whether or not the carrier is liable in damages to the shipper and consignee depends on whether the cause of the failure to deliver at the port of discharge amounted to a breach of, or an excepted peril in, the contract of carriage.

Where the carrier is by express contractual provision entitled to tranship it may insist on doing so. The carrier may then proceed with the goods to the port of discharge in another ship and claim the freight. The carrier is not obliged to deliver to the consignee at the place where the ship is stranded and waive the freight unless transhipment would involve an unreasonably long delay in making delivery.[88] It appears that the consignee cannot compel the carrier to tranship[89] although this has been doubted.[90] Where the failure of the ship to proceed to the port of discharge is due to an excepted peril, the carrier may avoid all liability by offering delivery at the place where the ship is stranded and waiving the freight. The carrier is entitled to tranship in any circumstances to the extent to which this is expressly permitted in the contract and, when so entitled, may tranship either on to another of its own ships, or to the ship of another carrier. If the goods are transhipped to the ship of another carrier, the first carrier nevertheless remains liable to the shipper as a carrier while the goods are being carried on the ship of the second carrier, in the absence of an express

[84] *Kulukundis v Norwich Union Fire Insurance Society* [1937] 1 K.B. 1.

[85] *Shipton v Thornton* (fn. 80).

[86] ibid.

[87] *Cook v Jennings* (1797) 7 T.R. 381.

[88] *Shipton v Thornton* (fn. 80).

[89] *De Cuadra v Swann* (1864) 16 C.B. (N.S.) 772.

[90] *Shipton v Thornton* (fn. 80).

provision in the contract to the contrary.[91] Even where the contract contains the statement "Transhipment at owner's risk", this may be interpreted as applying only to the actual operation of transhipping the goods from one ship to the other, and not as exempting the carrier from liability after transhipment.[92] The first carrier remains liable throughout to the shipper. The shipper generally has no contact with the second carrier, but may be bound by, and take advantage of, the second carrier's carriage conditions by the principles of sub-bailment on terms reviewed at 1.6.1.1. In such a case, the shipper or other owner of the goods may also have a right of action in tort against the second carrier in respect of any negligence by the second carrier in the performance of its obligations as a carrier.[93]

Where by the terms of the contract of carriage, the carrier is permitted to arrange for the transhipment of the cargo as agent of the shipper, the carrier may enter the contract of carriage with the second carrier as agent for the shipper.[94] In such a case, the first carrier will not be liable for the goods after transhipment if and to the extent that the original contract of carriage entered into between the first carrier and the shipper so provides. However, in this context, it should be noted that transport documents allowing transhipment may be rejected under a C.I.F. contract by the buyer (subject, of course, to contrary agreement or trade custom) unless the whole voyage is covered by the document[95] and by banks under U.C.P. 600 art.19(a)(iii), unless the transport document indicates the places of shipment and final destination stated in the credit.

3.1.4.3 General Average

The principle of the law of general average is that when any part of the cargo or of the ship is deliberately sacrificed in order to preserve the ship and cargo as a whole, all the parties whose goods or property were preserved by that sacrifice shall contribute to the loss suffered by the owner of the goods sacrificed. The loss is known as a general average loss and the contribution of the parties as general average contribution. Where there is no actual sacrifice of cargo or ship but expenditure is incurred in order to

[91] See *Stuart v British and African Steam Navigation Company* (1875) 32 L.T. 257.
[92] ibid.
[93] *The Termagant* (1914) 19 Com. Cas. 239 in which the owners of a barge into which the cargo had been transhipped were held liable in tort by reason of their supply of an unseaworthy vessel.
[94] *Matthews v Gibbs* (1860) 3 E. & E. 282.
[95] *Continental Imes Ltd v H.E. Dibble* [1952] 1 Ll.L.R. 220.

preserve the ship and cargo this is known as a general average expenditure, which is also governed by the law of general average and must be paid for by general average contribution.[96]

A general average loss has been described thus: "All loss which arises in consequence of extraordinary sacrifices made, or expenses incurred, for the preservation of the ship and cargo, comes within general average, and must be borne proportionally by all who are interested."[97] To constitute a general average loss, the goods lost must be deliberately sacrificed with the reasonable intention of preserving the ship and cargo.[98] If the goods are simply washed overboard or otherwise lost by the operation of the seas or of natural forces, they may not be the subject of a general average contribution.[99] Nor is there a general average loss where the goods sacrificed were already doomed in any event[100] (as where burning cargo is sacrificed in order to save the ship);[101] or apparently, even if the goods are not irretrievably doomed, they constitute a danger to the ship, as in the case of goods on fire.[102] The fact, however, that there was a probability that the goods sacrificed would shortly be lost does not prevent the sacrifice from being a general average loss, if the loss of the goods was not certain.[103] There is a general average loss where goods are damaged by water used to extinguish a fire on board,[104] or where part of the cargo was burned as fuel because no other fuel was available.[105] This only applies, however, where otherwise there is a probability of the cargo being lost. Action taken merely

[96] For the complicated law relating to general average expenditure, see *Svendsen v Wallace* (1885) 10 App. Cas. 404; *Chellew v Royal Commission on Sugar Supply* [1921] 2 K.B. 627 at first instance before Sankey J. whose judgment was upheld on appeal [1922] 1 K.B. 12.

[97] *Birkley v Presgrave* (1801) 1 East 220, 228, per Lawrence J.

[98] *The Bona* [1895] P. 125, 138, per Lord Esher M.R.; *Iredale v China Traders Insurance Company* [1900] 2 Q.B. 515, 519, per A. L. Smith L.J., with regard to what amounts to "reasonable intention".

[99] *Birkley v Presgrave* (fn. 97).

[100] *Annen v Woodman* (1810) 3 Taunt. 299; *Shepherd v Kottgen* (1877) 2 C.P.D. 585.

[101] *Annen v Woodman* (1810) 3 Taunt. 299; *Pirie and Company v Middle Dock Company* (1881) 44 L.T. 426.

[102] ibid.

[103] *Johnson v Chapman* (1865) 19 C.B. (N.S.) 563.

[104] *Whitecross Wire Company v Savill* (1882) 8 Q.B.D. 653; *Greenshields Cowie and Company v Stephens and Sons* [1908] A.C. 431.

[105] *Robinson v Price* (1877) 2 Q.B.D. 295.

in order to facilitate or hasten the progress of the ship cannot be a general average loss.[106]

Where the ship, or any part of it, is deliberately sacrificed in order to save the ship and cargo, this is a general average loss in respect of which the shipowner can claim general average contribution. Thus where the ship is scuttled in order to extinguish a fire, it is a general average loss.[107] The fact that the danger which necessitated a general average sacrifice was caused by the unseaworthiness of the ship, or by the negligence of the carrier or other person, does not prevent it from being a general average loss, and the owners of the cargo saved thereby are required to make general average contribution,[108] except that they are not obliged to contribute in respect of the loss incurred by the shipowner or other person in default.[109] The same applies where a general average loss occurs after the carrier has deviated.[110] However, where by the terms of the contract[111] or statute[112] the shipowner is exempted from liability for unseaworthiness or negligence, the shipowner is entitled to claim general average contribution in respect of a general average loss occasioned by unseaworthiness or negligence. This applies even if, by the law governing the contract, the obligation to make general average contribution is laid down by statute.[113]

There is a general average loss where the sacrifice is made by persons other than the master or crew[114] such as by the captor of a ship seized as prize,[115] or by any other person, provided that the person acted reasonably and with the intention of saving the ship and cargo. Where, however, the loss was suffered by a person not acting with such intent but in obedience to orders (e.g. as where the master, in obedience to a commodore commanding the convoy in wartime who in turn was obeying the orders of the

[106] *Royal Mail Steam Packet Company v English Bank of Rio de Janeiro* (1887) 19 Q.B.D. 362, 370, per Wills J.

[107] *Archard v Ring* (1874) 31 L.T. 647.

[108] *Strang, Steel and Company v Scott and Company* (1889) 14 App. Cas. 601.

[109] *Schloss v Heriot* (1863) 14 C.B. (N.S.) 59; *Fiumana Societa(g) di Navigazione v Bunge and Company* [1930] 2 K.B. 47.

[110] *Hain Steamship Company v Tate and Lyle* [1936] 2 All E.R. 597.

[111] *The Carron Park* (1890) 15 P.D. 203.

[112] *Dreyfus and Company v Tempus Shipping Company* [1931] A.C. 726.

[113] ibid.

[114] *Papayanni v Grampian Steamship Company* (1896) 1 Com. Cas. 418.

[115] *Price v Noble* (1811) 4 Taunt. 123

Admiralty, puts into port)[116] there is no general average expenditure as no one acts with the specific intention of saving the ship and cargo. The voluntary nature of the general average act is thus emphasised.

The obligation to make general average contribution rests on the owners of all cargo which has been saved by the sacrifice[117] but the owners of cargo which has been lost are not obliged to contribute.[118] The owners of cargo which was never endangered by the peril are also not liable to contribute to a general average sacrifice which averted the peril.[119] General average contribution is payable by the owner of the cargo.[120] It appears that the shipper is not liable to contribute if the shipper is not the owner of the goods, unless a contract to do so can be implied from the terms of the bill of lading or otherwise.[121] Where the consignee is not the owner of the goods, the consignee is not liable for general average contribution[122] unless it implicitly agrees to be liable (where, for example, the consignee takes delivery of goods on which the carrier claims a lien for general average contribution),[123] or where the obligation to make general average contribution is expressly included in the contract of carriage and there is a statutory transfer of the liabilities under that contract pursuant to the Carriage of Goods by Sea Act 1992, as discussed at 3.1.7.1 below. It appears that, in contrast to any contractual liability of the consignee arising by reason of such statutory transfer, the consignee cannot, simply as owner of the goods, be made liable for a general average contribution unless the consignee was already the owner at the time of the general average loss.[124]

The shipowner can claim, and is liable to pay, general average contribution both in respect of the ship and of the freight on the cargo carried. Where the ship or part of it is sacrificed, the shipowner is entitled to general

[116] *Athel Line v Liverpool and London War Risks Insurance Association* [1944] K.B. 87 where the master and the commodore acted in obedience to orders, and the Admiralty was motivated by questions of naval strategy.

[117] *Fletcher v Alexander* (1868) L.R. 3 C.P. 375, 382, per Bovill C.J.

[118] *Chellew v Royal Commission on Sugar Supply* [1921] 2 K.B. 627, per Sankey J. (affirmed on another point in the Court of Appeal, [1922] 1 K.B. 12); *Tate and Lyle v Hain Steamships Company* (1934) 151 L.T. 249, 256, per Greer L.J., in the Court of Appeal; *Morrison Steamship Company v Greystoke Castle (Cargo Owners)* [1947] A.C. 265, 283, per Lord Roche.

[119] *Nesbitt v Lushington* (1792) 4 T.R. 783, 787, per Lord Kenyon C.J.

[120] *Scaife v Tobin* (1832) 3 B. & Ad. 523, 529, per Littledale J.

[121] *Walford de Baerdemaecker v Galindez Brothers* (1897) 2 Com. Cas. 137.

[122] ibid.

[123] ibid.

[124] ibid.

average contribution[125] and where cargo is sacrificed, the carrier is entitled to general average contribution in respect of the freight lost on the carriage of the cargo.[126] The carrier is liable to contribution in respect of the ship where it was in danger and was saved by a general average sacrifice and in respect of the freight earned on cargo saved by the sacrifice. The carrier is liable to make general average contribution although the general average sacrifice was necessitated by an excepted peril for which the carrier is not liable.[127] In a charterparty, the charterer is liable to contribute, and may claim contribution, in respect of loss of the freight reserved by the charterparty.[128] The shipowner, or the charterer in a charterparty by way of demise, has a lien in respect of general average contributions due from the cargo owners and is obliged to enforce this lien in order to recover contributions due from other cargo owners to the owners of sacrificed cargo. The cargo owners may enforce their claims to contribution by action against the shipowner and other cargo owners.

Where a general average loss has been caused by the default of the carrier or a cargo owner, the party in default cannot recover contribution. The party in default (for example, the owner of another ship, where the general average sacrifice was occasioned by a collision caused by the negligence of the master of this ship)[129] is liable to indemnify the parties who were obliged to make general average contribution in respect of the sacrifice, although agreed contractual terms may limit the extent of such liability. Where cargo may, by established custom, be carried on deck, the cargo owner may claim and is liable for general average contribution.[130] This applies even where it is a term of the contract that the deck cargo is to be carried "at merchant's risk".[131] In all other cases deck cargo is not within the law of general average. If goods are stowed on deck without the express or implied consent of the shipper, the carrier is liable for loss or damage to the goods, albeit such carriage on deck will not amount to deviation.[132]

[125] *Hallett v Wigram* (1850) 9 C.B. 580, 601Ð02, per Wilde C.J.; *Svendsen v Wallace* (1885), 10 App. Cas. 404.

[126] *Pirie and Company v Middle Dock Company* (1881) 44 L.T. 426.

[127] *Schmidt v Royal Mail Steamship Company* (1876) 45 L.J. (Q.B.) 646.

[128] *Moran v Jones* (1857) 7 E. & B. 523.

[129] *Morrison Steamship Company v The Greystoke Castle (Cargo Owners)* [1947] A.C. 265.

[130] *Gould v Oliver* (1837) 4 Bing. N.C. 134; *Wright v Marwood* (1881) 7 Q.B.D. 62.

[131] *Burton v English* (1883) 12 Q.B.D. 218.

[132] *Kenya Railways v Antares Co Pte Ltd (The Antares) (Nos 1 and 2)* [1987] 1 Lloyd's Rep. 424 to be contrasted with *Royal Exchange Shipping Company v Dixon* (1886) 12 App. Cas. 11.

Passengers' luggage and provisions on a passenger ship are not within the law of general average, either as respects claim for or payment of general average contribution, as the law of general average applies only to merchandise.[133] The assessment of general average contribution is ordinarily to be made at the port of discharge of the goods concerned and to be computed according to the law or custom prevailing at this port.[134] However, it may be agreed between the parties that the assessment be made at the port of refuge and this will also be the case where an assessment at a port of refuge is compelled by necessity.[135] The basis of assessment of the value of the cargo for the purposes of a general average sacrifice and contribution is the value of the cargo at the time when the assessment was made. For the purposes of assessing the value of the cargo sacrificed, the value of the cargo lost is taken to be the value that such cargo would have had at the time of assessment, assuming it had not been sacrificed and taking into account any probable deterioration in the value of this cargo during the voyage.[136] The basis of assessment with respect to loss of the ship is the cost of repairing the damage, or, where the ship is a total loss, the value of the ship at the time of the loss less the value of the wreck. Where only part of the damage which caused the loss of the ship was a general average loss, the sum which it would have cost to repair this other damage, as well as the value of the wreck, must be deducted from the value of the ship at the time of the loss to ascertain the amount of the general average loss.[137] The assessment of loss of freight incurred by the carrier is the freight which the carrier would have obtained if the cargo sacrificed had been delivered, less the additional costs which would have been incurred in carrying it to the port of discharge if it had not been lost.[138]

Parties to contracts of carriage generally agree express contractual provision in relation to general average by the incorporation of particular rules which define the concepts of general average loss and general average expense and set out detailed rules for their calculation. The first such rules came into being in 1864 as the York Rules and have been revised and reissued many times. The most recent version is the York Antwerp Rules 2004. These were adopted by the 38th CMI conference that took place in Vancouver in June 2004. It is consequently most unusual for general

[133] *Brown v Stapyleton* (1827) 4 Bing. 119.
[134] *Simonds v White* (1824) 2 B. & C. 805.
[135] *Hill v Wilson* (1879) 4 C.P.D. 329.
[136] *Fletcher v Alexander* (1868) L.R. 3 C.P. 375.
[137] *Henderson Brothers v Shankland and Company* [1896] 1 Q.B. 525.
[138] *The Brigella* [1893] P. 189, 196, per Gorrell Barnes J.

average claims to be determined according to the common law, as they are far more commonly determined by whatever version of the York Antwerp Rules has been incorporated into the subject contracts of carriage and is contractually applicable to any dispute between the parties.

3.1.4.4 Salvage

Rights of salvage do not arise under contracts of carriage but do exist under the common law, as well as under many other legal systems. In essence, the common law principle is to the effect that where "maritime property" is in peril and is saved by the actions of an intervening party, that intervening party is entitled to a reward calculated by reference to the risks and costs incurred and limited to the salvaged value of the maritime property which had been imperiled. At common law the concept of "maritime property" is limited to "the ship, her apparel and cargo . . . .and the wreck of these and freight".[139]

The principles of marine salvage have been the subject of harmonisation by international public law in the form of the 1910 Brussels Salvage Convention, the 1967 Brussels Protocol and the 1989 London Salvage Convention. The 1989 London Salvage Convention has the force of law in the United Kingdom by virtue of s.224(2) of the Merchant Shipping Act 1995. The 1989 Convention extends the concept of property in relation to which salvage services may be rendered to a vessel ("any ship or craft, or any structure capable of navigation") and property ("any property not permanently and intentionally attached to the shoreline and . . . freight at risk") which is "in danger in navigable waters or in any other waters whatsoever".[140] Articles 12 to 19 prescribe the applicable rules for the assessment of any reward, which according to arts 13 and 14 comprises both a normal award for traditional salvage services in saving the vessel and her cargo (limited by art.13 to "the salved value of the vessel and other property") and special compensation for preventing or minimising damage to the environment (limited by art.14 to the salvor's expenses plus an uplift of up to 100 per cent). Special compensation is only payable where it exceeds any reward recoverable by the salvor as a normal award under art.13.

The mandatory effects of the 1989 Salvage Convention are however restricted by arts 6(1) and 7, which provide that those offering and

[139] *The Gas Float Whitton No.2* 1897 A.C. 337.
[140] Per art.19(a)–(d).

accepting salvage services may contract out of the convention provisions provided that: (a) such contract would not be voidable (by reason of undue influence or duress); or (b) the contractually agreed payment would not be "in an excessive degree" too large or too small for the services actually rendered. To achieve increased legal certainty those offering and accepting salvage services may agree that the salvage services will be provided on the basis of the well known Lloyds Open Form (LOF) arrangement which respects the "no cure no pay" concept of salvage law. The LOF came into being in the late nineteenth century and is now in common worldwide use. In its 2000 edition, LOF has an optional Special Compensation P&I Club's (SCOPIC) Clause to regulate those claims for special compensation envisaged by art.14 of the 1989 Convention.

3.1.5 Contractual Duties

3.1.5.1 Delivery

It is the duty of the carrier to deliver goods to the consignee. Where the port of discharge at which delivery is to be made is named in the bill of lading or otherwise agreed in the contract, the carrier must deliver the goods at this port. If it fails to do so, it cannot claim any freight.[141] For this reason, where at the request of the shipper the carrier undertakes to deliver to a named port, the carrier is likely to require an express warranty that the named port, or berth, is safe. It is likely that an express safe port warranty will give rise to an implied safe berth warranty;[142] terms will not otherwise be implied into a contract of carriage that a discharge port or berth is safe where the port or berth is actually identified by the contract since

> "... then the shipowner must take the responsibility of ascertaining whether he can safely berth his ship there or will take the risk of doing so. If he agrees upon the place, then, subject to excepted perils his liability to have his ship there is definite".[143]

[141] *Metcalfe v Britannia Ironworks Company* (1877) 2 Q.B.D. 423.

[142] Since were that not to be the case the port itself would not be safe within the description of a safe port by Sellers L.J. in *Leeds Shipping Co Ltd v Société Française Bunge (The Eastern City)* [1958] 2 Lloyd's Rep 127.

[143] Per Dixon C.J. in a dissenting opinion Dixon C.J. in the High Court of Australia in *Reardon Smith Line Ltd v Australian Wheat Board (The Houston City)* [1954] 2 Lloyd's Rep. 148 at p.153 approved by the Privy Council at [1956] A.C. 266.

However, where the shipper has reserved to itself the right to nominate a port or a berth, a safe port and/or berth warranty may be implied where such an implied term would do no more than simply "spell out what the contract actually means".[144] It would appear that such a warranty is likely to be implied more readily into a time charterparty[145] than it is in respect of a voyage charterparty or bill of lading contract.[146] This may be attributed to the increased degree of control exercised by charterers under contracts of carriage concluded by time charter, compared with that exercised under voyage charters or, for that matter, shippers under bills of lading.[147]

It is sometimes agreed that the carrier shall deliver the goods to the consignee at a named port "or as near thereto as the ship may safely get". In such a case, the carrier performs its duty to deliver the goods and may claim the freight if, when the port is unsafe, the carrier goes as near to it as is possible safely and offers to deliver to the consignee there.[148] The port is not safe, in the absence of any express agreement to the contrary, unless the ship can enter it as a laden ship carrying the cargo which is to be delivered to the consignee.[149] There is, however, some conflict of judicial opinion as to whether the port is safe where the ship could safely enter it after lightening the load in the approaches to the port and it is a custom of the port to lighten in the approaches.[150] Such issues are likely to be resolved by a determination as to whether such lightening is reasonable in the light of all the circumstances of the particular carriage.[151] Where it is a custom of the port of discharge to lighten the load in the approaches the contract of carriage may be subject to an implied term, imposing an obligation on the carrier to do so and then go on to proceed to discharge the remainder of the goods in the port. In these circumstances it would appear that the carrier cannot claim the port to be unsafe.

The port of discharge will be deemed unsafe where, in normal

[144] Per Lord Hoffman at para.27 of his judgment in Attorney General of *Belize v Belize Telecom Ltd* [2009] UKPC 10 discussed at 1.5.2.

[145] *Vardinoyannis v The Egyptian General Petroleum Corporation (The Evaggelos Th)* [1971] 2 Lloyd's Rep. 200.

[146] *Mediterranean Salvage & Towage Ltd v Seamar Trading & Commerce Inc (The Reborn)* [2009] EWCA Civ 531.

[147] The contrast between time and voyage charters is discussed at 3.2.

[148] *Dahl v Nelson, Donkin and Company* (1881) 6 App. Cas. 38.

[149] *Shield v Wilkins* (1850) 5 Exch. 304, 305, per Rolfe B.

[150] See *The Alhambra* (1881) 6 P.D. 68; *Capper v Wallace* (1880) 5 Q.B.D. 163; *Hillstrom v Gibson* (1870) 8 Sess. Cas. (3rd Series) 463 (in Scotland).

[151] *Owners of SS Athamas v Dig Vijay Cement Co Ltd (The Athamas)* [1962] 2 Lloyd's Rep. 120.

circumstances and for an indefinite or reasonably lengthy period when the vessel is ready to discharge the goods, the ship cannot reach, use and leave the port without being exposed to danger which cannot be avoided by good navigation and seamanship.[152] A temporary danger or obstruction such as ice[153] will not, however, render the port unsafe if the carrier could reasonably wait for the obstruction to be removed and then proceed to the port.[154] Any warranty that the discharge port is safe is a continuing warranty, which is to be construed as at the time it is made. There will be no breach of warranty where the safety of the port is undermined by an occurrence that would, when the warranty was given, have been considered abnormal, although if, when the warranty is given, the port is already unsafe from such abnormal occurrence the warranty will have been breached.[155] A port may be rendered unsafe by political factors[156] (e.g. war[157] or blockade[158]) as well as by natural dangers of the seas and is not a safe port when its authorities have prohibited the entry of ships owing to congestion of shipping, provided that the prohibition is not merely temporary.[159] When there was no indication of how long the prohibition was likely to last, it was held that the carrier could discharge the goods as near to the port as could safely be reached, and be entitled to the freight.[160] If access to the port is dangerous, owing to the operation of submarines in wartime, the port may be unsafe although there is no danger in the port itself.[161]

If by the contract of carriage the carrier has agreed to go as near to the named port as the ship may safely reach; then, although the port is unsafe, the carrier is not entitled to freight on proceeding to the nearest safe port and discharging there.[162] Instead, the ship must proceed as near to the port as it may go with safety and offer delivery of the cargo to the consignee at this place.[163] The carrier and the consignee may, however, always agree for

[152] *The Eastern City* [1958] 2 Lloyd's Rep. 127 at p.131, approved by the House of Lords in *The Evia (No.2)* [1982] 2 Lloyd's Rep. 307 at pp.310 col. 1 and 315 col. 1.

[153] *Steamship Knutsford Ltd v Tillmanns and Company* [1908] A.C. 406.

[154] *Schilizzi v Derry* (1855) 4 E. & B. 873; *Metcalfe v Britannia Ironworks Company* (1877) 2 Q.B.D. 423.

[155] *The Evia (No.2)* [1982] 2 Lloyd's Rep 307, per Lord Diplock at p.310 col. 1.

[156] *Ogden v Graham* (1861) 1 B. & S. 773.

[157] *The Teutonia* (1872) L.R. 4 P.C. 171.

[158] *Castel and Latta v Trechman* (1884) Cab. & El. 276.

[159] *Dahl v Nelson, Donkin and Company* (1881) 6 App. Cas. 38.

[160] ibid.

[161] *Palace Shipping Company v Gans Steamship Line* [1916] 1 K.B. 138.

[162] ibid.

[163] ibid.

the consignment to be delivered to the nearest safe port. Where it is an express term of the contract that, in the event of strikes at the agreed port of discharge, the carrier may discharge the cargo at any other port, the carrier is entitled to do so. Unlike a broad general liberty clause, a strike's liberty clause in a contract of carriage is not considered void as being contrary to the whole purpose of the contract of carriage.[164]

It is, of course, the duty of the carrier to deliver the cargo to the consignee who is entitled under the contract of carriage to receive it and this issue will be addressed in connection with bills of lading at 3.2.3.4 below, as particular issues arise in this respect with regard to bills of lading.

3.1.5.2 Loading and Discharge

In the absence of any express or implied agreement to the contrary the operations of loading and unloading are to be performed jointly by the carrier with, as regards loading, the shipper or, as regards unloading, the consignee.[165] In the case of loading, in the absence of agreement to the contrary, it is the duty of the shipper to bring the goods alongside the ship at the shipper's own expense; and it is the duty of the carrier to load the goods on to the ship from alongside with the ship's tackle at the carrier's expense. This does not apply where there is a custom of the port of loading to the contrary,[166] or where the nature of the cargo, or the carriage, requires loading by shore-based equipment. In the case of unloading, it is ordinarily the duty of the carrier either to unload the goods with the ship's tackle or to allow shore-based cranes to do so from alongside the ship and for the consignee to take delivery into lighters, or on the wharf.[167] However, other arrangements for loading and unloading may be agreed and "who owes what duties" is a question to be determined by the proper interpretation of the contract of carriage. These loading and discharging obligations are owed between the original contracting parties to the contract of carriage, i.e. the shipper and the carrier. The discharge obligations will only attach to a

[164] *Renton v Palmyra Trading Corporation* [1957] A.C. 149 (House of Lords) affirming the decision of the Court of Appeal [1956] 1 Q.B. 462.

[165] Per Lord Diplock *E.L. Oldendorff & Co GmbH v Tradax Export SA* [1974] A.C. 479 at 556 "Loading and discharging are joint operations. So the loading stage and the discharging stage call for acts of performance by the charterer as well".

[166] *Harris v Best* (1892) 68 L.T. 76, 77, per Lord Esher M.R.; *Aktieselkab Helios v Ekman and Company* [1897] 2 Q.B. 83; *Argonaut Navigation Company v Minister of Food* [1949] 1 K.B. 572, 580, per Bucknill L.J.

[167] *Petersen v Freebody and Company* [1895] 2 Q.B. 294.

consignee who becomes a party to the contract of carriage by reason of statutory transfer under COGSA 92 (see 3.1.7.1 below) or by reason of the common law principles previously discussed.[168] Notwithstanding any transfer (statutory or otherwise) of liability under the contract of carriage to anyone else, the shipper retains all its liabilities under that contract, including those relating to the discharge operation.[169] Accordingly, for this reason, the obligations of the consignee referred to below are in fact obligations of the shipper, which might also be owed by someone else receiving the goods as consignee.

It may be expressly agreed that the carrier shall discharge the goods at its own expense and carry them to the wharf or elsewhere, or that the consignee shall take delivery of the goods on deck or in the holds. Such an agreement will be implied where there is a custom of the port of discharge to this effect.[170] However, this agreement prevails (notwithstanding any custom of the port to the contrary) where there is an express provision in the contract that the goods are to be unloaded in a particular place at the expense of one or other of the parties, since the custom applies only in so far as it is not in conflict with the express terms of the contract.[171] It is sometimes expressly agreed in the contract that the ship shall discharge the goods at a named dock or berth in the port. In the absence of any such agreement, the consignee is entitled to direct where in the port the goods shall be unloaded[172] and the manner in which they are to be unloaded (e.g. whether into lighters, or on a wharf).[173]

Where it is agreed, in a charterparty or otherwise, that the consignee shall take delivery within a given time, the consignee is liable in damages (or, if so agreed, for demurrage) for detention of the ship where delivery is not taken within that time.[174] Where there is no provision in the contract with regard to the time for taking delivery, the consignee must take delivery within a reasonable time.[175] The time begins to run against the consignee as soon as

[168] See 1.3 and 1.6.1.

[169] See s.3(3) of the Carriage of Goods by Sea Act 1992 discussed at 3.1.7.1 below.

[170] *Catley v Wintringham* (1792) 1 Peake N.P.C. 202; *Smith, Hogg and Company v Louis Bamberger and Sons* [1929] 1 K.B. 150.

[171] *Akt. Helios v Ekman and Company* [1897] 2 Q.B. 83, 87, per Lord Esher M.R.; *Brenda Steamship Company v Green* [1900] 1 Q.B. 518.

[172] *Ireland and Sons v Southdown Steamship Company* (1926) 136 L.T. 412.

[173] *Bishop v Ware* (1813) 3 Camp. 360.

[174] *Moorsom v Bell* (1811) 2 Camp. 616.

[175] *Postlethwaite v Freeland* (1880) 5 App. Cas. 599; *Hick v Raymond and Reed Ltd* [1893] A.C. 22.

the ship has arrived at the port and is ready to deliver.[176] If the consignee requires the ship to proceed to a particular dock or berth or elsewhere to discharge, time runs against the consignee while the ship is proceeding there, or waiting to do so.[177] If, however, it is a term of the contract that the goods shall be delivered at a named dock or at a named berth in a dock, the carrier is not deemed to be ready to deliver until the ship has arrived at the stipulated dock or berth.[178] Where, owing to congestion of shipping, the port authorities have ordered the ship to anchor outside the area of the port, the time does not run against the consignee, unless this has been expressly agreed in the contract[179] or is the normal place selected by the port for ships to anchor, whilst awaiting a berth at the port and the ship is at the immediate and effective disposition of the charterer.[180]

When the ship has arrived and is ready to deliver, time begins to run against the consignee, whether or not the consignee has had notice of its arrival. The carrier is under no obligation to inform the consignee of the arrival of the ship,[181] but if the carrier actively misleads the consignee as to the arrival of the ship (e.g. by registering it in the port of discharge under a different name from that appearing in the bill of lading)[182] time will not begin to run against the consignee until the consignee has notice of its arrival. If owing to the failure of the carrier to comply with the regulations of the port authority the goods cannot be unloaded, the carrier is not deemed to be ready to deliver.[183] The duty of the consignee to take delivery within the time agreed in the contract, or within a reasonable time, is an absolute one[184] and the consignee is liable to the carrier for detention of the ship if the consignee fails to take delivery for whatever reason, unless it is because of the fault of the carrier.[185] Thus the consignee is liable for delay in taking delivery owing to the weather,[186] or to a strike at the port,[187] or

[176] *Leonis Steamship Company v Rank Ltd* [1908] 1 K.B. 499, 517–9, per Kennedy L.J.
[177] ibid.
[178] ibid.
[179] *Roland-Linie Schiffart v Spillers Ltd* [1957] 1 Q.B. 509.
[180] *E. L. Oldendorff & Co GmbH v Tradax Export SA* [1974] A.C. 479.
[181] *Harman v Clarke* (1815) 4 Camp. 159; *Houlder v General Steam Navigation Company* (1862) 3 F. & F. 170.
[182] ibid.
[183] *Good and Company v Isaacs* [1892] 2 Q.B. 555.
[184] *Postlethwaite v Freeland* [1880] 5 App. Cas. 599.
[185] *Budgett v Binnington* [1891] 1 Q.B. 35, 40, per Lindley L.J.
[186] *Thiis v Byers* (1876) 1 Q.B.D. 244.
[187] *Hick v Raymond and Reed* [1893] AC 22; *Budgett v Binnington* (fn. 185).

congestion of shipping,[188] or where the unloading is prevented by lawful[189] or unlawful[190] orders of the port authority. The consignee is liable if the carrier refuses to deliver because it is lawfully exercising its lien on the goods for freight due[191] or because of the delay of the consignee in producing the bill of lading.[192] Where the consignee's goods cannot be unloaded because another cargo owner has failed to take delivery of goods stowed above the consignee's goods, the consignee is liable for detention of the ship to the carrier,[193] although, in such circumstances, the consignee may claim damages either at common law[194] or pursuant to statute[195] from the other cargo owner whose goods have prevented the unloading. If the ship has arrived at the port of discharge and the carrier is ready to deliver, time continues to run against the consignee if the ship has to leave the port through no fault of either the carrier or the consignee. Accordingly, where a ship was ordered by the port authority to leave port for eight days for the safety of other ships in the port, the charterer was liable for demurrage during these eight days.[196] The consignee may be exempted from liability for all or any of these events by the express terms of the contract but, in the event of ambiguity, any such exceptions (unless in the carrier's standard terms) will be construed against the consignee, in accordance with the general principles discussed at 1.5.2.

Unlike the situation discussed above, where the consignee is bound, under the contract, to take delivery within an agreed time the consignee must do so, whatever circumstances are prevailing at the port.[197] Where the duty of the consignee is merely to take delivery within "a reasonable time", then all relevant factors existing at the port of discharge and otherwise are to be taken into account in determining what is "a reasonable time" for the consignee to take delivery.[198] Thus while the consignee is not excused for

[188] *Randall v Lynch* (1810) 2 Camp. 352.

[189] *Waugh v Morris* (1873) L.R. 8 Q.B. 202.

[190] *Bessey v Evans* (1815) 4 Camp. 131.

[191] *Lyle Shipping Company v Cardiff Corporation* (1899) 5 Com. Cas. 87, before Bigham J.; this point was not raised in the Court of Appeal, [1900] 2 Q.B. 638.

[192] *Erichsen v Barkworth* (1858) 3 H. & N. 894.

[193] *Porteus v Watney* (1878) 3 Q.B.D. 534.

[194] ibid. at p.544, per Brett L.J.

[195] The Civil Liability (Contribution) Act 1978 discussed at 1.8.1.

[196] *Compania Crystal v Herman and Mohatta Ltd* [1958] 2 Q.B. 196.

[197] *Postlethwaite v Freeland* (fn. 184), at p.608, per Lord Selborne L.C.; *Van Liewen v Hollis Brothers* [1920] A.C. 239.

[198] *Ford v Cotesworth* (1868) L.R. 4 Q.B. 127, 133, per Blackburn J.; *Postlethwaite v Freeland* (1880) 5 App. Cas. 599; *Hick v Raymond and Reed Ltd* [1893] A.C. 22.

failure to take delivery because of a strike, the strike will be taken into account in determining what is a reasonable time, in the circumstances, for taking delivery. Where the consignee has failed to take delivery within a reasonable time, the carrier may discharge the goods into a warehouse.[199] The carrier is only entitled to do this after waiting a reasonable time for the consignee to take delivery, unless, by an express term in the contract,[200] or by a custom of the port of discharge, the carrier is permitted to do so earlier.[201] The carrier is not obliged to discharge the goods into a warehouse[202] and may instead wait with them on board in the port of discharge and claim damages, or agreed demurrage, for the detention of the ship.

3.1.5.3 As Carrier and Warehouseman

Unless, extraordinarily, the carrier by sea should be a common carrier,[203] there is little significance in whether the carrier by sea holds the goods as carrier or warehouseman. However, it can probably still be said that the carrier by sea ceases to hold the goods as a carrier on expiry of the time fixed by the contract in which the consignee must take delivery of the goods, or, where no such time is fixed, on the expiry of reasonable time from when the consignee was first entitled to take delivery of the goods. The carrier is liable as a bailee whilst in possession of the goods as a warehouseman to the same extent as the carrier of goods by land at common law,[204] subject to the agreed, or statutory, terms of the contract of carriage. In the unlikely event that the time for taking delivery is not expressly provided for in the contract of carriage, even where no custom exists as to the taking of delivery, the consignee will be liable if it does not take delivery of the goods from the warehouse within a reasonable time.[205]

[199] *Erichsen v Barkworth* (1858) 3 H. & N. 601, 616, per Bramwell B., in the Court of Exchequer.
[200] *Alexiadi v Robinson* (1861) 2 F. & F. 679.
[201] *Marzetti v Smith and Son* (1883) 49 L.T. 580.
[202] *Hick v Rodocanachi* [1891] 2 Q.B. 626, 632, per Lindley L.J., in the court of Appeal (sub. nom. *Hick v Raymond and Reid* in the House of Lords).
[203] The concept of a common carrier by sea is discussed at 3.1.9 below.
[204] See 1.6.2.2.
[205] *The Clan Macdonald* (1883) 8 P.D. 178.

3.1.6 Incidents of Breach

3.1.6.1 Damage or Delay in Loading, Stowage and Discharging Operations

A shipper is of course under no liability to load or discharge until bound to do so by a contract with the carrier. In the case of a shipper other than a charterer, it is unusual for the contract of carriage to contain a term requiring the shipper to load or discharge. If a shipper is bound to load or discharge, it is liable for any failure to do so and may be liable for any damage caused subject to the terms of the contract. The extent of liability on the part of such a shipper is the same as that of a charterer who has undertaken under the charterparty to be responsible for loading and/or discharging.[206]

Claims arising in connection with loading and discharging may involve damage or delay each of which may be caused either to the ship or the cargo. Claims for damage more commonly arise to the cargo than the ship, whilst claims for delay more commonly concern the ship than the cargo. In an American case, where there was no stipulation as to the time for unloading, it was held that delay caused by congestion in the port was reasonable but, where bills of lading required "continuous discharge" by the consignee, the consignee was nonetheless required to unload the ship continuously irrespective of the port conditions and in consequence was held liable for delaying the ship.[207]

Where, in the case of a chartered ship, the goods are loaded or unloaded by stevedores, it is a question of fact in each case whether the stevedores are the servants of the shipowner or of the charterer. In a charterparty by way of demise (3.2.1.2) they are almost always the servants of the charterer. However, in a time or voyage charterparty not by way of demise (see 3.2.1.3 and 3.2.1.4) it depends on the proper interpretation of the charterparty concluded between the shipowner and the charterer.[208] The fact that the charterer is entitled to appoint the stevedores does not in itself necessarily mean that they are the charterer's servants.[209] Where goods are damaged by stevedores during loading, any shipper, other than the charterer, will have a

[206] The rights, duties and liabilities of charterers are discussed at 3.2.1 below.
[207] *Hellenic Lines v Embassy of Pakistan* [1973] 1 Ll.L.R. 363 U.S.C.A.
[208] *Harris v Best* (1892) 68 LT 76.
[209] *Sandeman v Scurr* (1866) L.R. 2 Q.B. 86.

right of action against whichever of the shipowner or the charterer employed the stevedores.[210]

If the ship is not cargoworthy at the beginning of the loading, the shipper is entitled to refuse to load despite being bound by contract (whether by charterparty or otherwise) to load.[211] If the shipper discovers, after beginning to load, that the ship was not cargoworthy at the beginning of the loading, the carrier may be required to unload the goods already loaded at the carrier's expense.[212] If, however, the ship was in fact cargoworthy at the beginning of the loading, the shipper is liable for breach of contract if it refuses to load, even though the shipper may have had reasonable grounds for believing that the ship was not cargoworthy.[213]

The carrier is entitled to stow the goods on board as it pleases, and the shipper has no right to stipulate how the goods shall be stowed. The carrier is, however, only entitled to stow the goods in those parts of the ship which are normally used for stowage.[214] The carrier must be careful not to stow the goods in such a way as to endanger the ship, as this may result in breach of warranty through the ship becoming unseaworthy.[215] The shipper is not entitled to require the carrier to stow goods in those parts of the ship which are not normally used for stowage.[216] Traditionally, the deck was not a part of the ship normally used for stowage, as cargo carried on deck is more likely to suffer damage. The carrier is therefore not entitled to stow goods on deck unless there is an agreement to do so with the shipper in the contract of carriage, or where, owing to the existence of a custom or otherwise, the shipper has implicitly consented to the goods being carried as deck cargo.[217] Where it is a recognised custom that goods of such a class are carried as deck cargo on the vessel and/or route in question (as is commonly the case in relation to the carriage of goods in containers), the carrier is entitled to stow the goods on deck.[218] The carrier will not succeed in establishing the existence of such a custom merely by proving that it is habitual for carriers on the route to carry goods of this class as deck cargo

[210] *Swainston v Garrick* (1833) 2 L.J. (Ex.) 255.

[211] *Stanton v Richardson* (1872) L.R. 7 C.P. 421; affirmed in House of Lords (1874) 9 C.P. 390; (1875) 3 Asp. M.L.C. 23.

[212] ibid.

[213] *Towse v Henderson* (1850) 4 Exch. 890.

[214] *Royal Exchange Shipping Company v Dixon* (1886) 12 App. Cas. 11.

[215] *Kopitoff v Wilson* [1876] 1 Q.B. 377.

[216] *Mitcheson v Nicol* (1825) 7 Exch. 929.

[217] *Gould v Oliver* (1840) 2 Man. & G. 208.

[218] ibid.

in breach of contract.[219] If it is impracticable to stow the goods elsewhere than on deck because of their nature, they may be stowed on deck.[220] The contract of carriage may, as commonly is the case, provide expressly that goods may be carried on or under deck at the carrier's discretion but an implied term to that effect might not arise even where the shipper, or its agent, has seen the goods being stowed on deck and has offered no objection.[221]

3.1.6.2 Loss, Damage, Delay or Misdelivery in Carriage

The carrier of goods by sea is under the same liability as the carrier of goods by land for damage, delay or misdelivery (1.7.1). Consequently, the carrier by sea may under common law resist claims for damage caused to cargo carried in a seaworthy ship where the loss or damage occurred notwithstanding the exercise by the carrier of reasonable care to safeguard the goods. Similarly the carrier will only be liable for delay caused to cargo if it fails to deliver the goods within a reasonable time on account of its negligence, unless of course there is a provision to the contrary in the contract (e.g. an expressly agreed date for delivery). It should be noted, however, that where delay results from unlawful deviation, the carrier will have committed a repudiatory breach of the contract[222] with the consequence that the shipper would have the right to "elect" to terminate the contract and sue the carrier free of obligations and exceptions contained in the contract of carriage as further discussed at 3.1.6.3 below.[223] Particular issues arise in connection with claims for misdelivery in connection with the carriage of goods by sea as the identification of multiple consignees for diverse consignments at ports worldwide is fraught with difficulty. These issues are discussed in connection with bills of lading at 3.2.3.4 below.

[219] *Royal Exchange Shipping Company v Dixon* (fn. 214).
[220] *Milward v Hibbert* (1842) 3 Q.B. 120, 136, per Lord Denman C.J.
[221] *Gould v Oliver* (fn. 217); but see *Royal Exchange Shipping Company v Dixon* (fn. 214), at p.13, per Lord Watson.
[222] As discussed at 3.1.4.2 above.
[223] *Hain Steamship v Tate & Lyle* [1936] 41 Com Cas 350; but note this principle is not consistent with the generally applicable principles of contract law following *Photo Productions v Securicor* [1980] AC 827 as discussed at 1.7.3 above and 3.1.6.3 below.

3.1.6.3 Repudiatory and Non-Repudiatory Breach

The distinction[224] between a repudiatory breach (which the other party may elect to accept as a termination of the contract) and any other breach (which does not give rise to termination unless fundamental)[225] is particularly important in connection with contracts of carriage. In part this is attributable to the fundamental nature of the implied duty on the carrier not to deviate, any breach of which would amount to a repudiation of the contract that the shipper, or the consignee, could accept as bringing the contract to an end. As carriage conditions generally relax the implied term by providing for a general liberty to deviate, the risk of any carrier finding itself in breach of the implied duty is much reduced. However, even more significant to contracts of carriage is the issue of time. Express contractual stipulations in mercantile contracts as to the time at which vessels, or cargo, should be available tend to be strictly construed and enforced.[226] Any delay in arrival or readiness of the ship or cargo is likely to be interpreted as a repudiatory breach of the carriage contract. Accordingly, when a voyage charterparty placed an obligation on charterers to narrow the available laycan (i.e. reduce the time for cancellation of the vessel after the earliest day for the commencement of loading) for the apparent benefit of the carrier the Court of Appeal held that a failure to do so amounted to a repudiatory breach, which the carrier was entitled to accept as a discharge of its own contractual obligations.[227] However, in contrast, a breach of the implied warranty of seaworthiness for instance is not a repudiatory breach

[224] See 1.7.3 for more discussion as to this distinction.

[225] In that, as previously discussed (ibid.) it goes to the root of the contract and substantially deprives the other contracting party of the entire benefit of the contract.

[226] *Bunge Corporation v Tradax Export SA* [1981] 2 Lloyd's Rep. 1 in which the House of Lords considered, in a contract concerning the sale of goods, that precise compliance with stipulations as to time was likely to fulfil the intentions of the parties in a "mercantile contract". See also the statement of the current principle in *Halsbury's Laws of England*, 4th/5th edn online version (LexisNexis Butterworths, 2008), vol.9 (Contract), para.932, that "the court will require precise compliance with stipulations as to time wherever the circumstances of the case indicate that this would fulfil the intention of the parties. Whilst the time of performance will not ordinarily be considered to be of the essence, it will readily be so construed in a 'mercantile contract…'".

[227] *Universal Bulk Carriers Ltd v Andre et Cie* [2001] 2 Lloyd's Rep. 65.

unless the breach is fundamental.[228] This apparent contrast under English law between obligations in mercantile contracts as to the time for performance (time obligations) and the manner of performance (performance obligations) is marked. In giving his judgment in the House of Lords in *Bunge Corp v Tradax*[229] Lord Wilberforce sought to draw a conceptual distinction between time and performance obligations by reference to the consequences of breach. He asserted that breach of a time obligation could only have one consequence (i.e. delayed performance), whilst breach of a performance obligation might have varying degrees of consequence (e.g. in respect of want of seaworthiness the consequences might be "extremely trivial, the omission of a nail; they might be extremely grave, a serious defect in the hull or in the machinery").[230] However, the contrast is better seen as one resulting from the exercise of contractual interpretation[231] carried out in a commercial context, in which, as described by Lord Roskill in the following terms,

> "the need for certainty in mercantile contracts is often of great importance and sometimes may well be a determining factor in deciding the true construction of a particular term in such a contract".[232]

Consequently, English law requires precise compliance with contractual stipulations as to the time for performance wherever the circumstances of the case are such that this would appear to have been intended by the parties.

As previously discussed, deviation appears to discharge the contract so absolutely that the carrier is left in possession of the goods as a wrongful possessor without the benefit of contractual limitations and exclusions to contain its liability.[233] However, this is now an aberrant principle in the light of subsequent decisions[234] since, whilst any fundamental breach discharges the parties from their future obligations, claims for breach of contract arising from a fundamental breach continue to be regulated by the

[228] *Hong Kong Fir Shipping Co Ltd v Kawasaki Kisen Kaisha Ltd* [1962] 2 Lloyd's Rep. 478; [1962] 2 Q.B. 26.
[229] fn. 226.
[230] ibid. p.5.
[231] Applying the principles discussed at 1.5.2.
[232] *Bunge Corporation v Tradax Export SA* (fn. 226), p.15.
[233] As already discussed above in 3.1.4.2 and 1.7.3.
[234] *Photo Production Ltd v Securicor Transport Ltd* [1980] A.C. 827 discussed at 1.7.3.

contractual terms, apart, perhaps, in sea carriage for claims arising from a deviation in the voyage.[235]

3.1.6.4 Exclusion of Liability—Excepted Perils

At common law, the carrier is entitled to exclude or limit its liability by express terms in the contract to any extent. In contracts to which the Hague-Visby Rules do not apply, it is usual for the carrier to exclude its liability for any loss or damage to the goods caused by certain specified causes, which were previously referred to as the excepted perils. The traditional excepted perils, many of which are still included in contracts of carriage, include such matters as: act of God; act of the Queen's enemies; restraint of princes and rulers; perils of the seas; fire; barratry; piracy; robbery and theft; collisions, strandings and accidents of navigation; and leakage and breakage. It is appropriate to consider their meaning. Not only do many of these excepted perils still appear as excepted perils in many contracts of carriage, they are also contained in the Hague-Visby Rules having statutory force in the United Kingdom in relation to bills of lading.[236]

"Act of God", frequently included in contractual stipulations, may be interpreted in a contractual context as having the same meaning as that given to it as a common law defence for a carrier exposed to the strict liability regime of a common carrier.[237] "Act of the Queen's enemies" may have a wider application when expressly included in the contract than at common law. Unlike the more literal meaning ascribed to the phrase at common law, the contextual meaning of "act of the Queen's enemies", when expressly included in the contract is determined by ascertaining the intention of the parties. Accordingly, where goods carried on a German ship were lost owing to seizure by Danish vessels during the Prusso-Danish War of 1864, it was held that the term in the contract exempting the carrier from liability for "act of the King's enemies" was to be interpreted as referring to the enemies of the Duke of Mecklenburg, the sovereign of the state of the ship's flag. In consequence the carrier was held not liable.[238] "Restraint of princes or rulers" covers any act of a sovereign state in

[235] Although, in the course of distinguishing the classic deviation cases from unlawful carriage on deck, Lloyd L.J. expressed critiscism of them in *Kenya Railways v Antaraes Co Pte Ltd (The Antares) Nos 1 and 2* [1987] 1 Lloyd's Rep. 42.

[236] Discussed at 3.3.1 below.

[237] Discussed at 1.10.3.1.

[238] *Russell v Niemann* (1864) 17 C.B. (N.S.) 163.

pursuance of its sovereign power. The carrier may rely on the defence if its master has submitted to the threat of force by the prince or ruler concerned, provided that there were reasonable grounds for believing that the threat would be implemented if the carrier did not submit.[239] Difficulties may arise in the interpretation of this exception where the exercise of power is not by a lawful ruler exercising powers de jure but by a de facto government exercising powers under its own authority and the issue will turn on whether the person exercising de facto authority is a prince or ruler for the purpose of the contract.[240]

"Perils of the seas" covers damage caused by any sudden and unexpected peril naturally arising in connection with a voyage by sea.[241] It may not cover perils of navigable rivers, as opposed to those of the open sea, unless expressly extended to apply to such a case.[242] The cause of the damage must be a sudden event and not a slow, prolonged occurrence, such as sea water seeping through the boards of the ship.[243] As the exception is "perils of the seas", and not "perils on the seas", it does not cover damage caused by an event which, while in fact occurring during the sea voyage, could equally well have occurred on land,[244] such as fire[245] or rain.[246] It applies to a collision with another ship at sea, provided that the collision was not caused by the negligence of the carrier's servants; notwithstanding that the collision may have been caused by the negligence of the master or crew of the other ship.[247] It does not protect the carrier where the damage was caused by the wilful act of third parties, such as the scuttling of the ship by a mutinous crew.[248] Even if a loss occurs due to a

[239] *Rodoconachi v Elliott* (1874) L.R. 9 C.P. 518; *Nobel's Explosives Company v Jenkins and Company* [1896] 2 Q.B. 326 (not overruled by *Becker, Gray and Company v London Assurance Corporation* [1918] A.C. 101).

[240] See *Luigi Monta of Genoa v Cechofracht Company* [1956] 2 Q.B. 552.

[241] *Wilson and Company v The Xantho (Cargo Owners)* (1887) 12 App. Cas. 503.

[242] See *Trent and Mersey Navigation Company v Wood* (1785) 3 Esp. 127; *Phillips v Barber* (1821) 5 B. & Ald. 161.

[243] *Sassoon and Company v Western Assurance Company* [1912] A.C. 561.

[244] *Wilson and Company v The Xantho (Cargo Owners)* (fn. 241) per Lord Herschell; *Hamilton Fraser and Company v Pandorf and Company* (1887) 12 App. Cas. 518, 527, per Lord Bramwell.

[245] *Hamilton Fraser and Company v Pandorf and Company* (1887) 12 App. Cas. 518, at p.527, per Lord Bramwell.

[246] *Canada Rice Mills Ltd v Union Marine Company* [1941] A.C. 55, 64, per Lord Wright.

[247] *Buller v Fisher* (1799) 3 Esp. 67; *Wilson and Company v The Xantho (Cargo Owners)* (fn. 241).

[248] *Samuel and Company v Dumas* [1924] A.C. 431.

peril of the sea, the exception will not protect the carrier from liability if due diligence has not been exercised in making the ship seaworthy at the beginning of the voyage.[249] As damage caused by fire at sea does not come within the exception of perils of the seas, it is usual to insert an express exception for "fire", in order to protect the carrier from liability for damage by fire in circumstances which are not within the provisions of s.186 of the Merchant Shipping Act 1995 (discussed at 3.1.7.2 below). The exception of "collisions, strandings and accidents of navigation" extends to all accidental collisions at sea, notwithstanding that the master and crew of the other ship were negligent, provided that the casualty was not caused by the negligence of the carrier's servants.[250]

"Barratry" is any act of open and wilful defiance by the crew of the master, or by the master and crew of the authority of the shipowner. Where the goods were damaged as a result of the action of the master and crew in trading with the enemy in time of war, or in smuggling,[251] the defence of barratry applied. The defence was not excluded by the fact that the master and crew intended to hand over the illicit profits to the carrier, provided that at the material time they acted in defiance of the authority of the carrier.[252] The words "piracy" and "pirates" are interpreted in their ordinary, and not in any strict legal, sense. They are therefore limited to acts by independent bands acting against the shipping of all states for private gain.[253] They do not extend to all acts of robbery with violence on the high seas, or to cases where the robbers are acting from a political motive.[254] "Robbery" is limited to robbery with open force and violence, as opposed to larceny by stealth.[255] The word "thieves" has also been interpreted as excluding furtive theft, and as applying only to robbery with violence.[256] The exceptions of robbery and theft do not extend to robbery and theft by the carrier's servants, even where the carrier is protected from liability for

[249] *Goodfellow (Charles) Lumber Sales v Verreault, Hovington and Verreault Navigation Inc* [1971] 1 Ll.L.R. 185 (Canadian Sup. Ct.).

[250] *Chartered Mercantile Bank of India v Netherlands India Steam Navigation Company* (1883) 10 Q.B.D. 521.

[251] *Vallejo v Wheeler* (1774) 1 Cowp. 143.

[252] *Earle v Rowcroft* (1806) 8 East 126.

[253] *Republic of Bolivia v Indemnity Mutual Marine Assurance Company* [1909] 1 K.B. 785.

[254] ibid.

[255] *De Rothschild v Royal Mail Steam Packet Company* (1852) 7 Exch. 734.

[256] *Taylor v Liverpool and Great Western Steam Company* (1874) L.R. 9 Q.B. 546, 551, per Archibald J.

stealing by "thieves of any kind".[257] The exception may, of course, expressly exclude the carrier from liability for robbery or theft by its servants.

In the absence of an express provision to the contrary in the contract, provisions excluding the liability of the carrier for an excepted peril are interpreted as exempting the carrier only where the carrier and its servants have not been guilty of negligence.[258] The carrier is liable if the negligence of the master and crew have contributed to the damage by the excepted peril. In the absence of an express provision in the contract, the carrier is similarly liable where damage by an excepted peril has been contributed to by a breach of the warranty of seaworthiness.[259]

The interpretation of contractual exceptions to liability in contracts of carriage is subject to the interpretative approaches discussed at 1.5.2; the statutory regulation of contractual exclusions and limitations afforded by the Unfair Contract Terms Act 1977 does not apply to the carriage of goods by sea other than in connection with consumer contracts.[260] Where a bill of lading is issued the contracts of carriage may be subject to the Hague-Visby Rules, which are given the force of law in the United Kingdom.[261]

3.1.7 Liability for Breach

3.1.7.1 Rights to Claim

The Carriage of Goods by Sea Act 1992 (COGSA 92) provides for the statutory transfer of rights and duties arising under contracts of carriage. COGSA 92 replaced the Bills of Lading Act 1855, which provided for statutory transfer only in respect of bills of lading and was considered inadequate to protect the interests of those shipping and receiving cargo. COGSA 92 adopts a revised mechanism of statutory transfer applying not only to bills of lading but also sea waybills and ship's delivery orders. By s.2(1) anyone who becomes either (i) the lawful holder of a bill of lading or

[257] *Taylor v Liverpool and Great Western Steam Packet Company* (1874) L.R. 9 Q.B. 546; *Steinman and Company v Angier Line* [1891] 1 Q.B. 619.

[258] *Wilson and Company v The Xantho (Cargo Owners)* (1887) 12 App. Cas. 503.

[259] ibid.; *Steel v State Line Steamship Company* (1877) 3 App. Cas. 72, 88 per Lord Blackburn.

[260] See s.1(2) and para.1(3) of Sch.1 to the 1977 Act. Contracts with consumers are regulated not only by the 1977 Act but also by the Unfair Terms Consumer Contract Regulations 1999 SI 1999/2083 discussed at 1.7.1.1.

[261] See 3.3.2 below.

(ii) a person to whom delivery of the goods is to be made by the carrier under a sea waybill or ship's delivery order, shall have transferred to and vested in them all rights of suit under the contract of carriage as if they had been the original contracting party. The lawful holder of the bill of lading is defined in s.2 as a person in possession of the bill of lading in good faith who is identified in the bill as the intended consignee or endorsee (or would so have been if they had possession of the bill before it ceased to be a document of title).

The transfer of liabilities under the contract is not simultaneous with the transfer of rights. Liabilities will, under s.3(1), only attach to the transferee of the rights where such transferee: (i) takes or demands delivery of the goods; (ii) makes a claim under the contract of carriage; or (iii) has already taken such steps prior to the transfer of rights *and* such steps were not withdrawn, unsuccessful or taken by others on their behalf without their authority.[262] This separation of rights from liabilities is significant, as it protects both banks (holding bills of lading simply as security for loan credits advanced to buyers) and agents (simply holding bills against payments due under the sale contract) from incurring liabilities under the contract of carriage, until such time as the bank or the agent might (in the course of enforcing its security on, or obtaining physical control of, the goods), seek delivery of the goods from the carrier, or seek to prosecute a claim against the carrier.

The contractual rights and liabilities are transferred under COGSA 92 from one person to another. The transfer of rights gives the transferee the same contractual rights under the contract of carriage as if the transferee had been the original contracting party to that contract and extinguishes the contractual rights of the shipper, or other intermediate transferor, save to the extent that the goods are rejected by the buyer and revert to the seller (and, in the case of a bill of lading, the seller regains possession of the bill). Similarly, the transfer of liabilities makes the transferee subject to the same contractual liabilities under the contract of carriage as if the transferee had been the original contracting party to that contract and extinguishes the contractual liabilities of any intermediate transferor, although by s.3(3) this release is without prejudice to the liabilities of the original party to the contract, so that the shipper always retains its liability under the contract of carriage. By way of further preserving rights for cargo interests to claim for goods lost, damaged or delayed during carriage, s.2(4) provides that persons with rights of suit who have not suffered personal loss or damage

[262] *The Berge Sisar* [2002] 2 AC 205.

from the carrier's breach of contract are entitled to exercise their rights of suit for the benefit of the person suffering the loss.

3.1.7.2 Value of Claim

The measure of damages for a breach of the contract of carriage, or for tort, is the same in regard to the carriage of goods by sea as in the carriage of goods by land.[263] Where a bill of lading is issued, carriers by sea may be able to assert the protection of the Hague-Visby Rules (discussed at 3.3.2 below) but, aside from the protection of such statutory terms, carriers by sea may be entitled to rely on more generally applicable legislative stipulations to exclude or limit their liability.

(i) Statutory protection for claims arising from fire or theft of valuables

The owners of UK registered vessels have for well over a century had the benefit of statutory protection against liabilities arising from fire or the theft of valuables. This protection is currently provided by s.186 of the Merchant Shipping Act 1995 which provides that the owner (and any charterer, manager and operator)[264] of a UK ship

> "shall not be liable for any loss or damage ... (a) where any property on board the ship is lost or damaged by reason of fire on board the ship; or (b) where any gold, silver, watches, jewels or precious stones on board the ship are lost or damaged by reason of theft, robbery or other dishonest conduct and their nature and value were not at the time of shipment declared by their owner or shipper to the owner or master of the ship in the bill of lading or otherwise in writing";

and extends its protection to the master and crew of the vessel whilst acting in the course of their employment.

However, liability is not excluded for any loss or damage resulting from a "personal act or omission" within art.4 of the 1976 Limitation Convention.[265]

[263] For an impression of how the courts set about assessing damages see *Jag Dhir and Jag Shakti* [1986] 1 Lloyd's Rep. 1; *The Aramis* [1989] 1 Lloyd's Rep. 213; and 1.8.2.

[264] By s.186(2)(b) of the 1995 Act, protection is also extended to anyone else who may be the employer of the master and crew of the vessel.

[265] The Convention on Limitation of Liability for Maritime Claims 1976 scheduled to the 1995 Act at Sch.7, Pt 1.

Accordingly, in order to render those operating a UK registered ship liable for loss or damage by fire or to valuables by dishonest means it must be proved that the conduct of the liable person was such that "the loss resulted from his personal act or omission, committed with intent to cause such loss, or recklessly and with knowledge that such loss would probably result".[266] Section 186 only gives protection for those liabilities which attach to the defined class of persons (i.e. the owner, part owner and any charterer, manager or operator of the ship or other employer of the master or crew and the master and crew themselves) expressly protected by the section for losses occurring on UK registered ships.[267]

As the current statutory protection broadly restates that previously applicable under prior legislation, it is appropriate to interpret s.186 by reference to antecedent authority. It does not apply to losses on foreign registered ships, nor to the liabilities of carriers by sea not within the defined categories of persons expressly protected by the section. The section applies in the case of any damage caused by fire on board ship. It does not therefore apply where the fire occurs in the lighters alongside the ship,[268] or anywhere other than in the ship herself. However, where goods are damaged by being swamped by water used in the process of extinguishing a fire on board ship, the section does apply. The fact that the ship is unseaworthy does not prevent the shipowner from relying on s.186 because the section refers to a "United Kingdom ship" and not to a "seaworthy United Kingdom ship",[269] unless, of course, the loss by unseaworthiness was caused by conduct within art.4 of the 1976 Limitation Convention as discussed above. The shipowner is not absolved by s.186 from making general average contribution with respect to a general average sacrifice necessitated by a fire on board ship.[270] The parties are free to contract out of the provisions of s.186 relating to fire on board ship,[271]

[266] Article 4 of the 1976 Convention, a provision restrictively interpreted as requiring foresight of the very loss actually occurring and not merely the general type of loss as discussed at (ii) below.

[267] See ss.186(1),(2)(a) and (b) and (5).

[268] *Morewood v Pollok* (1853) 1 E. & B. 743.

[269] *Virginia Carolina Chemical Company v Norfolk and North American Steam Shipping Company* [1912] 1 K.B. 229, 241, per Buckley L.J. decided under the old 1894 Act.

[270] *Dreyfus and Company v Tempus Shipping Company* [1931] A.C. 726.

[271] *Virginia Carolina Chemical Company v Norfolk and North America Steam Shipping Company* ibid. *Ingram and Royle Ltd v Services Maritimes du Treport Ltd* [1914] 1 K.B. 541, 555, per Buckley L.J.; *Dreyfus and Company v Tempus Shipping Company* ibid. at p.733, per Lord Dunedin.

which provisions are effectively displaced by the Hague-Visby Rules when they apply.

Section 186 applies with regard to valuables only where the loss or damage is caused by robbery or other dishonest conduct.[272] The provisions are therefore less extensive than those of the Carriers Act 1830, relating to carriage of goods by land discussed at 2.2.3. However, s.186 does apply to all valuables of the class stated, however small the value of the article. The provisions apply to valuables of the class specified carried in passengers' luggage,[273] unless the passengers carry the valuables on their persons, or otherwise in such a manner that they are deemed to retain possession of the valuables and not to have entrusted them to the carrier at all.[274]

The declaration of value, which has the effect of displacing the statutory exclusion, will not be invalidated because it is not in fact strictly accurate provided that the shipper has made a bona fide estimate of the approximate value.[275] However, to make a valid declaration the shipper must name some value in terms of money. Where the shipper stated merely that the box contained "about 248 oz. of gold dust", it was held that this declaration was insufficient to prevent the operation of a predecessor statute.[276] The value need not be declared in terms of British currency but may be made in the currency of the state of the port of loading.[277]

(ii) Statutory limitation by reference to vessel tonnage

The policy of fixing a maximum sum as a limit to the amount of damages recoverable against the owners of a British ship was first adopted by Parliament in the Responsibility of Shipowners Act 1734. The policy was re-enacted in many Merchant Shipping Acts but is now one which is applied in the context of public international law, in particular by the provisions of the Convention on Limitation of Liability for Maritime Claims 1976 (the LLMC 1976) revised pursuant to the 1996 Protocol. The LLMC 1976, as so revised, has some 35 contracting states which together account for some 40.52 per cent of the world's tonnage.[278] Section 185(1) of

[272] Section 186(1b).

[273] *Acton v Castle Mail Packet Company* (1895) 1 Com. Cas. 135; *Smitton v Orient Steam Navigation Company* (1907) 12 Com. Cas. 270.

[274] *Smitton v Orient Steam Navigation Company* ibid.

[275] *Williams v African Steamship Company* (1856) 1 H. & N. 300, 304, per Martin B.

[276] *Williams v African Steamship Company* ibid. .

[277] *Gibbs v Potter* (1842) 10 M. & W. 70.

[278] According to the International Martime Organisation depositary information *http://www.imo.org* (August 2009).

the Merchant Shipping Act 1995 (MSA 1995) gives the LLMC 1976, as revised,[279] the force of law in the United Kingdom.

By art.1 of the LLMC 1996 the owners, charterers, managers, operators and salvors[280] of all vessels (i.e. not only vessels registered in the United Kingdom or other contracting states but also vessels registered in non-contracting states) are entitled to limit their liability for certain claims. The claims attracting the right to limit are set out in art.2 and include, amongst others, claims for loss of or damage to property occurring on board or in direct connection with the operation of the ship, or with salvage operations and claims in respect of loss resulting from delay in the carriage by sea of cargo. By art.3 claims for salvage and general average are excluded from limitation, as are claims for nuclear damage (when limitation is governed or prohibited by international convention or national legislation)[281] and claims by employees where the applicable law does not permit limitation. Claims for oil pollution are only excluded where governed by other international limitation treaty regimes. The United Kingdom is a contracting party to two distinct such oil pollution treaty regimes: (a) the International Convention on Civil Liability for Oil Pollution Damage (the 1992 Liability Convention) and the International Convention on the Establishment of an International Fund for Compensation for Oil Pollution Damage creating a liability and compensation regime for oil pollution damage from oil tankers;[282] and (b) the International Convention on Civil Liability for Bunker Oil Pollution Damage (the 2001 Bunkers Convention) creating a liability and compensation regime for fuel oil pollution damage from vessels other than oil tankers.[283] The scheme of protection for those entitled to limit under these distinct regimes for oil pollution damage operates in much the same way as the scheme arising under the LLMC 1976.

The LLMC 1976 provides that all claims made for damage arising on any

[279] The 1996 Protocol was applied in the UK by the Merchant Shipping (Convention on Limitation of Liability for Maritime Claims) (Amendment) Order 1998, made under s.185(2A) of the MSA 1995.

[280] As well as, pursuant to art.1(4), any other persons for whose act, neglect or default such owners etc. are responsible.

[281] Statutory instruments made under s.76 of the Energy Act 2004 provide for such limitations in the UK implementing applicable public international law pursuant to the Paris Convention on Third Party Liability in the Field of Nuclear Energy of 29 July 1960.

[282] Given the force of law in the UK by Pt VI of the MSA 1995.

[283] Given the force of law in the UK by the Merchant Shipping (Oil Pollution) (Bunkers Convention) Regulations 2006 (2006 No.1244) amending Pt VI of the MSA 1995.

distinct occasion are subject to aggregate financial limitation. Three distinct aggregate "funds" are established for three different classes of claim. Each fund, valued in special drawing rights (SDR) for each class of claim, is calculated by reference to the tonnage of the vessel. The three classes of claim which are recognised by the LLMC 1976 for the purposes of the calculation of the funds are:

(i) claims at art.6(1)(a) for loss of life or personal injury;
(ii) claims at art.6(1)(b) for anything other than loss of life or personal injury; and
(iii) claims at art.7 for loss of life or personal injury to passengers of the vessel.

The general aggregate limits provided for all claims, for anything other than loss of life or personal injury, under art.6(1)(b) (as revised by the 1996 Protocol) are:

(i) 1 million SDR for a ship with a tonnage not exceeding 2,000 tons;
(ii) for a ship with a tonnage in excess thereof the following additional amounts:

— for each ton from 2,001 to 30,000 tons, 400 SDR;
— for each ton from 30,001 to 70,000 tons, 300 SDR; and
— for each ton in excess of 70,000 tons, 200 SDR.

Article 11(1) provides that the limitation fund may be established in a contracting state in cash or by guarantee. Pursuant to art.13, once a limitation fund has been constituted, any person with a claim against the fund is barred from exercising any right in respect of such claim against any other assets of the person by, or on whose behalf, the fund has been established. Article 12(1) provides that the claims of each class of claimant will rank equally with other claims within that class in proportion to their respective established values. However, art.6(2) particularly provides for the situation where the fund under art.6(1)(a) is insufficient to pay in full the non-passenger claims for loss of life or personal injury. In those circumstances, the unpaid balance of such claims will rank ratably with those of the claimants under art.6(1)(b) for claims other than loss of life or personal injury. Article 12(2) provides for the situation where claims are paid prior to the establishment of the fund. In that event, the person making payment of the claim is subrogated to the claimants' rights against the fund. In the context of claims arising in connection with the loss, damage or delay to cargo, it should be borne in mind that the value of any claim against the limitation fund is to be calculated by reference to, and as limited by, the contract of carriage.[284]

It is possible for the limitation right arising under LLMC 1976 to be lost in one or other of the following situations. First, if and to the extent that liability can be both determined and enforced in a state in which the right to limit is not recognised. Secondly, in the event it is proved pursuant to art.4 that the loss resulted from the defendant's "personal act or omission, committed with the intent to cause such loss, or recklessly and with knowledge that such loss would probably result". This provision was considered in the *Leerort*[285] when the Court of Appeal held, in the context of a collision between two vessels, that it required not only deliberate or reckless disregard of safety or navigation on the part of the defendant but also awareness that such disregard was likely to result in a collision. It is very difficult indeed to prove such conduct under English law.

However, not all carriers under contracts of carriage will be entitled to limit. Only carriers falling within the art.1 definition of those entitled to limit will have the right to benefit from the financial limitations calculated by reference to the tonnage of the carrying vessel. This definition, (encompassing owners, charterers, managers or operators of the vessel and other persons for whose act, neglect or default they are responsible)[286] will exclude many non-vessel owning contracting carriers who have no proprietary, possessory or contractual interest in the carrying vessel but have simply agreed to carry goods by sea.

3.1.7.3 Time to Claim

The time available under English law for the commencement of proceedings for breach of contractual or tortious obligations owed in connection with the carriage of goods by sea is generally the same as discussed at 1.8.3. The carrier may, however, be able to assert shorter periods of limitation pursuant to any scheme of mandatory regulation that is (as discussed in 3.3 below) applicable to the carriage. Furthermore, a ship owner is entitled to assert the benefit of the statutory protection provided

[284] As regulated by any applicable mandatory regulation such as the Hague-Visby Rules discussed at 3.3.2 below.

[285] [2001] 2 Lloyd's Rep 291.

[286] Article 1(1) and (4).

by s.190 of the Merchant Shipping Act 1995. Section 190 applies a two year suit time limitation to proceedings "to enforce any claim or lien against a ship or her owners" for damage or loss caused "to another ship, its cargo or freight or any property on board it" and "for damages for loss of life or personal injury"; although any court with jurisdiction over such a claim has an unfettered discretion under s.190(5) to extend the two year period.

3.1.8 Miscellaneous Carriage Contract Rights

3.1.8.1 Freight

The carrier is entitled to be paid freight for the goods carried in its ship, and the shipper of the goods is liable to pay the freight notwithstanding any counter claim against the carrier,[287] unless it is expressly agreed that freight shall not be payable, or shall only be payable subject to set off. However, if the carrier does expressly agree to carry the cargo freight free, or only subject to a set-off, such an agreement is binding on the carrier and on any assignee (such as any purchaser or mortgagee of the ship where the shipowner is the carrier) of the carrier's interest in the contract of carriage, none of whom can then claim freight for the carriage of the goods, or alternatively can only claim freight subject to set-off.[288] The master has no implied authority to agree to carry goods freight free on behalf of the carrier.[289]

The liability to pay freight rests on the shipper, even if the shipper is acting as agent for the consignee or for some other principal.[290] The consignee is not liable under the original contract of carriage to pay the freight at common law.[291] The consignee may become liable under the provisions of s.3(1) of the Carriage of Goods by Sea Act 1992 (see 3.1.7.1 above) where the obligation of the shipper to pay freight has been included as a term in a contract of carriage evidenced by a bill of lading, sea waybill or ship's delivery order and the liabilities under such contract have been transferred to the consignee. Under the 1992 Act, liabilities will be transferred to the consignee where the consignee is the person to whom delivery of the goods by the carrier is to be made under s.2(1) and the consignee has

[287] *Annen v Woodman* (1810) 3 Taunt. 299; *Fox v Nott* (1861) 6 H. & N. 630.
[288] *Wilson v Gabriel* (1863) 4 B. & S. 243.
[289] *Dewell v Moxon* (1808) 1 Taunt. 391.
[290] *Fox v Nott* (fn. 287).
[291] *Sanders v Vanzeller* (1843) 4 Q.B. 260.

under s.3(1) either taken or demanded delivery of the goods, or made a claim against the carrier pursuant to the contract of carriage. The consignee and any other person may also be liable to pay freight if taking possession of the goods, or acting in any other way which implies that such person has made a new contract with the carrier to be liable for the freight.[292] For example, if the consignee takes possession of the goods when the carrier is claiming the right to exercise its lien on the goods for payment of the freight due from the shipper, the courts may infer that a contract has come into existence between the carrier and the consignee for the delivery of the goods against the payment of the freight.[293]

The freight is payable to the carrier under the contract of carriage. The carrier may assign the right to receive the freight.[294] The carrier may also assign the right to receive future freight to be earned on contracts of carriage which have been made but not yet performed.[295] Where the shipowner sells the ship during the term of a charterparty, or other contract of carriage, the purchaser of the ship may thereby acquire the right to claim the freight with respect to the goods carried on the ship,[296] but the sale of the ship does not operate as an assignment of the charterparty, or other contract of carriage, to the purchaser unless, as is usual, the contract is also expressly assigned.[297] Where the carrier as shipowner mortgages the ship during the currency of a contract of carriage, the shipowner is nevertheless entitled to the freight[298] unless the mortgagee has entered into constructive possession of the ship, in which case the freight is payable to the mortgagee.[299] The master has no implied authority from the carrier to agree that the freight shall be paid to any person other than the carrier.[300]

Where the contract of carriage is illegal, as for example where the purpose of the voyage is to trade with the enemy in time of war, the carrier cannot recover the freight.[301] A distinction must be drawn between this situation and the situation where the carrier commits a criminal offence in

[292] ibid.
[293] *Brandt v Liverpool, Brazil and River Plate Steam Navigation Company* [1924] 1 K.B. 575; and *The Aramis* [1987] Lloyd's Rep. 58; *The Captain Gregos* [1990] 2 Lloyd's Rep. 395; *The Dominique* [1989] 2 W.L.R 440 and as discussed at 1.6.1.2.
[294] *The Ship Warre* (1817) 8 Pri. 269n., per Lord Eldon L.C.
[295] *Douglas v Russell* (1831) 4 Sim. 524.
[296] *Morrison v Parsons* (1810) 2 Taunt. 407; *Lindsay v Gibbs* (1856) 22 Beav. 522.
[297] *Splidt v Bowles* (1808) 10 East 279; *Morrison v Parsons* ibid.
[298] *Keith v Burrows* (1877) 2 App. Cas. 636.
[299] *Gumm v Tyrie* (1865) 6 B. & S. 298.
[300] *Reynolds v Jex* (1865) 7 B. & S. 86.
[301] *Muller v Gernon* (1811) 3 Taunt. 394.

the course of carriage, for example by overloading the ship. This does not make the contract of carriage illegal so as to prevent the carrier from recovering the freight of the goods so unlawfully loaded.[302]

In the absence of any express term in the contract to the contrary, the freight is payable to the carrier on delivery of the goods to the consignee[303] or when the carrier is ready to deliver subject to the payment of the freight and the satisfaction of the lien for contributions for general average. The obligations of the carrier to deliver the goods and of the shipper to pay the freight are simultaneous. Consequently, the consignee cannot insist that all the goods be unloaded before the freight is paid.[304] In the absence of an express provision in the contract to the contrary, freight is only payable if the goods are delivered to the consignee at the agreed port of discharge.[305] If the carrier fails to tender delivery of the goods at the port of discharge (or at any other place where the carrier may be entitled under the terms of the contract to discharge the goods) the carrier is not entitled to any freight.[306] Accordingly, unless the contrary is expressly provided for in the contract, the carrier is not entitled to freight where goods have been seized by an enemy in wartime,[307] or by pirates,[308] or where they have been lost by an excepted peril, or on account of their inherent vice.[309] Nor is the carrier entitled to freight where the voyage has been frustrated on account of ice which prevents the ship from proceeding to the port of discharge.[310] Even if the carrier has brought the goods to the port of discharge, freight cannot be claimed if the goods are destroyed before the carrier has offered to deliver them to the consignee.[311]

If the goods are delivered to the consignee, the carrier may claim to be paid the freight in full, even if the goods are damaged,[312] unless set off is expressly provided for in the contract of carriage. Accordingly, if goods are damaged in the course of carriage the owner of the goods must have

[302] *St John Shipping Company v Joseph Rank Ltd* [1957] 1 Q.B. 267.
[303] *London Transport Company v Trechmann* [1904] 1 K.B. 635, 643, per Collins M.R.
[304] *Möller v Young* (1855) 24 L.J. (Q.B.) 217, 220, per Lord Campbell C.J., in the Court of Queen's Bench (not overruled on this point in the Court of Exchequer Chamber, 5 E. & B. 755).
[305] *St Enoch Shipping Company v Phosphate Mining Company* [1916] 2 K.B. 624.
[306] *Osgood v Groning* (1810) 2 Camp. 466.
[307] *Curling v Long* (1719) 1 Bos. and P. 634.
[308] *Bright v Cowper* (1611) 1 Brownl. 21.
[309] *Acatos v Burns* (1878) 3 Ex. D. 282.
[310] *Metcalfe v Britannia Ironworks Company* (1877) 2 Q.B.D. 423
[311] *Duthie v Hilton* (1868) L.R. 4 C.P. 138.
[312] *Dakin v Oxley* (1864) 15 C.B. (N.S.) 646.

recourse to an action for damages. However, if the goods are not in fact delivered to the consignee in specie (i.e. as contemplated by the contract of carriage), no freight is payable.[313] In order to determine whether or not the goods have been delivered in specie, the court must

> "ascertain from the terms of the contract construed by mercantile usage, if any, what was the thing for the carriage of which freight was to be paid, and ... determine whether that thing, or any and how much of it, has substantially arrived".[314]

If the goods are no longer in a merchantable state, they are deemed not to have been delivered in specie, and no freight is payable.[315] "Merchantable state" means that the goods themselves still have the same commercial identity as that contemplated by the contract and have some commercial value. When a consignment of dates was immersed in the River Thames, it was held they no longer had the same commercial identity as that contemplated by the contract, or any commercial value.[316] Where part of the goods are delivered in specie, pro rata freight is payable on those goods which have been delivered. Where freight, other than advance freight, has been paid early prior to the delivery of the goods, the shipper may recover the freight if the cargo is not delivered to the consignee for any reason.[317]

Where goods are carried in bulk, the contract usually provides that freight shall be payable according to the weight of the cargo. This would generally be implied in any event, unless the contrary was indicated by the circumstances of, or some express provision in, the contract. Where the freight is assessed on the weight of the goods, the carrier is entitled to freight on the maximum weight of the cargo carried throughout the whole voyage from the port of loading to the port of destination. Consequently, where the weight of the goods has increased or decreased during the voyage, freight is actually payable on the lowest weight of the goods during the voyage.[318] In calculating the weight, the method of calculation in force at the port of loading must be adopted,[319] unless there is an express term in the contract, or a custom, to the contrary. The costs of weighing the goods

[313] ibid.
[314] ibid.
[315] ibid.
[316] *Asfar v Blundell* [1896] 1 Q.B. 123.
[317] *Krall v Burnett* (1877) 25 W.R. 305.
[318] *Gibson v Sturge* (1855) 10 Exch. 622; *Shand v Grant* (1863) 15 C.B. (N.S.) 324.
[319] *Pust v Dowie* (1865) 5 B. & S. 20.

must be borne by the party who wants to weigh them, and consequently if the carrier insists on weighing the goods the carrier must bear the cost,[320] unless there is an express agreement, or a custom,[321] to the contrary.

It was formerly the practice for the shipper to agree to pay a sum, known as "primage", to the ship's master for his personal remuneration. Where a provision for the payment of primage is included in the bill of lading and the master has signed it, the master is entitled to sue the shipper for the primage.[322] However, where the terms of the contract between the carrier and the master provide for the master to pay over the primage to the carrier in consideration of receiving a fixed salary from the carrier, neither the master nor the carrier can claim primage from the shipper. This may remain the case even though the bill of lading might contain a statement that primage shall be paid, since primage is, by its nature, a sum payable to the master for his own use.[323] If the master has notice that the carrier and the shipper have not included any provision for the payment of primage in the contract of carriage, the master is estopped from claiming primage.[324] In more recent times where shore-based agents arrange contracts of carriage for commission, the practice of paying a master primage has been abandoned. Where the master has signed the bill of lading and the bill of lading contains provisions with regard to the payment of freight, the master, as a party to the contract contained in the bill of lading, may sue the shipper[325] for the freight but if the master recovers the freight, it must be paid over to the carrier.

It is a clearly established principle that claims about cargo (non-delivery or damage) cannot be set off against claims for freight. Thus where a cargo of petroleum was short delivered and the owners deducted $30,000 from the freight payable, they were ordered to pay the entire freight due, even though they had lost the right to claim for short delivery; since, having deducted their claim from freight in purported satisfaction of their claim for loss, they had allowed time to pass and their claim had become statute-barred.[326] Section 3(3) of the Carriage of Goods by Sea Act 1992 provides that notwithstanding the statutory assignment of liabilities under the contract of carriage to the consignee or some other person, the original shipper

[320] *Annen v Woodman* (1810) 3 Taunt. 299; *Coulthurst v Sweet* (1866) L.R. 1 C.P. 649.
[321] ibid.
[322] *Best v Saunders* (1828) Mood. & M. 208.
[323] *Caughey v Gordon and Company* (1878) 3 C.P.D. 419.
[324] *Best v Saunders* (fn. 322), at p.212, per Lord Tenterden C.J.
[325] See *Brouncker v Scott* (1811) 4 Taunt. 1, 4, per Mansfield C.J.
[326] *Aries Tanker Corp. v Total Transport* [1977] 1 W.L.R. 185.

remains liable to the carrier under the contract. Accordingly, where such statutory transfer has taken place the carrier may seek to recover freight either from the shipper or the consignee (as statutory transferee). The carrier has a duty to mitigate its loss in respect of agreed, but unearned, freight by agreeing, where possible, to carry replacement cargo.

Generally, contracts of carriage make express written provision for the calculation and payment of freight which may be expressed payable in a number of ways such as: lump freight, advance freight, pro-rata freight, dead freight or as hire charges, the meanings of which terms are set out below.

(i) Lump freight is an arrangement where the parties agree that the shipper shall pay the carrier a fixed sum in lieu of freight in consideration of the carriage of the goods by the carrier. Where the contract provides for the payment of lump freight, the entire amount of the lump freight must be paid if the carrier delivers any part of the cargo carried in specie,[327] leaving the owner of the cargo to claim damages for the remainder of the cargo which is undelivered.

(ii) Advance freight constitutes an agreement that the shipper will pay the freight, or more often a certain agreed part of it, to the carrier in advance of delivery on the basis that such sum is to be payable in any event, even if none of the goods are delivered to the consignee. However, the fact that the shipper pays money for disbursements to the carrier[328] will not necessarily mean that this sum is to be regarded as advance freight, which the carrier could retain if the goods were lost during carriage. Similarly, where the contract provides that the freight shall be payable at the port of loading, this is not to be interpreted as meaning that the freight so payable shall be advance freight.[329] Conversely, a contractual arrangement giving the shipper the option of paying a lower rate of freight at the port of loading, or a higher rate at the port of discharge, was interpreted as meaning that, if the shipper chose to pay the lower rate, it was to be regarded as advance freight.[330] Where the shipper has agreed to pay advance freight, the liability

[327] *Merchant Shipping Company v Armitage* (1873) L.R. 9 Q.B. 99, 110, per Bramwell B.
[328] *Manfield v Maitland* (1821) 4 B. & Ald. 582.
[329] *Mashiter v Buller* (1807) 1 Camp. 84.
[330] *Andrew v Moorhouse* (1814) 5 Taunt. 435.

to pay it apparently arises, in the absence of an express agreement to the contrary, at the time when the ship sails from the port of loading.[331] The carrier is entitled to retain any advance freight paid, or due to be paid, if the goods are lost,[332] provided that the advance freight was paid, or that the liability to pay it arose, before the loss. However, where under the contract the carrier had an option to fix a certain proportion of the freight to be payable as advance freight, the carrier was held to be unable to claim any advance freight where this option had not been exercised before the time of the loss.[333] Where advance freight has been paid in respect of all the goods delivered to the carrier and part of the goods have been lost, the shipper may credit the sum paid as advance freight as being paid with respect to those goods that have not been lost, and not as being distributed pro rata between those lost and those not lost.[334] In consequence, the carrier effectively loses the protection of the advance freight in respect of the goods lost, as the shipper may credit the sum paid as advance freight towards the liability to pay freight only on the goods actually delivered to the consignee. However, all such issues concerning the interpretation of arrangements for advance freight and alternative freight arrangements are to be determined in the context and particular circumstances of the particular contract of carriage to which such issues relate.[335]

(iii) Pro rata freight is an arrangement whereby the shipper agrees to pay pro rata freight on goods which are not delivered to the consignee with respect to that part of the journey on which they have actually been carried. Such an agreement will generally not be implied and will require clear express agreement between the shipper and the carrier.[336]

(iv) Dead freight is effectively a liquidated damages provision obliging

[331] *Smith, Hill and Company v Pyman, Bell and Company* [1891] 1 Q.B. 742, 744, per Lord Esher M.R.

[332] *De Silvale v Kendall* (1815) 4 M. & S. 37; *Allison v Bristol Marine Insurance Company* (1876) 1 App. Cas. 209.

[333] *Smith, Hill and Company v Pyman, Bell and Company* (fn. 331).

[334] *Allison v Bristol Marine Insurance Company* (1876) 1 App. Cas. 209.

[335] Applying the principles referred to in 1.5.2.

[336] *Mitchell v Darthez* (1836) 2 Bing. N.C. 555; *St Enoch Shipping Company v Phosphate Mining Company* [1916] 2 K.B. 624.

a charterer, who is in breach of contract by failing to load a full cargo or indeed any cargo, to pay some or all of the freight lost.

(v) Hire charges effectively constitute charges for the carriage of goods where the arrangements for carriage are concluded by a contract of carriage in the form of a time charterparty, where the carrying vessel is hired for a period of time, rather than a voyage or succession of voyages. Such arrangements are reviewed at 3.2.1.

3.1.8.2 Carriers' Lien

At common law, the carrier by sea has a common law lien on the goods carried in respect of all sums due for freight properly so called[337] and for general average contribution.[338] He has no lien in respect of sums due as advance freight,[339] dead freight,[340] demurrage,[341] or for freight payable at an agreed date after delivery and not on delivery in the usual way. The carrier has no lien in respect of any other sums owed by the cargo owner in connection with other transactions.[342] The carrier may, however, acquire such a lien, commonly called a general lien, for all or any of such sums due in respect of other transactions by expressly agreeing in the contract of carriage a term providing for such a general lien.[343]

The carrier has a lien, at common law, not only in respect of the freight and general average contribution due in respect of the goods upon which the lien is exercised, but for sums due for freight and general average in respect of all the goods of the same owner in the same ship on the same voyage.[344] This applies even where the goods are carried under different bills of lading.[345] However, where the bills of lading have been endorsed, or delivered, to different endorsees or holders the carrier may not exercise, against one endorsee, a lien in respect of freight and general average

[337] *Anonymous* (1701) 12 Mod. Rep. 447 (Case 779), per Holt C.J.

[338] *Crooks v Allan* (1987) 5 Q.B.D. 38.

[339] *Kirchner v Venus* (1859) 12 Moo. P.C.C. 361; *How v Kirchner* (1857) 11 Moo. P.C.C. 21.

[340] *Philips v Rodie* (1812) 15 East 547; *Burley v Gladstone* (1814) 3 M. & S. 205.

[341] *Burley v Gladstone* (1814) 3 M. & S. 205.

[342] *Oppenheim v Russell* (1802) 3 Bos. & P. 42.

[343] *McLean and Hope v Fleming* (1871) L.R. 2 H.L. Sc. 128.

[344] *Bernal v Pim* (1835) 1 Gale 17.

[345] *Sodergren v Flight and Jennings* (1796) cited in *Hanson v Mayer* at 6 East 622.

contribution due on goods comprised in a bill of lading which has not been transferred, or has been transferred to another endorsee.[346]

The lien is lost if the carrier delivers the goods to the consignee, unless the carrier was induced to do so by fraud. The carrier may, however, deliver some of the goods on which it has a lien whilst continuing to exercise a lien on other goods retained in respect of sums owing on them.[347] If the carrier discharges the goods into one of its own warehouses, the lien continues to be held, as the carrier is still in possession of the goods.[348] However, where the carrier discharges the goods into a warehouse of a third party, the carrier loses the lien at common law,[349] although the lien may revive if the carrier obtains possession of the goods once more. If the carrier takes a bill of exchange in payment for goods in respect of which a lien is being exercised, the lien is lost, since taking the bill of exchange waives the carrier's right to be paid in cash forthwith, and thereby the carrier's right to exercise the lien.[350] Formerly the carrier also enjoyed a more extensive statutory lien arising under ss.492–501 of the Merchant Shipping Act 1894; but on the recommendation of the Law Commission these provisions were repealed, without re-enactment elsewhere, by the Statute Law (Repeals) Act 1993.

Where the carrier has acquired a contractual lien, which may specifically include a lien for dead or advance freight, such lien is only enforceable against the other party to the contract. Thus where, by the contract of carriage with the shipper, the carrier has acquired a lien in respect of advance freight, the lien cannot be enforced against the endorsee of the bill of lading (even if the endorsee had notice of the contractual lien when acquiring the bill of lading) unless the term as to the contractual lien is actually incorporated into the bill of lading.[351] Where the contractual lien is incorporated into the bill of lading (or sea waybill or ship's delivery order) it is enforceable against any consignee to whom contractual liabilities arising thereunder have been transferred by the Carriage of Goods by Sea Act 1992.

An agent who is in possession of the bill of lading has generally implied authority to pay the carrier the sums due to obtain the release of the goods

[346] ibid.
[347] ibid.
[348] *Mors-le-Blanch v Wilson* (1873) L.R. 8 C.P. 227.
[349] ibid.
[350] *Tamvaco v Simpson* (1866) L.R. 1 C.P. 363.
[351] *McLean and Hope v Fleming* (1871) L.R. 2 H.L. Sc. 128.

from the carrier's lien.[352] In such a case, the agent also has a lien on the goods in respect of the sum paid to the carrier.[353] Where the owner of the goods is indebted in respect of a general average contribution, the carrier may exercise its lien in order to obtain payment of the sums owed to the other cargo owners[354] as well as those owing to itself in respect of the general average contribution. Should the carrier fail to exercise its lien to recover such general average contribution, the carrier will itself be liable to the other cargo owners for any loss of the contribution due.[355] Where the carrier discharges goods into the custody of a warehouseman to hold them to the carrier's order and not to release them to the consignee in any circumstances, the warehouseman is bound to obey the carrier's instructions.[356] The carrier and warehouseman may, of course, be liable to the consignee if they are not justified in withholding delivery; in such circumstances the warehouseman should be entitled to an indemnity from the carrier for any loss it suffers through adhering to the instructions of the carrier.

3.1.8.3 Customers' Stoppage Rights

The right of an unpaid seller of goods to stop goods in transit where the buyer is insolvent is in general governed by the same principles where the goods are carried by sea as where they are carried by land. In the case of carriage by sea however, the issue may be complicated by the transfer of the bill of lading. The effect of such transfer on the seller's right of stoppage in transit is governed by s.47 of the Sale of Goods Act 1979. Section 47(1) provides that disposition or sale of the goods by the buyer shall not affect the unpaid seller's right of stoppage in transit. However, s.47(2) goes on to state that, where the buyer is in lawful possession of a document of title, the transfer by the buyer of that document to a person who takes it in good faith and for valuable consideration either defeats the unpaid seller's right under s.47(2)(a) (where such person acts as a buyer in taking over the document of title); or fetters the unpaid seller's right under s.47(2)(b) (where the transfer of the document of title was made by way of pledge, or

[352] *Hingston v Wendt* (1876) 1 Q.B.D. 367.
[353] ibid.
[354] *Crooks v Allan* (1879) 3 Q.B.D. 38.
[355] ibid.
[356] *Dennis and Sons v Cork Steamship Company* [1913] 2 K.B. 393.

other disposition for value), by making the exercise of such right subject to the rights of the transferee.

Thus, where the seller transfers the bill of lading to the buyer, the seller's right of stoppage in transit is not defeated. However, that right will be lost where the buyer makes a further delivery of the bill of lading, by way of transfer of the ownership of goods, to a holder for valuable consideration who has no notice of the seller's right of stoppage in transit. Where the buyer transfers the bill of lading not by way of property transfer but merely as security for a pledge, the seller's right of stoppage in transit remains in force subject to the rights of the pledgee or mortgagee. The seller's right of stoppage in transit is not in any way affected where the buyer transfers the ownership of the goods, or grants a pledge or mortgage on them, unless such transfer of ownership or pledge or mortgage is accompanied by the transfer of a bill of lading or other document of title to the goods.

3.1.9 Common Carriers by Sea

As with carriage by land, it was possible under the common law for a carrier by sea to have the status of a common carrier, although that status is easily avoided. Indeed, in the modern era, it would be as extraordinary for a carrier by sea as for a carrier by road to be invested with that status.[357] At common law there was uncertainty whether, in connection with carriage of goods by sea and/or inland waterway, there were two or three categories of carrier (i.e. common and contractual carriers; or common, public and incidental carriers). While there is no doubt that, with regard to the carriage of goods by land, any carrier who is not a common carrier is a contractual carrier, judges in former times sometimes[358] divided those carriers by sea and inland waterway who were not common carriers into: public carriers, who were not obliged to carry goods but if they did so were (in the absence of a special contract) liable as if they were common carriers; and private carriers, who did not generally carry goods but if they carried goods incidentally to their main business, or only for one consignor, would be in the same position as the contractual carrier of goods by land.[359] Since the Hague Rules were first incorporated into English law in 1924, there does

[357] See 1.1 and 1.10.1.

[358] See the judgments of Lord Esher in *Liver Alkali Company v Johnson* (1874) L.R. 9 Ex. 338, 343, and Brett J. in *Nugent v Smith* (1875) 1 C.P.D. 19; although the view was criticised by Cockburn C.J. in *Nugent v Smith* in the Court of Appeal (1876) 1 C.P.D. 423, 425.

[359] *Consolidated Tea and Lands Company v Oliver's Wharf* [1910] 2 K.B. 395.

not appear to be a single case applying this classification. Consequently, as with carriers by land, it is probably more appropriate simply to talk of common and contractual carriers.

The arcane principles relating to common carriers have little relevance to current shipping practices in which goods are invariably shipped pursuant to contracts of carriage with contractual carriers. If and to the extent that any carrier generally and as a matter of common practice were to undertake carriage of goods by sea for reward as common carriers and not pursuant to private contracts of carriage, they would be under the same duties and liabilities as the common carrier by land.[360] The common carrier by sea does have one additional defence to those five also enjoyed by the carrier by land: namely, the defence of jettison, which is available in the case of common carriers only for carriage by sea. The defence of jettison is open to the carrier where the goods have been intentionally sacrificed in order to preserve the safety of the ship and other cargo; however, whilst the ship owner is relieved of liability, the loss will constitute a general average loss to which all those participating in the marine adventure, including the carrier, are obliged to contribute (see 3.1.4.3). The jettisoning of the goods does not deprive the owner of ownership of the goods. If the goods are washed ashore and found, the finder does not acquire ownership of them,[361] but is obliged to hand them over to the receiver of wrecks. The common carrier by sea is under the same liability for negligence as is the common carrier of goods by land. Where any such negligence on the part of the common carrier by sea is a contributory cause of any loss or damage resulting from an act of God, the Queen's enemies, the fault of the cargo owner or shipper, inherent vice or jettison the carrier remains liable.[362]

3.2 Forms of Contract for Sea Carriage

3.2.1 Charterparty Contracts

3.2.1.1 Nature of a Charterparty Contract

A charterparty is a contract whereby a shipowner places its ship at the disposal of the charterer, either for the duration of a voyage or series of

[360] *Morse v Slue* (1673) 1 Vent. 238, per Hale C.J.; *Barclay v Cuculla y Gana* (1784) 3 Doug. K.B. 389, per Lord Mansfield C.J.

[361] *Tucker v Cappes* (1625) 2 Roll. Rep. 497, 498, per Dodridge J.

[362] *Siordet v Hall* (1828) 4 Bing. 607.

voyages (voyage charter) or for a given length of time (time charter). It is a type of contract that, as Lord Diplock remarked in 1973 (when giving judgment in the *Johanna Oldendorff* case[363] and as could still be said today), "has been the subject of minimal intervention by Parliament"[364] nor, indeed, by public international law.[365] A charterparty may be either a demise charter, by which possession of the ship is let to the charterer, or a non-demise charter, by which the ship remains in the possession of the ship owner whilst its economic use is placed at the disposal of the charterer. Whether a ship is chartered by voyage or time, the chartering arrangements may be by way of demise or non-demise. The distinction is that, where the charterparty is made by way of demise, the shipowner no longer has possession of the ship and, in consequence, the demise charterer and not the shipowner is exposed to vicarious liability for the actions of the master and crew of the vessel.[366]

Demise charterparty arrangements may involve the letting of possession to the charterer in one of two ways: either of the vessel alone, characterised as a bareboat arrangement, or of the vessel together with its master and crew, characterised as a demise arrangement. In either case, the vessel will have been let to the charterer for the charterer's own use, control and risk. Whilst a demise arrangement properly remains a contract of affreightment, it would be inappropriate to characterise a charterparty by way of demise as a contract of carriage, since in such circumstances the shipowner has not agreed to carry the bareboat or demise charterer's goods at all, rather the shipowner has simply leased its vessel to the demise charterer to use as it wishes subject to the terms of the charterparty. Consequently, where goods are shipped on board the vessel by persons other than the demise charterer pursuant to bills of lading, or other documents, signed by or on behalf of the master of the vessel, contracts of affreightment will come into being between those shippers and the demise charterer and not the shipowner.[367] In such a case, the demise charterer is the carrier of the goods shipped[368]

[363] *E.L. Oldendorff & Co GmbH v Tradax Export SA* [1974] A.C. 479.

[364] ibid. at p.554 in the context of a voyage charterparty.

[365] None of the Hague, Hague-Visby, Hamburg or Rotterdam Rules apply to contracts of carriage solely governed by charterparty; unless such international public law regimes are expressly incorporated into the charterparty by agreement between the parties by clause paramount as discussed in 3.2.1.3, 3.2.1.4 and 3.2.3.5 below.

[366] *Baumwoll Manufactur v Furness* [1893] A.C. 8.

[367] *Belcher v Capper* (1842) 4 Man. & G. 502.

[368] *Baumwoll Manufactur v Furness* (fn. 366).

and is liable accordingly to the owners of the goods under the contract of carriage. Should the demise charterer also ship its own goods on the vessel, the demise charterer will, effectively, be carrying its own goods.

Conversely, in a charterparty not by way of demise, the master and crew are the servants of the shipowner and it is appropriate to characterise the charterparty relationship as a contract of carriage (at least where it is for one or more voyages, rather than a period of time)[369] as the shipowner remains in charge of the vessel and is the carrier of all goods shipped by the charterer.[370] Where goods are shipped on board the vessel by persons other than the charterer, pursuant to bills of lading, or other documents, signed by or on behalf of the master of the vessel, it will be assumed that the master acts as agent of the shipowner and further contracts of carriage will come into being between those shippers and the shipowner and not the charterer of the vessel,[371] unless there is any indication to the contrary on the face of the bill of lading or other document evidencing the contract of carriage with the shipper.[372] Where there is any such contrary indication it will be a matter of interpretation of the face of the bill of lading, or other document evidencing the contract of carriage, to determine in what capacity and for whom the person who issued the relevant document was acting.[373] Issues relating to the effect of a bill of lading, issued to or by or transferred from a charterer, are discussed in relation to bills of lading at 3.2.3.5; whilst the effects of mandatory regulation on the terms of contracts of carriage are considered at 3.3 below.

The distinction between charterparties by way of demise and not has been judicially characterised as

> "the difference between hiring a boat in which to row yourself about, in which case the boat is handed over to you, and contracting with a man on the beach that he shall take you for a row, in which case he merely renders services to you in rowing you about".[374]

[369] *Hill Harmony* [2001] 1 A.C. 638, 653 where, in acknowledging non-demise voyage charters as contracts of carriage, Lord Hobhouse contrasted them from time charters which he characterised as "not a contract of carriage but a contract for the provision of the services of a crewed vessel".

[370] *Sandeman v Scurr* (1866) L.R. 2 Q.B. 86, 96, per Cockburn C.J.

[371] ibid.

[372] *Homburg Houtimport BV v Agrosin Private Ltd (The Starsin)* [2003] 1 Lloyd's Rep. 571.

[373] ibid.

[374] Per Mackinnnon L.J. in *Sea & Land Securities Ltd v William Dickinson & Co Ltd* [1942] 2 KB 65, 69.

The forms of charterparty used for these two categories of distinct relationships may be strikingly similar both in form and wording. For instance, both demise charters[375] and time charters not by way of demise[376] refer to the letting and the hiring of the vessel; but all that is meant by such wording in a time charter not by way of demise is that the charterer may ship goods aboard the vessel at load ports and have them carried by the owner to discharge ports for redelivery.[377] It is in every case a question of fact, dependent on all the relevant circumstances and the nature of the contractual obligations undertaken by the parties, whether a charterparty is by way of demise or not by way of demise.[378] The fact that the master and crew are to be appointed by the charterer does not necessarily mean that the charterparty is a charterparty by way of demise, for the fact that they are to be appointed by the charterer does not preclude them from being the servants of the shipowner.[379] Nor does the fact that the shipowner pays the master and crew necessarily preclude the charterparty from being a charterparty by way of demise.[380]

The majority of charterparties concluded in recent times are charterparties not by way of demise. Such non-demise forms of charterparty are very common in connection with the carriage of goods by sea. There may be several such charter arrangements in place in relation to any particular vessel on any particular voyage. This creates a chain of successive charterparty contracts extending a line of contractual entitlement to the vessel from its ultimate owner through successive disponent owners sub-chartering the vessel on to successive charterers. Each sub-charterer effectively

[375] See cl.2 of the BARECON 2001 standard bareboat charter recommended by BIMCO which states "... the Owners have agreed to let and the Charterers have agreed to hire the Vessel for the period ... ".

[376] See cl.1 of the NYPE 93 form of time charter recommended by BIMCO which states "The Owners agree to let and the Charterers agree to hire the Vessel from the time of delivery for a period ... ".

[377] As Mackinnon L.J. commented in the *Sea & Land Securities* case (fn. 374) at p.69, before defining the "essential nature" of a time charter not by way of demise as "a contract that the shipowners during a certain period of time agree to perform certain services for the charterers".

[378] ibid.

[379] *Harris v Best, Ryley and Company* (1892) 68 L.T. 76; *Sandeman v Scurr* (fn. 370), at p.98, per Cockburn C.J.; *Canadian Transport Company v Court Line* [1940] A.C. 934, 943, per Lord Wright.

[380] *Colvin v Newberry* (1832) 1 Cl. & F. 283.

becomes a disponent owner opposite its own sub-charterer under their own discrete chartering arrangements. Where the disponent owner is a demise charterer and has the authority of the owner to sub-charter the vessel by demise, those sub-chartering arrangements may be by demise. However, generally they are not; sub-charters frequently take the form of a time charter or of a voyage charter. The form of the sub-charter will not necessarily be determined by the form of charter held by the disponent owner and a time charter will commonly conclude sub-charters on a time or a voyage basis.

The master generally has no implied authority to sign charterparties as agent for the shipowner. Although isolated case authorities[381] from previous centuries indicate that masters have, by exception, been held to have such authority where the ship is in a distant port from which it is difficult to communicate with the shipowner, the factual circumstances, which gave rise to such authorities, are far more unlikely in more modern times. Nevertheless the authority to sign charterparties on behalf of the shipowner may be expressly given to the master[382] but is now far more likely to be given to chartering agents. The parties to a charterparty cannot obtain a decree of specific performance of the charterparty, but an injunction will be granted to the charterer restraining the shipowner, or a purchaser who has purchased the ship with notice of the charterparty, from putting the ship to a use which is inconsistent with the charterparty.[383] The applicable law and jurisdiction of a charterparty will be determined by the courts of England and Wales according to the principles set out at 1.4. Parties to a charterparty arrangement may have recourse to the procedure of ship arrest as a mechanism for establishing security or jurisdiction for their claims as described at 3.1.3; as claims under charterparties are included within the s.20(2) definition of admiralty actions supporting claims in rem.[384] Standard charterparty terms recommended by BIMCO generally provide for a choice of alternative law and jurisdiction clauses; a choice which should be exercised by the parties when agreeing the charter. Commonly available choices include English law and arbitration in London; or US maritime law and

[381] *The Fanny, The Mathilda* (1883) 48 L.T. 771.

[382] *Messageries Impriales Company v Baines* (1863) 7 L.T. 763.

[383] *Lord Strathcona Steamship Company v Dominion Coal Company* [1926] A.C. 108.

[384] Section 20(2)(h) of the 1981 Act expressly includes "h)any claim arising out of any agreement relating to the carriage of goods in a ship or to the use or hire of a ship".

New York arbitration;[385] or for some other law and jurisdiction to be chosen by the parties.[386]

It is usual for all charterparties, whether by demise or not, to contain certain factual stipulations such as the name of the ship; the nationality of the ship;[387] the class of the ship;[388] the carrying capacity of the ship; the registered tonnage of the ship; the names of the contracting parties (i.e. the owner or disponent owner of the ship and the charterer); the agreed hire or freight charges payable by the charterer; the dates for delivery[389] and redelivery[390] of the ship under the charterparty; and a cancellation date. These factual stipulations are generally incorporated within a summary frontsheet to which are appended detailed terms,[391] although it is a frequent occurrence for those terms to be amended by the parties.

Where charterparties are subject to English law, their proper construction in the event of dispute is subject to the principles outlined in 1.5. However, prior judicial interpretations of common clauses and stipulations in analogous charterparty arrangements are most likely to be followed, not least because English judges are concerned to safeguard contractual certainty in commercial relationships. In this context it is clear that a stipulation as to the nationality of the ship is likely to be construed as a warranty.[392] Accordingly, if a shipowner transfers ownership of the ship

[385] See cll.30(a) and 30(b) of Barecon 2001; 22(A) and 22(B) of Baltime 1939; 45(a) and 45(b) of NYPE 93 where they are the only choices proposed by the standard terms; and 19(a) and 19(b) of the Gencon charter.

[386] ibid., at sub-clauses (c) to each clause mentioned save as to NYPE 93.

[387] Being the state in which the vessel is registered (i.e. the flag state).

[388] Merchant vessels are classed by classification societies according to international rules that categorise merchant vessels according to type, e.g. Ro-Ro container; bulk container carrier; crude oil tanker, etc. The significance of ship classification and the roles, duties and liabilities of classification societies are further discussed in 5.3.5.

[389] Expressed in voyage charters as the date by which the vessel is exprected to be ready to load e.g. see cl.1 of the Gencon form of voyage charter.

[390] Although redelivery dates are not generally expressed in voyage charters as the chartering arrangement will only continue for the period of the agreed voyage, or voyages, which period will cease on discharge of the delivery of the cargo under the charter e.g. see Gencon cl.1 which contemplates delivery at the agreed discharge port or delivery place "or so near thereto as she may safely get".

[391] Although by no means invariably; indeed the commonly used NYPE 93 form of non-demise time charter is designed so that the information can be handwritten or typed within the body of the detailed terms.

[392] *Reusse v Meyers* (1813) 3 Camp. 475; *Isaacs and Sons v McAllum and Company* [1921] 3 K.B. 377.

during the period of the charter in circumstances which result in a change of the registered nationality of the ship, the owner commits a breach of contract for which the charterer may obtain damages.[393] In the absence of any contractual restriction on assignment, the shipowner is entitled to transfer the ownership of the ship during the charterparty where this does not involve a change in the nationality of the ship, save where by so doing, the shipowner prevents the performance of the charterparty.[394] Where ownership of the ship is transferred during the operation of the charter-party, the purchaser of the ship is *ordinarily* entitled to the freight in respect of the goods shipped on it.[395] However, the rights and liabilities under the charterparty and any other contracts of carriage are not transferred to the purchaser of the ship unless expressly assigned to him.[396] The stipulation as to the class of the ship is generally construed as a condition precedent to the charterparty taking effect[397] but may not necessarily be construed as a warranty that, at the date of the charterparty, the ship retains the classification.[398]

The stipulation as to the carrying capacity and registered tonnage of the ship may be a condition precedent to the charterparty where the charterer has undertaken to load a full cargo, and the carrying capacity or registered tonnage is relevant in determining what constitutes a full cargo; otherwise, it is unlikely to be construed as a condition precedent, and may not amount even to a warranty if it is irrelevant.[399] Any stipulation expressed as to the position of the ship is likely to be construed as a condition precedent or as a fundamental term. Where, at the time of the making of the charterparty, the ship was in fact 62 miles from the place where she was stated to be in the charterparty, the charterer was held entitled to treat the charterparty as repudiated, and refuse to load.[400] Modern charters generally make express provision as to the time at which the charter is to commence but there are significant distinctions in this respect between time and voyage charters which are explored at 3.2.1.3 and 3.2.1.4 below. Irrespective of whether the type of charterparty arrangement is by way of demise and/or for a period

[393] *Isaacs and Sons v McAllum and Company* [1921] 3 K.B. 377, per Rowlatt J.
[394] *Fratelli Sorrentino v Buerger* [1915] 3 K.B. 367, 371–2, per Buckley L.J.
[395] *Morrison v Parsons* (1810) 2 Taunt. 407; *Lindsay v Gibbs* (1856) 22 Beav. 522.
[396] *Morrison v Parsons* ibid.; *Splidt v Bowles* (1808) 10 East 279.
[397] *French v Newgass* (1878) 3 C.P.D. 163.
[398] ibid.
[399] *Hunter v Fry* (1819) 2 B. & Ald. 421, 424, per Abbott C.J.; *Barker v Windle* (1856) 6 E. & B. 675.
[400] *Behn v Burness* (1863) 3 B. & S. 751.

of time or for one or more particular voyage(s), charterparties will also generally incorporate express terms as to such matters as the seaworthiness of the vessel, the applicable law and jurisdiction for any dispute arising under the charterparty (as discussed above), the cancellation of the charterparty and the payment of hire or freight charges. With the sole exception of law and jurisdiction arrangements, all such provisions raise distinct issues in the contrasting contexts of time and voyage charterparty arrangements as discussed at 3.2.1.3 and 3.2.1.4 below; however, some general comments are appropriate as regards seaworthiness and cancellation.

Seaworthiness stipulations that the ship is fit for the purposes of the voyage will not generally be construed as conditions precedent,[401] nor, as already discussed at 3.1.4 and 3.1.6 above, are seaworthiness obligations likely to be construed as fundamental terms. Express contractual stipulations as to the fitness of the vessel should be distinguished from the implied warranty of seaworthiness arising, as previously discussed at 3.1.4 above, when the goods of the charterer are loaded and when the voyage, or the stages of the voyage, begin. An express stipulation that the ship is fit for the charter voyage or charter period is generally considered to refer to the condition of the ship at the time when it begins service under the charterparty.[402] Such an express stipulation may exclude or qualify the implied warranty of seaworthiness but in the absence of clear and express wording to such effect[403] charterers will also be entitled to the benefit of the implied warranty of seaworthiness at common law.[404] The charterparty will usually contain provisions excepting the shipowner from liability in respect of the usual excepted perils. It depends on the construction of the charterparty whether these excepted perils apply only with regard to the liability of the shipowner as a carrier of goods shipped or to be shipped under the charter, or whether they also apply to exempt the owner from liability where the ship fails to reach the port of loading, or of delivery. Where the charterparty contains a provision that the excepted perils are to apply "during the voyage", this will be construed, in the absence of any indication to the contrary, as applying to the period while the ship is proceeding to the port

[401] *Tarrabochia v Hickie* (1856) 1 H. & N. 183, 186, per Pollock C.B.

[402] *New York and Cuba Mail Steamship Company v Eriksen* (1922) 27 Com. Cas. 330.

[403] Since English law requires clear wording to be used to exclude rights or remedies existing at common law (see *Gilbert Ash (Northern) Ltd v Modern Engineering (Bristol) Ltd* [1974] A.C. 689).

[404] *Seville Sulphur and Copper Company v Colvils, Lowden and Company* (1888) 15 Sess. Cas. (4th Series) 616 (Court of Session, in Scotland).

of loading[405] but not while the ship is completing a previous voyage after the date of the making of the charterparty.[406] A penalty clause in a charterparty is void,[407] as in the case of all other contracts, but a provision for liquidated damages is valid.

Cancellation clauses generally give the charterer the option of cancelling the charter should the vessel not be delivered by an agreed date. Issues of interpretation arise as to whether or not cancellation pursuant to such provision arises simply as a contractual right, or by reason of breach of the owner's obligations to make delivery and/or give notice under the charter. These issues are addressed at 3.2.1.3 and 3.2.1.4 below in the distinct contexts of time and voyage charters and they should be distinguished from circumstances in which the charterparty has been frustrated. Where some intervening event wholly beyond the contemplation of the parties at the time when the charterparty was made has frustrated the whole purpose of the charterparty, the charterparty is frustrated, and both parties are excused from performing it.[408] The question as to what amounts to a frustration of the charterparty is governed by the principles of frustration in the law of contract.[409] Where the contract is frustrated, neither party is entitled to damages for the breach and repudiation of the charterparty[410] unless that frustration has been caused by the fault of one party. Thus, where the charterparty was frustrated owing to the outbreak of war in 1939 but the shipowner could have performed the charterparty before the outbreak of war (and did not do so by reason of the unseaworthiness of the ship) the shipowner was liable when the charterer accepted the shipowner's failure to perform as a repudiatory breach of the charterparty.[411] The onus of proving that the charterparty was frustrated rests on the party alleging it but where the shipowner established that the failure of the ship to be ready for loading by the agreed date was due to frustration, the onus of proof that the frustrating event was caused by the negligence of the shipowner was held to rest with the charterer.[412] Where a charterer failed to deliver cargo to the vessel because transport was not available, it was held that frustration had

[405] *Hudson v Hill* (1874) 30 L.T. 555.

[406] *Monroe v Ryan* [1935] 2 K.B. 28.

[407] *Watts, Watts and Company v Mitsui and Company* [1917] A.C. 227.

[408] *Jackson v Union Marine Insurance Company* (1874) L.R. 10 C.P. 125.

[409] See 1.7.3.

[410] *Associated Portland Cement Manufacturers v Houlder Brothers* (1917) 86 L.J. (K.B.) 1495; *Bank Line v Capel and Company* [1919] A.C. 435.

[411] *Monarch Steamship Company v Karlshamns Oljefabriker A/B* [1949] A.C. 196.

[412] *Joseph Constantine Steamship Line v Imperial Smelting Corporation* [1942] A.C. 154.

not occurred for the charterers had failed to make proper enquiries about transport before entering into the charterparty and hence it was not frustrated by "unavoidable hindrances".[413]

The rights of the parties with respect to payment of money, and the recovery of money paid where a contract has been frustrated, is generally governed by the Law Reform (Frustrated Contracts) Act 1943. However, this statute does not apply to the frustration of contracts for the carriage of goods by sea, except where such contracts are concluded by charterparty arrangements for the hire of a ship for a period of time (i.e. a time charterparty) or by way of demise (whether the demise charter is for a period of time or one or more voyages). Accordingly, the rights and liabilities of the parties in any voyage charterparty not by way of demise are governed by the common law as it applied before the enactment of the Law Reform (Frustrated Contracts) Act.[414]

The rights and liabilities of the shipowner and the charterer with regard to loading and discharge of the goods are, subject to the provisions of the charterparty, the same as those which apply with regard to the loading and discharge of the goods of other shippers. The charterparty may provide that the charterer is entitled to appoint the stevedores but this does not necessarily mean that the stevedores are the servants of the charterer rather than of the shipowner.[415] However, the issue as to who bears responsibility for the actions of the stevedores, where they are appointed by the charterer, is less likely to be determined against the owner in a dispute with the charterer under the charterparty than it is in dispute with third party shippers under other contracts of carriage made during the charter period.[416] Sometimes the port of discharge is not named in the charterparty, but the charterer is given the right to appoint it at a later time. In these cases, the charterparty usually empowers the charterer to name any port in a given area. Where the charterer fails to exercise the right to choose the port within a reasonable time, the master is entitled to proceed to any port within the given area.[417] Where the charterer is entitled to name a port, it may be an implied condition of the charterparty that a safe port will be

[413] *Trade and Transport Inc v Iino Kaiun Kaisha: The Angelia* [1973] 1 W.L.R. 210.

[414] With regard to the liabilities of the parties in a frustrated contract at common law, see *Fibrosa Spolka v Fairbairn Ltd* [1943] A.C. 32.

[415] See 3.2.1.3 below.

[416] *Swainston v Garrick* (1833) 2 L.J. (Ex.) 255.

[417] *Sieveking v Maass* (1856) 6 E. & B. 670.

named.[418] If such a warranty has been implied, or expressly agreed, and the charterer names an unsafe port, the shipowner is not entitled to repudiate the charterparty[419] but, must proceed to the nearest safe port, and discharge the goods there.[420] However, in such circumstances the charterer would be liable to the shipowner for any damage caused to the ship by sailing there;[421] unless the master ought to have been aware of the danger in the port named and to have exercised the right of proceeding to the nearest safe port since, where the master is at fault, the damage caused to the ship by sailing to the unsafe port will be attributed to the wrongful action of the master, which will be considered to be a novus actus interveniens breaking the chain of causation between the charterer's breach of warranty and the shipowner's loss.

The question as to what constitutes a safe port is determined by the same considerations as apply in the interpretation of a clause in a bill of lading that the ship shall sail to a named port or as near thereto as she may safely get. There are, however, certain differences between the interpretation of such a clause in the bill of lading and any term in a charterparty that the charterer shall name a safe port. If the port named by the charterer is unsafe, the shipowner is entitled to sail to the nearest safe port and is not obliged to proceed as near to the named port as is safe, for this has not been agreed in the charterparty. A charterer who is entitled to name a port and obliged to name a safe port cannot rely on any custom prevailing in the port of discharge by which the ship's load is lightened in the roads of the port. However, a consignee under a bill of lading contract may perhaps rely on such a custom where the carrier has agreed, in the bill of lading, to proceed to the port in question or as near thereto as the ship may safely get. The difference is attributable to the fact that in the case of a charterparty, the charterer had not named this port at the time when the charterparty was made and consequently the shipowner cannot under any circumstances be held to have agreed to lighten in accordance with the custom of the port. Conversely, in the case of a bill of lading contract or indeed a voyage

418 *Akt. Olivebank v Dansk Svovlsyre Fabrik* [1919] 2 K.B. 162: such a term can only be implied by applying the principles discussed at 1.5.2; and, as discussed at 3.1.5 above and 3.2.1.3 and 3.2.1.4 below, such warranty is less likely in contracts of carriage by voyage charterparty, or bill of lading, than a time charterparty.

419 *The Teutonia* (1872) L.R. 4 P.C. 171.

420 ibid.

421 *Lensen Shipping Company v Anglo-Soviet Shipping Company* (1935) 40 Com. Cas. 320; *Compania Naviera Maropan v Bowaters, Lloyd Ltd* [1955] 2 Q.B. 68; approved by the Privy Council in *Reardon Smith Line v Australian Wheat Board* [1956] A.C. 266.

charterparty identifying the discharge port, the shipowner generally assumes the risk of the port being safe. Where the charterer has the right to name the port of discharge, the port will never be held to be a safe port if the ship can only safely enter by lightening the load in the roads.[422] The fact that a strike is in progress at a port does not make it an unsafe port, for there is always the possibility that the strike may have been settled before the ship reaches the port. Where the charterer names a port at which a strike is in progress, the charterer is not precluded from relying on a clause in the charterparty exempting him from liability to load in the event of a strike.[423]

3.2.1.2 Demise Charterparty Arrangements

Before considering the contrasting nature of non-demise time and voyage charterparties, it is appropriate first to consider the essential nature of a demise charterparty relationship. In 1942, the view was expressed judicially that charterparties by way of demise had long been obsolete[424] but nowadays it is common for governments, shipowners and ship operators to let and hire ships by way of demise for reasons of commercial opportunity and operational necessity. Often such arrangements are concluded in relation to the ship alone and such demise charters are called "bareboat charters". The demise charterer of the vessel becomes to all intents and purposes the owner of the vessel as far as cargo interests are concerned, as demise charterers are invested with possessory title to the vessel.[425] As already mentioned, it is a question of fact as to whether a charter does or does not amount to a handing over of possession of the vessel so as to make the arrangement a charter by demise. By reference to the Barecon 2001 form of charter, the following can be seen to constitute significant attributes of a demise charter.

[422] *The Alhambra* (1881) 6 P.D. 68; *Shield v Wilkins* (1850) 5 Exch. 304, 305, per Rolfe B.; *Hall Brothers Steamship Company v Paul Ltd* (1914) 111 L.T. 811.

[423] *Reardon Smith Line v Minister of Agriculture, Fisheries and Food* [1962] 1 Q.B. 42 (reversed on another point in the House of Lords, [1963] A.C. 691).

[424] By Mackinnon L.J in the *Sea and Land Securities* case (fn. 374), at p.69 "That form of charter-party, which, as I say, was called a demise charter-party, has long been obsolete".

[425] In the *Stolt Loyalty* [1995] 1 Lloyd's Rep. 598 the Court of Appeal was content to accept that the word "owner" in an extension of time for the commencement of proceedings included not simply the owner of the vessel but also a demise charterer in possession of the vessel under a bareboat charter.

- The reiteration of the seaworthiness obligation, as in Barecon 2001 cll.3(a) and 3(c), to take effect only on the handover of the vessel with the delivery and taking over of the vessel on handover constituting a discharge of the owner's express and implied obligations as to seaworthiness.[426]
- The placing of wide-ranging restrictions on the charterer over a variety of matters, such as the vessel's use or employment, structural alterations, assigning or sub-chartering their possession of the vessel, reflagging or renaming etc.[427]
- The passing of full possession and control of the vessel to the charterer, together with full responsibility for the vessel's maintenance, repair, insurance, manning and operation etc.[428]
- Delivery and redelivery surveys to determine and agree the vessel's condition on handover and handback.[429]
- The provision for the payment of hire by the charterer continuously throughout the charter period whilst the vessel is not lost or missing,[430] although parties may agree alternative arrangements for the payment of hire such as a single lump sum payment for the entire charter period. Where hire has been paid in advance and the vessel is lost, the hire not earned must be repaid[431] but, of course, the charterer could assume the risk of the vessel being lost by agreeing to such lump sum freight being due and payable on commencement of the period of the charter.
- The provision for cross indemnity for any loss or damage suffered by the other party, by reason of arrest or detention of the

[426] Clauses 3(a) and 3(c) also limit the obligation to one of exercising due diligence, as at the time the vessel is delivered under the charter to ensure seaworthiness for the service contemplated by the charter; they go on to provide that owners will accept liability as to the costs of repairing latent defects existing as at handover which do not become apparent until within one year later.

[427] Barecon cll.6, 10 and 22.

[428] Barecon cll.10 and 13: shipowners, to safeguard their own financial interests, may elect under cl.14 to retain to themselves the responsibility for arranging insurance for their own and the charterer's respective interests in the vessel.

[429] Barecon cl.3, 7, 15; although these are also a feature of non demise time charters.

[430] Barecon cl.11, which provides at cl.11(a) for the time of payment to be *of the essence* and thereby allows any late payment of hire to be accepted by the owner as a repudiatory breach. This provision should be contrasted with hire under non-demise charters that generally distinguish between on-hire and off-hire periods.

[431] *Meling v Minos Shipping Co (The Oliva)* [1972] 1 L1.L.R. 458.

vessel, due to claims in rem attributable to claims against the indemnifying party.[432]

The effect on cargo owners of a demise charter are that any claims in tort for negligence or in bailment for want of reasonable care, in the event of loss or damage to the goods, are most likely to lie against the demise charterer, rather than the owner. Such contingent liability on the part of the demise charterer arises as it is the demise charterer (and not the ship owner) who will be in possession of the goods during the carriage and vicariously responsible for the actions of the master and the crew in connection with the carriage of the cargo and the rendering of any assistance as to loading or discharging operations. The demise charterer is also far more likely than the owner to be considered the carrier under any contracts of carriage that may be made with third party shippers during the period of the demise charter,[433] although, of course, this issue will be determined by an analysis of the contract of carriage to determine on whose behalf, as carrier, it was made.[434]

3.2.1.3 Time (Non-Demise) Charterparty Arrangements[435]

Where the shipowner, or the disponent owner, places the ship at the disposal of the charterer for a given period of time, this is known as a time charterparty. Time charterparties, like other charterparties, may either be by way of demise or not. It is far more common for them not to be by demise and the description of a charter as a "time charter" almost invariably indicates a non-demise arrangement. Common standard forms of time charter generally refer to the letting and hiring of the vessel. The terms of those forms of charterparty reveal that the ship owners, or other disponent owners in possession of the vessel by way of demise, actually retain effective possession of the vessel and remain responsible for its operation throughout the period of the time charter although, by reason of the time charter, the vessel must be operated for the business of the time charterer

[432] Barecon cl.17.

[433] Since the master of the vessel is generally assumed to be acting as the agent of the demise charterer in connection with the making of carriage contracts during the charter period.

[434] See the *Starsin* case (fn. 372).

[435] For a detailed analysis of rights, duties and liabilities arising in connection with time charters see Coghlin, Baker and Kenny, *Time Charters*, 6th edn (Informa Law, 2008).

and undertake carriage operations pursuant to the time charterer's orders.[436] This sharing of control in the vessel between charterers and owners, with the former managing the vessel's business for their own profit and the latter managing the operation of the vessel at their own cost, gives rise to an inherent tension in time charters. This tension is apparent from the careful balancing of obligations, in common standard forms of time charter, between the respective interests of owners and charterers in relation to such matters as: the seaworthiness of the vessel; the periods during which the vessel may be considered off hire; the contrasting obligations of the owner's master to follow the charterer's orders prosecuting voyages with all due despatch and to be responsible on behalf of the owner for the navigation and safety of the ship; the obligations and responsibility for cargo operations at the load and discharge ports; the safety of such ports; and as to the conclusion of, and liabilities arising under, carriage contracts concluded by the charterer with third party shippers.[437] These issues are discussed below in the context of two common standard form charterparty contracts, generally referred to as the Baltime 1939 (Baltime) and the NYPE 93 (NYPE) time charters.[438]

The essential bargain, in a time charter of a cargo vessel, is that the owner provides a working cargo vessel for the use of the charterer throughout the charter period and, in return, the charterer undertakes to pay the hire charge continuously throughout the period of the charter during which the vessel is placed at its economic disposal. The common law notion of seaworthiness is inappropriate for such a bargain, since the common law duty on the shipowner (as carrier opposite the time charterer) would be to ensure that the vessel was seaworthy only for each stage of any particular voyage, or on handover at the outset of the charter period. Accordingly, in stark contrast to the common law concept of stages, both the Baltime and the NYPE forms of time charter provide for the shipowner to be under duties both to provide a seaworthy vessel at the

[436] The vessel being operated for the charterer: under cl.9 of the Baltime 1939 charterparty form, as to "employment, agency or other arrangements"; and under cl.8 of the NYPE 93 form of charter, as regards "employment and agency".

[437] Lord Hobhouse acknowledged this tension in the *Hill Harmony* [2001] 1 A.C. 638 when he referred to the "conflict of interest between owners and charterers under a time charter" in a dispute over the master's selection of a longer route between load and discharge ports.

[438] Both Baltime 1939 and NYPE 93 being forms of non-demise time charter recommended by BIMCO and available from the BIMCO website.

commencement of the charter and to ensure that the vessel continuously remains seaworthy during service under the charter.[439] However, the content of the express seaworthiness obligation so created is, in substance, otherwise conceptually equivalent to the implied common law notion of seaworthiness.[440]

The vessel will only be effectively on hire to the charterer when it is at the economic disposal of the charterer and there will be circumstances when a vessel under time charter will not be available for use. The circumstances of the unavailability of the vessel may be such that the owner is, in any event, in breach of the charterparty (e.g. the vessel may be inadequately equipped for cargo operations and, in consequence, be unseaworthy) and in such circumstances, the charterer may seek damages from the owner for the loss of the vessel's earning potential. Alternatively there might be no breach. In this event, as the charterer remains liable for the hire charges, it would be the charterer who would effectively bear the loss. For this reason, time charters generally contain express provisions providing for the suspension of hire charges in certain circumstances. In the Baltime charter form those hire suspension circumstances are strictly limited to "necessary measures to maintain the efficiency" of the vessel or to repair damage, whilst the off hire circumstances under the NYPE charter form are more extensive in scope, encompassing such matters as ship arrest.[441] The application of these provisions, and of additional further such provisions particularly agreed by the parties, can raise difficult issues of interpretation and causation in many differing circumstances, as it is necessary to identify the agreed off hire circumstances and to determine

[439] Baltime 1939 cll.1 and 3 under which the owner is obliged to supply the vessel "in every way fitted for ordinary cargo service" and to "maintain her in a thoroughly efficient state in hull and machinery during service". NYPE 93 cll.2 and 6 under which the owner has obligations to supply the vessel "with clean-swept holds and tight, staunch, strong and in every way fitted for ordinary cargo service ..." and to "maintain the Vessel's class and keep her in a thoroughly efficient state in hull, machinery and equipment for and during the service ...".

[440] *Cheikh Boutros Selim El-Khoury v Ceylon Shipping Lines, Ltd (The Madeleine)* [1967] 2 Lloyd's Rep. 224 in which Roskill L.J. held that the words of cl.1 were not limited to the provision of the ship with adequate equipment, but required that the ship be seaworthy in terms of the required documentation.

[441] See cll.11 of the Baltime and 17 of the NYPE forms of time charter.

what part, if any, of the delay to the vessel has been caused by them.[442] The charterer is otherwise liable to pay the hire according to the terms of the contract. If this payment is late, the owner may exercise any right of withdrawal available in the contract, but late payment does not necessarily amount to a repudiation of the charterparty.[443]

Since the ship owner (or other disponent owner) under a time charter can reap no financial gain from the cargo operations performed by the vessel, the owner has little incentive to perform them with any despatch. This is particularly so when diligent performance will only serve to increase the vessel's exposure to those maritime perils capable of causing loss to the owner. Time charters generally address this by the imposition of express obligations on owners to prosecute voyages expeditiously and to adhere to the charterers' orders in terms of the economic management of the vessel, whilst leaving navigational matters to the seamanship of the master.[444] This distinction in the management of the vessel between the economic decisions to be taken by the charterers and the navigational decisions to taken by the master is a frequent source of dispute between owners and charterers since, whenever the ship is delayed by any reason not amounting to an off hire circumstance, or some repudiatory breach of the charter on the part of the disponent owner, it is the charterers who are primarily exposed to the financial consequence of such delay.[445] As Lord Bingham commented in the *Hill Harmony* case,[446] the legal distinction between economic

[442] As Rix L.J. commented in the *Doric Pride* [2006] 2 Lloyd's Rep. 175, 181, when considering such issues in the context of a particularly agreed hire suspension clause in an amended NYPE charter, one is "looking for an essential distinction made in the wording... between matters of responsibility for owners and matters of responsibility for charterers. The question still remains: 'On what side of the line, on the facts of this case, do these facts fall?' "

[443] *Tenax Steamship Co v Owners of the Motor Vessel Brimnes (The Brimnes)* [1972] 2 L1.L.R. 465; [1973] 1 All E.R. 769.

[444] See cl.9 of the Baltime form of charter which provides for voyages to be prosecuted "with the utmost despatch" under charterer's instructions "as regards employment, agency or other arrangements"; whilst cl.8 of the NYPE charter form obliges the Master to "perform the voyages with due despatch" and be under charterer's orders "as regards employment and agency".

[445] "My Lords, in merchant shipping time is money..." as Lord Mustill so accurately observed in *The Gregos* [1994] 1 WLR 1465, 1468.

[446] *Hill Harmony* [2001] 1 A.C. 638, 646 in the context of a decision to substitute a less hazardous, if longer, route in place of the shorter route ordered by charterers.

and navigational management is easy to perceive but difficult to apply.[447] The distinction is not whether decisions are taken on the vessel or the shore but one compared with that between strategic and tactical decisions.[448] Employing that distinction, it can be seen that it is the charterer who takes the strategic decisions as to the employment of the vessel (e.g. the cargo to be carried, the load and discharge ports at which calls are to be made and the routes to be taken etc.); and the disponent owner (deploying the seamanship and technical expertise available from its seagoing and shore-based personnel) who takes the tactical decisions as to how best to operate the ship to carry out the strategy in the light of paramount safety and security considerations as to the vessel, crew and cargo.

As time charterers exercise economic control over the vessel, it is they who decide what cargo to carry and where to load and discharge; but, not only are the owners responsible to ensure the seaworthiness of the vessel and the proper care of the cargo throughout all such operations, insofar as any assistance from the vessel is required such assistance can only be forthcoming from the owners' master and crew. All variable voyage costs (e.g. fuel, pilotage, tug assistance) and all port costs (e.g. stevedore charges, vessel overtime charges, harbour charges) which arise in respect of the operation of the vessel whilst on hire, are generally payable by charterers under time charterparty arrangements.[449] Furthermore, time charters generally place on charterers all obligations in relation to the loading and discharging of the vessel, albeit subject to owners being obliged to provide crew assistance for the operation of the vessel's cargo handling gear and the right of the master to exercise supervision to ensure the seaworthiness of the vessel.[450] Only the NYPE charter expressly refers to the right of the master to supervise the loading[451] but authority suggests this is a right which would ordinarily be implied where the owner is obliged to ensure seaworthiness.[452] In this context it is important to appreciate that the right

[447] "It is not hard to think of orders which plainly relate to the employment of the vessel and others which plainly relate to its navigation. It is much less easy to formulate any test which clearly distinguishes between the two", per Lord Bingham ibid.

[448] Davies, "Rights to Routes" (1999) LMCLQ 461.

[449] See Baltime cll.4 and 16; NYPE cll.7 and 29.

[450] See Baltime cll.3 and 4; NYPE cl.8(a).

[451] At NYPE cl.8(a) which provides for the charterer's cargo handling to be performed "under the supervision of the Master".

[452] *Court Line Ltd v Canadian Transport Co Ltd* [1940] AC 934, 937 where Lord Wright characterised it as "a right which in my opinion would have existed even if not expressly reserved".

to supervise does not create any duty on the owner towards the charterer to supervise.[453] Although the owner is responsible to the charterer for the seaworthiness of the vessel, English courts have rejected, as being a "remarkable construction", any interpretation which would result in the owner having responsibility to the charterer for unseaworthiness arising from the charterer's poor loading, as the charterer cannot rely on unseaworthiness arising from its own breach.[454] Owners may still be exposed to third party shippers in tort and bailment, however, for negligent supervision as discussed below.

By agreeing to a time charter, owners put their vessel at the disposal of the charterers. In return, charterers generally undertake obligations under the charter that any ports, berths and anchorages to which the vessel is sent will be safe. Such warranties are provided for in both the Baltime and NYPE forms of charter in similar terms, to the effect that the vessel "shall be employed" in "lawful trades" between "safe ports" or safe "places".[455] What constitutes a "safe" port or place has been judicially defined as being such a place that "in the relevant period of time, the particular ship can reach it, use it and return from it without, in the absence of some abnormal occurrence, being exposed to danger which cannot be avoided by good navigation and seamanship".[456] Where a time charterer has a wide discretion as to the ports or places to which the vessel may be directed, a warranty of safety may be implied,[457] but it will not necessarily be implied and the principles discussed at 1.5.2 will apply.

In the event of any loss, damage or delay being caused to cargo carried by the vessel during the period of the charter, the disponent owner will be exposed to claims, not only from the charterer, but also from third parties entitled to demand the cargo from the shipowner. These claims will arise in bailment and tort because such a disponent owner is in possession of the goods. Where the charterer has negotiated separate contracts of carriage

[453] *Court Line* ibid.; *The Imvros* [1999] 1 Lloyd's Rep. 848 and *Compania Sud American Vapores v MS ER Hamburg Schiffahrtsgesellschaft MBH & Co KG* [2006] 2 Lloyd's Rep. 66.

[454] Per Langley J. in *The Imvros* ibid. as approved by Morison J. in *MS Hamburg* ibid.

[455] See cl.2 of the Baltime, and cl.5 of the NYPE forms of charter.

[456] Per Sellers L.J. in *Leeds Shipping Co Ltd v Société Française Bunge (The Eastern City)* [1958] 2 Lloyd's Rep. 127, 133.

[457] *The Evaggelos Th* [1971] 2 Lloyd's Rep. 200, 204 where Donaldson J. implied a limited warranty as to war risks "because common sense and business efficacy require it in cases in which the shipowner surrenders to the charterer the right to choose where his ship shall go".

with third party shippers, or where rights under any bill of lading, ship's delivery order or sea waybill issued for the charterer's cargo are subject to statutory transfer,[458] claims may also arise in contract if and to the extent that the shipowner is considered carrier under such contract of carriage by reference to the principles of interpretation set out in the *Starsin*.[459] Time charters generally manage such liability by providing for the master to sign bills of lading and sea waybills as presented by the charterer, without prejudice to the charterparty and subject to an indemnity from the charterer to indemnify the disponent owner for any liability arising under any such bill of lading or sea waybill not in conformity with the charter.[460] Where disponent owners are obliged to issue bills of lading "as presented" and those bills expose disponent owners to a greater liability than that arising under the charter, an indemnity in favour of disponent owners may be implied.[461] The disponent owner remains responsible to the charterer for the due performance of the obligations, imposed by the charter, as to the carriage of the cargo and retains such liability for cargo claims as may be provided for by the charter but is entitled to be indemnified by charterers for any liability beyond that so provided in the charter. The extent of disponent owners' obligations for the carriage of cargo under the Baltime and NYPE charterparty forms is distinct. Although both impose substantively similar obligations as to seaworthiness, NYPE provides for "a clause paramount",[462] whilst the standard Baltime terms do not. The effect of the clause paramount is that any contract of carriage terms which are mandatorily applicable "by virtue of the origin or destination of the bill of lading" are incorporated into the terms of the charterparty. As a result, charterers under an NYPE charter can resist indemnity under cl.30(b) for cargo claims in circumstances where the applicable statutory terms, to the

[458] By the Carriage of Goods by Sea Act 1992 discussed at 3.1.7 above.

[459] [2003] 1 Lloyd's Rep. 571 discussed at 3.1.2 above and 1.5.2.

[460] See Baltime cl.9 and NYPE cl.30.

[461] *The Island Archon* [1994] 2 Lloyd's Rep. 227 where shipowners were held entitled to an indemnity for following charterers' instructions when that exposed them to liabilities beyond those arising under the charter.

[462] NYPE cl.31(a) providing "CLAUSE PARAMOUNT this bill of lading shall have effect subject to the Carriage of Goods by Sea Act of the United States, the Hague Rules, or the Hague-Visby Rules, as applicable, or such other similar national legislation as may mandatorily apply by virtue of origin or destination of the bills of lading ...".

extent of their incorporation,[463] impose liability on the disponent owner as carrier.[464] The disponent owners have, by the clause paramount in the NYPE charterparty, expressly undertaken towards the time charterer performance of the statutory obligations of a carrier under bills of lading.

As Lord Hobhouse explained in the *Hill Harmony*,[465] there are fundamental differences between a time charter and a voyage charter. By a time charter, as discussed above, the employment, potential earnings and variable trading costs of the vessel are transferred to the charterer, whilst by a voyage charter, as discussed below, the disponent owner is using the vessel to trade on its own account.

3.2.1.4 Voyage (Non-Demise) Charterparty Arrangements

Lord Diplock succinctly explained in the course of giving judgment in the *Johanna Oldendorff*,[466] that a voyage charterparty is a contract of carriage effectively divisible into four distinct operations, namely:

> "(1) The loading voyage, viz. the voyage of the chartered vessel from wherever she is at the date of the charterparty to the place specified in it as the place of loading. (2) The loading operation, viz. the delivery of the cargo to the vessel at the place of loading and its stowage on board. (3) The carrying voyage, viz. the voyage of the vessel to the place specified in the charterparty as the place of delivery. (4) The discharging operation, viz. the delivery of the cargo from the vessel at the place specified in the charterparty as the place of discharge and its receipt there by the charterer or other consignee".

[463] Issues of interpretation arise where the printed, or particularly agreed, terms of the charterparty conflict with the terms of the incorporated regimes. However, courts are generally content to manipulate the wording of the regimes to give effect to them in the context of the charterparty into which they have been incorporated. Accordingly, in *Adamastos Shipping Co Ltd v Anglo-Saxon Petroleum Co Ltd* [1959] AC 133 the express incorpoation of the US Carriage of Goods by Sea Act 1936 allowed shipowners to rely on statutory defences arising under the Act, notwithstanding the fact that such defences were by the express terms of the Act inapplicable to the charterparty.

[464] The incorporation (per Morison J in *Compania Sud American Vapores v MS ER Hamburg Schiffahrtsgesellschaft MBH & Co KG* [2006] 2 Lloyd's Rep. 66 at para.15) "requires the contract into which they have been incorporated to be read as though the Rules formed an integral part of the express terms".

[465] [2001] 1 A.C. 638, 652.

[466] *E. L. Oldendorff & Co GmbH v Tradax Export SA* [1974] A.C. 479 at 556.

As Lord Diplock acknowledged,[467] whilst the performance of the loading and discharge operations are by their nature joint operations of the disponent owner and the charterer,[468] the performance of the two distinct voyage operations (i.e. to the load port and from there to the discharge port) is wholly under the control of the disponent owner.[469] In consequence, the disponent owner has the absolute obligation to perform the two distinct voyage operations subject only to such exceptions in his contractual duty as may arise by: implication at law[470] or by express agreement under the charter. In this context, it is common for voyage charterparties to provide expressly for certain exceptions. The Gencon charterparty form, for example, restricts the disponent owner's obligations to the exercise of due diligence to make the vessel seaworthy and cargo-worthy (for each "stage" of the voyage recognised at common law),[471] as well as providing for a general liberty to deviate[472] and excuses the disponent owner from performance in the event exposure to war risks.[473] The joint shared cargo handling operations raise more complex isssues, both under the common law and by reference to the Gencon[474] voyage charter.

A charterparty often provides that the charterer will load at the port of loading, or discharge at the port of discharge, or both, within a given

[467] ibid.

[468] The joint nature of the cargo operations is emphasised by cl.5 of the Gencon form of charterparty, which provides at 5(a) for the cargo to be loaded and discharged "free of any risk, liability and expense whatsoever to the Owners" and at 5(b) for the owner to provide free use of the vessel's cargo handling gear and cranemen.

[469] As effectively confirmed in the case of the Gencon form of charterparty by cl.1 which provides that the vessel "shall, as soon as her prior commitments have been completed, proceed to the loading port(s) or place(s)", and after loading, "shall proceed to the discharging port(s) or place(s)" as stated in the charterparty.

[470] Lord Diplock suggested in *The Johanna Oldendorff* (fn. 466) at 557 that the common carrier exceptions of "Act of God or of the King's enemies or by inherent vice in the goods carried" would apply to all carriers by sea.

[471] See cl.2 of the Gencon charterparty form.

[472] Clause 3 ibid.; although as previously discussed such general liberty clauses are narrowly construed.

[473] Clause 17 ibid.

[474] The BIMCO uniform general form of voyage charter, as revised 1922, 1976 and 1994, that is recommended by BIMCO for trades in which there is no specially approved form of charter in place. The Gencon charter is available for download from the BIMCO website.

number of days.[475] These days are known as lay days. Where no days are provided for, the charterer is required to load and unload within a reasonable time.[476] The charterparty often provides that, if the charterer fails to load, or to unload, within the lay days, it shall be entitled to do so (in consideration of the payment of demurrage) within a given number of additional days, which are known as demurrage days.[477] Demurrage is usually made payable at a given rate per day of the demurrage days taken by the charterer to load or unload. A term for the payment of demurrage will be interpreted as referring only to the loading, or unloading, at the ports expressly mentioned in the charterparty in connection with demurrage.[478] Where the charterparty provides for demurrage, but no lay days are stipulated, the demurrage will be payable after a reasonable time for loading has elapsed.[479] Where lay days are stipulated, and the parties have not agreed to provide for demurrage days, the charterer is in breach of contract if it fails to load within the lay days. Where the parties have agreed to provide for demurrage days, failure to load within the lay days does not constitute a breach of contract, but merely entitles the disponent owner to demurrage under the charterparty; but if the charterer fails to complete the loading within the demurrage days, it is in breach of contract. The damages for a breach of the contract to load are frequently known as demurrage, and have even been so called judicially.[480] However, strictly the application of the term demurrage to damages for breach of contract is inaccurate. Where the charterer is in breach, the damages are measured in the usual way, and are not limited to the sum fixed as demurrage,[481] unless it is agreed that this sum shall also be payable as liquidated damages for the breach of contract.

At common law the lay days begin to run against the charterer when notice is given that the ship is ready to load or discharge.[482] In the absence of an express term to the contrary, the disponent owner is obliged to give notice to the charterer that the ship is ready for loading or discharging[483]

[475] Gencon box 16 and cl.6 facilitates the making of alternative agreements between the parties for separate laytime for loading and discharge or total laytime for both.

[476] *Postlethwaite v Freeland* (1880) 5 App. Cas. 599.

[477] Gencon box 20 and cl.7 provide for demurrage at the agreed rates to be payable in the event laytime is exceeded at the load or discharge ports.

[478] *Stevenson v York* (1790) 2 Chit. 570.

[479] *Postlethwaite v Freeland* (fn. 476).

[480] *Akt. Reidar v Arcos Ltd* [1927] 1 K.B. 352, 363, per Atkin L.J.

[481] ibid.

[482] *Fairbridge v Pace* (1884) 1 Car. & Kir. 317.

[483] *Stanton v Austin* (1872) L.R. 7 C.P. 651.

and the requirement of notice is expressly provided for by Gencon terms.[484] A notice that the ship will be ready to load at a certain future time is not notice of actual readiness, even if the ship was in fact ready.[485] If there is no berth available and the charterer is notified that the ship is ready for loading or discharge, the charterer may use some laytime lying at the nearest available point waiting for a berth and will not be liable for delay in providing a place for the vessel.[486] Where the master of a vessel gave notice that a ship was ready to load but in fact she was infested and the port authorities required her to be fumigated, the lay days did not begin until the day after fumigation was completed.[487] Where a ship was an arrived ship, and the charterers delayed in nominating a berth, it was held that the lay days had commenced from the time of arrival, although once a berth was nominated they could rely on a strike clause to suspend the lay days.[488]

Where it is a term in the charterparty that the ship will be ready to load by a given date, the charterer is under no obligation to begin loading before this date if the ship arrives early,[489] unless there is an express or implied term in the charterparty, or a custom of the port of loading,[490] to this effect. Ordinarily, time only begins to run against the charterer from the date agreed in the charterparty. The charterer is entitled to take all the lay days for loading and is under no obligation to load in less than this time.[491] Where lay days and demurrage days are provided for in the charterparty, it is a question depending on the terms of the charterparty and on the custom of the port whether the "days" are to be interpreted as running days, working days or weather working days.[492] When the ship has arrived at the port, and time has begun to run against the charterer, it continues to run if

[484] Gencon cl.6(c) provides that laytime for loading and discharging commences after notice of readiness to load or discharge is given to the shippers or receivers, or their respective agents, as identified by the charterparty.

[485] *Christensen v Hindustan Steel* [1971] 2 All E.R. 811.

[486] *Shipping Developments Corp. v v/o Sojuzneftexport (The Delian Spirit)* [1971] 2 W.L.R. 1434.

[487] *Compania de Naviera Nedelka SA v Tradex Internacional SA (The Tres Flores)* [1973] 3 W.L.R. 545.

[488] *The Prometheus* [1974] 1 All E.R. 597, Mocatta J.

[489] *Little v Stevenson and Company* [1896] A.C. 108.

[490] *Krog v Burns* (1903) 5 Sess, Cas. (5th Series) 1189 (in Scotland).

[491] *Margaronis Navigation Agency v Henry W. Peabody and Company* [1964] 3 W.L.R. 111.

[492] See *Niemann v Moss* (1860) 6 Jur. N.S. 775; *Commercial Steamship Company v Boulton* (1875) L.R. 10 Q.B. 346; *The Katy* [1895] P. 56; *Branckelow Steamship Company v Lamport and Holt Ltd* [1897] 1 Q.B. 570; *Bennetts and Company v Brown* [1908] 1 K.B. 490; *Alvion Steamship Corporation v Galban Lobo Company* [1955] 1 Q.B. 430.

the ship is ordered by the Port Authority to leave the port to prevent damage to other shipping; the days during which the ship is away from the port count as demurrage days. Provided that the days during which the ship was away from port were weather working days, on which the weather would have permitted the loading or unloading to have taken place if the ship had been in port, this continues to be the case although the charterparty provides that demurrage is only to be paid during weather working days.[493] Where the charterparty contains provisions for lay days (or for lay days and demurrage days) both at the port of loading and the port of discharge and the charterer either loads or unloads in less than the lay or demurrage days allowed, the days thus saved cannot be offset against the demurrage, or damages for breach of contract, due as a result of his exceeding the lay or demurrage days at the other port.[494] There may, however, be an express provision in the charterparty by which the disponent owner agrees to pay (or to credit) a sum for the time saved (known as despatch money) to the charterer if loading or unloading is completed in less than the lay days. A provision in the charterparty for "averaging demurrage" will be interpreted as an agreement for despatch money to be so credited.[495] Where the charterer fails to complete the loading within the lay days or the demurrage days (or within a reasonable time if there is no provision for lay days and demurrage days), the disponent owner is not entitled to repudiate the charterparty and depart[496] unless either the delay in loading is so great as to amount to a repudiatory breach or frustration of the charterparty,[497] or the charterer has given a definite refusal to load.[498]

It is an implied term of every charterparty that the charterer will do nothing to prevent the ship from reaching the port of discharge. In the *Aello*[499] a charterer was not ready to load by the due date and, in consequence, by the regulations of the port of Buenos Aires, ships were obliged to wait at an anchorage 22 miles outside the port until the charterer was ready to load. Owing to the charterer's failure to be ready, the ship was

[493] *Compania Crystal v Herman and Mohatta Ltd* [1958] 2 Q.B. 196.

[494] *Marshall v Bolckow* (1881) 6 Q.B.D. 231.

[495] *Molie(g)re Steamship Company v Naylor, Benzon and Company* (1897) 2 Com. Cas. 92; *Alma Shipping Company v Salgaoncar E Irmaos* [1954] 2 Q.B. 94 (Devlin J.).

[496] *Inverkip Steamship Company v Bunge and Company* [1917] 2 K.B. 193, 201, per Scrutton L.J., criticising earlier dicta to the contrary.

[497] *Matthews v Lowther* (1850) 5 Exch. 574; *Inverkip Steamship Company v Bunge and Company* ibid.

[498] *Danube and Black Sea Railway Company v Xenos* (1863) 13 C.B. (N.S.) 825.

[499] [1961] A.C. 135.

detained at this place for 15 days. The disponent owner was held entitled to damages from the charterer as the charterer, by not being ready to load at the agreed date, had prevented the ship from arriving at the port, such arrival being a condition precedent to readiness to load and, in consequence, demurrage. The particular finding of the House of Lords in the case of the *Aello*[500] that the ship could not be said to have arrived at the port when it reached the anchorage 22 miles away was reversed by the House in the *Johanna Oldendorff* in 1973.[501] In the *Johanna Oldendorff*, the House of Lords held that it was in error in 1961 in finding that a distance of 22 miles was too great to regard a ship as an "arrived" ship, finding that it was contrary to commercial commonsense to suggest that a ship had not arrived when it was anchored by order of the port authorities in a place where ships were ordinarily ordered to lie within the confines of the port, since, at such a place, in these days of steam, diesel power and instantaneous radio communications, the vessel could effectively be ordered by the charterer to a berth immediately one became available. Consequently, the ship was at the charterer's complete disposal whilst awaiting a berth and the geographical distance from the port, which may have been important in the days of sail, had been rendered immaterial by technological advance. Their Lordships held that the relevant test is whether or not the ship had "reached a position within the port where she was at the immediate and effective disposition of the charterers".

The charterparty usually contains, as does the Gencon charter,[502] a stipulation by the charterer that a full cargo will be loaded.[503] The obligation of the charterer to load is absolute.[504] The charterer is excused only where failure to load is due to the fault of the disponent owner,[505] or where it is covered by an express provision of the charterparty, or where the charterparty has been frustrated. If the disponent owner has broken any condition precedent in the charterparty, the charterer may refuse to load;[506] but where the disponent owner has broken stipulations that are not

[500] ibid.

[501] *E.L. Oldendorff & Co GmbH v Tradax Export SA* [1974] A.C. 479.

[502] Gencon cl.1 provides for a full and complete cargo to be loaded unless such has not been agreed when the words "part cargo" should be inserted at box 12.

[503] See *Hunter v Fry* (1819) 2 B. & Ald. 421.

[504] *Postlethwaite v Freeland* (1880) 5 App. Cas. 599, 620, per Lord Blackburn; *Bunge y Born Limitada v Brightman and Company* [1925] A.C. 799, 816, per Lord Sumner.

[505] *Bradley v Goddard* (1863) 3 F. & F. 638.

[506] See *Ritchie v Atkinson* (1808) 10 East 295, 306, per Lord Ellenborough C.J.; *Stavers v Curling* (1836) 3 Bing. N.C. 355, 368, per Tindal C.J.

conditions precedent to the charter, the charterer cannot refuse to load, although is entitled to claim damages.[507] Where, by the law of the port of loading, it is illegal to load the cargo contemplated, the charterer is excused from loading. In wartime, loading is illegal if the port of destination is controlled by enemies of the charterer's state,[508] or if the disponent owner is a subject of a state at war with the charterer's state.[509] This applies where the company owning the ship is in fact controlled by enemy aliens, although the ship is registered under the flag of a neutral state.[510] The charterer is excused from loading if the charterparty is frustrated.[511] The fact that the goods, which the charterer intended to load, have been destroyed or never existed,[512] does not amount to frustration unless it was a term of the charterparty that the cargo was to consist exclusively, or chiefly, of these goods.[513] The charterparty often contains provisions excusing the charterer from liability for failure to load in given circumstances. In accordance with the usual principles, these exceptions are interpreted against the charterer.[514] The charterer cannot rely on the excepted perils included in the charterparty to protect the disponent owner from liability for damage to the goods unless it is clear that these exceptions were also intended to except the charterer from liability for failure to load.[515]

Among the contractual exceptions that may be expressly agreed to protect the charterer are: (a) strikes, lock-outs and labour disputes; (b) riots and civil commotions; (c) accidents for which the charterer is not responsible; and (d) ice, frost, fog, snow and storm. Strikes and lock-outs are interpreted, in the absence of any contrary indication in the charterparty, as referring only to a cessation of work in connection with a labour dispute. The terms will not ordinarily cover a cessation of work by stevedores who have fled from the port in fear of a cholera epidemic.[516] The term "strikes" may be interpreted as excluding the case of a general strike, which may

[507] *Tarrabochia v Hickie* (1856) 1 H. & N. 183.

[508] *Reid v Hoskins* (1856) 6 E. & B. 953; *Esposito v Bowden* (1857) 7 E. & B. 763.

[509] *Clapham Steamship Company v Handels-en Transport-Maatschappij Vulcaan of Rotterdam* [1917] 2 K.B. 639.

[510] ibid.

[511] *Jackson v Union Marine Insurance Company* (1874) L.R. 10 C.P. 572.

[512] *Hills v Sughrue* (1846) 15 M. & W. 253.

[513] *Jones Ltd v Green and Company* [1904] 2 K.B. 275.

[514] *Hudson v Ede* (1867) L.R. 2 Q.B. 566, 578, per Blackburn J.; *Grant and Company v Coverdale, Todd and Company* (1884) 9 App. Cas. 470, 478, per Lord Watson.

[515] *Cantiere Navale Triestina v Russian Soviet Naphtha Agency* [1925] 2 K.B. 172.

[516] *Stephens v Harris and Company* (1887) 6 Asp. M.L.C. 192.

amount to a frustration of the charterparty.[517] The exception of strikes and lock-outs may possibly even be construed as excluding strikes by the charterer's own servants, and will certainly be interpreted as not excepting the charterer where the charterer has failed to use all reasonable efforts to end such a strike, or to engage other servants.[518] A clause exempting the charterer from the obligation to load or discharge the goods during a strike will not protect the charterer if the strike occurred after the end of the available time for loading (i.e. the "laytime" or "lay days") unless the clause expressly applies the exemption to the period continuing after the end of laytime when the charterer is obliged to pay damages for the detention of the vessel.[519] Where, under the charterparty, the charterer is entitled to load an alternative cargo, the charterer will not be protected if a strike only prevents one of the cargoes from being loaded and the charterer will be liable if it fails to load an alternative cargo.[520] The term "accidents" is interpreted as including only accidents caused by human factors and not those caused by operation of nature, such as snow, ice etc.[521] It is therefore usual to include an express exception of snow, ice, frost, fog and storm. The exception clause will be interpreted as referring only to the actual operation of loading, and will not apply to the failure of the charterer to bring the goods to the port of loading[522] unless a contrary intention is clearly shown in the charterparty. Where, however, it is a custom at the port of loading for cargo to be warehoused outside the area of the port and to be brought to the port only when the ship is ready to load, the process of bringing the goods to the port from the place where they are held will be considered to be part of the operation of loading and the exceptions will apply to excuse the charterer if the goods cannot be brought to the port from such customary place of storage.[523] Where it is clear from the terms of the charterparty that the exception refers to a period prior to the loading (e.g. by a reference to accidents in the mines)[524] the exception will also apply

[517] *The Penelope* [1928] P. 180.

[518] *Bulman and Dickson Ltd v Fenwick and Company* [1894] 1 Q.B. 179, 185, per Lord Esher, M.R.

[519] *Compania Naviera Aeolus SA v Union of India* [1964] A.C. 868. Such continuing period of delay is sometimes referred to as "the demurrage days".

[520] *South African Dispatch Line v Owners of S.S. Niki* [1960] 1 Q.B. 518.

[521] *Fenwick v Schmalz* (1868) L.R. 3 C.P. 313.

[522] *Grant and Company v Coverdale, Todd and Company* (1884) 9 App. Cas. 470; *Kay v Field* (1882) 10 Q.B.D. 241.

[523] *Hudson v Ede* (1867) L.R. 2 Q.B. 566.

[524] *Bunge y Born Limitada v Brightman and Company* [1925] A.C. 799, 817, per Lord Sumner.

to this expressly mentioned period. The relevant exceptions for the charterer contained in the Gencon charter are limited to strikes or lock outs affecting cargo operations at the load or discharge ports and ice rendering such ports inaccessible.[525]

Where, as is usually the case, the charterer has agreed to load a full cargo, the charterparty often contains provisions that, if it fails to do so, the charterer will pay freight at the agreed rate on that portion of the ship's stowage space which has not been filled. This is known as dead freight. However, where the charterer fails to load a full cargo and the sum payable as dead freight under the charterparty is actually higher than the maximum damages that could have been awarded for such breach of the charterparty the disponent owner is only entitled to the awardable value of such damages for breach of contract and the stipulation for the payment of dead freight will be void as being a penalty.[526]

At common law the disponent owner is obliged to exercise reasonable care to ensure that the vessel arrives at the load port in a reasonable time. An expressly agreed stipulation that the ship will proceed forthwith, or without delay, to the port of loading is not a condition precedent.[527] If the disponent owner breaks this term in the charterparty by reason of the ship delaying before proceeding to the port of loading, the charterer is entitled to damages for the breach,[528] unless the failure of the ship to proceed forthwith to the port of loading was due to an excepted peril in the charterparty which applies to excuse the disponent owner from liability,[529] or the delay is such as to amount to a frustration of the charterparty through no fault of the disponent owner.[530] The charterer is not, however, entitled to treat the delay in reaching the port of loading as a repudiation of the charterparty, and consequently is not entitled to refuse to load,[531] unless of course the circumstances of the delay are so great as to amount to a fundamental breach of the contract, or to result in frustration of the

[525] See cll.16 and 18, which effectively provide for a number of predetermined consequences in the event of such strike or ice events whilst relieving the charterer of responsibility for non-performance arising from such events.

[526] See *Watts, Watts and Company v Mitsui and Company* [1917] A.C. 227.

[527] *Tarrabochia v Hickie* (1856) 1 H. & N. 183.

[528] *M'Andrew v Adams* (1834) 1 Bing. N.C. 29.

[529] *Croockewit v Fletcher* (1857) 1 H. & N. 893, 912; *Geipel v Smith* (1872) L.R. 7 Q.B. 404.

[530] The concept of frustration is discussed at 1.7.3.

[531] *Clipsham v Vertue* (1843) 5 Q.B. 265; *MacAndrew v Chapple* (1866) L.R. 1 C.P. 643; *Dimech v Corlett* (1858) 12 Moo. P.C.C. 199.

adventure.[532] In the absence of any stipulation, there is nevertheless an implied warranty by the disponent owner that the ship will proceed without delay to the port of loading.[533] Where there is an express provision in the charterparty that the ship will be at the port of loading and ready to load by a given date, this amounts to a condition precedent and, if there is a breach of this condition, the charterer is entitled to treat the charterparty as repudiated, and to refuse to load.[534] The charterer is also entitled to damages for the breach of the stipulation unless the breach was caused by an excepted peril, which applies to excuse the disponent owner for the failure of the ship to reach the port of loading by the agreed date. Where the charterparty contains stipulations both that the ship will reach the port of loading (and be ready to load) by a given date and that the ship will proceed forthwith to the port of loading, these may be construed as two distinct stipulations. Where they are so construed as distinct obligations the disponent owner may, by failing to perform either one of them, be in breach of the charterparty: as for instance where the disponent owner was held liable in damages for failing to proceed forthwith to the port of loading, although the ship was ready to load at the port of loading by the agreed deadline.[535] A cesser clause will relieve the charterer from any liability after the time of loading.[536] In the case of any ambiguity, a cesser clause is interpreted as relieving the charterer only in respect of future breaches of the charterparty after this time, and not with regard to prior breaches committed before the time of loading.[537] A cesser clause may also provide for a "cesser of hire" should a vessel cease to be in an efficient state.

As with time charters, a voyage charter may oblige the disponent owner to authorise the master of the vessel to sign bills of lading at the request of the charterer. The status of such a bill in the hands of the charterer is that of a mere receipt for the goods, as the contractual relationship between charterer and disponent owner is governed by the terms of the charterparty.

[532] *Jackson v Union Marine Insurance Company* (1847) L.R. 10 C.P. 125.

[533] *M'Andrew v Adams* (fn. 528).

[534] *Shadforth v Higgin* (1813) 3 Camp. 385.

[535] *M'Andrew v Adams* (fn. 528).

[536] *Oglesby v Yglesias* (1858) E.B. & E. 930.

[537] *Clink v Radford and Company* [1891] 1 Q.B. 625, where at 627 Lord Esher M.R. attributed this to the fact that after goods have been loaded for shippers other than the charterer, the shipowner can rely on the contract of carriage with those shippers, whereas before the goods are shipped the shipowner's sole remedy lies against the charterer under the charterparty.

However, in the hands of some other shipper of the cargo, or some transferee, the bill of lading will represent a contract of carriage and this gives rise to the same issues of contractual construction that have been previously discussed.[538] To protect against this liability, Gencon cl.10 provides for the charterer to indemnify the disponent owner against all liabilities arising under the bill of lading in excess of those provided for in the charterparty and requires bills of lading to be issued in the "Congenbill" form,[539] which incorporates a clause paramount in favour of the Hague-Visby rules and seeks to incorporate by reference the terms of the charterparty pursuant to which it is issued.[540] The Gencon form of charterparty provides at cl.19 for any disputes to be determined by reference to English Law and London arbitration or US Federal Marine Law and New York arbitration in similar, although not identical terms, to the provisions in the Baltime and NYPE time charterparty terms.[541]

3.2.2 Sea Waybill and Delivery Order Contracts

In modern conditions there are many occasions when the legal properties (discussed at 3.2.3 below) of a bill of lading, as a document of title to goods that is capable of being transferred to third parties for value, is not required. Thus when dealing with an overseas subsidiary, or on "open-account" terms with a trusted customer, or in relation to roll-on/roll off short sea crossings, there is usually no intention of transferring goods to third parties, either at the time of loading or during the course of the sea carriage. In such cases a bill of lading is unnecessary. Its use may also give rise to difficulties arising from delay or increased administrative costs. These can be attributed to two factors. The inherent obligation on the carrier, when a bill of lading is issued, only to deliver the goods against an original bill of lading—given its status as an exchangeable receipt for the goods; and the difficulty of replicating the functions of a bill of lading in

[538] See the *Starsin* case (fn. 11) discussed at 3.2.1.3 above.

[539] The "Congenbill" bill of lading form edn 1994 recommended by BIMCO for use with the Gencon charterparty form.

[540] Such incorporated terms will only have effect in the context of the bill of lading contract to the extent that they are "germane" to the contract of carriage governed by the bill of lading as discussed at 3.2.3.5 below.

[541] It should be noted that law and jurisdiction clauses are typical examples of mutually agreed charterparty provisions considered not to be germane to bill of lading contracts and which thus require express words of incorporation to take effect in the context of such contracts.

electronic commerce, given its status as a document of title to the goods. Many carriers therefore offer non-negotiable sea waybills, ship delivery orders, or other forms of receipt or undertaking as alternative documents to the bills of lading for such carriage,[542] not least because such alternative documents may be more easily replicated in electronic form, for the facilitation of e-commerce.

Sea waybills may be "received for shipment" or "shipped on board" as required. Goods at destination will be released to the consignee or its agents on proof of identity and the waybill need not even be transmitted to the consignee as proof of ownership. This avoids delay and demurrage charges or warehousing costs associated with the non-arrival of documents. Although certain preconditions may be necessary (particularly the authorisation of bankers to accept the waybill as a valid document when letters of credit are being used, so that the banker is able to release payment on receipt of the documents),[543] the use of sea waybills (formerly called "liner waybills") is firmly established for a wide variety of sea trades. The sea waybill is non-negotiable, incapable of transferring title to the goods and generally does not confer any right to the possession of the goods, so that the carrier simply delivers them to whomsoever the shipper might identify as consignee.[544] Otherwise the non-negotiable sea waybill operates much like a bill of lading as it comprises evidence of the contract of carriage concluded by the shipper with the carrier and is likely to be issued subject to standard terms of carriage (which may either be incorporated into the sea waybill by reference or may, like a bill of lading, appear on its reverse

[542] For example see the *European Enterprise* [1989] 2 Lloyd's Rep. 185 in which, in a case concerning a sea waybill issued for carriage by Ro-Ro ferry on the short sea crossing between the UK and France, Steyn J. commented, at p.187, that "It is the invariable practice of all English cross channel operators not to issue bills of lading for the cross channel Ro-Ro ferry trade".

[543] Article 21 of the UCP 600 provides for the use of sea waybills in documentary credits.

[544] Although sea waybills may seek to limit the shipper's rights in this respect by incorporating provisions such as: the no disposal or NODISP clause where transfer rights are renounced on shipment; or the control clause where transfer rights are renounced on presentation under a letter of credit arrangement; or the transfer clause where the shipper can transfer rights to the consignee on shipment by notation on the sea waybill as under rule 6(ii) of the commonly adopted CMI Uniform Rules for Sea Waybills available at *http://www.comitemaritime.org/*.

side).[545] Contracts of carriage evidenced by sea waybills may be subject to the statutory transfer of rights and liabilities arising under COGSA 1992,[546] subject to the requisite criteria for transfer being fulfilled and to the document itself satisfying the statutory definition. This statutory definition is contained in s.1(3) of the Act, which defines a sea waybill as some document other than a bill of lading that comprises a receipt for the goods containing, or evidencing, a contract for the carriage of goods by sea; and identifies the person to whom delivery of the goods is to be made by the carrier under that contract.

In contrast a ship's delivery order operates like an instruction and simply records the contractual stipulation that the vessel is obliged to make delivery of the goods to a particular person or place. As Kerr J. commented in the *Dona Mari* there are various forms of delivery orders.[547] They may be issued by a seller to the buyer under the contract of sale (a merchant's delivery order) and have no effect on the contract of carriage unless the carrier has attorned to the buyer. However, a ship's delivery order is a document by which the carrier undertakes an obligation to deliver the goods to someone, or somewhere: with delivery either to a named person, or to the holder of the delivery order. The critical characteristic of ship's delivery orders is that they are

> "documents issued by or on behalf of shipowners while the goods are in their possession or at least under their control ... containing some form of undertaking that they will be delivered to the buyers (or perhaps to the bearer) on presentation of the documents".[548]

Contracts of carriage under which ship's delivery orders are issued may also be the subject of statutory transfer of rights and liabilities under COGSA 1992 where the criteria for transfer are satisfied and the document satisfies

[545] In the *European Enterprise* (fn. 542) the conditions of the waybill incorporated an amended version of the Hague-Visby Rules, which were applied (in their revised form) as the terms of the contract of carriage when the Rules were inapplicable as statutory terms in the absence of a bill of lading.

[546] As discussed at 3.1.7 above.

[547] *Cremer and Others v General Carriers SA* [1974] 1 W.L.R. 341, 349.

[548] Per Kerr J. in *Waren Import Gesellschaft Krohn & Co v Internationale Graanhandel Thegra NV* [1975] 1 Lloyd's Rep. 146, 155.

the statutory definition of a "ship's delivery order" contained at s.1(4) of the Act.[549]

These other forms of transport document are very different from bills of lading as they are not documents of title and do not operate as a gateway for the Hague-Visby Rules, unless the requirements of s.1(6)(b) of COGSA 71 are satisfied by a clause paramount in favour of the Rules,[550] or the issue of such alternative transport documents, in place of a bill of lading, amounts (in the context of s.1(6) of COGSA 71 and arts VI and III(8) of the Rules) to an unlawful derogation of the Rules.[551] In the context of charterparties they are construed in the same way as bills of lading and will simply operate as receipts in the hands of the shipper and, in the event of statutory assignment under COGSA 92 of contractual rights and liabilities, give rise to similar issues with regard to the incorporation of charterparty terms as do bills of lading.[552] Indeed, the duties arising under the common law on the part of the carrier (whether in contract, tort, or bailment) are largely unaffected by goods being consigned by one or other of these documents rather than under bills of lading save that (in the absence of express provision to the contrary) these documents (unlike bills of lading) neither imply that the carrier can only deliver the goods in exchange for the return of the carriage documentation it issued nor amount to a worldwide representation as to the shipment of the goods.

3.2.3 Bill of Lading Contracts

3.2.3.1 The Nature of Bills of Lading

A bill of lading is commonly issued by the carrier to the shipper of goods by sea, except in those trades where by custom (such as in the coasting trade) no bill of lading is generally issued or where the particular contract of carriage is concluded on a basis which does not contemplate the issue of a

[549] Those requirements being that the document comprises neither a bill of lading nor a sea waybill but contains an undertaking of the carrier, in respect of a contract for the carriage of goods by sea, to deliver such goods in whole or part to a person identified in the document.

[550] Section 1(6)(b) of COGSA 1971 provides that the Hague-Visby Rules have the force of law in relation to "any receipt" for goods containing, or evidencing, a contract of carriage which "expressly provides that the Rules are to govern the contract as if the receipt were a bill of lading".

[551] A possibility further discussed at 3.3.2.9 below.

[552] See 3.2.3.5 below.

bill of lading. There is no necessity for a bill of lading, or any other document, to be issued in connection with a contract for the carriage of goods by sea[553] but the shipper is always entitled to require the carrier to issue a bill of lading, unless the parties have expressly agreed in the contract of carriage that no bill of lading shall be issued.[554] The following aspects of bills of lading are addressed at 3.3.2 to 3.3.5 below: the processes by which they are issued; their various forms; their various functions; and their relationship with the terms of any charterparty pursuant to which they may have been issued.

3.2.3.2 The Issue of Bills of Lading

The bill of lading may be signed by the master as agent of the carrier. A master has authority to sign a bill of lading as agent for the shipowner[555] or, in a charterparty by way of demise, for the charterer. The authority of the master extends to confirming, by issuing a bill of lading, that the goods are shipped in good order and condition. This authority may be expressly denied to the master by the carrier but the carrier is bound by a bill of lading signed by the master on the basis of the master's ostensible authority, except as against persons who had notice that the master had no authority to sign it.[556] While the master has implied authority to sign the bill of lading as agent for the carrier, he has no implied authority to agree to carry goods without demanding any freight;[557] nor has he authority to sign the bill of lading as a receipt for goods which have not in fact been delivered to him.[558] It has for many years been the practice for bills of lading to be signed by the ship's broker as agent for the carrier.[559] However, the law with regard to the authority of the master to sign the bills of lading as agent for the carrier appears to be unaffected by this modern practice. Ships' brokers are responsible for signing and issuing bills of lading on the basis that they are apparently invested with the same ostensible authority as that enjoyed

[553] See *Vita Food Products v Unus Shipping Company* [1939] A.C. 277, 294, per Lord Wright.

[554] There appears to be no direct authority for this undoubted rule of common law. See art.III, rules 3 and 7 of the Hague-Visby Rules.

[555] *The St Cloud* (1863) 8 L.T. 54.

[556] *Manchester Trust v Furness* [1895] 2 Q.B. 539.

[557] *Dewell v Moxon* (1808) 1 Taunt. 391.

[558] *Grant v Norway* (1851) 10 C.B. 665.

[559] *Hayn, Roman and Company v Culliford and Clark* (1878) 3 C.P.D. 410, 414; and see *The Marlborough Hill v Cowan and Sons Ltd* [1921] 1 A.C. 444, 453.

by the master and, according to the face of the bill, frequently exercise such authority expressly "for the master".

A draft bill of lading may be prepared on the carrier's standard form on the basis of the information provided by the shipper. The front side of a bill of lading contains the commercial information (i.e. the details of the shipper, the consignee, the notify party at the discharge port, the load port, the discharge port and the goods) and the reverse side of the bill the carrier's standard terms of carriage. As cargo is received on the quay for loading onto a vessel, tallymen maintain a record briefly describing the goods in terms of quantity, weight and condition. That record is signed by the ship's officer or cargo superintendent supervising the loading of the cargo and given to the shipper in the form of what is generally called a "mate's receipt". The mate's receipt is compared with any draft bill of lading already prepared and multiple identical versions of the bill are signed by the carrier or the carrier's agent, in the form of the draft, or in an amended form, so that the details of the cargo appearing on the bill of lading are consistent with the details recorded on the mate's receipt. When this has been done, several original versions (normally in triplicate) of the bill of lading are given to the shipper. One of the original bills of lading delivered to the shipper should then be presented by the consignee to the carrier at the discharge port in return for delivery of the goods.

3.2.3.3 The Forms of Bills of Lading

The bill of lading may be classified either as "bearer", "order" or "straight consigned", depending on how the consignee is described. A bearer bill is one that does not name the actual consignee of the goods, simply making them deliverable "to bearer", the bearer being anyone in actual possession of the bill. An order bill may take the form of either a consignee order bill providing for delivery to the named consignee or to the consignee's order, thereby facilitating the endorsement and delivery of the bill by the consignee to a third party; or a shipper order bill providing for delivery to the shipper or to the shipper's order, thereby facilitating the endorsement and delivery of the bill by the shipper to a third party without naming a consignee. With either a consignee or shipper order bill the person entitled to immediate possession of the goods from the carrier on presentation of the bill will be the holder in due course of the bill of lading (i.e. the shipper, consignee or any party to whom the bill has been endorsed). Any endorsee may transfer the bill to subsequent endorsees by endorsement and delivery of the bill at any time until the bill has been exchanged for the goods on presentation to the carrier by the person entitled to delivery: at this point the bill is described as having been "accomplished". However, the carriage contract evidenced by a bill of lading will not be completed by being:

> "discharged by performance until the shipowner has actually surrendered possession (that is, has divested himself of all powers to control any physical dealing in the goods) to the person entitled under the terms of the contract to obtain possession of them".[560]

A straight consigned (sometimes called non-negotiable) bill of lading is one that makes the goods deliverable to the named consignee and does not (expressly or by implication) permit transferability, or else expressly negates transferability. Under a straight consigned bill of lading, the carrier is entitled and bound to deliver the goods to the consignee against the production of the bill of lading by that consignee; nonetheless a straight consigned bill remains a document of title for the purposes of art.1(b) of the Hague-Visby Rules, as an original bill of lading must still be presented by the identified consignee to obtain delivery of the goods from the carrier.[561]

There is another division in the classification of bills of lading not connected with delivery, but with shipment on board the carrying ship. Bills of lading may be described as "received for shipment", "ocean" or "combined transport" bills. A received for shipment or received bill merely states that the goods have been received by the carrier for shipment and provides no evidence of actual shipment. If the goods are in fact shipped after a received bill has been issued, this fact may be noted by the carrier on the bill thereby converting it into an ocean bill with effect from the date of shipment noted on it. An ocean bill of lading, or shipped bill is one that states that the goods have been shipped and constitutes a contract of carriage. A combined transport or through transport bill is a relatively modern development used with increasing frequency in multimodal transport by combined transport operators, particularly in the context of container shipments.[562] In the absence of international agreement on the

[560] Per Diplock L.J. in *Barclays Bank Ltd v Commissioners of Customs & Excise* [1963] 1 Lloyd's Rep. 81, 89 whilst holding that, notwithstanding discharge of the goods by the carrier and the storage of the goods by others for some seven months thereafter, the applicable bill of lading had not been accomplished.

[561] *The Rafaela S* [2003] 2 Lloyd's Rep. 113.

[562] Multimodal transport, combined transport operators and the documentation issued for such carriage is reviewed in more detail in 5.2.

difficult questions posed by the increase of modern containerised multimodal transport in an international regulatory regime created around unimodal carriage, the International Chamber of Commerce (ICC) has published a set of Uniform Rules for a Combined Transport Document[563] which could be adopted by a combined transport operator (CTO) as the basis of its conditions of carriage. These Uniform Rules were replaced on January 1, 1992 by the ICC/UNCTAD Rules for Multimodal Transport Documents,[564] which may be incorporated by agreement into contracts of carriage concluded between a shipper and a CTO. The terms of the ICC/ UNCTAD Rules, which are reviewed in further detail in 5.2.3.3 below, provide for the CTO to assume responsibility for the goods from the time of taking them until the time of delivery however the goods are carried.[565] Any such combined transport bill of lading is generally made available in the form of a received for shipment bill as soon as the goods have been taken over so that the documents can be lodged by the exporter at the bank to secure payment.

3.2.3.4 The Functions of Bills of Lading

The various forms of bills of lading referred to above all share five distinct qualities. They are exchangeable receipts for the cargo in the hands of the shipper, or any other person, who is entitled to possession of the goods as against the carrier; they are evidence of the making of the contract of carriage; they comprise documents of title to the goods in the hands of the sellers, buyers and their assignees; they are evidence to the world at large that the goods described in them have been shipped by the carrier (where an ocean bill is issued) or received by the carrier (where a received for shipment bill is issued); and the fact that the contract of carriage contemplates the issue of one of them is a prerequisite for giving the Hague-Visby Rules the "force of law" in the United Kingdom (see s.1(6) of the Carriage of Goods by Sea Act 1971 and art.1(b) of the scheduled Rules). Each of these five qualities is examined in detail below.

[563] ICC Brochure No.298 1975, reprinted March 1985.

[564] ICC Brochure No.481 1992.

[565] The liability of the CTO is determined by any mandatory rules applicable to any mode of carriage during which the loss, damage or delay in question is known to have occurred; or, in the absence of such knowledge, by the terms of the incorporated ICC/UNCTAD Rules.

3.2.3.4.1 The Bill of Lading as a Receipt

The bill of lading usually states the quantity, weight, measurements, etc., of the goods shipped. It frequently contains the statement that the goods are "shipped in good order and condition". As the master has no authority to sign the bill of lading for goods that have not been delivered to him, the carrier is entitled to deny receipt of any goods which are falsely represented by the bill of lading as having been received by the master, when such goods have not in fact been received.[566] The bill of lading is, however, prima facie evidence that the goods stated therein to have been delivered to the carrier have in fact been delivered and the onus of proving that the goods have not been delivered rests on the carrier.[567] This must be strictly proved by the carrier, and this onus cannot be discharged by merely establishing some extreme improbability in the contention that the goods had been delivered.[568]

However, where the bill of lading contains the statement that the goods are shipped in good order and condition, the carrier is estopped—as against any endorsee or holder of the bill of lading who, by acting on the statements contained in the bill of lading without notice that they are inaccurate, has changed position—from denying that the goods were in good order and condition with respect to all defects reasonably ascertainable by the carrier's servants at the time when the goods were delivered to them.[569] The statement, although constituting an estoppel, does not amount to a term in the contract.[570] Although it does amount to an estoppel at common law even if the statement was induced by the fraud of the shipper, provided that the endorsee of the bill of lading was not a party to the fraud.[571] Although the bill of lading is evidence of what is written in it in relation to the apparent quantity, order and condition of the goods, it is at common law only prima facie evidence of the quantity of the goods on the basis that it cannot be within a master's apparent authority to issue bills of

[566] *Bates v Todd* (1831) 1 Mood. & R. 106; *Grant v Norway* (1851) 10 C.B. 665. If the master states that the goods were shipped on a particular day, when in fact they were shipped on a later day, he will be deemed to have apparent authority to do so; *The Saudi Crown* [1986] 1 Lloyd's Rep. 261.

[567] *McLean and Hope v Fleming* (1871) L.R. 2 H.L. Sc. 128, 130, per Lord Chelmsford.

[568] *Hain Steamship Company v Herdman and McDougal* (1922) 11 Ll.L.R. 58.

[569] *Compania Naviera Vasconzada v Churchill and Sim* [1960] 1 K.B. 237; *Cremer v General Carriers SA* [1974] 1 All E.R. 1, Kerr J.

[570] *Compania Naviera Vasconzada v Churchill and Sim* ibid.

[571] *Evans v James Webster Ltd* (1928) 34 Com. Cas. 172, 179, per Wright J.

lading for goods which have never been shipped.[572] However, the carrier cannot contest the apparent condition of the goods as stated in the bill of lading as against a bona fide third party purchaser who has given value for the goods on the basis of the bill of lading (i.e. a consignee or endorsee of the bill).[573]

If the goods are damaged on loading the carrier should express a reservation as to their condition on the bill, thereby turning a "clean" bill into a "claused" or "fouled" bill.[574] The growth of container traffic in international trade has reduced the significance of clean bills of lading as bills are often stamped "shippers' load stow and count. Weight, condition and quality of the cargo unknown" precisely because on external inspection of the cargo all the shipowner can do is count the number of containers and confirm that they show no external damage.[575] If the carrier gives a clean bill of lading knowing that the goods are defective in return for an indemnity from the shipper, such indemnity will be void for fraud,[576] but if the carrier does not know the goods are defective and merely has misgivings about their condition, issuing a clean bill of lading against an indemnity from the shipper might be a perfectly reasonable step for the carrier to take.

However, notwithstanding the above common law rules, s.4 of COGSA 1992 provides that a person who has become the lawful holder of a bill of lading may rely on the bill, as against the carrier, as being conclusive evidence of the shipment of the goods or of their receipt for shipment. The right arises in so far as the bill represents that the goods have been shipped on board, or received for shipment on board, a particular vessel and the bill has been signed by the master of the vessel, or by someone else with the

[572] *Grant v Norway* (1850) 10 CB 665.

[573] *Canadian and Dominion Sugar Co Ltd v Canadian National (West Indies) Shipping Co Ltd* [1947] AC 46 where the shipowner would have been estopped from denying that sugar was damaged on loading had it not been for the fact that the bill had been qualified by a stamp which stated, in effect, that the issue of the bill was subject to the presentation of "clean" loading receipts.

[574] Although this will probably make the bill unacceptable to the buyer of the goods and the buyer's financing banks under documentary credit arrangements.

[575] It is for this reason that, under documentary credit arrangements, the buyer and the buyer's bankers often insist on sight of a packing list and container stuffing certificate to confirm the loading of the containers.

[576] *Brown Jenkinson & Co Ltd v Percy Dalton (London) Ltd* [1957] 2 Q.B. 621.

express, implied or apparent authority of the carrier to sign bills of lading.[577] The estoppel that is effectively created by s.4 COGSA 1992 only arises in favour of a "lawful holder" of the bill defined by s.5(2) of the 1992 Act as being a person who has become the holder in possession of the bill in good faith who is also (a) the consignee identified in the bill; (b) the person to whom possession of it has been transferred by delivery, endorsement or, in the case of a bearer bill, any other transfer; or (c) the person whose possession would have been within either of the above two categories if the transaction by which possession was transferred had taken place earlier at a time when possession of the bill still signified entitlement to possession of the goods against the carrier. The person who ships the goods with the carrier naming itself as consignee, or who relinquishes and subsequently retakes possession of the bill,[578] may, potentially, fall within this definition when the Hague-Visby Rules are inapplicable to the carriage.[579] Where the bill of lading states "Weight, quantity, quality unknown", it would appear that no estoppel will arise under s.4 COGSA 1992 as the bill of lading is not even prima facie evidence of the weight, quantity and quality stated in the bill of lading.[580] However, where the bill of lading contains statements both that the goods are shipped "in good order and condition" and that "the weight, quantity and quality are unknown", the latter statement will be interpreted as being qualified by the former, with the result that the carrier will be estopped from denying that the goods were shipped in good order and condition, with regard to any defect reasonably ascertainable on inspection.[581]

Where the bill of lading states that the weight, quantity and quality are unknown, the shipper is as much entitled as the carrier to deny the truth of

[577] Unlike the provision in s.3 Bills of Lading Act 1855, which s.4 COGSA 1992 replaced, such representations bind the carrier rather than merely the master or other agent signing the bill.

[578] A situation which may arise, for example, following rejection of the goods by the consignee under a contract of sale.

[579] The position is otherwise when the Hague-Visby Rules are applicable, as art.III(4) provides for a bill of lading to be conclusive evidence as to the description of the goods only when the bill of lading has been transferred to a third party acting in good faith.

[580] *New Chinese Antimony Company v Ocean Steamship Company* [1917] 2 K.B. 664; *Attorney-General of Ceylon v Scindia Steam Navigation Company* [1962] A.C. 60; *The Herroe and Askoe* [1986] 2 Lloyd's Rep. 281 being decisions made under the preceding, now repealed, provision at s.3 Bills of Lading Act 1855.

[581] *The Tromp* [1921] P. 337.

the statements in the bill of lading.[582] The parties may sometimes agree in the contract of carriage that the bill of lading shall be conclusive evidence with regard to the weight and quantity of the goods delivered to the carrier. Where the bill of lading contains a term that the statements in it are to be conclusive evidence and in fact the quantity of some goods delivered to the carrier is over-stated and the quantity of others understated, the carrier will be liable for failure to deliver to the consignee the full quantity of the goods which were over-stated in the bill of lading. The carrier cannot offset against this deficiency the extra quantity of goods which were understated in the bill of lading,[583] for the statements in it are conclusive with regard to each class of goods.[584] The provision in the bill of lading that the statements in it are to be conclusive evidence will not be effective as between the parties to a charterparty contract if such a provision is inconsistent with the terms of the charterparty[585] or any other contract of carriage pursuant to which the bill of lading may have been issued.[586] If the parties agree to issue a bill of lading containing statements which they know to be untrue, the contract may be found to be an illegal contract. Where the carrier, at the shipper's request, issued a clean bill of lading knowing that the goods were defective, the carrier was unable to rely on the shipper's agreement to indemnify it against any liability incurred to third parties by this untrue statement, as the indemnity was held to be unenforceable by the carrier, on the basis that the contract of indemnity was void for illegality.[587]

Of course, as discussed at 3.3.4.3 below in connection with the bill of lading as a document of title, the bill operates as an exchangeable receipt for the goods. It is issued by the carrier to the shipper as evidence that the carrier has the goods and, as an exchangeable receipt, it must be handed over by the consignee to the carrier by way of exchange for the goods to enable the consignee to obtain delivery of them. It is "a key which in the hands of a rightful owner is intended to unlock the door of the warehouse, floating or fixed, in which the goods may chance to be".[588]

[582] *Lebeau v General Steam Navigation Company* (1872) L.R. 8 C.P. 88.
[583] *The Nordborg* [1939] P. 121.
[584] *Mediterranean and New York Shipping Company v Mackay* [1903] 1 K.B. 297.
[585] *Oostzee Stoomvart Maatsshapij v Bell and Harrison* (1906) 11 Com. Cas. 214.
[586] *Lohden v Calder* (1898) 14 T.L.R. 311.
[587] *Brown Jenkinson and Company v Percy Dalton (London) Ltd* [1957] 2 Q.B. 621.
[588] Per Bowen L.J. in *Sanders Bros v Maclean & Co* 11 Q.B.D. 327, 341.

3.2.3.4.2 The Bill of Lading as Evidence of the Contract of Carriage

It is usual for the bill of lading to contain the shipowner's standard terms of carriage. At times there has been some conflict of judicial opinion as to whether, where a bill of lading is issued otherwise than to the charterer under a charterparty, it is itself the contract of carriage, or whether it is merely a document containing the terms of the contract and constituting evidence of the contract, but generally it can be seen as merely evidence of some prior oral or written contract for the carriage of the goods. For this reason, the parol evidence rule[589] is generally inapplicable to bills of lading and oral evidence is therefore admissible to vary the terms of the contract stated in the bill of lading if its terms are such that they do not reflect the contractual terms previously agreed.[590] In *The Ardennes* Lord Goddard C.J. held that the bill of lading was merely evidence of the contract and that where the carrier had verbally agreed with the shipper to proceed straight to London, he was liable for a breach of contract for calling at an intermediary port on the route, despite the fact that by the terms of the bill of lading he was permitted to call at any port.[591] The equivocal status of a bill of lading in this respect is now reflected by the statutory provision at s.5(1) COGSA 1992, which defines the contract of carriage as being "the contract contained in or evidenced by" the bill of lading, or as the case may be, the sea waybill.

Where under a charterparty, a bill of lading is issued to the charterer in respect of goods shipped by it, the bill of lading is ordinarily a mere receipt and document of title to the goods and does not contain, or evidence, the terms of the contract since these are contained in the charterparty.[592] As between charterer and shipowner or disponent owner it is the charterparty that governs the legal relationship and the terms of carriage. The charterer's and shipowner's rights and obligations as between each other are based solely on the charterparty unless, of course, the charterparty provides otherwise. If, extraordinarily, it appears that the parties intended to vary the

[589] The parol evidence rule being a common law rule to the effect that extraneous evidence cannot be adduced to contradict a written agreement, which on its own terms is entire and complete. Under English law, the rule is now subject to many exceptions in any event.

[590] See *Crooks v Allan* (1879) 5 Q.B.D. 38, 40; *Sewell v Burdick* (1884) 10 App. Cas. 74, 105, per Lord Bramwell; *Armour v Walford* [1921] 3 K.B. 473, 476–7, per McCardie J.

[591] *S.S. Ardennes (Cargo Owners) v S.S. Ardennes (Owners)* [1951] 1 K.B. 55.

[592] *Rodocanachi v Milburn* (1886) 18 Q.B.D. 67; *Temperley Steamship Company v Smyth* [1905] 2 K.B. 791, 801, per Collins M.R.

terms of the charterparty by provisions in the bill of lading, the terms of the bill of lading will prevail over those in the charterparty,[593] although this will only be the case to the extent that the terms in the new contract contained in the bill of lading are inconsistent with the provisions of the charterparty. Thus, where the bill of lading was clearly intended to contain the terms of a new contract between the shipowner and the charterer but contained no provision about arbitration, an arbitration clause in the charterparty was held still to be in force. The charterer could not enforce the terms of the bill of lading against the shipowner by an action in the courts but was obliged to resort to arbitration.[594]

As against the statutory transferee[595] of a bill of lading issued in respect of goods shipped by the charterer, the bill of lading contains the terms of the contract. Indeed, in that case the bill of lading does constitute the contract of carriage between the carrier as identified by it[596] and the statutory transferee of it.[597] In any dispute between those parties the terms of the bill may not be interpreted by reference to any charterparty or other contract of affreightment in place between the carrier under the bill and the shipper,[598] other than, to the extent that the terms of such a charterparty (or other contract) have been expressly incorporated into the terms of the bill of lading. In the hands of the statutory transferee the bill will comprise the contract of carriage as between the statutory transferee and the carrier under the bill of lading. Both will be bound by the terms of the bill.[599] However, where the endorsee or transferee of the bill happens also to be the charterer of the vessel, the provisions of the charterparty will

593 *Gullischen v Stewart Brothers* (1884) 13 Q.B.D. 317; but see *Kruger v Moel Tryvan Ship Company* [1907] A.C. 272, 278, per Lord Halsbury.

594 *The President of India v Metcalfe Shipping Company Ltd* [1969] 2 Q.B. 123.

595 Being such endorsee, holder, or other statutory transferee of the bill of lading as may be entitled to claim under the contract of carriage pursuant to s.2 COGSA 1992.

596 Pursuant to the decision of the House of Lords in the *Starsin* (2003) 1 Lloyd's Rep. 571 the identification of the contracting carrier under the bill of lading is made by interpreting the information provided on the front of the bill to determine on whose behalf, as carrier, it has been issued.

597 *Temperley Steam Shipping Company v Smyth*, at p.802, per Collins M.R.

598 *Leduc v Ward* (1898) 20 Q.B.D. 475.

599 ibid., where the endorsees of a bill of lading sought to recover damages for the loss of a consignment of rape seed and were able to rely on the bill of lading as conclusive evidence of the terms of the contract of carriage.

prevail[600] since the contractual relationship between shipowners and charterers is governed by the charterparty.[601]

3.2.3.4.3 The Bill of Lading as a Document of Title

When a bill of lading is delivered by the transferor to a transferee who gives valuable consideration for it, with the intention of transferring the ownership of the goods referred to in it to the transferee, the mere transfer of the bill of lading moves the ownership of the goods to the transferee.[602] However, title to goods passes from seller to purchaser under a contract of sale when, according to the contract, the parties intend it to pass;[603] so the real significance of the bill of lading lies in the right which it embodies to possession of the goods from the carrier. By the issue of the bill of lading, the carrier undertakes "to deliver, on production of the bill of lading, to the person entitled under the bill of lading";[604] and the rights to possession of the goods afforded by the bill of lading may be transferred through such mechanisms of negotiation or delivery as might be contemplated by the terms in which it is drawn.[605] In this respect, a bill of lading resembles a negotiable instrument. It is not, however, a conventional negotiable instrument, because the transferee cannot ordinarily acquire a better title to the goods than that held by the transferor[606] and the bill of lading must be expressly drawn so as to be negotiable, since no presumption arises at law as to its negotiability. It is therefore inaccurate to call a bill of lading a negotiable instrument for these reasons. Furthermore, where the transferee of a bill of lading does not give valuable consideration for it, no title whatever to the goods comprised in the bill of lading is acquired.[607] However, the bill of lading is often referred to as a semi-negotiable

[600] *President of India v Metcalfe* [1970] 1 Q.B.D. where it was held that the Indian government was unable to maintain litigation proceedings against the carrier under the terms of a bill of lading endorsed to them; since, as charterers of the vessel, the government was bound by the arbitration clause to which the charterparty but not the bill of lading was subject.

[601] As further discussed at 3.3.5 below.

[602] *Lickbarrow v Mason* (1794) 5 T.R. 683.

[603] Section 17 Sale of Goods Act 1979.

[604] Per Lord Denning in *Sze Hai Tong Bank v Rambler Cycle Co* Ltd [1959] AC 576.

[605] With bills drawn to bearer, or straight bills drawn only to the identified consignee, being transferable by delivery and bills drawn to order being transferable by negotiation as discussed in 3.3.3.

[606] *Newsom v Thornton* (1805) 6 East 17.

[607] *Sewell v Burdick* (1884) 10 App. Cas. 74, 80, per Lord Selbourne L.C.; *Chartered Bank of India v Henderson and Company* (1874) L.R. 5 P.C. 501.

instrument and it is in some ways considered to be a negotiable instrument for the purpose of the Hague-Visby Rules and statutes such as COGSA 1992.[608] A bill of lading may be transferred in order to give the transferee a mortgage, a pledge, or even ownership in goods; whether it actually does this depends entirely on the intention of the transferor.[609]

Where the transferor delivers a bill of lading in exchange for a bill of exchange drawn by the transferee, in the absence of an express agreement to the contrary it is implied that transfer of the ownership of the goods to the transferee is conditional upon the bill of exchange being accepted.[610] If it is not accepted, the transferee acquires no title to the goods; if, in such a case, the transferee of the bill of lading transfers it again, that transferee acquires no title to the goods unless it is received for value without notice that the transferor held only a conditional title to the goods.[611] If the second transferee had notice, at the time of acquisition of the bill, that the transferor was bankrupt, this is deemed to be notice that the transferor did not have a bona fide title to the goods.[612] However, this does not apply if the second transferee merely had notice that the transferor had not paid for the goods.[613] The holder of a bill of lading may deliver it to an agent with instructions to deliver it to a transferee when a certain condition has been performed. If the agent delivers the bill of lading to the transferee before the condition has been performed, the transferee nevertheless acquires a good title to the goods if the agent's authority to transfer the bill of lading can be implied, provided that the transferee had no notice, at the time when the bill of lading was delivered, of the transferor's instructions to the agent.[614]

At common law, the transfer of the bill of lading transfers only the ownership of the goods, and does not operate as an assignment of the contract contained in it.[615] However, as discussed at 3.1.7.1 above, a statutory assignment of the contract of carriage evidenced by a bill of lading is

[608] As discussed, respectively, at 3.3.2 below and 1.7.1 above.

[609] *Sewell v Burdick*; in *Kwei Tek Chao v British Traders and Shippers* [1957] 2 Q.B. 459.

[610] Section 19(3) Sale of Goods Act 1979.

[611] *Cahn v Pockett's Bristol Channel Steam Packet Company* [1899] 1 Q.B. 643, and s.25 and s.47 Sale of Goods Act 1979.

[612] *Cuming v Brown* (1808) 9 East, 506, 514, per Lord Ellenborough C.J.

[613] ibid.

[614] *The Argentina* (1867) L.R. 1 Ad. & Ec. 370. See also the Factors Act 1889.

[615] *Thompson v Dominy* (1845) 14 M. & W. 403; *Sanders v Vanzeller* (1843) 3 G. & D. 580.

provided for by COGSA 1992. The Act only assigns to the lawful holder[616] of a bill of lading the rights of suit and liabilities arising under the carriage contract as contained in, or evidenced by, it. No statutory transfer arises in respect of any other contract between the transferor of the bill of lading and the carrier, whether contained in a charterparty or elsewhere,[617] as the lawful holder of a bill of lading is not deemed to have constructive notice of the terms of the charterparty[618] unless such terms have been expressly incorporated into the terms of the bill of lading.[619] To the extent that these terms have been effectively incorporated into the bill of lading (and the effective operation of the statutory assignment) the lawful holder of the bill is bound by the terms of the charterparty.[620] If a bill of lading does not contain a reference to the shipper's "order or assigns", or otherwise indicate that the parties intend it to be a semi-negotiable instrument, the transfer of the bill does not transfer ownership of the goods[621] but may nonetheless be subject to the statutory assignment of rights and liabilities under the contract of carriage to the extent that the transferee is identified in the bill as the consignee of the goods to which the bill relates.[622]

It is ordinarily the duty of the carrier to deliver the goods to the holder of the bill of lading. If the carrier does this without notice that the holder is not entitled to the goods, the carrier is not liable to the person entitled to the goods for conversion or otherwise.[623] However, if the carrier delivers the goods to a consignee who is not in possession of the bill of lading, the carrier will be liable to the person entitled to the goods if this is not the person to whom the goods were delivered.[624] This remains the case even where the person entitled to the goods did not acquire the bill of lading until after the carrier had delivered the goods to the other person.[625] If the bill of lading states that the carrier's liability "shall be deemed to cease absolutely after the goods are discharged from the ship", the carrier will nevertheless be liable if the goods are delivered to the wrong consignee, who is not in

[616] As defined by s.5(2) COGSA 1992 and discussed at 3.1.7 above.

[617] *The Emilien Marie* (1875) 32 L.T. 435.

[618] *Manchester Trust v Furness* [1895] 2 Q.B. 539.

[619] See 3.2.3.5 below for discussion as to the incorporation of charterparty terms into bills of lading.

[620] *Wegener v Smith* (1854) 15 C.B. 285.

[621] *Henderson and Company v Comptoir d'Escompte de Paris* (1873) L.R. 5 P.C. 253.

[622] COGSA s.5(2)(a).

[623] *Barber v Meyerstein* (1870) L.R. 4 H.L. 317.

[624] *Glyn Mills and Company v East and West India Dock Company* (1882) 7 App. Cas. 591, 610, per Lord Blackburn; *Jag Dhir and Jag Shakti* [1986] Lloyd's Rep. 1.

[625] *Bristol and West of England Bank v Midland Railway Company* [1891] 2 Q.B. 653.

possession of the bill of lading. This applies even if the goods are customarily released at the port of discharge without requiring the bill of lading to be produced.[626] Where, however, the bill of lading is in the hands of a person who is not entitled to delivery of the goods, the carrier will not be liable if it delivers the goods to the person who is in fact entitled to take delivery,[627] and delivery to the person entitled will operate as a discharge of the bill of lading.[628] The bill of lading is in every case discharged when the goods are delivered to the consignee entitled to take delivery.[629]

It is common practice to execute the bill of lading in three parts, two of which are delivered to the shipper and one retained by the master. This practice has been condemned judicially as tending to facilitate fraud[630] but it is widely adopted. Often one part of the bill of lading is marked as the valid part, and the others as duplicates. Where a bill of lading is executed in three parts, it is often agreed in it that the delivery of one part shall render the other two parts void. The carrier is exempted from all liability if the goods are delivered to the holder of one of the parts of a bill, even though another part of the bill may have already been delivered to the person lawfully entitled to the goods.[631] However, while such delivery of the goods exempts the carrier from all liability, it neither operates to defeat the title of any person who had earlier received delivery of another original part of the bill of lading nor operates to pass any title to any person wrongfully in possession of the goods.[632]

3.2.3.4.4 The Bill of Lading as a Representation to the World at Large

The bill of lading is evidence of what is written in it in relation to the apparent quantity, order, condition and shipment of the goods.[633] It is also a representation, made by the carrier on whose behalf it is issued, as to the

[626] *Sze Hai Tong Bank v Rambler Cycle Company* [1959] A.C. 576.
[627] *London Joint Stock Bank v British Amsterdam Maritime Agency* (1910) 16 Com. Cas. 102, 107, per Channell J.
[628] ibid.
[629] ibid.
[630] *Glyn Mills and Company v East and West India Dock Company* (fn. 624), at p.599, per Lord Cairns.
[631] ibid.
[632] *Barber v Meyerstein* (1870) L.R. 4 H.L. 317.
[633] COGSA 1992 s.4 (as to quantity and shipment); *Compania Naviera Vasconzada v Churchill & Sim* [1906] 1 K.B. 237 and *Brandt v Liverpool, Brazil and River Plate Steam Navigation Company Ltd* [1924] 1 K.B. 575 being authority for the evidencial value of statements as to the order and condition of goods.

truth of the facts stated in relation to those matters. Such representation is made to anyone purchasing, or funding the purchase of, the goods in reliance upon the statements in the bill of lading since the carrier "intends that the bill of lading he issues should be relied upon by those into whose hands it properly comes: consignees, bankers and endorsees must be within his contemplation".[634] At common law the representation as to the quantity of the goods shipped was only prima facie evidence[635] but, pursuant to s.4 COGSA 1992, it is now conclusive evidence as to the quantity of the goods shipped as against a lawful holder of the bill.[636] These representations may not only have contractual effect but may also give rise to liabilities in tort for negligent misstatement or for deceit[637] as they constitute representations to those transacting business in relation to the goods and relying:

> "upon the veracity and authenticity of the bill. Honest commerce requires that those who put bills of lading into circulation do so only where the bill of lading, as far as they know, represents the true facts".[638]

3.2.3.4.5 The Bill of Lading as a Gateway to the Hague-Visby Rules

By s.1(6) of the Carriage of Goods by Sea Act 1971 (COGSA 71) and art.1(b) of the scheduled Hague-Visby Rules, the Hague-Visby Rules only apply by "force of law" where the carriage is subject to a bill of lading and one of the following criteria is met: the goods are shipped from a contracting state; the bill of lading is issued in a contracting state; or, the bill of lading contains a clause paramount applying the Hague-Visby Rules to it (or

[634] Per Mr Justice Cresswell in *Standard Chartered Bank v Pakistan National Shipping Corporation* [1998] 1 Lloyd's Rep. 684 whose decision in this respect was confirmed by the judgment of the Court of Appeal reported at [2000] 1 Lloyd's Rep. 218 and undisturbed by the judgment of the House of Lords reported at [2003] 1 A.C. 959.

[635] *Grant v Norway* (1850) 10 CB 665.

[636] *Alimport v Soubert Shipping Co Ltd* [2000] 2 Lloyd's Rep. 447.

[637] See 1.6.1.3, 1.8.1 and 1.8.2 for further discussion of such claims in tort for negligent misstatement and deceit.

[638] Per Cresswell J. *Standard Chartered Bank v Pakistan National Shipping Corporation* (fn. 634) in which case misdated bills of lading falsely representing that the goods had been shipped prior to the actual date of shipment were held to give rise to liabilities in tort for deceit on the part of the carrier and the carrier's agent: it being held by the House of Lords that the agent could not escape personal liability by reason of the fraud being committed in the course of employment by the carrier.

to a non-negotiable sea waybill providing that the Hague-Visby Rules are to apply as if such document was a bill of lading).[639] Accordingly, the applicability of the bill of lading is a prerequisite to the mandatory application of the Hague-Visby Rules, since the Rules only apply where the carrier's relationship with the shipper is (or should have been)[640] covered by a bill of lading or a similar document of title[641] It is for this reason that the Rules do not apply as far as the relationship between shipowner and charterer is concerned, since in English law, as explained above, that relationship is not covered by the bill of lading, but only by the charterparty provisions.[642]

3.2.3.5 The Relationship between the Terms of Bills of Lading and Charterparties

As considered above, a bill of lading in the hands of the charterer of the carrying vessel is merely a receipt. It is the charterparty that governs the relationship between the shipowner, or other disponent owner, and the charterer. This remains the case notwithstanding the issue of bills of lading to the charterer for the subject voyage. Only if such bills of lading are negotiated by the charterers to third parties providing value for the transfer of some legal or possessory interest in the cargo do they have contractual significance and, even then, their only contractual significance is between those third parties and the person identified by the bill of lading as the contractual carrier. The situation is more complex where the charterer contracts with other shippers for the carriage of goods since, in this event, there are two discrete types of contract of carriage, between the disponent owner and the charterer, and between the charterer and the shippers. If the vessel is carrying different parcels of cargo with some being shipped by the charterer and others by other shippers, the discrete bills of lading issued for each parcel may evidence contracts of carriage undertaken by different carriers, namely, the disponent owner and the charterer. Any transferee or endorsee of any bill issued for goods carried on a chartered ship cannot know whether the bill has been issued pursuant to contracts of carriage concluded between the charterer and the disponent owner or between the shipper with one or other of the disponent owner and the charterer. Where

[639] COGSA 1971 s.1(6)(b).

[640] See 3.3.2.9 below for a discussion as to when carriage otherwise than pursuant to a bill of lading might amount to an unlawful derogation of the Hague-Visby Rules.

[641] See art.1(b) of the Rules and s.1(4) COGSA 1971.

[642] The effect of the Hague-Visby Rules is considered at 3.3.2 below.

there is a chain of charterparties with various disponent owners sub-chartering the vessel to other disponent owners with many different shippers and transferees of cargo, as is commonly the case, identifying the party responsible for any loss or damage to the goods carried is complex. Obviously, the person who is responsible for the physical operation of the ship in terms of employing the master, officers and crew, maintaining the vessel in class and operating proper safe ship procedures may be liable in tort for negligence and in bailment. This will generally be the shipowner or the bareboat/demise charterer. Identifying the carrier for the purpose of a claim in contract, following their Lordships' decision in the *Starsin*,[643] now requires the front of the bill of lading to be interpreted to ascertain on whose behalf it has been issued.

In the *Starsin*[644] the House of Lords held that if the contractual carrier can be clearly identified from the front of the bill then any contrary indications on the reverse side should be ignored. All issued bills of lading are signed either manually, electronically or by printed stamp, and the signature and attestation clause need to be examined to see whether they evidence signature on behalf of the master of the vessel (who ordinarily will be the agent of the shipowner or bareboat/demise charterer by whom he is employed) or on behalf of some other person such as a time or voyage charterer. In the *Starsin* case the House of Lords was in no doubt that the bills of lading were the non-demise time charterers' bills as they had been expressly signed, on pre-printed forms bearing the name of the time charterers, by agents "As Agent for" the time charterers "As Carrier". As their Lordships considered the front of the bill unequivocally identified the time charterers as "carrier", their Lordships considered themselves justified in completely ignoring the contrary terms on the reverse side of the bill, even though those terms purported, by a so-called demise clause, to provide that the bill of lading bound only shipowners and charterers by demise (and not time or voyage charterers otherwise than by demise). Where the front of the bill is ambiguous such terms on the reverse may still be determinative, but in the first instance the front of the bill should be considered carefully to determine the identity of the contractual carrier under the bill of lading.

The bill of lading may seek to incorporate into its own terms the terms of the charterparty. The question arises as to what extent a third party transferee of a bill of lading should be bound by such incorporated terms.

643 [2003] 1 Lloyd's Rep 571.
644 ibid.

In the *Varenna*[645] the Court of Appeal adopted a stepped approach to this enquiry. First, operative words of incorporation must be found in the bill of lading. Secondly, those operative words must be carefully construed to assess precisely which charterparty terms are to be incorporated in the bill. Thirdly, those charterparty terms prima facie incorporated into the bill which "one might describe as surplus, insensible or inconsistent provisions" in the context of a bill of lading contract will "fall to be disincorporated, rejected or ignored as surplusage".[646] Fourthly, incorporated terms may be subjected to linguistic manipulation to adapt them for use in the bill of lading contract. Fifthly, binding judicial precedent or persuasive judicial opinion from existing case law should be applied in the interpretation of both words of incorporation in the bill of lading and the incorporated words in the charterparty.

There is considerable judicial authority in this area, which has given rise to much binding legal precedent of which the following are significant examples. General words of incorporation in bills of lading (i.e. "All other terms and conditions and exceptions as per charterparty . . .")[647] have been held to encompass only those charterparty terms that are directly germane to the shipment, carriage and delivery of the cargo and the payment of freight. Since charterparty arbitration clauses are not generally considered to be germane to a bill of lading contract, such an arbitration clause may only be incorporated into a bill of lading from a charterparty where: either the arbitration clause is the subject of specific and express incorporation by the bill of lading; or, if general words of incorporation in the bill of lading could be construed to include it, the arbitration clause itself expressly encompasses disputes under the bill of lading.[648] Charterparty words and clauses to be incorporated (whether by general or specific provision) must comprise terms that are consistent with the bill of lading contract; both in relation to the express terms of the bill[649] and the perceived intention of the parties to the bill.[650] In the event of inconsistency between the terms of the

[645] [1984] Q.B. 559.

[646] ibid. per Donaldson L.J.

[647] *T W Thomas & Co Ltd v Portsea Steamship & Co Ltd* [1912] A.C. 1.

[648] *The Delos* [2001] 1 Lloyd's Rep. 703.

[649] *Gardner v Trechmann* (1885) 15 Q.B.D. 154.

[650] *Miramar Maritime Corp v Holborn Oil Trading* [1984] 1 A.C. 676, where the House of Lords resisted the incorporation of demurrage provisions on the basis that such charterparty provisions were inconsistent with the intention of the parties to the bill of lading even though no inconsistency arose as to the bill's express terms.

bill and the terms of the charterparty, whichever document has contractual force as between the parties to the dispute will prevail. In consequence, whilst the contracting carrier will be bound by the terms of the bill of lading in any dispute with the transferee or endorsee of the bill notwithstanding contrary provisions in the charterparty,[651] the parties to the charterparty will be bound by the terms of the charterparty in relation to any claim for contribution or indemnity arising in respect of liabilities to third parties under such bill of lading terms.[652]

3.3 Mandatory Regulation of Contractual Terms

3.3.1 Nature of Mandatory Regulation

The contractual terms for the carriage of goods by sea may be subject to one of a number of various regimes of mandatory regulation deriving from one or other public international law treaty instruments. The applicability of any of these regimes in any particular carriage context will depend upon their express incorporation into the contractual terms of carriage,[653] or, alternatively, upon their application as instruments of mandatory law by the court or tribunal determining any dispute between the parties.[654] Of course, where such regimes are applicable as instruments of mandatory law they will apply irrespective of the agreement between the parties. The main treaty instruments particularly regulating the terms of contracts for the carriage of goods by sea (ignoring, for this purpose, treaties primarily relating to other modes of carriage that may, in particular circumstances, also have a mandatory effect on sea carriage contracts)[655] are, in

[651] *Kruger v Moel Tryvan Ship Co* [1907] AC 272.

[652] *The C Joyce* [1986] 2 All E.R. 177, where shipowners were unable to recover any indemnity from charterers for liabilities under the Hague-Visby Rules when the charterers were obliged by the charterparty to issue bills subject to the Hague-Visby Rules. The position may be otherwise when the shipowner is obliged to sign bills as presented since, as discussed at 3.2.1.3 above, a right to indemnity may then be implied.

[653] Issues of incorporation are discussed generally at 1.5.1.

[654] Issues of applicable law and jurisdiction are discussed generally at 1.4.

[655] The contrasting effects of the CMR and CIM conventions in connection with sea carriage contracts are respectively discussed at 2.3.1 and 2.6.2.1; whilst the issue of multimodal carriage is more particularly discussed at 5.2 below.

chronological order: the Hague Rules,[656] the Hague-Visby Rules,[657] the Hamburg Rules,[658] and the Rotterdam Rules.[659] The Hague and Hamburg regimes apply only to sea carriage and will be exclusively discussed in this Part Three. The Rotterdam Rules could apply not only to sea carriage but also to multimodal movements involving sea carriage and are therefore addressed not only in this Part Three but also in 5.2.3.4 in connection with multimodal carriage.

The original, unamended, version of the Hague Rules came into being following an international conference in Brussels in 1922, held in an attempt to resolve some of the difficulties in the carriage of goods by sea arising from the lack of uniformity in the laws of various nations with regard to bills of lading. These problems were adversely affecting international trade, since businesses were unwilling to accept bills of lading as they felt uncertain about their reliability. The conference agreed that if a set of rules acceptable to most nations with substantial maritime fleets could be adopted and enacted into the national systems of law applied by those nations, whenever a dispute arose, these international rules would be upheld by national laws and confidence in bills of lading would be restored. These Rules became known as the Hague Rules, as they were originally drafted by the International Law Association at a conference held at the Hague in 1921. The Rules were eventually ratified by most maritime trading nations, including the United Kingdom[660] but were found to give rise to ambiguities in the context of particular disputes, especially regarding such matters as the liabilities of servants or agents of the carrier and the calculation of the package limitation. Certain contracting states to the Hague Rules with significant interests in the ownership, operation and/or financing of sea carriage eventually agreed (by the Visby Protocol originally

[656] The International Convention for the Unification of Certain Rules of Law relating to Bills of Lading, signed in Brussels on August 25, 1924 known as "the Hague Rules" and discussed at 3.3.3 below.

[657] The Hague Rules as amended by the Protocol signed in Brussels on February 23, 1968 known as "the Hague-Visby Rules" and discussed at 3.3.2 below.

[658] The United Nations Convention on the Carriage of Goods by Sea signed in Hamburg on March 31, 1978 known as "the Hamburg Rules" and discussed at 3.3.4 below.

[659] The United Nations Convention on Contracts for the International Carriage of Goods Wholly or Partly by Sea signed in Rotterdam on September 23, 2009 known as "the Rotterdam Rules" and discussed at 3.3.5 below.

[660] The UK incorporated the Hague Rules into English law as a Schedule to the Carriage of Goods by Sea Act 1924, which has been repealed and replaced by UK COGSA 1971 now giving the Hague-Visby Rules the force of law in the UK.

signed in Brussels on February 23, 1968) to make various amendments to them with the revised version of the Rules, known as the Hague-Visby Rules, being incorporated into English law as a Schedule to the Carriage of Goods by Sea Act 1971 (UK COGSA 1971) and accorded the force of law in the United Kingdom. Conversely, those nations whose interest in maritime trading was predominantly that of exporters and importers of raw materials and finished goods considered themselves disadvantaged by the Hague regime and supported replacing it with an alternative international convention. This was eventually agreed (by the UN Convention signed in Hamburg on March 31, 1978) and these nations adopted the alternative regime of the Hamburg Rules. However, whilst the Hamburg Rules have entered into force as an instrument of public international law between many of those nations, they have not been adopted by the United Kingdom, nor by most other contracting states to the Hague-Visby Rules.

At the date of writing in August 2010, only the Hague-Visby Rules are ratified by and enacted in the United Kingdom. The provisions of the Hague-Visby Rules are accorded the force of law in the United Kingdom by COGSA 1971 and, when applicable, constitute mandatory statutory minimum contractual terms for the carriage of goods by sea under English law. Although the Hague-Visby Rules are essentially a revision of the 1924 Hague Rules by the 1968 Brussels Protocol, the 1968 Protocol has certainly not been ratified by all the trading nations who ratified the Hague Rules.[661] When traders are concerned with contracts for the carriage of goods by sea which are not subject to the Hague-Visby Rules,[662] the original 1924 Hague Rules may still be applied by reference to the law of some state other than the United Kingdom,[663] or by expressly agreed contractual terms incorporating the original Hague Rules into sea carriage contracts. As the 1924 Hague Rules and the 1968 Hague-Visby Rules are largely identical, textual differences between them will be highlighted in 3.3.2 (in the course of addressing the effect of the Hague-Visby Rules) leaving the succeeding 3.3.3 to address the contrasting effect of the Hague Rules in the light of those identified textual differences. The Hamburg Rules (which have the

[661] Those countries which still appear to be contracting states to the Hague Rules are identified in 3.3.3 below.

[662] For instance, when shipment is from a country that has not ratified the 1968 Visby Protocol and there is no clause paramount in favour of the Hague-Visby Rules.

[663] The law of such state being applicable either as the law governing the forum of the dispute, or by way of contractual incorporation of the law in force at the place of shipment.

force of law in various other countries) will be discussed at 3.3.4; the Rotterdam Rules (which are yet to take effect even in international law) are addressed at 3.3.5.

3.3.2 The Hague-Visby Rules

Article II of the Hague Rules (remaining unamended in its Hague-Visby form) summarises in a single sentence what the Hague and Hague-Visby regimes are all about when it provides:

> "Subject to the provisions of Article VI, under every contract of carriage of goods by sea the carrier, in relation to the loading, handling, stowage, carriage, custody, care and discharge of such goods, shall be subject to the responsibilities and liabilities, and entitled to the rights and immunities hereinafter set forth".

By stipulating as a matter of public international law on the one hand, the responsibilities and liabilities of the carrier and on the other hand, the carrier's rights and immunities the intention was to bring to an end the insecurity previously suffered by the holders of bills of lading. So long as a bill of lading came under the Rules, the security of the holder of that bill would not be undermined by whatever exclusions of liability the carrier might decide to incorporate into it as all such clauses evading responsibility would be null and void under the Rules, and the courts would not uphold them. Equally, the carrier had the security of being able to rely on certain rights and immunities under the Rules; so that, whilst the carrier had liability for its own errors and omissions, it would not have liability for matters beyond its control. However, notwithstanding the changes made to the Hague Rules by the 1968 Visby Protocol, the regimes laid down by these Rules seem to stand out (among the various other unimodal regulatory regimes) as conceptually under developed in the light of succeeding operational, commercial and legal developments.[664]

[664] For instance: international carriage is now largely multimodal and frequently containerised; several forms of transport document are now used in international trade which do not comprise documents of title and so fall outside the protection of the Rules; and the commonality of protection afforded by the Rules has been undermined by inconsistency in their implementation and interpretation across diverse legal systems.

3.3.2.1 Scope of Application

The Hague-Visby Rules were incorporated into UK law by the Carriage of Goods by Sea Act 1971. This Act was finally brought into force in June 1977, since which date the Act and 1968 Rules have been effective for the United Kingdom of Great Britain and Northern Ireland. The UK government has confirmed[665] that the Hague-Visby Rules apply to certain crown dependencies and present or former overseas territories[666] and that the following countries are also contracting states to the Hague-Visby Rules: Belgium, Croatia, Denmark, Ecuador, Egypt, Finland, France, Georgia, Italy, Lebanon, the Netherlands, Norway, Poland, Singapore, Spain, Sri Lanka, Sweden, Switzerland, Syria and Tonga. According to the 2007–2008 yearbook of the Comite Maritime International,[667] China, Germany, Greece, Latvia, Lithuania and Russia have also acceded to the Hague-Visby Rules.[668] The 1971 Act is a short Act, only six sections, but contains the full wording of the 1968 Protocol as a Schedule to the Act. This Schedule is given the force of law by s.1(2) of the 1971 Act.

While the chief concern of the Hague-Visby Rules was the regulation of contractual terms for the international carriage of goods by sea under bills of lading, the UK government was concerned that the Rules should also apply to coastal traffic around Great Britain and to the carriage of goods between Great Britain, Northern Ireland, crown dependencies and foreign territories. The 1971 Act achieved this through the mechanism of s.1(3) and s.5. The former provides that the scheduled Hague-Visby Rules

> "... shall have effect (and have the force of law) in relation to and in connection with the carriage of goods by sea in ships where the port of shipment is a port in the United Kingdom, whether or not the

[665] The Carriage of Goods by Sea (Parties to Convention) Order (SI 1985/443) as amended by SI 2000/1103 provides such confirmation.

[666] The Isle of Man, Bermuda, British Antarctic Territory, British Virgin Islands, Cayman Islands, Falkland Islands, Falkland Islands Dependencies, Gibraltar, Hong Kong, Montserrat, and the Turks and Caicos Islands.

[667] The CMI, under whose auspices the Hague Rules and the Hague-Visby Rules were agreed, is the depositary institution for state notifications of accession, denunciation and ratification and now publishes this information at *http://www.comitemaritime.org* together with the text of the Hague-Visby Rules.

[668] The ratification status of these countries is uncertain from the CMI depositary information.

carriage is between ports in two different States within the meaning of Article X of the Rules".[669]

The latter permits the Queen to make orders in Council extending the application of the Rules to encompass carriage from ports in specified crown dependencies (such as the Isle of Man, The Channel Islands etc.) and any specified country outside the Crown's dominions over which the Crown exercises jurisdiction. Section 1 also makes clear that the Rules do not apply to contracts for the carriage of goods by sea where no bill of lading is issued. The whole purpose of the Hague-Visby Rules was to give certainty to holders of bills of lading who take them in good faith for value. Where a bill of lading, or similar document of title, is not issued it is considered that the need for such certainty falls away, as third parties would not be purchasing a document of title to the goods. However, s.1(6) provides that if the parties to a contract wish to do so, they may expressly agree by clause paramount that the Hague-Visby Rules should apply to any non-negotiable document or receipt issued pursuant to a contract for the carriage of goods by sea, or to any bill of lading to which the Rules would not otherwise apply. This permits carriers and traders who approve of the Rules and agree to abide by them to adopt them into their contracts in circumstances where the Rules are not compulsory.

In certain circumstances however, the Rules are susceptable to being wholly or partly displaced by other unimodal regimes where sea carriage covered by a bill of lading is undertaken pursuant to contracts for the international carriage of goods by road, rail or air. The CMR convention applies to sea carriage from a port in the United Kingdom to a port in any foreign country (except Ireland) when undertaken pursuant to a contract for the international carriage of goods by road (other than in respect of funeral consignments and furniture removals) where the goods remain loaded on the road vehicle while they are on board the ship.[670] Similarly, the

[669] The wording of the opening section of the Act of 1924 was less careful than the quoted wording of s.1(3). Instead of referring to the "port of shipment is a port in the United Kingdom" it referred to "ships carrying goods from any port in Great Britain or Northern Ireland", which introduced uncertainty in the event of any intervening call at a UK port. The wording of s.1(3) of the 1971 Act makes it clear that, whilst the rules apply if the port of shipment is a port in the United Kingdom, an intermediate port of call within the UK will not by itself lead to the incorporation of the Rules.

[670] Pursuant to the Carriage of Goods by Road Act 1965 as discussed at 2.3.1.

CIM convention applies to sea carriage comprising supplementary transnational carriage by sea performed under a single contract for transfrontier carriage by rail.[671] The Montreal convention may also apply to sea carriage undertaken in derogation of a contract for the international carriage of goods by air as discussed at 4.2.1.1.

When the UK government enacted the Hague Rules in 1924 the use of a clause expressly incorporating the Rules into the bill was a mandatory requirement.[672] The clause in the bill of lading containing the required statement came to be known as the "clause paramount". The 1971 Act does not contain any reference to the need for a clause paramount in bills issued in Great Britain or Northern Ireland. Since a bill of lading to which the Rules apply is anyway subject to the Rules, the clause paramount has no real meaning in the context of the Hague-Visby Rules, except in relation to their voluntary incorporation discussed above. The significance of the clause paramount in the context of the Hague Rules lay chiefly in the fact that, by reason of the compulsory inclusion (pursuant to the law in force at the port of shipment, where shipment was from a contracting state to the Hague Rules) of a clause paramount into bills of lading, the Hague Rules were effectively incorporated into the contract of carriage[673] and could be applied with contractual force even though the 1924 Act only gave them the force of law when goods were shipped from a UK port. However, the effect of the 1924 Act was that where a bill of lading issued outside the UK failed to contain the clause paramount, a contract governed by English law would not be subject to the Hague Rules, although it would have been subject to the Hague Rules had the carriage contract been governed by the law of the state of the port of loading. This remained the case, even if the bill of lading had been issued without a clause paramount in defiance of the law in force at the port of loading.

Article X of the Hague-Visby Rules resolves such difficulties and explains why UK COGSA 1971 does not require bills of lading to be issued subject to a clause paramount. Article X provides as follows:

[671] Where such transfrontier carriage by sea is performed on designated services pursuant to CIM art.1.4 and COTIF art.24.1 as discussed at 2.6.2.1.

[672] Since s.3 of the Carriage of Goods by Sea Act 1924 provided that "Every bill of lading or similar document of title issued in Great Britain or Northern Ireland which contains or is evidence of any contract to which the Rules apply shall contain an express statement that it is to have effect subject to the provisions of the said Rules as applied by this Act."

[673] At least pursuant to English law as discussed at 1.5.1.

> "The provisions of these Rules shall apply to every bill of lading relating to the carriage of goods between ports in two different States if:
>
> (a) the bill of lading is issued in a contracting State, or
> (b) the carriage is from a port in a contracting State, or
> (c) the contract contained in or evidenced by the bill of lading provides that these Rules or legislation or any States giving effect to them are to govern the contract whatever may be the nationality of the ship, the carrier, the shipper, the consignee, or any other interested person."

As a result of Art.X the Hague-Visby Rules, as incorporated in English law by their inclusion in the Schedule to the 1971 Act, do cover all bills of lading issued in a contracting state, or issued elsewhere for shipment from a contracting state, as well as bills of lading into which the Hague-Visby Rules have been contractually adopted. As mentioned earlier, this wider application is further extended by s.1(6) of the 1971 Act, which extends the Rules (without prejudice to Art.X(c) of the rules) to cover: any bill of lading where the contract contained in it, or evidenced by it, expressly provides that the Rules shall apply; and also to any receipt which is a non-negotiable document marked as such, if the contract so provides. Accordingly, where goods are carried under a contract to which the Rules do not apply by virtue of art.X, the parties may nevertheless expressly agree to incorporate the Rules into the contract, and in this case the contract is subject to the Rules to the extent that is agreed between the parties. The fact that the governing law of the contract is English law will not, by itself, lead to the incorporation of the Hague-Visby Rules, as English law only requires the Rules to have the force of law in the circumstances provided for by art.X of the Rules and ss.1(3) and 1(6) of the 1971 Act. Where goods are shipped from a contracting state that has not ratified the Hague-Visby Rules, the contract of carriage evidenced by a bill of lading may be subject to the Hague Rules or the Hamburg Rules[674] where they are effectively incorporated into the terms of the bill of lading.[675]

[674] As discussed at 3.3.3 and 3.3.4 below.

[675] For instance, a clause paramount in favour of the Hague Rules or the Hamburg Rules, whether or not required under the law in force at the place of shipment, will lead to the contractual incorporation of, as the case may be, the Hague Rules or the Hamburg Rules if and to the extent that the Hague-Visby Rules do not have the force of law.

Article I(b) of the Hague-Visby Rules defines a contract of carriage to which the Rules apply as follows:

> "contracts of carriage covered by a bill of lading or any similar document of title, in so far as such document relates to the carriage of goods by sea, including any bill of lading or any similar document as aforesaid issued under or pursuant to a charterparty from the moment at which such bill of lading or similar document of title regulates the relations between a carrier and a holder of the same."

The words "covered by a bill of lading" are not to be interpreted as meaning only contracts in which a bill of lading is issued[676] and have generally been interpreted as referring to all contracts in which the shipper has the right to demand a bill of lading from the carrier;[677] even though the carrier might intend to deny that right.[678] The Rules apply to such contracts, even where the shipper has not exercised its right to demand a bill of lading and no bill of lading has in fact been issued.[679] As the right of the shipper to demand a bill of lading is always implied unless expressly excluded by the terms of the contract of carriage, the Hague-Visby Rules apply to all international shipments from contracting states (and all domestic shipments from the United Kingdom), except those where the parties may lawfully agree that a bill of lading shall not be issued, or where this is implied by custom.

Article I(c) of the Hague-Visby Rules defines the class of goods to which the Rules apply as including "goods, wares, merchandises and articles of every kind whatsoever, except live animals and cargo which by the contract of carriage is stated as being carried on deck and is so carried". Accordingly, contracts for the carriage of live animals are excluded from the operation of the Rules altogether. However, in order for deck cargo to be excluded, it is necessary both that the contract should state that the goods are to be carried on deck and that the goods are in fact carried on deck. Where the contract of carriage stipulates that the goods "may be carried on

[676] Not least because under art.III(3), the shipper is entitled to demand a bill of lading from the carrier, and if the Rules were not to apply at all until a bill of lading had been issued, art.III(3), would be rendered meaningless.

[677] See *Harland and Wolff v Burns and Laird Lines* [1931] S.C. 722, 728 (in Scotland); *Mack v Burns and Laird Lines* (1944) 77 L1.L.R. 377. 383 (in Northern Ireland).

[678] See *J I Macwilliam Co Inc v Mediterranean Shipping Co SA (Rafaela S)* [2005] 2 A.C. 423 as discussed at 3.3.2.9.

[679] *Pyrene Co Ltd v Scindia Steam Navigation Co Ltd* [1954] 1 Lloyd's Rep. 321.

deck" the Rules apply, since such a contract, by merely authorising the carrier to stow the goods on deck if it so chooses, does not comply with the provisions of art.1(c), which requires the carrier to be contractually obliged to carry goods on deck, for carriage on deck to be excluded from the Rules. Consequently, while a term in the contract authorising the carrier to stow the goods on deck is valid, it does not have the effect of excluding carriage on deck from the Hague-Visby Rules and such carriage pursuant to such a term remains subject to the Rules.[680] The exclusions from the Rules of the carriage of such deck cargo and live animals does not apply to the voluntary incorporation of the Rules pursuant to s.1(6) of the 1971 Act; as s.1(7) of the Act expressly disapplies such exclusions insofar as the contract, into which the Rules have been voluntarily incorporated, relates to such cargo.

Article I(e) of the Hague-Visby Rules limits the period during which the Rules are to apply to the "carriage of goods" which is defined as covering "the period from the time when the goods are loaded on to the time when they are discharged from the ship". It is clear that the Rules apply during[681] and throughout[682] the loading and unloading operations. Article VII of the Rules permits the shipper and carrier to agree to exclude the provisions of the Rules with regard to the liability of the carrier during the period "prior to the loading on and subsequent to the discharge from the ship on which the goods are carried by sea". This provision has been held by the House of Lords to permit the carrier to contract out of loading and discharging obligations.[683] In the course of refusing almost 50 years later to depart from their previous decision, the House of Lords confirmed that whilst the:

> "whole contract of carriage is subject to the Rules ... the extent to which loading and discharging are brought within the carrier's obligations is left to the parties themselves to decide. Thus, if the carrier has agreed to load, stow or discharge the cargo, he must do so properly and carefully"

in accordance with the Rules, but that "the Rules do not invalidate an agreement transferring the responsibility for these operations to the

[680] *Svenska Traktor Aktiebolaget v Maritime Agencies (Southampton) Ltd* [1953] 2 Q.B. 295; *The Tilia Gorthon* [1985] 1 Lloyd's Rep. 522.

[681] *Goodwin Ferreira and Company v Lamport and Holt* (1929) 141 L.T. 494.

[682] *Pyrene Co Ltd v Scindia Steam Navigation Co Ltd* [1954] 1 Lloyd's Rep. 321 in which Devlin J. held that "the rights and immunities under the Rules extend to the whole of the loading carried out".

[683] *Renton (G. H.) & Co v Palmyra Trading Corporation (The Caspiana)* [1957] A.C. 149.

shipper, charterer or consignee".[684] The concept of "loading on" for the purposes of arts I(e) and VII is interpreted as being the beginning of the loading operation of the goods for the shipper concerned and not as the moment when the goods in question cross the ship's rail.[685] Accordingly, where in a contract governed by the Rules the loading of the shipper's goods has begun and some of the goods which have not yet been loaded are damaged before they have crossed the ship's rail, liability for this damage is governed by the Hague-Visby Rules, and any term in the contract conflicting with the Rules is void for the purpose of determining the liability of the carrier for this damage.[686] Similarly, if goods are transhipped en route, the Rules will apply to the whole of the voyage (including the loading and discharging operations in connection with the transhipment) unless there is an agreement to the contrary.[687] However, determining the status of any such contrary agreement is critical since, whilst the carrier has contractual freedom to agree what services are or are not to be provided, the carrier is subject to the minimum requirements and liabilities provided for in the Hague-Visby Rules as to the performance of such services. Devlin J. summarised the position succinctly when he described the Hague-Visby Rules as defining "not the scope of the contract service but the terms on which that service is to be performed".[688]

The second sentence of art.V of the Rules provides that "The provisions of these Rules shall not be applicable to charterparties, but if bills of lading are issued in the case of a ship under a charterparty they shall comply with the terms of these Rules". This provision is supplemented by art.I(b), which provides that the Rules shall apply to a contract in which a bill of lading has been issued under a charterparty, from the moment at which the bill of lading regulates the relations between the carrier and the holder of the bill

[684] Per Lord Steyn in *Jindal Iron and Steel Co Ltd v Islamic Solidarity Shipping Co (The Jordan II)* [2005] 1 Lloyd's Rep. 57, 62 quoting pages 430–431 of the 20th edn of *Scrutton on Charterparties and Bills of Lading* as an accurate statement of the existing law.

[685] Devlin J. commenting in *Pyrene Company v Scindia Steam Navigation Company* [1954] 1 Lloyd's Rep. 321, 329 "Only the most enthusiastic lawyer could watch with satisfaction the spectacle of liabilities shifting uneasily as the cargo sways at the end of a derrick across a notional perpendicular projecting from the ship's rail".

[686] ibid.

[687] *The Anders Maersk* [1986] 1 Lloyd's Rep. 483; *Mayhew Foods Ltd v Overseas Containers Ltd* [1984] 1 Lloyd's Rep. 317.

[688] *Pyrene Co Ltd v Scindia Steam Navigation Co Ltd* [1954] 1 Lloyd's Rep 321, 322; such being described as the "accepted doctrine" by Longmore L.J. in *Trafigura Beheer BV v Mediterranean Shipping Company SA* [2007] 2 Lloyd's Rep. 622.

of lading. As discussed at 3.2.3.5 above, any bill of lading issued by a disponent shipowner in respect of goods shipped under a charterparty arrangement does not ordinarily contain the terms of the contract between such a disponent shipowner and the charterer, since the carriage of goods under such an arrangement is governed solely by the charterparty unless the parties intended, when the bill of lading was issued, to vary the terms of the contract contained in the charterparty. However, where according to the bill of lading the contractual carrier is the disponent owner, the bill will govern the relationship between the disponent owner and any third party to whom the bill has either been issued as shipper, or transferred or endorsed for value. Accordingly, where goods are carried on a chartered ship under bills of lading in circumstances covered by the Rules and those goods have been shipped by third parties, or shipped by the charterer and sold, charged or pledged to third parties, the Rules will apply to any contractual relationship between the disponent owner as carrier and such third parties. However, the contractual relationship between the disponent shipowner and the charterer will be unaffected by the Rules even if a bill of lading is issued, unless the parties have expressly or implicitly agreed to vary the contract contained in the charterparty by a contract contained in the bill of lading or by the provisions of the Rules.

Article I(a) states that the word "carrier" includes the owner or the charterer who enters into a contract with a shipper, but only if and to the extent that such an owner or charterer is bound as carrier to the contract of carriage covered by a bill of lading falling within the Rules. The shipowner will have no liability under the Rules unless it is the contractual carrier, since the Rules have been held to create no statutory duty independent of a contractual relationship. When the Hague-Visby Rules first came into force, academic and judicial contentions were originally advanced to the contrary;[689] but such contrary views have not prevailed. In the 1990 *Captain Gregos* case[690] the Court of Appeal held that the wording of the 1971 Act and the Hague-Visby Rules should be interpreted as only regulating the rights and duties of those persons who were parties to contracts of carriage evidenced by the bill of lading. When contractual rights are being asserted under a bill of lading by anyone other than the original shipper, the identity

[689] See the article "The Hague-Visby Rules" [1978] 2 LMCLQ 225 at 248–249 by Anthony Diamond Q.C. and the obitur dictum of Lord Denning M.R. in *Gillespie Bros v Roy Bowles Ltd* [1973] 1 Lloyd's Rep. 10, 15.

[690] *Compania Portorafti Commerciale SA v Ultramar Panama Inc (The Captain Gregos)* [1990] 1 Lloyd's Rep. 310.

of the contractual carrier is a matter to be determined by proper construction of the bill of lading, particularly the face of the bill of lading.[691]

The scope of the Rules was extended by art.IVb, inserted by the 1968 Visby Protocol. Article IVb(1) of the Hague-Visby Rules applies the "defences and limits of liability" arising under the Rules to "any action against the carrier in respect of loss or damage to goods covered by a contract of carriage whether the action be founded in contract or in tort". Article IVb(2) extends the protection of the "defences and limits of liability" available to a carrier under the Rules to "a servant or agent of the carrier (such servant or agent not being an independent contractor)". This provision has some similarity with the Himalaya Clause developed by the common law and discussed at 1.6.1.2. It applies the exclusions and limitations of liability to the servants and agents of the carrier; enabling such individuals, if sued personally, to claim the benefits of the Rules as far as those exclusions and limitations of liability are concerned. Irrespective of whether such claims, either against the carrier or its servants and agents, are made in contract or tort, the Rules will apply and the wording of art.IVbis will protect them but the protection will not extend so far as to protect independent contractors.[692] Independent contractors (such as ship owners or operators who are not carriers and third party stevedores) are not expressly protected by the Rules, but where they are performing services contemplated by the bill of lading they may be able to secure the protection of the Rules by reference to the principles of bailment and agency as previously discussed at 1.6.1 above.

3.3.2.2 Documentation

Article III(3) provides that "After receiving the goods into his charge, the carrier or the master or agent of the carrier shall, on demand of the shipper, issue to the shipper a bill of lading". The information to be shown on the bill must include: "(a) The leading marks necessary for identification of the goods";[693] "(b) Either the number of packages or pieces or the quantity or weight"; and "(c) The apparent order and condition of the goods".

[691] According to the principles applied by the House of Lords in the *Starsin* case [2003] 1 Lloyd's Rep. 571 variously discussed elsewhere including at 3.1.2 above.

[692] *Scruttons Ltd v Midland Silicones* [1962] A.C. 446 decided in relation to an identical provision of the United States Carriage of Goods by Sea Act 1936.

[693] As both furnished in writing by the shipper before commencement of loading commences and as stamped (or shown) on the goods so as to be legible at the end of the voyage.

However, the carrier is relieved of any obligation to state any marks, number, quantity or weight regarding goods as to which the carrier either has reasonable grounds for suspicion or has had no reasonable means of checking. Article III(4) provides that the "bill of lading shall be prima facie evidence of the receipt by the carrier of the goods as therein described in accordance with paragraph 3 (a), (b) and (c)". The Hague-Visby version of the Rules goes on to provide: "However, proof to the contrary shall not be admissible when the bill of lading has been transferred to a third party in good faith". These words were added to remove the implication of the Hague Rules wording that the carrier was entitled, even as against a third party purchaser of the goods for value relying upon the bill of lading, to seek to rebut the prima facie evidence of the bill to prove that it did not in fact receive the goods. The revised Hague-Visby version of the Rules prevents the carrier from disproving a bill of lading that has come into the possession of an innocent third party for value; since clearly such a party would be disadvantaged if a carrier were able to do this. This means that the carrier would be liable to any such third party under the Hague-Visby Rules for any disparity as to description, weight or condition between the goods as shipped and as stated in the bill of lading. The carrier will of course seek compensation from the original shipper of the goods in respect of any liability incurred by the carrier to any subsequent holder of the bill of lading in this regard and the carrier's claims in this respect are facilitated by art.III(5) which provides:

> "The shipper shall be deemed to have guaranteed to the carrier the accuracy at the time of shipment of the marks, number, quantity and weight as furnished by him, and the shipper shall indemnify the carrier against all loss, damages and expenses arising or resulting from inaccuracies in such particulars. The right of the carrier to such indemnity shall in no way limit his responsibility and liability under the contract of carriage to any person other than the shipper".

The carrier is not, however, obliged to issue a bill of lading that complies with art.III(3) unless the shipper demands it, and if the carrier issues a bill of lading which does not comply with these provisions, and the shipper accepts it without objection, the terms of the bill of lading will nevertheless form the contract between the parties and will be binding on the transferees of the bill of lading.[694] The common law relating to the operation of the bill

[694] *Canada and Dominion Sugar Company v Canadian Steamships* [1947] A.C. 46, 57, per Lord Wright.

of lading as an estoppel with regard to statements as to the weight, quantity and quality of the goods shipped applies to bills of lading issued under contracts governed by the Rules[695] as supplemented by rights arising in favour of statutory transferees of bills of lading under s.4 COGSA 1992.[696] Article III(7) of the Rules provides that the carrier is obliged to issue "a 'shipped' bill of lading" after loading upon request by the shipper provided that the shipper surrenders any prior document of title already received[697] in exchange for the "shipped" bill of lading. However, the carrier may elect to note such prior document of title at the port of shipment with the names of the vessels and the dates of shipment, in which case the prior document of title so noted constitutes a "shipped" bill of lading.

3.3.2.3 Liability of Carrier

Articles III and IV of the Rules regulate the liability of the carrier with regard to the goods during the carriage. Article III(1) provides that:

> "The carrier shall be bound, before and at the beginning of the voyage, to exercise due diligence to: (a) Make the ship seaworthy; (b) Properly man, equip and supply the ship; (c) Make the holds, refrigerating and cool chambers, and all other parts of the ship in which goods are carried, fit and safe for their reception, carriage and preservation".

The meaning of "before and at the beginning of the voyage" was discussed in *Maxine Footwear Co Ltd v Canadian Government Merchant Marine Ltd*, where it was determined that the expression denotes a continuous period from loading to departing.[698] By art.III(1) the absolute duty of seaworthiness on the carrier at common law to provide a seaworthy ship at the commencement of each separate stage of a voyage is displaced by a qualified obligation on the carrier to exercise due diligence to provide a seaworthy ship throughout a continuous period, starting at the commencement of loading and continuing until the vessel departs for the commencement of

[695] *Silver v Ocean Steamship Company* [1930] 1 K.B. 416.

[696] By s.4 COGSA 1992, as already discussed, representations by bills of lading as to the shipment of goods constitute under English law conclusive evidence of the shipment of the goods in favour of any lawful transferee or endorsee of the bill as against the carrier.

[697] Such as any prior received for shipment bill of lading.

[698] [1959] A.C. 589.

the voyage. It is described as an "overriding obligation" as it takes effect notwithstanding the defences arising under art.IV(2) and has the effect of overriding them.[699] Article IV(1) of the Rules provides that:

> "Neither the carrier nor the ship shall be liable for loss or damage arising or resulting from unseaworthiness unless caused by want of due diligence on the part of the carrier to make the ship seaworthy, and to secure that the ship is properly manned, equipped and supplied, and to make the holds, refrigerating and cool chambers and all other parts of the ship in which goods are carried fit and safe for their reception, carriage and preservation, in accordance with the provisions of paragraph 1 of Art.III".

The provision also stipulates that where unseaworthiness causes loss or damage the carrier bears the burden of proving the exercise of due diligence; although, of course, the claimants have the burden of proving the vessel was unseaworthy "before and at the beginning of the voyage" within the meaning of art.III(1) and of proving that unseaworthiness was the cause of the loss or damage alleged.[700]

The concept of unseaworthiness under the Rules is the same as at common law; the vessel should be seaworthy relative to the characteristics of the voyage in any particular case.[701] However, the above provisions of the Rules make clear that the absolute warranty of seaworthiness otherwise implied at common law becomes, under the Rules, a qualified duty of the carrier to exercise due diligence to make the ship seaworthy. However, the difference between the absolute common law duty and the qualified statutory duty has been described as "a limitation or qualification more apparent than real"[702] as the carrier is liable, not only for its negligence, but also the negligence of its servants and agents and any independent contractors engaged by, or on behalf of, the carrier as the statutory duty, although limited to the exercise of due diligence, is non-delegable.[703] In the

[699] ibid. p.603.
[700] *The Europa* [1908] P 84, 97 to 98.
[701] As discussed at 3.1.4.1 above.
[702] Per MacKinnon L.J. in *Smith Hogg & Co Ltd v Black Sea & Baltic Gen. Ins Co Ltd* (1939) 64 Ll.L.Rep. 87, 89.
[703] *Riverstone Meat Company v Lancashire Shipping Company (The Muncaster Castle)* 1961 A.C. 807.

event of unseaworthiness the res ipsa loquitur concept is applicable,[704] as "a ship should not be unseaworthy if proper care is taken".[705] Accordingly, in most cases where a vessel is unseaworthy, due diligence will not have been exercised; if it had been exercised, the vessel would have been seaworthy. Only where the defect causing unseaworthiness is of a latent nature which the due diligence of the shipowner exercised by itself, its servants, agents and independent contractors could not have discovered, can the shipowner point to the qualified duty as having been discharged notwithstanding the unseaworthiness of the vessel.[706] The carrier is not responsible for latent defects already existing in a ship at the time it is acquired from a shipbuilder or shipowner where the carrier has exercised due diligence in commissioning or purchasing it.[707] As the carrier's duty to make the ship seaworthy under the Rules is stated by art.III(1), to exist "before and at the beginning of the voyage"; the principles of the common law relating to stages of the voyage, with regard to the warranty of seaworthiness, have no application to the carrier's duty with regard to seaworthiness under the Rules.[708] The carrier is not liable under art.III(1)(a) if the ship becomes unseaworthy during the course of the voyage. Neither can the carrier rely, in such a case, on the defence provided by art.IV(1)[709] and must instead claim protection by reference to the exceptions arising under art.IV(2) in the event the claimant establishes breach of the duty arising under art.III(2).

Article III(2) provides that: "Subject to the provisions of art.IV, the carrier shall properly and carefully load, handle, stow, carry, keep, care for and discharge the goods carried". This provision refers only to the manner in which the goods are dealt with by the carrier, and has no reference to the place of discharge. A clause in the bill of lading permitting the shipowner, in the event of a strike at the agreed port of discharge, to discharge the cargo in some other port, is valid, as it does not contravene art.III(8) by

[704] *Amstelslot, The; Union of India v NV Reederij Amsterdam* [1963] 2 Lloyd's Rep. 223, 235 per Lord Devlin.

[705] *The Fjord Wind* [2000] 2 Lloyd's Rep. 191, 205 per Stuart-Smith L.J.

[706] Per Mackinnon L.J. in *Smith Hogg & Co Ltd v Black Sea & Baltic Gen. Ins Co Ltd* (fn. 702).

[707] *Angliss and Company v Peninsular and Oriental Steam Navigation Company* [1927] 2 K.B. 456; *Riverstone Meat Company v Lancashire Shipping Company* [1961] A.C. 807.

[708] *Maxine Footwear Company Ltd v Canadian Government Merchant Marine Ltd* [1959] A.C. 589.

[709] *Leesh River Tea Company v British Indian Steam Navigation Company Ltd* [1967] 2 Q.B. 250.

relieving the carrier of its liabilities under art.III(2).[710] Article III(2) does not oblige the carrier to load or discharge the goods, but if the carrier does so then goods must be loaded and discharged "properly and carefully". This provision has been interpreted by the English courts to mean that the carrier must load and discharge both in accordance with a system, which is sound "in light of all the knowledge which the carrier has or ought to have about the nature of the goods"[711] to be carried and with reasonable skill and care.[712] Whether the carrier's obligations under the Rules have been discharged will be a question of fact in each instance.[713] The onus of proof that this duty has been satisfactorily performed rests on the carrier when cargo is damaged in the course of the carriage,[714] since under art.III(2) where:

> "cargo ... was shipped in good order and condition and was delivered damaged, in a manner which was preventible and ought not to have been allowed to occur, there was sufficient evidence of a breach by the carrier of his obligations".[715]

The carrier may, however, avoid liability under the Rules for any breach of art.III(2) which can be proved by the carrier to have been caused specifically by one of the permitted exceptions provided for in art.IV(2).[716] The provisions of art.IV(2) are to the following effect:

> "Neither the carrier nor the ship shall be responsible for loss or damage arising or resulting from: (a) Act, neglect or default of the master, mariner, pilot, or the servants of the carrier in the navigation or in the management of the ship; (b) Fire, unless caused by the actual fault or privity of the carrier; (c) Perils, dangers and accidents of the

[710] *Renton v Palmyra Trading Corporation* [1957] A.C. 149 (House of Lords), affirming the decision of the Court of Appeal [1956] 1 Q.B. 462.

[711] Per Lord Reid in *Albacora Srl v Westcott & Laurance Line Ltd* [1966] 2 Lloyd's Rep. 53, 58.

[712] ibid. in which Lord Reid commented at p.58 that "...'properly' in this context has a meaning slightly different from 'carefully' ... that here 'properly' means in accordance with a sound system ... and that may mean rather more than carrying the goods carefully".

[713] *Albacora SRL v Westcott and Laurence Line Ltd* [1966] 2 Ll.L.R. 53; *The Lucky Wave* [1985] 1 Lloyd's Rep. 80.

[714] *Gosse Millerd v Canadian Government Merchant Marine* [1929] A.C. 223.

[715] ibid. per Viscount Sumner.

[716] The carrier bearing "the onus of bringing the cause of the damage specifically within Art.IV., r. 2" per Viscount Sumner ibid.

> sea or other navigable waters; (d) Act of God; (e) Act of war; (f) Act of public enemies; (g) Arrest or restraint of princes, rulers or people, or seizure under legal process; (h) Quarantine restrictions; (i) Act or omission of the shipper or owner of the goods, his agent or representative; (j) Strikes or lock-outs or stoppage or restraint of labour from whatever cause, whether partial or general; (k) Riots and civil commotions; (l) Saving or attempting to save life or property at sea; (m) Wastage in bulk or weight or any other loss or damage arising from inherent defect, quality or vice of the goods; (n) Insufficiency of packing; (o) Insufficiency or inadequacy of marks; (p) Latent defects not discoverable by due diligence; (q) Any other cause arising without the actual fault or privity of the carrier, or without the fault or neglect of the agents or servants of the carrier, but the burden of proof shall be on the person claiming the benefit of this exception to show that neither the actual fault or privity of the carrier nor the fault or neglect of the agents or servants of the carrier contributed to the loss or damage".

In view of the provisions of art.IV(2)(a), the carrier's duty to exercise due diligence to make the ship seaworthy assumes considerable importance as, irrespective of the art.IV(2) exception relied upon, the exception will not relieve the carrier of the overriding qualified duty of seaworthiness to which the carrier is subject under the Rules. Accordingly, if the goods are damaged through the negligence of the master and crew, the question as to whether or not the carrier is liable will turn on three issues: first, whether the negligent act or omission was committed in the "navigation or management of the ship" so as to entitle the carrier to rely on the exception and shift the onus to the claimant to prove unseaworthiness; secondly, whether the negligent act or omission did in fact render the ship unseaworthy so as to shift the onus back to the carrier to establish the exercise of due diligence; and thirdly, whether the carrier did or did not exercise due diligence "before and at the beginning of the voyage" to ensure the seaworthiness of the vessel so as to determine liability. Where a defective valve caused a cargo of phosphate to be damaged by water it was held that the valve was unserviceable before the ship sailed, and that the crew had failed to exercise due diligence to ensure a seaworthy vessel.[717]

A general issue arising in respect of art.IV(2) is whether the exceptions apply to claims for economic loss arising from delay in delivery in

[717] *Fisons Fertilizers v Thomas Watson Shipping* [1971] 1 Ll.L.R. 141.

circumstances in which the exceptions are only expressly applied to "loss or damage". Similar issues arise in the context of other provisions of the Rules including the non-derogation and financial limitation provisions at arts III(8) and IV(5)(a) although such provisions are expressly applied to liability "for loss or damage to, or in connection with" the goods. The additional words "or in connection with" were critical to the reasoning applied by the House of Lords in *GH Renton & Co Ltd v Palmyra Trading Corp of Panama*[718] and *Adamastos Shipping Co Ltd v Anglo Saxon Petroleum Co Ltd*[719] in deciding that the loss or damage contemplated in those articles included financial loss suffered in connection with the goods. It would be consistent with each of those decisions, and the general approach adopted at common law towards exceptions,[720] for the art.IV(2) exceptions to be interpreted more narrowly as meaning only "loss" or "damage" to the goods, in which case the carrier's liability for financial loss arising from delay would not be subject to any of the exceptions at art.IV(2). However, there seems no logical reason why the Rules should distinguish claims for loss or damage to goods from claims for other loss or damage and a broader construction of the exceptions, to embrace all claims for loss or damage however arising, would appear to better reflect the legislative purpose behind art.IV(2).[721]

"Management of the ship" is construed as meaning acts wholly or primarily committed with the object of managing the ship herself as opposed to the cargo. If the carrier's servants act negligently in the management of the cargo, the exception will not benefit the carrier and the carrier will remain liable for the claim. The test is whether the object of the action was primarily to manage the ship or cargo. The distinction is between:

> "damage resulting from some act relating to the ship herself and only incidentally damaging the cargo, and an act dealing ... solely with the goods and not directly or indirectly with the ship herself".[722]

Management of the ship means "management of the ship ... [and not] ...

[718] [1957] A.C. 149 as to art.III(8) in the context of a claim for misdelivery due to labour disputes at the discharge port.

[719] [1959] A.C. 133, as to art.IV(5)(a) in the context of voyages lost, by reason of unseaworthiness, from a charterparty expressly incorporating the Hague-Visby Rules.

[720] See 1.5.2.

[721] ibid.

[722] *Hourani v T & J Harrison* (1927) 27 Ll.L. Rep. 415.

the general carrying on of the business of transporting goods by sea".[723] Thus the carrier was liable where the goods were damaged by rain owing to the negligent failure of the carrier's servants to shut the hatches when the ship was in dock;[724] also where the goods were stolen by stevedores owing to negligent care of the goods by the crew;[725] as these acts of negligence did not occur in the course of management of the ship. However, the carrier was not liable where goods were damaged by water being negligently pumped into the ballast tank to strengthen the ship;[726] nor where, on the claimant's case, a cargo exploded due to excessive heating of an adjacent bunker tank beyond what was required for the optimum storage of fuel oil.[727] Similarly, the failure of the carrier's servants to take periodic soundings that might have revealed that the ship's storm valves were defective was, if negligent at all, an act of negligence in the management of the ship.[728] However, negligent stowage is not negligence in the management of the ship;[729] so that where stevedores stole the cover plate of a storm valve at a port where the ship called on the voyage, and as a result the ship became unseaworthy after leaving the port, this was not an act of management of the ship.[730] However, where the negligence in the "navigation or management of the ship" amounts to the deliberate running of an unnecessary risk such as to constitute recklessness the exception is not available.[731] The withdrawal of the defence in such circumstances is attributable to the paramount duty on the carrier to take care of the cargo and carry it safely and there is no defence to that paramount duty save in the event of "(1) negligence in caring for the safety of the ship; (2) failure to take care to prevent damage to the ship, or some part of the ship; or (3)

[723] ibid.

[724] *Gosse Millerd v Canadian Government Merchant Marine* [1929] A.C. 223.

[725] *Hourani v T & J Harrison* (1927) 27 Ll.L. Rep. 415.

[726] *The Glenochil* [1896] P. 10.

[727] *Compania Sud American Vapores v MS ER Hamburg Schiffahrtsgesellschaft MBH & Co KG* [2006] 2 Lloyd's Rep. 66.

[728] *Riverstone Meat Company v Lancashire Shipping Company* [1961] A.C. 807.

[729] *The Ferro* [1893] P. 38.

[730] *Leesh River Tea Company Ltd v British Indian Steam Navigation Company Ltd* [1967] 2 Q.B. 250.

[731] See the New Zealand Court of Appeal decision in *Tasman Orient Line CV v New Zealand China Clays (The Tasman Pioneer)* [2009] 2 Lloyd's Rep. 308.

failure in the management of some operation connected with the movement or stability of the ship, or otherwise for ship's purposes."[732]

Where terms are used in the Rules which are either familiar to the English common law or identical to those used in earlier English statutes, the courts of England should not simply interpret these terms in accordance with the principles of common law or English statutes. The purpose of the Rules was to lay down an international code, so as to assimilate contrasting legal principles operating in those states which became contracting states to the international treaties containing the Rules. Accordingly:

> "it is desirable in the interests of uniformity that their interpretation should not be rigidly controlled by domestic precedents of antecedent date, but rather that the language of the rules should be construed on broad principles of general acceptation".[733]

However, earlier decisions of the English courts as to the interpretation of terms in earlier statutes have on occasion been taken as a guide to the interpretation of similar terms in the Rules.[734]

In art.IV(2) provision (p), a "latent defect" is apparently any defect which is not apparent, and which cannot be discovered by due diligence;[735] the words "not discoverable by due diligence" appear, at least for the purposes of English law, to be superfluous. If the latent defect is not discoverable by due diligence, the carrier is apparently not liable, even if it failed to exercise due diligence in attempting to discover the latent defect.[736] In art.IV(2) provision (q), the word "or", where it occurs for the second time, is to be interpreted as meaning "and".[737] Consequently the carrier cannot rely on exception (q) unless the carrier can prove that neither its own actual fault or privity, nor the fault or neglect of its agents or servants, contributed to the damage. The carrier's liability for the fault and neglect of its agents applies

[732] *Gosse Millerd v Canadian Government Merchant Marine* [1928] 1 KB 717 for the dissenting Court of Appeal judgment of Greer L.J., which was approved by Viscount Sumner in the House of Lords [1929] A.C. 223, 236.

[733] *Stag Line v Foscolo Mango* [1932] A.C. 328, 350, per Lord Macmillan.

[734] *Gosse Millerd v Canadian Government Merchant Marine* at p.237, per Lord Sumner. See also *Compania Columbiana de Seguros v Pacific Steam Navigation Company* [1965] 1 Q.B. 101.

[735] See *Brown v Nitrate Steamship Company* (1937) 58 L1.L.R. 188, 191, per Porter J.

[736] *Corporation Argentina v Royal Mail Lines* (1939) 64 L1.L.R. 188, 192, per Branson J.

[737] *Hourani v T & J Harrison* (1927) 27 Ll.L.Rep. 415

only with regard to agents employed by the carrier in its capacity as carrier. The carrier is therefore not liable for the negligence of reasonably competent shipbuilders who were engaged to build or repair the ship.[738] Where stevedores, employed by the carrier to load goods at an intermediary port on the voyage, stole the cover plate of a storm valve with the consequence that the ship became unseaworthy after leaving the port, and goods carried on board the ship were damaged, the carrier was not liable for the damage to the goods. The claimant could not rely on art.IV(1), or art.IV(2)(a), as the ship was not unseaworthy at the beginning of the voyage; whilst the carrier could not rely on art.IV(2)(a) as the theft by the stevedores was not an act of management of the ship, the carrier was exempted from liability under art.IV(2)(q). The act of the stevedores in stealing the cover plate was considered to be wholly outside the scope of their employment, and it was held, therefore, that they were not the "agents or servants" of the carrier for the purpose of art.IV(2)(q).[739] The previous decisions[740] as to the narrow meaning of "actual fault or privity" for the purpose of the now repealed ss.502 and 503 of the Merchant Shipping Act 1894[741] might be applied to the interpretation of the words in art.IV(2)(b) and (q) but, in view of the fact that the carrier is vicariously liable for the negligence of its servants as well as liable for personal fault or privity, the issue is unlikely to arise.

Article IV(4) provides:

"Any deviation in saving or attempting to save life or property at sea,

[738] *Angliss and Company v Peninsular and Oriental Steam Navigation Company* [1927] 2 K.B. 456, 463, per Wright J.

[739] *Leesh River Tea Company Ltd v British Indian Steam Navigation Company Ltd* [1967] 2 Q.B. 250.

[740] See the case of *Lennard's Carrying Co Ltd v Asiatic Petroleum Co Ltd* [1915] A.C. 705 where Viscount Haldane L.C. held that in order to address the shipowner's defence under s.502 (i.e. that fire causing loss had occurred without the shipowner's "actual fault or privity") it was necessary to identify the person or persons being "the directing mind and will" of the shipowning company as to the performance of its shipowning function; and the *Lady Gwendolen* [1965] P.294 where in applying s.503 (i.e. that claims arising from a collision without the shipowner's "actual fault or privity" were subject to limitation by reference to the tonnage of the subject vessel) Sellers L.J. said (p.333) "In their capacity as shipowners they must be judged by the standard of conduct of the ordinary reasonable shipowner in the management and control of a vessel or of a fleet of vessels".

[741] The tonnage limitation now provided for by the LLMC 1976 refers to "personal act or omission"; which, as discussed at 3.1.7.2, has a very restrictive meaning.

or any reasonable deviation, shall not be deemed to be an infringement or breach of these Rules or of the contract of carriage, and the carrier shall not be liable for any loss or damage resulting therefrom".

The question as to what is a reasonable deviation for the purpose of art.IV(4) is probably a question of fact in every case.[742] The concept of reasonable deviation is not limited to those departures from the original route which was actually being contemplated by the parties at the time when the contract was made.[743] However, it is not sufficient that the departure should be reasonable from the point of view of the carrier alone. The interests of all the parties concerned, including those of all the cargo owners and not only those of the particular cargo owner concerned in the dispute, must be considered.[744] It has been suggested that a deviation might be reasonable if it were in the national interest; for example, to assist in the arrest of a fugitive from justice, or to land an important statesman in an emergency[745] but a deviation to land two engineers who had been working in the ship was held not to be reasonable.[746]

It had previously been assumed in the English courts that an unreasonable deviation, which is not permitted by art.IV(4) of the Rules, amounts to a repudiation of the contract of carriage and precludes the carrier from relying on the Rules; placing the carrier, as a wrongful possessor of the goods, under the full liability faced by the carrier who has deviated at common law.[747] The foundations for such an assumption have not been firm for many years and have been undermined by recent authorities such as the *Antares*[748] and the *Kapitan Petko Voivoda.*[749] As previously discussed the Court of Appeal declined in 1987, and again in 2003, to extend the concept of "deviation properly so called" to unlawful carriage on deck and allowed the carrier variously, in each of the cases mentioned, to claim the benefit of the suit time and financial limitation provisions,

[742] *Stag Line v Foscolo Mango* [1932] A.C. 328, per Lord Warrington (p.339) and Lord Russell (p.346), Lord Atkin dub. (p.344).

[743] ibid.

[744] ibid.

[745] ibid.

[746] ibid.

[747] *Stag Line v Foscolo Mango*, at p.340, per Lord Atkin.

[748] *Kenya Railways v Antares Co. Pte Ltd (The Antares)* [1987] 1 Lloyd's Rep. 424 discussed at 1.7.1.4.

[749] *Daewoo Heavy Industries Ltd v Klipriver Shipping Ltd (The Kapitan Petko Voivoda)* [2003] 2 Lloyd's Rep. 1.

provided for in the Rules, to defeat the claimants' actions. In the *Kapitan Petko Voivoda* the Court of Appeal held that, even if the case had concerned deviation properly so-called, any common law principle requiring loss of contractual protection for the carrier could not abrogate rights under an international treaty such as the Hague Rules.[750] The parties could probably agree by an express term in the contract that the carrier may deviate in circumstances not permitted under art.IV(4), since such a term would probably be considered as being a valid specification of the scope of the carrier's duties and not an unlawful derogation of the Rules, notwithstanding the provisions of art.III(8).[751] However, the House of Lords refused to decide the point in 1956 and has not subsequently been afforded the opportunity of doing so.[752]

3.3.2.4 Value of Claims

Under the original version of the Hague Rules, the liability of the carrier was limited "to £100 per package or unit". As discussed at 3.3.1 this aspect gives rise to a number of difficulties under the unamended version of the Hague Rules. Those difficulties are now largely avoided by the 1968 Visby Protocol applied into English law by the Carriage of Goods by Sea Act 1971. Article IV(5)(a) of the Hague-Visby Rules provides as follows as to limitation:

> "Unless the nature and value of such goods have been declared by the shipper before shipment and inserted in the bill of lading,[753] neither the carrier nor the ship shall in any event[754] be or become liable for

[750] Longmore L.J. commenting in the *Kapitan Petko Voivoda*, at para.14, "that the principle for which the deviation cases are authority is very far from being a principle 'of general acceptation'. It is a question of some controversy whether they now exemplify even a principle of English law".

[751] *Foreman v Federal Steam Navigation Company* [1928] 2 K.B. 424, 431, per Wright J.; *Stag Line v Foscolo Mango* [1932] AC 326; *Renton v Palmyra Trading Corporation* [1956] 1 Q.B. 462, 505, per Jenkins L.J. (neither approved nor disapproved by the House of Lords, [1957] A.C. 149).

[752] *Renton v Palmyra Trading Corporation* [1957] A.C. 149.

[753] By art.IV(5)(f) such a declaration where "embodied in the bill of lading, shall be prima facie evidence, but shall not be binding or conclusive on the carrier".

[754] The phrase "in any event" was interpreted by the Court of Appeal in *Daewoo Heavy Industries Ltd v Klipriver Shipping Ltd (The Kapitan Petko Voivoda)* [2003] 2 Lloyd's Rep. 1 as meaning "in every case" and was applied in that case to claims arising from unlawful carriage on deck.

> any loss or damage to or in connection with the goods in an amount exceeding the equivalent of 666.67 units of account per package or unit or 2 units of account per kilo of gross weight of the goods lost or damaged, whichever is the higher".

By the SDR Protocol agreed in Brussels on December 21, 1979, the SDR (as defined by the International Monetary Fund) was adopted as the relevant unit of account and art.IV(5)(d) of the Hague-Visby Rules was revised to reflect this, providing that the SDR "shall be converted into national currency on the basis of the value of that currency on a date to be determined by the law of the Court seized of the case". Accordingly, claims for loss or damage to cargo, which are brought under the Hague-Visby Rules subject to the law of those states that have adopted the SDR protocol is:[755] 666.67 SDRs per package or 2 SDRs per kg of gross weight of the goods actually lost or damaged. Difficulties arise for cargo interests where only part of a consignment is damaged and the damage to part has deleteriously affected the value of the undamaged portion. As far as the weight limitation is concerned it would appear that, under the Hague-Visby Rules, the claimant can only recover the value of the damaged portion of the goods limited by reference to the weight of the damaged portion alone.[756]

However, as far as the package limitation is concerned, the issue is expressly provided for by the art.IV(5)(c) provision that:

> "Where a container, pallet or similar article of transport is used to consolidate goods, the number of packages or units enumerated in the bill of lading as packed in such article of transport shall be deemed the number of packages or units for the purpose of this paragraph as far as these packages or units are concerned. Except as aforesaid such article of transport shall be considered the package or unit".

[755] *The Comite Maritime International Yearbook 2007—2008*, available at the CMI *http://www.comitemaritime.org/* reveals that the following states have ratified the SDR protocol: Belgium, Finland, France, Hong Kong, Italy, Japan, Netherlands, Norway, Poland, Spain, Sweden, Switzerland, United Kingdom (for itself, crown dependencies and overseas territories).

[756] *Serena Navigation Ltd v Dera Commercial Establishment (The Limnos)* [2008] 2 Lloyd's Rep. 166 in which Burton J. summarised the position (at para.42) as follows: "what is permitted in art.IV.5(a) is a claim in respect of (lost or) damaged goods, and a claim for loss or damage in connection with those (lost or) damaged goods, but in the second part of the clause the weight of those (lost or) damaged goods is then taken as the limit".

The wording of this provision suggests strongly that it is the enumeration of the packages (i.e. separate parcels of goods) or units (i.e. separate units, boxed or unboxed, in which goods are shipped) on the bill of lading that is determinative, rather than the number of packages or units that are actually shipped (save, of course, to the extent that an action lies for rectification of the bill). This approach was adopted firmly by the Federal Court of Australia in *El Greco (Australia) Pty Ltd v Mediterranean Shipping Co SA*[757] after reviewing various international authorities.[758] On this basis the actual description of the goods in the bill of lading is crucial. If the words used in the bill:

> "can be seen to be an enumeration of a number of articles of cargo as packed then there will be that number of units as packed. In that sense 'units' means shipping units, which can include unboxed and unpackaged articles if packed in the container as such, and if that is made clear in the bill. This would be so even if the units were small . . . ."[759]

In the light of the non-derogation provision at art.III(8), the carrier may not (having enumerated the number of "packages" or "units" on the bill) be able to avoid the effect of such enumeration by stating "shipper's load, stow and count", or expressing reservation as to the number of packages or units shipped in some other way.[760]

Article IV(5)(b) provides a mechanism for the valuation of the claim subject to limitation by stating that:

> "(b) The total amount recoverable shall be calculated by reference to the value of such goods at the place and time at which the goods are discharged from the ship in accordance with the contract or should have been so discharged. The value of the goods shall be fixed according to the commodity exchange price, or if there be no such price, according to the current market price, or, if there be no

[757] [2004] 2 Lloyd's Rep. 537.

[758] The issues addressed (see 3.3.3 below) by the Court of Appeal in the *River Gurara* [1998] 1 Lloyd's Rep. 225 in connection with the Hague Rules require quite distinct analysis; since, "the Hague-Visby Rules apply … a very different limitation regime", per Lord Phillips in *River Gurara*, ibid., 234.

[759] Allsop J. in the *El Greco* case (fn. 757), para.286.

[760] ibid. para.265.

commodity exchange price or current market price, by reference to the normal value of goods of the same kind and quality".

According to art.IVb(3) "The aggregate of the amounts recoverable from the carrier, and such servants and agents, shall in no case exceed the limit provided for in these Rules"; but just as the carrier and its servants and agents are entitled to the benefits of the limitation provisions of the Hague-Visby Rules, they are both susceptible to losing that benefit in the event of recklessness. Article IV(5)(e) provides that:

> "Neither the carrier nor the ship shall be entitled to the benefit of the limitation of liability ... if it is proved that the damage resulted from an act or omission of the carrier done with intent to cause damage, or recklessly and with knowledge that damage would probably result."

Article IVb(4) makes similar provision for the "servants or agents" of the carrier (not independent contractors who have no right under the Rules to claim their protection) who may lose the entire protection of the Rules, and not just the right to limit, in the event of recklessness, since art.IV(b)(4) is couched in the following terms:

> "Nevertheless, a servant or agent of the carrier shall not be entitled to avail himself of the provisions of this article,[761] if it is proved that the damage resulted from an act or omission of the servant or agent done with intent to cause damage or recklessly and with knowledge that damage would probably result".

The criteria under arts IV(5) and IVb(4) for breaking the financial limitation provided for in the Rules are obviously extremely restrictive. There must be deliberate or reckless[762] action or omission by the carrier

[761] Article IVb.

[762] Recklessness under English law is generally understood to involve an act or omission creating an obvious risk committed by someone who "either has not given any thought to the possibility of there being any such risk or has recognised that there was some risk involved and has nonetheless gone on to do it" per Lord Diplock in *R. v Caldwell* [1982] A.C. 341, 354, in connection with s.1(1) Criminal Damage Act 1971.

itself[763] committed in the knowledge that damage is likely to happen as a result.

3.3.2.5 Time to Claim

Article III(6) of the Rules restricts the period during which claims may be made against the carrier in relation to cargo in two respects. First, the carrier has the benefit of a rebuttable presumption that goods are not lost or damaged where such loss or damage has not been the subject of an immediate written claim. Secondly, the carrier is released from liability absolutely unless proceedings are issued within one year of discharge.

In relation to the operation of the rebuttable presumption art.III(6) provides that:

> "Unless notice of loss or damage and the general nature of such loss or damage be given in writing to the carrier or his agent at the port of discharge before or at the time of the removal of the goods into the custody of the person entitled to delivery thereof under the contract of carriage, or, if the loss or damage be not apparent, within three days, such removal shall be prima facie evidence of the delivery by the carrier of the goods as described in the bill of lading".

The carrier and the receiver are obliged, in the event of "any actual or apprehended loss or damage" to give the other "all reasonable facilities for inspecting and tallying the goods". No notice in writing need be given however, in the event of the goods being the subject of a "joint survey or inspection" on their receipt. As the failure of the consignee to give notice in writing of the claim, under the provisions of the first and second paragraph of art.III(6), only constitutes prima facie evidence that the goods were delivered in the condition in which they were shipped, such failure does not constitute a bar to successful proceedings against the carrier in the event of the claimant rebutting the presumption by credible convincing evidence and proving the existence of loss or damage on receipt of the goods from the carrier.

763 *Browner International Ltd v Monarch Shipping Co. Ltd (The European Enterprise)* [1989] 2 Lloyd's Rep. 185, 191; *Grand Champion Tankers v Norpipe A/S (The Marion)*, [1984] 2 Lloyd's Rep.1; and *Lennard's Carrying Co Ltd v Asiatic Petroleum Co Ltd* [1915] A.C. 705, 713–715; which in the case of a body corporate requires culpability on the part of the "alter ego" or "controlling mind" of the corporation itself.

As to the time bar provision, art.III(6) provides that:

> "the carrier and the ship shall in any event be discharged from all liability whatsoever in respect of the goods, unless suit is brought within one year of their delivery or of the date when they should have been delivered".

In the event delivery takes place after the date when the goods should have been delivered, the period of limitation runs from the date of actual delivery.[764] However, where actual delivery is made pursuant to some other transaction that is entirely separate and distinct to the contract of carriage, the limitation period should be calculated not from the date of actual delivery under that other transaction, but from the intended date of delivery under the contract of carriage.[765] By the express wording of art.III(6) in the Hague-Visby Rules (inserted by the Visby Protocol) the suit time limitation period may be extended by agreement between the parties after the cause of action has arisen. The Visby Protocol also revised the Rules to provide for an extension of suit time to accommodate claims for indemnity and art.III (6bis) of the Hague-Visby Rules makes provisions for an "action for indemnity against a third person" to be brought within the time allowed "by the law of the court seised of the case"[766] subject to a minimum period of:

> "not less than three months, commencing from the day when the person bringing such action for indemnity has settled the claim or has been served with process in the action against himself".

This provision permits a carrier, who has been sued by a cargo owner or who has satisfied the claim of a cargo owner whose goods were damaged, to bring an action for indemnity against the person who caused the damage, even if the one-year period has expired.

Expiry of the permitted one-year suit time limitation period[767] without an agreed extension, or without proceedings being commenced in the selected

[764] *Trafigura Beheer BV v Golden Stavraetos Maritime Inc* [2003] 1 W.L.R. 2340; where the Court of Appeal held that delivery at a substituted port, when the original receiver refused to accept delivery at the original discharge port, constituted delivery for the purposes of art.III(6).

[765] ibid. per Clarke L.J. at para.53.

[766] English law allows (under the Civil Liability (Contribution) Act 1978 discussed at 1.8.3) a period of two years for the bringing of such an indemnity claim.

[767] Or the period as extended by art.III(6bis) for indemnity actions.

jurisdiction, bars all new proceedings against the carrier thereafter. Accordingly, in a case where the charterer failed to pay the balance of freight due because damage to the cargo had been sustained, not only was it reiterated that freight is payable according to the contract without any right of set-off (unless set-off is expressly permitted) but the charterer alleging set-off was barred by the expiry of the one-year suit time from making any counter claim for the damage to the goods.[768] The relevant "suit" for the purposes of art.III(6) is the subject action in which relief is being sought against the carrier.[769] Thus, where the carrier was sued in the English courts, and proceedings were begun more than one year after delivery of the goods, the carrier could rely on the defence that the action in the English courts was barred under the time limit imposed by art.III(6), despite the fact that the claimant had in fact begun proceedings in connection with the same claim, within the time limit of one year, in the courts of New York.[770]

Where the shipowner claims general average contribution from a cargo owner and the cargo owner resists the claim on the grounds that the general average loss was caused by the shipowner's failure to exercise due diligence to make the ship seaworthy, this defence by the cargo owner does not come within the provisions of art.III(6), and the cargo owner may raise this defence although more than one year has elapsed.[771]

3.3.2.6 Carriage by Multiple Carriers

The scope of the Hague-Visby Rules does not extend to protect independent sub-contractors of the carrier undertaking any part of the carriage obligation. However, where such independent sub-contractors undertake their obligations pursuant to a separate contract of carriage also evidenced by a bill of lading satisfying the requirements of the Hague-Visby Rules, or the Carriage of Goods by Sea Act 1971, the Rules will apply to that further contract of carriage entered into between the contracting and the performing carrier. Alternatively, the Rules may be incorporated into the terms of any sub-bailment of the goods by the contracting carrier to its subcontractor as performing carrier. Such terms will govern not only the

[768] *Henriksens Rederi A/s v Rolimpex (T.H.Z.) (The Brede)* [1973] 3 W.L.R. 556.
[769] *The Amazona and Yagamaria* [1989] 2 Lloyd's Rep. 130.
[770] *Compania Columbiana de Seguros v Pacific Steam Navigation Company* [1965] 1 Q.B. 101.
[771] *Goulandris Ltd v B. Goldman Ltd* [1958] 1 Q.B. 74.

bailment relationship between those parties, but also the sub-bailment relationship between the sub-contractor as performing carrier and the shipper, or any person to whom the performing carrier may have attorned.[772]

3.3.2.7 Rights to Claim

No provision is made by the Hague-Visby Rules as to the persons entitled to claim against the carrier for loss or damage to the goods being carried, so that claimants must establish contractual or non-contractual causes of action under the law applicable to the carrier's contractual and non-contractual obligations.[773] Accordingly, pursuant to English law, for claimants to establish a right to claim under the Hague-Visby Rules causes of action must be established by the claimant in contract, tort or bailment.[774]

3.3.2.8 Jurisdiction and Recognition

Similarly, the Hague-Visby Rules contain no jurisdictional rules and issues of jurisdiction are subject to the private international law of the forum in which any proceedings are brought. For claimants to establish jurisdiction within England and Wales for any claim subject to the Hague-Visby Rules, the normal jurisdictional rules of the courts of England and Wales must be applied.[775] However, it should be noted that the effect of any express agreement as to applicable jurisdiction, or indeed any applicable law, may only take effect subject to the mandatory application of the Hague-Visby Rules in the United Kingdom.[776] Any express choice of law or jurisdiction that would in practice result in the Hague-Visby Rules not being applied to any dispute (in circumstances in which they would have the force of law in the United Kingdom) will be considered, by the courts of England and

[772] Such issues are discussed at 1.6.1.1.

[773] The applicable law concept in the carriage context is discussed at 1.4.3.

[774] As to such causes of action in the carriage context see 1.6.1, 1.8.1 and 3.1.7.1.

[775] For the application of such jurisdictional rules in the carriage context see 1.4 and 3.1.3.

[776] Pursuant to s.1(3) of UK COGSA 1971 the Hague-Visby Rules have the *force of law* in the United Kingdom.

Wales either, to be void and of no effect,[777] or, only to take effect subject to the mandatory application of the Hague-Visby Rules.

3.3.2.9 Contractual Derogation

Article III(8) provides that:

> "Any clause, covenant or agreement in a contract of carriage relieving the carrier or the ship from liability for loss or damage to or in connection with goods arising from negligence, fault or failure"

in the performance of the art.III duties "or lessening such liability otherwise than as provided" in the Hague-Visby Rules "shall be null and void and of no effect". Consequently, any clause in a contract designed to reduce the carrier's liability is invalid under the Hague-Visby Rules whether it expressly relieves the carrier from liability or has that effect by giving the carrier some positive right such as a "benefit of insurance ... or similar clause". However, art.V provides that:

> "A carrier shall be at liberty to surrender in whole or in part all or any of his rights and immunities or to increase any of his responsibilities and liabilities under the Rules contained in any of these Articles, provided such surrender or increase shall be embodied in the bill of lading issued to the shipper".

It is thus open to the parties to increase the liabilities of the carrier under the Rules, but not to limit the liability imposed on the carrier by the Rules.

Article III(8) has no application to a contract relieving the carrier from liability in respect of matters which are not dealt with in the Rules. Thus terms in the contract relating to jurisdiction,[778] or an arbitration clause,[779] are valid insofar as they do not amount to any contracting out of the Rules; as is a term giving the carrier liberty to tranship the goods,[780] or the right to discharge the goods at another port in the event of a strike at the agreed

[777] The *Hollandia* (sub nom *Morviken*) [1982] 3 W.L.R. 1111 where an exclusive jurisidiction clause was held to be prohibited under art.III(8) where it would have had the effect of subjecting the dispute to a law affording the claimant less protection than required by UK COGSA 1971.

[778] See *The Media* (1931) 41 L1.L.R. 80.

[779] *Maharani Woollen Mills v Anchor Line* (1927) 29 L1.L.R. 169.

[780] *Marcelino Gonzalez v Nourse* [1936] 1 K.B. 565.

port of discharge;[781] and so, probably, is a term giving the carrier liberty to deviate in circumstances not permitted by art.IV(4) of the Rules.[782] Article V of the Rules expressly provides that the parties are free to insert in the bill of lading any provision dealing with general average. Similarly, as discussed at 3.3.2.1 above, art.VII has been interpreted by the courts of England and Wales as constituting liberty for the carrier to contract out of loading, stowage and discharge obligations.

Contracts not subject to the Hague-Visby Rules by the force of law, but into which the Rules are contractually incorporated by agreement with only contractual effect may incorporate the Rules without overriding effect. Thus, where goods were carried from a port of loading in a foreign state to a port in the United Kingdom and the original Hague Rules did not have the force of law and could only have taken effect by reference to a pre-printed clause paramount, such clause paramount could be disapplied by a clause stamped over the printed clauses in the bill of lading, when it was clearly intended by the parties that the erstwhile incorporation of the Rules should be ousted by the clause.[783] Similarly, where the Hague-Visby Rules were incorporated in an amended form into a non-negotiable sea waybill, which clearly stated that the Rules were not to take effect as if the waybill was a bill of lading,[784] the Hague-Visby Rules were given effect in their contractually amended form.[785]

The effective contracting out of the Hague-Visby Rules by the simple expedient of issuing non-negotiable receipts, rather than bills of lading, is confirmed by the express provisions of the Rules, although the contractual freedom is couched in language that only "caters for an exceptional situation".[786] Article VI refers to four factual pre-conditions for such contractual freedom in relation to the shipments to which the Hague-Visby Rules would otherwise have the force of law, namely: (1) that "no bill of lading has been or shall be issued"; (2) the agreed terms are "embodied in a receipt which shall be a non-negotiable document"; (3) the non-negotiable

[781] *Renton v Palmyra Trading Corporation* [1957] A.C. 149.

[782] *Foreman v Federal Steam Navigation Company* [1928] 2 K.B. 424, 431, per Wright J.; *Stag Line v Foscolo Mango* [1932] A.C. 328; *Renton v Palmyra Trading Corporation* [1956] 1 Q.B. 462, 505, per Jenkins L.J., and in House of Lords [1957] A.C. 149.

[783] *Varnish and Company v The Kheti (Owners)* (1949) 82 L1.L.R. 525.

[784] The sea waybill, in consequence, not fulfilling the requirements of s.1(6) of the 1971 Act.

[785] *The European Enterprise* [1989] 2 Lloyd's Rep. 185.

[786] Per Lord Steyn at para.42 of the House of Lords judgment in *J I Macwilliam Co Inc v Mediterranean Shipping Co SA (The Rafaela S)* [2005] 2 A.C. 423.

receipt "shall be marked as such"; (4) the subject goods are not "ordinary commercial shipments made in the ordinary course of trade"; and (5) the nature of the goods or the circumstances of the carriage "are such as reasonably to justify a special agreement". Only where such pre-conditions are satisfied does art.VI give the carrier:

> "liberty to enter into any agreement in any terms as to the responsibility and liability of the carrier for such goods, and as to the rights and immunities of the carrier in respect of such goods, or his obligation as to seaworthiness..."

and provide for such agreement to "have full legal effect". This provision has previously received scant attention from the courts of England and Wales, where consideration of the effect of the Hague-Visby Rules in the context of non-negotiable sea waybills has focused on the effect of s.1(6) of UK COGSA 1971;[787] but, in giving judgment in the *Rafaela S* in the course of holding straight bills of lading to constitute documents of title, Lord Bingham remarked that together s.1(6) and art.VI:

> "were intended, subject to the charterparty exclusion already mentioned, to govern the great majority of ordinary commercial shipments"

and that

> "the concern of those negotiating the Hague Rules was not to restrict the scope of the Rules but to prevent their circumvention".[788]

Accordingly, in the event of claims being made in respect of shipments under non-negotiable sea waybills to which the Hague-Visby Rules would otherwise apply, the issue of the non-negotiable sea waybill may itself be considered an unlawful agreement to contract out of the Rules and be rendered "null and void and of no effect" under art.III(8) whenever the art.VI pre-conditions are unfulfilled.

787 Steyn J. in the *European Enterprise* (fn. 785), at pp.187–188; although, as the case involved a short sea Ro-Ro shipment, the five art.VI pre-conditions also appear to have been satisfied.

788 *The Rafaela S* (fn. 786) para.18 where Lord Bingham, in compartmentalising its criteria into the five stated pre-conditions, referred to art.VI as being "very restrictive and hard to satisfy".

Article VIII expressly stipulates that that the Rules:

> "shall not affect the rights and obligations of the carrier under any statute for the time being in force relating to the limitation of the liability of owners of sea-going vessels".

Consequently, all sea carriage contracts regulated by the Hague-Visby Rules are subject to the limitation provisions arising under ss.185 and 186 of the Merchant Shipping Act 1979 and other legislation discussed at 3.1.7.2. The Visby Protocol inserted a new art.IX (displacing the gold value provision discussed in 3.3.3 below) providing that the Rules "shall not affect the provisions of any international Convention or national law governing liability for nuclear damage": as discussed in 3.1.7.2 above.

3.3.2.10 Rights of Carriers

Article IV(6) provides the carrier with certain contractual rights in connection with the carriage of dangerous goods: such goods being defined as any goods "of an inflammable, explosive or dangerous nature to the shipment" (i.e. by reference to their general nature in the context of the contemplated marine adventure, as under the common law, rather than their particular designation).[789] The extent of the substantive right depends upon whether the carrier had knowledge of the dangerous nature of the goods when the carrier consented to the shipment of the goods. Where the carrier has not been made aware of their "nature and character" there are the following consequences: (i) the carrier is entitled "at any time before discharge" to land the goods at any place, or to destroy them, or to render them innocuous without compensation; and (ii) the shipper of the dangerous goods is expressed to be "liable for all such damages and expenses directly or indirectly arising out of or resulting from such shipment". Where the carrier has "such knowledge" of the nature and character of the goods but the dangerous goods "become a danger to the ship or cargo", they may similarly be "landed at any place or destroyed or rendered innocuous by the carrier without liability on the part of the carrier except to general average, if any". However, in this second case where the carrier has knowledge, "the

[789] The extent of the common law concept of "dangerous" (applied by the House of Lords to art.IV(6) of the Hague-Visby Rules in *Effort Shipping Co Ltd v Linden Management SA* [1998] AC 605) is discussed at 1.9.1.3.

shipper is not liable in damages to the carrier".[790] As discussed at 3.3.2.2 above, the carrier is also entitled by Art.III(5) to be indemnified by the shipper in respect of "all loss, damages and expenses arising or resulting from inaccuracies" in the particulars of the goods furnished by the shipper, since by that provision the shipper is deemed to guarantee the accuracy of those particulars.

However, art.IV(3) expressly releases the shipper from any responsibility:

> "for loss or damage sustained by the carrier or the ship arising or resulting from any cause without the act, fault or neglect of the shipper, his agents or his servants".

Prior to the decision of the House of Lords in *Effort Shipping Co Ltd v Linden Management SA*,[791] it was considered that this provision might exclude the shipper from any liability where the shipper did not know, and was not negligent in not knowing, that the goods were dangerous or the bill of lading particulars inaccurate, at the time of the shipment. The *Effort Shipping*[792] case is now clear authority for art.IV(6) to be interpreted as a free-standing provision, which:

> "is neither expressly, nor by implication, subject to art.IV, r. 3. It imposes strict liability on shippers in relation to the shipment of dangerous goods, irrespective of fault or neglect on their part".[793]

Article III(5) ought now to be read subject to a similar construction.

Under a contract of carriage regulated by the Hague-Visby Rules, the carrier's rights to freight or lien remain governed by the common law provisions discussed at 3.1.8 above.

[790] *Effort Shipping Co Ltd* ibid., per Lord Steyn 621.

[791] ibid.

[792] ibid.

[793] Per Lord Lloyd ibid. 614; although in his dissenting judgment Lord Cooke preferred to interpret art.IV(3) "on a fair reading of the Rules as a whole" as taking priority over art.IV(6) in the event of inconsistency between the two provisions.

3.3.2.11 Claims among Carriers

The Hague-Visby Rules make no particular provision for claims between carriers, save for the provision inserted by the Visby Protocol at art.III (6bis) of the Hague-Visby Rules extending suit time to accommodate claims for indemnity as discussed at sub-part 3.3.2.5 above.

3.3.3 The Hague Rules

The *CMI 2007–2008 Yearbook*[794] refers to many nations as still being contracting states to the original Hague Rules and as not having ratified the Visby Protocol.[795] Consequently, contracts of carriage, covered by bills of lading, for shipments from those contracting states may still be governed by the original unamended Hague Rules. Textual differences between the original and amended forms of the Rules have been highlighted at 3.3.2 above and the substance of the unamended original rules as regards those differences is discussed below. Where no differences are referred to regarding the issues in 3.3.2.1 to 3.3.2.10, it may be assumed that no material change was made by the 1968 Visby Protocol and that the provisions of the 1924 Hague Rules are substantially the same as those Rules discussed at 3.3.2 above. Nevertheless, when significant matters arise, reference should be made to the terms of the unamended convention, which is available online at various sites.[796]

The scope of application of the Hague Rules was designed around the compulsory contractual incorporation of the Rules, by the contracting parties, into the bill of lading pursuant to the national law in force at the

[794] Published at *http://www.comitemaritime.org* by Comite Maritime International as the depositary institution for state notifications of accession, denunciation and ratification of the Hague Rules from whose site the text of the unamended convention is also available.

[795] The following are those contracting states so referred to as continuing parties to the original unamended Hague Rules: Algeria, Angola, Antigua and Barbuda, Argentina, Bahamas, Belize, Bolivia, Cape Verde, Cuba, Cyprus, Fiji, Ghana, Grenada, Guyana, Iran, Ivory Coast, Jamaica, Kiribati, Kuwait, Macao, Malaysia, Mauritius, Monaco, Mozambique, Nauru, Nigeria, Papua New Guinea, Paraguay, Peru, Portugal, Sao Tomé and Principe, Sarawak, Seychelles, Solomon Islands, Somalia, St Kitts and Nevis, St Lucia, Timor, Trinidad and Tobago, Turkey, Tuvalu, United States of America, Zaire.

[796] See fn. 794.

place in which the bill was issued.[797] The technique of mandatory contractual incorporation of the Hague Rules into bills of lading was found to be ineffective where the clause paramount was omitted and the contract of carriage governed by English law, since, although such omission might be illegal under the national law in force at the place of shipment, English law considered such illegality to be irrelevant to the contractual construction of the bill.[798] However, where a foreign statute has been contractually incorporated into a bill of lading the courts of England and Wales will give full effect to it (unless displaced by UK mandatory law in the form of COGSA 1971 and the Hague-Visby Rules), even though the contract would otherwise be subject to some other governing law,[799] such as English law. This frequently occurs in connection with disputes arising in relation to the carriage of goods involving the USA. The USA incorporated the Hague Rules into federal law in an amended form by the United States Carriage of Goods By Sea Act 1936 (US COGSA), applying the Hague Rules in this amended form to all shipments from and to the USA and requiring all bills of lading issued for such shipments to contain a clause paramount incorporating the terms of US COGSA into the terms of the bill.

The Hague Rules do not extend their protection to servants or agents of the carrier (unlike art.IV(bis)(2) of the Hague-Visby Rules) and, as interpreted by the courts of England and Wales, are applicable only to the relationship between the contracting parties. Consequently, the carrier's servants are not protected by the Hague Rules in their unamended form and the limitation, imposed by art.IV(5) of the old Convention on the amount of damages recoverable, does not apply to protect the carrier's servants or agents if they are sued personally for negligence, although any such negligence would ordinarily be committed in the course of their employment by the carrier.

The status of the bill of lading, and the scope of the carrier's liability under the Hague Rules, were broadly unchanged by the Visby Protocol,

[797] Article X of the unamended Hague Rules.

[798] *Vita Food Products Inc v Unus Shipping Co Ltd* [1939] A.C. 277 where at p.296 Lord Wright explained that if a court "has before it a contract good by its own law or by the proper law of the contract, it will in proper cases give effect to the contract and ignore the foreign law". Similarly, in *OT Africa v Magic Sportswear* [2005] 2 Lloyd's Rep. 170 the Court of Appeal refused to allow the Canadian Marine Liability Act 2001, in force at the place of shipment, to displace an exclusive jurisdiction clause in favour of the English courts.

[799] *Stafford Allen & Sons Ltd v Pacific Steam Navigation Company* [1956] 1 Lloyd's Rep. 104.

apart from the significant amendment to art.III(4) to afford greater protection to a third party transferee of a bill of lading acting in good faith, by making the bill of lading conclusive evidence of the particulars of the goods shipped. However, the financial limitation provisions were amended significantly as these had caused the greatest trouble in the interpretation and application of the Rules. Article IV(5) of the original Hague Rules provided that:

> "Neither the carrier nor the ship shall in any event be or become liable for any loss or damage to or in connexion with goods in an amount exceeding 100 pounds sterling per package or unit, or the equivalent of that sum in other currency ...".

As the value of pounds sterling has changed significantly on the foreign exchange market since 1924, there has been significant divergence in the interpretation and application of this provision across the contracting states, both as to the value of "100 pounds sterling" and as to the meaning of a "package or unit". Some countries have decided that the limit is the fluctuating present value of the quantity of gold that in 1924 would have been represented by the sum of £100, thereby giving effect to the original art.IX which provided that: "The monetary units mentioned in this Convention are to be taken to be gold value". Some countries converted the £100 limit into a sum expressed in their own national currency by reference to the currency exchange values prevailing in 1924 (e.g. the limit under US COGSA was and remains $500)[800] in accordance with para.2 of art.IX. Other countries, such as the United Kingdom, have simply applied the "100 pounds sterling" limit and interpreted the phrase literally. However, in the significant decision of the *Rosa S*,[801] the English High Court held in 1988 that the art.IV(5) £100 limit was qualified by the art.IX gold value provision and that the two articles had to be interpreted together to provide the measure of the carrier's obligation and not merely indicate the mode of payment. In the *Rosa S* Hobhouse J. valued £100 in gold by reference to UK legislation, defining the gold content of £100 sterling[802] to produce a Hague Rules per package limitation value of £6491.25. A similar calculation

[800] US COGSA does not contain any reference to gold value.

[801] *The Rosa S* [1988] 2 Lloyd's Rep. 574.

[802] The gold content of sterling was defined at 798.805 grammes of gold of a millesimal fineness 916.66 (equating to 732.238 grammes of fine gold) by the Coinage Acts 1870 and 1971.

of the currently prevailing value of gold as at November 2009 would have produced a per package limitation of £16,525.08, were such calculation still considered to be appropriate in light of revisions made to UK coinage legislation and if any contractual incorporation of the Hague Rules were to include art.IX. As to the latter proviso, it should be noted that any such contractual incorporation is frequently limited to arts I to VIII of the Hague Rules: "a formulation that avoids the 'gold clause trap' ".[803]

A further difficulty under the Hague Rules is the question of what constitutes a package or unit. In order to achieve the lowest possible limitation fund, carriers seek to persuade courts to call a container a package, although its contents manifestly exceed £100 in value. Conversely, in order to secure the highest possible limitation fund, cargo owners seek to contend that each carton stuffed into a container should be considered an individual package, even though, without further packaging, it is manifestly unable to withstand the rigours of carriage. What constitutes a package was not made clear in the original Convention and has been the subject of varying interpretations in international jurisprudence. In the US courts various approaches have been taken over the years, with courts postulating a variety of contrasting tests to determine the issue, including the following: addressing whether the units in question were those in which the shipper packed the goods, or else functionally part of the ship, in the course of deciding that 99 bales of leather packed in one container were to be regarded as 99 packages;[804] distinguishing between packages capable of being shipped overseas and units which required other packing for export shipment and, in respect of the latter, placing the onus on the shipper to produce other evidence to prove such units themselves constitute packages,[805] in determining that a container of machinery constituted one package although it contained 350 adding machines;[806] determining what constitutes "packages" in the context of the particular shipment by reference not to the parties' respective intentions but the factual context, in holding that cartons of colour television sets inside containers were to be considered as the packages (notwithstanding an express provision to the effect that "where cargo has been packed in containers it is agreed that the

[803] Per Keith J. the *Tasman Discoverer* [2002] 2 Lloyd's Rep. 528, New Zealand Court of Appeal.

[804] *Leather's Best Inc v The Mormaclynx* [1970] 1 L1.L.R. 527 U.S.D.C.

[805] The so-called "functional economics" test.

[806] *Royal Typewriter Co v M.V. Kulmerland and Hamburg-Amerika Linie* [1973] 1 L1.L.R. 318 U.S.D.C.

number of such containers shall be considered as the number of packages").[807] These cases illustrate the confusion inherent in the Hague Rules over the meaning of "package or unit". The courts in many jurisdictions, now including the US,[808] have allowed the parties contractual freedom to resolve the issue by the description of the cargo in the bill of lading, with the consequence that, if the bill of lading clearly defines the concept of package or unit by description (e.g. freight rates per ton or container), the express description in the bill of lading will be allowed to prevail. However, in 1988 the English Court of Appeal adopted a contrasting approach in the *River Gurara*,[809] and "dissented from the approach of attempting to deduce an agreement of the parties as to limitation from the face of the bill of lading".[810] In that case the Court of Appeal held that, unamended by the Visby Protocol, the package limitation under the Hague Rules could not be solely determined by the bill of lading to the exclusion of other evidence,[811] since art.III(4) provided for the bill of lading only to be prima facie evidence of the goods shipped. The consequence of this decision in England and Wales is:

> "that the Hague Rules limit of liability falls to be calculated by reference to the particulars of the cargo and its packaging as it is proved to have been on loading, not by reference to the description in the bill of lading".[812]

In terms of temporal limitation, as to the available suit time for the commencement of proceedings, art.III(6) of the Hague Rules contains no

807 *The Aegis Spirit* (1977) 1 Lloyd's Rep. 93 U.S. District Ct.

808 For example see *Binladen BSB Landscaping v M.V. Nedlloyd Rotterdam* 759 F. 2d 1006 (1985) where Judge Mansfield said "that the touchstone of our analysis should be the contractual agreement between the parties as set forth in the bill of lading".

809 [1998] 1 Lloyd's Rep. 225.

810 Per Phillips L.J. ibid. 234 with the agreement of Mummery L.J., Hirst L.J. dissenting.

811 Rejecting the conclusion reached by Colman J. at first instance (which was supported by the dissenting judgment of Hirst L.J. on appeal) that, in the interest of international uniformity (and following the current trend evident in US, Canadian, Australian, French and Dutch decisions) the package concept under the unamended Hague Rules should be determined (alike with the Hague-Visby Rules) by construing the description of the goods on the face of the bill of lading.

812 Per Phillips L.J. ibid. 233 with the agreement of Mummery L.J., Hirst L.J. dissenting.

relaxation of the one-year suit time provision and, unlike the Hague-Visby Rules, affords claimants neither any express right to extend the time limit by agreement; nor any extra time to assert claims for indemnity or contribution against others in respect of liabilities incurred under the contract of carriage. In other respects the Hague Rules, where incorporated by agreement into contracts of carriage and not displaced by the mandatory effect of the Hague-Visby Rules, will be interpreted by the courts of England and Wales in accordance with the principles referred to at 3.3.2 above.

3.3.4 The Hamburg Rules

The Hamburg Rules constitute a further set of rules for the international carriage of goods by sea. They emanate from the United Nations Commission on International Trade Law (UNCITRAL) and were adopted by the United Nations Conference on the Carriage of Goods by Sea, held at Hamburg in 1978. They can be downloaded from various websites.[813] In comparison with the Hague regime (i.e. the original and amended Hague Rules), the substance of the Hamburg Rules has less affinity with the jurisprudence and legislative approaches of the common law legal systems. Indeed, it seems to have far more affinity with the regulatory structure of the CIM and CMR conventions on the international carriage of goods by rail and road. The Hamburg Rules were intended to tilt the balance of rights and obligations in connection with the international carriage of goods by sea towards cargo interests and to increase the extent of liability falling on carriers for loss, damage and delay to the goods carried. They entered into force as an instrument of public international law on November 1, 1992 between the first 20 contracting states to ratify the convention.[814] The Hamburg Rules are now in force between some 34 contracting states;[815]

[813] In particular from that of UNCITRAL, being the depositary institution for the receipt of notices from contracting states of accession, ratification and denunciation, at *http://www.uncitral.org* from which the current status of the convention including details of all state ratifications is available.

[814] ibid.

[815] ibid., the contracting states as at November 24, 2009 being: Albania, Austria, Barbados, Botswana, Burkino Faso, Burundi, Cameroon, Chile, Czech Republic, Dominican Republic, Egypt, Gambia, Georgia, Guinea, Hungary, Jordan, Kazakhstan, Kenya, Lebanon, Liberia, Lesotho, Malawi, Morocco, Nigeria, Paraguay, Romania, St Vincent, Senegal, Sierra Leone, Syria, Tunisia, Uganda, Tanzania, Zambia.

significantly in terms of the continuing applicability of the Hague regime, few of them are major maritime nations. However, the Hamburg Rules will be applied by the courts of England and Wales whenever they are incorporated by clause paramount into bills of lading as long as they are not displaced by the mandatory effect in the United Kingdom of the Hague-Visby Rules.

3.3.4.1 Scope of Application

Article 2 frames the scope of the Hamburg Rules to apply to any contract for the international carriage of goods by sea for particular shipments excepting charterparties, which by art.2(3) are excluded; although the Rules still apply to any bill of lading issued pursuant to a charterparty but nevertheless governing the relationship between the carrier and any holder of the bill of lading other than the charterer. The particular international shipments to which the Rules apply are those where either the port of loading or discharge (as provided for in the contract of carriage) is in a contracting state; or the documentation evidencing the terms of carriage is issued in a contracting state, or contains a clause paramount in favour of the Hamburg Rules. Accordingly, unlike the Hague regime, the Hamburg Rules apply to shipments from and to contracting states, whatever documentation is issued to evidence the contract of carriage. By art.4(1) the Rules govern the responsibility of the carrier during the period the carrier is in charge of the goods "at the port of loading, during the carriage and at the port of discharge" with such period commencing from when the carrier "has taken over the goods" and continuing until "the time he has delivered the goods". Consequently, the period of responsibility is not the period from loading to discharge during which the goods are under ship's tackle as provided for in the Hague regime, but instead the period during which the carrier has constructive possession of the goods whilst they are at the port of loading, during the carriage and at the port of discharge.

The Hamburg Rules apply to all cargo other than passenger luggage and unlike the Hague regime extend to live animals and deck cargo; although particular liability provisions are made in respect of live animals, deck cargo and dangerous goods as discussed at 3.3.4.3 and 3.3.4.10 below. The carrier and the shipper are broadly defined. Article 1(1) defines the carrier as being:

> "any person by whom or in whose name a contract of carriage of goods by sea has been concluded with a shipper".

Article 1(3) defines the shipper as being:

> "any person by whom or in whose name or on whose behalf a contract of carriage of goods by sea has been concluded with a carrier, or any person by whom or in whose name or on whose behalf the goods are actually delivered to the carrier in relation to the contract of carriage by sea".

By art.7 the defences and limitations provided for in the Rules in relation to claims for loss, damage or delay to the goods carried are applied not only to actions against the carrier in contract but also in "tort or otherwise" and to any such action against any servant or agent of the carrier proved to have "acted within the scope of his employment". Unlike the Hague regime, the Hamburg Rules also expressly regulate the relationship between the shipper (as defined) and the performing carriers defined by art.1(2) as being:

> "any person to whom the performance of the carriage of the goods, or of part of the carriage, has been entrusted by the carrier, and includes any other person to whom such performance has been entrusted".

By art.10(2) the actual carrier and its servants and agents are subject to all those provisions of the Rules "governing the responsibility of the carrier" as regards the carriage performed by the actual carrier and art.10(4) provides for any liability of both the carrier and the actual carrier to be joint and several. However, the definition of "contract of carriage" at art.1(5) confirms that the Hamburg Rules only encompass the carriage by sea (extended to include the period of possession of the goods by the carrier at the load and discharge ports but not any prior or subsequent land carriage) as it provides that a contract for multimodal carriage is only deemed a contract of carriage by sea "in so far as it relates to the carriage by sea".

3.3.4.2 Documentation

Article 14(1) of the Hamburg Rules provides that when the carrier takes over the goods "the carrier must, on demand of the shipper, issue to the shipper a bill of lading". Whilst art.14(2) provides that where the master of the carrying ship signs the bill of lading it is "deemed to have been signed on behalf of the carrier"; this provides no assistance in determining the identity of the carrier, which would still be determined by the English courts by reference to the principles outlined in the *Starsin* case.[816] The contents of the bill of lading must include the information described in art.15. For the most part, this comprises the commercial information traders would normally expect to see. However, it also requires the inclusion in any transport document, evidencing carriage under the Hamburg Rules, of the statement at art.23(3) to the effect that:

> "the carriage is subject to the provisions of this Convention which nullify any stipulation derogating therefrom to the detriment of the shipper or the consignee".

The absence of any of the required particulars from the bill does not affect its status as a bill of lading,[817] provided that, as required by art.1(7), it remains a document "by which the carrier undertakes to deliver the goods against surrender of the document". However, omissions may be of evidential significance. By art.16(2) any failure to note the apparent condition of the goods is deemed to be a notation to the effect "that the goods were in apparent good condition".[818] Failure to make express stipulations as to freight or demurrage due from the consignee is, under art.16(4), "prima facie evidence that no freight or such demurrage is payable" to the carrier; and proof to the contrary is not admissible when the bill of lading has been transferred to a third party acting in good faith in reliance on the absence of such stipulation. Otherwise the evidential value of a bill of lading under the Hamburg Rules is stipulated at art.16 as being that of "prima facie evidence of the taking over or, where a 'shipped' bill of lading is issued, loading, by the carrier of the goods as described in the bill of lading" pursuant to art.16(3)(a). By art.16(3)(b)

> "proof to the contrary by the carrier is not admissible if the bill of lading has been transferred to a third party, including a consignee, who in good faith has acted in reliance on the description of the goods therein".

As discussed above, application of the Hamburg Rules is not dependent upon the issue of a bill of lading, but under art.18 the evidential value of

[816] [2003] 1 Lloyd's Rep. 571; discussed at 3.1.2.
[817] Article 15(3).
[818] Apparently in favour of the shipper as well as any transferee or endorsee of the bill.

any other transport document issued by the carrier is merely "evidence of the receipt of the goods to be carried" and "prima facie evidence of the conclusion of the contract of carriage by sea and the taking over by the carrier of the goods as therein described".

3.3.4.3 Liability of Carrier

The structure of the liability provisions of the Hamburg Rules appears similar to that of the CMR Convention discussed in 2.3 in relation to the international carriage of goods by road. As with the CMR Convention,[819] art.5 of the Hamburg Rules provides that:

> "The carrier is liable for loss resulting from loss of or damage to the goods, as well as from delay in delivery, if the occurrence which caused the loss, damage or delay took place while the goods were in his charge as defined in art.4, unless the carrier proves that he, his servants or agents took all measures that could reasonably be required to avoid the occurrence and its consequences".[820]

However, whilst the onus lies on the carrier to prove that loss, damage or delay occurred without fault on its part, the extent of the duty of care appears somewhat less than the duty of utmost care required of CMR road carriers.[821] Annex II to the Hamburg Rules Convention, which should be considered part of the travaux préparatoires and used as an aid to the construction of this provision, states: "It is the common understanding that the liability of the carrier under this Convention is based on the principle of presumed fault or neglect ...".[822] This suggests that, in the case of the Hamburg Rules, the intended extent of the duty is one of reasonable care; however, the wording of art.5(1) does tend to suggest that the duty might be more onerous, even though the carrier cannot be required to undertake measures that would not be "reasonable" in the circumstances.

Unlike the CMR Convention, or the Hague regime, the Hamburg Rules do not furnish the carrier with many other defences except in cases concerning deck cargo, live animals, fire or measures to save life or property.

[819] In particular art.17 of the CMR.

[820] The period of responsibility under the Hamburg Rules is discussed at 3.3.4.1 above.

[821] As discussed at 2.3.3.

[822] As made available online by UNCITRAL at *http://www.uncitral.org.*

Deck cargo is addressed by art.9, with art.9(1) providing that the "carrier is entitled to carry the goods on deck" where such carriage is agreed with the shipper, or is in accordance with "the usage of the particular trade or is required by statutory rules or regulations". The fact that the carrier is, by art.9(3), made "liable for loss of or damage to the goods, as well as for delay in delivery, resulting solely from the carriage on deck", where goods are carried on deck otherwise than pursuant to art.9(1) suggests that the carrier should not be liable for any loss, damage or delay that is solely occasioned to goods because they were carried on deck in accordance with art.9(1). However, by art.9(2) the carrier loses any such defence against any third party acquiring a bill in good faith when the fact of such carriage on deck is not stated in the bill. The carrier is "not liable for loss, damage or delay in delivery resulting from any special risks inherent in" the carriage of live animals under art.5(5). Apart from this provision, the concept of inherent vice, which is such a notable feature both of other carriage conventions and the common law, does not feature in the Hamburg Rules. Under art.5(4) the onus of proof is transferred to the claimant in the event of a claim for loss, damage or delay to goods caused by fire; since, in respect of such a claim, "fault or neglect on the part of the carrier, his servants or agents" must be proved for the carrier to have any liability. By art.5(6) the carrier is relieved of any liability (other than in general average) for loss, damage or delay resulting "from measures to save life or from reasonable measures to save property at sea".

The concept of seaworthiness, so central to the common law and the Hague regime, is absent from the Hamburg Rules; save, perhaps, to the extent that unseaworthiness constitutes a manifestation of any "fault or neglect" on the part of the carrier, for the consequences of which the carrier remains liable under art.5(7), notwithstanding the defences referred to above.

3.3.4.4 Value of Claim

The financial limitation provisions of the Hamburg Rules provide separately for loss and damage and for delay. In regard to loss of or damage to goods, art.6(1)(a) provides for a limitation calculated at the higher of: 835 SDRs per "package or other shipping unit"; or 2.5 SDRs "per kilogramme of gross weight of the goods lost or damaged". Article 6(2)(a) provides that where goods are consolidated into a larger transport unit, such as a container, the number of packages or shipping units is deemed to be the number of packages "enumerated" (either in any bill of lading issued, or in "any other document evidencing the contract of carriage by sea") as having been "packed in such article of transport".[823] In the absence of such enumeration "the goods in such article of transport are deemed one shipping unit".[824] With regard to claims for delay in delivery, art.6(1)(b) provides for a limitation:

> "to an amount equivalent to two and a half times the freight payable for the goods delayed, but not exceeding the total freight payable under the contract of carriage of goods by sea"

albeit the limit for loss and damage at art.6(1)(a) is made an overriding aggregate limit for any claims involving both delay and loss and/or damage.[825] The carrier may, by agreement with the shipper, submit to higher limits than those referred to above.[826] The carrier only loses the right to limit claims under art.8 where the loss, damage or delay is proved to have

> "resulted from an act or omission of the carrier done with the intent to cause such loss, damage or delay, or recklessly and with knowledge that such loss, damage or delay would probably result".[827]

Unlike the Hague regime,[828] the Hamburg Rules contain no valuation provisions for the calculation of claims subject to limitation. Accordingly, where any such valuation is a matter to be determined by English law, the principles discussed at 1.8.2 apply.

3.3.4.5 Time to Claim

Article 19 concerns the giving of notices to the carrier in the event of any loss, damage or delay being caused to the goods carried; whilst art.20

[823] A provision which is both similar and dissimilar from the Hague-Visby Rules since the number of packages is determined by their enumeration on carriage documentation, but such documentation is not limited to bills of lading.

[824] Irrespective of such enumeration, the article of transport itself, where not owned or supplied by the carrier, is taken as being "one separate shipping unit" as provided for at art.6(2)(b).

[825] Article 6(1)(c).

[826] Article 6(4).

[827] The onus of proof that the claimant must discharge in seeking to prove such conduct was discussed above, in relation to the similar provision to be found in the LLMC 1976, at 3.1.7.2.

[828] See Art.IV(5)(b) of the Hague-Visby Rules discussed at 3.3.2.4 above.

concerns the issue of proceedings in relation to any consequent claims. Article 19 requires that written notice, "specifying the general nature of" loss or damage to the goods, be given to the carrier[829] by the consignee "not later than the working day after the day when the goods were handed over to the consignee"; unless the damage is latent, when such period is extended to "15 consecutive days" after the day of handing over.[830] In the absence of such written notice "such handing over is prima facie evidence" of redelivery of the goods in the condition described in the bill of lading (or other transport document); or, in the absence of such description, of redelivery in good condition.[831] However, by art.19(3), notice in writing need not be given of loss or damage ascertained during any survey or inspection jointly carried out. The parties owe apparently synallagmatic obligations under art.19(4) to provide each other with "all reasonable facilities ... for inspecting and tallying the goods". Where any failure by the claimant to give notice arises from any breach by the carrier of this provision, the claimant may be able to rebut the presumption otherwise arising as to the redelivery of the goods. In relation to delay, art.19(5) has the effect of discharging the carrier from liability for delay unless written notice is given to the carrier[832] "within 60 consecutive days after the day when the goods were handed over to the consignee". Unlike the Hague regime, art.19(7) of the Hamburg Rules stipulates a time period for claims against the shipper for any loss or damage sustained by "fault or neglect of the shipper, his servants or agents". Any such loss or damage must be the subject of a written notice given to the shipper "not later than 90 consecutive days after the occurrence of such loss or damage or after the delivery of the goods ... whichever is later" and the absence of such notice is prima facie evidence that no such loss or damage has been sustained by the carrier or any actual carrier.

Article 20 provides for "any action relating to carriage of goods" under

[829] Article 19(8) provides that notices may be given by, or to, persons acting for (as the case may be) the shipper or the carrier and art.19(6) provides that such notices may either be directed to the contracting carrier or any other carrier actually delivering the goods.

[830] Articles 19(1) and 19(2).

[831] Article 19(1).

[832] The carrier being defined for this purpose as the contracting carrier, or any other carrier actually delivering the goods as per art.19(6).

the Rules to be time-barred unless proceedings[833] are commenced within two years: with such period commencing

> "on the day on which the carrier has delivered the goods or part thereof or, in cases where no goods have been delivered, on the last day on which the goods should have been delivered"

excluding the day on which such limitation period commences. Unlike the Hague regime,[834] the limitation period under the Hamburg Rules may be prolonged simply by written declarations of the claimant's entitlement.[835] Claims for indemnity may be pursued even after expiry of the art.20(1) limitation period "within the time allowed by the law of the State where proceedings are instituted", although such a period may not be less than 90 days commencing from when the indemnity claimant settles, or is served with proceedings in relation to, the underlying claim.[836]

3.3.4.6 Carriage by Multiple Carriers

As discussed at 3.3.4.1 above art.10 expressly applies the Hamburg Rules not only to the contracting carrier but also to the actual carrier as defined by art.1(2). However, under art.10(3), the actual carrier does not have liability to cargo interests pursuant to any "special agreement under which the carrier assumes obligations not imposed by ... [the Rules] ... or waives rights conferred by ... [the Rules] ..." except where the actual carrier has expressly agreed in writing to such obligations or to the waiver of such rights; although art.10 expressly provides that it does not "prejudice any right of recourse as between the carrier and the actual carrier". Accordingly, whilst the actual carrier is exposed to claims under the Rules for "loss, damage or delay in delivery caused by an occurrence which takes place while the goods are in his charge",[837] the actual carrier is not exposed to liabilities falling on the contracting carrier outside the Rules. The contracting carrier meanwhile retains responsibility for the performance of the entire carriage and, by art.10(1), is made responsible "for the acts and

[833] The proceedings stipulated by art.20(1) encompassing both litigation and arbitration proceedings.
[834] But alike with the CMR and CIM regimes for the international carriage of goods by road and rail respectively, variously discussed at 2.3.5 and 2.6.2.5.
[835] Article 20(4).
[836] Article 20(5).
[837] Article 11(2).

omissions of the actual carrier and of his servants and agents acting within the scope of their employment" in the context of such carriage. The contracting carrier is permitted by art.11(1) to exclude such responsibility for the performance of the carriage by the actual carrier where the carriage contract "provides explicitly that a specified part of the carriage" is to be performed by an expressly named actual carrier, provided that judicial proceedings can be instituted against the actual carrier in one of the jurisdictions provided for by the Rules[838] and the contracting carrier can discharge the burden of proving that any loss, damage or delay has been caused by an occurrence that took place when the actual carrier was in charge of the goods.

3.3.4.7 Rights to Claim

The Hamburg Rules make no stipulations as to the identity of the person entitled to claim for loss damage or delay to goods. Whilst the Rules expressly provide for the making of such claims against the contracting and/or actual carrier, the question of who has the right to claim must, apparently, be determined by whichever law is chosen by the forum of the dispute as governing the substantive obligation (contractual or non-contractual) in question.[839] Accordingly, where the Hamburg Rules have been incorporated into a contract of carriage to which English law is applicable as the governing law of the contract: claims for loss, damage or delay to goods may be pursued in contract, tort or bailment according to the principles discussed at 1.8.1 and 3.1.7.1.

3.3.4.8 Jurisdiction and Recognition

Unlike the Hague regime, the Hamburg Rules seek to regulate the choice of forum for the determination of any dispute relating to the carriage of goods under the Rules. The Rules purport to regulate the choice of both national court jurisdiction by art.21, and the applicable seat of arbitration[840] by

[838] Being one of the jurisdictions provided for at arts 21(1) and 21(2).

[839] The English law rules of private international law applicable to contractual relationships are discussed at 1.4.3.

[840] The Rules do not refer to the arbitration seat as such but, since art.22(1) expressly permits the parties to enter into written agreements referring future disputes to arbitration, it is submitted that the reference by the Rules to "the place" in which "arbitration proceedings" are "instituted" must be a reference to the legal seat of the arbitration, rather than simply where submissions are heard.

art.22. The claimant has the choice of selecting, at their sole option, any one jurisdiction, or seat, from the following list provided for at art.21(1) or 22(3):

- the place where the defendant's principal place of business is situated;[841] or
- the place where the defendant's place of business, branch or agency, through which the contract was made, is situated; or
- the place in which the port of loading or the port of discharge is situated; or
- any additional place designated for that purpose in the contract of carriage by sea.

Incorporating an exclusive jurisdiction agreement into a contract of carriage governed by the Hamburg Rules cannot deprive the claimant of the entitlement to choose an applicable jurisdiction or arbitration seat from the above list of permitted places.[842] However, the Hamburg Rules will only be applied by the courts of England and Wales when, according to the applicable law of the contract of carriage, they have been contractually incorporated. Accordingly; Canadian legislation, effectively introducing into domestic Canadian law in force at the place of shipment jurisdictional provisions equivalent to those contained in the Hamburg Rules, was incapable of disapplying an exclusive jurisdiction agreement in the bill of lading in favour of the English courts when that agreement was effective according to the governing law of the contractual obligation.[843] A jurisdiction, or place of arbitration, agreement made by the parties "after the claim under the contract of carriage by sea has arisen"[844] is valid under the Hamburg Rules and unaffected by arts 21 and 22. The Hamburg Rules also expressly permit claimants to exercise jurisdiction elsewhere to obtain

[841] Or, in the absence of such a place, the habitual residence of the defendant.

[842] As derogation from the Rules is prohibited by art.23.

[843] *OT Africa Line Ltd v Magic Sportswear Corporation* [2005] 2 Lloyd's Rep. 170. More complex issues of contractual construction (informed by the principles reviewed at 1.5.2) would have arisen had there been a contractual incorporation not only of the exclusive jurisdiction agreement but also of the Canadian legislation, or indeed the Hamburg Rules. In that event the exclusive jurisdiction agreement might have been interpreted as having been overridden by the non-derogation provisions of the Rules.

[844] Pursuant to arts 21(5) and 22(6).

security by ship arrest;[845] to secure provisional or protective measures;[846] or for the purposes of enforcement.[847] By art.22(4) any arbitrator or arbitration tribunal is required to apply the Rules in the determination of disputes under carriage contracts governed by the Hamburg Rules; and the provisions of arts 22(3) and 22(4) are incorporated by art.22(5), with overriding effect when the Hamburg Rules have the force of law or contractual effect[848] into any agreement to refer disputes to arbitration.

3.3.4.9 Contractual Derogation

Like the Hague regime, the Hamburg Rules (when applicable) have overriding effect to the extent that: the carrier cannot avoid or reduce the extent of its obligations or liabilities, or increase those of the shipper provided for in the Rules, otherwise than as expressly permitted by the Rules themselves. Article 23 of the Rules provides that:

> "Any stipulation in a contract of carriage by sea, in a bill of lading, or in any other document evidencing the contract of carriage by sea is null and void to the extent that it derogates, directly or indirectly, from the provisions of [the Rules]";

although a carrier is permitted, by art.23(2), to "increase his responsibilities and obligations" under the Rules. Articles 23(3) and 23(4) require a statement to be included in any bill of lading, or other document evidencing the contract of carriage, that any terms inconsistent with the Hamburg Rules will be overridden by the Rules and those articles also entitle the claimant to compensation for any loss suffered by reason of the absence of that statement.

3.3.4.10 Rights of Carrier

The Hamburg Rules afford the carrier with certain limited rights against the shipper in relation to information provided as to the goods shipped and as to dangerous goods; other rights commonly stipulated in bills of lading by carriers for the protection of their interests are not addressed. In particular

[845] Article 21(2); the nature of ship arrest is discussed at 3.1.3.
[846] Article 21(3).
[847] Article 21(4).
[848] Since any term inconsistent with arts 22(3) and 22(4) is rendered "null and void".

provision is not made for the carrier to exercise any lien over the goods in respect of claims for unpaid freight, or for damage caused to the vessel. As previously discussed in relation to the other transport conventions,[849] the Hamburg Rules should be seen as only a partial code regulating, when applicable, those matters which they address but leaving the parties free to make their own arrangements in respect of other matters. In this context, as the Rules make no provision for the exercise of liens over the goods,[850] there seems no reason why an expressly agreed general lien should not be effective.[851]

Dangerous goods are subject to the special rules provided for at art.13 by which the shipper is subject to the obligation of marking or labelling "as dangerous", those goods which are dangerous, "in a suitable manner"[852] and of informing the carrier, or the actual carrier, "of the dangerous character of the goods and, if necessary, of the precautions to be taken" when the shipper hands the goods over to it.[853] Where, in breach of art.13(2), the shipper fails to inform the carrier of the dangerous nature of the goods and the carrier does not otherwise have knowledge of their dangerous character, then:

> "(a) the shipper is liable to the carrier and any actual carrier for the loss resulting from the shipment of such goods, and (b) the goods may at any time be unloaded, destroyed or rendered innocuous, as the circumstances may require, without payment of compensation".[854]

Where the carrier has been informed, or is otherwise aware, of the dangerous character of the goods but they nevertheless "become an actual danger to life or property" the carrier is given the express right to unload, destroy or render innocuous such dangerous goods.[855] However, such right is subject, in the event of the carrier's knowledge of the dangerous character

[849] See, in particular, 1.6.1.2.
[850] Unlike the CMR convention on the international carriage of goods by road (which, as discussed at 2.3.10, does make provision for a particular lien).
[851] See 1.9.1 as to general and particular liens.
[852] Article 13(1).
[853] Article 13(2).
[854] ibid.
[855] Article 13(4).

of the goods, to the carrier's obligation to pay general average contributions and/or liabilities arising under art.5.[856]

According to art.17 of the Rules the shipper is:

> "deemed to have guaranteed to the carrier the accuracy of particulars relating to the general nature of the goods, their marks, number, weight and quantity as furnished by him for insertion in the bill of lading"

and is obliged to indemnify the carrier in respect of any "loss resulting from inaccuracies" in such particulars. Article 17(2) provides for the carrier's liability for inaccuracies in bills of lading to anyone other than the shipper to remain unaffected by any indemnity, whether implied or express, from the shipper. Furthermore, where the carrier commits any intentional mis-description of the goods in the bill of lading to defraud a third party, any such indemnity will be rendered void under art.17(3), as at common law,[857] and the carrier will have no right to claim limitation under the Hamburg Rules for loss incurred by a third party acting in reliance upon the description of the goods in the bill of lading.[858]

3.3.4.11 Claims among Carriers

The Rules do not make any separate provision as to the liabilities between the contracting carrier and actual carriers *inter se*. Accordingly, where those arrangements constitute contractual arrangements "whereby the carrier undertakes against payment of freight to carry goods by sea from one port to another", so as to constitute a "contract of carriage by sea" within the meaning of art.1(6) of the Rules, the arrangements between the carriers *inter se* will be governed by the Rules just as would any other contract of carriage.

[856] Accordingly, under art.5(1), the carrier will be liable for the loss, damage or delay of the dangerous goods unless it can prove that "he, his servants or agents took all measures that could reasonably be required to avoid" the goods becoming, or the consequences of the goods becoming, such an actual danger to life or property.

[857] As discussed at 3.2.3.4 above.

[858] Article 17(4).

3.3.5 The Rotterdam Rules

The Rotterdam Rules[859] have been signed by 21 contracting states but as at July 31, 2010 none have yet ratified the convention nor apparently completed the necessary steps to give the convention the force of law in their jurisdictions. Although many important maritime nations, including the United States of America, have signed the convention, the United Kingdom has not done so and its future status remains uncertain. Pursuant to art.94, it will not come into force as an instrument of public international law unless and until ratified by at least 20 signatory states giving the convention the force of law under their respective national laws. Should it come into force it will, for those states adopting it, have the effect of displacing whichever of the other international sea carriage conventions previously discussed at 3.3.2, 3.3.3 or 3.3.4 might currently have the force of law in those jurisdictions.[860] The genesis of the Rotterdam Rules was the work of the CMI working group established in 1998 at the request of UNCITRAL to consider the law and practices of the international carriage of goods by sea, which culminated in the submission by the CMI of the Draft Instrument on Transport Law.[861] The Draft Instrument was considered at length, and amended, by the further working group convened in 2001 under the auspices of UNCITRAL before being presented to the UN General Assembly and adopted in amended form on December 11, 2008. It is an ambitious convention seeking not only to replace the previous sea carriage regimes[862] but also to embrace any multimodal carriage by sea, facilitate electronic commerce and regulate certain tangential issues of international trade, such as constructive possession of goods and the assignment of contractual rights, that have previously been left to the applicable laws applied by the forum of any dispute. Although the Rotterdam Rules have not been signed by the United Kingdom and have neither entered into

[859] The United Nations Convention on Contracts for the International Carriage of Goods Wholly or Partly by Sea adopted by the UN on December 11, 2008 and published by UNCITRAL at *http://www.uncitral.org/uncitral/en/uncitral_texts/transport_goods/2008rotterdam_rules.html.*

[860] It is pertinent to note that the current signatory states to the Rotterdam convention include contracting states to each of the prior international conventions.

[861] See Stuart Beare "Liability regimes: where we are, how we got there and where we are going" [2002] LMCLQ 306 for a more detailed history of this genesis.

[862] Article 89 obliges states ratifying the Rotterdam Rules to denounce the 1924 Hague Rules, the 1968 Hague-Visby Rules and their amending 1979 SDR protocol and the 1980 Hamburg Rules.

force as public international law, nor yet been ratified by any of the signatory states, it is still possible that they may be widely adopted in the future. For that reason it is appropriate to review the substantive provisions of the convention.

3.3.5.1 Scope of Application

The scope of application of the Rotterdam Rules is complex. Article 5 provides for the application of the Rules to contracts for the carriage of goods by any means, as long as the contract provides for part of the carriage to be performed by sea,[863] where both the places of receipt and delivery, and the ports of loading and discharge for the same sea carriage, are in different states; provided that "according to the contract of carriage, any one of the following places is located in a Contracting State: (a) The place of receipt; (b) The port of loading; (c) The place of delivery; or (d) The port of discharge". Charterparty contracts and other contracts for the use of a ship or space on a ship are excluded by art.6 as are contracts of carriage in "non-liner transportation"[864] unless (i) a "transport document or an electronic transport record is issued" and (ii) a charterparty, or other excluded, contract is *not* issued. Whilst not applying between the original contracting parties to the excluded contracts, the Rules are, by art.7, applied as between the carrier and any "consignee, controlling party or holder that is not an original party" to the excluded contract.

Carriers contracting with a shipper for the carriage of goods by sea (or by sea *and* any other mode or modes of transport),[865] maritime performing parties,[866] their respective employees and any person performing services on board a ship are all afforded the protection of the Rules in relation to any claim

> "in contract, in tort, or otherwise, that is instituted in respect of loss of, damage to, or delay in delivery of goods covered by a contract of

[863] Whether this provision includes a contractual liberty to carry goods by sea is discussed at 5.2.3.4.

[864] "Liner transportation" being defined by art.1(3) as a transportation service "offered to the public".

[865] Carriers being defined at art.1(5) by reference to whether the contract entered into is a contract of carriage within art.1(1).

[866] Defined by art.1(7) as any party performing any of the carrier's obligations between the goods' arrival at the port of loading and departure from the port of discharge.

> carriage or for the breach of any other obligation under this Convention".[867]

The Rotterdam Rules comprise a much more comprehensive regulatory code for contracts of carriage. They not only address issues of liability for the entire period of carriage, including carriage by other means as well as carriage by sea, they also address such matters as the exercise of rights and transfer of rights and liabilities under negotiable transport documents[868] and delivery obligations under negotiable and non-negotiable transport documents and receipts.[869]

The Rotterdam Rules, unlike the Hague-Visby Rules, apply to carriage on deck and the carriage of live animals[870] and, given their intended multimodal scope, carriage performed by, or on behalf of, the carrier (or the "maritime performing party")[871] before or after the sea carriage. According to art.26, the Rotterdam Rules expressly give way to "any international instrument that, at the time of such loss, damage or event or circumstance causing delay" would have applied to the other mode of carriage "where the loss of, or damage to goods, or an event or circumstance causing delay" occurred had the shipper made a "separate and direct contract with the carrier" for such other mode of carriage.[872] Article 82 makes specific provision to preserve the effects of the existing unimodal conventions[873] on multimodal carriage. This provision is further discussed at 5.2.3.4 below.

[867] Per art.4(1); the shipper, documentary shipper and respective subcontractors, agents and employees all enjoy similar protection.

[868] See arts 50 to 58 of the Rotterdam Rules: the current position under English law in respect of such issues is addressed at 3.1.7 above.

[869] See arts 43 to 49 of the Rotterdam Rules: the current position under English law in respect of such issues being addressed at 3.1.6 and 3.2.3.4 above.

[870] The carrier's liability for such carriage (on deck or of live animals) is subject to particular regulation as discussed at 3.3.5.3 below.

[871] Defined by art.1(7) as being a performing party as to those of the carrier's obligations that fall to be performed "during the period between the arrival of the goods at the port of loading of a ship and their departure from the port of discharge" and includes an inland carrier when operating "exclusively within a port area".

[872] Provided such international instrument has mandatory effects on "the carrier's liability, limitation of liability, or time for suit" pursuant to art.26(b) and (c).

[873] Including the CMR, CIM and Budapest conventions (as to road, rail and inland waterway carriage respectively) discussed at Part Two above and the Warsaw and Montreal Conventions (as to air carriage) discussed at Part Four below.

3.3.5.2 Documentation

The Rotterdam Rules apply to all contracts of carriage irrespective of the form of documentation, so long as the contract is not one of the excluded art.6 contracts. The form of documentation issued is significant in terms of its potential evidential effect.[874] Articles 36–39 provide for certain information to be included in the transport document giving particulars of the shipment of the goods (contract particulars) and the identity of the carrier. By art.39 the "absence or inaccuracy" of such information does not detract from "the legal character or validity of the transport document", but may permit certain evidential conclusions to be drawn.[875] In broad terms the types of documentation provided for by the Rotterdam Rules comprise negotiable, non-negotiable and surrendable non-negotiable transport documents and negotiable and non-negotiable electronic transport records.[876] Pursuant to art.35 the shipper has the option to demand a negotiable document:

> "unless the shipper and the carrier have agreed not to use a negotiable transport document or negotiable electronic transport record, or it is the custom, usage or practice of the trade not to use one".

The nature of the negotiable, surrendable and non-negotiable transport documents provided for in the Rotterdam Rules derives largely from the negotiable bills of lading, straight bills of lading and non-negotiable sea waybills previously discussed at 3.2.2 and 3.2.3 above. The nature of electronic transport records is discussed subsequently at 5.1 below.

3.3.5.3 Liability of Carrier

The basis of liability under the Rotterdam Rules, similarly to the Hague-Visby Rules, is one of fault, although the onus is on the carrier to disprove

[874] Whilst any transport document comprises "prima facie evidence" of the receipt of the goods in the condition stated by art.41, proof to the contrary is not admissable at all as against a third party transferee, acting in good faith, of a negotiable or a surrenderable transport document.

[875] For instance, pursuant to arts 39(2) and 39(3), that goods were shipped in apparent good order and condition on the dates indicated by the document.

[876] See art.1(14) to (22) for their respective definitions; arts 8 to 10 as to their electronic nature; art.35 for their issue; arts 45 to 47 for their respective status as to delivery; art.51 for their respective status as to control; and art.57 as to their respective transferablity.

fault. By art.17 of the Rotterdam Rules the carrier is made liable "for loss of or damage to the goods, as well as for delay" where the claimant proves that such loss or damage, or the event causing or contributing to it, took place during the period in which the carrier was responsible for the goods. Where the carrier "proves that the cause or one of the causes of the loss, damage, or delay is not attributable to its fault", the carrier will be wholly or partially relieved of liability. The period of responsibility is defined by art.12 as beginning on the receipt of the cargo by "the carrier or a performing party" for carriage and ending on delivery.

The concept of "fault" under art.17 is undefined; ordinarily, it would be assessed by reference to the express obligations imposed by arts 13 and 14. These obligations are for the carrier to "properly and carefully receive, load, handle, stow, carry, keep, care for, unload and deliver the goods" and:

> "before, at the beginning of, and during the voyage by sea to exercise due diligence to: (a) Make and keep the ship seaworthy; (b) Properly crew, equip and supply the ship and keep the ship so crewed, equipped and supplied throughout the voyage; and (c) Make and keep the holds and all other parts of the ship in which the goods are carried, and any containers supplied by the carrier in or upon which the goods are carried, fit and safe for their reception, carriage and preservation of the cargo".

As previously discussed, the English courts interpret the Hague-Visby Rules as regulating the performance and the consequences of breach by the carrier of loading and discharging obligations, but not as restricting party autonomy as to the undertaking of such obligations by the carrier.[877] The tenor of that distinction is retained in the Rotterdam Rules by art.13(2), which provides that:

> "the carrier and the shipper may agree that the loading, handling, stowing or unloading of the goods is to be performed by the shipper, the documentary shipper or the consignee".

Article 17(3) provides for the carrier to be relieved of all or part of its liability where, although not proving the absence of fault, it proves that the loss, damage, or delay were caused or contributed to by one or more

[877] See 3.3.2.1 above and also the House of Lords decision in *Jindal Iron and Steel Co Ltd v Islamic Solidarity Shipping Co Jordan Inc (The Jordan II)* [2005] 1 Lloyd's Rep. 57.

specified circumstances. These circumstances are stipulated at (a) to (o) of art.17(3) as follows:

> "(a) Act of God; (b) Perils, dangers, and accidents of the sea or other navigable waters; (c) War, hostilities, armed conflict, piracy, terrorism, riots, and civil commotions; (d) Quarantine restrictions; interference by or impediments created by governments, public authorities, rulers, or people including detention, arrest, or seizure not attributable to the carrier or any person referred to in art.18; (e) Strikes, lockouts, stoppages, or restraints of labour; (f) Fire on the ship; (g) Latent defects not discoverable by due diligence; (h) Act or omission of the shipper, the documentary shipper, the controlling party, or any other person for whose acts the shipper or the documentary shipper is liable pursuant to art.33 or 34; (i) Loading, handling, stowing, or unloading of the goods performed pursuant to an agreement in accordance with art.13, paragraph 2, unless the carrier or a performing party performs such activity on behalf of the shipper, the documentary shipper or the consignee; (j) Wastage in bulk or weight or any other loss or damage arising from inherent defect, quality, or vice of the goods; (k) Insufficiency or defective condition of packing or marking not performed by or on behalf of the carrier; (l) Saving or attempting to save life at sea; (m) Reasonable measures to save or attempt to save property at sea; (n) Reasonable measures to avoid or attempt to avoid damage to the environment; or (o) Acts of the carrier in pursuance of the powers conferred by arts 15 and 16".

This list is clearly comparable with the art.IV(2) liability exceptions under the Hague-Visby Rules discussed at 3.3.2.3 above. However, entirely new exceptions are included for damage arising from reasonable measures to protect the environment or safeguard the ship (by sacrificing goods or rendering dangerous goods harmless), or from loading, handling, stowing, or unloading by the shipper or consignee,[878] whilst the wording of other exceptions has been changed.[879] Only the Rotterdam exceptions at (a), (b), (g) and (j) of art.17(3) precisely reflect the Hague-Visby exceptions at

[878] See paras (n), (o) and (i) at art.17(3) of the Rotterdam Rules.

[879] For instance, the exception "(b) Fire, unless caused by the actual fault or privity of the carrier" at art.IV(2) of the Hague-Visby Rules is restated as "(f) Fire on the ship" by art.17(3) of the Rotterdam Rules.

art.IV(2).[880] Furthermore, by art.17(4) of the Rotterdam Rules the carrier remains liable for loss, damage, or delay proved to have been caused or contributed to by the fault of the carrier, or of anyone for whom the carrier is responsible;[881] or of other circumstances not listed in art.17(4) where "the carrier cannot prove that this event or circumstance is not attributable to" fault on the part of itself or any person for whom the carrier is responsible. As with the Hague-Visby exceptions, the art.17(3) exceptions do not apply in the event of unseaworthiness being causative of "the loss damage or delay".[882]

Whilst these obligations appear to mirror those already included in arts III(1) and III(2) of the Hague-Visby Rules (discussed at 3.3.2.3 above), the mirror does not show a true reflection and there are some critical differences. First, the period during which the obligation as to seaworthiness must be performed is different. Under the Hague-Visby Rules the relevant period was only "before and at the beginning of the voyage";[883] under the Rotterdam Rules, this period is extended throughout the duration of the voyage, obliging the carrier to exercise due diligence to make and keep the ship seaworthy under art.14 "before, at the beginning of, and during the voyage by sea". Secondly, as discussed, the art.17(3) exceptions differ significantly from those arising under art.IV(2) of the Hague-Visby Rules. Thirdly, the art.17(3) exceptions may be disapplied: not only pursuant to art.17(5), in the event of unseaworthiness but also pursuant to art.17(4), where either the carrier is otherwise at "fault", or some other event caused or contributed to the damage in question and the carrier cannot disprove "fault".

Specific provision is made for deviation, deck cargo and live animals.[884] By art.24 whether deviation amounts to a breach of the carrier's contractual obligations is an issue left to the applicable law, but the effect of deviation is

[880] See Hague-Visby paras (d), (c), (p) and (m) of art.IV(2).

[881] The carrier being responsible pursuant to art.18 for the acts or omissions of "(a) Any performing party; (b) The master or crew of the ship; (c) Employees of the carrier or a performing party; or (d) Any other person that performs or undertakes to perform any of the carrier's obligations under the contract of carriage, to the extent that the person acts, either directly or indirectly, at the carrier's request or under the carrier's supervision or control".

[882] See art.17(5) of the Rotterdam Rules. Pursuant to art.17(6), where unseaworthiness is proved, the burden is on the carrier to disprove causation or prove the exercise of due diligence.

[883] Article III(1) Hague-Visby Rules.

[884] Dangerous goods are also subject to specific provisions, but these are discussed at 3.3.5.10 below.

made expressly subject to the defences and limitations of the Rules.[885] Carriage of goods on deck is expressly permitted in one of three circumstances:

> "(a) Such carriage is required by law; (b) They are carried in or on containers or vehicles that are fit for deck carriage, and the decks are specially fitted to carry such containers or vehicles; or (c) The carriage on deck is in accordance with the contract of carriage, or the customs, usages or practices of the trade in question".[886]

Where carriage on deck is permitted the carrier is relieved by art.25(2) of liability for loss, damage or delay to goods caused by the "special risks involved in their carriage on deck". Where goods are carried on deck other than in the permitted circumstances:

> "the carrier is liable for loss of or damage to the goods or delay in their delivery that is exclusively caused by their carriage on deck, and is not entitled to the defences provided for in art.17".

The carrier also loses its right to limit liability where such carriage on deck occurred despite an express agreement between the carrier and the shipper for carriage underdeck.[887] The carriage of live animals may be the subject of particular derogation as discussed at 3.3.5.9 below.

3.3.5.4 Value of Claim

The measure of damages in respect of claims for loss, damage or delay is to be calculated by reference to art.22 and limited pursuant to arts 59 and 60.

The application of these provisions in respect of claims for loss[888] or damage to goods appears straightforward. Article 22(1) provides that "compensation payable by the carrier for loss of or damage to the goods is

[885] Departing from the traditional common law effect of deviation as discussed at 3.1.4.2 above.

[886] Article 25(1); although by art.25(4), circumstance (c) cannot be relied upon as against a third party holder in good faith of a negotiable transport document or record unless the contract particulars state "that the goods may be carried on deck".

[887] Articles 25(3) and 25(5).

[888] Including loss arising due to misdelivery as the Rotterdam Rules do not differentiate loss by misdelivery from any other kind of loss.

calculated by reference to the value of such goods at the place and time of delivery"[889] with the value of the goods being fixed by art.22(2):

> "according to the commodity exchange price or, if there is no such price, according to their market price or, if there is no commodity exchange price or market price, by reference to the normal value of the goods of the same kind and quality at the place of delivery".

Subject to the permitted derogation discussed at 3.3.5.9 below, art.22(3) provides that the carrier is not liable for other compensation beyond the value of the goods as so determined in respect of claims for the "loss of or damage to the goods". Article 59 provides for such claims to be limited to the higher of 875 SDRs "per package or other shipping unit" or three SDRs "per kilogram of the gross weight of the goods that are the subject of the claim or dispute".[890] The definitional issue as to the identification of the number of packages discussed at 3.3.2.4 above, where goods are shipped in consolidation units such as containers or vehicles, is determined by reference to the enumeration on the applicable contract particulars of the number of packages shipped; or, failing such enumeration, by the number of such consolidation units actually shipped.[891]

The application of these provisions in respect of other claims is not so clear. Article 60 provides that:

> "compensation for loss of or damage to the goods due to delay shall be calculated in accordance with art.22 and liability for economic loss due to delay is limited to an amount equivalent to two and one-half times the freight payable on the goods delayed. The total amount payable pursuant to this article and art.59, paragraph 1, may not exceed the limit that would be established pursuant to art.59, paragraph 1, in respect of the total loss of the goods concerned".

[889] The time of delivery determined by art.43 being either when the consignee accepts delivery at the time and place agreed with the carrier under the contract of carriage; or, in the absence of such agreement, at the time and place delivery would "reasonably be expected" under the contract.

[890] Article 59 applies this limit to "the carrier's liability for breaches of its obligations under this Convention" but the carrier may, by art.59(1), agree a higher limit with the shipper.

[891] Article 59(2) providing: "If not so enumerated, the goods in or on such article of transport or vehicle are deemed one shipping unit".

However, the concept of "economic loss" is undefined and art.22 only refers to claims "for loss of or damage to goods" while claims for delay under English law may include claims for physical damage to other goods or direct revenue losses.[892] If the Rotterdam Rules do enter into force in the United Kingdom, contrasting constructions of these provisions may be anticipated. Whilst a purposive interpretation, respecting the international application of the Rules,[893] would suggest any claim arising in relation to the carriage of the goods under the Rules should be encompassed within their limitation provisions, the particular obligations, breach and claims would nevertheless have to be considered to fall within the Rules' regulatory scope.

The right to limit may only be lost pursuant to art.61 where it is proved that the loss resulted from a breach

> "attributable to a personal act or omission of the person claiming a right to limit done with the intent to cause such loss or recklessly and with knowledge that such loss would probably result".

3.3.5.5 Time to Claim

The suit time provided for at art.62 of the Rotterdam Rules ("for claims or disputes arising from a breach of an obligation under this Convention")[894] is a period of two years commencing on the date of delivery, or in the case of non-delivery "the last day on which the goods should have been delivered" with the date of commencement being excluded from the period.[895] The practice of the carrier extending suit time by agreement is expressly permitted by art.63; which provides that, whilst suit time "shall not be subject to suspension or interruption",[896] any person against whom a claim is made may (for as long and so often as they might elect) extend the period "by a declaration to the claimant". However, expiry of the permitted two-year suit time does not prejudice reliance, pursuant to art.62(3), on any claim "as a defence or for the purpose of set-off against a claim asserted by the other party". Neither does it prejudice claims for indemnity under art.64, nor claims under art.65 against any bareboat charterer or other carrier identified

[892] See *Hadley v Baxendale* (1854) 9 Exch. 341 discussed at 1.8.2.
[893] See 1.5.2.
[894] Article 62(1).
[895] ibid.
[896] Unlike under the CMR or CIM Rules for the carriage by road and rail; in respect of which the claimant may extend suit time by written notice.

by the registered owner of a vessel as carrier, provided that such claims are brought within the later of the time allowed by the applicable law of the forum or 90 days from the day either "when the person instituting the action for indemnity has either settled the claim or been served with process in the action against itself, whichever is earlier",[897] or "when the carrier has been identified, or the registered owner or bareboat charterer has rebutted the presumption that it is the carrier".[898]

3.3.5.6 Carriage by Multiple Carriers

The Rotterdam Rules do not provide for successive carriage. By art.18 the carrier is made responsible for the acts and omissions of any person performing the contractual obligations (whether as "performing party",[899] master or crew of the ship, employee of carrier or performing party or any other person). However, the obligations arising under the Rotterdam Rules only attach to a "performing party" as so defined where that party is a "maritime performing party"[900] which received, or delivered, the goods in a contracting state, or otherwise performed its activities as to the goods in a port in a contracting state; and the:

> "occurrence that caused the loss, damage or delay took place: (i) during the period between the arrival of the goods at the port of loading of the ship and their departure from the port of discharge from the ship; (ii) while the maritime performing party had custody of the goods; or (iii) at any other time to the extent that it was

[897] Article 64(b).

[898] Article 65(b): the presumption that the registered owner is the carrier arises pursuant to art.37(2), where the contract particulars fail to identify the carrier, but do "indicate that the goods have been loaded on board a named ship".

[899] Defined by art.1(6) as being "a person other than the carrier that performs or undertakes to perform any of the carrier's obligations under a contract of carriage ... directly or indirectly, at the carrier's request or under the carrier's supervision or control" provided that such person is not retained by a shipper, documentary shipper, controlling party or consignee.

[900] Defined by art.1(7) as being a performing party as to those of the carrier's obligations that fall to be performed "during the period between the arrival of the goods at the port of loading of a ship and their departure from the port of discharge" and includes an inland carrier when operating "exclusively within a port area".

> participating in the performance of any of the activities contemplated by the contract of carriage".[901]

To that extent the maritime performing party, but no-one else other than the carrier itself, is made subject to the contract of carriage with the shipper. However, the maritime performing party only becomes a party to the original carriage contract to the extent that such contract is governed by the Rules, since art.19(2) clearly provides that the maritime performing carrier is not bound by any ancillary obligations or higher limits that may have been agreed by the carrier "unless it expressly agrees to accept such obligations or such higher limits". Article 20 provides that the carrier and any maritime performing party shall have joint and several liability for the overall value of the aggregated claims, limited pursuant to the Rules.

However, art.4 also provides that:

> "(a) The carrier or a maritime performing party; (b) The master, crew or any other person that performs services on board the ship; or (c) Employees of the carrier or a maritime performing party"

may themselves claim the protection of any provision of the Rules that would have the effect of affording the carrier with a defence or a right to limit. The protection of such provisions may be asserted

> "in any judicial or arbitral proceeding, whether founded in contract, in tort, or otherwise, that is instituted in respect of loss of, damage to, or delay in delivery of goods covered by a contract of carriage or for the breach of any other obligation under this Convention"

against those parties. Accordingly, under art.12 such persons may always claim the protection of the Rules throughout the entire period of multi-modal carriage from receipt to delivery of the goods by or on behalf of the carrier. However, other inland carriers[902] remain fully exposed to claims in tort or bailment, or under collateral contractual arrangements without the benefit of limitation or exclusion under the Rules, whether pursuant to the Rules or principles of sub-bailment, since the Rules do not purport to

[901] Article 19(1).

[902] Being land carriers by road, rail or inland waterway (or even air carriers) when not providing services as a maritime performing party.

afford such independent contractors their protection unless they are maritime performing parties.[903]

3.3.5.7 Rights to Claim

The Rules do not generally regulate who has the right to assert claims against the carrier, or the maritime performing carrier, with the consequence that such matters are generally left to be determined by the rules applied by the forum of the dispute;[904] however, unlike the Hague-Visby Rules, they do afford certain specific rights to claim. In particular, art.47 provides that when carriage is undertaken under a negotiable transport document, or a negotiable electronic transport record, the holder of such a negotiable transport document, or negotiable electronic transport record, is entitled to claim delivery of the goods from the carrier after they have arrived at the place of destination. Pursuant to art.47(2)(e) "a holder that becomes a holder" after delivery of the goods:

> "that did not have and could not reasonably have had knowledge of such delivery at the time it became a holder, acquires the rights incorporated in the negotiable transport document or negotiable electronic transport record".

Clearly, were the Rotterdam Rules to take effect in the United Kingdom, very careful consideration would have to be given to their relationship to the rights arising under COGSA 1992 discussed at 3.1.7 above.

3.3.5.8 Jurisdiction and Recognition

Unlike the Hague-Visby Rules, the Rotterdam Rules contain detailed jurisdictional provisions. Applicable jurisdictions are prescribed for the

[903] See 1.6.1.1. The position under the Rotterdam Rules in this respect apparently contrasts with the position arising under the CMR, discussed at 2.3.6, by which all successive carriers and most sub-bailees will be able to claim the protection of the CMR.

[904] Rights to claim arising under English law are discussed at 1.6.1, 1.8.1 and 3.1.7.

commencement of proceedings against both the carrier at art.66[905] and any maritime performing party at art.68.[906] There is no requirement (unlike all the other transport conventions that contain jurisdictional provisions) that such courts must be within contracting states to the convention. The commencement of proceedings elsewhere is prohibited under art.70 except where such proceedings are issued for the purpose of "provisional or protective measures, including arrest". Although, under art.72, the parties may agree after a dispute has arisen to resolve that dispute exclusively in a different jurisdiction to those prescribed, any such exclusive agreement made in anticipation of a future dispute is only permissible under art.67 for carriage under "volume contract" arrangements, and only when such agreement:

> "clearly states the names and addresses of the parties and either (i) is individually negotiated or (ii) contains a prominent statement that there is an exclusive choice of court agreement and specifies the sections of the volume contract containing that agreement"[907]

and designates courts of a particular contracting state. Article 67(2) provides that third parties may be bound by such an exclusive jurisdiction agreement in a volume contract: where the court is in one of the places designated in art.66(a), the agreement is contained in the transport document or electronic transport record; timely and adequate notice of the agreement is given to the third party; and the applicable law applied by the forum "recognizes that that person may be bound".

Arbitration is particularly regulated by arts 75 to 78 largely with similar effect to that described above, although there are some significant differences. Whilst the place at which arbitration proceedings against the carrier

[905] Subject to arts 67 and 72, such proceedings being only permissable: (a) within a jurisdiction in which one or other of the following is situated; the domicile of the carrier, the places of receipt or delivery of the goods under the contract of carriage, the ports of initial loading or final discharge; or, (b) within some other jurisdiction designated, otherwise than as an exclusive jurisdiction, by agreement between the parties.

[906] Such proceedings being permissable only in courts having jurisdiction over: the place of the maritime performing party's domicile; or, the ports where the goods were received or delivered by, or the relevant activities performed by, the maritime performing party.

[907] A "volume contract" is defined by art.1(2) as a contract for the carriage of a "specified quantity of goods in a series of shipments during an agreed period of time".

are to be conducted is regulated by art.75(2),[908] no provisions address the commencement of arbitration against maritime performing parties, except to the extent they are made subject, as non-parties, to arbitration agreements under volume contracts pursuant to art.75(4).[909] The provisions of sub-paragraphs 1 to 4 of art.75 are, by art.75(5), incorporated into any arbitration agreement with mandatory effect, thereby facilitating challenge to any arbitration commenced in breach of those provisions, although art.76 completely excludes arbitration in non-liner transportation unless the arbitration agreement is contained in a transport document or electronic transport record and is being relied upon as against a "consignee, controlling party or holder that is not an original party to the charter party or other contract of carriage excluded from the application of this Convention" under art.7. As against such a person an arbitration agreement in non-liner transportation remains subject to the provisions of art.75

> "unless such a transport document or electronic transport record: (a) Identifies the parties to and the date of the charter party or other contract ...; and (b) Incorporates by specific reference the clause in the charter party or other contract that contains the terms of the arbitration agreement".[910]

3.3.5.9 Contractual Derogation

The provisions as to derogation under the Rotterdam Rules comprise a general prohibition of derogation for all contracts of carriage subject to the Rules,[911] special provisions for volume contracts and further special provisions for the carriage of live animals and certain other goods. Article 79(1) provides the basic prohibition, rendering void any contractual stipulation to the extent that it directly or indirectly either excludes or limits the obligations, or the liabilities, of the carrier, or of the maritime performing party, or purports to assign insurance benefits to the carrier or any

[908] To similar effect as provided for at art.66 (fn. 905) as regards jurisdiction.

[909] To similar effect as provided for at art.67(2) as regards jurisdiction.

[910] This provision reflects the current approach taken by English law, which is discussed at 3.2.3.5 above.

[911] Of course, certain contracts of carriage are wholly excluded from the Rules. In particular, art.6 excludes from the Rules carriage contracts comprising: charter-parties; other contracts for the use of, or for the use of space in, a ship; and non-liner transportation not performed pursuant to a transport document.

person for whose acts or omissions the carrier is responsible;[912] or excludes, limits or increases the obligations and liabilities of the "shipper, consignee, controlling party, holder or documentary shipper".[913]

In the case of volume contracts, derogation is valid when all the conditions stipulated by art.80(2) are met, namely that:

> "(a) The volume contract contains a prominent statement that it derogates from this Convention; (b) The volume contract is (i) individually negotiated or (ii) prominently specifies the sections of the volume contract containing the derogations; (c) The shipper is given an opportunity and notice of the opportunity to conclude a contract of carriage on terms and conditions that comply with this Convention without any derogation under this article; and (d) The derogation is neither (i) incorporated by reference from another document nor (ii) included in a contract of adhesion that is not subject to negotiation."

Article 80(3) restricts the concept of a volume contract by providing that it may not comprise the "carrier's public schedule of prices and services, transport document, electronic transport record or similar document", although the volume contract may, by reference, incorporate the contents of such documents. By reason of art.80(4), the right to derogate in respect of volume contracts neither: entitles the carrier to decrease its obligations and liabilities as to either seaworthiness, or such conduct as would under art.61 disentitle the carrier from asserting limitation under the Rules; nor permits the carrier to increase the shipper's obligations and liabilities as to either the provision of information, or in relation to the shipment of dangerous goods. To the extent derogation is permitted under volume contracts: such derogation will, pursuant to art.80(5), apply to the carrier's relationship, not only with the shipper but also any other person provided that such person "... gave its express consent to be bound by such derogations", otherwise than by simply accepting "a carrier's public schedule of prices and services, transport document or electronic transport record". By art.80(6) the party claiming the benefit of any derogation has the onus of proving not only that the derogation has been agreed but that all the prescribed conditions for such derogation are satisfied.

Article 81 provides that where the goods comprise live animals or other goods the character or condition of which, or the terms and conditions for

[912] Article 79(1).
[913] Article 79(2).

the carriage of which, "reasonably ... justify a special agreement" the contract of carriage may exclude or limit the obligations and/or the liability of both the carrier and a maritime performing party. In the case of live animals any such exclusion or limitation of liability will not take effect to the extent the claimant proves loss, damage or delay resulted from conduct that would under art.61 disentitle the carrier from asserting limitation under the Rules;[914] in the case of other goods, no special agreement may be justified where the contract of carriage is related to ordinary commercial shipments in the ordinary course of trade, or where a negotiable transport document or negotiable electronic transport record is issued.[915]

3.3.5.10 Rights of Carriers

Carriers are afforded various rights by the Rotterdam Rules. The shipper has obligations as to the provision of various types of information, including: "reasonably necessary" information, instructions and documents for the carrier as to the goods to be shipped; "accurate information required for the compilation of the contract particulars and the issuance of the transport documents or electronic transport records"; dangerous goods information "in a timely manner before they are delivered to the carrier or a performing party"; and, in respect of dangerous goods, the shipper is obliged to "mark or label dangerous goods in accordance with any law, regulations or other requirements of public authorities that apply during any stage of the intended carriage of the goods".[916] In the event of any failure to perform those obligations the shipper is liable for, and/or liable to indemnify the carrier in respect of, any loss or damage sustained by the carrier pursuant to arts 30, 31(2) and 32. This is so whether the breach is that of the shipper or, pursuant to art.34, that of "any person, including employees, agents and subcontractors, to which it has entrusted the performance of any of its obligations" other than the carrier or a performing party acting on behalf of the carrier. These obligations and liabilities attach both to the person (the shipper) entering into the contract of carriage with the carrier and any person other than the shipper who agrees to be named as shipper in the transport document or electronic transport document (documentary shipper).[917] In respect of goods that may become a danger to

[914] Article 81(a).
[915] Article 81(b).
[916] See arts 29(1), 31(1) and 32.
[917] See the definition of these terms at arts 1(8) and 1(9) of the Rules.

"persons, property or the environment" the carrier and any performing party have particular rights under art.15 to "decline to receive or to load, and may take such other measures as are reasonable, including unloading, destroying, or rendering goods harmless".

The carrier also has an express right to make what is, in effect, a general average[918] sacrifice of goods at sea "for the common safety or for the purpose of preserving from peril human life or other property involved in the common adventure" pursuant to art.16. The rights of carriers to assert global limitations for casualties by reference to tonnage or some other mechanism is preserved by art.83. Rights of lien arising under the contract of carriage or the applicable law "to secure the payment of sums due" are expressly preserved by art.49. However, such rights are not regulated by the Rotterdam Rules, except where the contract particulars state that the freight has been paid, when art.42 provides that the carrier is not entitled to "assert ... the fact that the freight has not been paid" against either the holder of the negotiable transport document or record, or the consignee, unless such parties are also the shipper.

By arts 43 to 47, the Rotterdam Rules also afford the carrier particular rights to refuse delivery where the consignee refuses to acknowledge receipt of the goods, or fails to identify itself properly, or fails to produce any surrendable non-negotiable transport receipt, or fails to surrender any negotiable transport document, or fails to demonstrate that it is the holder of any negotiable transport record. Those articles also entitle the carrier to obtain a good discharge (i.e. release) of its obligations under the contract of carriage by delivering goods upon the instructions of the shipper or documentary shipper in circumstances in which delivery is not, for particular specified reasons,[919] made to the person otherwise entitled to the goods under any transport document or record; save that, where a negotiable transport document or record is issued, such discharge is only possible under art.47(2):

> "where the negotiable transport document or the negotiable electronic transport record expressly states that the goods may be delivered

[918] Rights in general average are discussed at 3.1.4.3 above.

[919] Such reasons comprising circumstances such as: the refusal of delivery by the carrier in particular circumstances; refusal of delivery by the consignee; instructions not being forthcoming from the consignee, despite the giving of notice of arrival of the goods; or the consignee not being located after reasonable enquiry.

without the surrender of the transport document or the electronic transport record".

Article 48 provides the carrier with particular rights to store, unpack, sell or destroy the goods "at the risk and expense of the person entitled to the goods ... as circumstances may reasonably require"; subject to the carrier giving reasonable notice and holding any net proceeds of sale for the person entitled to the goods. The carrier is expressly exempted by art.48(5) from liability for loss or damage to undelivered goods unless the claimant proves both: that such loss or damage was caused by the carrier's failure to take reasonable steps to preserve the goods; "and that the carrier knew or ought to have known that the loss or damage to the goods would result from its failure to take such steps". The operation of these provisions, if the Rotterdam Rules take effect in the United Kingdom, is unlikely to be straightforward; they have been criticised by commentators both for their potential effect on international trade and their complexity.[920]

3.3.5.11 Claims among Carriers

Claims among carriers are not subject to discrete regulation, other than in respect of the time limit for indemnity claims under art.64 discussed at 3.3.5.5 above. Accordingly, issues of liabilities arising between carriers *inter se* will be subject to the Rules' general provisions to the extent that the arrangement between the carriers constitutes a "contract of carriage" in the terms defined by art.1(1) as discussed at 3.3.5.1 above. If not, issues of liability between carriers *inter se* will be determined by the express terms of the contractual arrangement concluded between them; subject, of course, to any mandatory regulation arising under the applicable law.

3.3.6 Carriage of Passengers' Luggage

By s.183(1) of the Merchant Shipping Act 1995, the Athens Convention on the carriage of passengers and their luggage by sea[921] is given the force of law. The scope of application of the Athens Convention is by art.2

[920] See the article "The next sea carriage convention" by Anthony Diamond Q.C. L.M.C.L.Q. (2008) 2 (May) 135–187; although, as discussed above, art.47(2) of the Rotterdam Rules now protects the integrity of surrendable transport documents (i.e. bills of lading) unlike the prior draft of the convention reviewed in that article.

[921] Appended to the Merchant Shipping Act 1995 at Sch.6.

restricted to international carriage; pursuant to delegated legislation now taking effect under s.184 of the 1995 Act, the scope of the convention's provisions are extended to any domestic carriage of passengers and luggage by sea within the United Kingdom.[922] The basis of liability under the convention is not one of strict liability but of negligence. Pursuant to art.3 the carrier is liable where the loss of or damage to luggage "occurred in the course of the carriage and was due to the fault or neglect of the carrier or of his servants or agents acting within the scope of their employment". Whilst the onus of proof lies on the claimant, the claimant has the benefit of a rebuttable presumption that the carrier was at fault, subject to the contrary being proved by the carrier; although, in the case of cabin luggage, the presumption only applies where the loss or damage "arose from or in connection with the shipwreck, collision, stranding, explosion or fire, or defect in the ship". The carrier is not liable for loss of or damage to "monies, negotiable securities, gold, silverware, jewellery, ornaments, works of art, or other valuables" except when expressly deposited with the carrier for their safe-keeping.[923]

Save where the carrier agrees a higher level of limitation under art.10, the carrier's liability for loss of or damage to luggage is limited by art.8 to 833 SDRs "per passenger, per carriage" in respect of cabin luggage; 3,333 SDRs "per vehicle, per carriage" for loss of or damage to vehicles including all luggage carried by the vehicle; and 1,200 SDRs "per passenger, per carriage" for all other luggage.[924] By art.8(4) claims may, by agreement between the parties, be subjected to deductibles provided that such deductibles do not exceed 117 SDRs per vehicle for damage to vehicles and 13 SDRs per passenger for loss of or damage to other luggage. The carrier's right to limit may be lost under art.13 if it is proved, the onus of proof being on the claimant:

> "that the damage resulted from an act or omission of the carrier done with the intent to cause such damage, or recklessly and with knowledge that such damage would probably result".

[922] Pursuant to Carriage of Passengers and their Luggage by Sea (Domestic Carriage) Order 1987 (SI 1987/670).

[923] See art.5.

[924] These limits were all significantly increased by the 2002 Protocol to the Athens Convention, but as at February 8, 2010 that 2002 Protocol has neither come into force as an instrument of public international law nor yet been ratified by, and given the force of law in, the UK.

By art.16 the Athens Convention stipulates a time period of two years for the commencement of proceedings for claims as to the loss of or damage to passengers' luggage, with the stipulated period commencing on the actual or intended date of disembarkation, whichever is later. Furthermore the passenger must, pursuant to art.15, give written notice to the carrier of claims within certain stipulated periods; otherwise the claimant is rebuttably presumed, unless the contrary is proved by the claimant, to have received the luggage in an undamaged condition. The relevant time periods differ according to whether the damage is apparent or not. For apparent damage, the written notice must be given before, or at the time of, disembarkation of the passenger in the case of cabin luggage; or before, or at the time of, re-delivery in case of any other luggage. For non-apparent damage to, and for the loss of, luggage written notice must be given within 15 days of the date of disembarkation or actual (or intended) re-delivery.

The provisions of the convention apply, by art.4, to claims against the contracting or performing carrier, with the contracting carrier being responsible for the entire carriage and the performing carrier responsible for the carriage performed by it. The contracting carrier is made responsible for the "acts and omissions of the performing carrier and of his servants and agents acting within the scope of their employment". The convention provides that claims may only be brought within the jurisdiction of a contracting state to the convention and, at the claimant's option, such proceedings must be brought in one of the competent jurisdictions stipulated by art.17. Those competent jurisdictions are as follows: the defendant's place of permanent residence or principal place of business; the place of departure or destination under the contract of carriage; the place of domicile or permanent residence of the claimant (provided that the defendant also has a place of business in, and is subject to jurisdiction of, that state); and the place where the contract of carriage was made (provided that the defendant has a place of business in, and is subject to the jurisdiction of, that state). Article 18 prohibits carriers and passengers from derogating from the provisions of the convention and makes any purported derogations "null and void".

PART FOUR: CONTRACTS FOR THE CARRIAGE OF GOODS BY AIR

4.1 Overview of Air Carriage

4.1.1 Nature of Air Carriage Contracts

The English courts seemed ready to extend the principles of carriage of goods by land, in so far as they are applicable, to carriage of goods by air, in the same way as the principles of carriage by horse-drawn vehicles were previously extended to railway and motor vehicles. However, there have been comparatively few reported decisions on the carriage of goods by air under the common law. It soon became apparent that, since most flights were likely to be between countries, problems arising from a "conflict of laws" would be inevitable and an international conference was held in Warsaw in 1929 to address these problems in connection with the carriage of both goods and passengers. This conference resulted in the Convention for the Unification of Certain Rules Relating to International Carriage by Air (the Warsaw Rules) being signed at Warsaw on October 12, 1929. The Convention required the application of the Warsaw Rules to any international carriage by air between places of departure and destination situated in two contracting states (or in one contracting state with an agreed stopover in another state). It was implemented by the enactment of legislation in the countries ratifying the Convention, which made the Warsaw Rules part of the law of the state concerned. Most countries have gradually come to ratify the 1929 Convention.

From the perspective of some states, the original 1929 Warsaw Convention has been amended and eventually superseded by subsequent conventions. However, none of the subsequent conventions has been ratified by all the contracting states to the 1929 Warsaw Convention and states ratifying subsequent conventions have not denounced their obligations under prior conventions. Accordingly, various different versions of international rules can apply to the carriage of goods by air with the version applicable to any particular carriage being determined (pursuant to s.1(4) of the Carriage by Air Act 1961 as amended) by whichever is the most recent version in force between the states of departure or destination.[1] In any

[1] Or whichever is the most recent convention in force in the state of departure and destination, where the state of departure and destination are the same but the air carriage is international carriage (pursuant to art.1(2), which is common to all the various versions of the rules), by reason only of some agreed stopping place in some other state.

dispute involving international carriage of goods by air, it is crucial to ascertain which, if any, particular convention has been agreed by the states of the places of departure and destination; the high contracting states to each of the relevant air carriage conventions are shown in Table 1 at 4.2.8 below.[2]

Subsequent to the original 1929 Warsaw Convention, further international conventions addressing the international carriage of goods by air have included the following: (a) an amending protocol signed at the Hague in 1955 giving rise to the Amended Convention; (b) a convention opened for signature at Guadalajara in 1962 to revise both the original and amended conventions to extend regulation to the air carriage by performing carriers other than the contracting or successive carriers; (c) amending protocols signed at Montreal in 1975 to introduce the SDR in place of the French gold franc for the purposes of financial limitation (protocols 1 and 2) and to address the limitations for passengers (protocol 3) and for goods (protocol 4 giving rise to a so-called Reamended Convention); and (d) the Montreal Convention of 1999, which completely supersedes the Warsaw Convention, radically revising its provisions in relation to the carriage of passengers and less radically revising the rules for carriage of goods.

These instruments of public international law have resulted in a succession of domestic UK primary and secondary legislation implementing the various international conventions. Since the incidence of ratification varies from country to country, implementation has been on the basis that it is possible for carriage with different countries variously to be under carriage with the Montreal Convention, the Reamended Warsaw Convention, the Amended Warsaw Convention, or the original unamended Warsaw Convention (with or without Montreal Protocol 1). It is also possible, in relation to each of the Warsaw regimes, that the applicable convention may be subject to the performing carrier extension arising under the Guadalajara Convention. Some carriage activities are not subject to any of these rules[3] but are governed by derivative UK rules for "non-international"

[2] In Table 1 the high contracting states to each relevant convention are designated by the symbols "☑" or "*" being shown in the appropriate column and row. The symbol "☑" indicates those states identified as high contracting states by the ICAO as at August 8, 2010, whilst the symbol "*" indicates those states certified as high contracting states in the UK by the authority of the Crown: fnn. 9–14.

[3] Due to such circumstances as: the places of departure and/or destination not being within contracting states to any of the conventions; the flights being entirely domestic; or the goods being carried comprising only postal items and thus not constituting "international carriage" within the meaning of the various conventions.

carriage.[4] A series of Carriage by Air (Parties to Convention) Orders issued from time to time conclusively certify identified states as high contracting state parties to the Original Warsaw Convention and the various amended versions of it. In the absence of certification for any particular contracting state, the status of its agreement and ratification may, probably, be proved by evidence.[5] The chain of legislation in the United Kingdom has been as follows.

(1) The Carriage by Air Act 1932 implementing the Original Warsaw Convention. The 1932 Act was repealed by the Carriage by Air Act 1961 Act, which enacted the Amended Convention. However, the Original Convention was and remains effective for carriage from and to those countries that have not ratified the 1955 Hague Protocol. The currency of the Original Convention was preserved by the Order in Council bringing the 1961 Act into force and is now preserved by SI 2004/1899, referred to at para.10 below.
(2) The Carriage by Air (Non-International Carriage) United Kingdom Order 1952. This applied the rules of the Original Convention (on international carriage) to non-international flights. It was repealed in 1967 and has subsequently been reenacted in successive amended forms.
(3) The Carriage by Air Act 1961 implementing the Amended Convention of 1955. The 1961 Act has been frequently amended and remains the principal operative statute regulating the contractual terms for carriage by air at the present time. By the terms of the 1955 Hague Protocol it could not be implemented until a quorum of nations had ratified the Amended

[4] Carriage by Air Acts (Application of Provisions) Order 2004 (SI 2004/1899) reg.4.

[5] The precise status of such delegated legislation certifying the high contracting states to the Air Carriage Conventions was addressed by the House of Lords in *Philippson v Imperial Airways Ltd* [1939] A.C. 332, when their Lordships decided Belgium was a contracting state to the Warsaw Convention, despite no order in council having been issued as required by the Carriage by Air Act 1932. However, it should be noted that this case actually concerned a contractual incorporation of the Warsaw Convention and Lord Atkin indicated (ibid., p.351) that their Lordships might have reached a different conclusion had they been asked to apply the convention through the force of law rather than contractual incorporation.

Convention, and consequently the 1961 Act only took effect on June 1, 1967.

(4) The Carriage by Air (Supplementary Provisions) Act 1962 applied the relatively minor amendments required by the 1961 Gualdalajara Convention so as to extend the provisions of the Warsaw Convention and the Amended Convention to cases where the carrier makes a sub-contract with another carrier to perform the whole or part of the carriage and the goods are therefore carried by a carrier who has no contractual relationship with their owner. The Act of 1962 applies the provisions of the Warsaw Convention and the Amended Convention both to the "contracting carrier" and the "actual carrier", giving the passenger and the owner of the goods the same rights against both, and affording both, whenever the Guadalajara Convention is applicable, the same exceptions from liability granted by the Warsaw Convention and the Amended Convention.

(5) The Carriage by Air Acts (Application of Provisions) Order 1967 (SI 1967/480), which brought the 1961 Act into effect and also repealed the Non-International Carriage Order of 1952 replacing it with the Non-International Carriage Rules of 1967 and which was itself amended by various Amendment Orders in 1969, 1979, 1981, 1998 and 1999.

(6) The Carriage by Air and Road Act 1979, which implemented the protocols signed at Montreal on September 25, 1975 by enacting amendments to the 1961 Act.

(7) The Carriage by Air (Parties to Convention) Order 1999 (SI 1999/1313) certifying the High Contracting Parties to the 1929 Warsaw Convention, the 1955 Hague Protocol and the 1975 Montreal Additional Protocol No.1 and revoking prior Parties to Convention Orders.

(8) The Carriage by Air Acts (Implementation of the Montreal Convention 1999) Order 2002 (SI 2002/263), which implemented the convention signed at Montreal on May 28, 1999 by enacting amendments to the 1961 Act to give the force of law to the Montreal Convention, whilst preserving the application of the 1955 Hague Amended Convention and the 1975 Montreal Protocol Reamended Convention.

(9) The Carriage by Air (Parties to Protocol No.4 of Montreal, 1975) Order 2000 (SI 2000/3061) certifying the High

Contracting Parties to the 1955 Hague Protocol and the reamending 1975 No.4 Montreal Protocol.

(10) The Carriage by Air Acts (Application of Provisions) Order 2004 (SI 2004/1899), which repealed SI 1967/480, enacted revised UK rules for "non-international" carriage in Sch.1 and preserved the application of the original Warsaw Convention in both unamended form at Sch.2 and as amended by the 1975 Montreal SDR Protocol No.1.

(11) The Carriage by Air (Revision of Limits of Liability under the Montreal Convention) Order 2009 (SI 2009/3018), which applies into the laws of the UK the periodic increase in financial limits provided for at art.24 of the Montreal Convention as from December 30, 2009.

This impressive chain of legislation naturally makes the law of carriage by air somewhat complex, although such complexity has, to a certain extent, been alleviated by the reform introduced by s.3 of the 1979 Act. This reform facilitated making statutory revision consequent upon amendment to the air carriage conventions by a simplified procedure under which existing UK legislation is reformed by statutory instrument. However, the EU has also been active in the regulation of air carriage and EU as well as UK legislation must be addressed. Through EU Regulations 2027/1997 and 889/2002, the EU has imposed particular liability obligations with regard to carrying passengers and their luggage on community air carriers (air carriers with a valid operating licence granted by an EU Member State). Subject of course to future EU and UK modifications, the status of air carriage conventions under UK law is as follows.

The Carriage by Air Act 1961 gives the force of law[6] to:

- the 1999 Montreal Convention (Sch.1B to the Act) for flights between contracting states to the Montreal Convention;
- the 1929 Warsaw Convention as amended by the 1955 Hague Protocol and reamended by the 1975 Montreal Protocol No.4 (Sch.1A to the Act) for flights between

6 Save to the extent displaced by the provisions of EU Regulations 2027/1997 and 889/2002, as so provided by s.1(2) and s.14(2) of the 1961 Act.

contracting states to the Reamended Warsaw Convention; and

- the 1929 Warsaw Convention as amended by the 1955 Hague Protocol alone (Sch.1 to the Act) for flights between contracting states to the Amended Warsaw Convention.

The Carriage by Air Acts (Application of Provisions) Order 2004 (SI 2004/1899) applies[7] into UK law three further scheduled versions of statutory terms comprising:

- an amended version of the 1999 Montreal Convention (Sch.1 to the Regulations) for carriage by air not constituting "international carriage" within the meaning of the conventions by reason of the carriage being either domestic (i.e. internal to the UK) or international with non-convention states (i.e. from or to countries which are not convention contracting parties);
- the 1929 Warsaw Convention as amended only by the 1975 Montreal Protocol No.1 (Sch.3 to the Regulations) for flights between states contracting only to the unamended version of the Warsaw Convention and Montreal Protocol No.1;
- the unamended 1929 Warsaw Convention (Sch.2 to the Regulations) for flights between states contracting only to the unamended version of the Warsaw Convention.

The Carriage by Air (Supplementary Provisions) Act 1962, which gives the force of law to the performing carrier extension provided for by the Guadalajara Convention in the context of whichever version of the Warsaw regime is applicable, to the extent only that the flight is also between contracting states to the Guadalajara Convention.

Accordingly, as a result of the Carriage by Air Act 1961 (as amended), Carriage By Air (Supplementary Provisions) Act 1962 (as amended) and the Carriage by Air Acts (Application of Provisions) Order 2004 contracts of carriage by air in the United Kingdom have, since August 6, 2004,[8] been governed by various different statutory codes (the air carriage rules) as follows:

[7] Save to the extent displaced by the provisions of EU Regulations 2027/1997 and 889/2002, as so provided by reg.3(2) of the 2004 Order.

[8] Save to the extent displaced by the provisions of EU Regulations 2027/1997 and 889/2002, as so provided by s.1(2) and s.14(2) of the 1961 Act and reg.1(2) of the 2004 Order.

i. The 1999 Montreal Convention (The Montreal Convention) for international carriage between places in the United Kingdom and elsewhere in high contracting states to the Montreal Convention;[9]
ii. the Reamended Warsaw Convention of 1929, as amended by the 1955 Hague and Protocol No.4 of Montreal 1975 (the Reamended Convention), for international carriage between places in the United Kingdom and elsewhere in high contracting states to the Warsaw Convention as so amended and reamended;[10]
iii. the Amended Warsaw Convention of 1929, as amended by the 1955 Hague Protocol (the Amended Convention), for international carriage between places in the United Kingdom and elsewhere in high contracting states to the Warsaw Convention as so amended;[11]
iv. the Original 1929 Warsaw Convention, as revised by the 1975 Montreal Protocol No.1 (the Warsaw MP1 Convention) for international carriage between places in the United Kingdom and elsewhere in high contracting states to the Warsaw Convention as so revised;[12]
v. the Original Warsaw Convention of 1929 as unamended

[9] The composite table of contracting states published by the International Carriage by Air Organisation at *http://www.icao.int/icao/en/leb/treaty.htm* reveals the high contracting parties to the 1999 Montreal Convention to be, as at December 9, 2009, the states indicated by the ☑ in the 6th column of Table 1 at 4.2.8.

[10] The Carriage by Air (Parties to Protocol No.4 of Montreal 1975) Order 2000 (SI 2000/3061) certifies the high contracting parties to the Warsaw Convention as amended at the Hague 1955 and as further amended by Protocol No.4 of Montreal 1975 to be the states indicated by the * in the 4th column of Table 1 at 4.2.8, in addition to the UK and its dependent territories.

[11] The Carriage by Air (Parties to Convention) Order 1999 (SI 1999/1313) certifies the high contracting parties to the 1955 Hague Protocol to be the states indicated by the * in the 3rd column of Table 1 at 4.2.8, in addition to the UK and its dependent territories.

[12] The Carriage by Air (Parties to Convention) Order 1999 (SI 1999/1313) certifies the high contracting parties to the Warsaw Convention as amended by the Montreal Protocol No.1 1975 to be the states indicated by the * in the 2nd column of Table 1 at 4.2.8, in addition to the UK and its dependent territories.

(the Unamended Convention) for international carriage between places in the United Kingdom and elsewhere in high contracting states to the Warsaw Convention as unamended;[13]

vi. with the exception of the Montreal Convention at (i) above, the possible application of the Guadalajara Convention of 1961 will also need to be addressed in respect each of the above international conventions at (ii) to (v); the terms of the Guadalajara Convention having, when applicable, the force of law pursuant to The Carriage by Air (Supplementary Provisions) Act 1962 to which it is appended at Sch.1;[14]

vii. all other cases of carriage by air are now governed by the UK rules for "non-international" carriage (the UK Non-international Rules), which now appear at Sch.1 to The Carriage by Air Acts (Application of Provisions) Order 2004 (SI 2004/1899).

Each version of the air carriage rules is considered at 4.2 below. They are of paramount importance in considering contracts for the carriage of goods by air. Since June 1, 1967, no contract for carriage by air has been entirely governed by the common law. According to English law however, these statutory air carriage codes take effect within a contractual matrix formed and interpreted according to the principles of the common law. For that reason it is important not to consider them in isolation as if they constituted some complete exhaustive contractual code for air carriage. Certain derogations from the regulations are prohibited; apart from those prohibitions, further or additional terms may be agreed between the parties and their agreement will be formed and interpreted according to the common law applying those principles reviewed at Part One above.

13 The Carriage by Air (Parties to Convention) Order 1999 (SI 1999/1313) certifies the high contracting parties to the Unamended Warsaw Convention to be the states indicated by the * in the 1st column of Table 1 at 4.2.8, in addition to the UK and its dependent territories.

14 The composite table of contracting states published by the International Carriage by Air Organisation at *http://www.icao.int/icao/en/leb/treaty.htm* reveals the high contracting parties to the 1961 Guadalajara Convention to be, as at December 9, 2009, the states indicated by the ☑ in the 5th column of Table 1 at 4.2.8.

4.1.2 Parties and Practices

The parties shipping and receiving goods by air are respectively known as the consignor and consignee. Goods for carriage by air are consigned either through airlines or freight forwarders. Such airlines are likely to be members of the International Air Transport Association (IATA), which is the global trade organisation for the aviation industry. IATA admits airlines as full members and also operates training programmes for freight forwarders which it may accredit. Any forwarder involved in the carriage of goods by air and satisfying the applicable regulatory requirements can apply to be registered as an IATA cargo agent. Since the membership of IATA extends to 230 airlines carrying some 93 per cent of the world's international scheduled air traffic,[15] IATA has had a significant impact on the harmo nisation of international practices in connection with the carriage of goods by air. A large part of this impact is due to IATA's promulgation of standard form documentation, the most significant of which is the IATA approved form of air waybill, most recently revised in 2008 and adopted in its revised form by Cargo Services Conference Resolution 600b for use as from March 17, 2008. The waybill is the central transport document issued for the carriage of goods by air. The IATA revised form incorporates:

> "the rules relating to liability established by the Warsaw Convention or the Montreal Convention unless such carriage is not "international carriage" as defined by the applicable Conventions"[16]

and defines the Warsaw Convention by reference to whichever of its various forms might be applicable. Where neither the Warsaw or the Montreal Convention is applicable, the IATA revised form of air waybill provides for its own scheme of liability; in the United Kingdom this can only take effect in relation to matters not regulated by UK non-international carriage rules.[17]

Chartering aircraft for the carriage of goods by air is a relatively common practice. In the same way as sea vessels, airplanes may be chartered by way of voyage charter for one or more flights, or by time charter for a period of time. In the terminology of the air industry charters may be "dry leased" (in

[15] IATA website at *http://www.iata.org* (accessed December 13, 2009).

[16] IAIA 600b approved air waybill clause 2.1.

[17] Carriage by Air Acts (Application of Provisions) Order 2004 (SI 2004/1899) reg.4 Sch.1.

which case the charterer operates the aircraft itself under its own operating licence and is entirely responsible for all aspects of the aircraft's operation, including such matters as crewing, maintenance and insurance);[18] or it may be "wet leased" (in which case the owner remains responsible for operating the aircraft under an ACMI[19] arrangement, where aircraft, crew, maintenance and insurance are all provided by the owner for the charterer, although the charterer may have to provide other services such as the fuel).[20] Conceptually dry leasing arrangements appear to have much in common with vessel chartering arrangements concluded by way of demise, whilst wet leasing has more in common with vessel time and voyage charters other than by way of demise.[21]

In the context of such air chartering arrangements as well as cargo booking activities by freight forwarders and airlines for the carriage of goods on aircraft operated by others, air waybills are frequently issued not simply by the performing air carrier but also by the contracting carrier. The form of air waybill issued by the performing air carrier has become known as the master air waybill (commonly referred to by the initials MAWB), whilst the version issued by a contracting carrier who is not to be the performing air carrier has become known as the house air waybill (commonly referred to by the initials HAWB). As both performing and contracting carriers have the same duties, liabilities and rights under the applicable regulations,[22] no distinction is drawn in the applicable regulations between these distinct forms of air waybill.[23] IATA now promotes the use of air waybills with a more significant distinction between contracting air carriers and non-contracting air cargo booking agents by reference to contrasting air waybills described as the airline air waybill (referred to by the initials AWB) for use by contracting airlines and the neutral air waybill

[18] Such dry leasing arrangements may be in the form of an operational or a finance charter, with the key distinguishing characteristics of the latter being that the duration of the charter is likely to extend over most of the operational life of the aircraft and, at the end of the term, the charterer will have the option of purchasing the aircraft.

[19] The mnemonic stands for Aircraft, Crew, Maintenance, Insurance.

[20] See *Novus Aviation Ltd v Onur Air Tasimacilik AS* [2009] 1 Lloyd's Rep. 576 for an example of a wet leased chartering arrangement.

[21] Vessel chartering by way of demise and otherwise is discussed at 3.2.1.

[22] As applied in the UK by the 1961 and 1962 Acts as amended and the 2004 Order.

[23] See *Western Digital Corporation v British Airways Plc* [2000] 2 Lloyd's Rep. 142 for discusion of the liabilities of contracting and performing air carriers under HAWB.

(referred to by the initials NAWB) for use by anyone other than a contracting air carrier. The AWB identifies the issuing air carrier who accepts a contractual obligation to carry goods by air; this obligation is subject to whichever version of the international regulations or UK non-international regulations is applicable to the carriage. The NAWB does not identify any particular air carrier as the contracting carrier and the issuer purports merely to undertake an obligation to arrange for the carriage of the cargo by air, without accepting any obligation of carriage; the intention is that the issuer will thereby avoid being subject to the regulations that would otherwise be applicable.[24]

4.1.3 Jurisdiction and Law

Each version of the air carriage rules (other than the UK non-international rules) contains mandatory jurisdictional provisions which take effect subject to the EU jurisdiction regime discussed at 1.4.2. Where, in accordance with the EU regime, the UK courts exercise jurisdiction pursuant to the air carriage rules the provisions of those rules will be applied. Such provisions will take effect irrespective of the law applicable to the contractual or tortious obligations in question by reason of their status as mandatory laws, or overriding mandatory laws, of the forum.[25]

4.1.4 Contractual Terms

Notwithstanding their statutory force, the air carriage rules must be construed by "a purposive construction to the Convention looked at as a whole"[26] to achieve a meaning that gives effect to the underlying purpose of whichever convention provision (in the context of the convention as a whole) might be the subject of dispute, whilst reflecting any international consensus that may have been reached in that respect, and having regard to the interpretative rules for public international law provided for at arts 31 to 33 of the Vienna Convention on the Law of Treaties. That this is indeed the case has been confirmed by various decisions of the English courts

[24] Under English law the scope of the obligations undertaken will be determined by reference to the principles outlined at 1.5.2 and 5.2.2.1. See para.16 of the judgment of Mance L.J. in *Western Digital Corporation* ibid. for the application of these principles to forwarders in the context of carriage by air.

[25] As discussed at 1.4.3.

[26] Per Lord Diplock in giving judgment in *Fothergill v Monarch Airlines Ltd* [1981] A.C. 251, 278.

addressing various provisions of the air carriage rules, such as the permitted time period for making claims, the carrier's right to limit liability for claims and the claimant's right to claim.[27] A particular interpretative issue which has arisen in various cases is that the Warsaw Convention was only drawn up in the French language,[28] and the French language versions of the original, amended and reamended Warsaw conventions are the only authoritative versions for the purposes of public international law. This has been reflected in national UK legislation implementing the conventions into UK law. Whilst both official French texts and English translations have been scheduled to the Carriage by Air Act 1961, s.1(8) provides that in the event of any inconsistency "the French text shall prevail". In contrast, the English text of the Montreal Convention is as authoritative as the French text.

The air carriage rules do:

> "... not purport to deal with all matters relating to contracts of international carriage by air. But in those areas with which [they deal]—and the liability of the carrier is one of them—the code is intended to be uniform and to be exclusive also of any resort to the rules of domestic law".[29]

Accordingly, although one version of the air carriage rules will apply to any contract for the carriage of goods by air, the common law principles reviewed in Part One continue to be applicable to issues falling outside the scope of the applicable code. Even in relation to those issues which generally fall within the scope of the statutory regulation, such as liability, the air carriage rules only establish a general framework and operate "with some flexibility, and as allowing a role for the relevant domestic law ... in situations where the Convention is not in terms exclusive".[30] Clearly, however, it is to the air carriage rules that one must first turn in addressing liability issues in connection with any contract of carriage by air.

[27] ibid. (as to claim notification); *Sidhu v British Airways Plc* [1997] A.C. 430 (as to the carrier's right to limit); and *Western Digital Corporation v British Airways Plc* [2000] 2 Lloyd's Rep.142 (as to the claimants' title to sue).

[28] See art.36 of the Warsaw Convention.

[29] Per Lord Hope (*Sidhu v British Airways Plc* (fn. 27), at p.453) regarding the Amended Warsaw Convention.

[30] Per Mance L.J. in *Western Digital Corporation* (fn. 27), at para.59, in the course of applying common law principles to issues of title to sue under the Amended Warsaw Convention.

4.2 Statutory Regulation

The rules provided for in the Montreal Convention, being the most recent version of the international air carriage rules, are reviewed in detail at 4.2.1 below. When applicable, these rules displace the other versions which can only apply as and when the Montreal Convention is inapplicable. The Reamended Convention, the Amended Convention, the Unamended MP1 Convention and the Original Unamended Convention are respectively reviewed at 4.2.3 to 4.2.6 below as this is the order in which the application of these versions of the remaining air carriage rules should be considered.[31] The UK non-international rules are reviewed at 4.2.2.

4.2.1 The Montreal Convention

4.2.1.1 Scope of Application

Article 1(1) of the Montreal Convention provides:

> "This Convention applies to all international carriage of persons, baggage or cargo performed by aircraft for reward. It applies equally to gratuitous carriage by aircraft performed by an air transport undertaking".

The Montreal Convention and the Warsaw Convention (in all its various forms) contain substantively the same definition of "international carriage" at art.1(2). Being carriage in which the places of departure and destination, as agreed in the contract, are within the territory of two different states, both of which are parties to the Convention (whether or not there is an agreed stopping place in the territory of a third state); also carriage between places of departure and destination in the territory of one state which is a party to the Convention, where there is an agreed stopping place in the territory of another state, whether or not this other state is a party to the Convention. For the purpose of this definition forced landings, in places other than as agreed between the parties to the contract of carriage, are disregarded. Included within this common concept of international carriage is carriage by a succession of air carriers which will be deemed one undivided carriage, where the parties to the contract of carriage regard it as a

[31] See s.1(4) and (5) of the Carriage by Air Act 1961 and regs 3–6 of SI 2004/1899.

single operation, even if a particular flight, or series of flights, is performed entirely within the territory of the same state.[32]

Consequently, a flight between two states which have ratified the Montreal Convention is international carriage as defined in the amended Convention and is governed by the rules of the Montreal Convention. However, a flight between two contracting states to the same version of the Warsaw Convention[33] where only one, or neither, has ratified the Montreal Convention, will be international carriage only as defined by the applicable version of the Warsaw Convention (and not as defined by the Montreal Convention). Section 2 of the Carriage by Air Act 1961 provides for the Carriage by Air (Parties to Convention) Orders[34] to be conclusive evidence as to which states are deemed to be parties to which conventions. In the absence of such orders, other evidence may be adduced as to the status of ratification. The International Carriage by Air Organisation (ICAO), although not the depositary institution for the notification of state accessions, denunciations and ratifications, collates, retains and publishes this information online.[35]

Thus a flight from London to Paris is governed by the Montreal Convention, as it has been ratified by both the United Kingdom and France.[36] A flight from London to Uganda is governed by the original Warsaw Convention; although Uganda is a party to the original Convention,[37] it has not yet ratified any further versions of it, nor has it ratified the Montreal Convention.[38] A flight from London to Glasgow is governed by the Non-International Carriage Rules, because it is a flight within the territory of the same state. However, a flight from London to Glasgow via Dublin is governed by the Montreal Convention because, whilst the places of departure and destination are within the territory of the UK, there is an

[32] As provided by art.1(3); both of the Montreal Convention, and all versions of the Warsaw Convention.

[33] Being whichever of the Reamended, Amended, Unamended MP1, or Original Unamended is the most recent version of the Warsaw Convention to have been ratified by both states (ibid.).

[34] See fnn. 10–13.

[35] See fn. 9 and *Philippson v Imperial Airways Ltd* (fn. 5).

[36] See fn. 9.

[37] See fn. 13.

[38] See fnn. 9–12.

agreed stopping place in the territory of another state.[39] A flight from London to Somalia is governed by the UK Non-International Carriage Rules, because Somalia is party to neither the Montreal Convention nor the Warsaw Convention in any of its various forms.[40]

The Montreal Convention (by art.57) and the Warsaw Convention in all its various forms (by Additional Protocol) provide that contracting states may exempt from the operation of the Conventions flights in their own state-owned aircraft. In the case of the Montreal Convention only, they may also exempt flights performed for their military authorities in aircraft registered in, or leased by, their state where "the whole capacity" of the aircraft has been reserved by the state for such purposes. This right of derogation has been exercised by Canada, The People's Republic of the Congo, the Republic of Cuba, Ethiopia, the Republic of the Philippines and the United States of America in respect of the Warsaw Convention.[41] Accordingly, flights in the state-owned aircraft of any of these six states are not governed by whichever version of the Warsaw Convention might otherwise have applied; however, for the purpose of English law, any such flights are governed by the UK Non-International Carriage Rules. The air carriage rules are applied to carriage by the Crown, except as to:

> "gratuitous carriage by the Crown ... of members of Her Majesty's naval, military or air forces undertaken during a time of actual or imminent hostilities or of severe international tension or of great national emergency".[42]

Article 2 of the Montreal Convention excludes the carriage of "postal items"; save to the extent permitted, "in accordance with the rules

[39] Whether or not Ireland has ratified the Montreal Convention is irrelevant in this context, as such carriage constitutes "international carriage" under art.1(2), even if the agreed stopping place is situated in a state which is not a party to the Montreal Convention.

[40] See fnn. 9–13.

[41] As so certified by Sch.2 to the Carriage by Air (Parties to Convention) Order 1999 (SI 1999/1313).

[42] Pursuant to regs 4 and 8 of the Carriage by Air Acts (Application of Provisions) Order 2004 (SI 2004/1899).

applicable to the relationship between the carriers and the postals administrations", in the state concerned.[43]

The phrase "air transport undertaking" used in art.1(1) of all the air carriage rules is not defined by any of them; a statutory definition of the phrase, which is now contained in s.155(1) of the Air Navigation Order 2005 (SI 2005/1970), provides that an air transport undertaking is "an undertaking whose business includes the undertaking of flights for the purpose of the public transport of passengers or cargo". In *Disley v Levine*[44] the Court of Appeal applied this definition[45] in holding that the proprietor of a paragliding school was not an air transport undertaking (for the purposes of an earlier version of the UK Non-International Air Carriage Rules)[46] as the proprietor could not be said to be undertaking flights for public transport of passengers or cargo for which "he would have needed an air operator's certificate, and a certificate of airworthiness for each paraglider".[47] However, it is only where air carriage is undertaken gratuitously that the involvement of a performing air carrier holding an air operator's licence appears to be essential. Contracts for the carriage of goods by air for reward will, in any event, be subject to one or other version of the air carriage rules, pursuant to the commonly worded provision at art.1(1).

Article 18(1) makes provision for the carrier to be liable for "loss of, or damage to, cargo" caused during "the carriage by air". The period of "the carriage by air" is defined by art.18(3) as "the period during which the cargo is in the charge of the carrier"; although such period "does not extend to any carriage by land, by sea or by inland waterway performed outside an airport".[48] The Convention does not apply while the goods are

[43] By the original Warsaw Convention only carriage performed under "any international postal Convention" was excluded, whilst under the Amended Convention the carriage of "mail and postal packages" was entirely excluded. The UK non-international rules are identical to the Montreal Convention in this respect.

[44] [2002] 1 W.L.R. 785.

[45] Previously contained in the preceding Air Navigation Order 2000 (SI 2000/1562).

[46] Schedule 1 to the now repealed Carriage by Air Acts (Application of Provisions) Order 1967 (SI 1967/480).

[47] Per Henry L.J., fn. 44, at p.796.

[48] Per art.18(4) of the Montreal Convention, which, in contrast to the Warsaw Convention in all its various forms, does not apply its liability provisions to any period of carriage by land, sea or inland waterway in the event of any forced or other landing outside an airport.

being carried on land (including inland waterways) or by sea. Consequently, carriage of the goods to and from the aerodrome, and from and to the air terminal or other place, is not governed by the Convention. In English law, the air carrier's liability while it is carrying the goods to and from the air terminal and to and from the airport, in England is the same as the carrier of goods by land.[49] As with the various versions of the Warsaw Convention, where carriage by land or sea

> "takes place in the performance of a contract for carriage by air, for the purpose of loading, delivery or transhipment, any damage is presumed, subject to proof to the contrary, to have been the result of an event which took place during the carriage by air".[50]

The Montreal Convention has significantly extended the scope of the air carriage rules by providing at art.18(4) for the period of "the carriage by air" to include carriage by any other mode, when substituted by the carrier "without the consent of the consignor ... for the whole or part of a carriage intended by the agreement between the parties to be carriage by air". This provision might be thought to conflict with the provisions of various international conventions which also have the force of law in the United Kingdom, for the international carriage of goods by road, rail and sea.[51] However, although those conventions are not applicable simply by virtue of goods having been carried by other modes. Instead, for their application, they require such carriage to have been made pursuant to agreements concluded for the carriage of goods by, as the case may be, road, rail or sea.[52] For that reason, where the contract requires carriage by air and does not permit carriage by other means, any such carriage by other means will not fall within the scope of the carriage rules prescribed by the CMR, CIM or Hague-Visby Conventions. Mance L.J. dismissed such a "clash of

[49] See 2.1; although, since any carriage of goods by land performed by an air carrier will be ancillary to its air carriage occupation, it is difficult to envisage circumstances in which an air carrier could ever be considered to be a common carrier.

[50] Montreal Convention art.18(4), Warsaw Conventions art.18(3).

[51] Such conventions comprise the CMR, CIM and Hague-Visby Rules discussed at 2.3, 2.6 and 3.3.1.

[52] ibid.

conventions" as being merely an esoteric possibility in *Quantum Corporation Inc v Plane Trucking Ltd*[53] when he applied the CMR Convention to road carriage performed under an air waybill expressly entitling the air carrier to "without notice substitute alternate carriers or other means of carriage" for the contemplated air carriage. However, since that case concerned the Reamended Warsaw Convention, the Court of Appeal's judgment did not address the above extension to the period of "the carriage by air" introduced by art.18(4) of the Montreal Convention. It is submitted that the application of this provision might have affected the outcome of the case as the contractual liberty claimed by the air carrier to carry goods by road ought, in the context of art.18(4), to be interpreted as a contractual provision rendered "null and void" by art.26, as being a provision purporting to relieve the air carrier of liability.[54] The prospects for a "clash of conventions" might now be seen not as a purely theoretical issue but as a real possibility. The issue may in future have to be addressed by courts determining, as a matter of overall characterisation, by which mode the parties had agreed the goods were to be carried.[55]

4.2.1.2 Documentation

The Montreal Convention and the Reamended Warsaw Convention take account of modern trends to document air carriage contracts electronically by providing at art.4, not only for the possibility of the carrier issuing an air waybill or passenger ticket to record the details of the air carriage contract, but also for the substitution of the air waybill by "[a]ny other means which preserves a record of the carriage to be performed" (e.g. an electronic record). However, where any such other means are used, the carrier is obliged by art.4(2) to issue to the consignor on request "a cargo receipt permitting identification of the consignment and access to the information". Article 5 provides that the air waybill or cargo receipt must include:

53 *Quantum Corporation Inc v Plane Trucking Ltd* [2002] 2 Lloyd's Rep., para.28. Under the Reamended Warsaw Convention, and prior versions of the Warsaw Convention, the possibility of any actual conflict could be thus discounted by virtue of the factual implausibility of having consensual carriage of the same cargo by different modes at the same time.

54 See 4.2.1.9 below.

55 Even though in the *Quantum Corporation Inc* case (fn. 53) Mance L.J. dismissed (at paras 14 to 36) the need for such overall categorisation in the context of the operation of the various versions of the Warsaw Convention and the CMR Convention.

> "(a) an indication of the places of departure and destination; (b) if the places of departure and destination are within the territory of a single High Contracting Party, one or more agreed stopping places being within the territory of another State, an indication of at least one such stopping place; and (c) an indication of the weight of the consignment".[56]

The carrier is, by art.6, expressly excused from any "duty, obligation or liability" in relation to further documentary requirements imposed by national authorities on the consignor; consequently the carrier's documentary obligations opposite the consignor under the Montreal Convention are confined to the air waybill or cargo receipt. Article 7 provides that the consignor shall make out the air waybill, when issued, in three original parts. The first is to be marked "for the carrier" and signed by the consignor; the second "for the consignee" and signed by the consignor and the carrier; and the third is to be signed "by the carrier" and delivered to the consignor, once the cargo has been accepted by the carrier. The signatures of both the consignor and the carrier may be printed or stamped. Where the carrier makes out the air waybill "at the request of the consignor", a rebuttable presumption arises that the carrier has done so on behalf of the consignor. When the consignment comprises more than one package, separate air waybills may be required by the carrier; where the carriage is recorded other than by an air waybill, separate cargo receipts may be required by the consignor.[57] However, pursuant to art.9 of the Montreal Convention, non-compliance with the documentary requirements stipulated by arts 4 to 8 does

[56] The specification of the air waybill (at that time called air consignment note) in art.8 of the Original Convention of 1929 required far more detailed particulars, which still appear on many standard form air waybills. The requirement in the original Convention that failure to issue a "baggage check" (i.e. the air waybill) invalidated the contract of carriage and disapplied the rules of the Convention was discarded in 1955 when the Amended Convention was adopted. The originally onerous documentary burdens on carriers was reduced by subsequent versions of the Warsaw Convention and is now satisfied for the Montreal Convention by these simple particulars.

[57] See art.8 of the Montreal Convention.

> "not affect the existence or the validity of the contract of carriage, which shall, nonetheless, be subject to the rules of this Convention including those relating to limitation of liability".[58]

Article 10 provides that the consignor is responsible for the correctness of the particulars supplied in the air waybill or inserted in the cargo receipt, which is to be issued by the carrier when "other means" are used to maintain a record. The consignor must indemnify the carrier for any loss suffered, either directly or as a result of claims made against it, caused by a defect in the particulars supplied. Equally, if the consignor supplies correct particulars but the carrier inserts incorrect particulars (either into the records kept by "other means", or the cargo receipt) the carrier must indemnify the consignor, or any other person to whom the consignor is liable, for any loss suffered. Article 11(1) provides that the air waybill, or cargo receipt, constitutes "prima facie evidence of the conclusion of the contract, of the acceptance of the cargo and of the conditions of carriage" to which it refers. Statements contained in the air waybill, or cargo receipt, as to "the weight, dimensions and packing of the cargo, as well as those relating to the number of packages" also constitute prima facie evidence of the factual matters so stated.[59] This means, of course, that such evidence can be overturned by proof to the contrary.

The Montreal Convention does not contain the provision included at art.15(3) of the Amended Convention of 1955 to the effect that "[n]othing in this Convention prevents the issue of a negotiable air waybill". Nevertheless, the ability to issue negotiable air waybills[60] may be inferred from art.15(1) of the Montreal Convention, which provides that neither "the

[58] This is not so for carriage under the original unamended, the MP1 or the Amended Warsaw Convention, since under these conventions, in the event of non-complaince with documentary requirements, air carriers are disentitled by art.9 from relying on Convention provisions to limit their liability. The Reamended and Montreal Conventions are more favourable to carriers since, despite being in breach of documentary requirements, a carrier may still claim the protection of the liability limitation provisions they contain.

[59] Pursuant to art.11(2), which goes on to provide that statements as to "quantity, volume and condition of the cargo" only constitute prima facie evidence as against the carrier, where they either relate to "the apparent condition of the cargo", or the carrier has actually checked the veracity of the statements and this checking is confirmed by the air waybill.

[60] Being air waybills capable, pursuant to some special agreement of the consignor and the carrier, of transferring constructive possession of the cargo from the consignor to the consignee, as further discussed in 4.2.1.7 below.

relations of the consignee and consignor with each other", nor the derivative rights of third parties, are affected by arts 12, 13 and 14, which deal with the rights of both consignor and consignee in their relations with the carrier.

4.2.1.3 Liability of Carrier

Under art.18 of the Montreal Convention, the carrier is liable for loss or damage to cargo caused by an event taking place during the "carriage by air";[61] and, under art.17(2), for destruction of and loss or damage to checked baggage which occurs on board the aircraft, or during any period when the carrier is in charge of the checked baggage. Pursuant to art.18(2), the carrier is exempted from liability for cargo where it can prove, the onus of proof being on it, that:

> "the destruction, or loss of, or damage to, the cargo resulted from one or more of the following: (a) inherent defect, quality or vice of that cargo; (b) defective packing of that cargo performed by a person other than the carrier or its servants or agents; (c) an act of war or an armed conflict; (d) an act of public authority carried out in connection with the entry, exit or transit of the cargo".[62]

These exemptions vary considerably from the liability exemptions under the various forms of the Warsaw Convention, which, to avoid confusion, are discussed at 4.2.3 to 4.2.6 below. Article 19 provides for the carrier to have liability for damage occasioned by delay, but exempts the carrier from such liability where it proves, the onus again being on the carrier, that "it and its servants and agents took all measures that could reasonably be required to avoid the damage or that it was impossible for it or them to take such measures".

In addition to the above exemptions the carrier may also be wholly or partly exonerated from liability pursuant to art.20 of the Montreal Convention where it proves, the onus of proof again being on the carrier, that

[61] The relevant period of the carriage by air, for art.18, is discussed above at 4.2.1.1.

[62] Baggage liability exemptions are only available under art.17(2) for "inherent defect, quality or vice of the baggage"; for unchecked baggage, liability fault must be proved on the part of the carrier, its servants or agents.

> "the damage was caused or contributed to by the negligence or other wrongful act or omission of the person claiming compensation, or the person from whom he or she derives his or her rights".[63]

In the context of art.20 it seems appropriate to interpret "damage" in the wide sense as being any financial loss, rather than in the narrow sense of physical damage; otherwise the carrier would not be exonerated from liability even in the event of a total loss of the goods in consequence of such negligence, wrongful act or omission on the part of any claimant, consignor or consignee.[64]

4.2.1.4 Value of Claim

The Warsaw Convention fixed certain sums as the maximum payable in compensation by a carrier for loss, damage or delay and until 1975 the limit of liability was stated in gold francs. The 1975 Montreal Protocol No.1 introduced a variation to the currency units used for the calculation of the limit of liability, from gold francs to Special Drawing Rights (SDR).[65] This variation is effective for the purposes of the Reamended, Amended and MP1Warsaw Convention. The basis on which the limit of liability for cargo claims is calculated under those versions of the Warsaw Convention is identical to the basis stipulated for the calculation of such claims under the Montreal Convention,[66] subject to the operation of the periodic review of limits under the Montreal Convention and consequent increase in the

[63] The carrier being exonerated to the extent of the damage so caused, by such negligence, wrongful act or omission.

[64] *Fothergill v Monarch Airlines* [1981] A.C. 251 in which the House of Lords accorded such a wide interpretation to "damage" under art.26 of the Amended Warsaw Convention.

[65] The nature of the SDR as a notional currency unit, now used in the context of many international conventions, is discussed in the context of the CMR at 2.3.4.2.

[66] As discussed at 4.2.3 to 4.2.6 below; whilst the cargo liability limitations under the Reamended Warsaw and Montreal Conventions apply irrespective of the nature of the breach, the limits under the Amended, MP1 and Unamended Warsaw Conventions are disapplied where damage results from recklessness (under the Amended Convention) or wilful misconduct (under the MP1 and Unamended Warsaw Conventions) on the part of the carrier or those for whom it is responsible.

amount of the limit.[67] Article 22 of the Montreal Convention specifies the limits of liability for cargo claims as follows:

> "... in the case of destruction, loss, damage or delay is limited to a sum of [19][68] Special Drawing Rights per kilogramme, unless the consignor has made, at the time when the package was handed over to the carrier, a special declaration of interest in delivery at destination and has paid a supplementary sum if the case so requires ...".[69]

Article 22 goes on to provide that the weight to be taken into account in calculating the limit "... shall be only the total weight of the package or packages concerned ...", except where the destruction, loss, damage or delay of such package or packages affects the value of other packages covered by the same air waybill,[70] when the total weight of such package or all such packages is also to be taken into account pursuant to art.22(4) in determining the limit.[71] In addition to the above, courts are entitled under art.22(6) to exercise any power afforded to them by the governing law of the forum to award "... the whole or part of the court costs and of the other expenses of the litigation incurred by the plaintiff, including interest ...",[72] except where the damages awarded (excluding court costs and other litigation expenses) do not exceed the value of any sum offered in writing by the carrier to the claimant prior to the action, or "... within a period of

[67] Article 24 provides for the Montreal Convention limits to be revised at five-year intervals and the latest such revision took effect, as from December 30, 2009, pursuant to The Carriage by Air (Revision of Limits of Liability under the Montreal Convention) Order 2009 (SI 2009/3018).

[68] See fn. 67, with the limit being 17 SDRs prior to December 30, 2009 and remaining at 17 SDRs for claims under the Warsaw regime.

[69] Article 22(3), which confirms declared values will not be applied, if and to the extent the carrier proves "the consignor's actual interest in delivery at destination" is less than that declared.

[70] Or, in the absence of an air waybill, any art.4(2) cargo receipt or carriage record.

[71] The financial limitation for baggage under art.22(2) is limited to 1,131 SDRs (as from December 31, 2009, with the limit previously being 1,000 SDRs) for each passenger in the absence of declaration of special interest and payment of additional charges. The limit in respect of baggage may be disapplied under art.22(5) (unlike cargo, in respect of which the limit may not be disapplied) where the damage results from some intentional or reckless act or omission committed, in the knowledge that damage would probably result, by the carrier, or its servants or agents proved to have been acting within the scope of their employment.

[72] In England and Wales statutory rights to interest arise under s.35A of the Supreme Court Act 1981 and s.69 of the County Courts Act 1984.

six months from the date of the occurrence causing the damage …". Pursuant to art.23(1) of the Montreal Convention, the value of the SDR liability limit payable as a result of judicial proceedings is to be converted into national currencies at the rate prevailing as at the date of judgment.

The financial limitation (and other liability provisions) stipulated by the Montreal Convention in respect of any liability on the part of those responsible for carrying cargo by air for the destruction, loss, damage or delay to cargo (arising from occurrences taking place during the period of the carriage by air, as defined) is absolute, irrespective of the basis of the claim.[73] Article 29 of the Montreal Convention provides that any action brought for damages (whether the action is founded on the Convention, or contract, or tort, or any other cause) can only be brought subject to the limitations of liability outlined above, which are maximum limits and may not be exceeded, whatever the circumstances giving rise to the liability. Any jurisdiction of the forum to award "punitive, exemplary or any other non-compensatory damages" is expressly excluded. The benefit of the financial limitations may be claimed by the contracting air carrier and the actual performing carrier.[74] Their respective servants or agents who prove they "acted within the scope of their employment" at the material time may also claim the benefit of such limitation.[75]

Accordingly, claims for destruction, loss, damage or delay to cargo during any period of the carriage by air, subject to the Montreal Convention, are calculated in England and Wales by reference to the applicable law of the contract or the tort (as the case may be). However, the maximum amount payable may only exceed the limit of liability provided for in the Montreal Convention where the consignor's interest in delivery of the cargo exceeds the value of the limit and the consignor not only declared such interest to the carrier as a "special interest" when the cargo was handed over to the carrier, but also paid any supplementary sum demanded by the carrier for such increased liability. In all other cases such cargo claims will be subject to the financial limitation applied by the Montreal Convention.

[73] Whilst art.22(5) entitles courts to disapply financial limitations in respect of claims for delay to passengers or for destruction, loss, damage or delay to passenger baggage, where damage is caused by deliberate or reckless conduct; this provision does not apply to claims relating to the carriage of cargo.

[74] See in particular arts 30, 36 and 39 to 41.

[75] See in particular arts 29 and 43.

4.2.1.5 Time to Claim

Article 31 of the Montreal Convention provides that no action shall lie against the carrier unless the person entitled to take delivery of the goods has made a complaint to the carrier in writing within a stated time limit,[76] except where the carrier has been guilty of fraud. Receipt of cargo or baggage without complaint, by the person entitled to take delivery of them, is prima facie evidence that they were delivered in good condition and in accordance with the contract of carriage. If this subsequently proves not to be the case, notice must be given forthwith, either on the document of carriage or in a separate letter, within the applicable time limit. This is 14 days from the receipt of the goods in the case of damage to cargo.[77] In the case of delay to either goods or baggage, the time limit is 21 days from the date when the goods or baggage are placed at the disposal of the person entitled to take delivery. In addition to this time limitation for giving written notice to the carrier of any claim, the Montreal Convention stipulates that any action must be brought against the carrier within a period of two years. This stipulation appears in art.35, which is expressed in the following terms:

> "(1) The right to damages shall be extinguished if an action is not brought within two years reckoned from the date of arrival at the destination or from the date on which the aircraft ought to have arrived or from the date on which the carriage stopped. (2) The method of calculating the period of limitation shall be determined by the law of the court seised of the case".

Accordingly, where the aircraft is delayed or deviates and the carriage ultimately ceases at a place other than the agreed place of destination for the goods (and at a date later than that on which the aircraft ought to have arrived), the period of limitation only begins to run from the date at which the carriage of goods ceased.

Action in terms of legal proceedings before the courts of England and Wales is commenced for the purposes of suit time limitation when the claim form is issued and not when it is served. For this reason, where

[76] In this context it should be noted that art.52 provides that the expression "days" when used in the Convention, means calendar days, not working days.

[77] Being reduced, pursuant to art.31(2), to seven days from receipt, for damage to passengers' checked baggage.

action is to be brought before the courts of England and Wales, it will be time barred under the provisions of the Montreal Convention if the claim form is not issued within two years of the date when the aircraft arrived, or ought to have arrived, at its destination. For the avoidance of doubt, it should be noted that s.5 of the Carriage by Air Act 1961 applies the art.35 time limitation provision to actions brought against the carrier's servants or agents personally. It expressly provides that this statutory time limit for the commencement of such actions against servants or agents applies to arbitration as much as to litigation.[78]

4.2.1.6 Carriage by Multiple Carriers

For the purposes of the Montreal Convention and the Warsaw regime, successive carriage is defined by art.1(3) as "one undivided carriage" performed by several successive carriers, where the carriage has been regarded by the parties as a "single operation", regardless of whether the contractual arrangements for such a single carriage operation are in the form of a single contract or a series of contracts. If they are in the form of a series of contracts, any individual contract within such a series must be regarded as "international carriage" under art.1, although it is to be performed entirely within the territory of a single state. By art.36(1) any carrier accepting "passengers, baggage or cargo" for successive carriage, as so defined by art.1(3), does so subject to the Montreal Convention; such a carrier is deemed to be one of the contracting parties to the carriage contract for that part of the carriage which it is to perform.[79] Rights to claim against successive carriers are governed by art.36(3) and are discussed at 4.2.1.7 below.

Where international carriage by air is performed by someone who is neither a contracting carrier nor a successive carrier, as defined by art.1(3), the provisions of Chapter V (at arts 39 to 48) of the Montreal Convention apply, subject only to such carriage being performed with the authority of the contracting carrier, which authority is presumed under art.39 in the

[78] Whilst "action" under art.35 of the Montreal Convention is not expressly defined, it must be the case that it includes both litigation and arbitration. When arbitral proceedings are to be regarded as commenced for the purposes of the art.35 and s.5 suit time limitations is determined in the UK by reference to s.14 of the Arbitration Act 1996.

[79] The Montreal Convention contains no pre-condition (such as that contained in art.34 of the CMR in relation to the international carriage of goods by road) that a successive carrier must also have accepted the consignment note (or air waybill) for the entire carriage.

absence of proof to the contrary. Under art.40, whilst the contracting carrier remains liable for the performance of the entire contractual carriage, actual carriers are made subject to the provisions of the Montreal Convention as regards that part of the contractual carriage which they perform;[80] however, by art.41 the actual carrier is only affected by any special agreement, waiver of rights or special interest in delivery accepted by the contracting carrier to the extent that it also agrees to them. These Chapter V provisions reflect the provisions of the 1961 Guadalajara Convention, which is applicable to the various versions of the Warsaw regime whenever international carriage takes place between, or within, states that are high contracting parties to the Guadalajara Convention.

4.2.1.7 Rights to Claim

Articles 12 and 13 confer rights to claim on, respectively, the consignor and the consignee. Pursuant to art.14, each of them may enforce its own respective rights in its own name whether "acting in its own interest or in the interest of another". There does not appear to be a decision of the courts of England and Wales which expressly confirms that this apparent notional right to sue can be exercised, notwithstanding the absence of loss on the part of the consignor or consignee, for the benefit of others outside those categories of notional claim generally permissible under English law.[81] However, such a broad interpretation appears to be both appropriate and supported by certain judicial observations, indicating that the notional right of consignors and consignees may be pursued outside the generally permitted categories of notional claim.[82]

Article 12 confers all rights on the consignor to dispose of the cargo by withdrawing it at any time; whether at the airport of departure, airport of destination, or at any intermediate landing place. The consignor may require the cargo to be delivered to another address, or to be returned to the airport of departure. The carrier, if requested to stop goods in transit in

80 Being responsible under art.41 not only for their own acts or omissions but also for those of the contracting carrier and its respective servants and agents, whilst acting in the course of their respective employments.

81 Such as claims pursued by insurers, trustees and bailees, which may respectively be pursued under principles of subrogation, equity and bailment.

82 Such as the reference by Gatehouse J. in *Gatewhite Ltd v Iberia Lineas Aereas de Espana SA* [1990] 1 Q.B. 326, 334 (in relation to the identically worded provisions of the Amended Warsaw Convention) to such notional rights of suit being exercised by "a customs clearing agent, a forwarding agent or the buyer's bank".

this way, should require the consignor to produce its copy (i.e. the copy referred to by art.7(2) as "the third part", which has been signed by the carrier) of any air waybill or cargo receipt (if any) issued for the carriage, as proof that it is still entitled to stop the goods and re-direct them.[83] Where the carrier carries out the consignor's instructions without requiring production of any air waybill or cargo receipt (if any) issued to the consignor, art.12(3) provides the carrier will be liable to any other person lawfully in possession of such an air waybill or cargo receipt, subject to the carrier's rights of recourse against the consignor. The rights of the consignor to stop goods or assert rights under the contract of carriage cease when those of the consignee begin under art.13.[84] Thus, the provisions of arts 12 and 13 have the effect of facilitating the use of negotiable air waybills, to which reference was made at 4.2.1.2 above, although a negotiable air waybill is not negotiable as such: it is simply that its physical transfer from the consignor to the consignee has the effect of divesting the consignor of its right to control the disposition of the cargo by the carrier. In the light of these provisions the right of an unpaid seller to stop goods in transit under the Sale of Goods Act 1979 (as discussed in 1.9.2) is of little, if any, significance in the context of international carriage by air.

Pursuant to art.13, the consignee's rights begin on arrival of the goods at the airport of destination. Unless otherwise agreed, it is the duty of the carrier to give notice to the consignee as soon as the goods arrive. Provided the consignor has not exercised its art.12 rights to stop or divert the goods in transit, the consignee is entitled to require the carrier to deliver the cargo to it, on payment of the charges due and compliance with any other condition of the carriage. If the carrier admits the loss of the cargo, or if the cargo has not arrived within seven days of the due date, the consignee may proceed to enforce against the carrier the rights flowing from the contract of carriage either (as discussed above) on its own behalf, or on behalf of another as stipulated in art.14.

Whether these Convention rights of the consignor and consignee are exclusive (and, in consequence, have the effect of ousting rights to claim otherwise applying under the contract, tort, agency or bailment principles

[83] Such proof of entitlement is apparently unnecessary in the event that no air waybill or cargo receipt is issued for the carriage, there being no requirement under art.4 for the delivery of an air waybill where "other means" are used to preserve a record of the carriage; in such a case, the carrier is only obliged to issue a cargo receipt on request by the consignor.

[84] Pursuant to art.12(4) the consignor's rights will resume if the consignee cannot be communicated with, or refuses to accept the cargo.

normally arising under English law)[85] has been the subject of detailed judicial consideration in England and Wales. Although such consideration has been given in the context of various versions of the Warsaw Convention, such consideration is also material to the provisions of the Montreal Convention, since the wording (and numbering) of arts 12, 13 and 14 in all the air carriage conventions is identical. The issue was considered by Gatehouse J. in the *Gatewhite v Iberia Airlines* case,[86] in the context of a claim by the purchaser of a consignment of chrysanthemums, in respect of the delay of the consignment. The purchaser had acquired the property in the goods on its shipment by air; the air waybill named the vendor as consignor and the purchaser's customs' clearing agents as the consignee; and the sole issue was whether the purchaser was entitled to sue the carrier in tort as the owner of the goods. Recognising the importance of considering the issue purposively from an international perspective in light of the aims and purposes of the applicable Convention, rather than from the "parochial" viewpoint of the English lawyer, Gatehouse J. nonetheless decided (since the Convention did not deal expressly with the position by excluding such a right of action and there was no international consensus as to the interpretation of these provisions) that there was no reason why English tort law principles could not be applied and afford the owner a right of action against the carrier.[87] Despite doubt being cast on this decision by the House of Lords in *Sidhu v British Airways Plc*,[88] the decision of Gateway J. was endorsed by the decision of the Court of Appeal, given by Mance L.J., in *Western Digital Corporation v British Airways Plc*,[89] to the effect that claims may be pursued against air carriers undertaking international carriage subject to the applicable Convention under the normal

[85] See 1.8.1 for a discussion of these principles.
[86] See fn. 82.
[87] On the basis that, in the words of Gatehouse J. ibid. p.334, "the lex fori could fill the gap".
[88] [1997] A.C. 430, 450 when Lord Hope commented that it seemed "more consistent with the purpose of the Convention to regard it as providing a uniform rule about who can sue for goods which are lost or damaged during carriage by air, with the result that the owner who is not a party to the contract has no right to sue in his own name"; in the course of deciding that passengers carried, under contracts for the international carriage by air regulated by the applicable Convention, had no separate and distinct right under English law to remedy falling outside the scope of the applicable Convention.
[89] [2000] 2 Lloyd's Rep. 142.

English law principles of contract, tort, agency or bailment.[90] According to the detailed and insightful judgment of Mance L.J. in the Court of Appeal in that case, such claims would be subsumed within the scheme of liability provided for by the applicable Convention, with Mance L.J. concluding "that the scheme of the Warsaw and Guadalajara Conventions is to read as permitting such claims, where they would be allowed under the relevant domestic law".[91] It is submitted that the Montreal Convention, as well as other applicable versions of the Warsaw Convention, should be susceptible to the same interpretation, despite the obiter dictum in the House of Lords to the contrary.[92]

Article 36(3) makes further express provision for rights to claim in the case of successive carriage stipulating that: the consignor can sue the first carrier; the consignee, who is entitled to delivery, can sue the last carrier; and that each of the consignor and the consignee may sue the carrier performing the carriage when the destruction, loss, damage or delay to the cargo took place.[93] In *Western Digital Corporation*[94] Mance L.J. confined the equivalent provision in the Warsaw Convention to

> "a perceived need to regulate and distribute the rights of claim between two sides in the very specific situation of successive carriage, rather than being aimed at any identification or limitation of those entitled to present themselves either as, or through, the consignor or consignee".[95]

There seems no reason to interpret art.36(3) as disentitling persons other than the consignor and consignee from exercising their rights to claim under English law. However, it seems appropriate to seek to categorise such claims as being equivalent to consignor or consignee claims to achieve the practical allocation of responsibility, required by art.36(3), for claims in successive carriage, as between first, last and performing carriers.

90 Apparently, in addition to those rights of the consignor and consignee to claim, which are expressly provided for in arts 12 to 14.

91 See fn. 89, at p.164.

92 See fn. 88.

93 With such carriers being jointly and severally liable to the consignor or consignee.

94 See fn. 89.

95 ibid. per Mance L.J. para.47.

4.2.1.8 Jurisdiction

Articles 33, 34 and 46 of the Montreal Convention provide for a self-contained jurisdiction regime for cargo claims. Like the other international carriage jurisdiction regimes, the Montreal jurisdiction regime takes effect in the United Kingdom within the context of the EU jurisdiction regime.[96] Article 33(1) of the Montreal Convention provides that any

> "action for damages must be brought at the option of the plaintiff in the territory of one of the States Parties, either before the Court of the domicile of the carrier or of its principal place of business, or where it has a place of business through which the contract has been made or before the court at the place of destination".

Thus the courts of England and Wales are entitled to have jurisdiction in an action arising from a contract of international carriage by air, which is subject to the Montreal Convention: if the liable carrier's domicile or principal place of business is within England or Wales; or if the contract was made at an English or Welsh office of the liable carrier; or in any case where the final destination for the carriage by air of the goods is at an airport within England or Wales. Such cases are governed by English legal procedure, since art.33(4) provides for "Questions of procedure" to be governed by the forum of dispute. The Montreal Convention, by art.34(1), expressly permits agreements to resolve disputes by arbitration subject to the arbitration proceedings taking place, at the claimant's option, in one of the art.33 jurisdictions and the arbitration tribunal applying the provisions of the Montreal Convention to determine the dispute.[97]

Where cargo claims lie against a performing actual carrier, as well as the contracting carrier; the claimant is entitled by art.45 to proceed against either or both of them. By art.46 any such action may, at the claimant's option, be brought in one of the art.33 jurisdictions, or before the court of one of the "States Parties" which has jurisdiction at the place where the actual carrier has its domicile or principal place of business. Article 49 provides that any contractual stipulation or special agreement, made prior to the occurrence of the damage at issue, by which the parties purport to

[96] Accordingly, the EU jurisdiction regimes, particularly discussed at 1.4.2, will need to be considered and applied where the jurisdictional issues arising are not conclusively determined by the Montreal Convention.

[97] Pursuant to sub-clauses 2, 3 and 4 of art.34.

infringe the Convention rules "whether by deciding the law to be applied, or by altering the rules as to jurisdiction, shall be null and void". Accordingly, unlike the EU jurisdiction regime, exclusive jurisdiction agreements are not permitted and are rendered void unless they are entered into after the occurrence of the damage, which is to be the subject of the claim.

4.2.1.9 Contractual Derogation

Derogation from the provisions of the Montreal Convention by agreement between the consignor and the carrier is only permitted to the extent that such derogation is to the prejudice of the carrier. Article 27 expressly preserves the rights of the carrier to waive any defences arising under the Convention. The carrier is entitled by art.25 to commit to higher limits of liability than those afforded by the Convention, or to undertake carriage without any entitlement to limit. However, derogation to the prejudice of the consignor, or any other claimant, is not permitted: with art.26 expressly providing that any such provision, otherwise relieving the carrier from the liabilities provided for by the Convention, is rendered "null and void" without detracting from the validity of the carriage contract which remains subject to the Convention provisions. The carrier by air can only avoid the contingent liabilities arising under the Montreal Convention by refusing to enter into the carriage contract and its contractual autonomy to do so is expressly preserved by art.27,[98] which also expressly provides that the carrier is not prevented "from laying down conditions which do not conflict with the provisions" of the Montreal Convention.[99]

4.2.1.10 Rights of Carriers

There is no stipulation in the Montreal Convention, nor in any of the various applicable versions of the Warsaw Convention, making express provision with regard to the carrier's lien, although the consignee's express right under art.13(1) of the Convention to require delivery of the cargo

[98] Under art.33(5) of the Reamended Warsaw Convention, the carrier is prohibited from any refusal to carry due to the inoperability of systems (i.e. integrated computerised documentation systems) at the airports of destination, or transit, for the preservation of records of carriage by means other than an air waybill, but such prohibition does not arise under the Montreal Convention.

[99] The Warsaw Convention, in all its various forms, is rather more ambiguous as to contractual derogation, as discussed at 4.2.3 below.

from the carrier at the place of destination is expressed as being conditional upon "payment of the charges due and on complying with the conditions of carriage". Accordingly, it seems appropriate to assume that the carrier is therefore free to agree with the consignor that it has a right to exercise a particular lien against the cargo (i.e. a lien for the carriage costs incurred in relation to the subject cargo) although art.12(4) imposes no conditionality on the consignor's contingent delivery right where the "consignee declines to accept the cargo, or cannot be communicated with". The fact that no such conditionality is expressly provided for by any of the applicable air carriage regulations suggests (in the absence of any such lien being implied by the common law)[100] that the carrier has no right to exercise a particular lien against the consignor in the absence of an express contractual stipulation to that effect. However, as the art.13(1) provision referred to above appears to contemplate only the exercise of a particular lien against the consignee, any agreement for a general lien (i.e. a lien for any amount whatever due from the consignor to the carrier)[101] is most likely rendered null and void under art.26.[102]

The carrier is entitled to be indemnified for any loss it suffers due to the absence or inadequacy of information and documentation supplied, or to be supplied, to Customs, police and other public authorities, as the consignor has a duty to supply such information and documentation pursuant to art.16. By art.10 the consignor is also made responsible for the accuracy and completeness of the particulars of the cargo inserted into the air waybill, or provided to the carrier for the purposes of the record of the carriage by other means and any cargo receipt. Whether the particulars are supplied by the consignor, or by some agent acting for the consignor (and even where such agent is also an agent for the carrier), an obligation arises on the part of the consignor to indemnify the carrier in relation to any damage or liability it suffers, which is attributable to "the irregularity, incorrectness or incompleteness" of those particulars. The Montreal Convention makes no particular stipulation in relation to dangerous goods. However, as the carriage of dangerous goods by air is tightly regulated under national law[103] (with such national regulation implementing decisions

[100] As discussed at 1.9.1.2.
[101] ibid.
[102] See the discussion in relation to liens under the CMR at 2.3.10.1.
[103] In the UK the applicable regulations are The Air Navigation (Dangerous Goods) Regulations 2002 (SI 2002/2786) as amended.

of the ICAO Council)[104] arts 10 and 16 of the Montreal Convention have the effect of passing responsibility and liability for the proper classification, packing, labelling and documentation for dangerous goods onto the consignor.

4.2.1.11 Claims among Carriers

Article 37 of the Montreal Convention provides that the liability of any person under Convention provisions does not prejudice any right of recourse of the liable person against any other person. Otherwise, the Convention does not particularly address either the relationship of successive carriers between themselves, or the relationship referred to at Chapter V[105] between actual and contracting carriers who are not successive carriers, since art.48 provides that such relationships are unaffected by the other Chapter V provisions governing only the relationship between cargo and passenger claimants on the one hand and carriers on the other.[106] This does not mean that there is any freedom for successive carriers (and actual and contracting carriers) to apportion liability between themselves[107] on some non-Convention basis, since such sub-contract carriage relationships must remain subject to the provisions of the Convention insofar as they constitute contracts for the international carriage by air falling within art.1.[108]

[104] Namely, the Technical Instructions for the Safe Transport of Dangerous Goods by Air, 2009–2010 Edition, as amended.

[105] Chapter V comprises arts 39 to 49, which appear to constitute a self-contained regime subject to its own jurisdiction and non-derogation provisions at arts 46 and 47, reflecting the incorporation of these provisions from the 1961 Guadalajara Convention.

[106] Apart from art.45, which provides that, where action could have been commenced against the contracting and performing carrier by joint action, either of them has the right to require the other to be joined to the proceedings when sued alone.

[107] Or to have such liability apportioned by applicable national law in default of agreement.

[108] The Montreal Convention being applicable, by art.1, to any "international carriage ... performed by aircraft for reward" defined by reference to the contract made between the contracting parties.

4.2.2 Non-Convention Carriage Regulated by the UK Non-International Carriage Rules

The UK Non-International Carriage Rules of 2004[109] apply to every case of carriage by air which is neither governed by the Montreal Convention nor any of the various versions of the Warsaw Convention: in consequence they are applicable to any domestic UK carriage by air and any carriage by air to, or from, places in non-Convention states. In most respects they are identical to the provisions of the Montreal Convention, albeit with consequential revision such as to their scope of application. However, there are certain significant differences, which are set out below.

(i) The Non-International Carriage Rules do not include the articles of the Montreal Convention relating to the issue of an air waybill, nor any other provisions attending the air waybill such as those imposed on the consignor by art.10. The parties to the contract may, if they wish, issue an air waybill; but they are not required to do so by the Rules, and no legal consequences result from the absence of an air waybill. The requirement for the issue of a baggage check at art.3(3) is retained, but no legal significance attaches to it, other than as a mere receipt.

(ii) The provisions of arts 12, 13 and 14 with regard to delivery, stoppage of the goods and the attendant rights of the consignor and consignee are not included in the Non-International Carriage Rules.

(iii) The provisions of arts 33, 34(2) and 46 with regard to jurisdiction, do not apply to non-international carriage; and questions of jurisdiction are therefore determined by the jurisdictional rules outlined at 1.4.2.

In all other respects, the provisions of the Montreal Convention apply to non-international carriage as from August 6, 2004 when SI 2004/1899 came into effect; since which time the different provisions contained in the Non-International Carriage Rules of 1967 have had no further application.[110]

[109] Applied by reg.4 and Sch.1 of the Carriage by Air Acts (Application of Provisions) Order 2004 (SI 2004/1899).

[110] SI 1967/480 as subsequently amended and now revoked.

4.2.3 The Reamended Warsaw Convention

The Reamended Warsaw Convention, which appears as Sch.1B to, and is applied by s.1(5)(b) of, the amended Carriage by Air Act 1961 comprises the Warsaw Convention as amended by the 1955 Hague Protocol and the 1975 Montreal Protocol No.4. In substantive terms it is very similar to the Montreal Convention and most of its provisions identical, despite differences in the way they are numbered. Accordingly, the majority of the points made at 4.2.1 above in relation to the Montreal Convention apply equally to the Reamended Warsaw Convention. However, there are a number of significant differences which (in the context of the evaluation made at 4.2.1 above) are highlighted below, by reference to the relevant articles of the Reamended Warsaw Convention.

i. Differences in the scope of application at 4.2.1.1 above: the period of carriage by air "in the case of a landing outside an airport" extends to any period during which the carrier is in charge of cargo or baggage at "any place whatsoever"[111] but, unlike the Montreal Convention, does not otherwise extend to carriage undertaken by other means without the consent of the consignor.[112]
ii. Differences in the documentary requirements at 4.2.1.2 above: the substitution of "other means", other than an air waybill or passenger ticket, for the preservation of a record of carriage is, under the Reamended Convention, not possible in the case of baggage and only possible in the case of the carriage of cargo with the consent of the consignor.[113]
iii. Differences in the liability provisions at 4.2.1.3 above: the carrier is not excused from liability for damage caused by delay through merely taking all measures "reasonably required" to avoid the damage, only by taking "all necessary measures" for such purposes as provided by art.20 of the Reamended Convention.

[111] Pursuant to art.18(4) of the Reamended Convention.

[112] Albeit it is still rebuttably presumed, under art.18(5) of the Reamended Convention, that any damage occurring in the course of "loading, delivery or transshipment", resulted from an event taking place during the carriage by air.

[113] See arts 5.2 and 5.3 of the Reamended Convention which also restricts the carrier from refusing to accept cargo for carriage, because the use of such other means (i.e. computerised carriage records) is impossible at the destination and transit airports.

iv. Differences in the financial limitations at 4.2.1.4 above: the same financial limitations applied under the Reamended Convention until December 30, 2009; however, unlike the Montreal Convention, they are not subject to review at five yearly intervals and still remain at 17 SDRs per kg for cargo and 1,000 SDRs per passenger for baggage.

v. Differences in the non-derogation provisions at 4.2.1.9 above: the wording of these provisions at arts 23, 32 and 33 of the Reamended Convention is somewhat different. Significantly, there is no clear equivalent of the Montreal art.27 preservation of contractual autonomy in respect of "conditions" not in conflict with the Convention. Article 33 of the Reamended Convention does preserve the right of the carrier to make "regulations", but it is not clear whether the reference to "regulations" in that article is to be interpreted as meaning that the carrier is entitled to insist on further non-conflicting contractual terms or whether it is confined to such regulations as the air carrier may be authorised to make by delegated statutory power. The former less literal and more purposive interpretation appears more consistent with the prevailing judicial view in England and Wales that the Warsaw regime comprises a partial statutory code, preserving the contractual freedom of the contracting parties in relation to those matters not regulated by Convention provisions.[114] Furthermore, the parties would otherwise have no contractual autonomy, other than for the liberty of the carrier, to refuse to enter into the contract of carriage; accept higher limits of liability; or, to agree with the consignor in connection with the carriage of cargo to refer disputes to arbitration.[115] Accordingly, whilst not entitled to contract out of the provisions of the Convention in any other respect, the parties may by agreement insert terms into the contract of carriage with regard to matters not dealt with by the Convention, for example as to any entitlement of the carrier to a particular lien, this being a matter on which the Convention is silent.[116]

[114] For example, see the view of Mance L.J. in the *Western Digital Corporation* case (fn. 89), at para.59.
[115] See arts 22(2), 32 and 33 of the Reamended Convention.
[116] However, as regards any attempt to secure a general lien see the discussion at 4.2.1.10 above.

vi. Differences in the jurisdictional provisions at 4.2.1.8 above: these are distinct in that the Reamended Convention contains no further provision relating to arbitration; apart from the provision at art.32, which permits "arbitration clauses" in the carriage of cargo where such arbitration is to take place within any one of the jurisdictions stipulated for litigation.[117]

vii. Differences in the status of actual carriers at 4.2.1.6 and 4.2.1.11 above: whilst the status of successive carriers (as reviewed at 4.2.1.6 above) is the same, the Reamended Convention does not incorporate the self-contained provisions of Chapter V, which were incorporated into the Montreal Convention from the 1961 Guadalajara Convention. Consequently, there are possible differences in the status of the actual carriers performing air carriage (otherwise than as successive or contracting carriers) in terms of liability as they are not expressly protected by the terms of the Reamended Convention.[118] In order to claim rights to exclude, limit or recover liability under the Reamended Convention, any actual carrier, not being a contracting or successive carrier, must rely on the Guadalajara Convention to assert rights under the Reamended Convention, or else assert rights arising under English law in bailment to rely on the rights of the principal air carriage contractor.[119] Such an actual carrier would also be entitled to assert contractual, tortuous or statutory rights arising under English law to recover contributions or indemnity to any liability to which it was exposed.[120]

[117] Such jurisdictions being, by art.28, identical to those under the Montreal Convention.

[118] By art.25A any "servant or agent" of the carrier proved to have "acted within the scope of his employment" can claim the protection of the Reamended Convention; this protection does not extend to an independent contractor, such as a non-successive actual carrier.

[119] By reference to principles of agency, bailment and contract at common law as particularly discussed at 1.6.1.

[120] See, in this context, art.30A of the Reamended Convention, providing that nothing in the Convention prejudices rights of recourse in respect of Convention liabilities and see the Civil Liability and Contribution Act 1978 discussed at 1.8.1.

4.2.4 The Amended Warsaw Convention

The Amended Warsaw Convention (which appears as Sch.1A to, and is applied by s.1(5)(a) of, the amended Carriage by Air Act 1961) comprises the Warsaw Convention as amended by the 1955 Hague Protocol. There are some significant differences between it and the Reamended Convention which, despite most of the commentary at 4.2.2 above as to the Montreal Convention being nonetheless relevant to the Amended Convention, it is appropriate to highlight by reference to the relevant articles of the Amended Convention.

i. Differences in the scope of application at 4.2.1.1 above: the period of carriage by air is the same as that provided for in the Reamended Convention.[121]
ii. Differences in the documentary requirements at 4.2.1.2 above: there is no provision in the Amended Convention for the substitution of any "other means" and the only record of the carriage provided for is that of an air waybill or passenger ticket. Article 34 of the Amended Convention disapplies the documentary requirements in respect of "carriage performed in extraordinary circumstances outside the normal scope of an air carrier's business".[122] Most significantly, whilst the Amended Convention continues to apply notwithstanding the absence or irregularity of an air waybill or passenger ticket,[123] such absence (and any irregularity consisting of a failure to give the required notice of the applicability of the Amended Convention)[124] results in the carrier losing its rights to claim the protection of the financial limitations provided for by the Convention.[125]
iii. Differences in the liability provisions at 4.2.1.3 above: under the Amended Convention the carrier has a general liability exemption for damage where the carrier and its servants or agents have

[121] Pursuant to art.18(2) and (3) of the Amended Convention.

[122] The Original Warsaw Convention disapplied the Convention entirely in respect of such flights; in contrast, the Amended Convention applies to such flights, except as to the issue of tickets and air waybills.

[123] By virtue of, respectively, arts 5(2) and 3(2) of the Amended Convention.

[124] Such notice being required as to passenger tickets and air waybills, respectively, by arts 3(1)(c) and 8 of the Amended Convention.

[125] Such loss of the right to limit as against passengers and cargo claimants being provided for, at arts 3(2) and 9 respectively, of the Amended Convention.

"taken all necessary measures to avoid the damage", or it was impossible for them to take such measures; however, the carrier can only be exonerated from liability for damage caused or contributed to, "by the negligence of the injured person", pursuant to the provisions of the law of the forum.[126]

iv. Differences in the financial limitations at 4.2.1.4 above: the same financial limitations apply in respect of the Amended Convention as under the Reamended Convention (i.e. since they are not subject to review at five yearly intervals they remain 17 SDRs per kg for cargo and 1,000 per passenger in respect of baggage).[127] However, like the original Warsaw Convention, it is possible in respect of claims for the loss, damage and delay of both cargo and baggage to break through the financial limitations when such claims are caused by particularly reprehensible conduct on the part of the carrier.[128] For limitation to be disapplied, the act or omission at issue must have been committed deliberately or recklessly "and with knowledge that damage would probably result".[129]

v. Differences in the non-derogation, jurisdictional and actual carrier provisions at, respectively, 4.2.1.9, 4.2.1.8, 4.2.1.6 and 4.2.1.11 above: the differences in these respects are the same under the Amended Convention as under the Reamended Convention.

[126] Pursuant to arts 20 and 21 of the Amended Convention (requiring the application in the UK of the Civil Liability Contribution Act 1978); which should be contrasted with the more comprehensive treatment of these issues under the same revised articles in the Reamended Convention and arts 19 and 20 of the Montreal Convention.

[127] In the UK these financial limits were substituted in the Amended Convention (for the limits arising under the MP1 and Unamended Warsaw Conventions: respectively discussed at 4.2.5 and 4.2.6 below), by s.4(1)(a)(i) of the Carriage by Air and Road Act 1979.

[128] Or, of its servants or agents, provided that they were acting within the scope of their authority as provided at art.25 of the Amended Convention.

[129] Pursuant to art.25 of the Amended Convention, which was considered by the Court of Appeal in *Goldman v Thai Airways International Ltd* [1983] 1 W.L.R. 1186, where a passenger was unseated during unexpectedly severe air turbulence and the Court of Appeal held that, even if the pilot's failure to illuminate the fasten seatbelt sign was subjectively reckless, the pilot could not be fixed with foresight of injury from what was found to be an unexpected contingency.

4.2.5 The MP1 Warsaw Convention

The rarely applicable MP1 Warsaw Convention[130] comprises the original Warsaw Convention as amended only by Montreal Protocol No.1 with the effect that, apart from the issue of limitation under art.22, it is identical in all respects to the original unamended Warsaw Convention. In relation to limitation the MP1 Warsaw Convention applies a claim limitation value for the carriage of baggage and cargo of 17 SDRs "per kilogramme".[131] But such limits are claimed, calculated and disapplied by provisions that are otherwise identical to those arising under the original unamended Warsaw Convention; the provisions of which are discussed at 4.2.6 below.

4.2.6 The Unamended Warsaw Convention

The Unamended Warsaw Convention, applied in the UK by reg.6 and Sch.2 of the Carriage by Air Acts (Application of Provisions) Order 2004 (SI 2004/1899), comprises the original Warsaw Convention unamended by any subsequent conventions. As discussed at 4.2.5, the Unamended Convention is, save as to limitation, identical to the MP1 Convention, but they are both significantly different from the Amended and Reamended versions of the Warsaw Convention and consequently also from the Montreal Convention. Those differences are highlighted below, in contrast to the commentary as to the Montreal Convention at 4.2.2 above and by reference to the relevant articles of the Unamended Convention.

i. Differences in the scope of application at 4.2.1.1 above: the period of carriage by air is the same as that provided for in the Amended Convention.[132]
ii. Differences in the documentary requirements at 4.2.1.2 above: the provisions of the Unamended Convention as to the issue of

[130] Applied by reg.6 and Sch.3 of the Carriage by Air Acts (Application of Provisions) Order 2004 (SI 2004/1899); but applicable only to flights between countries (such as Honduras and Cuba) that are contracting states to *both* Warsaw and MP1, whilst not *both* being contracting states to other conventions.

[131] In addition to which passenger claims for objects of which the passenger remains in charge, are limited to 332 SDRs per passenger under art.22(3) of the MP1 Warsaw Convention.

[132] Pursuant to art.18(2) and (3) of the Unamended Convention.

air waybills and passenger tickets are identical to those contained in the Amended Convention and discussed at 4.2.4(ii) above.[133]

iii. Differences in the liability provisions at 4.2.1.3 above: under the Unamended Convention the carrier not only has the general liability exemption and liability exoneration rights discussed at 4.2.4(iii) above[134] but also enjoys further such rights. As it was drawn up in the days when neither aircraft nor pilots were as reliable as today, the Unamended Convention also provides that the carrier is not liable for negligent pilotage, negligence in the handling of the aircraft, or negligence in navigation, provided that "in all other respects, he and his servants or agents have taken all necessary measures to avoid the damage".[135] However, such exemptions and exonerations from liability will be denied to the carrier in the event of the documentary irregularities referred to at 4.2.4(ii) above,[136] or in the event of such wilful misconduct as is referred to at (iv) below.

iv. Differences in the financial limitations at 4.2.1.4 above: the financial limitations arising under the Unamended Convention are "250 francs per kilogramme" in relation to claims for both cargo and registered baggage,[137] although this limitation is defined by reference to the gold content of the French franc, which is stated by art.22(4) as being "65 milligrammes gold of millesimal fineness 900".[138] The carrier may accept the goods for carriage subject to a special declaration of value and increased air freight, in which case the limit of liability is increased to the declared value.[139] However, in all cases the right to claim limitation may be lost by reason of documentary irregularities relating to air waybills

[133] Pursuant to arts 3, 5, 9 and 34 of the Unamended Convention.

[134] Pursuant to arts 20 and 21 of the Unamended Convention.

[135] Pursuant to art.20(2) of the Unamended Convention.

[136] Article 9 of the Unamended Warsaw Convention providing that, in the absence or irregularity of the air waybill, "the carrier shall not be entitled to avail himself of the [Convention] provisions ... which exclude or limit his liability".

[137] Pursuant to art.22(2) of the Unamended Convention.

[138] Article 22(4) provides for "these sums" to be converted into any national currency in round figures permitting a similar approach to be taken to the calculation of the limitation fund under the Unamended Warsaw Convention as was adopted by the English High Court (in *The Rosa S* [1988] 2 Lloyd's Rep. 574) in relation to the Hague Convention for the carriage of goods by sea as discussed at 3.3.3.

[139] See fn. 137.

or passenger tickets.[140] Otherwise, the carrier may only lose the right to limit in the circumstances provided for in art.25 of the Unamended Convention, which provides that:

> "(1) The carrier shall not be entitled to avail himself of the provisions of this Convention which exclude or limit his liability if the damage is caused by his wilful misconduct, or by such default on his part as in accordance with the law of the Court seised of the case is considered to be equivalent to wilful misconduct. (2) Similarly the carrier shall not be entitled to avail himself of the said provisions if the damage is caused as aforesaid by any agent of the carrier acting within the scope of his employment."[141]

v. Differences in the non-derogation, jurisdictional and actual carrier provisions at, respectively, 4.2.1.9, 4.2.1.8, 4.2.1.6 and 4.2.1.11 above: the differences in these respects are the same under the Unamended Convention as under the Reamended Convention.

4.2.7 Carriage of Passengers' Luggage

The liabilities of the carrier in respect of passengers' luggage are discussed above in the context of liability for damage to cargo. The scheme of liability under each of the applicable air carriage conventions is similar for cargo and baggage, save as to the calculation of the time to claim and the financial limitation provisions, the application of some of the exclusions and (albeit only in the case of the Montreal and Reamended Conventions) the disapplication of such limitations and exclusions. Such differences, as and when arising, are highlighted at 4.2.1 to 4.2.6 above. However, in respect of the carriage of passengers and their luggage, the liability of air carriers (community air carriers) with a valid operating licence issued by an EEA Member State is also the subject of EU Regulation 2027/97 as amended by Regulation 889/2002. This legislation, directly applicable within the United Kingdom (and capable of direct effects in the contractual and tortious relationship of passengers and carriers) provides for the liability of community air carriers, in respect of passengers and their baggage, to be

[140] See fn. 136.

[141] The meaning ascribed by the courts of England and Wales to the phrase "wilful misconduct" was generally discussed, in the context of the CMR, at 2.3.4.3.

governed always by the Montreal Convention.[142] The legislation also provides that:

- the carrier is obliged when selling carriage by air at all points of sale to provide passengers with a summary of the main liability provisions of the Convention (including the possibility of passengers declaring a special value for their baggage in place of the limitation fund) in the terms of the annex appended to the legislation;
- the amount of the supplementary sum that may be demanded by the carrier for any such declaration of special value must be based on a tariff, to be made available to passengers on request, which must be proportionately related to the additional costs arising; and
- in the event of an accident, the carrier is obliged to provide advance payments to claimants to meet immediate economic needs.[143]

4.2.8 Table 1: Contracting States to the Air Carriage Conventions

Denoting: by *, certification by UK Statutory Instrument; and by ☑, identification by ICAO, as referred to at 4.1.1 and fn. 2 of this Part Four.

Contracting State	(1) Unamended Warsaw	(2) MP1 Warsaw	(3) Amended Warsaw	(4) Reamended Warsaw	(5) Guadalajara Convention	(6) Montreal Convention
Afghanistan	☑*		☑*			
Albania						☑
Algeria	☑*		☑*			
Angola	☑*		☑*			
Antigua & Barbuda	*					
Argentina	☑*	☑*	☑*	☑*		☑
Armenia	☑					☑
Australia	☑*		☑*	☑*	☑	☑
Austria	☑*		☑*		☑	☑
Azerbaijan	☑	☑	☑	☑*	☑	

[142] Pursuant to art.3 of R2027/97 as replaced by R889/2002/EC.
[143] Pursuant to arts 6, 3a and 5 of R2027/97 as replaced by R889/2002/EC.

Contracting State	(1) Unamended Warsaw	(2) MP1 Warsaw	(3) Amended Warsaw	(4) Reamended Warsaw	(5) Guadalajara Convention	(6) Montreal Convention
Bahamas	☑*		☑*		☑	
Bahrain	☑*	☑*	☑*	☑*	☑	☑
Bangladesh	☑*		☑*			
Barbados	☑*		*			☑
Belarus	☑*		☑*		☑	
Belgium	☑*		☑*	☑	☑	☑
Belize	*		*			☑
Benin	☑*		☑*			☑
Bolivia	☑					
Bosnia & Herzegovina	☑*	☑*	☑	☑*	☑	☑
Botswana	☑*					☑
Brazil	☑*	☑*	☑*	☑*	☑	☑
Brunei Darussalam	☑*					
Bulgaria	☑*		☑*			☑
Burkina Faso	☑*				☑	
Cambodia	☑*		☑*			
Cameroon	☑*		☑*			☑
Canada	☑*	☑*	☑*	☑*	☑	☑
Cape Verde	☑		☑		☑	☑
Chad	*		*		☑	
Chile	☑*	☑*	☑*	☑		☑
China	☑*		☑*			☑
Colombia	☑*	☑*	☑*	☑*	☑	☑
Comoros	☑*					
Congo Rep.	☑*		☑*			
Cook Islands						☑
Costa Rica	☑*		☑*			
Côte d'Ivoire	☑*		☑*			
Croatia	☑*	☑*	☑*	☑*	☑	☑
Cuba	☑*	☑*	☑*			☑
Cyprus	☑*	☑*	☑*	☑	☑	☑
Czech Rep.	☑*		☑*		☑	☑

Contracting State	(1) Unamended Warsaw	(2) MP1 Warsaw	(3) Amended Warsaw	(4) Reamended Warsaw	(5) Guadalajara Convention	(6) Montreal Convention
D.P.R. Korea	☑		☑			
Congo Dem. Rep.	☑*					
Denmark	☑*	☑*	☑*	☑*	☑	☑
Dominica	*					
Dominican Rep.	☑*		☑*			☑
Ecuador	☑*		☑*	☑*		☑
Egypt	☑*	☑*	☑*	☑*	☑	☑
El Salvador			☑*		☑	☑
Equatorial Guinea	☑*					
Estonia	☑*	☑*	☑*	☑*	☑	☑
Ethiopia	☑*	☑*	*	☑*		
Fiji	☑*		☑*		☑	
Finland	☑*	☑*	☑*	☑*	☑	☑
France	☑*	☑*	☑*		☑	☑
Gabon	☑*		☑*		☑	
Gambia	*					☑
Germany	☑*		☑*		☑	☑
Ghana	☑*	☑*	☑*	☑*	☑	
Greece	☑*	☑*	☑*	☑*	☑	☑
Grenada	*		☑*		☑	
Guatemala	☑*	☑*	☑*	☑*	☑	
Guinea	☑*	☑	☑*	☑*	☑	
Guyana	*					
Honduras	☑*	☑*		☑*		
Hungary	☑*		☑*	☑*	☑	☑
Iceland	☑*		☑*	☑	☑	☑
India	☑*		☑*			☑
Indonesia	☑*					
Iran	☑*		☑*		☑	
Iraq	☑*	☑	☑*		☑	
Ireland	☑*	☑*	☑*	☑*	☑	☑
Israel	☑*	☑*	☑*	☑*	☑	
Italy	☑*	☑*	☑*	☑*	☑	☑

Contracting State	(1) Unamended Warsaw	(2) MP1 Warsaw	(3) Amended Warsaw	(4) Reamended Warsaw	(5) Guadalajara Convention	(6) Montreal Convention
Jamaica	*				☑	☑
Japan	☑*		☑*	☑*		☑
Jordan	☑*	☑	☑*	☑*		☑
Kazakhstan			☑			
Kenya	☑*	☑	☑	☑*		☑
Kiribati	*		*			
Kuwait	☑*	☑*	☑*	☑*	☑	☑
Kyrgyzstan	☑		☑			
Laos P.D.R.	☑*		☑*			
Latvia	☑*		☑			☑
Lebanon	☑*	☑	☑*	☑	☑	☑
Lesotho	☑*		☑*		☑	
Liberia	☑*					
Libya	☑*		☑*		☑	
Liechtenstein	☑*		☑*			
Lithuania			☑*		☑	☑
Luxembourg	☑*		☑*	☑	☑	☑
Madagascar	☑*		☑*			☑
Malawi	☑*		☑*		☑	
Malaysia	☑*		☑*	☑	☑	☑
Maldives	☑*		☑*			☑
Mali	☑*		☑*		☑	☑
Malta	☑*					☑
Mauritania	☑*				☑	
Mauritius	☑*		☑*	☑*	☑	
Mexico	☑*	☑*	☑*		☑	☑
Monaco			☑*			☑
Mongolia	☑*					☑
Montenegro	☑	☑	☑	☑	☑	☑
Morocco	☑*		☑*		☑	☑
Myanmar	☑*					
Namibia	*		*			☑
Nauru	☑*		☑*	☑*		
Nepal	☑*		☑*			
Netherlands	☑*	☑*	☑*	☑*	☑	☑

Contracting State	(1) Unamended Warsaw	(2) MP1 Warsaw	(3) Amended Warsaw	(4) Reamended Warsaw	(5) Guadalajara Convention	(6) Montreal Convention
New Zealand	☑*	☑	☑*	☑	☑	☑
Niger	☑*	☑	☑*	☑*	☑	
Nigeria	☑*		☑*		☑	☑
Norway	☑*	☑*	☑*	☑*	☑	☑
Oman	☑*		☑*	☑*		☑
Pakistan	☑*		☑*		☑	☑
Panama	☑*		☑*			☑
Papua New Guinea	☑*		☑*		☑	
Paraguay	☑*		☑*		☑	☑
Peru	☑*	☑*	☑*		☑	☑
Philippines	☑*		☑*		☑	
Poland	☑*		☑*		☑	☑
Portugal	☑*	☑*	☑*	☑*		☑
Qatar	☑*		☑*			☑
Rep. of Korea	*		☑*			☑
Rep. of Moldova	☑*		☑*		☑	☑
Romania	☑*		☑*		☑	☑
Russia	☑*		☑*		☑	
Rwanda	☑*		☑*		☑	
St Kitts. & Nevis	*					
St Lucia	*					
St Vincent & Gren.	☑*		☑			☑
Samoa	☑*		☑*			
Saudi Arabia	☑*		☑*		☑	☑
Senegal	☑*		☑*			
Serbia (FYR)	☑*	☑*	☑*	☑*	☑	☑
Seychelles	☑*		☑*		☑	
Sierra Leone	☑*					
Singapore	☑*		☑*	☑*		☑
Slovakia	☑*		☑*		☑	☑

Contracting State	(1) Unamended Warsaw	(2) MP1 Warsaw	(3) Amended Warsaw	(4) Reamended Warsaw	(5) Guadalajara Convention	(6) Montreal Convention
Slovenia	☑	☑	☑	☑*	☑	☑
Solomon Islands	☑*		☑*		☑	
South Africa	☑*		☑*		☑	☑
Spain	☑*	☑*	☑*	☑*		☑
Sri Lanka	☑*		☑*			
Sudan	☑*		☑*			
Suriname	☑*		☑*			
Swaziland	*		☑*		☑	
Sweden	☑*	☑*	☑*	☑*	☑	☑
Switzerland	☑*	☑*	☑*	☑*	☑	☑
Syria	☑*		☑*			☑
Tajikistan	*					
F.Y.R. Macedonia	☑*	☑*	☑*	☑*	☑	☑
Togo	☑*	☑*	☑*	☑*	☑	
Tonga	☑*		☑*			☑
Trinidad & Tobago	☑*		☑*			
Tunisia	☑*	☑*	☑*		☑	
Turkey	☑*		☑*	☑*		
Turkmenistan	☑*					
Tuvalu	*		*			
Uganda	☑*					
Ukraine	☑*		☑*		☑	☑
UAE	☑*		☑*	☑*		☑
UK	☑*	☑*	☑	☑*	☑	☑
United Rep. Tanzania	☑*					☑
USA	☑*		☑	☑*		☑
Uruguay	☑*					☑
Uzbekistan	☑*	☑	☑	☑*	☑	
Vanuatu	☑*		☑*			☑
Venezuela	☑*	☑*	☑*			
Vietnam	☑*		☑*			
Yemen	☑*		☑*			
Zambia	☑*		☑		☑	

Contracting State	(1) Unamended Warsaw	(2) MP1 Warsaw	(3) Amended Warsaw	(4) Reamended Warsaw	(5) Guadalajara Convention	(6) Montreal Convention
Zimbabwe	☑*		☑		☑	
European Union						☑

PART FIVE: UNDERTAKING CONTRACTS OF CARRIAGE

5.1 Electronic Carriage Records

5.1.1 Introduction

Concluding contractual arrangements electronically is increasingly common in the twenty-first century. However, progress in replacing carriage documentation with electronic records has been hampered by the absence of a secure legal environment for the creation and use of such electronic records in international trade. Consequently, traditional paper documentation is still the norm, particularly in connection with the carriage of goods by sea,[1] in spite of the increased cost, delay and administrative inconvenience of transferring transport documentation in hard copy between carriers, consignors, consignees, sellers, buyers and their respective agents, bankers and insurers across the world.[2] In recent years there has been much international effort towards creating a more stable platform for electronic commerce generally[3] and electronic carriage documents in particular.[4] Despite these efforts and notwithstanding the general absence under English law of any formal documentary precondition or requirement for the formation or evidencing of contracts of carriage,[5] it is still difficult for

[1] See the UNCTAD Secretariat enquiry report *The Use of Transport Documents in International Trade* of November 26, 2003, published at *http://www.unctad.org*, which reveals that only 22 per cent of the responding traders, bankers and carriers substituted electronic records for carriage documents.

[2] Delay in delivery, or delivery against indemnity, in the absence of a bill of lading (e.g. *Sze Hai Tong Bank v Rambler Cycle Co Ltd* [1959] A.C. 576), is still a common feature in sea carriage.

[3] Facilitated by the UNCITRAL Model Laws on Electronic Commerce 1996 and Electronic Signatures 2000 which have been widely influential on national law worldwide, also EU single market initiatives, such as the Electronic Commerce Directive (D2000/31 EC), art.9 of which facilitates making contracts by electronic means by requiring the removal, throughout the EU, of legal obstacles to electronic commerce.

[4] As discussed at 5.1.3 below.

[5] The Civil Evidence Act 1995 makes no distinction between hearsay evidence recorded in paper or electronic form, defining "document" at s.13(2) as "anything in which information of any description is recorded"; s.7(1) Electronic Communications Act 2000 ensuring the validity of electronic signatures "in any legal proceedings"; and the Interpretation Act 1978 Sch.1 providing: "'writing' includes typing, printing, lithography, photography and other modes of representing or reproducing words in a visible form ...".

contracting parties to maintain electronic records which are functionally equivalent to traditional transport documentation.

5.1.2 Transport Documentation Types and Functions

Functional equivalence must be addressed with regard to the function of each particular type of documentation issued for the carriage of goods. This varies partly according to the different modes of transport (for reasons of commercial practice and distinct unimodal regulation) and partly according to their transferability and negotiability. All travel documents share two common features; evidence of the making of the contract of carriage and evidence of the receipt of the goods by the carrier and sometimes the consignee. The other potential functions of transport documents attach to particular categories of carriage document and can be briefly described as follows: being a representation to third parties as to the consigning and condition of the goods;[6] being a necessary gateway to the applicable unimodal regime of mandatory carriage terms;[7] taking effect as an exchangeable receipt, which must be exchanged in return for taking, or retaking, possession of the goods;[8] and taking effect as a document of title in disputes with third parties.[9]

Most of these functions can now be replicated by electronic records. Nevertheless, whilst there is no distinction under English law between electronic and non-electronic contracts of carriage in terms of their formation[10] and evidential status,[11] electronic records do suffer from deficiencies in terms of their legal status. The essential difficulty under English law is the absence of any implication at law that electronic records for the carriage of goods by sea perform any of the following functions:

[6] Discussed at 3.2.3.4.4.

[7] Discussed at 3.2.3.4.5 as to the Hague-Visby Rules, 2.3.6 as to successive carriage under the CMR and 4.2.4 as to inability to limit under the Amended Warsaw Convention and the similar issue at 4.2.5 and 4.2.6 arising under the MP1 Original and the Original Unamended Warsaw Convention.

[8] Discussed at 3.2.3.4.1.

[9] Discussed at 3.2.3.4.3.

[10] Even transactions concluded by electronic data interface (EDI) must be concluded under English law pursuant to some overarching agreement concluded by the traditional objective notion of *consensus ad idem* (i.e. matching offer and acceptance), although, subject to the conclusions of such agreement, cascading discrete contractual arrangements could be concluded by electronic interface using structures such as UN-EDIFACT for standard electronic messaging.

[11] See fn. 5.

representations towards third parties on which those third parties may reasonably rely; an exchangeable receipt for the goods; or a document of title effective against third parties. Difficulties also arise as to their legal status under certain unimodal conventions that do not refer to electronic records such as the Hague-Visby Rules, the Warsaw regime (apart from its Reamended version) and the CMR.[12] The problems posed by the uncertain legal status of electronic carriage records and the available solutions offered for each carriage mode are discussed below.

5.1.3 Problems and Solutions

5.1.3.1 Carriage of Goods by Land

Under English law there are no issues as to the functionality of electronic records in place of traditional carriage documents in domestic carriage by land. The use of such documents is unlikely to be extended further than their function as evidence of the making of the contract of carriage; the receipt of the goods by the carrier; the delivery of the goods, when such documents are appropriately acknowledged (whether by counter signature or some inputting of electronic data) by the consignee. The terms of the contract and collection of the goods can be proved just as easily by durable electronic records as by paper documentation, provided that appropriate data storage systems are in place.[13]

As to international carriage, the CMR does not require the road consignment note to be in any particular form; however, pursuant to art.5(1) it should be made out in "three original copies", one of which should accompany the goods, so it would be difficult for it to be replicated by electronic means. As discussed at 2.3.4 and 2.3.6, this is only of real significance for successive carriage under the CMR, since the CMR note neither constitutes an exchangeable receipt for the goods[14] nor a document of title to them. Furthermore, it is only prima facie evidence as to the making of the contract of carriage and is not a prerequisite to the application of the CMR. An additional protocol recognising the now common practice of issuing and transmitting the consignment note in electronic

[12] See fn. 7.

[13] See fn. 5.

[14] Although, pursuant to CMR art.12 as discussed at 2.3.7, the consignor may lose its right to control delivery of the goods by endorsing the CMR consignment note to the effect that such rights are transferred to the consignee.

form was agreed on May 27, 2008, although only by certain states;[15] it is yet to enter into force. Under the CIM, full functional equivalence is achieved for electronic rail consignment notes by art.6(9). However, the functionality of the through rail consignment note is in many respects similar to that of the road consignment note, although two significant distinctions are apparent. First, the physical transfer of the consignment note is capable of transferring certain rights to control the rail carrier's disposition of the goods, since, pursuant to the CIM as discussed at 2.6.2.7, simple transfer by the consignor of possession of the rail consignment note to the consignee (or by the consignee to one alternative identified recipient) has the effect of transferring to the consignee (or the one alternative recipient identified by the consignee) rights to modify delivery arrangements under the contract of carriage. Secondly, pursuant to art.44(5) and (6) of the CIM, the physical presentation of the rail consignment note to the carrier is a pre-condition to making a claim against the rail carrier and, if it cannot be produced, the claimant must justify its absence or loss. Nevertheless, similarly to the CMR note, the CIM rail consignment note is neither an exchangeable receipt for, nor a document of title to the goods, neither is its existence a prerequisite to the application of the CIM to the contract for the carriage of goods by rail.

5.1.3.2 Carriage of Goods by Sea

As discussed at 3.2 the transport documentation issued in connection with sea carriage may comprise contracts of affreightment (in the form of demise or non-demise charterparties for the use of a ship, or space on a ship), sea waybills, ship's delivery orders and bills of lading. The bill of lading is the only one of these documents capable of constituting a document of title and exhibiting all the functions described above. The functions of the other documents, insofar as they relate to the making of the contract of carriage or the receipt of the goods by the carrier, can easily be replicated electronically; it is electronic replication of the bill of lading that poses particular difficulty.

The functionality of an exchangeable receipt can be replicated contractually by subscription-based facilities, such as Bolero and GlobalTrade,[16] where the hosting associations control access to knowledge of a unique code (commonly known as a "personal key"), which passes the contractual

[15] Such states comprising Belgium, Finland, Latvia, Lithuania, Netherlands, Norway, Sweden and Switzerland as at February 24, 2009.

[16] *http://www.bolero.net/index.htmland* and *http://www.globaltradecorp.com/*.

right to the possession of the goods as against the carrier, and facilitates the transfer of such right to others. The problem is that participating carriers, sellers, purchasers and bankers must subscribe to the system. Limitations of liability imposed by the host might also detract from the security intended for those wishing to control constructive possession in the goods. The same exchangeable receipt function can be replicated by importing into the contract of carriage terms (such as the CMI Rules for Electronic Bills of Lading)[17] which achieve functional equivalence by authorising and obliging the carrier to: issue an electronic personal key to the shipper on shipment; transfer the personal key on the instructions of the shipper or any subsequent holder; and deliver against electronic presentation of the personal key.

Of course, such arrangements only operate as a mechanism to pass constructive possession of the goods between the carrier and the shipper (or anyone else to whom the carrier may have attorned)[18] and any other parties who may have agreed to the arrangement. The extent to which such arrangements would be respected by any applicable law as equally effective as the negotiation, or transfer, of a bill of lading to secure a transfer of legal title binding on all third parties (as well as the contracting parties), is an issue that can only be addressed by reference to the particular rights claimed by the third party in the context of the particular applicable law. This represents a significant functional deficiency in these contractual arrangements which can only be corrected either by the systems of applicable law giving effect to any developing custom and practice employed by merchants,[19] or by mandatory regulation. The UNCITRAL Model Law on Electronic Commerce sought to promote the introduction of appropriate mandatory law at a national level by including provisions, at arts 16 and 17, towards achieving such functional equivalence. However, very few states have been willing to implement arts 16 and 17 into their legal systems and these articles have not been introduced in the United Kingdom, or elsewhere in the EEA.

Currently it is a prerequisite for the application of the Hague-Visby Rules, pursuant to art.I(b), that the contract pursuant to which the goods are carried by sea is "covered by a bill of lading". It seems consistent with

[17] Which can be accessed from the CMI at *http://www.comitemaritime.org/*.

[18] See 1.6.1.1.

[19] Under English common law, effect can only be given to any such custom and practice that is notorious, certain and reasonable within the context of any particular trade.

the decision in *The Rafaela S*,[20] however, that an electronic record, capable of controlling constructive possession of the goods as against the carrier, should be regarded as a document of title by the English courts for the purposes of art.I(b). The Carriage of Goods by Sea Act 1992, discussed at 3.1.2, provides at s.1(5) that its provisions may be extended to the transfer of rights and liabilities under "an electronic communications network or any other information technology" as well as bills of lading, sea waybills and ship's delivery orders. Despite the absence of any such order to date, electronic records are not excluded from the provisions of the 1992 Act for the reasons discussed at 5.1.1 above.

The Rotterdam Rules (discussed below at 5.2.3.4 and at 3.3.5 above) do seek to provide a secure legal environment for the issue of negotiable and non-negotiable electronic records of carriage. Were they to enter into force, they would specifically provide, pursuant to art.8(b), that "The issuance, exclusive control, or transfer of an electronic transport record has the same effect as the issuance, possession, or transfer of a transport document".

5.1.3.3 Carriage of Goods by Air

The Reamended Warsaw Convention and the Montreal Convention both facilitate the replication of air waybills by electronic means, since art.4(2) provides "Any other means which preserves a record of the carriage to be performed may be substituted for the delivery of an air waybill"; although where the consignor requests, the carrier must provide "a cargo receipt" (which may, where the consignor agrees, be electronic) to identify the consignment and provide access to the information in the record "by other means". However, in any event, the air waybill neither comprises a document of title to nor an exchangeable receipt for the goods, although by arts 12 and 13 the retention by the consignor of possession of the air waybill does show the consignor's right to control delivery of the goods by the carrier and the physical transfer of the air waybill will result in the loss of that right by the consignor. Whilst the issue of the air waybill is not a prerequisite for the application of the Original and MP1 Unamended, and Amended, Warsaw regimes, its issue is a precondition to the air carrier's right to limit liability under them, since the carrier loses any right to limit

[20] *Macwilliam Co Inc v Mediterranean Shipping Co SA* [2003] 2 Lloyd's Rep. 113 deciding that a document of title for art.I(b) included a straight consigned bill as well as a negotiable bill.

under art.9 in the absence of the air waybill. The UK Non International Carriage Rules impose no documentary requirements at all for cargo.

5.1.3.4 Carriage of Goods by Multimodal Transport

In the absence of a multimodal regime for the mandatory regulation of multimodal carriage terms, the status of electronic multimodal transport documentation must be considered in the context of the common law and any applicable unimodal regimes. Where multimodal transport documents are issued as bills of lading and include carriage by sea, they are certainly capable of constituting exchangeable receipts and negotiable documents of title by implication under the common law, since, whenever the goods are still in the possession (actual or constructive) of the sea carrier under an ocean bill of lading, possession of the bill of lading gives rights of constructive possession over the goods irrespective of their physical location.[21] However, as discussed at 5.1.2 above, where they are issued in electronic form, it is difficult to replicate such functionality.

5.2 Multimodal Performance

5.2.1 Introduction

Where goods are required to be carried from one place to another, whether in the course of their sale or for some other reason, more than one mode of carriage may well be involved. In particular, goods carried by sea, air, rail or inland waterway will almost invariably need to be carried by some other mode or modes of transport as well: to and from the port, airport, rail terminal or other place where the sea, air, rail or inland waterway carriage is to begin and end. The resulting multi-modal transport (by sea and land, air and land, or various modes of land carriage) may be carried out either using several discrete contracts of carriage, each of which relates only to one method of carriage (unimodal carriage). Alternatively, one or more contracts of carriage relating to carriage by more than one mode (multimodal carriage) may be used. Arrangements for unimodal carriage fit neatly within the various, currently applicable, schemes of mandatory regulation for

[21] *Barclays Bank Ltd v Commissioners of Customs & Excise* [1963] 1 Lloyd's Rep. 81, where Diplock J. held possession of bills of lading gave rights of constructive possession over goods throughout an extended six month period of warehouse storage on behalf of the carrier following discharge.

contracts of international carriage (whether by road, rail, inland waterway,[22] sea or air). Arrangements for multimodal carriage, however, cut across those schemes and, consequently, create difficulties for carriers (multimodal transport operators) concluding contracts for multimodal carriage across international borders. Prior to addressing those difficulties, it is appropriate first to consider the role and liabilities of those providing freight forwarding services in connection with carriage.

5.2.2 Freight Forwarding Services

5.2.2.1 Role and Status

Freight forwarding services are essentially the provision of intermediary services for consignors and consignees in relation to a range of logistical arrangements for the carriage, export and import of goods, including route and transport mode selection, labelling and packaging, consolidation, carriage contract negotiation and conclusion, preparation and negotiation of carriage documentation, export and import clearance, insurance and associated services. Freight forwarding services may be provided by specialist intermediaries (freight forwarders) who simply provide those services and do not carry goods on their own road or rail vehicles, ships or aircraft, although they may still undertake the obligation of carriage and subcontract its performance to others.[23] Of course, freight forwarding services may also be provided by businesses that do operate their own road or rail vehicles, ships or aircraft. Indeed, that is invariably the case when those businesses operate their transport fleet for multimodal carriage operations. The freight forwarding industry is represented in the United Kingdom, by the BIFA organisation[24] (which provides services to its members including the standard BIFA 2005A Conditions trading conditions) and internationally, by the FIATA organisation.[25]

In connection with the provision of freight forwarding services, a significant difficulty arises under English law in relation to resolving the question as to whether the services are being provided as an agent on behalf of a client consignor, or consignee, or as a principal contractor

[22] Although, in respect of carriage by inland waterway, the UK is not a contracting state to the applicable international convention in the form of the Budapest Rules discussed at 2.7.

[23] *Aqualon (UK) Ltd v Vallana Shipping Corp* [1994] 1 Lloyd's Rep. 669.

[24] The British International Freight Association *http://www.bifa.org.*

[25] International Federation of Freight Forwarders Associations *http://www.fiata.com.*

undertaking the carriage. Certainly, freight forwarders may act as agents in arranging, on behalf of their clients, carriage contracts with third party carriers; alternatively, freight forwarders may themselves agree to carry and sub-contract performance of all, or part, of their contractual obligations to third party carriers.[26] As carrier, the freight forwarder will be liable for the performance of the carriage and is exposed to claims by anyone having the right to claim for damage, loss or delay to the goods in contract, tort or bailment, subject, of course, to the rights and duties to which the contract of carriage is subject under the applicable mandatory regulation. Conversely, as agent, the freight forwarder is liable only for arranging the carriage; it is generally only exposed to its client, or any third party, where it acts outside the terms of its authority, or is negligent in the exercise of its authority as agent.

Identifying whether a freight forwarder is an agent or carrier is not straightforward and is a matter of fact that courts have addressed on many occasions. The issue must be analysed against the entire factual matrix in each particular case. In *Aqualon (UK) Ltd v Vallana Shipping Corp*,[27] Mance J. considered that such analysis required enquiry to made as to each of the following particular issues: the terms of the contract, to ascertain what the forwarder was obliged to do; the description by the parties of the forwarder's role, to ascertain the parties' intentions; the extent and performance of any previous course of dealing, to ascertain the shared understanding of the parties; the nature and basis of charging, to ascertain whether the forwarder charged freight as the cost of carriage or commission for agency services; the nature and terms of any documentation issued and the status of that documentation. Evans J. held in *Bardiger (H.) Ltd v Halberg Spedition ApS*[28] that it was possible for a forwarder also to contract as principal, rather than agent, to procure a contract a carriage for a client. In the *Aqualon* case, Mance J. accepted "... that it must be possible for a contractor to undertake" such an intermediate role between that of carrier and agent; but commented that such a role was not "likely or lightly to be inferred".[29] Conversely, in French law a freight forwarder is normally

[26] The nature of agency relationships is discussed briefly at 1.6.1.4.

[27] See fn. 23, in which case a forwarder was found to be a CMR carrier notwithstanding that the CMR note accompanying the goods had been amended to name the collecting road haulier as carrier, since such amendment had been made by the forwarder without the consignor's agreement.

[28] Unreported October 26, 1990.

[29] See fn. 23.

considered to have such an intermediate role and has a particular status as a *commissionaire de transport*.

The role and liability of a *commissionaire de transport* under French law was considered by Rix L.J. in *Royal & Sun Alliance Insurance Plc v MK Digital Fze (Cyprus) Ltd.*[30] He distinguished the status of a *commissionaire de transport* from that of a freight forwarding agent as follows: "... unlike an English freight forwarding agent, who prima facie contracts only as an agent so far as the actual carriage is concerned, the French *commissionaire de transport* is an agent who contracts with personal liability throughout ...".[31] That is clearly not the position according to English law, under which freight forwarding services are either provided in the course of a party agreeing to carry as principal contractor, having liability for the performance of the carriage, or alternatively agreeing to arrange carriage as agent, with liability for the performance of its agency services but no liability for the actual performance of the carriage. In either case, it is common for freight forwarders which do not operate their own transport fleet to seek to incorporate[32] the standard trading conditions recommended by BIFA into their contractual arrangements with clients.

5.2.2.2 BIFA 2005A Conditions[33]

The BIFA 2005A Conditions, most recently updated on January 13, 2010, are the forwarding conditions recommended by BIFA. At cll.4(A) and 5, they particularly acknowledge the central ambiguity in the status of freight forwarders referred to above. In consequence of their intermediary role in the actual performance of the carriage, freight forwarders have no real risk of being exposed to the liabilities of a common carrier. Hence, it is not surprising that the BIFA 2005A Conditions do not even address such a remote contingency.[34] Unlike the RHA and FTA road carriage conditions,[35] the benefit of the BIFA freight forwarding conditions is not extended to sub-contractors, although, by cl.3 of the BIFA 2005A Conditions, any customer warrants that it is either the owner of the goods, or the authorised

30 [2006] 2 Lloyd's Rep. 110, paras 31 and 32.
31 ibid. para.32.
32 The principles of contractual incorporation under English law are discussed at 1.5.1.
33 *http://www.bifa.org.*
34 Other than by providing at cl.2(A) that all the activities of the freight forwarder are carried out subject to BIFA 2005A Conditions.
35 RHA 2009 and FTA 2002 Conditions discussed at 2.2.2.

agent of the owner and that it is accepting the standard conditions on behalf of both itself and the owner. The liability provisions are radically distinct from the road carriage conditions; BIFA 2005A Conditions only impose duties on freight forwarders, whether acting as agents or carriers, to act with reasonable "care, diligence, skill and judgment" in their contractual performances.[36]

Exemptions from liability are available in certain circumstances: under cl.24(A), where the consequence of a "strike, lock-out, stoppage or restraint of labour" cannot be avoided by "reasonable diligence"; under cl.24(B), where "any cause or event" cannot be avoided and its consequences cannot be prevented by "reasonable diligence". In addition, BIFA 2005A Conditions purport to impose various indemnity obligations on the customer aimed at relieving the forwarder of liability. Such indemnities are purported to arise in many diverse circumstances including: under cl.20(A); where liability, losses or costs are incurred by reason, either of the freight forwarder acting on the customer's instructions, or of any breach of warranty or negligence on the part of the customer;[37] under cl.20(B), where liability is incurred simply by reason of the freight forwarder carrying out the customer's instructions; under cl.20(C), for any liabilities arising in excess of the liability provided for in BIFA 2005A Conditions; under cl.20(D), for "claims of a general average nature"; under cl.13, where liability is incurred to third parties, by reason of the customer passing on to them advice or information from the forwarder; under cl.18, in respect of dangerous goods;[38] and under cl.19, in respect of the consequences of claims being brought against directors or employees of the forwarder. As the freight forwarder may never be in physical or constructive possession of the goods, there is no concept of any period of responsibility for it.

As with the RHA and FTA road carriage conditions, any liability on the part of the freight forwarder is subject to financial limitation. The financial

[36] Clause 23 of BIFA 2005A Conditions effectively mirroring the statutory obligations under s.13 of the Supply of Goods and Services Act 1982, discussed at 1.6.1.2.

[37] Clause 17 of BIFA 2005A Conditions provides that the customer warrants that supplied information is accurate and equipment is fit for purpose; that all goods have been properly packed, stowed and labelled and that transport units supplied or loaded by the customer are suitable: but BIFA 2005A Conditions contain other significant promises on the part of the customer breach of which may trigger indemnity (such as cl.3 as to the customer's authority).

[38] Broadly defined by cl.18, in terms apparently co-extensive with the common law concept discussed at 1.9.1.3.

limitations are calculated in the notional SDR currency.[39] Limitations are calculated as follows: (i) claims for loss or damage to goods at the rate of 2 SDR per kilo of the gross weight of the goods lost or damaged, which limitation is applicable whenever the value of any loss or damage would otherwise exceed that limitation; and (ii) claims for anything else, at the lower of the value of the goods, or of the above limitation fund (calculated on the consignment weight of the goods at the above 2 SDR rate per kg of the goods carried), or 75,000 SDR.[40] These limitations are subject to an aggregation provision for all losses attributable to any one "original error, and/or omission" applying an aggregate financial limit of 75,000 SDR in any one trading year commencing from the "original error, and/or omission".[41] Furthermore; claims for delay in delivery, or arranging delivery, of goods are limited in value to twice the value of the freight forwarder's charges under cl.26(B) and claims for indirect or consequential loss (as defined) are excluded under cl.26(C). Increased values may be requested by the customer and agreed by the carrier on the customer agreeing to pay increased charges.

The absolute common law right to the payment of freight is extended by cl.21(A) to freight forwarding charges of any kind; the customer remains liable for the payment of such charges, even where goods are consigned on a freight collect basis under cl.12. Unlike the RHA and FTA road carriage conditions, BIFA 2005A Conditions purport to impose a general lien on, and power of sale over, any goods and any documents. Such general lien can be exercised against not only the customer but also any owner, or any other person, otherwise entitled to possession of the goods.[42] Claims must not only be the subject of notification within a period of 14 days from awareness of the loss event[43] but must also be the subject of proceedings commenced within nine months of that loss event.[44] Clause 28 of BIFA 2005A Conditions provides for English law to apply and for the exclusive jurisdiction of the English courts.

39 The notional SDR currency is described at 2.3.4; it should be noted that under BIFA 2005A Conditions cl.26(A), the value of the SDR is to be calculated when the written claim is received.

40 See cl.26(A)(i)–(ii).

41 See cl.26(A)(iii).

42 See cl.8(A).

43 Or, as per cl.27(A), when they ought reasonably to have become aware of the loss event, unless notification was "impossible" for the claimant.

44 By cl.27(B) it is necessary not only for proceedings to be commenced but for notice of those proceedings to be given, within the nine month period.

Obviously, where the forwarder has agreed to carry pursuant to BIFA 2005A Conditions, the resulting contract of carriage will be subject to any applicable mandatory regulation of the carriage terms arising in the case of international carriage by road, rail, sea or air and any domestic UK carriage by air.[45] This is explicitly recognised by BIFA 2005A Conditions at cl.2(B).

5.2.3 Multimodal Carriage Services

5.2.3.1 Overview of Problems and Solutions

The essential problem in undertaking the contractual performance of multimodal carriage (within the context of the current diverse unimodal regulatory regimes for carriage contract terms) is that the contracting parties' rights and duties under single contracts for the multimodal carriage of goods from A to B will not be fixed and definite but variable and indefinite. When loss, damage or delay are caused to the goods, or the carrier, during carriage it will be necessary to determine at which stage of the carriage the act, omission or event (causing such loss, damage or delay) occurred and which, if any, of the various regimes of mandatory regulation is applicable.

This problem creates a number of difficulties (evident in decided cases and much discussed in academic literature)[46] not only for contracting parties entering into contracts for multimodal carriage, but also for any court or tribunal determining disputes under them. On the one hand, since each of the applicable unimodal regimes imposes contrasting requirements, the contracting parties encounter difficulties (both when the contract is originally concluded and when any claim arises) in correctly applying such diverse and varied mandatory terms. On the other hand, since they are not coherently linked in their scope and application, the unimodal regimes produce uncertainty, gaps and overlaps in the mandatory regulation of contractual terms for multimodal carriage: these must be carefully negotiated by courts when applying the identified mandatory terms.

To understand their contractual rights, duties and liabilities fully, the contracting parties must undertake detailed analysis of the scope,

[45] See 1.2.

[46] Particularly informative discussions can be found in the judgment of Mance L.J. in *Quantum Corporation Inc v Plane Trucking Ltd* [2002] 2 Lloyd's Rep. and Malcolm Clarke, "The transport of goods in Europe: patterns and problems of uniform law" (1999) L.M.C.L.Q. p.36.

application and terms of the diverse regulatory regimes: such analysis must be pursued in the light of the route, logistics and documentation of any multimodal movement. It is the results of such analysis, rather than their agreed contractual terms, that will have the most significance on such matters as: the selection of documentation required to record the contract of carriage; the identification of the parties' rights, duties, liabilities and defences as and when any claim arises; the claim values and financial limitations the parties are entitled to assert in the light of such claims; the procedures and timescales for claim notifications; the applicable jurisdictions for the commencement of proceedings; the discharge of the evidential burden as to the claim generally; and, in particular, the discharge of the evidential burden as to the cause of the alleged loss, damage or delay and when, how and during what stage of the carriage such cause occurred. As and when disputes arise, it is the courts or tribunals before whom proceedings are commenced that will have to resolve the uncertainties, gaps and overlaps produced by the interaction, in multimodal carriage, of the various unimodal regimes.

Uncertainties arise when the stage of the carriage at which the loss, damage or delay occurred is unknown (e.g. where goods on being destuffed from an undamaged container are found to have been damaged). In such cases, English law demands that the party making the allegation must prove it on the balance of probability. Whilst the court or tribunal determining the matter must be convinced that the loss, damage or delay was more likely than not to have been caused in the circumstances alleged, it may, in reaching that conclusion, place reliance on inferences drawn from the evidence.[47] However, where goods have been handed over to a multimodal carrier in good condition, a claimant may (in the absence of contractual terms, or evidence, to the contrary) rely, under English law, on any redelivery of the goods in a damaged condition (or on any non-delivery of the goods) as rebuttable proof of liability in tort or bailment on the part of the multimodal carrier.[48] The onus would then shift to the carrier to prove either that such loss or damage had occurred notwithstanding the exercise by it of reasonable care (thereby defeating the common law claim), or that it

[47] *Datec Electronics Holdings Ltd v United Parcels Service Ltd* [2007] 2 Lloyd's Rep. 114, where an inference, drawn by the Court of Appeal, of theft by the carrier's employees was upheld by the House of Lords, and distinguished by Lord Mance, at para.50, from the impermissible "trap" of engaging in "a process of elimination leading to no more than a conclusion regarding the least unlikely cause of loss".

[48] See 1.6.1.

was attributable to a cause or event within the scope of one or other of the applicable mandatory regimes, thereby ensuring the application of such particular unimodal regime. Alternatively, the multimodal carrier may seek to rely on agreed contractual terms to defeat the claim; in which case the onus would be on the claimants to assert the applicability of any unimodal regime that might be more favourable to their case.

Gaps are left when goods are not actually in the course of carriage under any of the applicable regimes at the time the loss, damage or delay occur. For instance, where goods are to be carried by road across international borders under the CMR to a load port and subsequently carried by sea subject to Hague-Visby, then carried onward from the discharge port by road, storage at the load and discharge ports will not be subject to any of the applicable mandatory unimodal regimes. However, if the goods were to remain loaded to a road vehicle throughout, the CMR would be applicable.[49] Similar gaps in the application of mandatory codes arise when goods are stored outside an airport in connection with international carriage by air under the Warsaw regime, or when they are the subject of internal domestic road movements and carriage by air under the Montreal regime. In such circumstances liability for loss, damage or delay caused during the gaps in the mandatory regime will be determined by any agreed terms and the law applicable to the multimodal carriage contract.

Overlaps occur when, at the material time, more than one regime is applicable. This may occur in relation to any mode of carriage. The CMR, relating to international carriage by road, may continue to apply during carriage by rail, inland waterway, sea or air when the road vehicle, to which the goods remain loaded, is carried in such a way.[50] The CIM, as to international carriage by rail, may continue to apply both to domestic carriage by road or inland waterway and to transnational carriage by sea or inland waterway on designated services.[51] Each of the Warsaw and Montreal Conventions on international carriage by air continue to apply during carriage by any other mode at an airport and apply rebuttable presumptions that loss or damage occurred during the carriage by air. The Warsaw Convention (although not the Montreal Convention) also applies to land or sea carriage undertaken in the event of a forced landing outside an airport. The Montreal Convention provides that it shall apply to any carriage by

[49] See CMR art.2(1) discussed at 2.3.1.
[50] ibid.
[51] See CIM arts 1.3 and 1.4 discussed at 2.6.2.

land or sea undertaken in breach of a contract for the carriage of goods by air.[52] In connection with the international carriage of goods by sea, whilst the Hague-Visby Rules can only apply from *ship's tackle* on loading to release of *ship's tackle* on discharge, the Hamburg Rules also apply to any carriage by road, rail, or inland waterway that is undertaken, by or for the sea carrier, within the confines of the ports of loading or discharge.[53] In the context of overlapping regulation, it has been contended that the relevant instruments of public international law (and the UK legislation implementing them) conflict, although, to date, UK courts have resisted such contentions.[54]

The international community has been considering for many years what the most appropriate solutions might be to these various difficulties, given the significance of international carriage arrangements for world trade. The potential for uniform, network, or modified solutions has been acknowledged.[55] The concept of a uniform solution has at its heart a vision of a widely adopted international instrument of public international law imposing common terms for multimodal carriage irrespective of the modes of carriage employed; this would displace the unimodal regimes when multimodal carriage is undertaken. Conversely, the concept of a network solution envisages the imposition of common terms for multimodal carriage, subject to the application of the unimodal regimes: essentially, liability would be determined by whichever unimodal regime was applicable to the carriage at the time when the act, omission, or event giving rise to the cause of action occurred; or, in the absence of any regime being applicable at that time, by the mandatory terms of the multimodal carriage. The modified approach applies the network solution, but modifies that solution by revising the existing network of unimodal regimes. This approach was taken by the UN Convention on International Multimodal Transport of Goods 1980 discussed at 5.2.3.2 below, which received insufficient support to enter into force even as an instrument of public international law. In the absence of international agreement as to a uniform or modified solution, the

[52] See art.18 of the Warsaw & Montreal Conventions discussed at 4.2.1.1.

[53] See art.I(e) of the Hague-Visby Rules and art.4(1) of the Hamburg Rules, discussed at 3.3.2.1 and 3.3.4.1 respectively.

[54] See judgment of Mance L.J. in *Quantum Corporation Inc v Plane Trucking Ltd* [2002] 2 Lloyd's Rep., para.28 discussed at 4.2.1.1.

[55] See the reports prepared by the UNCTAD secretariat on *Implementation of Multimodal Transport Rules* and *Multimodal Transport: The feasibility of an international legal instrument* respectively dated June 25, 2001 and January 13, 2003, *http://www.unctad.org*, which chart back to the 1930s the international efforts to resolve the difficulties in multimodal carriage regulation.

international business community has, by the agreement of standard terms for multimodal carriage in the form of the UNCTAD/ICC Rules for Multimodal Transport Documents discussed at 5.2.3.3 below, effectively adopted the network solution. The Rotterdam Rules on the carriage of goods by sea (discussed at 3.3.5 above and at 5.2.3.4 below) now introduce a further piece into this already complex jigsaw of provisions; if they were ever to enter into force, they would prescribe mandatory terms (on the basis of a network solution) for contracts of multimodal carriage involving any carriage by sea.

5.2.3.2 Multimodal Transport Convention

This international convention, adopted by the UN General Assembly on December 20, 1978 and open for signature from September 1, 1980, has to date only received support from some 13 states.[56] According to art.36, it will not enter into force internationally until it has been ratified by at least 30 states. Nevertheless, it is appropriate to consider briefly the modified network solution which it embodies and which has been influential in the development of the UNCTAD/ICC Rules addressed at 5.2.3.3 below.

The Multimodal Transport Convention applies common rules to multimodal carriage, defined by art.1(1) as

> "carriage of goods by at least two different modes of transport on the basis of a multimodal transport contract from a place in one country at which the goods are taken in charge by the multimodal transport operator to a place designated for delivery situated in a different country"

although "pick-up and delivery" operations facilitating unimodal carriage are excluded from that definition. The convention was designed specifically to accommodate the Hamburg Rules and imposes a similar liability regime for multimodal carriage to that of the Hamburg Rules. Under art.14(1) the multimodal transport operator[57] is not only made responsible for the goods "from the time he takes the goods in his charge to the time of their delivery", but is also liable under art.16(1) "if the occurrence which caused

[56] Those states being: Burundi, Chile, Georgia, Lebanon, Liberia, Malawi, Mexico, Morocco, Norway, Rwanda, Senegal, Venezuela and Zambia.

[57] Defined by art.1(2) as being "any person who ... concludes a multimodal transport contract and who acts as a principal ... and who assumes responsibility for the performance of the contract".

the loss, damage or delay in delivery took place while the goods were in his charge as defined in art.14". This applies unless it can be proved that the multimodal transport operator and its agents "took all measures that could reasonably be required to avoid the occurrence and its consequences".

The convention would limit claims against the multimodal transport operator to common uniform financial limits equivalent to those provided for by the Hamburg Rules, except where the multimodal carriage contemplated by the contract did not include carriage by sea or by inland waterway, in which case the applicable limits would have been equivalent to those imposed by the CMR.[58] However, whilst imposing this common scheme of liability on multimodal transport operators, the convention provides at art.19 that, where loss or damage occur during a particular stage of the multimodal transport for:

> "which an applicable international convention or mandatory national law provides a higher limit of liability . . ., then the limit of the multimodal transport operator's liability for such loss or damage shall be determined by reference to the provisions of such convention or mandatory national law".

Accordingly, the common scheme of liability for multimodal carriers to be imposed by this convention would accommodate a networked scheme of financial limitations based on whichever of the unimodal regimes or mandatory national legislation might be applicable in the particular circumstances of any claim.

5.2.3.3 UNCTAD/ICC Rules for Multimodal Transport Documents

These rules were developed by a joint UNCTAD/ICC working group and first published by the ICC in their current form on January 1, 1992 as ICC Publication No.481. They comprise standard terms for multimodal carriage which may be adopted by those undertaking such carriage and, by agreement with shippers, incorporated into multimodal carriage contracts. These rules have been widely adopted by multimodal transport operators (such as forwarders and multimodal carriers), particularly through the auspices of FIATA and BIMCO, who each publish standard multimodal transport

58 See arts 18(1) and 18(2)(3).

documentation based on them.[59] Multimodal transport is simply defined by cl.2 of the rules as being "a single contract for the carriage of goods by at least two different modes of transport": a multimodal transport operator is called an MTO; and defined as:

> "any person who concludes a multimodal transport contract and assumes responsibility for the performance thereof as a carrier".

Clause 4.1 states that the MTO is responsible for the goods "from the time the MTO has taken the goods in his charge to the time of their delivery"; clause 4.2 makes the MTO responsible for the acts or omission of any person whose services it uses to fulfil the multimodal contract.

Clause 5.1 provides for the MTO to be liable for any loss, damage or delay occurring during the period in which it is, by cl.4.1, responsible for the goods: "unless the MTO proves that no fault or neglect of his own", or any person for whom it is responsible, caused or contributed to the loss, damage or delay. However, where goods are carried by sea or inland waterway, the MTO also has the benefit of exclusions mirroring the Hague-Visby art.IV(2)(a) and IV(2)(b) exceptions. Clause 6.1 entitles the MTO to limit its liability for loss or damage to the same amounts provided for by Hague-Visby art.IV(5)(a), except when the multimodal transport does not involve carriage by sea or inland waterway, when, pursuant to cl.6.3, the limitation is set at the amounts prescribed for international road carriage by CMR art.23(3). Liability for delay is limited by cl.6.5 to the value of the freight payable under the multimodal transport contract. No provision is made for the disapplication of the limits provided for by the rules. Liabilities attaching to the consignor under the rules are similar to those attaching to a shipper under the Hague-Visby Rules and, as with the Hague-Visby Rules, the UNCTAD/ICC rules include no jurisdictional provisions; non-apparent loss or damage must be notified within six days of delivery and claim proceedings must, under cl.10, be commenced within nine months of actual delivery, due delivery, or the expiry of 90 days following the due date of delivery.

As the UNCTAD/ICC rules simply comprise standard contractual terms they must be incorporated and interpreted according to the

[59] FIATA and BIMCO publish standard documents subject to UNCTAD/ICC Rules, comprising negotiable multimodal bills of lading and non-negotiable waybills code-named: FIATA "FBL" and "FWB"; and BIMCO "MULTIDOC 95" and "MULTIWAYBILL 95".

applicable law, so that, as and when English law is applicable, the principles outlined at 1.5 must be applied. As simple contractual terms the rules will be displaced by any contrary mandatory regulation. This is expressly acknowledged by cl.13, which provides that the rules only take effect to the extent they are not contrary to applicable mandatory international conventions or national law. The network concept that underpins the rules is further supported by cl.6.4 which provides that, when loss or damage occurs during any particular stage of the multimodal carriage to which:

> "an applicable international convention or mandatory national law would have provided another limit of liability if a separate contract of carriage had been made for that particular stage"

the MTO's liability will be limited by reference to such convention or national law and not the rules, irrespective of whether a higher or lower limit would then result.

5.2.3.4 Rotterdam Rules

If and when the Rotterdam Rules enter into force they would effectively comprise a further network solution to the regulation of contractual terms for multimodal carriage but one that would not be reliant on contractual incorporation, and would only apply where the contract for multimodal carriage provides for carriage by sea.[60] There is apparent uncertainty as to whether a contractual option, or liberty, on the part of a multimodal carrier to carry goods by sea would "provide for carriage by sea" within the meaning of the Rotterdam Rules,[61] not least because the conditionality embodied by such a liberty actually prevents the contract from providing, in an obligatory sense, for carriage by sea. The requirement that the contract should "provide for carriage by sea" contrasts starkly with other transport conventions that simply require performance of carriage by the relevant mode pursuant to contract.[62] The network solution envisaged by the Rules takes effect pursuant to arts 26 and 28.

Article 26 provides that, in relation to claims for loss or damage

[60] Pursuant to art.1(1) of the Rotterdam Rules, as discussed at 3.3.5.1.

[61] See the commentary on the Rules in "The next sea carriage Convention" by Anthony Diamond Q.C., L.M.C.L.Q. 2008 2 (May) 135–187 at 141.

[62] See discussion of this issue regarding the CMR, by Mance L.J. at para.20 of his judgment in *Quantum Corporation Inc v Plane Trucking Ltd* [2002] 2 Lloyd's Rep. 25.

occurring (or claims for delay caused by circumstances occurring) "solely" before loading on, or after discharge from, the carrying vessel, the Rules will not prevail over provisions of "another international instrument" that: (a) would have applied had the shipper made "a separate and direct contract with the carrier" for the relevant stage; (b) stipulate "the carrier's liability, limitation of liability, or time for suit"; and (c) are mandatory in their effects. Article 82 specifically provides that the Rules shall not affect the application of:

> "the following international conventions ... that regulate the liability of the carrier for loss of or damage to the goods: (a) Any convention governing the carriage of goods by air to the extent that such convention according to its provisions applies to any part of the contract of carriage; (b) Any convention governing the carriage of goods by road to the extent that such convention according to its provisions applies to the carriage of goods that remain loaded on a road cargo vehicle carried on board a ship; (c) Any convention governing the carriage of goods by rail to the extent that such convention according to its provisions applies to carriage of goods by sea as a supplement to the carriage by rail; or (d) Any convention governing the carriage of goods by inland waterways to the extent that such convention according to its provisions applies to a carriage of goods without trans-shipment both by inland waterways and sea".

These provisions appear to have been designed so as to ensure that the Rules would take effect as a pure network solution giving way to the existing unimodal regimes as and when, according to their own provisions, they would apply to multimodal carriage. However, a literal interpretation of their provisions suggests that they might not have that effect.[63] In the event of the Rotterdam Rules entering into force in the United Kingdom, it is certainly to be hoped that they would be interpreted so as to take effect as a pure network solution, since they do not require contracting states to denounce existing conventions relating to carriage modes other than by sea and any other interpretation could hardly be said to be consistent with notions of international comity.

[63] See fn. 61 at 142–143.

5.3 Regulatory Environment

5.3.1 Introduction

The performance of contractual obligations in all modes of carriage is now subject to a considerable volume of mandatory regulation. Such mandatory regulation frequently derives from international public law obligations and informal understandings entered into by the United Kingdom and/or the EU.[64] These obligations are imposed on the contracting parties by mandatory UK regulation or mandatory and directly effective EU regulation with breach sounding in criminal sanctions,[65] administrative sanctions,[66] contractual illegality[67] and/or civil liability[68] sanctions. The resulting harmonisation of statutory requirements for the operation of contractual carriage across international borders greatly facilitates the performance of international carriage obligations, since carriers are enabled to take advantage of qualified rights of access, egress and transit to, from and within states other than their own domicile, provided such states are contracting parties to the relevant treaty or understanding and subject to compliance with the harmonised requirements.

In the EEA such regulation takes effect within the context of the European internal market, which has always (since the creation of the European Economic Community (EEC) in 1957 by the Treaty of Rome) anticipated a common policy for transport by road, rail and inland waterway; this has since been extended to transport by sea and air.[69] Initially progress towards a common transport policy was slow; indeed it was so

[64] By formal international treaties and informal memoranda of understandings agreed under the auspices of the relevant international agency for the particular mode of carriage concerned.

[65] For various specific offences under UK statutory provisions such as the criminal offence on an owner or master under s.98 Merchant Shipping Act 1995 for having a "dangerously unsafe" ship in a UK port or, where it is a UK ship, in any port.

[66] Pursuant to various instruments of UK or EU statutory regulation such as the prohibition orders, which can be issued under s.262 Merchant Shipping Act 1995, prohibiting a ship from undertaking certain activities or from going to sea.

[67] Pursuant to English common law, subject (in the case of breach of EU law) to the EU law principles of equivalence and effectiveness applied in the enforcement of EU legislation, as discussed at 5.3.7 below.

[68] ibid.

[69] See, in this regard art.100(2) of the Treaty on the Functioning of the European Union (TFEU) revising art.80(2) of the EC Treaty (ECT).

slow that the European Parliament felt constrained in 1983 to bring an action in the European Court of Justice against the Council for its failure to implement such a policy. The ECJ held both that the Council was, as at that time, in breach of its Treaty obligations (by having failed to introduce measures to ensure that transport services could be freely provided by EEA domiciled carriers outside the state of their domicile) and that it should introduce such measures within a reasonable period.[70] Subsequently, and particularly in consequence of the 1986 Single European Act, the common transport policy has become a reality for transport by land, sea and/or air. The policy was initially focused on the harmonisation of national rules and regulations that restricted EEA carriers from using ships, aircraft, rail and/or road vehicles to carry goods and passengers outside the state of the carrier's domicile—a practice widely referred to as "*cabotage*"; however, the focus has now widened to include the development of a trans-European transport network[71] and the promotion of sustainable development, safety enhancement, operational competitiveness and international co-operation.[72]

Transport and trans-European networks now fall within the shared competence of the EU and its Member States under art.4(2) of the Treaty on the Functioning of the European Union (TFEU); the TFEU is the amended version of the EC Treaty (ECT).[73] Title VI to the TFEU authorises the institutions of the EU to facilitate: (a) international transport across Member States; (b) the operation of transport services by EEA domiciled carriers in EEA states other than that of their domicile (c) the improvement of transport safety; and (d) other appropriate provisions within the framework of a common transport policy.[74] TFEU art.56 (ex 49 ECT) provides for the abolition of restrictions on the freedom of EEA domiciled persons to provide services within the EEA subject to the

[70] Case C-13/83 *European Parliament v Council* [1986] 1 C.M.L.R. 138.

[71] Pursuant to arts 170 to 172 (ex 154 to 156) of the revised version of the Treaty on European Union ("TEU"); introduced by the Treaty of Lisbon on December 1, 2009, by which the EU is committed to the establishment and development of trans-European networks in the areas of transport, telecommunications and energy infrastructures.

[72] European Commission's Communication Paper *A sustainable future for transport: Towards an integrated, technology-led and user friendly system* of June 17, 2009 (COM(2009) 279 final).

[73] The TFEU entered into force under the Treaty of Lisbon on December 1, 2009.

[74] See in particular arts 90 and 91 of the TFEU (ex 70 and 71 ECT).

application of TFEU arts 90 to 100 at Title VI (ex 70 to 80 ECT).[75] TFEU art.56 is capable of being directly effective, which means that any rights afforded by it may be enforced and protected by the national courts of any Member State;[76] however, although a carrier may claim freedom to provide transport services in another Member State, that freedom, inevitably, is subject to compliance with the regulatory requirements of the common transport policy. This policy has arisen under EU legislation and conforming national law and has been implemented in the UK legal systems through primary and delegated legislation introduced by the Department for Transport (DfT), which is the relevant UK governmental agency.[77]

Such cascading mandatory regulation is most conveniently summarised by referring separately to each mode of carriage and to each of the relevant legislative levels, as discussed below.[78]

5.3.2 Road Carriage

5.3.2.1 International Regulation

There is no worldwide regulating body for road carriage but the UN has five regional agencies, including the United Nations Economic Commission for Europe (UNECE), that seek to foster international co-operation on a regional basis in such matters as road and rail transport. In connection with the carriage of goods by road, UNECE has effectively assumed the co-ordinating role that was previously performed by the Council of Europe under the auspices of which the CMR was originally agreed in 1956. Now 56 countries liaise under the auspices of UNECE on transportation issues such as the facilitation of border crossing under the *Transports Internationaux Routiers* (TIR) global Customs' transit system (underpinned by the issue of the TIR Carnet for carriage of goods under guaranteed duty suspension arrangements in secure vehicles or containers);[79] dangerous goods

[75] TFEU art.58 (ex 51 TEC).

[76] See Case C-26/62 *Van Gend en Loos* [1963] E.C.R.1.

[77] Detailed information about existing and forthcoming UK regulation for carriage by aviation, rail, road and shipping is available at the DfT website *http://www.dft.gov.uk/*.

[78] Namely international regulation and EEA and UK regulation.

[79] Discussed at 1.11.

(underpinned by the GHS,[80] TDG,[81] and most significantly the ADR);[82] and also vehicle and road safety, with UNECE working through the World Forum for Harmonisation of Vehicle Regulations and the Road Safety Forum.[83]

5.3.2.2 EEA and UK Regulation

Whilst there is no specialist agency within the European Commission, other than that of the European Commissioner for Transport,[84] responsible for regulating road carriage, a considerable body of EU legislation has been passed in this respect and implemented into UK law.[85] The current regulatory environment for the carriage of goods by road in the EEA and the United Kingdom can be examined by reference to distinct measures for the regulation of cabotage, operators, vehicles, drivers and road safety.

Cabotage is governed by Regulation 881/92/EEC, which provides that international carriage of goods by road[86] for hire or reward within the EEA

[80] The Globally Harmonised System of Classification and Labelling of Chemicals (republished in July 2009 in its 3rd revised edn) that facilitates the communication of physical and toxicity risk information along supply and transportation chains.

[81] The "Model Regulations on the Transport of Dangerous Goods" proposing a basic regulatory scheme for the classification, packing, testing, labelling and documenting of dangerous goods for voluntary adoption into national law in respect of carriage by road or rail.

[82] The 1957 European Agreement on the International Carriage of Dangerous Goods by Road annexing conditions with the force of international public law (as per the reissued 2009 edition) for the packaging and labelling of the goods (Annex A) and for the construction, equipment and operation of the carrying vehicle (Annex B). The ADR (which is in conformity with the TDG and the public international law requirements for carriage by inland waterway, sea and air) is currently applied into UK laws by The Carriage of Dangerous Goods and Use of Transportable Pressure Equipment Regulations 2009 (SI 2009/1348).

[83] The UNECE website is at *http://www.unece.org/trans/welcome.html*.

[84] From whom detailed information about existing and forthcoming EU road carriage regulation is available at *http://ec.europa.eu/transport/index_en.htm*.

[85] When, for instance: the EU legislation is not capable of having direct effect in English law; criminal sanctions are required; or some measure of discretion, as to implementation, has been left to Member States.

[86] International carriage is defined at art.2 as being any laden journey between different Member States (with or without transit through any other country); or from a Member State to a non-member country or vice versa (with or without transit through any other country); or between non-member countries with transit through any territory within the EEA; and any unladen journey undertaken in conjunction with such carriage.

and undertaken, subject to "community authorisation",[87] by a motor vehicle registered in the EEA is permitted for all journeys. The concept of "community authorisation" is governed by arts 3, 5 and 7, which provide for the issue of such authorisation for a period of five years to any haulier established in a Member State carrying goods by road for hire or reward and authorised (or entitled to be authorised) by that Member State to perform international carriage of goods by road.[88] Such authorisation is subject to a number of requirements as follows: it must be issued in the form and subject to the conditions[89] annexed to R881/92/EEC; it must be retained by the haulier and also retained, in the form of certified copies, in each vehicle used by it for the international carriage of goods;[90] it must be made out in the haulier's name; it cannot be transferred to any third party; and the certified true copy retained in the vehicle must be produced whenever required by an authorised inspecting officer. The vehicles used subject to such community authorisation or UK operator's licence need not be owned by the operator and may be hired from other organisations,[91] provided that they are registered in the state of the operator's domicile, hired without a driver, at the sole disposal of the operator during the period of hire and driven by the operator's personnel.[92] Article 11 provides for Member States to give each other mutual assistance in the application and monitoring of the authorisation regime. In the event of any infringement of this Regulation, the Member State within which the haulier is established, being the state responsible for the issue of the authorisation, must be informed and will be invited to impose sanctions. Such sanctions may, pursuant to art.8, extend (in the event of serious, or repeated minor,

[87] Directive 2006/94/EC, by way of amendment to prior EU legislation, exempts certain limited types of international carriage (such as where the goods being carried are the property of the carrier or have been sold, bought, let out on hire or hired, produced, extracted, processed or repaired by the carrier) from having to be carried out subject to community authorisation.

[88] In the UK such "authorisation" takes the form of an operator's licence issued pursuant to the Goods Vehicles (Licensing of Operators) Act 1995.

[89] Those annexed conditions, inter alia, requiring the holder of any authorisation to comply with the "laws, regulations and administrative provisions in force in that State, in particular with regard to transport and traffic".

[90] The number of such vehicles may not exceed the maximum number specified in the operator's licence pursuant to s6 of the Goods Vehicles (Licensing of Operators) Act 1995.

[91] Directive 2006/1/EC on the use of vehicles hired without drivers for the carriage of goods by road.

[92] ibid. art.2(1).

regulatory infringements) to the suspension of the authorisation. Regulation 484/2002/EC introduces a system of Member State attestation for drivers from outside the EEA who are lawfully employed by a community haulier holding a community authorisation for road haulage services.

An undertaking (i.e. a natural or legal person) intending to transact business as a road haulage operator in the EEA for the transportation of goods "for hire or reward" using a motor vehicle, or a combination of vehicles, must satisfy the requirements of Directive 96/26/EC (as amended by Directive 98/76/EC) according to its implemention by conforming Member State legislation.[93] Article 3 of D96/26/EC requires that such undertakings must: "(a) be of good repute; (b) be of appropriate financial standing; and (c) satisfy the condition as to professional competence".[94] The requirement of good repute will not be satisfied if the person or persons in question:

> "(a) have been convicted of serious criminal offences, including offences of a commercial nature, (b) have been declared unfit to pursue the occupation of road transport operator under any rules in force, (c) have been convicted of serious offences against the rules in force concerning: the pay and employment conditions in the profession, or ... the rules relating to drivers' driving and rest periods, the weights and dimensions of commercial vehicles, road safety and vehicle safety, the protection of the environment and the other rules concerning professional liability"

subject to rehabilitation of offender provisions.[95] There are also specific provisions for the satisfaction of the financial standing and professional competence requirements.[96] In the event of compliance issues in the United Kingdom, careful consideration should be given not only to the implementing legislation under the Goods Vehicles (Licensing of Operators) Act 1995 (as amended), but also the provisions of the applicable EU directives

[93] Such directives, not being capable of direct effects, have been implemented in the UK by the Goods Vehicles (Licensing of Operators) Act 1995 as amended.

[94] Although a natural person not otherwise satisfying requirement (c), may do so by designating continuous and effective management of transport operations to another satisfying both (a) and (c).

[95] Article 3(2) D96/26/EC as amended by art.1(3) of D98/76/EC.

[96] Article 3(3) and (4) D96/26/EC as amended by art.1(3) of D98/76/EC.

in conformity with which, as far as possible, the implementing UK legislation must be interpreted.[97]

For a vehicle to be used in the EEA for the international carriage of goods, it must be registered for that purpose in a Member State pursuant to Directive 1999/37/EC and the registration certificate (in paper, or pursuant to Directive 2003/127/EC, microprocessor smart card format) must be carried in the vehicle. The vehicle must also satisfy the road vehicle roadworthiness tests required by Directive 96/96/EC (as amended). Drivers should ensure they can satisfy authorities, undertaking any technical roadside inspection, that all required roadworthiness tests have been satisfactorily performed. Even where they are able to do so such authorities are entitled, where they consider there are deficiencies in the maintenance of a commercial vehicle which represent a safety risk, to undertake further examination and more elaborate testing at a designated testing facility. Where it is "clear that a commercial vehicle presents a serious risk to its occupants or other road users", use of the vehicle may be prohibited until the identified dangerous deficiencies have been rectified.[98] In the United Kingdom, implementation of these provisions has been achieved by The Road Vehicles (Construction and Use) Regulations 1986 as amended, which have been enacted pursuant to s.41 of the Road Traffic Act 1988.[99]

Performance of international road carriage is subject to the driver undertaking performance holding a valid community driving licence for the vehicle concerned, pursuant to Directive 91/439/EEC as amended. This provision, implemented into UK law by The Motor Vehicles (Driving Licences) Regulations 1999 (SI 1999/2864) pursuant to the Road Traffic Act 1988, has been recast by Directive 2006/126/EC, which is due to be transposed into national law by January 19, 2011. D2006/126/EC provides, at art.1, for Member States to issue driving licences in the form of the community model licence at Annex I and, at art.2, for there to be mutual recognition of licences across the community, irrespective of the country of issue. Regulation 3820/85/EEC lays down mandatory regulation of driving times and rest periods for drivers providing for: maximum driving periods at art.6; a compulsory weekly rest period at art.8; and mandatory daily breaks and rest periods at art.7. The calculation of each of these periods in any given case varies according to circumstances (such as the places at

[97] *Marleasing* (Case C-106/89) [1990] ECR I-4135.

[98] Pursuant to art.5 Directive 2000/30/EC.

[99] See SI 1986/1078 and amending instruments: SIs 1995/2210, 1996/2085, 1998/1563, 2000/1434, 2002/227 and 2003/3145.

which weekly rest periods are taken, the inter-relationship of daily breaks and rest periods, the number of drivers manning the vehicle, any carriage of the vehicle by rail or sea, and other factors), which all require careful consideration and calculation in the context of the logistics for any particular carriage operation.

In connection with road safety regulation, national road safety measures of the host Member State in which the services are performed prevail; difficulties arise with respect to cross-border enforcement of offences to which the European Arrest Warrant is inapplicable.[100] The Commission considers existing bilateral measures of Member States to be ineffective and insufficient and has proposed various initiatives to address these and other road safety issues.[101] The inland carriage of dangerous goods by road, rail and inland waterway is now subject to Directive 2008/68/EC, which applies into European law the international convention for the international carriage of dangerous goods by road (ADR).[102]

5.3.3 Rail Carriage

5.3.3.1 International Regulation

As with road transport no single entity is responsible for facilitating harmonised regulation for the carriage of goods by rail on a worldwide basis. For rail carriage from the European shore of the North Atlantic Ocean to the Siberian shore of the North Pacific Ocean[103] facilitating such harmonisation is undertaken under the auspices of the Intergovernmental Organisation for International Carriage by Rail (OTIF). OTIF was established on May 1, 1985 under the Convention on International Carriage by Rail of 9 May 1980 (COTIF); it replaced the Central Office for International Carriage by Rail (which had been set up in 1893 to administer the CIM Convention). OTIF provides a forum for international agreement in relation to the carriage of goods by rail for the 44 states that are members of OTIF and contracting states to COTIF; it encompasses not only the

[100] Where, for instance, the maximum penalty for the offence is less than a year in prison.

[101] See, in particular the European Road Safety Charter details of which are available at *http://www.erscharter.eu/*.

[102] As well as the international conventions for the carriage of dangerous goods by rail (RID) and inland waterways (ADN) referred to below.

[103] Throughout most of Europe, Russia and several states in North Africa and the Middle East.

CIM and CIV conventions, but also the RID convention on the carriage of dangerous goods by rail.[104]

5.3.3.2 EEA and UK Regulation

Within the EEA regulation of carriage of goods by rail is primarily still a matter for the governmental authorities of each Member State,[105] although the EU has now established the European Railway Agency (ERA) pursuant to Regulation 881/2004/EC, which has been tasked with implementation of the common transport policy in respect of the "European railway system" (to use the terminology of R881/2004/EC to describe the various national railway systems of EU Member States).[106] The high level aims of the ERA are described at art.1 as being those of

> "improving the competitive position of the railway sector by enhancing the level of interoperability of railway systems and at developing a common approach to safety on the European railway system, in order to contribute to creating a European railway area without frontiers and guaranteeing a high level of safety".

The ERA is tasked with developing the common safety methods, safety targets and technical specifications for interoperability[107] that Member States are required, by various European directives,[108] to introduce. The ERA has established joint working groups with OTIF on various issues, such as the vehicle keeper marking register, suggesting that the ERA may, over time, move towards membership of OTIF. The issue of cabotage

[104] RID is an abbreviation for the Convention entitled *Reglement concernant le transport International ferroviare des merchandises Dangereuses par chemin de fer*, which is currently applied into UK laws by The Carriage of Dangerous Goods and Use of Transportable Pressure Equipment Regulations 2009 (SI 2009/1348).

[105] The Department for Transport (DfT) is the relevant national agency in the UK, details of which are available at the DfT website *http://www.dft.gov.uk/*.

[106] Detailed information as to the activities of the ERA is available at *http://www.era.europa.eu/Pages/Home.aspx*.

[107] Being the ability for trains to operate safely and without interruption across national borders over those parts of the European railway system that are designated as international lines (see, in particular, art.2 of Directive 2008/57/EC).

[108] See, in particular, D2008/57/EC and D2007/32/EC as to interoperability; D2004/49/EC as to safety; D2007/59/EC as to the licensing of train drivers; and D2008/68/EC as to the transportation of dangerous goods.

within the EEA is addressed by various EU legislative instruments,[109] providing for the issue and recognition throughout the EEA of a European rail freight operator's licence for the operation of rail freight services (other than in relation to regional rail freight services, or own freight operations on privately owned railway infrastructure). Such legislation has been implemented in the United Kingdom, where the Office of the Rail Regulator (ORR) is responsible for the issue of licences and the provision of such a rail service without a European licence is a criminal offence.[110]

5.3.4 Inland Waterway Carriage

As there can be no carriage by UK inland waterways across international borders, regulation remains a domestic matter.[111] The UK regulatory environment is very similar to that applicable to the carriage of goods by sea insofar as inland waterway craft fulfil the statutory definition of a "ship". The relevant definition is contained at s.313(1) of the Merchant Shipping Act 1995, which provides that "ship includes every description of vessel used in navigation". The concept of using vessels in "navigation" has generally been defined under English law as being restricted to those vessels "used to make ordered progression over the water from one place to another",[112] whether at sea or over inland waterways. Certain provisions of the Merchant Shipping Act 1995, such as Part III concerning the employment of masters and seamen, only apply to a "seagoing ship": a concept that has no clear statutory definition, but which the Court of Appeal considers means no more than a ship setting out on a sea voyage.[113] Accordingly, a ship using an inland waterway may be a seagoing ship for the purposes of the applicable regulation only where it is setting out on a sea voyage from an inland port.

Pursuant to the common law, public rights of navigation exist over all

[109] Directive 95/18/EC on the licensing of railway undertakings (as amended by Directives 2001/13/EC and 2004/49/EC).

[110] Pursuant to s.8 of the Railways Act 1993 and the Railway (Licensing of Railway Undertakings) Regulations 2005.

[111] Accordingly, the UK regulation of inland waterway carriage remains largely unaffected by the growing body of regulation at EU level as to cross border carriage by inland waterway.

[112] *R v Goodwin* [2006] 1 W.L.R. 546, para.33 per Lord Phillips C.J. in the course of deciding that a jet ski used on the sea was not a ship.

[113] ibid. para.38.

navigable tidal waterways[114] and, pursuant to s.33 of the Harbours Docks and Piers Clauses Act 1847, the use of any public harbour, dock or pier is open to all persons for the shipping and unshipping of goods subject to the payment of the rates (and compliance with the bylaws) applicable to their use. However, rights of navigation over non-tidal inland waterways are not generally available and depend upon the existence of express statutory rights (which exist in relation to certain particular waterways),[115] express grant of public rights by the riparian owner of the riverbed, or public user rights arising under the common law by reason of continuous use since "time immemorial".[116]

5.3.5 Sea Carriage

5.3.5.1 International Regulation

International regulation of the performance of contracts of sea carriage under the auspices of the International Maritime Organisation (IMO)[117] is highly developed and increasingly effective, as evidenced by declining ship casualty rates.[118] The relevant governmental agencies have co-operated together with various non-governmental organisations (including such

[114] See *Orr-Ewing v Colquhoun* (1876–77) L.R. 2 App. Cas. 839.

[115] By s.105 Transport Act 1968, a right of public navigation is created over the 2,200 mile canal and river network operated by the British Waterways Board; albeit such rights are limited to vessels of dimensions not exceeding those of the vessels which customarily used "that waterway or part during the period of nine months ending with 8th December 1967"; unless the waterway has been since "restored or improved" so that the vessel is in fact suitable.

[116] The original common law, and subsequent statutory public rights of navigation, which have existed over the non-tidal waters of the River Thames, were considered by the Court of Appeal in *Rowland v Environment Agency* [2005] Ch.1.

[117] The IMO (*http://www.imo.org/*) was created pursuant to the 1948 Convention on the International Maritime Organisation (the IMO Convention) and now operates under the auspices of the United Nations. It was established when the IMO Convention came into force on March 17, 1958 and its membership now extends to 168 states by whom some 97.22 per cent (calculated by reference to vessel tonnage) of the world's merchant shipping fleet is registered.

[118] IMO Library Services online publication *International Shipping and World Trade Facts and figures* (ibid. accessed on January 31, 2009) provides figures suggesting a decline in the ratio of ship casualties per registered vessel from 0.5 per cent in 1959 to 0.1 per cent in 2004.

bodies as BIMCO,[119] the ISC,[120] and the related ISF[121]) and other international bodies (such as the UN ILO)[122] in the development and agreement of minimum standards for ship safety, marine pollution, liability and compensation, seafarer's welfare and other issues. The IMO now operates within the international framework provided by the 1982 UN Convention on the Law of the Sea (UNCLOS), which provides all states with "the right to sail ships flying its flag"[123] on the high seas (i.e. the right of free navigation for peaceful purposes) and territorial waters (i.e. the right of innocent passage) and regulates the relationship between the state whose flag is flown and the ship which flies it. In particular: there must be a "genuine link" between the state and the ship; the ship must be registered in the state and sail under the flag of only that state; and, whilst on the high seas, the ship is generally subject to that state's exclusive jurisdiction.[124]

Article 94 places any flag state under the general duty to "effectively exercise its jurisdiction and control in administrative, technical and social matters over ships flying its flag". Article 94 particularly requires every such flag state to:

> "(a) maintain a register of ships containing the names and particulars of ships flying its flag... and (b) assume jurisdiction under its internal law over each ship flying its flag and its master, officers and crew in respect of administrative, technical and social matters concerning the ship"

with every flag state also being required to take all measures necessary to ensure the "safety at sea" of ships flying its flag. Ensuring "safety at sea" must include measures as to the following:

119 The Baltic International Marine Cargo Organisation (*https://www.bimco.org/*) which was founded in 1905 to provide a worldwide international forum for both ship and cargo interests.

120 The International Chamber of Shipping (*http://www.marisec.org/*) representing the various national associations of merchant ship operators.

121 The International Shipping Federation (*http://www.marisec.org/*) representing the interests of marine employers.

122 The International Labour Organisation (*http://www.ilo.org/global/lang--en/index.htm*).

123 UNCLOS art.90 relating to the right of free navigation.

124 UNCLOS arts 91–93.

> "(a) the construction, equipment and seaworthiness of ships; (b) the manning of ships, labour conditions and the training of crews ...; (c) the use of signals, the maintenance of communications and the prevention of collisions";[125]

and

> "(a) that each ship, before registration and thereafter at appropriate intervals, is surveyed by a qualified surveyor of ships, and has on board such charts, nautical publications and navigational equipment and instruments as are appropriate for the safe navigation of the ship; (b) that each ship is in the charge of a master and officers who possess appropriate qualifications ... and that the crew is appropriate in qualification and numbers for the type, size, machinery and equipment of the ship; (c) that the master, officers and, to the extent appropriate, the crew are fully conversant with and required to observe the applicable international regulations concerning the safety of life at sea, the prevention of collisions, the prevention, reduction and control of marine pollution, and the maintenance of communications by radio".[126]

The measures adopted by flag states to ensure "safety at sea" must "conform to generally accepted international regulations, procedures and practices",[127] such as those various ship safety, pollution control, safe navigation, seafarer training and welfare conventions made under the auspices of the IMO or the ILO, insofar as they can be proved to be "generally accepted".[128] The considerable body of international public law concluded in respect of such issues (much of which actually predates UNCLOS, although it should now be considered under the general

[125] UNCLOS art.94(3).
[126] UNCLOS art.94(4).
[127] UNCLOS art.94(5).
[128] Complex issues arise in connection with the relationship between public international law obligations under UNCLOS and the various substantive IMO conventions as to such issues as ship safety etc. The paper "IMO interface with the Law of the Sea Convention" presented by Agustín Blanco-Bazán at the 23rd Annual Seminar of the Center for Ocean Law and Policy, University of Virginia School of Law, IMO, 6–9 January 2000, published online by the IMO (fn. 117), contains a useful discussion of such issues.

legislative UNCLOS umbrella) is available online[129] from the IMO (or, as to certain seafarer welfare conventions, the ILO). Where, as generally is the case, the United Kingdom is a contracting state, the relevant instrument of public international law is appended, in the form of one or more schedules, to UK legislation. The following are some of the most significant public law instruments to have been implemented into UK legal systems in this area.

- The 1974 SOLAS convention[130] (as amended) in relation to ship safety. The 1974 version is the fifth incarnation of the original SOLAS convention, which resulted from the *Titanic* disaster and was concluded in 1914. SOLAS specifies minimum standards for the construction, equipment and operation of ships according to their type[131] and prescribes particular certification to prove compliance. SOLAS incorporates the ISM Code 1998[132] and the ISPS Code 2002.[133]
- The combined MARPOL 73/78 convention[134] on the prevention of ship pollution. MARPOL 73/78 imposes certain operational procedures to reduce the risk of accidental pollution, prohibits deliberate pollution, requires punishment for deliberate and reckless pollution and regulates emissions.[135]
- The 1972 COLREG convention in relation to ship navigation, which is aimed at the avoidance of ship collisions for safe

[129] See fnn. 117 and 122.

[130] The 1974 International Convention for the Safety of Life at Sea, which entered into force on May 25, 1980 and is implemented in the UK by delegated legislation generally under s.85 of the Merchant Shipping Act 1995.

[131] Merchant vessels are classed according to type. There are several broad categories (i.e. container, tanker, bulk, Ro-Ro (freight), Ro-Ro (passenger ferry), cruise ship and general cargo) each having several sub-categories.

[132] The International Safe Ship Management Code, against which the prescribed on-board and on-shore ship safety management procedures of the ship operator will be audited.

[133] The International Ship and Port Facility Security Code, against which prescribed on-board and on-shore security procedures of the ship operator and port terminal operator will be audited.

[134] The 1973 International Convention for the Prevention of Pollution from Ships as amended by the 1978 Protocol, which is implemented in the UK by delegated legislation generally under s.128 of the Merchant Shipping Act 1995.

[135] MARPOL 73/78 applies to pollution from a variety of noxious substances, whether carried as part of the vessel's cargo or the vessel's supplies.

navigation and comprises detailed mandatory rules for ship navigation on international seaways.[136]

- The 1978 STWC convention[137] regulating the training and certification required for seafarers, imposing minimum international requirements on such matters as training, certification and watchkeeping.

Each of the various IMO conventions provides, as does UNCLOS, for the flag states to have primary responsibility for ensuring that ships under their flag comply with the requirements of public international law. Compliance is certified by whichever of the various ship classification societies has been engaged by ship owners to: carry out the inspections necessary to audit compliance with these internationally agreed standards; issue the appropriate certification, to the owner and the flag state, for the purposes of the original registration, any re-registration with another state and any renewal. Control provisions also allow the governments of contracting states other than flag states to inspect ships within their territory to monitor compliance. This procedure is known as port state control and was introduced as a result of the "ineffectiveness" of flag state control by certain states.[138] The US spearheaded the port state control initiative, but the IMO has also promoted and facilitated the worldwide spread of port state control and has encouraged regional co-operation by states in exercising it. Such regional co-operation has been secured in various regions by memoranda of understanding (MOU) between neighbouring states in various regions,[139]

[136] The 1972 Convention on the International Regulations for Preventing Collisions at Sea, which entered into force on July 15, 1977 and has been implemented in the UK by The Merchant Shipping (Distress Signals and Prevention of Collisions) Regulations 1996 (SI 1996/75) under ss.85 and 86 of the Merchant Shipping Act 1995.

[137] The 1978 International Convention on Standards of Training, Certification and Watchkeeping for Seafarers, implemented in the UK by The Merchant Shipping (Training and Certification) Regulations 1997 (SI 1997/348) under s.47 of the Merchant Shipping Act 1995.

[138] Sir Anthony Clarke "Port state control or sub-standard ships: who is to blame? what is the cure?" 1994 2 L.M.C.L.Q. pp.202–209.

[139] Including the Asia Pacific Region (Tokyo MOU), the Caribbean Region (Carribean MOU), the Latin American Region (Viña del Mar Agreement), the Indian Ocean Region (Indian Ocean MOU), the Mediterranian Region (Mediterranian MOU) and the Black Sea Region (Black Sea MOU).

including the European Region by the Paris MOU.[140] This co-operation facilitates the systematic inspection of ships whilst at port, explicitly targeting those ships that are considered most likely to exhibit non-compliance. The risk factors taken into account vary from region to region and over time, but include such matters as the performance record of: that type of ship; the ship itself; its owner or manager; its flag state; and its classification society. Where the inspection procedure reveals non-compliance with the internationally agreed standards, states exercising port state control may detain ships pending repairs, report such non-compliance to flag states and prosecute any criminal offences uncovered.

5.3.5.2 EEA and UK Regulation

As discussed above, the United Kingdom implements the internationally agreed standards to which it has subscribed by delegated legislation largely introduced under the Merchant Shipping Act 1995.[141] Such implementation must now take effect within the context of a variety of EU policy and legislative initiatives affecting carriage by sea and the marine environment.[142] The EU has established the European Maritime Safety Agency (EMSA), which is particularly tasked with assisting Member States in the performance of their responsibilities as flag and port states, and assisting the Commission in the development of EU law with regard to maritime safety and prevention of pollution by ships.[143] The ambit of the current regulatory environment for the carriage of goods by sea in the EEA is very broad indeed, encompassing seafarer welfare, competition, port infrastructure and many other matters; for the purposes of this summary, it is grouped by reference to certain distinct measures for the regulation of cabotage, ship safety and marine pollution.

Regulation 4055/86/EC legislates for the freedom to provide services between Member States, and between Member States and third countries. The general freedom is provided for in art.1 in the following terms:

[140] The Paris MOU on port state control under which 27 state maritime authorities (including those of the UK) agree to co-operate on measures of port state control; details at *http://www.parismou.org/*.

[141] See fnn. 130, 134, 136 and 137.

[142] The most recent of which is the Integrated Maritime Policy for the European Union anticipated by the Commission Communication of 10 October 2007 [COM(2007) 575 final].

[143] Regulation 1406/2002/EC as amended pursuant to which EMSA is established. Details of EMSA's current activities are available at *http://www.emsa.europa.eu/*.

> "1. Freedom to provide maritime transport services between Member States and between Member States and third countries shall apply in respect of nationals of Member States who are established in a Member State other than that of the person for whom the services are intended. 2. The provisions of this Regulation shall also apply to nationals of the Member States established outside the Community and to shipping companies established outside the Community and controlled by nationals of a Member State, if their vessels are registered in that Member State in accordance with its legislation.".[144]

Regulation 3577/92/EEC provides for the freedom for "Community shipowners",[145] operating ships registered in, and flying the flag of, a Member State to: provide maritime transport services within any Member State (which activity is defined by the Regulation as "maritime cabotage");[146] provided, as required by art.1, there is compliance with "all conditions for carrying out cabotage in that Member State". To date, proposals for a European ship registry have not been supported by Member States and are not within the EU's current legislative agenda.

The EU has a broad legislative framework in connection with maritime safety, with a range of measures having been adopted to require Member States, as a matter of community law, to comply with their flag state[147] and port state[148] obligations under public international law and adopt common standards for ship inspections and ship classification societies.[149] In relation to pollution, various legislative measures have been adopted, including provisions to: require compliance with international standards as to the

[144] All national restrictions of these freedoms were required to be phased out by, at the latest, January 1, 1993.

[145] The concept of a Community shipowner is defined by art.2 as "(a) nationals of a Member State established in a Member State …; (b) shipping companies established in … and whose principal place of business is situated, and effective control exercised, in a Member State; or (c) nationals of a Member State established outside the Community or shipping companies established outside the Community and controlled by nationals of a Member State, if their ships are registered in and fly the flag of a Member State …".

[146] A narrower definition of cabotage than used elsewhere in this book.

[147] Directive 2009/21/EC on flag state control.

[148] Directive 2009/16/EC on port state control.

[149] Regulation 2009/391/EC on common rules and standards for ship inspection and survey organisations; Directive 2009/15/EC on common rules and standards for ship inspection, survey organisations and Member State flag/port state activities.

prevention of pollution;[150] require criminal sanctions for deliberate, reckless or seriously negligent pollution;[151] and require civil liability, for the damage and clean up costs consequent upon pollution, on a strict liability basis in accordance with the basic principle that the "polluter pays". This basic principle is established by various legislative measures[152] that combine together to produce a complex liability picture discussed at 5.3.7 below.

5.3.6 Air Carriage

5.3.6.1 International Regulation

International carriage by air is the most tightly regulated mode of carriage. International regulation is facilitated by the ICAO,[153] which was established in 1944 pursuant to the Chicago Convention[154] to achieve an ordered worldwide expansion of the civil aviation industry. The opening preamble of the Chicago Convention defines the aim and purposes of the ICAO as being:

> "that international civil aviation may be developed in a safe and orderly manner and that international air transport services may be established on the basis of equality of opportunity and operated soundly and economically".

The Chicago Convention provides the general public international law framework for the undertaking of international carriage by air on a worldwide basis. Article 5 obliges contracting states to allow civil aircraft

[150] Directive 2002/84/EC.

[151] Directive 2005/35/EC on ship-source pollution and on the introduction of penalties for infringements and Council Framework Decision 2005/667/JHA on the strengthening of the criminal-law framework for the enforcement of the law against ship-source pollution.

[152] See Directive 2004/35/EC on environmental liability for prevention and remedy of environmental damage and Directive 2008/98/EC (replacing D2006/12/EC, which replaced D1975/442/EC) on waste initiated by the Commission's Environment Directorate-General.

[153] The ICAO came into being on April 4, 1947 and now has 190 contracting states and operates as a specialised agency of the United Nations.

[154] The Convention on International Civil Aviation, which was signed on December 7, 1944 by 52 states and is now in its 9th revision. Originally adopted in English, all the French, Russian, Spanish and English language versions are equally authentic.

from other contracting states to fly over their territories ("subject to the right of the State flown over to require landing") and to stop without prior permission and take on or discharge passengers, cargo, or mail ("subject to the right of the State where such embarkation or discharge takes place to impose such regulations, conditions or limitations as it may consider desirable");[155] although art.7 permits contracting states to refuse permission for domestic internal (i.e. non-international) carriage by air. Article 11 obliges contracting states to apply aviation regulations to all civilian aircraft "without distinction as to nationality", whilst art.15 provides, to similar effect, that public airports should permit aircraft of all contracting states to use their facilities on the basis of "uniform conditions" applicable to all. The flight regulations, or air flight rules, applicable over the high seas are those made under the auspices of the ICAO, whilst each contracting state is obliged by art.12 to keep its own such regulations for flights over its territory "uniform, to the greatest possible extent, with those established from time to time" under the Convention.

Aircraft must be registered and adopt the nationality of the state in which they are registered (art.17); although that registration may be changed, an aircraft cannot have dual nationality and can only be registered in one state at any one time (art.18). States in which aircraft land are entitled by art.16 to "search aircraft of the other contracting States on landing or departure, and to inspect the certificates and other documents prescribed" by the Convention. By art.29 those documents must include the prescribed certification of: registration; airworthiness; pilot and crew competence; all of which must, by art.31, be issued by the state of registration which has the primary responsibility for such matters. In addition, a cargo manifest and other specified documentation must be included. Article 33 provides for mutual recognition of all certificates issued in accordance with the minimum standards prescribed by the Convention. Article 37 requires contracting states:

> "to collaborate in securing the highest practicable degree of uniformity in regulations, standards, procedures, and organisation in relation to aircraft, personnel, airways and auxiliary services in all matters in which such uniformity will facilitate and improve air navigation"

and mandates the ICAO to:

[155] Although scheduled air services require special permission under art.6.

> "adopt and amend from time to time, as may be necessary international standards and recommended practices and procedures dealing with"

the many and varied air carriage issues referred to in art.37; as well as all "such other matters concerned with the safety, regularity, and efficiency of air navigation as may from time to time appear appropriate". As a result of extensive and continually developing regulation by the ICAO, air carriage is certainly the most internationally harmonised mode of carriage of goods and such international public law takes effect in the United Kingdom pursuant to primary and delegated legislation.[156] However, such harmonisation is of the minimum applicable requirements for carriage by air. States are entitled under the Chicago Convention to impose further, more onerous, safety requirements, provided that such further mandatory standards are made generally applicable and are not overtly discriminatory.

5.3.6.2 EEA and UK Regulation

The United Kingdom implements the internationally agreed standards to which it has subscribed by delegated legislation generally made pursuant to the Civil Aviation Act 1982. As with carriage of goods by sea, the national UK law must be implemented in the context of a highly developed EU legislative framework relative to aviation. The EU has established the European Aviation Safety Agency (EASA),[157] which is particularly tasked with responsibility for harmonising the technical rules applied by Member States as to aviation safety and their uniform application by Member States. The scope of EU air carriage regulation covers such matters as harmonisation of technical safety standards for aviation infrastructure and operational procedures, environmental issues, air security, passenger rights, air traffic management in the "Single European Sky", compulsory liability insurance, development of regional airports, arrival and departure slot allocation rights and so on. However, for present purposes, attention will be focused only on issues of cabotage, air operation licences and the certification of airworthiness.

[156] Requirements for air carriage prescribed by the ICAO are generally implemented in the UK by the making of Air Navigation Orders pursuant to s.60 of the Civil Aviation Act 1982.

[157] EASA, which was established pursuant to Regulation 1592/2002/EC, provides information on its non-confidential activities at *http://www.easa.europa.eu/ws_prod/index.html.*

Since November 1, 2008, both cabotage and operator licensing have been governed by R1008/2008/EC on common rules for the operation of air services in the Community; this has recast the previous regulations applicable to these issues (i.e. R3407/92 and R20408/92). As to rights of cabotage within the EEA, art.15 of R1008/2008/EC provides:

> "(1) Community air carriers shall be entitled to operate intra-Community air services.[158] (2). Member States shall not subject the operation of intra-Community air services by a Community air carrier to any permit or authorisation. Member States shall not require Community air carriers to provide any documents or information which they have already supplied to the competent licensing authority, provided that the relevant information may be obtained from the competent licensing authority in due time".

Article 19 does permit Member States to exercise some control over air traffic distribution between airports and the exercise of air traffic rights: art.19(1) provides that the exercise of air traffic rights is

> "subject to published Community, national, regional and local operational rules relating to safety, security, the protection of the environment and the allocation of slots".

However, Member State regulation of the distribution of air traffic between airports is constrained by art.19(2), which provides that such regulation must be "without discrimination among destinations inside the Community or on grounds of nationality or identity of air carriers"; and must fulfil prescribed criteria aimed at ensuring a "level playing field" for competing air carriers, as well as respecting community principles of "proportionality and transparency" and being "based on objective criteria".

The concept of a "community air carrier" is defined by art.2 as "an air carrier with a valid operating licence granted by a competent licensing authority in accordance with" the Regulation. The competent licensing authorities are those authorities in each Member State entitled to "grant, refuse, revoke or suspend an operating licence"; there is full harmonisation of the criteria for the taking of such action within the EEA. The criteria for

[158] The concept of "intra-Community air service" is defined by art.2 as "an air service operated within the Community".

granting or refusing an operating licence are provided for at art.3, which also provides at 3(1) that

> "No undertaking established in the Community shall be permitted to carry by air passengers, mail and/or cargo for remuneration and/or hire unless it has been granted the appropriate operating licence".

Article 9 prescribes the criteria to be applied by the competent licensing authorities when addressing any issues of suspension and revocation in relation to an operating licence.

Airworthiness of aircraft and their components is now also subject to full harmonisation, by reason of the activities of EASA, pursuant to Regulation 1592/2002/EC on common rules in the field of civil aviation. Article 5 of R1592/2002/EC provides that aircraft registered in a Member State shall comply with the "essential requirements for airworthiness laid down in Annex I". The regulatory framework for airworthiness requires: all component products (satisfying such harmonised airworthiness requirements) to be issued with "a type-certificate"; all parts and appliances (also satisfying such requirements) to be issued with "specific certificates" of airworthiness; and each registered aircraft to be issued with an "individual certificate of airworthiness" on proof of conformity "with the type design approved in its type-certificate and that relevant documentation, inspections and tests demonstrate that the aircraft is in condition for safe operation". The validity of such a certificate of airworthiness continues for as long as:

> "it is not suspended, revoked or terminated and as long as the aircraft is maintained in accordance with the essential requirements related to continuing airworthiness"

as prescribed by Annex I. Organisations responsible "for the design, manufacture and maintenance of products, parts and appliances" must be approved: personnel responsible "for the release of a product, part or appliance after maintenance" may be obliged to hold a "personnel certificate", and the competences of maintenance training organisations to issue "personnel certificates" may need to be recognised by the issuance of an approval. In implementing the detailed rules as to the "essential requirements for airworthiness" the Commission is mandated by art.5(5) to "take specific care" that such detailed rules:

> "(a) reflect the state of the art and the best practices in the field of airworthiness; (b) take into account worldwide aircraft experience in

service, and scientific and technical progress; (c) allow for immediate reaction to established causes of accidents and serious incidents".

Certificates issued in accordance with the Regulation issued by competent national licensing authorities must be recognised by Member States pursuant to art.8 "without further technical requirements or evaluation". This should be contrasted with the procedures required throughout the community, pursuant to Directive 2004/36/EC, for third-country aircraft[159] landing within the Community, which are suspected of non-compliance with international safety standards. Such aircraft are subject to physical inspection to confirm their safety.

5.3.7 Effect of Regulatory Breach on Contractual Carriage

In the context of contracts for the carriage of goods, it is normally only necessary to consider the impact of mandatory regulation relating to the physical undertaking of the carriage, where goods have been lost, damaged or delayed and regulatory non-compliance is suspected of having been a contributory cause. Sanctions operating in the public law arena that impose criminal and administrative penalties on carriers and their employees are unlikely to provide cargo owners with adequate redress; private civil sanctions arising in contract and tort will need to addressed. These private civil sanctions are addressed below in the context of the contrasting effects of UK and EU legislation.

5.3.7.1 UK Legislation

The first and overriding question posed by English common law, when addressing the contractual effect of legislative prohibitions imposed by UK legislation or any foreign applicable law in the context of contractual duties, is whether the contract, as well as the act, is prohibited.[160] An affirmative answer can only be given where either the contract is illegal, because it is

[159] Defined by art.2 of D2004/36/EC as being "an aircraft which is not used or operated under the control of a competent authority of a Member State".

[160] In the words of Baron Parke in *Cope v Rowlands* (1836) 2 M. & W. 149 "It is perfectly settled, that where the contract which the plaintiff seeks to enforce, be it express or implied, is expressly or by implication forbidden by the common or statute law, no court will lend its assistance to give it effect ... The sole question is, whether the statute means to prohibit the contract".

prohibited and could never be lawfully performed,[161] or where an otherwise lawful contract was performed, or was to be performed, in a manner which was prohibited.[162] In the latter case the illegality operates against the party performing, or intending to perform, the contract in a prohibited manner.[163] It only operates against all contracting parties where there is an illegal conspiracy among them to perform the contract in an illegal manner (all of them having, or having had, a common and fixed intention towards such illegal performance).[164] An enquiry as to the fact of illegality demands investigation both as to the scope of the statutory prohibition and the nature of the contractual obligation to be performed. Such investigation involves careful textual analysis of the legislative provision at issue[165] and factual enquiry of the contractual context in which the allegation of illegality has arisen.[166] English law does not necessarily require criminal intent for contractual illegality. Contravention of a statutory prohibition is sufficient to render contractual performance illegal, irrespective of knowledge of the prohibition or of its contravention. Only in the case of intended future performance, by illegal means, of an otherwise lawful contract would actual

[161] See *Phoenix General Insurance Co v Halvanon Ins Co Ltd* [1986] 2 Lloyd's Rep. 552 where the Insurance Companies Act 1974 (now repealed) was held to make unenforceable any contract of insurance entered into by an insurer outside the scope of their authorisation.

[162] See *Ashmore Benson Pease & Co Ltd v Dawson Ltd* [1973] 2 Lloyd's Rep. 21, where consignor and consignee acted in concert in overloading a vehicle pursuant to an otherwise lawful contract of carriage with the consequence that the contract was rendered void through illegality.

[163] In *Archbolds (Freightage) Ltd v S Spangfeldt* [1961] 1 Q.B. 374 the consignor was able to recover damages for the loss of a consignment of whisky unlawfully carried by the carrier in an unlicensed vehicle as the consignor was unaware of the illegality and the carriage could have been carried out lawfully in another vehicle.

[164] *Ashmore Benson Pease & Co Ltd v Dawson Ltd* [1973] 2 Lloyd's Rep. 21.

[165] See for example *Phoenix General Insurance Co v Halvanon Ins Co Ltd* [1986] 2 Lloyd's Rep. 552 where the prohibition placed on insurers extended to "carrying out" unauthorised insurance, so that contracts for such insurance were void for illegality as they could not lawfully be carried out.

[166] See, for example, *St John Shipping Corp v Joseph Rank Ltd* [1956] 2 Lloyd's Rep. 413, in which Devlin J. held that overloading a vessel, in breach of the prohibition in s.44 Merchant Shipping (Safety and Load Line Conventions) Act 1932 (to the effect that the ship "shall not be so loaded as to submerge" the appropriate load-line) did not necessarily make contracts of carriage illegal.

knowledge of the prohibition be required for the contract to be considered illegal.[167]

Illegality operates under English law as a barrier to a private civil law claim. The barrier can be raised by the court itself but is generally raised by a litigant by way of defence. The barrier operates to the prejudice of all contracting parties, irrespective of fault, and its effect is to render any prohibited contract, or any other contract tainted by such illegality,[168] void and unenforceable to the prejudice of all parties, irrespective of responsibility for the statutory non-compliance.[169] Accordingly the principle of illegality can be seen to operate to the prejudice of wholly innocent parties under English law. Reasons why this should be the case under English common law were expressed in the following terms by Lord Mansfield[170] in the eighteenth century.

> "The objection, that a contract is immoral or illegal as between plaintiff and defendant, sounds at all times very ill in the mouth of the defendant. It is not for his sake, however, that the objection is ever allowed; but it is founded in general principles of policy, which the defendant has the advantage of, contrary to the real justice, as between him and the plaintiff, by accident, if I may so say. The principle of public policy is this; ex dolo malo non oritur actio. No court will lend its aid to a man who founds his cause of action upon an immoral or an illegal act".

[167] As in *Waugh v Morris* 1873 LR 8 Q.B. 202, where Blackburn J. held that the jointly held intention of charterer and owner to land French hay in London, in ignorance of a statutory prohibition against the import of French hay, was insufficient to render the charter illegal where the required contractual performance was that of loading alongside in London. In the event, the hay was transhipped in London and exported elsewhere.

[168] A contract is considered "tainted" where despite ostensible legality it is so connected with the prohibited contract as to be tainted with illegality. In *Group Josi Re v Walbrook Ins Co Ltd* [1996] 1 Lloyd's Rep. 345 Saughton L.J. considered that letters of credit opened to pay sums arising under illegal contracts would be unenforceable as against any bank otherwise liable to make payment under them by reason of the illegality of the contractual debt.

[169] See *Mahmoud v Ispahani* (1921) 6 Ll. L. Rep. 344, where the sale of linseed oil without a licence was prohibited and the contract was held illegal by the Court of Appeal, although responsibility for the failure lay with the vendor rather than the purchaser.

[170] *C.J Holman v Johnson* (1775) p.1 Cowp.

It is only in the event of illegality in the performance by one of the parties (the contract not itself being prohibited and the other parties not intending, or participating in, such illegal conduct) that the barrier might operate only to the prejudice of the party responsible for the illegal performance.[171]

Clearly there is considerable scope for illegality in the context of regulatory non-compliance in the performance of contracts of carriage by land, sea and air, since such contracts cannot be performed unless the road, rail, ship or aircraft is compliant with the applicable regulations, required security and transport procedures are followed and, in respect of certain modes, the carrier itself is duly authorised. In every case where such issues arise as to regulatory non-compliance, in the context of a contractual dispute, an enquiry must be made as to whether there has been a breach of a statutory prohibition and, if so, whether the contract, as well as the act, is prohibited; since in that event issues of contractual illegality under the common law will need to be addressed. The contract is unlikely to be saved by the doctrine of severance (by which judges are able to sever from contracts provisions which are void as being against public policy when the offending provision or obligation is not the entire consideration moving from one party to another),[172] as this doctrine ought not to be applied to contracts rendered illegal by reason of statutory contraventions where "the illegality is criminal, or *contra bonos mores*".[173]

Breach of UK legislation does not inevitably lead to any private civil law liability in tort. The tort of breach of statutory duty only lies, according to English common law, when the legislature not only imposes a statutory duty on some person or persons but can be proved to have intended that private law rights of action should be afforded to those claiming against any such person acting in breach of the statutory duty imposed on them.[174]

[171] Once illegality is proven, the common law barrier operates in response to various principles developed by the common law to balance the right of the state to have the prohibition upheld; and the duty of the court to uphold legal rights that are not, as a matter of law, dependent on the illegal contract. See *The EC REACH Regulation and Contractual Supply Obligations* by B.E. Harris JBL [2010] 5, 394–419.

[172] See *Goodinson v Goodinson* [1954] 2 Q.B. 118 (concerning a clause purporting to oust the jurisdiction of the court) and *Goldsoll v Goldman* [1915] 1 Ch.292 (concerning a clause in unlawful restraint of trade).

[173] Per Somervell L.J. in *Goodinson* [1954] 2 Q.B. 118.

[174] See judgment of the House of Lords in *Hague v Deputy Governor of Parkhurst Prison* [1992] 1 A.C. 58 in two conjoined cases; where prisoners unsuccessfully sought damages in tort for breach of statutory duty and/or false imprisonment, for segregation decisions taken under the Prison Rules by the governors of their prisons.

Difficult issues of statutory construction arise where the UK statute makes no such express provision and the court needs to ascertain the intention of the legislature as to the capacity of the statute to create a civil right of action. However, following the judgment of the House of Lords in *Hague v Deputy Governor of Parkhurst Prison*,[175] it now seems clear that claims for breach of statutory duty in tort only lie when:

> "... upon the true construction of the legislation in question that the intention was to confer on members of the protected class a cause of action sounding in damages occasioned by the breach.".[176]

Except where a UK statute makes express provision for civil claims, non-contractual civil liability is a most unlikely consequence of regulatory breach. There is no presumption that the legislature intends to give a private right of action in tort simply because the legislation protects some particular class of individuals. Civil law claims for breach of statutory duty cannot be created from a statutory duty not intended by the legislature to be owed to individuals.[177] Where civil claims for breach of statutory duty do lie, it is the statute rather than the common law that will control the standard of care and the extent of the losses that can be recovered by reason of breach;[178] there appear to be no instances of Parliament expressly creating such causes of action for cargo claimants against the carrier for breach of those various statutory duties imposed on the carrier, which are referred to above.

For that reason, aside from issues of illegality, the effect of regulatory breach on issues of liability, for loss, damage or delay to goods carried under the carriage contract, has to be considered in the context of the contractual terms. Where a contract of carriage is subject to seaworthiness obligations it is clear that this imports an obligation of regulatory compliance to ensure that the vessel is legally seaworthy and not simply seaworthy in a physical sense.[179] Where the regime of liability is basically

[175] ibid.

[176] Lord Bridge in *P. v E Liverpool Daily Post and Echo Newspapers Plc* [1991] 2 A.C. 370, 420 approved by Lord Jauncey in *Hague* ibid. 170–171.

[177] *Gorringe v Calderdale MBC* [2004] 1 WLR 1057; especially analyses of Lord Hoffman at 1068–1069 and Lord Scott at 1078–1079.

[178] K. M. Stanton L.Q.R. 2004, 120 (Apr), 324–341.

[179] *Golden Fleece Maritime Inc v ST Shipping and Transport Inc (The Elli)* [2009] 1 All E.R. (Comm) 908 discussed at 1.2.

strict,[180] excepting only particular exclusions,[181] liability caused by the consequences of regulatory non-compliance will not fall within the scope of the exceptions.[182] Similarly, in the context of domestic carriage of goods by land or sea, general obligations to exercise reasonable care may be imposed by the contract, either expressly or by implication;[183] introducing the possibility that breach of regulation might be considered evidence of breach of such qualified contractual duty.[184] Furthermore, the circumstances of regulatory breach may be asserted by claimants in efforts to set financial limitations aside. In particular, when circumstances of regulatory non-compliance are causative of loss, and are such as to amount to wilful misconduct (by responsible employees of the road carrier) or recklessness (by responsible employees of the rail, sea or air carrier), such road, rail, sea, or air carrier will lose the right to limit under contracts for the international carriage of goods by road or rail.[185] In the case of tonnage limitation for carriage by sea, recklessness as to regulatory compliance (and foresight of the particular damage suffered) on the part of the responsible alter ego of the carrier itself would have to be established in order for the financial limitations to be set aside.[186]

[180] As under the CMR and CIM conventions (in connection with the international carriage of goods by, respectively, road and rail) discussed at 2.3.3 and 2.6.2.3 and under the Warsaw and Montreal regimes (for the international carriage of goods by air) discussed at 4.2.1.3.

[181] Such as the exclusion under CMR art.17(2), discussed at 2.3.3, excluding the carrier from liability for "circumstances which the carrier could not avoid and the consequences of which he was unable to prevent".

[182] Since the loss would not have been caused by one of the particularly excluded events; but by reason of the regulatory non-compliance, to the extent such is proved to have been causative of the subject loss, damage or delay.

[183] For instance, pursuant to s.13 Supply of Goods and Services Act 1982, and at common law as discussed at 1.6.1.

[184] As the Privy Council commented in *Tan Chye Choo v Chong Kew Moi* [1970] 1 W.L.R. 147, any breach of statutory obligations requiring a particular standard of care, may be considered evidence of negligence.

[185] Pursuant to: art.29 of the CMR; art.36 of the CIM; art.IV(5)(e) of Hague-Visby; and art.25 of all versions of the Warsaw regime, apart from the Reamended Warsaw Convention; as discussed, respectively, at: 2.3.4.1 and 2.6.2.4; 3.3.2.4; and 4.2.1.4.

[186] Pursuant to The Convention on Limitation of Liability for Maritime Claims 1976 scheduled to the Merchant Shipping Act 1995, discussed at 3.1.7.2.

5.3.7.2 EU Legislation

Whilst instruments of public international law are not capable of direct effect in the United Kingdom without being directly applied into UK legal systems by implementing legislation, EU law is directly applicable in the United Kingdom by the European Communities Act 1972.[187] EU legislation takes effect within the national legal systems of the EU Member States as overarching legislative instruments capable of having supremacy[188] over national law, with the result that a national court, or indeed an arbitration tribunal,[189] is obliged to give full effect to it—even to the extent of suspending, or setting aside, its own national law rules.[190] The difficulty is that not all EU legislative provisions have direct effect within national legal systems and only in the event that such legislation has direct effect will it be considered supreme to national law. However, even where EU legislation is not capable of direct effects, national courts are obliged to construe national law, as far as possible,[191] in conformity with EU legislation.

In the absence of direction by the Community legislature, the direct effect of any EU legislation is left to be determined by the Community courts on a case by case basis under the ad hoc referral system operating under TFEU art.267 (ex art.234 ECT). By this system particular issues of EU law (as and when they require determination in connection with litigation before national courts), may be referred to the Community courts

[187] Having been applied into the laws of the UK by s.2(1), subjected to the interpretation of the Community Courts by s.3(1) and accorded supremacy by s.2(4).

[188] As established by the Community Courts in numerous cases, including: *van Gend en Loos* (Case 26/62) [1963] ECR 13, *Costa v ENEL* (Case 6/64) [1964] ECR 585 and *Simmenthal SpA* (Case 106/77) [1978] ECR 629, in respect of EU legislation having direct effects.

[189] At least where EU legislation should be regarded as being "a fundamental provision which is essential for the accomplishment of the tasks entrusted to the Community and, in particular, for the functioning of the internal market" (*Eco Swiss China Time Ltd v Benetton International NV* (Case C-126/97) [1999] ECR I-3055, at para.36 of the ECJ judgment).

[190] See the judgment in *Simmenthal* (Case 106/77) [1978] ECR 629, para.24 and, as far as the laws of the UK are concerned, the judgment of Lord Bridge in *Factortame Ltd v Secretary of State for Transport (No.2)* [1991] 1 Lloyd's Rep. 10, 13.

[191] What is possible in relation to particular UK legislation is an issue ultimately determinable by the UK Supreme Court; it would appear from decisions such as *Litster v Forth Dry Docks* [1989] 1 All E.R. 1194 and *Webb v EMO Air Cargo* [1995] 4 All E.R. 577 that courts may exercise a broad interpretative discretion in favour of reading such UK legislation in conformity with non-directly effective EU legislation.

for a definitive ruling; but the Community courts do not accept references unless their legal and factual context is clear[192] and the question arises out of an actual, and not a hypothetical, dispute.[193]

The EU legislation referred to at 5.3.1 to 5.3.6 largely comprises directives and regulations and these legislative forms have contrasting effects. EU Directives require national implementation by Member States. Direct effect of a Directive in national law is only possible on expiry of the period allowed for national implementation or, if earlier in time, when national measures of implementation have been enacted.[194] Directives are only capable of direct effects as between public bodies (i.e. emanations of the state) and private persons (i.e. natural or legal persons not being emanations of the state).[195] This is categorised as the EU legislation having direct effect at the *vertical level* as the state and citizen are at different levels in terms of the nature of the legal powers they exercise. Directives are not capable of direct effects as between private persons and are only relevant to the interpretation and application of national law. However, in contrast, an EU Regulation is a legislative measure, which applies throughout the EU and is capable of giving rise to direct effects not only between public bodies and private persons at the vertical level, but also as between private persons in their own contractual, tortious and proprietary relationships.[196] This is categorised as the EU legislation having direct effect at the *horizontal level* as such private persons are at the same level in terms of the legal powers they exercise. It does not need to be transposed into national law nor does it have any conditionality as to its effect, other than so far as it might itself provide such conditionality. However, the extent to which any particular EU legislative provision, whether by directive or regulation, is likely to have direct effects is very difficult to predict. Over the last 40 years, since the principle of "direct effects" was first established by the Community courts,[197] certain recognisable criteria for such direct effects have been established. These are that the legislation must be of a type that is capable of giving rise to direct effects in the material legal relationship; the

[192] *Telemarsicabruzzo SpA v Circostel, Ministero delle Poste e Telecommunicazioni and Ministerio della Difesa* (Cases C-320–322/90) [1993] ECR I-393.

[193] *Gasparini* (Case C-467/04) [2006] ECR I-9199.

[194] *Pfeiffer v Deutsches Rotes Kreuz, Kreisverband Waldshut eV* (C-397/01) [2004] ECR I-08835.

[195] Case 152/84 *Marshall v Southampton and South West Area Health Authority (Teaching) No.1.*

[196] See *Muñoz* (Case C-253/00) [2002] ECR I-7289.

[197] In the seminal judgment in *Van Gend en Loos* (Case 26/62) [1963] ECR 13.

legislative provision in question must itself be intended to confer rights on parties to such legal relationships, and corresponding duties; and such duties must satisfy certain justiciability requirements of being clear, precise and unconditional in their effects.[198] The Community courts adopt a teleological interpretative approach to this enquiry, pursued in the context of what they divine to be the intended purposes of the legislation.

Where EU legislation is directly effective in the context of particular legal relationships, any breach of that legislation must be enforced by national courts. Those national courts are obliged by EU law to enforce any breach of EU legislation in such a way that there is both equivalence and effectiveness in the sanctions imposed. The concept of equivalence requires sanctions for infringements of EU law to be equivalent to sanctions applied by the national courts for "comparable infringements of like seriousness"[199] of national law.[200] The concept of effectiveness requires that the sanctions applied for breach of EU law are effective, proportionate and have deterrent effect.[201] Judicial application of *equivalence* requires little more than the non-discriminatory application of EU legislation to ensure it is as effective as a similar right arising under domestic national law. The difficulty for national courts in applying this principle lies not in determining the extent of the sanctions to be applied but in determining when to apply which sanction; the doctrine of equivalence only has application when the rights created by EU law and national domestic law are similar.[202] Judicial application of *effectiveness* requires English courts to ensure that EU legislation is applied effectively in the achievement of its essential purposes and appears to comprise a twofold enquiry ensuring that Member States both

[198] *Muñoz v Frumar Ltd* (Case C-253/00) [2002] ECR I-7289.

[199] Paragraph 54 of Advocate General Geelhoed's Opinion in *Muñoz* (Case C-253/00) [2002] ECR I-7289.

[200] The ECJ, at para.93 of the judgment in *Manfredi v Lloyd Adriatico Assicurazioni SpA* (Cases C-295–298/04) [2006] ECR I-6619, has clearly stated that procedural and substantive equivalence must exist in respect of any public, private, criminal or civil sanctions.

[201] *Courage v Crehan* (Case C-453/99) [2001] ECR I-6297, in which the ECJ relied upon the "effectiveness" principle in deciding that damages should be recoverable for breach of competition regulation arising under art.81 EC Treaty.

[202] *Levez v Jennings Ltd* (Case C-326/96) [1998] ECR I-7835, in which the European Court of Justice held any determination of *similarity*, for the application of the principle, should be made by reference to what was described at para.43 of the judgment as, "both the purpose and the essential characteristics of allegedly similar domestic actions".

effectively enforce compliance with EU law and give effective judicial protection for those disadvantaged by breach of EU law.[203]

The Community courts have, by judgments applying effectiveness in a series of cases,[204] effectively reserved for themselves the discretion to consider any national law provision, or omission obstacles to: either the effective fulfilment of the aims of EU legislation, or to the effective protection of those disadvantaged by non-compliance with EU legislation. In consequence, Community courts have applied the principle of effectiveness in various cases to require national courts to afford certain private civil remedies for breach of EU legislation, when such remedies would not have been available for breach of national legislation and notwithstanding such remedies being inconsistent with the applicable law of the contract.[205] The contrasting effects of EU and national UK regulation on contractual rights are generally complex but particular complexity arises in relation to contracts of international carriage, because such regulation cascades down from the level of public international law into EU and UK legislation. Two ECJ cases, both addressing the consequences of seaborne pollution, illustrate the difficulties arising in this respect.

In one, the *Intertanko* case,[206] it was argued that Directive 2005/35/EC on ship-source pollution should not be implemented into UK legal systems as it did not comply with the UK's international obligations under the Marpol 73/78[207] and UNCLOS[208] conventions. The ECJ decided that the

[203] Paolisa Nebbia "*Damages actions for the infringement of EC competition law: compensation or deterrence*" E.L Rev. 2008 33(1), 23–43.

[204] See in particular the decisions of *Courage* (Case C-453/99) [2001] ECR I-6297; *Manfredi* (Cases C-295–298/04) [2006] ECR I-6619 in the context of issues of EC competition law arising under arts 81 of the EC Treaty, and *Muñoz* (Case C-253/00) [2002] ECR I-7289 in the context of agricultural product regulation.

[205] ibid.

[206] *International Association of Independent Tanker Owners (Intertanko) v Secretary of State for Transport* (Case C-308/06) ECR I-04057.

[207] Article 4 of D2005/35 required Member States to introduce criminal offences for ship-source pollution "committed with intent, recklessly or by serious negligence" in relation to: not only the internal waters of Member States but also to their territorial waters, straits used for international navigation, the exclusive economic zone of Member States and the high seas. The relevant international obligations under Marpol 73/78 only referred to deliberate or reckless discharges.

[208] Article 3(1) of D2005/35/EC purported to disapply defences available under Marpol 73/78 in relation not only to the internal waters of Member States; but also as to their territorial waters, over which the relevant international obligations under UNCLOS provided for the right of innocent passage.

validity of D2005/35/EC could not be assessed in the light of either convention. As regards Marpol 73/78, the ECJ considered that, although all its Member States were contracting parties to the convention, since the EU was not a contracting party to it, the EU had not assumed any obligations under it and was not bound by it. As regards UNCLOS, the ECJ accepted that the EU was a party to UNCLOS but considered that its provisions were not generally capable of direct effects (other than in relation to actions against a flag state for damage resulting from a failure to fulfil its obligations as a flag state). Accordingly, the ECJ determined that the United Kingdom was obliged to implement D2005/35/EC, notwithstanding contrary public international law obligations; and it has now done so despite its wider international obligations under Marpol 73/78 and UNCLOS.[209]

In the *Total* case,[210] relating to the *Erika* casualty in 1999 off the Brittany coast of France, the ECJ considered the relationship between international obligations as to the limitation of liability for marine claims,[211] and Directive 75/442/EC on waste.[212] The ECJ held that:

> "oil accidentally spilled at sea following a shipwreck, mixed with water and sediment and drifting along the coast of a Member State until being washed up on that coast, constitute waste"[213]

within D75/442/EC; and that, despite Member States being obliged in accordance with their international obligations to limit the liability of the carrier for the clean up of such waste, they would

> "have to make provision for that cost to be borne by the producer of the product from which the waste thus spread came".[214]

[209] D2005/35/EC was implemented by The Merchant Shipping (Implementation of Ship-Source Pollution Directive) Regulations 2009 (SI2009/1210) pursuant to, inter alia, s.95 and s.96 Merchant Shipping Act 1995 and s.2(2) European Communities Act 1972.

[210] Case C-188/07 *Commune de Mesquer v Total France SA and Total International Ltd.*

[211] In particular, by the International Conventions on Civil Liability for Oil Pollution Damage 1992 and on the Establishment of an International Fund for Compensation for Oil Pollution Damage 1992.

[212] Now repealed and, as discussed at 5.3.5.2 above, re-enacted as Directive 2008/98/EC.

[213] See fn. 210 at para.63.

[214] ibid. at para.82.

However, the court went on to say, in the same paragraph, that:

> "such a producer cannot be liable to bear that cost unless he has contributed by his conduct to the risk that the pollution caused by the shipwreck will occur"

giving as an example of such conduct the wrong choice of ship. The decision effectively exposes charterers of vessels by non-demise time or voyage charter and shippers of cargo to liability for marine pollution consequent upon maritime casualties, without the benefit of financial limitation under public international law.

The effect, in each of these cases, was that public international law obligations implemented into national law apparently had to give way to conflicting obligations under EU legislation. Given the reasoning of the ECJ in these cases, it seems that similarly complex issues touching upon the relationship of statutory regulation at different levels in the legal hierarchy, and upon the interaction of such regulation (particularly arising pursuant to EU legislation) with contractual and tortious duties arising under the common law are now set to become an established feature of English law relating to the carriage of goods by land, sea and air in the EEA. This seems assured as, whatever happens internationally, the pace of harmonisation within the EEA single market is increasing across all modes of carriage, towards fulfilment of the common transport policy. Further EU legislation to achieve that policy is inevitable.

INDEX

LEGAL TAXONOMY
FROM SWEET & MAXWELL

This index has been prepared using Sweet and Maxwell's Legal Taxonomy. Main index entries conform to keywords provided by the Legal Taxonomy except where references to specific documents or non-standard terms (denoted by quotation marks) have been included. These keywords provide a means of identifying similar concepts in other Sweet & Maxwell publications and online services to which keywords from the Legal Taxonomy have been applied. Readers may find some minor differences between terms used in the text and those which appear in the index. Suggestions to *sweetandmaxwell.taxonomy@thomson.com.*